LOS ANGELES BEFORE HOLLYWOOD

JAN OLSSON

LOS ANGELES BEFORE HOLLYWOOD

JOURNALISM AND AMERICAN

FILM CULTURE, 1905 TO 1915

NATIONAL LIBRARY OF SWEDEN

P. O. BOX 5039, 102 41 STOCKHOLM, SWEDEN

© JAN OLSSON & NATIONAL LIBRARY OF SWEDEN

DESIGNED BY JENS ANDERSSON/WWW.BOKOCHFORM.SE

PRINTED IN SWEDEN BY KRISTIANSTADS BOKTRYCKERI, 2008

ISSN 1654-6601

ISBN 978-91-88468-06-2

MEDIEHISTORISKT ARKIV 10

CONTENTS

ACKNOWLEDGEMENTS

TIMELY AND MUCH appreciated research grants for this study have been provided by the Swedish Research Council (VR), the Swedish Foundation for International Cooperation in Research and Higher Education (STINT), the Bank of Sweden Tercentenary Foundation (RJ), and the Lauritzen Foundation for Research in Film History, all based in Stockholm.

The research was carried out during a protracted period of commuting between Los Angeles and Stockholm. Over the years, a select group of friends have made living in Los Angeles and its environs highly entertaining—short-listed in random order are Lynn Spigel, Doris Baizley, Jeffrey Sconce, Ed Woll, Robert Israel, Todd Boyd, Rudolf Kammerer, Sieglinde Gottschalk-Vahldiec, and the Renov family. Michael Renov in addition co-chaired an exchange program between our schools at Stockholm University and the University of Southern California within the framework of STINT, throughout with unfailing éclat. In an inspiring spirit of generous friendship and intellectual companionship, Lynn and Jeff have endured legions of discussions of the project in Los Angeles, Chicago, and New York City during teaching and archival ventures. Ed and Dorie, also with a true genius for friendship, held the ground when I have been away from Los Angeles. Dorie has graciously received countless book deliveries on my behalf and turned part of her home into a

7

storage facility. By inviting me to numerous readings of her plays in progress in kitchens and living rooms all over Los Angeles, she has introduced me to the rich local theater scene. Ed has generously shared his vast architectural knowledge and Los Angeles expertise besides helping out with all kinds of mundane matters. Robert Israel, illustrious raconteur, bartender, and chef when not composing, compiling, or conducting, has been a steadfast provider of fun, mischief, and music on both continents. Dining with Todd Boyd is the most entertaining way of keeping track of popular culture with a Los Angeles slant; his insights into the game we love are unrivaled. For poolside chat, Rudi and Siegi are the best.

Robert Vaughn, Supervising Library Specialist at the University of Southern California during my most intense research period—currently Music Librarian—and his former staff have been untiring in their efforts to bring in material for my research. Dace Taube, Regional History Librarian at USC, has offered numerous advice and suggestions, and Senior Library Assistant Ned Comstock at the Cinematic Arts Library at USC has been helpful far beyond the call of duty. Kristen Anderson, Dino Everett, and Michele Torre assisted during various phases of the research process; Michele has in addition been the savviest TA imaginable. Barbara Hall and the efficient staff at the Margaret Herrick Library at the Academy of Motion Picture Arts and Sciences, Beverly Hills, have most graciously facilitated access to archival materials. The staff at the History Department at the Los Angeles Public Library has patiently expedited a phalanx of requests for material, as did the librarians at the Microform and Media Services Division at the Young Research Library of the University of California, Los Angeles, the staff at the microfilm room at the New York Public Library, as well as the archivists at the Billy Rose Theatre Collection of the Lincoln Center Library for the Performing Arts Library. John M. Cahoon, Collections Manager at Seaver Center for Western History Research at Natural History Museum of Los Angeles County, has been a most skillful guide through the collections. Jay Jones, City Archivist at Los Angeles City Archives, enthusiastically shared his expertise during my delving into the city collections and promptly answered scores of e-mail queries. Brent C. Dickerson has generously provided access to material from his wonderful collection of vintage Los Angeles postcards. Marc Wannamaker, Bison Archives, has with impressive dispatch tracked down odd requests for visuals. Film

8

material was viewed at the UCLA Film and Television Archives, Library of Congress, Museum of Modern Art, the Academy of Motion Picture Arts and Sciences, the Danish Film Institute, the British Film Institute, and the Nederlands Film Museum—assistance from friends and archivist in conjunction with viewing was highly appreciated: Mark Quigley (UCLA), Mike Mashon and Madeline F. Matz (LoC), Charles Silver (MoMA), Snowden Becker (AMPAS), Thomas C. Christensen and Dan Nissen (DFI), Elaine Burrows, Bryony Dixon, and Fleur Buckley (BFI), and Nico de Kleck (NFM). Bo Berglund, Bertil Friberg, John Fullerton, Bart van der Gaag, Elaine King, Jakob Olsson, and Henrik Schröder have in multiple ways and always with good cheer assisted the project. I am much indebted to Steve Wilder for his stellar copyediting of the manuscript. His keen diligence, sharp eyes, and wit have been indispensable in the final phase of the work. Spela Mezek efficiently prepared the index. Over the years, I have benefited immensely from the friendship and scholarship of Richard Abel, Tom Gunning, and Charles Musser and their inspiring intellectual generosity.

More than anyone, however, Marina Dahlquist has added flair, intellectual companionship, and *savoir vivre* to this project and its two home bases, not to mention Monterey, New York City, and scores of other places. This book is for her and all "our" wonderful children.

Marina di Ragusa and Marina del Rey
July and August 2007

LIST OF ILLUSTRATIONS

Front Cover
Tally's New Broadway at 554 S. Broadway advertising *Roosevelt in Africa* in 1910 (Courtesy of the Los Angeles Public Library)

Back Cover
Tally's Phonograph and Vitascope Parlor at 311 S. Spring Street (Courtesy of Marc Wanamaker)

Introduction
Figure 1: College Theater (Courtesy of Brent C. Dickerson)
Figure 2: Operating Room at the College Theater, *Motography*, Vol. 6, No. 2 (August 1911): 86.
Figure 3: Interior of the Hyman, *Moving Picture World*, Vol. 8, No. 16 (22 April 1911): 880-81.

Chapter 1
Figure 4: *Chicago Daily News*, 3 May 1907, 1.

Chapter 2
Figure 5: Vitascope projection during election night 1896. Cartoon from *New York Herald*, 4 November 1896, 2.
Figure 6: Non-theatrical exhibition. An audience viewing film at the Hiram Playground in Cleveland. *Playground*, Vol. 5, No. 8 (November 1911): 270-71.
Figure 7: *Billboard*, Vol. 20, No. 26 (27 June 1908)

Figure 40: Harry C. Carr on the attempts of banning the screenings of *The Clans-man*. *Los Angeles Times*, II February 1915, III:1.

Image restoration and retouching: Jakob Olsson

INTRODUCTION

"This has come to be the age of the reporter. In even its simplest
form, news is the nerves of the modern world."[1]

THIS BOOK ABOUT American film culture during the years 1905–1915
was written in an intimate dialog with contemporary journalism. Toward
the end of that period, cinema's rapid inroads on the amusement market
and complex processes of transformation took the industry to suburban
Los Angeles, a relocation applauded by boosters in the local newspapers.
In contrast to previous studies of the period before Hollywood, we will
approach film culture predominantly if not exclusively from the West
Coast and Los Angeles.

Newspaper discourses, the nervous system of the modern world, form
the backbone of this inquiry. Just like the human nervous system, the
press monitors and coordinates events and processes in addition to ini-
tiating action by way of its complex, adaptive system. From the Vitascope debut in 1896 through the nickelodeon boom around 1906 to the
years of serials and features in the mid-1910s, the press negotiated and
interacted with all aspects of film culture in what can be described as a
series of adaptive stages. The medium of film, a conveyance-like apparatus mysteriously attuned to the neural flow of modernity, whether rapid
or leisurely, has never, I would argue, experienced a decade more critical
than the one singled out here. As made evident by the news flow, production practices, film formats, exhibition strategies, theater architecture, modes of spectatorship, and marketing methods were fundamen-

tally reconfigured. And in the mid-1910s Los Angeles had become the undisputable center of the industry. Transition has become the key scholarly term for analyzing not only the relocation of the industry, but also the complex web of transformations and negotiations of film culture from the nickelodeon boom to the emergence of the feature era.

Studies of pre-1905 cinema and its attractions align the medium with amusement parks and their thrills by invoking a perceptual regime closely tied to modes of transportation. Panoramic vision, with its constant reframing of landscape views from inside train compartments and the perception of time and space produced by train travel, offered a veritable education of the eye further elaborated upon by filmmakers. From such a perspective, it is hard to overestimate the impact Wolfgang Schivelbusch's groundbreaking study of railway travel had on the scholarship concerning early cinema.[2] Around 1910, when cinema was firmly established in the Los Angeles cityscape—the primary locus of this book—automobiles entered the equation, be it in descriptions of the vicissitudes of moving about downtown, automobile patronage signaling the film medium's strides, or building booms driven in tandem by mushrooming garages and moving-picture theaters.[3]

This study revisits a constellation of discourses from cinema's so-called transitional period. Such forays have been undertaken by others, but pivoted differently. The materials addressed here form an eclectic discourse mixing enthusiasm for the new with critical engagement and concerns for its cluttered cultural brouhaha. In this work such discourses coalesce around Los Angeles and its film culture as well as the more abstract place of films and movies within a larger cultural sphere. The topics singled out for discussion all bear on a sensibility decidedly Los Angeles-specific on a discursive level, but with inevitable excursions to gain broader perspectives. The inquiry is all about discourses, about cultural constructions for coming to terms with the multiple conceptions of film culture during a protean decade when the medium's features were still changing in rapidly overlapping successions, just like the city of Los Angeles.

We will touch base with a set of problems hotly debated between scholars over the last few decades: These discussions involved approaches to spectatorship and the complex relations between modernity and cinema in particular. The method is comparative in several respects. Not only is news material bearing on film culture mobilized from different cities in the U.S., the European press scene is occasionally invoked to provide perspectives on film cultures with salient differences compared to the American, for instance concerning programming, censorship, and the feature format. These discourses—foremost in the form of newspapers, but also maps, license records, directories, legal documents, general-interest magazines, and trade papers relating to theatrical or filmic matters—are the key remnants, apart from surviving films, from this volatile decade of American film culture.[4]

The operative hypothesis scaffolding the project is that a constellation of local newspapers provides a productive, nay indispensable, discursive repository for understanding film culture's repositioning within the overall amusement geography. Dystopian and utopian aspirations for cinema were intertwined in the debate, and the medium was simultaneously chastised as a school of crime and celebrated as an educative visual tool for navigating the modern world. For better or for worse, writers concluded, cinema offered lessons, particularly impacting children's susceptible minds via the eyes.

The overwhelming majority of films from this decade have been lost, and the paper trail for gauging spectatorship, the makeup of audiences in terms of class, race, gender, and age, is thin, while actual programming in theaters is difficult to tease out prior to the appearance of regular advertising with serial films and early features in 1914. Yet, as this inquiry suggests and seeks to demonstrate, a turn to newspaper morgues might help us fill in some of the blanks concerning the many facets of film culture during the period. Newspapers can be seen as a predominantly reactive arena, albeit offering a refracted mirroring of the world's work, which is charged with political outlooks and cultural predilections. The papers created policies, and not only editorially, but by instituting campaigns, crusades or promotions, or by offering space to such ventures. Scholars have configured these endeavors as a metonymy for the elite's policing of a budding form of popular entertainment, both risky and risqué, that was allegedly embraced foremost by the most susceptible of audience constituencies.[5]

The focus on policing, and its assumption of middleclass fears and anxieties concerning popular culture, tend to obfuscate the promotional efforts championed by the newspapers in terms of progressive reform and uplift initiatives. Overall, the columns effortlessly housed seemingly contradictory responses to film culture both between and during campaigns. As Paul Starr tersely phrased it in his overview of turn-of-the century American journalism and its diversity in terms of address, content, and style: "A newspaper is not a single item, but a collection of things."[6] In order to create a mass market, he argues, diversity, rather than homogeneity, offered the only viable approach—just like in vaudeville, one could add. Early film culture is part of such a diversity of expressions, which spawned novel forms of journalism and an expanded field of periodical literature and magazines.

The interplay between cinema and daily print culture at critical junctures during the transitional era represents a discursive domain calling for analysis as a phenomenon in its own right, apart from being yet another trove of source material to add to the panoply of paper sources otherwise mobilized by film historians for fleshing out film culture. In this respect newsprint speaks volumes. Crudely put and with eminent exceptions, film historians have often settled for a derivative approach to newspaper material. Primarily preoccupied with culling the trade discourse, scholars have to an overwhelming extent contented themselves with the press items the trade weekly *Moving Picture World* elected to reprint in its columns, thus removing the press material from its context proper and simultaneously ignoring material disregarded by the trade press. Regarding film-related material in general-interest magazines, discussions seldom move beyond the articles referenced by *Readers' Guide to Periodical Literature*, besides focusing their energy on the exhibition context in New York City. Fair enough, Gotham was after all the nation's leading film market.

Data marshaled from scores of maps and directories in addition to snippets of intelligence garnered from a host of sources complement the newspaper and trade-paper sources.[7] City directories, readily available for the entire period, and the city clerk's license records have been a productive combination to consult. The yearly directories initially made no distinction between theaters and moving-picture houses, and a yearly publication stood no chance of keeping pace with the capricious meandering of venues for film exhibition. The stenographic license records provide a precise chronicle of payments month by month for the privilege of operating places of amusement as regulated by a local ordinance. When I was invited to try to unearth old license ledgers occupying scores of pallets in a warehouse adjacent to the Records Management Division in downtown Los Angeles, only the volumes for 1903, 1904, 1906, 1907

18

cropped up—slow start-up years for film exhibition outside the vaude-ville theaters—and 1911, when a wide variety of houses were already legion.[8] Records for the key years, 1908–1910, are missing.

While the realm of film production is given short shrift, a cacoph-ony of journalistic voices from the past that addressed film culture in its broadest sense will help us discursively map the exhibition terrain, for example the concrete relocation of film exhibition in Los Angeles from the city's exotic fringe to the business center. Being predominant-ly dependent on newsprint means that the source material we can glean comes with an agenda for urban development, more so, perhaps, in Los Angeles than in any other American city. Here, the *Times*' unflinching advocacy for the open shop and a city free from the putative tyranny of organized labor most certainly played into the equation when the *Los Angeles Times*' building was dynamited in 1910. General Otis, the *Times*' controversial publisher, regarded the open shop as a panacea for all social ills.[9]

The newspaper scene in Los Angeles was partisan and prone to hard-nosed infighting, but united in boosting the region at a time of unprec-edented growth. All papers published yearly issues basking in the city's recent progress and glorious outlook. More often than not, editorial policies spilled over into the reporting of news. William Randolph Hearst's *Los Angeles Examiner* was one of many cogs in the Chief's polit-ical machine, and he also enlisted the film medium for campaign purpos-es in a broad sense.[10] The progressive forces were represented by the *Los Angeles Express* and later the *Los Angeles Tribune* also, both under the management of local business tycoon Edwin T. Earl. Unbeknownst to most readers, the *Times* was the clandestine force behind the *Los Angeles Herald*. The latter's transformation from morning paper to evening sheet prompted Earl in the summer of 1911 to launch the *Tribune* as a one-cent morning paper intended to compete with the *Times* and the *Examiner*, both of which sold for a nickel. Lastly, the *Los Angeles Record* was one of the Scripps-McRae League's numerous low-price ventures catering primarily to working-class readers.[11] During the heyday of progressive leadership in Los Angeles, after the downfall of Mayor Arthur C. Harper in March 1909 and the subsequent reign of progressive Mayor George Alexander, the city published the *Municipal News* for one year. Frank E. Wolfe was one of the forces behind this paper.[12] He had previously worked for the *Herald* and was soon to emerge as a socialist filmmaker who chronicled the most controversial political issue in Los Angeles, the trial after the bombing of the *Los Angeles Times*' plant, in the film *From Dusk to Dawn* (Occidental Motion Picture Co. of California, 1913).[13]

This inquiry provides a preliminary blueprint for the reporting on and negotiation of film culture in the American press. The objective is therefore to analyze local film culture in Los Angeles in relation to the overall changes of American film culture from 1905 to 1915—hence the excursions to the bigger cities along the newspaper trails. Furthermore, multiple functions are ascribed to the press. Apart from being a source that reflects film culture's strides and transgressions from the perspective of news, journalism is perceived as a forceful agent for striking a balance between the three concepts Raymond Williams proposed for coming to grips with the dynamics of cultural processes.[14] Over time newspapers, I argue, thus discover, position, and reposition cinema's cultural purchase within William's flexible register of the *residual*, *dominant*, and *emergent*. In fact, newspapers might be the best available arena for reading cultural changes in line with Williams' analytical grid and the interplay between his three intertwined, dynamic cultural layers. Toward the end of the period these processes moved full circle as the film medium developed a genre of cine-reporting, the newsreel, as a regular programming slot, which survived as a genre until made obsolete by television's faster news cycle.

Williams' dynamic terms were ventured to account for cultural spans of considerable duration in contrast to the mere decade under scrutiny here—and within the framework of a Marxist analysis of society. Thus, Williams analyzed a relatively slow trajectory from a pre-capitalist folk culture to a full-fledged mass market for commodified culture. The repositioning within the limited realm of film culture, in contrast, took place within a firmly established market for cultural commodities, albeit stratified due to admission prices and numerous other determinants, just like the press. Shortly after 1905 film exhibition developed with unprecedented dispatch from a marginal phenomenon on the vaudeville bills into a veritable mass medium as a result of the nickelodeon boom.

In spite of the compressed time frame covered by this study, one can adopt Williams' terms for two purposes: analyzing the (imaginary) place and position of film culture within the overall dynamics of the cultural fabric, and for a restrictive analysis of the internal dynamics within the realm of film culture proper. In this inquiry, these two perspectives overlap. In partial alignment with Williams' protracted focus some lengthy historical flashbacks will help set the stage for the mere decade under consideration.

Film attractions, as discussed by Tom Gunning most prominently, can, in the light of Williams' terms, be seen as residual elements incorporated into the emergent production dynamics of narrative films far beyond the period when the regime of attractions dominated cinema. The designation cinema of attractions, coined by André Gaudreault and Tom Gunning, generated a wealth of analytical energy for the burgeoning field of early cinema.[15] Amidst the success of the approach, Charles Musser championed a different analytical category, screen practice: Rather than highlighting ruptures and changes, it stresses the historical continuity of screen entertainment. Tom Gunning's influence is not restricted to the felicitous term cinema of attractions. A series of studies from his pen has provided pointed analyses of film culture, including beyond the period it posits, not least his book-length study of D.W. Griffith's years at the Biograph Co., which is built around what he calls the narrator system, a cinema of voice and correlated incidents.[16]

In the aftermath of the cinema of attractions several scholars talk about attractions as contained and integral devices in models of transformation, or as moments of intense excitement in film narratives, for example Ben Singer concerning thrilling elements in cliffhanging serial films.[17] More generally, the devices of style and storytelling Kristin Thompson labels excess, seemingly falling outside or working against a work's unifying forces, can perhaps be read as residual elements vis-à-vis a predominant model of storytelling operating with otherwise invisible devices.[18] Such lines of reasoning for describing the internal dynamics of cinema, giving formerly dominant forms a residual afterlife by processes of incorporation, are clearly in tune with Williams' analytical blueprint for the overall dynamics and inner workings of cultural processes.

Charles Musser's detailed account of early American cinema references Raymond Williams' conceptual triad in its title: *The Emergence of Cinema*.[19] Musser's study, published in a multi-volume series on the history of American cinema, takes us through September 1907, and the baton is picked up by a book Eileen Bowser authored. While continuity in relation to other forms of screen practice defines Musser's point of departure, transformation is the salient designation in Bowser's inquiry spanning the period 1907–1915.[20] The following volume, penned by

Richard Koszarski, covers 1915–1928 and is subtitled *The Age of the Silent Feature*.[21] Thus, in the book series' historiographic architecture, a trajectory moves from an emergent, marginal phenomenon, which after a period of transformation and heightened cultural visibility is organized around an increasingly predominant commodity, the feature film, and a new type of programming, with a penetration and leverage meriting the inclusion of cinema among dominant cultural practices. Phrased differently, and in line with Miriam Hansen's influential analysis, cinema, as an alternative public sphere in which marginalized groups for a short time collectively enjoyed and acted out their experiences in a kind of free zone, were in the processes of transition supplanted by a privatized mode of spectatorship removed from its alternative roots and participatory audience engagement.[22] Judging from the discursive material, however, residual pockets and tactics of resistance—as is always the case with cultural practices—lingered in audiences' engagement with cinema outside the new, ritzy palaces for spectatorship.

The press organizes the world according to a daily hierarchy of news, some of it falling into preset, albeit plastic and locally inflected, beats and sections in addition to feature material and editorials. Bouncing between beats and sections while generating news, buzz, and outrage prior to the 1910s, cinema eventually was reported on as a major American industry, garnering attention in both editorials and feature texts. The medium was then perceived as a truly emergent cultural factor and a theatrical entertainment which regularly advertised its programs, meriting review, while its stars and personalities were awarded attention in more or less gossipy columns.[23] To boot, film screenings were offered for educational purposes in venues outside the theatrical context. And from the perspective of Los Angeles, film had emerged as a forceful agent for showcasing the region, thus the concerns expressed by the Merchants' and Manufacturers' Association when Universal, at a critical juncture in media development, threatened to take its businesses elsewhere.[24]

At the end of the period under consideration, cinema had reached a culturally mature stage, on the verge of moving to a position within the dominant culture due to its economic clout and inclusive cultural practices. The medium of film could therefore partake in campaigns in alliances with newspapers instead of being targeted in crusades. Hearst's news empire, for example, instigated such a campaign together with the Selig film company for the purpose of bolstering California's assets after the Panama Canal opened. The obvious traction of film culture in the mid-1910s is evidenced by the journey intrepid traveler Grace Darling undertook via waterways, starting from New York City, to promote California during the exhibition year of 1915. Reporter Grace Darling, a Hearstian newspaper construct and *nom de plume*, was grafted onto and acted out by an actress. This media event will be analyzed in multiple dimensions in order to highlight the bleed between series, newsreels, and serials in the mid-1910s and their marketing in the press. This campaign clearly marks the medium's affinity with dominant culture after a decade of intense negotiations in the press. Hearst and Selig's joint effort coincided with important steps in the relocation of the film industry out west.

From 1907, American cities began regulating the exhibition of what had briskly turned into a full-fledged mass medium organized in such a manner that the government dismantled its monopolistic business structure in the mid-1910s, which at that point was more diverse than when the legal proceedings began. The films produced during 1905–12 were predominantly short subjects in different genres, exhibited in nickel shows' variety programs or in combination programs at vaudeville theaters, exhibition models for which spectatorship was put into verbal form by audience observers in the press. The fledgling story format across genres provided models for changing perceptions of film acting besides yielding rudimentary conceptions of film direction—and a narrator system to boot within a dominating variety format for exhibition of single-reel films.[25] Apart from split reels accommodating several topics within 1,000 feet, longer films found a market parallel to the standardized format, most often in legitimate venues outside the nickel-and-dime realm. In the mid-1910s serial films and features emerged at the forefront of exhibition in the new movie palaces located on the white ways of big cities. These and other changes will be charted in a dialog with newsprint sources and their mercurial manner of and strategies for addressing and interacting with film culture.

A sustained focus on Los Angeles grounds and propels this book, but we will resort to parallel editing by incorporating strands from outside Los Angeles for the purpose of highlighting connections significant for the bigger picture of film culture. Chicago and New York City loom large, not least due to the attention paid these metropolises in the scholarly discussion of exhibition practices and regulations and because of the extent of the two cities' press scenes.[26] American newspapers voiced both fears and hopes for what moving pictures could achieve within a larger framework of modernity characterized by an upgraded tempo and mobility in all realms of society. Overall, this book reads cinema within modernity's mobilities, changes in pace, and meltdowns of traditions—which were more or less shocking. Simultaneously, modernity incurred rationale management writ large for the organization and distribution of a wide range of experiences, processes, and products. The industrialization of film production, which happened in France first, was thus a prerequisite for the nickelodeon boom. Out of this industrialized structure came the one-reel story film, exemplified by *Escape from Sing Sing* (Vitagraph, 1905), which will be dealt with in the next chapter. Moving pictures and film culture, as negotiated in the press under the auspices of news, found a place within a discursive domain transacting general patterns of sociocultural change wrought by modernity, be it immigration, consumerism, trust capitalism, graft and corruption, or the effervescent patterns of everyday life in the urban centers. The aim of this book is to study aspects of the historical reception of American film culture within the framework of modernity as a series of shifting interfaces with print culture during an intense ten-year period.

Cinema's relation to modernity has been a bone of contention among scholars. Patterns of audience formation and spectatorship, especially in Manhattan, have been analyzed and intensely debated. Transitional cinema has enjoyed currency as an overarching designation for a period marked in its very name by instability and fluidity, spanning the onset of the nickelodeon boom and lasting roughly until the definitive consolidation of Hollywood. The term transitional cinema implies an orderly process of gradual changes far removed from the explosiveness characterizing film exhibition during the period. Even the very the notion of a transitional cinema has been disputed, and among its champions there is no universal agreement as to its delimiting dates. Virtually all aspects of changes during the transitional years have been passionately contested: issues of style, program formats, modes of production and distribution, the burgeoning star system, and the impact of the emerging feature format. And film exhibition shifted countenance at a pace far beyond the spurious stability of data presented in business yearbooks and city directories, which is clearly evidenced in several of the case studies in this volume.

In the protracted debate regarding the so-called modernity thesis, which is central to the conceptualization of transitional cinema, the key issue seems to be primarily the proponents' alleged inability to explain changes within the late 1900s' and early 1910s' film style. If early films, albeit in far from pellucid manners, somehow mirror modes of vision indicative of modernity—as the popular discourse of the time clearly suggests—must one not then posit changes in the overall perceptual fabric of the era in order to account for subsequent changes in film style? Thus, if the cinema of attractions, with its distractions, non-continuities, and in-your-face spectatorial address, were correlated to hard-wired perceptual changes wrought by modernity, why did this film regime gradually peter out or drift towards a transitional cinema of narrative integration charged with strategies aimed at coherence, ask both David Bordwell and Charlie Keil.[27] Even if some form of causality, as Ben Singer claims, appears to be the only viable way of understanding the thesis, the patterns are still complex, multilayered, and virtually impossible to disentangle. Changes in film style are however paradoxical only in a decidedly trenchant formulation of the maze of causal mechanisms impacting norms for film representations. The thesis, qua thesis, is however seemingly in search of proponents; those adopting modernity as a reading frame entertain more modest claims. This is obvious from one of the most productive analyses of stylistic changes—Richard Abel's discussion of film style and narration in French cinema, which proceeds from a regime of attractions to a group of models of transformation and pre-features.[28] And as Singer and many others convincingly argue, attractions were not auctioned away, but rather integrated into story films, and soon enough narratives in different genres came to cultivate the excitements and perceptual assaults bolstering early cinema in line with Raymond Williams' triad. Thus, the gradual emergence of a predominantly story-based cinema offered new genre formats for reframing the perceptual functioning of attractions. Story films were in this respect part of an integrative cinema of absorption, albeit still capable of operating in the residual register of shocks, thrills, and perceptual mayhem. Still, convincingly analyzing patterns of causality in order to reach a more fine-grained understanding of mechanisms of changes bearing not only on film style, but film culture's makeup by and large, requires more research devoted to the cultural conversations from the time.

In Tom Gunning's recent (and perhaps definitive) retort in the debate concerning the modernity thesis he carefully reformulates his arguments to clarify shared basic assumptions concerning the correlations between early cinema and modernity as well as the importance of heightened levels of societal rationality as the flip side to modernity's perceptual volleys. Gunning proceeds from a group of avant-gardists and their succinct response to cinema, formulations clearly in line with the cornucopia of popular material fleshing out cinema from the perspectives of modernity picked up from the press for this inquiry.[29] Given that we cannot form focus groups for discussions with audiences and publics back then, we can only resort to more or less porous records, surviving films, and theoretical models. Still, it seems that multiple correlations between mediated experiences and overall features of modernity, however we elected to spell them out, were posited as part of a widespread and wide-ranging discursive spectrum readily available for making sense of new technologies.

Most of the popular spins were certainly soft, slippery, and more playful than shocking, still part of a rational negotiation of experiential realities contesting and stretching pre-modern worldviews. Obviously, contemporary writers believed that cinema affected a form of overall cultural processing of perceptions, without necessarily incurring a mental re-wiring on the individual level, but rather a cultural accommodation or adaptation—novel metaphors and schemata—based on perceptual experiences inside and outside film shows. How malleable the perceptual apparatus might be and how it absorbs and processes such changes falls outside this inquiry. In line with the pervasive educative metaphors enveloping transitional cinema—schools of crime—one can argue that cinema offered a perceptual education suggesting schemata for reading and acting upon aspects of modern reality and its representations, cinematic or otherwise. Complaints about overblown shot scales, fast-paced editing, and shocking gore are part of this curriculum for producing meaning from "correlated scenes of melodramatic incidents." We will return to this formula repeatedly.

The street and film culture addressed by my text have been wrestled with by an erudite group of film historians since the late 1970s.[30] When access to archival film prints became less stringent in the aftermath of the legendary FIAF conference in Brighton in 1978, a whole generation of scholars turned their attention to early cinema. Subsequently, ambitious film festivals were launched to showcase rarely seen and recently restored silent films. Pordenone in particular emerged as a beacon in the mid-1980s, attracting a coalition of archivists and scholars. The consolidation of the field of the early and transitional cinemas as important areas for research is further evidenced by the formation of an international research organization, Domitor, which is dedicated to pre-classical cinema. Publication of an encyclopedic volume covering all aspects of early cinema and its scholarship provides another indication of an academically mature research area, a project which has come to fruition thanks to Richard Abel's editorial dexterity in mobilizing the field.[31]

Among academic efforts to shed light on the transformations of filmmaking's industrial context and the establishment of normative practices for filmic storytelling, the key study comes from the Madison school, spearheaded by David Bordwell. In an impressively systematic volume Bordwell, Janet Staiger, and Kristin Thompson analyze the formation of classical Hollywood.[32] A later generation trained in Madison and sharing Bordwell's anti-culturalist stance and emphasis on narration and film style further elaborated this approach, most prominently Charlie Keil in his meticulous study of American cinema's transitional era followed up in an influential, co-edited volume featuring leading scholars in the field.[33]

Studies engaged with the period under consideration here range from Eileen Bowser's standard tome to more narrowly tailored inquiries, for example Jane Gaines' and Jacqueline Najuma Stewart's discussions of race cinema and black spectatorship,[34] William Uricchio and Roberta Pearson's discussion of strategies for uplift,[35] Shelley Stamp's and Lauren Rabinovitz's inquiries into women's engagement with cinema.[36] Exhibition practices, not least the ethnic, gender, age, and class profiles of metropolitan nickel audiences, have been a highly contested field of inquiry. In the last few years one can detect an upsurge in the interest in small-town film exhibition inspired by a study by Gregory Waller of the amusement culture in Lexington, Kentucky, and Kathryn Fuller's book on traveling exhibition outside metropolitan areas.[37] Waller's profile of a not-so-small city offers a keen model in terms of scope and methodology for reading local film culture. The studies authored by Waller and Fuller have fueled the recent boom in examinations of local exhibition, not least within the framework of the Homer project, where scholars take on both big cities and rural and small-town exhibition both inside and outside the U.S. Recently, and from a more theoretical perspective, Robert C. Allen has published an excellent reappraisal of the role of empirical studies in regional audience research, which, among other aspects, complicates the analysis of black spectatorship by looking at film exhibition in the South.[38]

Richard Abel is the leading authority on French film culture of the period under consideration. Closer to home, he has focused on how Pathé's dominance on the American market generated a plethora of counter-strategies to thwart the Red Rooster's leading role prior to 1910. This 1999 study has been followed up from a decidedly American perspective in his most recent work, which is also indicative of the press' importance for analysis of film culture.[39] The pioneer in exploiting newspaper material is otherwise Charles Musser; his preeminent analysis of the first decade of American film culture relies heavily on newsprint. My study moves on to the daily press from a later period, a timeframe productively discussed from a regulatory perspective by Lee Grieveson.[40] Miriam Hansen has convincingly studied issues of spectatorship and cinema's role in relation to the public sphere, or as an alternative public sphere. Her analytical perspective has however been partly challenged by Shelley Stamp.[41] The melodramatic mode and its underpinning of several genres has been studied by Ben Singer in relation to issues of modernity in an examination of the serial films, and within the confines of body genres by Linda Williams in a volume addressing the representation of race in key works from the era, from the numerous versions of *Uncle Tom's Cabin* to *The Birth of a Nation*. Griffith's chronicle of the Civil War and its aftermath is a watershed film which has generated an array of important discussions; the broadest analytical scope for the film can be found in Jane Gaines' study of race cinema.[42]

In 1905, where this investigation begins, French films and particularly Pathé dominated the global market, as Richard Abel makes clear in his authoritative work on French cinema. As he shows, the chase films offered a key model of transformation from attractions to rudimentary story films. When the nickel phenomena began littering American inner cities with no-frill exhibition venues for moving pictures from circa 1905, New York City soon had more such houses than any other. In Los Angeles a few nickel houses were established in 1906, a process which will be outlined within the overall volatility of the amusement geography and in dialog with flaneurs, a new generation of man-about-town reporters with the eyes of urban dwellers.

Without devaluing the importance of non-metropolitan film culture, this book rarely looks outside the big cities, albeit Los Angeles at the time can hardly be described as a metropolis on a par with Chicago or New York City. We will however move outside the period of inquiry proper by acknowledging the early steps of a flaneurian discourse in the *Times*, which sets the stage for later flaneur reporters and their discovery of nickel shows. The flaneur genre's incidental city reporting during the nickelodeon period provided a foundation for subsequent writings on film matters and cinema. This flashback takes us to the 1880s, when modernity began to put its stamp on Los Angeles, which is evident from the ambivalent exploits penned by the Saunterer. This puritan flaneuse observed a cityscape in flux. She subscribed to the idea of a manifest mission for the city and underwrote its processes of change while nostalgically bemoaning the loss of old Los Angeles. While the Saunterer was conflicted, the editorial page of the *Times* voiced Los Angeles' purchase on the future vocally and unequivocally. Eventually, moving pictures became important enough to merit the attention of the *Times*' editorialists as a local industry and partner in boosterism capable of effectively and most vividly showing off the city's vocation and splendor. The motion-picture people's "value to the community as national and international advertisers is inestimable," wrote the *Times*. Nonetheless, the editorial considered film actors to be something of a "pest" early in 1911, not least for having invaded the city's sylvan parks. "Griffith Park," the editorialist lamented, "has become a sentiment factory in which sweet nonsense is canned."[43] A few years down the road, mammoth studio complexes obviated the need to occupy city parks, freeing the local papers for sizing up the number of dollars invested in the industry, the magnitude of the local studios' weekly payrolls, the many miles of negative film used—and the number of automobiles owned the by the film companies.[44]

The early 1910s was a period when social scientists and progressive reformers began mapping the amusement and recreational geographies in America. In the spring of 1911 renowned social scientist Dr. Emory S. Bogardus was summoned to Los Angeles at the behest of the University of Southern California's president. The mission: establishing a department of sociology at USC. The result: a highly regarded and in several respects groundbreaking academic institution crafted during Bogardus' long tenure at the helm.[45] According to a small news item from December 1911, Dr. Bogardus, during his first year as a professor at USC, had thirty-five students in a civic-education course prepare two maps of downtown Los Angeles marking all its places of amusement and recreations based

29

on a systematic inventory of 3,600 blocks. The dots on the maps were gathered under different headings, one including commercialized amusements comprising movie and other theaters, hotel cafes selling liquor, and saloons; their aggregate figure amounted to 322. At the students' own initiative, twenty "gambling dens and many vice resorts" provided additional color to the maps. The maps marked 425 places, if commercialized recreations were added to the amusements, without exception located within eighteen so-called social amusement centers.[46]

FIGURE 1: College Theater
(Courtesy of Brent C. Dickerson)

FIGURE 2: Operating Room
at the College Theater,
Motography, Vol. 6, No. 2
(August 1911): 86.

Bogardus slotted the amusements and recreations into three categories, the first being city playgrounds and recreation centers, churches and schools comprised category two, while commercialized amusements made up the final category. According to the *Examiner* article, Bogardus' objective was to establish a basis "from which to work for an idealized, but practical bettering of social conditions, so that more adults may have a chance for the amusements they need, and children for the recreations necessary for their development," a bona fide blueprint for progressive-era activism and civic aspirations. A literal grounding of Bogardus' research and teaching in relation to Los Angeles and its ethnic makeup bolstered a sustained research focus bearing on issues of diversity and Americanization, which laid the foundation for future enterprises devoted to local and regional history at his new alma mater.[47] In addi-

FIGURE 3: Interior of the Hyman, *Moving Picture World*, Vol. 8, No. 16
(22 April 1911): 880–81.

tion to numerous local-recreation surveys, many conducted by Rowland
Haynes, field secretary at the Playground and Recreation Association
of America, more general studies approached amusements and recreations from the imaginary perspective of "our town," for instance Richard Henry Edwards' well-documented *Popular Amusements* from 1915,
which rests on the entire corpus of recreation surveys from the early
1910s.[48] This is a genre that, of late, has attracted ample attention from
film scholars.[49]

In several chapters attention will be given specific time periods, primarily 1909, 1911, and early 1914. During the momentous year of 1911,
when professor Emory S. Bogardus' students mapped the amusement
culture in Los Angeles, the City of Angels almost elected a socialist may-
or in the first municipal election in which women had the right to vote.
According to a common perception, socialist Job Harriman would have
won if it had not been for female voters.[50] Women figure prominently in

this work: The case study devoted to the Mozart Theater in Los Angeles, a venture operated by women only, looks at the trials and tribulations of high-class exhibition practices and how the unforgiving amusement geography counteracted the Mozart's ambitious undertaking.

In the early nickelodeon days and well into the palace era women patrons were sought after by exhibitors to lend legitimacy to the new, unruly, and oftentimes besieged mass medium. Statistical accounts ran rampant when the nickel culture was covered by the press. Apart from trade figures regarding feet of film exported or imported, estimates about the amount of nickelodeons and the tickets sold were marshaled as evidence of the overwhelming magnitude of the seemingly unstoppable phenomenon. The presence of women in the storefront houses was repeatedly emphasized, both in neighborhood houses with friends and family, and in shows on the busy thoroughfares after downtown shopping sprees. Exhibitors repeatedly tried to woo a female clientele to acquire a veneer of family entertainment. When E.J. Tally (not to be confused with his brother Thomas Lincoln Tally) opened Tally's on West Colorado Street in Pasadena, a trade notice informed, "the new place caters especially to ladies and children."[51] When cinema approached the feature age, young women came across as the prototypical fans propelling screen entertainment predicated on recognizable stars. A 1913 novel painted a somewhat different, more escapist picture: "[A] moving picture show," the narrator claims, is "an institution [harboring] many lonely women."[52] James Oppenheim's short story *Saturday Night* (1910), which we will return to, is built around one such woman's far-from-habitual movie experience.

In the early 1910s the prototypical film fan was undoubtedly a young woman. In 1915 Guy Price, in charge of the film column at the *Los Angeles Herald*, even gave the female film fan a name, "Movie Molly," and pronounced her a more ubiquitous species than "stage-door Johnnie" of old. Mollie allegedly lavished her affection by way of sending letters, thus operating in a detached manner matching the indirect presence of screen idols. And letters were sent not only to the idols and their companies, but also the new fan pages in the newspapers.[53] Mae Tinee in the *Chicago Tribune*, more about her later, headed one such inquiry section.

Women were conspicuously active in the regulation of film culture. From the discursive discovery of the nickelodeons to the gradual establishment of standing press genres for more or less daily copy about film matters, women played decisive roles, as progressive activists, police officers, pioneering film journalists, and exhibitors. And early appraisals of spectatorship oftentimes zoomed in on women. Mary Heaton Vorse's account of an immigrant woman's engagement with the screen, perhaps the most frequently discussed and reprinted of all metaspectatorial reports, offers a prototypical case.[54] When men were singled out, they were, just like Vorse's spectatrix, often aliens, and ethnicity explained their culturally deviant mode of spectatorship. When film culture in New York City finally won full acceptance in the press, organized mothers, as we will show, tellingly played a decisive role.

The campaigns mounted to counteract the nickel syndrome displayed a distinct gender code: The activists were predominantly women and the anxieties—alongside fears boys would emulate behaviors in crime films—centered on the audience segment allegedly most vulnerable, young girls. Issues of female sexuality represented a hotly debated concern at a time when the public sphere was undergoing a dramatic series of changes due to far-reaching upheavals in industry, housing, labor, and recreation conditions. Vice, consumerism, and amusements overlapped on the reformers' radar, and young workingwomen represented an unsettled factor in public social life as avid consumers and inveterate patrons of amusements. The discussion of regulatory efforts will lead up to the early career of Alice Stebbins Wells, the first policewoman in the U.S., who was responsible for monitoring girls' amusements habits in Los Angeles. She soon emerged as a national spokesperson for this particular model.

This study, fashioned from a wealth of discourses, constructs a retrospective version of film culture from the nickelodeon breakthrough to early 1915, toying with mechanisms and practices overall intended to address, align, negotiate, promote, and regulate film culture during this particular time frame, though reading them in a trickle-down process due to the local focus. In the absence of real objects to unearth the archeological rag-picking process is decidedly discursive-driven—it is texts and documents we are looking for in order to build and fashion the story of an unfathomable world, as it were.

Discourses crisscross and encircle figures of time and space, in manners grounded in a multiplicity of interests, ideologies, and worldviews. Such matters have to be taken into account and made visible. As Janet Staiger pointedly notices in a recent intervention, time travel is indeed a lost art in the absence of theoretical assumptions and a broader situating of moving pictures as part of media culture (or the even broader framework of amusements and recreations) as well as in relation to social forces and era-specific configurations of class, race, and gender.[55] Methodological and theoretical assumptions offer guideposts for designing research processes, and for slotting the results into productive headings and cases under which to discuss the findings. In this fashion, persistently toying with discourses, historians run the gauntlet of lost times and intangible spaces in order to design blueprints for discussing a once-palpable world, here American film culture in 1905–1915 with an emphasis on Los Angeles and some flashbacks to the time before 1900. At best, the end result mounts a story that in an informed fashion addresses such a stripped-down parallel universe, a story attempting to offer explanatory adequacy vis-à-vis a progressively receding and discursively depleted time slot due to the withering away of documents and films. If this sounds like an exercise in futility, this is because the funneling of historical practices and processes in retrospect never yields an imprint of a global or definitive meaning. In this sense history, as a haptic experience, is as unattainable as lost times and lost films.[56] Needless to say, hands-on presence at the actual scene offers no guarantee for access to a putative capital meaning, since events and processes occupy a multitude of places and migrate between sets of explanatory sequences, which again throw us back on discourses and schemata for making sense from the material at hand, eyewitnessed or not.

A grand motto like *wie es eigentlich gewesen ist* ("how things really were") was long perceived as a—if not *the*—viable ideal to strive toward when engaging with the past. Perennial as Leopold von Ranke's approach to historiography once was, in all modesty we can only juggle discursive traces and devise explanatory sets, but which discourses we deem relevant, pertinent, and worth visiting depends on the questions we pose, the assumptions we make, the scholarly company we keep, and the source routes we are prone to traveling along. There is, indeed, not one and only one yellow brick road. The inevitable result will be a narrative, a story—here about the establishment of film culture in Los Angeles—anchored in discursive fragments of the past, a voice that already formed part of a time warp then, albeit less elusively than now, a century later. This does not mean that anything goes in retrospect; there must be a concerted effort to harmonize mediated and decentered discursive data—often conflicting—under the banner of explanatory adequacy, in this case by resorting to Raymond Williams' concepts, but for a brand of short-term cultural analysis within a capitalist production structure. The key issues are to chart the repositioning of cinema within the overall cultural realm as well as the inner regrouping of cinema as cultural form. These processes are gauged predominantly on the basis of press material. In truly modern fashion the repositioning of film culture took place at lightning speed over the course of a mere decade. Still, the traces left behind can be productively analyzed in terms of the residual, emergent, and dominant, originally mobilized by Williams for understanding more slow-paced changes in overall culture.

Ideally, one would side with Ranke and his desire to have the archives and discourses speak about the past unequivocally and tellingly propel or unravel an account of how things really were by adding up and connecting pertinent slices of everyday life and practices in redux-like fashion. An assemblage of discourses concerning players in the field—local exhibitors, filmmakers, and the people in the industry—the signs of the time, the *Zeitgeist*, and the indexes of the prevalent mass mentality are perhaps what we are after when placing film culture under the slippery standards of modernity. The newspaper beats might be our best shot at sifting out a set of common denominators for the salient terms of the era. Then again, not only newspapermen and female journalists' understanding of the period under consideration is at stake. Determinants at higher levels—be they capitalism and commodity fetishism, or acceleration, constant transformation, incessant change, the melting away of so lidity, Taylorism, Fordism, progressive-era activism, woman suffrage, or racism—provide backdrops against which the agents engaged in their everyday practices during this period of upheavals.

Film culture materialized from a profit-driven business structure that, due to its interfaces with society and alleged impact on its audiences, became regulated and circumscribed in a complex interactive process with local variations. Since hosts of patrons congregated in front of the screens at what were often makeshift venues, and the films were potentially hazardous, which devastating theater fires had proved—from the Parisian Bazaar conflagration in 1898 to the Iroquois Theater fire in Chicago in 1903, reenacted in a Pathé film, to the disasters in Boyerstown, Cannonsburgh, Mexico City, and St. Petersburg, for example—public authorities put strictures on the design of the houses and the booths harboring the projectors, and the flammable nitrate films.

35

Age limits for entering places of amusement became regulated via ordinances after campaigns of different lengths in various cities. In 1909 a body with nationwide impact, the National Board of Film Censorship, was formed in collaboration between civic groups in New York City and the companies licensed to inspect film representations prior to distribution, but not to exercise censorship proper. In the process entrepreneurial brashness turned into circumspect business under the auspices of this self-imposed regulatory body. In addition to this seal of approval many cities and later states adopted regular censorship bodies. A censorship bill on the state level in California was however defeated after the interventions of exhibitors in 1911. The civic vigilance concerning moving pictures was gradually reframed, and in 1915, for example, a leading women's magazine, *Woman's Home Companion*, inaugurated a campaign for better films, adamantly clarifying that the aim was positive promotion of the best films and exhibition practices instead of clamoring for censorship or other regulatory measures.

Teasing out the careers of prominent local exhibitors in order to highlight mechanisms for success and failure entails moving back to the Vitascope years in the late 1890s. Irrespective of efforts and travail, accounts of bygone days of film culture are destined to furnish sketchy and lopsided chronicles in the absence of meaty records and marrowy documents offering information beyond the bare bones. By definition, the transitional years of film culture straddle a protean timeframe. The buoyant corporate structure for dealing with moving images during the loosely defined transitional era was initially frail and limited in scope and size, at least on the exhibition level, but even global production giants like Pathé neglected to preserve records and documents beyond dry financial documentation. Consequently, the exhibition tycoons in Los Angeles, such as Tally or Clune, entertained no ambitions of keeping records for posterity for the benefit of the unlikely future interest group we now at times term new film historians. To those involved in the game at the time, future academic cred or cultural accolades seemed highly improbable propositions. Thus, no diaries or memoirs were penned and no business ledgers or correspondence files were saved or donated to archives. Further adding to a sense of being left between a scholarly rock and studiously hard place, we are even bereft of the film fans' experiences of movie-going from the era, apart from the indirect accounts, which will be liberally quoted for flavor and to flesh out descriptions. Therefore, this is at best a discursive patchwork providing street coordinates for a world merrily running away from itself and in the process erasing its past with a finality that thwarts the historian's efforts at animating this slice of bygone everyday life and its amusement practices. Film culture in this respect is as elusive as most of yesteryear's quotidian practices, perhaps more so than most due to its contested status at the time.

Early film exhibitors negotiated a highly circumscribed field: Cultural proclivities voiced by progressive interest groups in the press called for regulatory measures; audience composition and various subgroups' fickle preferences and capricious patterns of attendance had to be gauged, and the licensed film companies tried to streamline production processes and exchange practices while the independent camp added further volatility to a business which was scrutinized simultaneously under the legal lens of the Sherman Act as well as the copyright laws and framework for free speech. The burgeoning trade press opened up a realm for an ongoing debate across the entire spectrum of the business and the emerging film culture—with shifting emphasis between factions—on conditions both inside the business and its interface with society at large. The latter aspect gave a shared direction for all the trade papers, fan magazines, and house organs.

Researchers seek patterns and adequacy in relation to explanatory models when marshalling data more or less received from previous scholarly efforts. Initially, scholars devoted their energy primarily to the biggest pictures—national cinemas and their relationships over time, and big men, perhaps emulating Carlyle's dictum that "there is properly no history, only biography." At first, inventors and their machines provided focuses for writings on the history of the medium, and later the auteur titans commanded attention even prior to coinage of the term for celluloid geniuses. Piecemeal approaches have of late sparked endeavors geared to more modest surveys, which often entail an expansion of the biographical realm—here, for example, the attention devoted to exhibitors Tally and Clune. In fact, the sheer ubiquity of studies of local exhibition has made them a vigorous subfield within the larger area of research on early and transitional cinemas. As John Collier so poignantly put it: "Everything about the picture show, except the picture, is a local product," besides the fact that in Los Angeles the pictures too were shot around the corner.[57]

At best, a focus on local film exhibition yields an understanding of

film culture with a high level of specificity in understanding how practices trickled down from one rung in the institution, production, to exchanges and then exhibitors and their audiences, and how society overall interacted and engaged with cinema. The repertoire of documents
bearing on historical spectatorship and film exhibition are cumbersome
to glean, but the editorial choices regarding what was newsworthy offer
a discursive domain for film culture's place in society over time in the
dynamic interplay between residual, emergent, and dominant features.
Together, the book's chapters address the tensions and shifting balances
a rapidly changing film culture enjoyed in relation to dominant culture,
with newspapers as the central arena for negotiation.

Metaspectatorship, the double-faced reporting from visits to nickel theaters, focusing both on screen representations and audience members'
bodily and physiognomic engagement with screen matters, will be elaborated upon throughout all chapters. Metaspectatorship represented a
mainstay of virtually all campaigns against moving pictures, combining
saturnine accounts of the events depicted on the screen with more or
less fine-grained audience portraiture. To reverse the perspective, newspapers at times actively promoted film culture, for example by giving
away coupons for shows, thus underwriting the nickel houses' contributions as being wholesome and socially valuable; Hearst's *Los Angeles Examiner* is a case in point here. Such mutually reinforcing schemes culmi-
nated in the printing of synopses of serial films from early 1914 onward
by the *Chicago Tribune* and the Hearst press. This is a process intimately correlated with concerted efforts by the press to attract a potentially
important group of advertising clients, local film exhibitors, at a time
when newsreels offered a novel form of celluloid journalism. The interplay between the press and local film culture provides a sustained focus
of this book, both in terms of mobilizing data in print form lifted from
long-neglected columns as part of an explanatory framework, but perhaps even more so in terms of detecting policy and the shrewd business
tactics involved in picking up advertising clients.

The nickelodeons and the emerging film culture presented themselves
as problematic issues for a progressive sensibility striving to build—in
current vernacular—better or more beautiful cities. In the cleanup process alcohol, vice, graft, and cheap amusements were targeted in a complex partnership with city officials and the press. The commercial authorities capitalized on this sensibility, and soon enough the movie col-

ony managed to blend in. In Los Angeles the city and the movies mutually reinforced each other; spectacular filmic backgrounds for celluloid tales lured Easterners to the Southland, or Greater Los Angeles, while the city helped promote the film colony in all kinds of ways. Socially, the colony sought social "incorporation" in the mid-1910s by organizing clubs and building clubhouses, and the Screen Club, the most prominent organization, hosted parades, pageants, and balls, generally putting movie people on the social map. From the start Selig's Zoo, which opened a few months after Universal in 1915, emerged as a venue for outings and picnics, bringing together a wide variety of communities as a playground and thus forging bonds between generations, ethnicities, denominations, and classes.

Rate wars between the competing railroad companies facilitated the buildup of a tourist industry and turned Los Angeles into a resort in addition to an industrial town and the center of an agricultural region. A labor force comprised predominantly of Mexicans or Asian ethnicities carried the latter aspect. A cultural and ethnic mix filled the historical city center, and the yellow and brown faces that populated the Plaza in the past continued to provide downtown with color when the nickel houses began to crop up.

Offhand racial slurs formed part of the first round of accounts from inside these nickel shows. Amusements were highly segregated in several respects however: Steep price ranges whitewashed certain houses and their types of bills, while the nickel houses at least initially catered to more colorful constituencies apart from attracting younger patrons; the latter aspect was partly remedied when progressive interventions were rewarded with regulatory ordinances. Skin color had profound implications for the overall amusement geography in Los Angeles, which will be obvious from the press material that forms the basis of this book. First, however, we will turn our attention to contemporary amusement theory.

CHAPTER 1

ESCAPE FROM SING SING AND NICKELODEON-ERA AMUSEMENT THEORY

"Moving Pictures—They Are the Historians
of the Ages from This Time On."[1]

TWO FILMS SERVE as symbolic bookends for the decade under investigation and for this book: a lost one-reel title from 1905 discussed below
and a controversial 1915 blockbuster in feature format, which is the
centerpiece of the closing chapter. *Escape from Sing Sing* (Vitagraph, 1905)
was a narrativized spin-off of a popular vaudeville act developed by a
magician and was produced at a studio run by a team comprised of a former magician and a sketch artist. *The Clansman*, later *The Birth of Nation*
(Epoch, 1915), was based on Thomas F. Dixon's highly controversial
novel and stage play.[2] The latter film's director, D.W. Griffith, was
willing to shoulder personal responsibility for virtually all storytelling
devices added to the cinematic vocabulary in the period between the
two films. His long tenure at Biograph had won him no official credit, so
he placed ads in trade press to set the record straight concerning his own
accomplishments.[3] In this context, the two films function as pretexts for
engaging with some of the discourses they inspired. As will be evident,
Escape from Sing Sing and other early story films ushered in winning formulas with cultural reach far beyond the nickel houses.

Apart from embodying a trajectory of film production from Manhattan
to Los Angeles, from outdoor shooting and makeshift "studios" to proper ones sealed off from the city's fabric, contemporary observers heralded
these bookend films as novelties indicative of new eras in the develop-

ment of the medium—whether this is accurate or not is of course beside the point. From a novelty perspective, *Escape from Sing Sing* represents a film type that took the medium to an arena of instant emergence, virtually unrivaled in the history of culture—the nickelodeons. In a similar fashion—symbolically but also in practice—*The Birth of a Nation* undisputedly placed domestic feature production within the realm of dominant culture. It opened and played for months in a sumptuous theater with few counterparts in the country: Clune's Auditorium in Los Angeles.

By 1905, to be sure, American cinema had been telling stories for several years, and the press had reported on film shootings prior to Theodore Waters' piece chronicling the production of *Escape from Sing Sing*.[4] There was already, for example, a condensed 1900 version called *Escape from Sing Sing*, produced by American Mutoscope & Biograph. Similarly, domestic feature films had enjoyed considerable success before Griffith's divisive Civil War epic, prominent titles including *The Spoilers* (Selig, 1914), *The Virginian* (Lasky, 1914), and Griffith's own *The Escape* (Majestic, 1914).

The reallocation of the industry to the West Coast can be read as an escape from a hotbed of modernity, New York City and its environs, to an Eden-like pastoral milieu associated with the aftermath of the pioneering spirit of the rugged West. As more and more film companies discovered, natural splendor and beauty around Los Angeles were readily at hand for framing. Soon enough, the era of movie stars wreaked havoc in the otherwise dull social life in the City of Angels. In the process, the medium and the city, in a fascinating series of transformations, eventually merged into Hollywood—representing a mindset in lieu of a place discursively set off against the backdrop of the mental landscape of the Midwest symbolically represented by Iowa.

Travelers arriving in Los Angeles often compared certain squalid downtown arteries to New York City's Bowery, while others only noted the resort culture in the beach communities. The film community scattered around Los Angeles turned into Hollywood more or less when we will sign off, early 1915. At the time D.W. Griffith was one of many film pioneers who had moved over from the East Coast—in his case from Biograph's studio in Manhattan to one on Sunset Boulevard. Griffith's inflammatory magnum opus, *The Clansman/The Birth of a Nation*, epitomizes a hardcore version of reading history in terms of race. As Michael Rogin aptly puts it apropos Griffith's film, "American movies were born, then, in a racist epic."[5] The production of longer, multi-reel subjects had been pioneered several years earlier in Europe, foremost in Italy and Denmark. In the U.S., the domestic feature production launched by Famous Players, Lasky, Ince, Warner Features, and later Triangle materialized in the wake of the success of Italian features not distributed by the general release organizations and exhibited at upscale venues otherwise offering theatrical attractions proper.[6] We will, however, suspend discussion of *The Birth of a Nation* until the last chapter.

In 1905 the alliance between cinema and modernity was easier to decipher from Manhattan's skyline than from downtown Los Angeles. In order to explain a putatively new phenomenon, a renowned journalist specializing in popular science, Theodore Waters, devoted a long essay to the shooting of *Escape from Sing Sing*.[7] Waters' how-it's-done approach—a trademark of his journalism—later turned into a staple of the discourse concerning trick films and their fantastic effects.[8] Waters' text was however not published in a newspaper, but in one of Hearst's flagship magazines, the January 1906 issue of *Cosmopolitan*.[9] Waters' intention, after acting in the film for hands-on insights—a practice later emulated by the first generation of film critics, which we will return to—was to explain, for his middle-class magazine readership, the nuts and bolts of the production of a new form of film commodity.

In his opinion, this type of film marked a new phase for the medium and for audiences allegedly fed up with the attractions of old. "The public taste in moving pictures (which has been sated with scenes of foreign travel)," he writes, "now demands 'stories,' i.e., correlated scenes of melodramatic incidents, comic or tragic," vehicles that soon came to dominate the nickelodeon bills. The film he reported on was later singled out among a group of sensational titles in the much-discussed crusade against the movies in Chicago in 1907, which attests to its longevity on the market.

Waters' text evidences the medium's leverage for attracting a gawking mass audience—an "army"—for the shooting, which took place on the roof of a high-rise structure in New York City's business district, on a building "dwarfed" by surrounding skyscrapers. During the shooting, "an army of typewriters and office clerks [...] had been enjoying the nooning with a view of the hair-raising melodrama." The audience identified by Waters mirrors the patronage for movies later posited by theorists like Siegfried Kracauer, shop girls and white-collar workers. Here

43

cinema, even for films in the making, comes across as an exciting metropolitan interlude, witnessed free of charge as an urban attraction adding yet another thread to the perceptual fabric of the teeming metropolis. Consequently and irrespective of the film's gruesome content—Waters was one of the gunned-down convicts—he connects the spectacle of shooting to romance and contrasts the marvels of making film with the disenchanting street life below. Meanwhile, "in the street below," and thus as part of the overall urban montage, "the tide of prosaic business ebbed and flowed, all unconscious of the proximity of romance. Only those fortunate souls with box seats in the proscenium of the skyscrapers were aware of the almost daily occurrence of sights and sounds which the theater-going public for the most part imagines takes place far from the maddening crowd." This haphazardly constituted audience's interest in the production of movies found its industrial emulation when Universal opened its studio in 1915 in a city of its own outside Los Angeles. According to Waters' informant, filmmakers resorted to shrewd tactics to be able to operate on city streets and had to "bribe, or jolly, or even fool the crowd out of range." Still, at times people interfered, believing "we were perpetrating a crime." Shooting on the streets added yet another layer of puzzling enigmas for those not up to speed concerning film culture as a plausible reading frame for street occurrences that were slightly off key.

Misrecognition and unscripted, uncalled-for acting soon turned into a fixture in literary accounts of film shooting as well as in metafilms. Studio head William N. Selig was not only wounded by a Japanese gardener who simultaneously killed director Francis Boogs at the Edendale studio in 1911, as early as 1904 a tourist near Colorado Springs shot Selig in the arm when he was acting out a stagecoach robbery: Somebody misreading the scene interfered in the form of real bullets, wounding Mr. Selig. A 1906 headline in the *New York World* addressed a puzzling situation in a more reflective mode, asking, "Was It Revenge or a Moving Picture?"[10] What, then, had happened? The byline explains: "Woman Sees Clerically-Clad Man Dragged from Flatbush Church and Mauled." At that time, in contrast to 1904, when outdoor shooting still was a rarity to come across, a plausible hypothesis for the unlikely, or bizarre or enigmatic, in 1906 was a film shoot, which attests to an emerging schematic mindset related to film culture at the onset of the nickelodeon boom and the swift emergence of story films.

By adding gore as a residual element of attraction to the resolution of *Escape from Sing Sing*, Vitagraph offered a rigorous variation on the hare-brained chase theme, pronounced the "latest feature of the moving picture game." Chase films, predominantly in a comedic mode, had however been in vogue for at least a year; a key film in this "genre" is the much-copied newspaper film *Personal* from mid-1904 (American Mutoscope and Biograph, Co.), in which women chase a man who has advertised for a wife. His ad generates a lively response far beyond his expectations.

The grim film formula delineated by Waters, with gunplay aplenty during a protracted chase, several dead wardens, two dead convicts, and the third convict's child killed in the crossfire, garnered immediate cultural purchase and was thus a readily available format for outlining tragic events, including outside cinema. Waters discussed the films in relation to vaudeville exhibition, but it was the success of the nickel shows in 1906 and afterward that turned cinematic storytelling into a cultural model with widespread cachet.

In that spirit, "genre events" in scenario form illustrate a pervasive register for mobilizing film form for the presentation of melodramatic events. The *Chicago Daily News*, for example, elected to headline and outline a real-enough tragedy as a "series of moving pictures," seven in all in the synopsis. Young Mrs. Ida Applegate's suicide was thus framed as "a kinetoscopic tragedy." Readers were told that "the suicide of a 19-year-old mother" was "surrounded by strange scenes of horror, pathos and excitement which followed each other in rapidity of succession equaled only by the whirling film." The reporter then transfers the "sad details" to "the world of flashing canvas," concluding, "it resembles a series of motion pictures which occurred in rapid order." The seven pictures, in a circular composition, moved between several spaces, and apart from the suicide featured an explosion scene, when a policeman "struck a match" in a gas-filled apartment. Film form was apparently perceived as an appropriate format for giving vivid detail to an everyday tragedy in all its grim, Grand Guignol-like (un)reality. Moreover, the opportunity for editing pointedly contracts the various threads of the events inside and outside the apartment and compresses the time frame for the tragedy's unfolding. Hence, the triumphant cinema of "correlated scenes of melodramatic incidents" provided a viable cultural schema to aid readers in making sense of the gruesome realities of everyday life.

45

A kinetoscopic tragedy was enacted in Chicago to-day—the suicide of a 19-year-old mother being surrounded by strange scenes of horror, pathos and excitement which followed each other in rapidity of succession equaled only by the whirling film. The relation of the sad details which frame the death . of the young mother as probably enacted could be transferred to the world of flashing canvas. It resembles a series of motion pictures which occurred in a rapid order.

First Picture.

Mrs. Ida Applegate frantically kisses her baby in a room at her home, 6610 Evans avenue. With tears streaming from her eyes she places the child on a couch and with one heartrending backward look. passes out of the door. The door is shut tight and locked.

Second Picture.

It is the bedroom of Mrs. Applegate. The woman enters with her face buried in her arms. She falls at her bedside and raises her eyes. Then she rises to her feet. She looks about her with clinched fists and frightened countenance. Then with a lurch she springs on a chair. Both hands grasp the curving arms of the chandelier. With a tremendous jerk she pulls the entire brass affair from the ceiling. She falls to the carpet amid a shower of loose plaster. The air grows dim . and after a few feeble tremors her body becomes still.

Third Picture.

It is the hall outside Mrs. Applegate's room. Several persons are sniffing the air and pounding at the door. One peeks through the keyhole and gazes in horror-stricken fascination. A policeman enters He pushes the people aside and applies his shoulder to the door. Other officers join him and the door falls inward. The first policeman, who is Officer Bryan O'Connell of the Grand Crossing station, enters.

Fourth Picture.

It is Mrs. Applegate's apartment once more. Through the haze the star and buttons of O'Connell's uniform can dimly discerned. He bends over a dark object Then a tiny spark tells that he has struck a match. A blinding flare fills the apartment. The gas has exploded and O'Connell is carried out. Some bend over the blackened body of the mother.

Fifth Picture.

It is the exterior of the Applegate home A group is seen coming down the steps bearing the limp form of O'Connell. A physician hurries up, bearing a black satchel. He applies a restorative to O'Connell and nods assurance that he is not dangerously hurt. Then he leaps up the steps.

Sixth Picture.

Again the bedroom of Mrs. Applegate. The doctor enters and the people kneeling about the body of the woman make way for him. He is about to bend over, when he turns his head and places his hand to his ear. Apparently he had heard a strange sound. He rushes from the room by another door from that which he had entered.

Seventh Picture.

It is the scene of the first picture In the corner, on the couch, a little white bundle is seen to move. The physician enters and takes the bundle up in his arms. It is the infant, whom the mother had taken precautions to preserve before she took her own life.

So ; [illegible] tragedy.

FIGURE 4: *Chicago Daily News*, 3 May 1907, 1.

Social theorist Simon N. Patten addressed the enormous drawing power of films like *Escape from Sing Sing* and nickelodeon culture in general in a booklet from 1909. Reading it alongside his 1905 Kennedy lectures on economic theory (published in 1907) sheds light on how fundamentally the nickel shows had changed the cityscape and the perception of its amusement geography. Regeneration and education of the eye occupied a privileged place in Patten's economic analysis of the hard conditions experienced by toilers. His writing is by far the most articulate and theoretically circumspect nickelodeon-era attempt at analyzing the mechanisms underlying the emergence of cinema as a widely embraced cultural form.

A progressive economist educated at Northwestern University and in Halle, Germany, Patten integrated amusements as key realms in his analysis of a shift away from what he called "pain to pleasure economy." His texts from 1905 and 1909 respectively highlight a crucial shift in that in 1909 he can elaborate on a popular cultural form having turned into a form of folk culture, albeit for the people rather than by the people, since it was industrially produced and distributed. The nickel shows, glaring and vulgar perhaps, have emerged, he maintained, as an affordable pleasure outlet where dominant cultural institutions are out of touch with the people. In Patten's analysis the ample natural resources available for distribution in the 20th century sufficed in theory for providing a good life for everyone if exploitation could be eliminated or at least minimized. Patten's most influential outline of his theory was delivered as the Kennedy Lectures in 1905 and published as *The New Basis of Civilization* in 1907.[11] For Patten, the ancient pain economies grappled with deficit and insufficient resources, while contemporary society could and should "utilize the surplus for common good, not to undermine energy and productive ability or to create parasitic classes, but to distribute the surplus in ways that will promote general welfare and secure better preparation for the future" (9). When taking Karl Marx to task, Patten summoned "the misery-wrung toiler of [Jean François] Millet's picture and [Edwin] Markham's poem ["The Man With the Hoe"]" (70). Patten disputed that Millet's toiler would be resurrected instantaneously if the pressure of the economic system were lifted from his back. Millet's emblematic painting was invoked as a model for victimization in Griffith's *A Corner in Wheat* (Biograph, 1909).

Patten, instead of Marx's quick fix as it were, argued for a much slower shift, as in geology, and that more complex casual patterns rooted in the longevity of social determinants were at play. "Men are moulded into their classes by the pressure of social things accumulating generation after generation, which finally sums themselves into an acquired heredity binding men firmly to their places." Moreover, "[t]he social is at once a record and a continuation of the methods that were necessary in vanished economic environments, telling us how and when forces were in action, and its dominance indicates that static are stronger than dynamic conditions" (71). Patten's recipe for a gradual change of the economic and political realm mobilizes amusements as an arena for alleviating pent-up energies without alternative outlets for those hard pressed by industrial conditions in the cities. Cut off from nature, the worker's "organism painfully seeks adjustments" (121).

Patten's "geological" perspective zooms in on discomforts unknown to the hunter of old, stirred by thrills when interacting with an environment, however harsh. For the industrial-age baker or tailor, in contrast, the unnatural work environment "checks rather than arouses their bodily and mental activities" (121). Overall, the uprooted city toiler's response is still rooted in "race memories," though toned and diminished by "the protesting organism [...] forced to adapt itself to bad air, poor light, fixed position, and routine occupation" (122). The toiler thus turns to drinking, smoking, and vices to "sate appetite and deaden acute pain" (123). Thus, the $64,000 question: "How shall activity be made pleasurable again, and how shall society utilize the workingman's latent vitality in order to increase his industrial efficiency and give to him the rewards of energies, now ineffective, within his body and mind?" (123). Unchallenged by mechanized work, it is the communal in its broad sense that ought to arouse the toiler as a path to the more advanced stages of abstract regeneration. Intense release of tensions and emotions triggered by amusements and recreations—be they Coney Island, department stores, or settlement houses—are arenas for negotiating and alleviating such straits. Patten describes the process as an "education of the eye," since the hand only is engaged at the workplace and in purposeless activity (125). Patten's program was intended to eventually integrate toilers into urban civilization and produce a spirit of association and a pride in "coöperative communal institutions" (126). A tripartite division between work, pleasurable leisure, and sleep in eight-hour blocks should mark each day as being complete, which will provide incentive for sustained efforts to cash in on the next day's pleasures.[12]

From the vantage point of 1905, Patten singles out melodrama as the prime agent and emotional corrective for assimilating a heterogeneous urban population cut off from its traditions and regenerating roots. Even "[t]he cheap magician of a vaudeville can excite the primitive curiosity of the mass and his claptrap thrill it into thought" (133). Patten was of course destined to discover the nickelodeons and the film melo-

48

drama and integrate them into the theoretical framework outlined in his lecture series.

In his 1909 pamphlet *Product and Climax*, the subject of less discussion than his classic *The New Basis of Civilization*, the street and its two sidewalks represent a cultural spectrum linked to the ills of wage labor and the promises of consumerism. One sidewalk in his symbolic city, he muses when walking along the street, is brightly lit, lively, and replete with popular amusements and nickelodeons, a veritable smorgasbord of affordable pleasure outlets, while the other side stays gloomily dark in the evenings and on weekends when its venerable institutions, schools, libraries, churches, museums, etc., are closed. Valorizing opportunities for release from the dreary side of existence after long hours of dull work, Patten celebrates what the light side of the street has to offer the toilers, and hails the nickelodeons as beneficial institutions in the same price bracket as the saloons, but without the latter's costly and anticlimactic aftereffects. The imposing and uninviting institutions on the dark side leave the toilers to fend for themselves after hours, and when in full swing preach the gospel of restraint rather than their sought-after release, the latter a synonym for the climactic and pleasurable in Patten's vocabulary. However, as a policeman informs the stroller, the school is worth visiting "if only for the sake of the public-spirited committee of leading ladies who opened it daily from two to five."[13] Patten's analysis distances itself from the brunt of the progressive discourse which, in a sense, wanted to move the people across the street, from the light and pleasurable amusements to the dark side and its civilizing institutions, under the banner of education after hours and dampening the bright side's glare. Apart from opening schools for educational play, the progressives, as we will show, desired to organize playgrounds and recreation centers combining physical activities with educational amusements.

Taking in soda fountains and ice-cream parlors in passing along the street, Patten arrests his glance and tellingly sets up the nickelodeon and its enveloping sounds in cleverly pointed contrast to the "barren school yard" across the street.

Opposite the barren school yard was the arcade entrance to the Nickelodeon, finished in white stucco, with the ticket seller throned in a chariot drawn by an elephant trimmed with red, white, and blue lights. A phonograph was going over and over its lingo, and a few picture machines were free to the absorbed crowd which circulated through the arcade as through the street. Here were groups of working girls—now happy 'summer girls'—because they had left the grime, ugliness and dejection of their factories behind them, and were freshened and revived by doing what they like to do. There were nothing listless, nothing perfunctory here (18–19).

For Patten, schools and churches stand as repressive institutions unable to furnish the vitalizing antidote for those subjected to the "merciless grinding out of product." The dark side of the street is thus read as an adjunct to the factories, given the institutions' inability to offer "the climaxes of satisfaction that renews men and makes them throng the bright side" (29). Moral agencies, philanthropies, and schools serve only negatively as "devices for protection," Patten claims. Furthermore, they are not "expressions of happiness, security and pleasure in life. At present, they actively deprecate the development of men through pleasure as the Church does, or they ignore it, depending upon discipline and penalty as does the school" (28). Patten was by no means adverse to religion, education, and culture. His point was that the set of fixed core values these institutions embodied and preached was more or less unattainable for the most needy, since "civilization is failing through its success, for it has created a class too low to be moved by it" (66–67). According to Patten, strenuous physical activity, strong willpower, and vivid intensity in life in combination constitute climax, which, in turn, "form a natural ladder" leading "to the plane where religion and culture acts." The agent for elevation in life spells the "increase of its climaxes" (61). However, for the over-worked populace, religion and morality "do not act," and the only available agents for climax are sports and amusements. In his analysis "sport is the beginning of inspiration, amusements is the lower round of regeneration," both activities occupying a place lower on the ladder than the desired elevated level of complete development, and hence functioning as progressive forces (67). Passionate citizenship resides at "the complex end of a series of preparatory climaxes," and in this respect the commercialized streets and especially nickel culture play an important role as a stepping stone. Patten dismisses the complaints concerning the cheap shows; to his mind, their alleged suggestiveness can only, albeit rarely, be found in the films' intertitles. More importantly, he reflects in an aside on spectatorship, "the watcher thinks with purpose, following a story which either has a plot or else holds his attention by showing novel scenes of travel among alien people" (46).

Patten's essay was inspired by his experience hiking in the summer. Such outings and regeneration in the company of others offer avenues to real democracy, he claims. For the toilers, summer camps, Sunday picnics, and park dances stimulate variegated impressions and an increasing curve of climaxes, forging a link to the underlying ideology of the playground movement. Apart from discounting moralizing and disciplinarian tendencies, Patten shares key values with the progressives. He is however openly critical of the underlying momentum of capitalism and its merciless engineering of exploitation of the many for the benefit of the few in the brutal era of trusts, child labor, and scientific management—the pain economy in his vocabulary. The salient factor in the equation, distancing Patten from the garden-variety brand of progressivism, is his cheerful celebration of street excitements and the nickel culture by and large, not as ends in themselves but as rungs on the ladder to higher realms of culture. In Patten's analysis it takes truly drastic measures to usher in real change for the working class, foremost workdays with at least a minimum of built-in climaxes for the toilers. Patten's stances, underpinned by his economic theories of consumption and abundance, drew retorts from several prominent social workers. The bone of contention was primarily the value of a philanthropic approach to social work and whether social problems like unemployment resulted from a lack of moral fiber or had its predominant causes in an environment that could be bettered by government action.[14]

Patten's amusement theory was penned at a time after the most intense phase of anti-nickel agitation had petered out. The broad scope of his analysis offered a unique contribution to the debate concerning progressive-era amusements. More than anybody else, Patten provided a socioeconomic context for understanding the magnetic pull nickel culture exercised on both toilers and others. Patten's discovery of nickel culture was no accident. His replication of "sauntering" journalists' discoveries of nickel shows a few years earlier was part of a program of academic intervention and a conviction that economists had to leave the libraries for the streets to "engage with current economic events." Thus, "our real affinity," Patten claimed in a 1909 lecture for his peers, is with "the journalist, the magazine writer, and the dramatist." In order to be of relevance, "we need fresh observations, not fine arguments; we need clear contrast, not the accumulation, arrangement, and restatement of antiquated obsolete data." His own *Product and Climax*, published a couple of months later, vividly showed that "economist[s] should work in the open and get their inspiration from the struggle and evolution which passing events reveal; for where change is there should also the economist be." His defense of economy as an interventionist, street-smart discipline and an agent for change summarizes the basic tenor of progressive-era policies, which underpinned much of the writing we will engage with in coming chapters. A whole generation of social reformers would certainly underwrite his conclusion: "What we do for college our allies can do for the nation. First the economist, then the journalist, and finally the legislator; this is the order of progress and key to success."[15]

In an article in *Survey* Lewis E. Palmer briefly commented on Patten's amusement analysis as an attempt at negotiating a brand of amusement with a global following, film culture. The point of departure for Lewis' text is the unprecedented success of the medium, not only on brightly lit streets in the U.S. Films like *Escape from Sing Sing* has shaped a brand of global spectatorship, as it were, a point invoked by a montage of far-flung vistas featuring "exiled lepers of Molokai" on remote islands in the Pacific Ocean symbolically connected in celluloid appreciation with "excited Eskimos" applauding cowboy heroics. Lewis tries to strike a balance between Patten's celebration of street excitements and the criticism leveled at film culture by members of the clergy and social workers as extremes, with the middle-ground efforts to transform the medium evidenced by the industry's support of the National Board of Film Censors. Lewis underwrites Patten's position that physical sports offer the ideal corrective for the indoor worker, and he simultaneously endorses the playground movement's analysis that the number of playgrounds and parks is insufficient; Lewis, too, therefore considers the commercialized street offerings a "temporary substitute." For the future, he hopes the cities will provide "wholesome outdoor amusement and [that] the moving picture show will become in reality the 'people's theater.' "[16] Patten's dictum, formulated in numerous texts, resonated in the Chicago reform efforts in 1907. One of the leading reform figures noted apropos the Hull House initiative to open a counter-nickelodeon that "[i]t is gratifying to know of these efforts along the lines of Dr. Patten's suggestion, that to release virtues is better than to suppress vices."[17]

Simon N. Patten developed his theory in a trajectory connecting rural recreation to the small town, while Lewis emphasized the medium's global penetration. In D.W. Griffith's *A Corner in Wheat* the diegetic geography is highly complex and the film's key achievement is to devise a method for constructing an abstract whole, an economy, from spatially separated strands that in turn bear on the global market. This economy features small-time farmers, ruthless middlemen, and customers buying bread, and the key aspect is the abstract marketplace for trading in commodity futures, localized in Chicago.[18]

The nickel shows and their offerings, from *Escape to Sing Sing*, with its straightforward chase geography, to *A Corner in Wheat*, with its editorial dexterity in abstracting space, provided only an intermediary type of entertainment for Patten's toilers. Patten's theory addressed the institution in general and not the films. In a book also published in 1909 Rollin Lynde Hartt's discussion of leisure activities focused more on the films and their viewing context and spectatorship. In *The People at Play* Hartt dwells on contemporary film culture in a chapter titled "The World in Motion." His approach to cinema was comparative, and his observations are ventured against the backdrop of dominant culture and thus address a medium involved in cultural transactions. Hartt's text exemplifies a form of burgeoning criticism, but still without analytical tools outside the field of dominant culture. Consequently, he weighs in on cinema in relation to theater and its flesh-and-blood interface to audiences, besides invoking painting and literature. From this intermedia perspective he offers numerous perceptive insights. The film medium, he claims, has left behind practices akin to impressionist painters' proclivities and the entire realm of works he acerbically labeled "Nobody in Particular Doing Nothing." In lieu of such rambling practices, filmmakers have turned literary and "dared to return to the philosophy of the old masters, all of whom risked 'storytelling pictures.' " Moreover, this new type of film has "carried out the philosophy to its logical conclusion. Instead of catching a mere instantaneous scene in the story, it caught the story entire. It became dramatic, not figuratively, as the painters had done, but literally." In a first round, Hartt tells us, the films have "summoned the Comic Muse" and hailed "the villains and angelic heroines of melodrama" (126). Hartt here echoes the "correlated scenes of melodramatic incidents" Theodore Waters noted apropos *Escape from Sing Sing*. *A Corner in Wheat*, on the other hand, is dramatic in a figurative, allegorical fashion. From the perspective of cinema in 1909, *A Corner in Wheat* comes across as a quintessential effort by an unafraid director risking a storytelling picture with grand scope, irrespective of its small, one-reel format, by resorting to abstraction and a narrator system with an implied voice beyond character agency.

When reflecting on the future of cinema, and, in a sense, features *avant la lettre*, Hartt factors in the "inevitable unresponsiveness of muslin and film"—the longstanding debate concerning the nature of film representations, given that the material is mediated via machines and thrown onto a screen. For many, the dependence on an apparatus obviated creative treatment and positioned the medium outside the sphere of art proper. In addition, the inevitable time shifting brought about by the technology due to the lag between the shooting and projecting of films introduces a set of rifts bearing on acting in the cinema, resulting in a double homelessness for the actors. During the recording the performance takes place for the camera only, and when audiences eventually experience the acting, the actors are divested from their own bodies and no longer there. Hence, at both junctures, actors are unable to physically connect or directly engage with audiences. The film actor is doomed to execute his or her art severed from the audience. This lack of vitalizing contact has often been perceived as a drawback for all parties concerned: The actor is not animated by connecting sparks from the audience, while audiences are deprived of the physical illusion involving actor and character and have to be content with images often described as shadows and ghosts, projected substitutes for flesh-and-blood characters. These vicissitudes of screen acting were later probed most poignantly in Luigi Pirandello's remarkable novel *Si gira*.[19]

So no salvo of applause during a first entrance on screen, writes Hartt, and no calls for encores, and no speeches delivered by the "wigless idols" after the show—that is out of character. Theatrical audiences' power to cancel the illusion by "ripping asunder the continuity of an artistic creation" is not an option in film theaters, even if clueless audience members at times try to physically engage with the story world thrown on the unresponsive muslin. Meanwhile, theater audiences can quash the rationality of the performance by embarking on accepted audience participation. "As a matter of pure aesthetics, the biograph's adorers have the better of us here, and that is why they may one day weary of the biograph" (146–147).

The actors and the fictional world's immunity during recording and projection represented a different type of concern in 1909 prior to the advent of credit sequences and star billing a few years later. When films aspired to an artistic form by way of the feature format, famous players, and literary material with more or less canonical pedigree, the medium developed scores of strategies for navigating the hypothetical drawbacks and differences identified by Hartt. To be sure, the wigless idols gave no speeches, but at times they stepped out from the story and engaged the audience by addressing the camera, especially in the first seasons of feature production.

The education of the eye, mentioned in passing by Patten, bolster the changes in cinematic storytelling discussed by Hartt. The year 1909 was a critical juncture, inspiring a diverse range of writers to negotiate cinema in relation to metropolitan visuality. Perceptual vicissitudes were addressed head-on in a 1909 editorial published in the *New York Evening Post*. It outlined the predicaments of modern sightseeing as a form of perceptual frenzy, a gulping down of sights, indicative of the age.[20] This facetious attempt to appraise a readily identifiable condition of modernity fuels the *Evening Post*'s editorial intervention in its focus on sightseeing, but without making the obvious connection to cinema or the yellow press' shock aesthetics. For the touristic gaze, the editorial in the *Evening Post* informs us, one impression after the other is briskly wiped from the retina to be replaced by yet another sight, be it a cathedral, engineering feat, or a cascade rushing by. In the process the mind is bracketed, as it were, and "less and less an adjunct of the vision." Mindful contemplation vanishes from the ocular scene and gives way to "an almost feverish craving after the sight for the sight's sake." This new mode, readers were told, "induces the rather doubtful advantage of speed." Henry M. Hyde, in an 1910 article entitled "Most Men Are Blind," comes up with the critical metaphor that hovered over the editorial on sightseeing without emerging. Hyde writes:

> Under modern conditions, most of us look at so many things in the course of the day that we have no time to really see anything. Rushing about in automobiles, street cars, elevated trains we turn the whole world into a moving picture show. We come home at night with a lot of blurred impressions and a pair of very tired optic nerves.[21]

According to Hyde's appraisal, the rush of urban impressions overwhelms the perceptual apparatus. Denied time for contemplation, impressions blur and strain our optic nerves. We look at many things but do not see. The look is here associated with quick glances on the fly, while seeing represents a contemplative mode of vision affording the mind time enough to absorb the impressions. The look is the result of modes of vision associated with urban transportation, an analysis closely aligned with Schivelbusch's account of railway journeys. For Hyde, panoramic vision from inside vehicles transformed the world to a moving-picture show. Such shows were predicated on variety across multiple genres, while the individual films sported more and more shots per reel. As evidenced by the trade-paper discourse, critics voiced misgivings about an overly brisk pace of editing in the early 1910s. Dr. Stockton's famous empirical survey of the number of shots per reel in *The Moving Picture World*—he covered seventeen films—fuelled one of the first debates on the reception of film style. Given this cinematic velocity, Epes Winthrop Sargent concludes apropos Stockton's material: "Acting is not possible. Clarity of story is not possible. Unfolding of plot is not possible."[22]

Hyde's succinct reflection programmatically highlights a basic tenet of the discourse we will engage with throughout this study. Fittingly, his adage is taken from a newspaper column. In the next chapter we will show how cinema emerged as a cultural form and reading frame. For this purpose, we will analyze the press' engagement with moving-picture culture from the debut of the Vitascope in 1896 to Griffith's monumental screen epics of the mid-1910s.

CHAPTER 2

NEWSPRINT AND NITRATE, COLUMNS AND CRITICS

"He who is without a newspaper
is cut off from his species."[1]

NEWS ORGANIZATIONS REGARD themselves as eyewitnesses, nonpartisan, unbiased chroniclers positioned virtually on the cusp of unfolding events. During the late 19th and early 20th centuries this perception gradually gained currency as newspapers came to be regarded as being in a pact with modernity at large as brisk disseminators of information collected from an ever-broader field and mediated to the news desks with unprecedented dispatch. In this regard, newspapers turned into virtually panoptic machines capable of seeing everything.

On January 10, 1915, the *Los Angeles Times* published a Sunday issue consisting of 466 columns of advertising and 389 of text, which shows the paramount importance of the former for a mass-market-driven consumer society.[2] As the paper explained, looking back at the challenge of publishing the world's most extensive newspaper that particular day, distance was annihilated for the reader, as all four corners of the world were pulled together and served on the breakfast tray. The press, represented here by the *Los Angeles Times*, thus harbored global ambitions by delivering news with a cosmopolitan touch for its local readership.

This appreciation of the press' resourcefulness in scooping up information and its prowess in serving the world on a daily basis as news was recurrently debated and self-consciously reflected upon in the columns. In numerous prophecies of the future state of affairs—often looking a century ahead—journalists took time to speculate on postmodern conditions for reading in general. In 1909, a crucial year as previously noted, an unsigned piece in the *Los Angeles Times* proclaimed that 2009 would be a "tabloid era," anticipating that a novel with more than 300 words would stand little chance of finding a readership. Ideally, one should be able to read a novel in its entirety during an airship flight from Los Angeles to San Francisco. Tom Wolfe, John Irving, and others have not taken notice, or rather, contemporary air transportation is much slower than anticipated in 1909 and novels are still of appropriate length for air travel, albeit intercontinental rather than local. It was further self-consciously prophesied that the historians of 2009 would bypass the writings of the historians of 1909. The prime source for anthropological insights regarding everyday life in 1909 will instead be the press—given archival efforts for preserving newsprint.[3] In 1909 *Atlantic Monthly* expressed a similar conviction in a piece on newspapers as historical sources penned by John Ford Rhodes, an article that stirred up editorial comments in numerous newspapers.[4] W. Stephen Bush, in *Moving Picture World*, directed future historians to celluloid sources instead, thus claiming reel renderings more real and revealing than material remnants: "If the future historian, whose duty it shall be to describe the manners, customs and ways of living of the plain American people, has about six well-selected Selig films, his task will be an easy one. No need of excavating the suburbs of Chicago or digging into the ruins of Indianapolis or Omaha or Des Moines."[5] Here, material history is abandoned for an understanding of the past and its everyday life in anthropological terms on the basis of information fixed on celluloid. In this spirit, the Chicago Historical Society put a film shot at the Chicago & Northwestern station by Essanay in a glass jar together with full documentation concerning the provenance; the time capsule was to be opened in 1936. In an optimistic belief stretching even farther into the future, archivists hoped that "by the magic of science the people of 2011 will be able almost literally to turn back the hand of time and view Chicago and Chicagoans as they lived and moved in 1911."[6] What happened to the jar remains a mystery, which hopefully will be resolved by 2011.

The appreciation of both the screen's and the press' historiographic wherewithal in accounting for the neural flow of world affairs was far from novel around 1910. Bush's contention echoes an enthusiastic musing by Edison from 1895 which speculated about the impact of combining the kinetoscope with the phonograph: "What a way to write history. [...] How much more effectively one could convey to future generations an idea of the President than word and writing could. In fact, written words would cease to have their historical importance," which, in turn, relayed the glowing appreciation of future media constellations based on his previous predictions.[7] In 1895 Edison also proclaimed that the newspapers of the future would be delivered by phonographs—"the eyesight of people was becoming poorer, the time of busy people was becoming more and more occupied, and many of the newspapers were now so large that it was impossible to read them through."[8]

Before the era of moving pictures, newspapers were perceived by some commentators as panoptic machines laying out daily grids—or nerve fibers—between the local and global. The prominent Reverend Thomas De Witt Talmage of the Brooklyn Tabernacle pondered a couple of Bible passages along such lines. The Reverend ventured a media-savvy reading of a couple of verses from Ezekiel 10 which were riveted to vision and sight:

> 9 Then I looked, and behold, four wheels beside the cherubim, one wheel beside each cherub; and the appearance of the wheels *was* like the gleam of a Tharshish stone. 10 As for their appearance, all four of them had the same likeness, as if one wheel were within another wheel. 11 When they moved, they went in *any of* their four directions without turning as they went; but they followed in the direction which they faced, without turning as they went. 12 Their whole body, their backs, their hands, their wings and the wheels were full of eyes all around, the wheels belonging to all four of them.[9]

The passage calls, of course, for hermeneutics, and the reverend suggested the following interpretation via an analogy. The many wheels of the press are replete with optic nerves from axis to periphery and constantly on the alert for the purpose of monitoring the whirling wheels of reality. They watch up-close and afar, notice matters big and small, and observe in all directions. The press is therefore the prime democratic institution, particularly for the illiterate masses deprived of the resources at public libraries, an insight that evoked the lords of the yellow press and their visual reporting, not least in New York City. A generation later, film reformers inside the industry and out defined cinema's true mission as cultural education for the masses due to the pleasure incurred by lessons steeped in a universally readable visual vernacular.

In a circumspect essay discussing the relationships between cinema and newspapers Paul S. Moore proposes maps and menus as productive metaphors for the ways papers cover the ground or serve up the city à la carte within the framework of modernity's new consumerist geography. The changing face of journalism, its new types of columns, its larger scope of interest for metropolitan occurrences, its shrewd tactics in attracting advertising clients, all this marked a time when the readership had become more diverse, not least in the big cities due to immigration. In describing the role of the metropolitan press, Moore relies on Gunther Barth's analysis of metropolitan newspapers as a prime agent for integrating the "divided space of cities segregated by class, ethnicity, race, and male privilege."[10] In the process, Barth claims, newspapers engender a form of common identity for city people straddling spatial divisions bearing on class, etc., by offering a common placeless space, be it a map or menu. Mass readership is thus a prerequisite for turning city people into consumers in a society fueled by advertising. Moore subscribes to Barth's assumption that the modern press offers a language for communication across divides, at the same time voicing reservations concerning the "assumption of awareness and perception" of such processes. Still, one might add, this posited common identity did not always translate smoothly into integrative practices straddling differences. Segregated seating in metropolitan theaters, which we will return to, made differences blatantly obvious.

Daily print media offers a fertile ground for negotiating the everyday fabric of reality in the many genres of writing that emanate from the desks in newspaper buildings. Hardly any aspect of life, least of all the impact of moving images, was left uncommented upon by journalists in an era of rapid newspaper expansion predicated on adding visual material to wordage and favoring the spectacular aspects of reality by accounts from flaneurian or globetrotting eyewitnesses. Newsprint had its roots in pre-modern soil, irrespective of attempts at branching out, but when the *Chicago Herald* began producing a weekly newsreel, the city itself turned star, its trappings—"skyscrapers, parks, railroads, and homes"—stage properties, and the residents turned extras "to be used in the thousands of comedies and tragedies to be plucked from real life by the camera man."[11] Such alliances and exchanges between media ushered in a wider conceptualization of news and coalitions between newsprint and newsreels.

Monitoring the world and the local city space are hardly innocent mediations. Newspapers are therefore agents acting on the local urban fabric by framing an ever-changing metropolitan scene—or, to pick up Moore's metaphors, newspapers offer an atlas-like rendering of the world from the perspective of the local, or an eclectic menu incorporating multiple cuisines. As businesses making revenue from advertising, newspapers had a vested interest in turning all commercial ventures into clients. Two of the primary machines of modernity, automobiles and moving pictures, for example, were gradually awarded increasing amounts of newspaper space and soon incorporated into sections awash with advertisements, to the benefit of all parties.

As a legend for upcoming chapters, the intricate dynamics between the press and the imprints in the city fabric left by the burgeoning realm of moving images can be slotted into a series of palimpsest-like movements. By boiling down and compartmentalizing the complex interaction between two prime agents of modernity—printer's ink and nitrate film—one doubtless dilutes the colorful media exchange during a period ranging from the mid-1890s up to the threshold of the classical era in the mid-1910s. The last of these heuristic stages, discernible from early 1914, propelled film culture—housed in film palaces regularly advertising programs predominantly built around serial films and features—into the respectability of standing press columns, daily and weekly, parallel to the emergence of sprightly fan magazines and trade sheets more sober in tone. In the mid-1910s cinema was on the threshold of the dominant culture. A film magazine could thus report that the School of Journalism at Columbia University assigned topical films "as a permanent means of instructing the students in reporting actual events first hand." According to the headline, journalism was "taught by the movies." This controlled environment functioned as a remedy, since instructors now could "check up the students' stories."[12]

Like the film medium, the newspaper industry underwent momentous changes around the turn of the century, not only editorially and in terms of layout, but also as the result of improved printing technologies, novel methods for turning both rags and pulp into paper, the telegraphic and telephonic relaying of news via press bureaus, and the attempts to regulate the advertisement market. Thus, the page looked distinctly different in 1915 than it did in 1896.[13] The Postal Act of 1912 made it mandatory for publications to clearly differentiate between editorial matter and advertisements in order to obtain the lower postage rate for second-class mail. In 1913 the establishment of the Audit Bureau of Circulation forced publishers to disclose accurate circulation figures, which previously were often doctored in order to overcharge advertisers impressed by big numbers. These measures resulted from longstanding complaints concerning unclean methods in procuring ads together with advertisers' attempts to influence editorial policies; this was fueled by some papers' willingness to offer editorial write-ups in exchange for hefty advertising accounts.

When the press, once foremost an unfettered medium for publicly voicing political opinions on the editorial page, turned news into its premium focus and simultaneously broadened the scope to groups of readers previously not catered to by publishers—women, mechanics, and immigrants, to put it simply—the market moved away from a select readership to a mass market, which, in turn, made the papers totally dependent on advertising, not least from department stores.[14] Consumerism was embodied mainly by women, the most frequent patrons of its high temple, the department store, so the newspapers' increasing dependence on department store ads for their revenue necessitated an address which was on the whole attractive to female readers. The nickelodeons' variety programs emerged as department stores for popular amusements—offering cheap, unpretentious, and easy accessible visual excitement with broad audience appeal, explicitly wooing female patrons in a pitch for at least a modicum of gentility.

The overall turn to a mass readership was most conspicuous in New York City. Building up wide circulation necessitated a low price, often a penny, a gospel preached by Adolph Ochs when he took over the *New York Times* and immediately moved his paper into the penny league. By slashing the price, Ochs distanced his paper from the *Sun*, which cost two pennies, and the *Herald* at three, a move that paid off in greater circulation for the *Times* a few years down the road. Journalism historians generally concur that the *New York Herald* and James Gordon Bennett pioneered the emphasis on news in a broader fashion, while the writing style in the *Sun* under Charles A. Dana "became the standard and criterion; the old, stilted, highfalutin style retreated to the country and the frontier," writes Will Irwin.[15] The stage was thus set in 1896 for lively reporting of moving pictures as a theatrical news item and even more so—

but from a different perspective—when the papers and flaneur reporters discovered the nickel culture after 1905.

The transformation of the American press scene around the turn of the century reflected an expanded base of prospective readers for which low-priced sensationalist tabloids served as a cultural gateway, particularly for those only semi-fluent in English. Daniel F. Kellogg put the observation more bluntly: "The aim is no longer to produce literature at all, but to produce cheap reading-matter meant to be read, apparently, by cheap people." Moreover, in his discouraged opinion "[n]ews matter and editorials are set forth chiefly as the dress and allurement of advertising matter. The newspaper is most successful now that has the most advertising. [...] [T]he advertising department now controls the newspapers of our country."[16]

A vivid visual style combined with inventive illustrations—photographs profusely amalgamated with diagrams and charts, albeit with a highly sensationalist veneer; circulation wars ran rampant in New York City in particular—arguably revolutionized the press. The resulting tabloid era and the most successful papers' increasingly yellow mode of address, foremost in the *New York World*, exerted pressure on all papers, to either hold on to traditional methods of layout and styles of reporting or implement changes in order to compete with the low-price sheets and their sensationalist clamor. In the process new sections emerged, particularly in the evening papers' Saturday editions and the morning papers' Sunday editions, featuring sports, automobiles, fashion, popular accounts of science, and eventually moving pictures.

Will Irwin's groundbreaking 1911 series of articles on the American press scene, published in *Collier's*, provided in-depth analysis of and a critical perspective on these processes, though in a style far removed from the muckraking crusades so prevalent in magazines during the period under consideration. Perhaps the most perceptive and innovative aspect of Irwin's installments is his comprehensive discussion of the complex transformation of the press to a predominant focus on news, a fluid concept whose contours Irwin attempts to outline in an installment replete with poignant observations. The slippery nature of the mechanisms for turning events into news and bestowing news status upon the seemingly commonplace are still with us in the information era, when "facts" and fabrications in intricate patterns of "newsworthyness" blend with entertainment, gossip, and investigative reporting.

63

Irwin's text was grounded in meticulous research. Although there was precious little scholarship for him to draw upon, he convincingly documents the historical processes and their trajectories and the unscrupulous methods used by some papers to attract advertisers and readers. The most flagrant tactics he singled out concern the theatrical advertising in Hearst's *New York Evening Journal* in the years around 1910. Irwin shows in detail that certain theaters buying a full- or half-page ad were rewarded with editorial write-ups or featured articles on their productions within a framework discounting critique proper for "constructive" criticism.[17] Irwin's critical stance can be characterized as a form of auteur theory; the papers under discussion invariably seem to reflect the personality of their respective publisher and his structural ideas and news style, from Bennett and Dana to Pulitzer, Hearst, and Ochs.

The press scene in New York City changed drastically in the mid-1890s when Hearst took over the *New York Evening Journal* and Adolph Ochs acquired the *New York Times*. Michael Scudson makes a useful distinction, contrasting on the one hand the action journalism of Pulitzer's *New York World* (acquired in 1882) moving from one crusade to the next—a mode at the heart of the yellow press and bolstering the Hearst papers as well, especially the *New York Evening Journal*—and on the other what he calls "journalism as information." The latter is Scudson's banner for a standard embodied by the *New York Times* during Adolph Ochs' stewardship. Scudson's analysis of the *New York Times* is underwritten by the contemporary assessment of Will Irwin from his *Collier's* series: "[T]he nearest of any newspaper to presenting a truthful picture of life in New York and the world at large."[18] When all the other big dailies in New York City began publishing synopses for serial films, it is perhaps telling that the *New York Times* shied away from a genre pioneered by the *Chicago Tribune* for *The Adventures of Kathlyn* (Selig, 1913–14), which was picked up in New York by the *Sun* and in Los Angeles by the *Times*.

Journalistic practices turned the key concepts touched upon here—facts, news, information, literature, opinions, and crusades—into operational genres for progressively more diverse readerships, and film material in various forms impinged upon all those categories over time. A flaneurian style of news reporting, hovering somewhere between literary modes and factual chronicling, gained prominence in the process. Stephen Crane's journalism is a case in point, which focused on street life in New York City in tandem with his work as short-story writer and

novelist. Crane did not address the nickelodeon culture for obvious reasons, given the timeframe of his writing prior to his premature death
in 1900, though he did note the phenomenon of moving images.[19] The
genre Crane and a whole generation of would-be authors developed in
the columns—for instance his colleague Abraham Cahan, though with a
distinct ethnic inflection—emerged as a form of metropolitan portraiture, often highly specific in its take on situations and protagonists comprising the dramas of the street. This mode of journalism coalesced into
what Lennard Davis and Michael Robertson have fittingly categorized
as a fact-fiction discourse. Its leading champion among editors was Lincoln Steffens at the *Commercial Advertiser*.[20] Steffens actively recruited
journalists like Crane and Cahan, "fresh, young, enthusiastic writers
who would see and make others see the life of the city. This meant individual styles, and old newspaper men wrote in the style of their paper,
the *Sun* men in the *Sun* style, *Post* men in the Godkin manner."[21] If the
Post was all about facts, delivered without intervening fingerprints from
reporters, Steffens' crew, recruited from Eastern colleges, adopted more
of a hands-on approach, "benefit[ting] from the experience of city life
as a spectacle, and they contributed to it. They provided their readers a
running account of the marvels and mysteries of urban life."[22]

In the following chapters we will regularly return to one writer matching Lincoln Steffens' ideal for writing up the excitements of modernity's
city life: Harry C. Carr of the *Los Angeles Times*. His brand of chronicling
Los Angeles street life had its predecessor in a column from the pre-nick-
el period signed The Saunterer. An analysis of its author's manner of
writing about the city at a critical juncture in Los Angeles' development
away from the sleepy garden days steeped in lingering mission culture to
a lively metropolis identifies all the genre elements indicative of the
latter era of city portraiture. As a series of transitions, the Saunterer's
writing was engrossed by the tribulations of the bustling young city
boosted in the columns of the *Los Angeles Times*. The Saunterer's conflicted column and her many nostalgic escapades often clamped down on
young women's new mobility, an issue taking on added urgency when
the nickelodeons dominated the amusement scene. Already in the late
1880s, the Saunterer had voiced her concerns when women allegedly
turned themselves into spectacles in the proximity of places of amusement, a traffic which was regulated decades later when policewomen
were hired for the job. A closer look at her column reveals the style and

content indicative of the peripatetic mode of writing, which discovered the nickel shows as both street and screen ventures around 1905. At that time, the Saunterer's puritan engagement had been refashioned into flippant, street-smart detachment à la Carr.

A Prelude: Walking the City—Writing the City

Angelina Patti's opera concert in 1887 at Mott Hall in downtown Los Angeles inspired an early intervention associated with what, in relation to film audiences, can be dubbed metaspectatorship. In the Patti case, the account penned by "The Saunterer" in the *Los Angeles Times* deviates in two aspects from the core depictions later ventured for moving pictures and their patrons: The observations do not focus on audience members in the act of taking in representations, here an opera concert rather than a film, and the text verbally bypasses the offerings on stage, instead portraying members of the audience as they leave Mott Hall. Positioned at the foot of the stairs, the Saunterer arrests the patrons at a threshold-like passage leading away from the excitement of the performance to the street, and her account zooms in on female audience members only. The piece is defined as "a study" of "the different faces of the ladies" of all ages. Due to the strong "electric glare," made-up complexions "were easy to discover"; the alleged female artificiality turns out to be the text's critical feature. All generations of women apparently sport heavy makeup in Los Angeles, which is particularly unbecoming for young women, the Saunterer quips. "The glare of the electric light magnified all their foolish art, and made them look like a long line of moving ghosts."[23] The text makes no connection between the stage offerings and the lingering impression of the audience as they left. The scrutinizing observation, which turns the female patrons into an uncanny spectacle due to the combination of electric light and makeup, later developed into a genre for reporting on early modes of film spectatorship.

Berating women for artifice and tampering with nature's course resonates with the puritan sensibilities advocated not only in the *Times*' columns in the aftermath of the rowdy Gold Rush days. Allegorical pleasures with a distinct moral, in tandem with the wholesome natural environment that represented Southern California's primary draw for the burgeoning film industry decades later, offered an antidote to the metropolitan excitements intended to provide superficial thrills. Masquer-

66

ading behind the flaneurian signature was the editor's wife, Eliza Wetherby Otis. Besides her two columns, "The Saunterer" and "Susan Sunshine," Mrs. Otis was "in charge of religion, society, fashion, literature, drama, and the 'women's' section," while the General himself, Harrison Gray Otis, more or less edited and penned the rest of the paper in the early days.[24] The unique atmosphere of Southern California inspired an eclectic promotional discourse from the 1870s onwards, perhaps best represented by Charles Fletcher Lummis (1859–1928). Fittingly, Lummis wrote for the *Los Angeles Times* initially, later editing his own magazine, *In the Land of Sunshine*, apart from publishing numerous books.

The Saunterer's brand of peripatetic journalism chronicled Los Angeles' rapid transformation from an idyllic small town enveloped in the romantic mission culture from the adobe days to a modern cityscape filled with excitements and opportunities and briskly heralding its future mission. The electric streetlights, which added to her impression of the women in makeup, were only one aspect of the transformed city. In her weekly installments running from late 1884 to mid-1898 Mrs. Otis served up small scenes from a cityscape demarcated by Pearl Street and the river west to east and the Plaza and Sixth Street north to south in the 1880s, which however expanded in all directions on her watch. In addition to impressions from the sidewalks, background color and perspective were added by views from outlying vistas reached by cable cars and streetcars, the latter initially horse-drawn. As the city turned increasingly complex and busy, the Saunterer repeatedly escaped to the country to indulge in the pastoral coloration and sensory richness that once belonged to the old orchard city. In her discourse laments at the loss of the old romantic life rub shoulders with the gospel of progress, but the downsides and careless mindsets of a sprawling city form part of her negotiation of the many-sided changes. Mrs. Otis, for example, clamps down on uncleanliness in all forms, stinking butcher shops, filthy trash collecting, and streets littered with dirt and horse manure. As was the case with all flaneurs, the streets provided the primary scene for observations and reflections. Mrs. Otis closely monitored the metropolitan developments and, in addition to calling for clean streets, advocated a system of beautiful parks and trees planted along the new or widened lanes and avenues in order to preserve the atmosphere previously provided by the numerous orchards, which were sacrificed to meet the expanding city's needs. In the process, numerous residences were replaced by business development. Land, she observes, "became too valuable for mere residence purposes, owing to its proximity to the business center."[25] As she puts it, "the glory of a city is its streets. Public buildings may be costly and triumphs of architectural skill; private residences may be modern and elegant, and gardens and parks may be attractive and beautiful, but if the streets are bad, poorly kept and poorly graded, the reputation of a city will suffer."[26] In this respect, Los Angeles' progress has been "metropolitan" she concludes, only to chide authorities for a series of eyesores. The main artery for the Saunterer was Spring Street, always busy and teeming with metropolitan life, and consequently it was here that phonograph parlors and arcades were established in the 1890s. Interestingly, the feminine chronicler kept her gender under wraps, and most of the cartoons above her column sport men in the classic flaneur outfit, even if one can find an occasional stray drawing depicting a flaneuse.

If feminine vanity is scolded on a regular basis, progressive activism within the context of the women's clubs is lauded for "helping to make Los Angeles what she is today, a progressive city with modern tendencies and ever-increasing culture."[27] The historical city center around the Plaza, with its Latin atmosphere and historical buildings, such as the Pico house and the Church of Santa Maria, or Lady Queen of the Angels, are beacons of the romantic past and the old mission culture now surrounded by the modern cityscape where "the cable cars are running swiftly along the shining rails."[28] Around the time moving pictures debuted, the Saunterer recurrently deliberated on Los Angeles as the city of the future. In the Saunterer's negotiation of progress—fueled by building booms and transportation developments bringing in people from the Midwest—romantic impulses blend with a touch of eschatological modernity. Contemporary splendor is set off against the backdrop of a lost romantic vision, but she hears the pulse of the future in the rhythm of today's enchantments. The Los Angeles of the future, she prophesizes, will retain the paradisical quality of long-gone days and, in her characteristic version of boosterism, Otis proclaims: "It is here that the glory of our civilization shall culminate and an empire of progress be established."[29] Or, as she more soberly phrased it a couple of months earlier: "That old life had its charm, but today is grander, and being here has infinitely broadened. Who would go back to the world's yesterday? Today! Today! that is what we would make glorious and out of it we hope to carve a future that shall be sublime."[30]

In a reversal of the rhetoric of Manifest Destiny, the Saunterer claims that the "aggressive Yankee" never entertained an ambition to push "so far toward the sunset slopes of the continent" as Los Angeles. The sleeping adobe city therefore long rested content in its comfortable past. However, a "new race and a new civilization possesses the land, and the tide of the empire has flowed hither from the East." Moreover, in yet another vision of the future, in which the Saunterer gauges its advances "step by step, as art and science and culture, wealth and invention gather their forces here [. . .] he [sic—still masquerading] would like to look upon the tomorrow of a quarter of a century hence, for beyond a doubt it will witness the culmination of far greater advances than we have yet seen, and find here a city beautiful enough to make the conquest of the world."[31] Little did she suspect that the prime vehicle for this conquest would be motion pictures, which she paid no heed in her columns in her last few years as the Saunterer. Her negotiation of a cityscape transformed by modernity looked elsewhere for agents of progress.

The romantic impulses from the Edenic days of the past and the transformations wrought by speculation and industrial developments coalesced into discursive frames for describing the influx of film companies to the area in the early 1910s. Prior to reporting on local film production, the audience criticism pioneered by the Saunterer in her text from Mott Hall turned into a fixture in accounts of the threshold between street excitements and nickel shows, primarily on Main Street. The *Times'* particular blend of puritan boosterism and open-shop advocacy together with Hearst's populism, the *Record*'s working-class profile, and Earl's papers' progressive inclinations thus provide prime sources for the coming chapters.

ENTERING THE COLUMNS—FIVE STAGES OF MEDIA INTERACTION

I. A Machine for Seeing Differently

Obviously, in the first stage of reporting after Vitascope debuted on the vaudeville circuit in April 1896, the new phenomenon of projected moving images commanded attention per se as a regular news item—and yet another spectacular technical marvel to reflect upon. This Edisonian discourse, to wit, linearized the phenomenon of projected moving images within a series of inventions and wondrous technical novelties indicative of modernity. An era which, in the shorthand of popular discourse and imagination, was embodied by Edison and the steady flow of marvelous products emanating from his laboratory, some of them however only repackaged, upgraded, and branded by his staff, like the Vitascope. The wizard himself was an unrivaled master in appropriating gadgets of the future and marketing them well in advance of their technical practicability. In this sense, Edison was a true visionary, or an early incarnation of the press agent. In several respects the press attention devoted to the kinetoscope and Latham's projecting panopticon, which has been partly documented by Terry Ramsaye, functioned as a journalistic genre pilot in relation to the subsequent press coverage of the Vitascope's debut.[32]

In Los Angeles, the Vitascope was introduced on the Orpheum bill on July 6, 1896, for a two-week turn in; Edwin S. Porter, the legend to be, was one of the machine operators.[33] After the Vitascope's success at the Orpheum, Thomas L. Tally purchased the machine and turned projected film images into a regular fixture at his Tally's Phonograph Parlor located at 311 South Spring Street.[34] When the Vitascope films opened as an attraction at the Orpheum in July 1896, the press release expounded on the technology by relating it to a familiar Edison machine, the kinetoscope:

> The Vitascope is Edison's latest and most shining triumph. It is a miracle of human ingenuity in the realm of electricity and photography. It is on the same order as the kinetoscope, with the difference that in the kinetoscope one person at a time peeps into a hole and sees a tiny moving picture, while in the Vitascope the picture is thrown upon a screen, and shines forth of more than life-size, so that the entire audience can see the spectacle at once.

A string of different types of films made up the bill:

> The things shown by the Vitascope are of many different kinds. A bit of Broadway in New York is very striking. The audience can see the swarms of people hurrying along, the jostle of the horses, carriages, trucks etc. in the street, all moving and changing, and so real one almost expects to hear the street noises. A snowstorm, a skirt dance, and a sea beach scene are some of the things shown. The life-like reality of the pictures is said to be

startling. In San Francisco and elsewhere, one of the most popular scenes was a reproduction of the famous bit of acting in which May Irvin [Irwin] is kissed by John C. Rush [Rice]. The changing expression of their faces, their graceful movements, the play of hand and lip and eye, are said to be faultlessly reproduced.[35]

The promotional release from the Orpheum in July singles out the machinery, while the brand name further endorses the premium value of the attraction by linking it to the well-established wizardry associated with Edison. That the Vitascope was primarily the result of the ingenuity of others and acquired by Raff & Gammon with Edison's name as a selling point seemed to be of no consequence.

The text underscored the machine's capacity to capture modern life: The lively busyness in the frame, the hectic pace of city life and its frantic traffic, and the variety of items on display were presented in a theatrical context instead of the individual viewing afforded by the kinetoscope. Single-shot films were soon to be captured with cameras mounted on various means of transportation in order to achieve a panoramic effect, a continuing expansion of landscape or cityscape visually shaped by this alliance between camera and a moving vehicle. The impression elicited, that of imaginary travel, became a lasting genre, called phantom rides. While enlarged later to a multi-shot format, they still predominantly favored extended shots to capture a panoramic frame of experience. Such films were popular well into the 1910s and for some seemingly had a dreamlike, almost hypnotic quality, with ingenious editing showing off scenic travel routes and spectacular vistas.[36]

The *Los Angeles Herald* also offered its readers an outline of the miraculous Vitascope based on the same press release from the Orpheum, again underscoring the variety aspect of the bill: "On a huge white curtain one can see the dash of ocean billows [this film was shot by Robert Paul in England] or watch the endless procession of a New York street pass by or see a skirt dancer go through her graceful evolutions, all with so much reality it is hard to believe one sees only a shadow and not the substance." The multiplicity of topics here suggests an all but haptic sense of reality, while the mode of projection and the effect of reality achieved is elaborated upon in detail: "The theater will be darkened. Suddenly a piece of Broadway in New York at the busiest hour will be flashed out upon the white curtain. The audience can see the hurrying throng of people, the jam of carts, trucks, carriages, horses and all perfect and real life, except that one cannot hear the noises of the street."[37] The ad for the Orpheum show emphasized the "life-size" photographs, the natural movements, and the life-like quality of the display—Vitascope was thus no misnomer for a show priced at 10, 25, or 50 cents.

In Los Angeles as elsewhere, the Vitascope was marketed as a theatrical attraction whose realistic and uncanny play in the gray area between shadow and substance was perceived as mediation—in lieu of a live attraction—only due to its hardly perceptible lack of substance. Numerous commentators singled out sound as the only missing component in the face of movement and color—not that all Vitascope films were colored. The Vitascope "shows life and color, with speech and the noise of movement the only thing missing," an impression from New York echoed in Los Angeles.[38]

> Edison's invention, the Vitascope, the wonderful mechanism which projects upon a white drop curtain bits of real life, in their natural size, in their own colors, and moving and changing continually so that the spectator seems to see reality and not a shadow.[39]

Besides placing the effect within the framework of modernity, gauged by its rapidity, the brunt of the review was devoted to the Rice-Irwin film kiss in the *Herald*'s enthusiastic account:

> Only its productions are seen, and these, were it not for the rapid age in which we live, would be rightly termed marvelous. Thrown on a screen, in life-size figures, one sees Anna Belle [Annabelle Moore] in the sun, serpentine and butterfly dances; the Venezuela imbroglio, in which Uncle Sam comes out the winner; Herald square, New York, with its mighty traffic, its elevated trains rushing by, its cable cars, its horse-drawn drays, and the surging throng of men and women—every movement natural as in actuality; Cissy Fitzsimmon's dance, in which she shows a bewildering amount of fine muslin and hosiery and flying, dainty and shapely feet; and lastly, the famous May Irwin and John Rice kiss. Well, the latter could be described, but space forbids. It is immense. Let this general term suffice. One sees it, and one is almost inclined to blush for the participants. One sees the jolly May's lips move as her face is nestled against that of John, and one almost hears her speak. Suddenly John Rice prepares for the kiss

proper—and such a kiss it proves to be! Well, the glorified and perfected
kinetoscope, named the vitascope, is a big thing.[40]

The review situates the technologically mediated spectacle as pure display cut off from the invisible machinery by its paradoxical mode of presentation, given that the machine was the advertised attraction. The severing induces an effect of quasi-independence between films and machine. The overall effect imparted by the moving images was heralded as
a product of the age, primarily characterized in terms of speed. The in-
cessantly changing street scenes brimming with activity and busy traffic
evidenced the varied character of the program, while the uncontrolled
flow of movement and the multitude of bodies in the frame offered a
contrast to the regulated dancers in some of the scenes. The female bodies, highly eroticized in a display of underwear and body parts, bewil-
dered the reviewer, which led up to the troubling, let alone indescribable, but still elaborated, intimacy of the Rice-Irwin kiss. Overall, the
nature of gazing combined with the nature of the display—hidden and
thus mysterious in its source-less suppression and thus coming to the
fore as "reality" minus sound—offers the most food for thought.

The *Los Angeles Express* singled out the "lifelike view of the waves" for
particular praise as the "most wonderful" of the six films displayed during the second week. In comments on the films the shifting patterns of
movement and speed in the frames provide focal points for the description. The machine is succinctly characterized as a "kinetoscope on a heroic scale throwing upon a screen on the stage by means of electricity a
multiplicity of photographs in such quick succession that they portray
every motion of real life most truthfully." In focusing on a street scene in
New York City, a "wagon drawn by two horses is coming along leisurely. Then appears an electric car going in the same direction, which soon
overtakes the wagon and then disappears from view. From the opposite
direction comes another trolley car and speeds on its way, while people
afoot are walking on the sidewalks and crossing the street."[41] The condensed, but detailed, description of the multiple layers of movement in
the frame is centered on the horse-drawn wagon. Its slow and regulated
speed and movement in the frame ground faster vehicles coming and going in different directions so rapidly that they either disappear from or
enter the frame at a late point in the shot. The pedestrians offer a mere
afterthought for even slower parallel movement across the street. The

streetcars are by no means behemoth forces here, but represent the upper echelon of speed in the gamut delineated in the description, ranging from electrical locomotion to animal and then human.

The change, shifts, and transformations alluded to also capture salient qualities of the vaudeville "machine," especially the continuous version's regulated turns. The reviewer at the *Los Angeles Herald* ventured a reflective take on the "nature" of vaudeville and considered its success an index of the restlessness of the era, with new appliances in store for the immediate future. A conception of modernity as a never-ending succession of upgrades, improvements, and progress reinforced the reception of the Vitascope, which was placed within a series of technical marvels as a perfection of the kinetoscope "on a heroic scale," promising increasingly global forms of reproduction in addition to scores of other gadgets outside the realm of capturing reality.

> It must be obvious that the clue to the whole thing lies in the nervousness and desire for change that is characteristic of nineteenth century mankind. Sitting in a theater for three hours at a stretch, looking at the same faces, hearing the same voices and waiting for the denouement of a play, is apt to become monotonous to most people. They prefer a constant change, both of actors and acts, and this they get in a theater where vaudeville is presented. After a while we will not go to the theater at all. We will stay quietly at home or go to the club or visit the houses of our friends, and by aid of electrical appliances we will be enabled to enjoy as much or as little of a performance as we desire.[42]

A novelty like the Vitascope found its place on the vaudeville bills as one attraction among a string of others, and was therefore partly modeled on the spectatorial interface elicited by the vaudeville format and orchestrated as a series of continuous attractions, though without entertaining any ambitions of building a coherent program structure. Instead, each act had its own logic, rhythm, and tempo, and the shifts between turns were often breathtaking. Differences, changes, and clashes between attractions were tailored to effect, if not outright shocks, at least jolts produced by a brisk shifting of gears, backgrounds, and modes of attention. The audience was treated to a mental roller-coaster ride, as it were. Overall, the popular branch of the turn-of-the-century aesthetics aimed at inducing astonishment, with fast-paced action prompting instant reactions from the audience. Buildup had no place here; slow-paced psychology belonged to the legitimate theater and long-gone days, as contemporary critics opined. Variety was the crucial billing ideal that trickled down to the attractions' micro-level besides permeating the mix of genres the Vitascope offered in its turn on the bill, which lasted around 15 minutes. The turns were cut progressively shorter: "Brevity is not only the soul of wit, but the very life of vaudeville, which is making its acts shorter every year."[43] Felicitously, Edwin Milton Royle concluded: "The vaudeville theater belongs to the era of the department store and the short story. It may be a lunch-counter art, but then art is so vague and lunch is so real."[44] In an oft-cited essay William Dean Howells bemoans a gradual move away from the fast-paced turns when aspects of legitimate drama began to infest big-time vaudeville as playlets or dramatic sketches in pocket format, a development appreciated by Royle, but acerbically described by Acton Davis as featuring "dramatic extinct volcanoes."[45] In Howell's words "the fine superiority of the continuous performance is beginning to suffer contamination from the plays where there are waits between the acts."[46] His stance prefigures Hutchins Hapgood's fine analysis of the ethos of vaudeville and his beautifully succinct adage: "Vaudeville puts together what does not fit."[47]

A notice in the *Los Angeles Times* the day of the first show neatly sums up the program mode and the Vitascope's relationship to live attractions and their exhibition practices. Then again, the impression of a live performance created by the Vitascope was a prerequisite for rubbing shoulders on the bill with live attractions. When the life-like quality became institutionalized as positively machine-made in the minds of audiences, moving images lost some of their window-like magical appeal, which might explain the chaser perception and the negative take on moving images prior to a gradual conversion of the medium to storytelling.[48]

The last day of Vitascope magic at the Orpheum was July 19th; after two weeks the apparatus was no longer on the bill. The machine did not, however, leave Los Angeles, finding its way to Tally's Phonograph Parlor. The vaudeville houses remained important venues for moving pictures for years to come, even when the medium had secured a place of its own in the entertainment universe—the nickelodeons—albeit a contested one due to the sheer ubiquity of these new outlets and the nature of the representation in relation to the perceived audiences.[49] But after 1896, individual film titles in vaudeville programs were seldom mentioned in the theatrical pages.

Some papers elected to totally ignore the novelty of moving pictures in 1896. The *New York Tribune*, for example, took no notice whatsoever of the bill at Koster & Bial's, a couple of weeks later even disputing the newness and thus news status of the Vitascope by reprinting an account of the Aletorama published "more than fifty years ago!" for the purpose of belittling the novelty value of Edison's projector.[50] In an overview of the sorry state of the legitimate stage the *New York Tribune* singled out two causes, the first being the omnipresence of middle-class bicycle riders. Though they carried the theaters in the past, bike riding was apparently preferred when money was short. The second cause put forward was the popularity of vaudeville, described as cheap "makeshift" entertainment, hence no account from Koster & Bial's.[51] Other papers immediately allied themselves with the world of moving images. We will look at one spectacular media event that moved the Vitascope out onto the street on election night.

In November the *Chicago Tribune* managed to enlist the two Vitascopes in operation in Chicago at Hopkins' South Side Theatre; one machine was moved to the newspaper's offices and the other to the Coliseum, a venue rented by the *Tribune* for the benefit of its readership on election night. At the Coliseum a multitude of screens were in place for constantly updating the audience on the election returns via "stereopticons," projected slides, as the counting of votes progressed. In between election returns the Vitascope projected films as entertaining diversions. This service was offered free of charge, as was transportation to the Coliseum on trams from all over Chicago.

In the meantime, the Vitascope machine at the newspaper office was not idle. Two screens were attached to façades at the intersection where the *Tribune*'s headquarters was located for projecting slides as soon as returns were relayed via telegraph and telephone. In addition, people on the streets were treated to films projected onto a third screen fixed on ropes crossing the street diagonally. The Vitascope projected the films from inside the *Tribune*'s office, and the streetlights had been turned off so as not to interfere with the projection. The screen's placement made it possible to watch the films from all four corners at the intersection. Apart from the visual display of election returns, barkers recruited from circuses voiced the results on the streets, and for those unable to attend an intricate system of smoke bombs indicated the direction in which the count was leaning. Bombs were set off at the top of every hour from the roof terrace at the

Great Northern Hotel—one of the tallest buildings in Chicago—according to a color code: blue smoke indicated that the Democratic/Populist alliance had the upper hand, red that the GOP was in the lead. *One* smoke bomb referred to the election returns in the Cook County, *two* indicated the results in the state of Illinois, *three* informed about national returns.[52]

Prior to radio and television there was a vexing lag in getting election results to the constituencies. Print is an extremely slow medium, even when newspapers put out extra editions. The advent of telegraphy had speeded up news-collecting processes, and the informational flow intersected at the news desks, motivating multiple editions for continuous update. The *Tribune*'s multimedia show in 1896 represented an elaborate attempt at minimizing the time span between the information's arrival at the office and news' delivery to the public before being written up in the columns.

Removing the Vitascope from its vaudeville context and placing the films in the public sphere represented part of a radically different bill substituting the liveness of the otherwise enveloping vaudeville shows for an alliance with the hoped-for immediacy of red-hot news wired or called in and briskly transformed into slides projected onto screens mounted on building façades. The initiative offered a novel form of public, non-theatrical film exhibition, which resurfaced when films were screened in parks for educational purposes or at makeshift outdoor venues or airdromes. Inside the theaters, in the company of vaudeville acts, film actors could be read as being akin to stage artists with a virtual presence convincing enough to wipe out the real absence, a common discursive interface in the early Vitascope reception. On the streets, the projected slides opened a gateway to events taking place elsewhere in realtime. The distance traversed by the news before being delivered was wiped out by the minimized time lag between events' occurrence and their being cast as news. The information was doubly mediated before it reached the façades, after being called in or telegraphed and then put on slides. If context matters—and, more importantly, rubs off—the films shown in conjunction with the 1896 election could be read as if broadcasted from afar rather than performed in the here and now, which the vaudeville frame apparently suggested otherwise. Both variations of liveness—if at all applicable as reading strategies—downplayed the storage aspect of film images by favoring reception modes associated with either physical presence, here à la vaudeville, or liveness à la "broadcasting" over wires.

Chicago was not the only city offering projected Vitascope films on the street. In New York City a crowd of 125,000 congregated in Lower Manhattan's City Hall Park near Park Row in the vicinity of the newspaper offices: "[A]ll classes were represented [...] and it looked as though all theaters in New York had suddenly closed, and a hundred audiences had been turned into the street." Election returns were projected as slides, just like in Chicago, and "between bulletins on one screen there was an exhibition of the Vitascope, and as the scenes were flashed upon it the shouts of laughter and merriment rose above the din of horns and rattles."[53] The show hosted by the *New York Herald* mixed news slides projected onto a gigantic white sheet attached to the Herald Square building with Vitascope films of the Grand Canyon, a dentist's office, whirling dancers, breaking surf, "melon eating darkies," and, of course, May Irwin's kiss, which made the crowd "roar with laughter."[54] This alliance between the Vitascope and publishing enterprises in 1896 provides a historiographic point of departure for a series of intersections during the transitional era where the press either offers salient source material or emerges as a foe or partner in different respects to the film industry.

IN FRONT OF HERALD BUILDING WHEN M'KINLEY'S VICTORY WAS ANNOUNCED.

FIGURE 5: Vitascope projection during election night 1896.
Cartoon from *New York Herald*, 4 November 1896, 2.

In April 1896, the Vitascope month, the *New York World* presented scores of humorous sketches of X-ray images—cathode photography was the favored term—showcasing amusingly deconstructive observations of everyday situations through a novel lens, as it were, for instance, a symphony orchestra "seen" in Roentgen's penetrating light zooming in on box office, orchestra pit, audience, and performers. Among the featured performers were Sandow—of Edison fame—and May Irwin at the Bijou stage. Interestingly, the *World* ran the Roentgen material in its Colored Supplement.[55]

The John C. Rice – May Irwin Kiss, the most talked about of all Vitascope films, was slotted into this discourse of seeing differently, but resides at the other end of the spectrum. While the cathode camera strips away the flesh, the Vitascope focuses on it—perhaps even fetishizing it—by portraying bodies and body parts up-close, at least in this particular film. One observer was however totally disgusted by the display and wanted to destroy the very mechanism.

> Now I want to smash *The Vitascope*. The name of the thing is in itself a horror, but that may pass. Its manifestations are worse, *The Vitascope*, be it known, is a sort of magic lantern which reproduces movement. Whole scenes are enacted on its screen.

The piece, even if unsigned, was surely written by the editor of *The Chap-Book*, Herbert S. Stone. After describing the machine, Stone then relatively innocently moves on to the Vitascope films, scoffing at the public before clamping down on the Irwin-Rice vehicle:

> La Loie dances, elevated trains come and go, and the thing is mechanically ingenious, and a pretty toy for a great child, the public. Its managers were not satisfied with this, however, and they bravely set out to eclipse in vulgarity all previous theatrical attempts.
>
> In a recent play called *The Widow Jones* you may remember a famous kiss which Miss May Irwin bestowed on a certain John C. Rice, and *vice versa*. Neither participant is physically attractive, and the spectacle of their prolonged pasturing on each other's lips was hard to bear. When only life-size it was pronouncedly beastly. But that was nothing to the present sight. Magnified to Gargantuan proportions and repeated three times over it is absolutely disgusting. All delicacy remnant of charm seems gone from

Miss Irwin, and the performance comes very near being indecent in its emphasized vulgarity.[56]

Irwin and Rice were recognizable stage stars and billed as such in the title, and the film was advertised as a pregnant scene from a well-known play, but in Stone's opinion, the process of shooting grotesquely transformed the moment. As such, the film came to the fore as an attraction, gilding the titillating aura of the kiss with star billing. Even worse, the stylistic choice, the close shot displayed in "Gargantuan proportions," an attraction in its own right, was nothing but a "beastly" spectacle in the eye of this particular beholder.

Both machines, the Roentgen apparatus and the Vitascope, thus toy with the current body politics from different vantage points and offer strangely fascinating—or repulsive—ways of seeing the hitherto familiar in unfamiliar ways, which partly accounts for the instructive ambition behind the kiss film as well as the amusing appropriation of Roentgen views. When the exhibition market for moving images had stabilized and the Cinématograph and the Biograph outrivaled the Vitascope, the press' interest predictably cooled off in the absence of significant novelties to report on. The press was after all in the business of—news. This dull state of affairs more or less lasted until the nickel houses began to surface with film genres like the chase film, which turned into a billing fixture in the flourishing venues.

II. Glancing while Walking—Flaneurs and the Nickelodeons

In a second movement the flaneurian city scribes discovered the nickelodeon phenomenon within a fact-fiction discourse in a mode of refracted, peripatetic journalism. This *flanerie* of the inkwell picked up oblique fragments of street culture and city life for belletristic spins. Sauntering journalists randomly explored the streets and put a personal, idiosyncratic imprint on matters attracting their attention in a genre very much in the male ilk, even if a very few female reporters were added to some newspaper rosters. The frame of mind in these interventions was detached, and this semi-reluctant mode of observation further underscored a sense of ennui or spleen. Its mobilized glance turned modernity's occurrences into strange fact-fiction snapshots bordering on the bizarre, often filtered through a flippant, distracted style. Metropolitan topics stumbled upon in this manner were incidental discoveries and thus removed from the regular influx to the news desk of happenings and events on which all papers reported: disasters small and large, national and local politics and events, sports and the like. The stylistic flavor deemed appropriate for addressing the emerging nickelodeon phenomenon was the result of this peripatetic mode of unraveling accidentally discovered metropolitan oddities.

The flaneur discourse runs more or less in tandem and blends with the interventions from phase III, when the true purveyors of progressive modernity put a radically different spin on the ubiquity of moving pictures. Agenda-driven surveys replaced contingent essays, brisk and determined mapping substituted the slow pace of detached detection, superintended monitoring supplanted literary portraiture. To be sure, articles oftentimes mixed discovery, phase II, and dismay, a mode underpinning the surveys from phase III, but the prototypical discoveries were purely flaneurian and untainted by condemnation or cautionary caveats. The demarcation between these phases—and at times the order of phases II and III was reversed—is therefore grounded in mode—glance versus gaze—and emphasis rather than chronology. Interventions from other countries hence observe different timelines for film culture's shifts. The pervious time span for this breed of journalism lasted from approximately 1904 to late 1907, when the nickelodeon craze had reached ubiquity and was no longer visible to flaneurs, but all too visible to the reform-minded with their instrumental mode of attention. Since accounts by flaneurs oscillated between journalism proper and literary essays that happened to be published in newspapers, only metropolitan centers could offer a city fabric saturated with enough amusements and a newspaper environment sufficiently rich and varied to encourage and sustain this particular mode of writing—and by definition only for a short time. A piece by Hjalmar Söderberg, the quintessential flaneur in Swedish literature, published in the conservative morning paper *Svenska Dagbladet* in 1904, incorporates the whole gamut of the flaneurian discourse as well as textual strategies indicative of phase III well in advance of the nickelodeon boom's onset in the U.S.[57] Placing his lone voice next to a phase III text from the *New York Evening World* clearly illustrates the shift from a flaneurian mode to vigilant activism, although the impressions from inside the shows are animated by virtually identical screen content.

When Hjalmar Söderberg happened to take in a film show in April of

81

1904, his visit was triggered by a chance meeting with two boys; the piece was consequently titled "En barnförestàllning" ("A Matinee for Children"). The peripatetic mood is colored by a feeling of gloom and tediousness, the sky is blue, but there is a black, stationary cloud in front of the sun, which gives the firmament a tint reminiscent of corpse-like blueness, further reminding him of the picture postcards sold at cigar shops. Toying with metaphors allied with mechanical reproduction, the houses are described as emanating from a commercial catalog of chromolithographs, and, even worse, people look like poor photographs of themselves. While pondering the forlorn Sunday feeling, Söderberg suddenly notices a child crying at his feet. The kid is three or four years old, and there is an older brother too, perhaps around seven. When our flaneur searches for a coin in his pocket, the older one pinches his brother to increase the volume and, hopefully, the size of the consolation coin. A nickel gives solace to the smaller kid; the older one asks if he, too, can have one so they can watch *levande teater* (living theater). The boy points toward a former art gallery, now a theater for moving pictures. Our flaneur recollects being amused by moving images when the Lumières visited the Stockholm Exposition in 1897—divers cranked backwards were particularly entertaining. So, why not? Inside, the auditorium is packed with children; it smells like graduation day and a man bangs on the piano. Olfactory and aural impressions already garnish the comments on the visual display.

Now it starts: 'Storming a Fortress.' An arranged and entirely impossible staging including fencing with sabers, climbing a wall, and so forth. But the young ones gaze horror-stricken and enchanted, pale and with wide-open mouths. Next an old woman taking snuff is seen caressing a cat. The girls laugh out loud, but the boys long for more loss of men. And they are rewarded. Next item shows Manchurian spies captured and executed by Russians. Yes, they are apprehended, lined up against a wall, shot and fall to the ground like sacks of potatoes, while a man still bangs on a piano. The scene is, of course, staged, but it seems almost real to me, and undoubtedly to the children. Thus—on a Sunday afternoon, I have treated two small boys to an execution. I am beginning to feel nauseated. But children have strong nerves, and all around me the delight abounds.

Next the highlight of the show, 'Spanish Bull Fight.' Already the first scenes evidence that this is not staged—it must have been captured during a real event. I have never been to Spain, never visited a ring, and my cheeks grow hot when the bull enters the arena and in amazement stops and looks around. This is brisk business, and all of a sudden he has buried his horn in the belly of a white horse that rears, mad with pain and horror. One flank is black-speckled with blood and the hide dangles in rags, or perhaps it is guts...

I glanced at the program leaflet and read—'The bull is stabbed to the accompaniment of the audience's exultation.' This is however way ahead, and before more horses are disposed of, I looked for the exit. I watched the small ones in the auditorium: wide-eyed, black, open mouths. I try to avoid the white screen, where the photographically produced images still relieve each other, but I cannot, and again a horse with open belly falls down, and a man bangs on a cracking piano.

This is too much for the flaneur. He flees, and when passing the usher, throws the crumpled program leaflet in his face, leaving behind a very young audience enthralled by the screen, especially the boys; the girls at least sometimes laugh.

A similarly graphic description of a bullfight film formed part of the long crusade against such shows in the *New York Evening World* in the fall of 1910. The quite different frame illustrates a salient shift from the discovery phase associated with the flaneurian genre's accidental discoveries, triggered by the glance, to a systematic, gaze-based inventory regarding the sociological conditions of film culture. Dissatisfied with the New York City-based National Board of Censorship, then a year and a half into its mission, the *Evening World* explained the background for the text: "In order to find out conditions to-day as to the character of the films shown, The World has had its investigators visit moving picture establishments with the following result":

A bullfight in its most repulsive realism is what was served up for a large crowd of school children at the Chelsea, No. 49 Flatbush avenue, Brooklyn on Saturday afternoon. It was a Pathé film and ran for about fifteen minutes. As the investigator went into the Chelsea a mother came out leading three children under ten. In the front row of seats were a dozen little girls and in the same row with the investigator were three lads about ten.

The picture begins with the arrival of the crowd and picadors at the coliseum, and proceeds swiftly to the entry of the bull into the ring. In a few moments the excitements begin with the bull catching one of the horses on its horns and throwing it. The horse attempts to rise, with the blood gushing from it, but the picture is mercifully shifted. The bull's madness when taunted with the red cloaks of the toreadors is graphically shown, and then another horseman attacks him. This horse is disemboweled, and a large picture is thrown on the screen showing the horse, almost life-size, in its dying agony.

Quiet a little time is devoted to 'feats of the ring.' The picadors have thrown about ten darts into the shoulders of the bull, the hide is torn off and blood is dripping. The panting and exhaustion of the animal are horrible and it finally lies down. The picadors advance and attempt to make it rise. It staggers to its front feet with the blood gushing from its mouth, nose and eyes, then sinks back. The matador, brandishing his sword, kills the animal, and not to leave the picture unfinished, the limp carcass of the noble creature is dragged about the arena by a team of horses.

The matador is carried in triumph on the shoulders of the crowd, and, no doubt to teach children that they must be kind to animals, and that cruelty is a characteristic of the base, handsomely dressed women shown laughing, applauding wildly and drinking wine in a box.[58]

In the *Evening World* article the outline of the bullfight film was followed by descriptions of other titles showed at the same establishment before the investigative team moved on to other houses. Statements from an array of concerned social workers, clergy, and magistrates further reinforced the findings within the framework of this multi-installment campaign. The two accounts of bullfight films provide a clear example of a genre shift predicated on textual motivation—fact-fiction snapshot versus systematic campaign—in turn the result of being penned at two radically different junctures in the course of film culture. In a sense, both texts report findings, but the discoveries are by no means of a comparable nature: Söderberg accidentally discovers a nickel venue and is shocked by representations far removed from his memories of the wholesomely amusing Lumière shows in 1897. The investigators in 1910 distrusted the effectiveness of the Censorship Board, especially in relation to its touted educational agenda. Reports from other sources concerned the ubiquity of crime films; the harshest description, perhaps, was from Magistrate House, which branded film shows "sinks of iniquity" and

84

called for investigation. The field investigators' mission was to find out if the Board was doing its job or asleep at the switch by looking at films approved by the Board in everyday theatrical environments in New York City, and further reporting on audience composition.

The timelines between the phases pigeonholed here indeed fluctuate greatly, the motivations for the texts however—accidental discovery versus field investigation—make salient the difference even when discovery, as in Söderberg's case, is couched in disapproval.

III. Regulatory Interventions and the Reform Gaze

Arguably, the *Chicago Tribune* orchestrated one of the most conspicuous cross-promotional endeavors by enlisting the Vitascope during that momentous year of film's debut on American vaudeville stages, 1896. A decade later film culture had donned a new countenance due to the emerging nickelodeon boom, only marginally stymied by the 1907 recession. The visibility in the cityscape of these no-frills store-front venues, and the brazen promotion of their screen offerings via glaring posters, powerfully voiced barkers, and booming music, were conspicuous in more ways than one, besides soliciting a veritable deluge of nickels, further spawning the phenomenon which prompted crusades in both the *Chicago Tribune* and the *New York Evening World*. Not only the representations and conditions inside the theaters attracted attention. Harrowed citizens as well as coalitions of traditional businessmen even took exhibitors to court, asking for regulations of the intrusive music outside the theaters that literally forced passersby to take notice. In Harlem, for example, businessmen and neighbors unsuccessfully tried to stop the Nicolet's phonograph from blaring outside the establishment daily from 1:30 to 11:00 p.m. Lacking legal authority, the magistrate could not stop the proprietor, identified only as having "a Greek name," of the establishment at 37 West 125th Street from blanketing the neighborhood with rousing phonograph music.[59]

The preponderance of progressive reform interventions to appropriate the fact-fiction discourse in campaigns for regulatory measures characterized phase III in the manner of the quoted text from the *New York Evening World*. Efficient reformers reversed the flaneur perspective by way of systematic inquiries and mapping procedures when riveting their gazes to a wide assortment of social problems putatively related to the nickel culture. Moreover, they effectively managed to mobilize the press for crusades targeting a cultural form that allegedly corrupted young minds, albeit not without entertaining hopes for the medium as a vehicle for wholesome instruction. The haphazard backdrop for texts fashioned in the spirit of discovery is here supplanted by a body of resolute writing which serves as a precursor to the recreational surveys and their systematic inventory of the entire field of commercialized amusements. This genre shift is far removed from the casual motivation for the flaneur pieces and a style steeped in spleen or glibness. For reformers, *au courant* or trained in social sciences, the phenomenon of moving pictures was processed in a far from novel manner and integrated into an ongoing campaign mode against a wide set of social problems, for instance representations in slot machines, crime novels, saloons, dance halls, child labor, graft, etc. More importantly, reformers campaigned not only *against* social ills, but also *for* uplifting distractions and recreations; the playground movement will be discussed as a key progressive field for implementing active, beneficial leisure outside, and as an alternative to, commercialized amusements. Concerning moving pictures, reform and repositioning were perceived as boons for appropriating the promising features of a widely popular branch of commercial amusement.

The reformers undoubtedly visited more than one nickel house, in contrast to the casual flaneurs, and did not leave in the middle of the show. Local newspapers therefore offer a set of scattered coordinates for outlining a progressive trajectory of the monitoring and policing of film exhibition from a multitude of vantage points, roughly during the period 1906-11; the crucial years are mainly 1907 and 1908. The agenda-driven writing, accompanied by interventions targeting government bodies, eventually led to ordinances regulating film exhibition. In Los Angeles, for example, a number of regulations came into effect in 1907, when a city ordinance made it unlawful for unaccompanied children younger than fourteen years of age to visit places of amusements. It seems as if a petition to the City Council was instrumental in bringing about the ordinance, but it was predated by interventions in the press. The petition, dated May 20th, in fact only a week before the ordinance was passed by the Council, was co-signed in the name of the Los Angeles District of the Federation of Women's Clubs and by the Juvenile Court Association.[60] A local censorship ordinance, fended off by exhibitors in 1909 but adopted during a new campaign in 1911, crowned the regulatory frenzy. The petition of May

1907 was part of a campaign that took off in the columns of the *Los Angeles Times* late in 1906, when members of various civic organizations visited nickelodeons, vaudeville houses, and penny arcades in order to analyze audience composition and the nature of the representations on display, thereby articulating a phase III sensibility prior to the publishing of texts in the flaneur genre in 1907. The most famous crusade, which began in the columns of the *Chicago Tribune* in the spring of 1907, offered the broadest cultural framework for situating the reform movement. The *New York Evening World* championed the most sustained campaign efforts, though during the otherwise discursively mixed phase IV.

IV. Just Taking a Look (at Film Culture)

Phase IV represents an intermediary stage featuring a multitude of tentative approaches to a film culture on the uplift after successful calls for reform. Flaneurian essays still cropped up, albeit in upgraded forms, and undercurrents of nickel policing continued to enjoy currency. In fact, some of the most intense campaigns emerged in the early 1910s, at a time when trade papers had opened a business-friendly avenue for monitoring and admonishing the trade from an array of perspectives. Widely divergent exhibition contexts explain the holdover from the crusade era proper. New York City, where the late crusades were published, was very much a special case in its trenchant exhibition scene due to dual license requirements. The flaneurian note in some pieces bordered on making them surveys, at the same time sporting a benign tone predicated on a new type of glance, or rather, look. This look is distinct from both the flaneurian glance and the reformers' penetrating gaze; together, these three visual modes define salient aspects of metaspectatorship distributed between texts from phases II, III, and IV. Visual awareness permeates this casual observer's stylistic maneuvering in 1909: "A glance of this gathering convinces the chance onlooker that the moving picture show is not what it used to be, and here the chance onlooker gets his first eye opener. 'Just dropped in to take a look at the audience,' he confides to the usher."[61] This latter-day flaneur in a few strokes upgrades the discourse to a mode of furtive metaspectatorship ideally suited to the shift of venues and thus discursive phase, here an elegant theater on New York City's 14th Street far removed from the common-show dives discovered during phase II. Tellingly, this piece has no agenda beside merely taking a look.

87

Film culture gradually adopted less sensationalist modes of exhibition, and reporters and magazine writers unearthed progressive and upscale exhibition sites for moving pictures. Italian features made cultural inroads, and expedition films exploring Siberia, Africa, and other exotic vistas in production missions backed by venerable cultural institutions tapped into an educational discourse also visible in film campaigns outside theatrical exhibition.[62] These campaigns were hosted by a wide assortment of authorities or agencies for a multitude of social purposes, not least for health instruction, and overall sponsored by progressive interest groups or authorities familiar from the crusades. While expedition films and features were shown in upscale theaters for moneyed patrons,

FIGURE 6: Non-theatrical exhibition. An audience viewing a film at the Hiram Playground in Cleveland. *Playground*, Vol. 5, No. 8 (November 1911): 270–71.

educational efforts took moving pictures to the most unexpected venues. At times, one could also find forms of counter-exhibition, for instance in churches or charitable institutions. So, film culture had turned into a diverse phenomenon difficult to pin down in an era brimming with displays of moving images for purposes of entertainment, education, and instruction. Furthermore, the domestic film industry, legitimized by the Board of Censorship, had successfully taken over a market previously dominated primarily by French films, but now contained within the regulating embrace of the trust. Pathé's exodus from the licensed corral coincided with the breakthrough for serial films and was prompted by clashes around the newsreel market at the onset of next phase.

V. On the Same Page: Advertising and Reviewing

Taking the interaction full circle, lasting alliances were formed between newspapers and cinema. In phase V, finally, early in 1914, film culture and the program bills emerged as discursive fixtures in the press worthy of standing columns. By the mid-1910s the film industry and the press were natural bedfellows for spawning circulation and boosting attendance. Films were gradually perceived as works warranting review, and a cultural and theatrical phenomenon that had to be acknowledged and reckoned with. For the press, film theaters were highly attractive advertising clients, which had significant journalistic repercussions at a time when features, serials, and newsreels began to dominate the screens. Still, it was difficult to persuade the production companies to place ads in local newspapers, as evidenced by the concerted efforts by the *Baltimore News*. According to its advertising manager, Frank D. Webb, the volume of local advertising prompted an expansion from two columns to a full page, which had proved valuable from the perspective of circulation. In spite of intense overtures to the producers, no manufacturer considered it reasonable to spend money for advertising on local markets in 1913; this changed to a degree with the tie-ins for serials a year later.[63]

Certain papers, for instance the *New York Telegraph* from 1909 on, displayed a level of engagement with film material on par with the amount of space devoted to film issues in theatrical trade weeklies like *Billboard*, *Variety*, the *New York Dramatic Mirror*, the *New York Clipper*, and *Show World*. For all intents and purposes, the *Sunday Telegraph*'s Theatre Supplement was a regular trade paper, available as a separate item at newsstands. In January 1910 moving pictures were severed from the Theatre Supplement and awarded a supplement of their own. A few newspapers had devoted space to film on an irregular basis from around 1910, for instance papers published by the McRae-Scripps' League, among them the *Los Angeles Record*. Others offered their readers coupons for local film theaters, for instance the *Los Angeles Examiner*, while a select group of papers managed to attract substantial advertising volume for local picture houses, for example the *St. Louis Republic* and the *Cleveland Leader*.[64] Such flurries apart, it was not until the success of the serial films and their companion pieces in the press in 1914 that a more general snowstorm of coverage emerged, reflecting significant changes in film formats and exhibition practices—as well as a vested interest from the press concerning advertising.

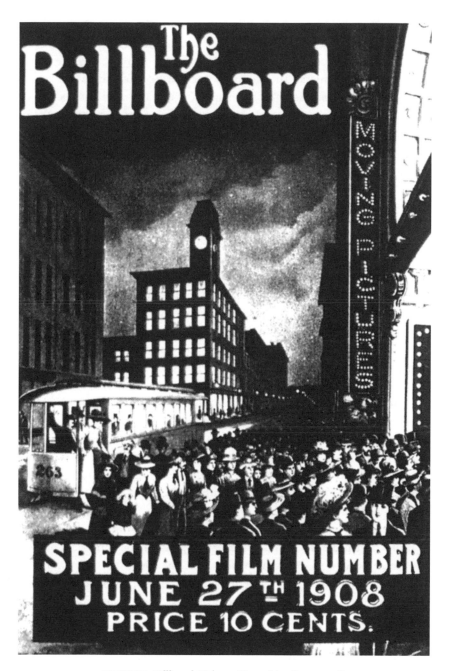

FIGURE 7: *Billboard*, Vol. 20, No. 26 (27 June 1908)

In attempts to avoid state censorship, the film medium sought protection under the law and constitution. A case sponsored by the Mutual organization ended up before the Supreme Court early in 1915, and the unanimous verdict dismissed the claim for such protection, since the "moving picture is a business, pure and simple, originated and conducted for profit" and hence not "part of the press of the country, or as organs of public opinion."[65] When, in 1915, *Woman's Home Companion* inaugurated its standing column devoted to "Better Films," an endeavor highly supportive of film culture, Helen Duey in the second installment seemingly took the Supreme Court to task when asserting: "The motion picture deserves the freedom that is accorded the press. While it is an expression of dramatic art, it is also a kind of journalism for free public discussion. Pure milk, tuberculosis, and the fly nuisance have been discussed on the screen; in like manner, big moral problems are being discussed at every film show, and at the same time the audience is being entertained."[66] Duey's column did not mark a new era, but was still a clear indication of a comfortable balance between progressive sensibilities and a mature film culture playing a decisive role in society and individuals' lives.

A year earlier the progressive weekly *Independent* had established its film column, "The Moving World. A Review of New and Important Motion Picture." The column was published once a month and focused on "films of educational value such as those in natural history, physical science, travel, industries, hygiene, social reform and the like, and we shall include only such photoplays as have some special historical, literary or religious interest." In explaining the background for the column, the editorial invokes Henri Bergson's philosophy and succinctly sums up aspects of modern life under the heading "The Birth of a New Art":

> Bergson has shown us what a paralyzing influence static conceptions of reality have had upon the history of philosophy and how futile have been all attempts to represent movement by rest. The scientist of today thinks in terms of movement. All modern thought is assuming kinetic form and we are coming to see the absurdity of the old ideas of immutability and immobility.

This focus on movement as the key factor of modern life that will revolutionize the arts and cinema has allegedly, "in fact already overtaken the older art in some respects." In contrast to the literary realm with its critical institution, film patrons have "no such guidance" to consult. Fishing out the good films from among the flow of trash presupposes criticism: "The way to do it is doubtless the same as that which has been found most effective in the case of books, pictures, and plays, that is independent and conscientious criticism from the standpoint of the public."[67]

This sketchy press trajectory in five layered movements, lopsided and motley for sure, still reflects dominant strands in the fourth estate's grappling with key junctures in American exhibition practices, which for a long time were geared to predominantly daily program changes. Such protean politics of billing dissuaded exhibitors from placing advertisements in their local newspapers, not without exception and in particular prior to the formation of the licensed trust.[68] Audiences expected constant novelty and, according to conventional wisdom, posters, handbills, and barkers provided enticement sufficient to attract patrons. It seems, however, as if the smaller houses in Los Angeles operated with longer exhibition windows, at least during 1908 and 1909; the lack of systematic programming information makes it however well-nigh impossible to ascertain the overall practices. When the *Los Angeles Examiner* provided its readers with free coupons to the nickel shows, the theaters offered concentrated descriptions of their bills and in many cases noted how often they changed program, most of them less frequently than daily.[69] In Europe in contrast weekly program changes were the norm, and longer films encouraged exhibitors to advertise, which often produced editorial payback in the news columns. After a visit to Berlin in 1911 Carl Laemmle reported with surprise that the local exhibitors changed program only twice a week, and some big houses only once a week.[70] Hence, newspapers in countries like Denmark and Sweden paid more attention to film exhibition than their American counterparts, and the high volume of advertising helped inaugurate standing film columns well in advance of the U.S.

The discussion in the following chapters will not chart film culture in the American press in the systematic fashion suggested above. This intermedial field is simply too overwhelming to be ferreted out in a convincing manner within a single study, so the approach cannot be anything but case-based and tentative. Still, the crudely engineered phases will provide direction and guiding points. During phase IV, several trade papers commenced publication, reprinting material from the press and in numerous ways engaging in a dialog on film culture in tandem with the newspaper reporting.

Film Criticism and the Trade Discourse

When reprinting an editorial from New York's *Sun*, the *Film Index* claimed in June 1909 "that it is not unusual nowadays to find long editorials on the subject in the leading daily papers of the country." Underscoring 1909 as a critical year, "the magazines, too, are giving large sections of their valuable space to really interesting articles on moving pictures."[71] On a different but gloomier note, the *Film Index* maintained early in 1910 that "picture theatre managers are not wildly enthusiastic upon the idea of local advertising," but confidently predicted that advertising would eventually be a necessity.[72] Among prominent exceptions to the rule of non-advertising were exhibitors in St. Louis, which the trade papers observed.[73] In December 1912 *Moving Picture World* contrasted the lack of film advertising in the daily press to the situation in Europe, remarking that "[h]ere in New York there is scarcely a line of cinematographic advertising in the daily press, and the same deplorable condition prevails in most of the populous centres of the country."[74] The trajectory underlying the trade observations is in the main accurate and even applies to 1913, but with a few notable exceptions however, for instance the *Baltimore News*, as previously mentioned. The gradual breakthrough for feature films in 1914 with their predominantly weekly exhibition span encouraged theaters to advertise their programs. Parallel to this development, the emergence of serial films triggered advertising and tie-ins, and publication of story installments became an integral part of the launch of serials. *Moving Picture Story Magazine*, and to a certain extent *Photoplay Magazine*, had by then already garnered track records in providing film fans with fictionalized accounts of films, and some newspapers published film stories on an irregular basis.

In November 1911 *Billboard* found it newsworthy—which attests to the general lack of film reporting at this time—to inform its readers that the Scripps-McRae press group was collecting material for an article on the film industry. A journalist had visited the Eclair plant at Fort Lee and witnessed the shooting of *Hands Across the Sea in '76*, which was the studio's first title produced in the U.S.[75] Apart from bulletin-like accounts on the theater page for upcoming attractions at the houses that advertised, newspapers gradually started to plug individual films under separate headings in the form of story synopses, predominantly without added critical observations. Film matters were seldom addressed in the daily press in 1911, and therefore *Moving Picture World* and *Film Index*, in the early days, often elected to reprint the few articles that found their way to the columns. The *Cleveland Leader*, under editor Ralph Stoddard, was one of the first newspapers to publish a film page, "Photo-Plays and Players," in December 1911. During the first half of the 1910s, the term photoplay provided an appealing concept for taking on an industry and a film culture in transition. A future critical institution for reviewing films in the lay press presented itself as a possible avenue of writing, according to trade-paper editors.[76]

Around the time trade papers devoted exclusively to moving pictures emerged—*Views and Films Index* in 1906 and *Moving Picture World* in the spring of 1907—and the theatrical trade weeklies instituted standing columns dealing with film matters. *Billboard* inaugurated its film column on February 2, 1907, mixing trade notes with plot synopses from bulletins for new film releases. On December 3, 1910, an editorial informed readers about an upcoming review section promised for January 7, 1911, but the start was delayed for a week. The unsigned reviews were curt and overall appreciative.

Adopting a critical discourse and a proper format for addressing individual films rather than straightforward promotion presented itself as something of a problem for the trade papers. More or less from the outset, the film-trade weeklies reprinted synopses of released films, material emanating directly from the producers' publicity departments. The bulletins prepared by the Biograph Company, for example, represent one such release genre, and they found their way into the trade columns virtually unedited. Gradually, the film companies began to publish their own house organs and even exhaustive accounts of films often illustrated with production stills: *Edison's Kinetograms*, *Universal Weekly*, *Essanay News*, etc.[77] Stills were also being published in the trade papers, most frequently in *Film Index*.

The *New York Dramatic Mirror* began reviewing films on a modest scale in June 1908; in the June 6th issue only three were reviewed under the heading "Reviews of Late Films," which in a couple of months became "Reviews of New Films," headlining a more ambitious level of coverage. Initially, the criticism was highly condensed; the Pathé title *The Athletic Woman*, for example, received only two dismissive short lines: "This is a rather dreary subject and not up to the high mark set by the Pathe company."[78] The following week, the editorial policy for reviewing was explained:

In reviewing late films, foreign or American, it is the purpose of THE MIRROR to cover only those that have been seen on exhibition by one of THE MIRROR staff. It will not be possible therefore to review all the new films as fast as they are produced. Nor are THE MIRROR reviews of films to be considered in the light of the press notice or advertisements. They will aim rather to be unprejudiced criticisms of the pictures and the story they tell, giving praise where praise is due and pointing out faults where faults may appear. An intelligent treatment of new subjects along this line should be of benefit to the moving picture art or profession in the same degree that able press criticism benefits the drama.[79]

Eight titles were covered this second week. *Variety* had been reviewing films on a limited scale in addition to new vaudeville acts since early 1907 in columns signed Sime (Simon J. Silverman, the paper's founder and editor) and Rush (Alfred Rushton Grearson), and for a time started reviewing not only films but the entire bill at one New York City house per week. This new policy and the shift from product to exhibition contexts were announced on December 5, 1908; the initiative did not however preclude reviewing additional film titles outside the context of a full program. The reviews of houses and program bills were soon abandoned and the dominant focus for reviews in *Variety* remained individual films rather than programs. The reviewers, however, conscientiously informed readers at which theater the title had been viewed. The number of films reviewed by *Variety* was lower than in the *New York Dramatic Mirror*, but the articles were somewhat longer and the tone often decidedly acerbic.

On August 21, 1909, Epes Winthrop Sargent (Chicot) was hired by *Views and Film Index* as a reviewer.[80] Sargent had recently worked for *Variety* after having established himself in the drama supplement of the *New York Telegraph*, writing predominantly about vaudeville. By hiring Sargent and instituting a review section, *Film Index* curtailed the space available for reprints of manufacturers' advance notices, which henceforth appeared in condensed form. The *New York Dramatic Mirror* had pioneered the review form in 1908, but continued to publish only very terse criticism. When commenting upon the hiring of Chicot, the *Mirror* reminded readers about its track record and that the review concept had been instituted by the *Mirror* and later emulated by *Moving Picture World* before *Film Index* jumped on the bandwagon.[81] Sargent's reviews in *Film*

Index devoted more space and attention to each film, however, and thus renewed the genre.

In October 1908 *Moving Picture World* enlisted "two capable newspaper men" to visit local theaters in New York City together with a staff writer. The outsiders "were asked to be guided in the expression of their opinions by the remarks overheard among the audience and to note particularly how the film was received or applauded." The experiment of publishing "comments on film subject" was not taken lightly by the paper. It was the result of "yielding to requests of many of our readers" and guarded with caveats. According to the lead-in, the comments were edited, still "some statements may not agree with the opinion of the manufacturers." As a "defense of the critiques we say that they must be taken as an expression of public opinion." This indirect feedback from the public, as it were, would benefit the manufacturer, "as it is or should be the aim of the film manufacturer to please the public, we will try to hold up the mirror of public opinion as the surest and safest guide to the success of and future stability of the business." The opening column reviewed ten titles plus a split reel from Essanay. Most of the manufacturers were featured and named, though there was no mention of the Biograph Co. for *Ingomar, the Barbarian*, which was however a "first-class film." This initial round favored historical subjects: Vitagraph's *Richard III* and Pathé's *Samson and Delilah* were both praised, while Kalem's *As You Like It* lacked "the finishing touches." Edison's *The Devil* garnered laurels for "acting and scenic effects," while the critics did not mince words concerning Vitagraph's *The Wages of Sin*, which apparently lacked redeeming qualities.[82]

Late in 1909 *Moving Picture News* blatantly dismissed a request from a reader proposing a section for film criticism. According to the editor, "the motion picture industry is going ahead too rapidly for such nonsensical things as film criticism to interfere with or unduly fill up our columns." Further elaborating on the matter, the editor fears he would be accused of being partisan, this irrespective of whether a film is chastised or praised. Furthermore, he considers criticism futile if not delivered well in advance of the film's opening. In a putatively decisive retort the editor quips: "[N]o two criticisms are alike."[83] A review of Imp's *Destine* published "in a contemporary" periodical—in all likelihood *Show World*—was reprinted as an example of the futility of critical activities in the face of an alternative account penned by the *News'* writer. After having demonstrated the critical institution's lack of consensus, he concludes: "Our position is thus fully defined, and we feel sure that after criticism is eliminated the trade will be happier." The columns devoted to criticism in the *New York Dramatic Mirror, Billboard, Variety, Moving Picture World,* and *Show World* were not to be eliminated, a change of heart had to take place elsewhere—at the editorial desk of the *News.*

The editor of *Moving Picture News* returned to the topic a few weeks later, this time enlisting support from an editorial in the St. Louis, Mo., *Republican,* which mocked the stenographic manner of criticism in *Show World.* Its author, Alfred E. Saunders, concluded that the attempts razzed by this and other high-class papers are indeed a "ridiculous manner of film criticism."[84] Soon enough, *Moving Picture News* had second thoughts and began to publish succinct reviews, first signed by Colin (only twice), later Walton, and then Jean on the Curtain.

In the early days of picture criticism audience reactions were considered a vital aspect of the endeavor advocated by both the *Mirror* and the *Moving Picture World.* A similar sensibility motivated *Variety*'s decision to review full programs in the manner of the *World.* The critical initiatives thus offered merely a vessel-like channeling of audience reactions in lieu of a critic's personal opinions. In a balanced discussion of "picture criticism" and reviewing Harvey Harris Gates rebukes the perception that the critic's sole obligation was to report on audience reactions and instead argues for what to his mind appears to be the decisive matter: "the question of whether it is a good picture or a bad one." To embark on such a critical mission requires good taste and "analytical talent."[85] An institution of picture criticism conducted under such auspices, he claims, would serve audiences and producers alike. Gates' contention in 1913 reflected a film culture distinctly different from the offerings reviewed in 1908. His call to pen was partly answered in the columns of the *Chicago Tribune* in 1914 by Kitty Kelly. The pioneering efforts of Kelly and her colleagues will be addressed later. In the next chapter we will turn to the amusement geography in Los Angeles and chart it in several registers, from the calls for theater construction in the 1880s to the palatial film theaters for features in the mid-1910s. The latter's programs were both advertised and reviewed.

CHAPTER 3

AMUSEMENT MOBILITY IN LOS ANGELES: GEOGRAPHY, VENUES, AND EXHIBITORS

"I don't mean that kind of history."[1]

Amusements before the Nickelodeons

A CHARTING OF the theatrical geography from the early days to the era of film palaces will literally set the stage for the complex amusement fabric tying in with general patterns of business mobility in Los Angeles. The structure of business life reflects multiple interests and interacts with consumer mobility in compounded constellations, which in turn are defined by the overall urban flow and transportation networks. After beginning with the establishment of a theatrical scene before 1900, we will follow the paper trail from the nickelodeons initially dotting the dense yet culturally peripheral part of the city that once was its absolute center, the Plaza area. Gradually, and fueled by popular demand, film culture widened its circle of exhibition, but in the process, just a few years down the road, moved into palatial venues for predominantly licensed films. Meanwhile, longer films were booked by legitimate houses centered in a part of town on the verge of losing its grip as the business hub. Within the confines of the fledgling business center, intersecting further south in the vicinity of Spring Street and Seventh, new movie palaces loomed large.

Los Angeles was an entertainment-driven city, and the influx of "colonists" and winter tourists provided a stabile market for high-class amusement offerings. Homeownership, a crucial factor for the census in Los Angeles, largely placed the patrons for pricey theatrical offerings in neighborhoods outside the city center, which presupposed first-rate transportation options for shopping sprees as well as evening entertainments. Theaters located slightly off the beaten track in relation to the transportation nodes suffered in the competition. This was the bitter lesson learned by hosts of managers at the Walker Theater on Grand Avenue, even if the rapidly increasing number of automobiles made patrons more mobile. This chapter leads up to a case study of the many futile attempts at finding a viable formula for this particular house and especially the exhibition strategies implemented by the Mozart family.

In the 1870s, back in the days when the Saunterer penned accounts of life in the city, traveling stage attractions were offered at only one venue in Los Angeles, the Merced Hall close to the Plaza. Here "three civilizations meet," as Robert Grau discerningly observed: "[T]he Chinese and Japanese at one corner of the triangle, the Spanish and Mexican at the second, and the 'Gringos,' or Americans at the third." This mix of civilizations proved to be highly important for the emergence of film culture in Los Angeles. Merced Hall, at 418 North Main Street, functioned as a community center, hosting, in addition to occasional traveling performances, lectures, funerals, weddings, and other ceremonies.[2] As the "building boom continued without diminution," all signs indicated that Los Angeles was destined to develop into "a large city." Still, certain key features were sorely missed in the burgeoning city in 1883: Hotel facilities were inadequate for accommodating incoming visitors, there were no public parks for leisurely strolls, and—important for civic and cultural aspirations—the city could boast no theater building.[3] Downtown was electrified that year, and 250 lamps on tall masts were set up along the busiest thoroughfares. Ambitious sewer projects were finished in 1890, and running water became accessible in outlying districts also. As Robert M. Fogelson has shown in his classical study, Los Angeles was consciously planned as a city scattered and fragmented.[4] Railroad tracks tied far-flung districts to downtown, and telephone services, schools, and later playgrounds were available throughout the area.

Census reports for 1900 document the penchant for living in suburbia, listing 42% of household heads in Los Angeles as homeowners. For colonists arriving in droves, not least from the Midwest and the metonymic Iowa, the prospect of owning a home provided a major incentive for relocation. By the time it was connected to the rest of the country via

Southern Pacific's line to San Francisco in 1876, Los Angeles' population had more than doubled: from over 5,000 in 1870 to over 11,000 in 1880. The number of residents reached 50,000 in 1890, a figure which had doubled again by the turn of the century; in 1910 it touched the 320,000 mark. The unprecedented real-estate and development boom from 1886 to mid-1888 was mainly triggered by a second railroad connection to Los Angeles, the Santa Fe Railroad, and the ensuing rate war between the lines. While the market outlook turned considerably gloomier in the early 1890s, the economy gradually bounced back at the end of the decade. The industrial backbone of the local economy in 1910, two years before the harbor had opened in San Pedro after a protracted battle, was agribusiness, manufacturing, and oil. It was at this particular juncture, in 1911, that local boosters discovered the clout of the burgeoning local film industry as an advertising agent for the Southland as well as an economic behemoth in the making.

The absence of a proper theater building did not preclude stage entertainment at several venues in the pre-railroad era: foremost the old Merced, housed on the second story of a building close to the Pico house at the Plaza—the historic city center. The Turnverein Hall, one of many developments in 1887, occasionally hosted theater performances, as Mott Hall did more regularly; like the Merced, it was on the second story, though over the market in Mott's case. Hazard's Pavilion, a barn-like structure that was home to fairs, pageants, lectures, conventions, poultry shows, prizefights, and political rallies—plus all forms of theatricals; in that capacity it seated 4,000—was erected at the corner of Olive and Fifth in 1887 when the expanding city outgrew the small Merced. Henry T. Hazard, the mayor of Los Angeles, built the pavilion in collaboration with entrepreneur George Pike. The Baptist Church later acquired the lot and built the long-standing Temple Auditorium, which opened with much pomp in 1906, offering church services on Sundays and high-class musical attractions the rest of the week presented under the auspices of legendary impresario L.E. Behymer.[5] In 1914 the house became Clune's Auditorium and later Philharmonic Auditorium. The structure was used as a venue for music until 1964—today, the site is dominated by a parking lot across the street from Pershing Square.

In October 1884 the first purpose-built theater opened, the Chinese Theater located at 212 Marchessault Street just northeast of the Plaza between Alameda Street and the so-called Negro Alley; it was reported to accommodate 1,200 patrons. The theater operated until just after the turn of the century and ended its tenure by screening moving pictures.[6] In 1887 visual entertainment was provided by the Los Angeles Panorama Company, and its debut panorama on a lot on South Main was *The Siege of Paris*. Earlier that year, another panorama had been erected at Washington Gardens, an extensive park-like tract located on the outskirts of the city at the southwest corner of South Main and Washington Street.

Washington Gardens, in its different guises, turned into a popular park and outdoor resort before its demise late in 1912. In 1901 Washington Gardens became Chutes Park, which advertised itself as park, theater, zoo, and midway. The theater presented small-time vaudeville acts interspersed with films, initially billed as Vitascope films. In November 1910 Arthur S. Hyman acquired the theater's lease, offering vaudeville and films at what was then the newly opened Luna Park, which featured an array of novel attractions and an enlarged zoo after a year in virtual "hibernation."[7] The midway attractions, previously under attack, were relegated to a segregated area in the park, liquor was banned, and the dance pavilion was transformed into a skating rink. When the new managers took over the lease, they, as everybody else, sought patronage from women and children foremost.[8] Luna closed down in the spring of 1911 for additional improvements and reopened in June, but not for long. Washington Gardens also hosted a baseball park. Chutes Park was where the Los Angeles Tourists—several name changes later the Angels— played their first game in the Pacific Coast League in March 1903 against Seattle. When Luna Park was sold late in 1912, the buildings were flattened to give room for an expanded ballpark.

When the theatrical season opened in 1894, a decade after the call for a theater building, the Burbank Theater offered melodrama, the Los Angeles Theater society drama, while the Grand Opera House opened its dramatic season in November after an initial round of opera. Vaudeville had found a home at the recently opened Imperial Music Hall, on Main Street between First and Second in the old Chamber of Commerce building. According to the *Times*, "the opening [of the Imperial] promised to be the amusement event of Los Angeles."[9] The old auditorium had been refurbished with the latest stage equipment and comfortable opera chairs for the audience. The hall, modeled after the music halls in London and Paris, was decorated in white and gold. A frivolous cartoon

published a few days after the debut put a dancing lady in front of an audience, captioned "La Fiesta De Los Baldheads." Apart from bald men,
the audience included several women in gaudy hats, hinting at frivolous
interaction between the groups. Other than the Imperial Music Hall,
vaudeville was offered at Mott Hall in 1895 by the trio Gottloeb, Lehman, and Ellinghouse; Lehman was also affiliated with the Orpheum circuit. The Orpheum Vaudeville Circuit—that is the Meyerfeld syndicate
which operated together with Martin Beck—opened its own branch in
Los Angeles on December 31, 1895, by moving into the Grand Opera
House at 110 South Main. The house, built by O.W. Child with 1,440
seats, had opened in May 1884 in response to the previous year's call for
a regular theatrical venue. The house was torn down in 1936 after having closed with "a nudist show."[10]

The founder of the Casino Theater, J.E. Waldeck, once local manager
of the Orpheum, started off with burlesque at 344 South Spring Street
and was initially met with a good following. His establishment in fact
had three legs: Apart from the live attractions on stage, another section
of the building displayed sixty-eight waxwork scenes under the familiar
name Eden Musee, while the second floor housed a luxury billiard parlor as well as slot machines for visual attractions. The house opened late
in 1903, but when problems mounted due to escalating costs for attractions and unpaid construction bills, Waldeck apparently saw no way to
alleviate the straits; he died after being found in a canyon near Santa
Monica in 1904.[11]

The first stock house in Los Angeles, the Burbank, opened in 1891
(1,580 seats). Dr. David Burbank, a legendary Southland developer with
a city named after him to boot, built the theater. Fred A. Cooper was
among a string of more than a dozen unsuccessful Burbank managers in
the early days. His demise as manager, however, happened to coincide
with the presentation of the Vitascope at the Orpheum in July 1896.[12]
Oliver Morosco picked up the lease for the Burbank in 1898, which initiated an era in Los Angeles theatricals. In 1908 the new Majestic Theater (1,650 seats) in the Hamburger building, 845 South Broadway, was
opened under Morosco's management and booked by the John Cort
Syndicate. The opening of the Majestic redefined the amusement geography and functioned as a bellwether for upcoming developments. Soon,
movie palaces nestled around Morosco's house. The link to the newfangled business center was marked by Hamburger's Department Store,

which in addition housed a small film theater for the shoppers and their children, the Arrow.

The Mason Opera House, built by John Mason, opened on June 18, 1903 (1,552 seats), under the management of H.C. Wyatt, a seasoned impresario who previously managed the Grand Opera House during several seasons. Klaw & Erlanger took over the bookings at Mason in August 1911. The house stood until 1955, but was turned over to film in the 1920s.

In August 1904 the Belasco Theatre, seating 1,200, opened the door for legitimate drama under Frederick Belasco and John Blackwood. After the Burbank, this was the second prominent stock company in Los Angeles. On May 22, 1911, it was reported that the Belasco, the Burbank, the new Belasco (under construction; opened as Morosco's Theater in early 1913), the Majestic, and the Lyceum (renamed when the Orpheum moved out) were all operating under the management of Morosco-Blackwood. The extent of their business empire prompted an incorporation, which took place on June 3.[13]

In 1903 the Orpheum proceeded to a new location, formerly the Los Angeles Theater (1,425 seats) at 227 South Spring, a house built in 1888 by Juana Neal. Moving pictures remained on the bill at the new house on South Spring, though under various designations: Orpheum Motion Pictures, High-Class Moving Pictures, Daylight Pictures; the latter technology was adopted when dark auditoriums became a concern. On June 26, 1911, the Orpheum again relocated, this time to a purpose-built house at 624 South Broadway which seated 2,000. Moving pictures were on the bill at all three Orpheum venues.[14] After August 14, 1911, newsreels were the only type of films screened by the Orpheum, initially the *Pathé Journal*, billed as "Motion Views of the World's News."[15] The elegant new Orpheum was built to meet the competition from the rivaling vaudeville stages, not least the Pantages Theater, 532–36 South Broadway, which had opened on September 26, 1910, more or less the same day as Clune's Theater next door at 528 South Broadway. While Clune offered vaudeville and first-run licensed pictures, Pantages interspersed its vaudeville turns with films as a standing item on the bill, under the rubric Pantageoscope. Overall, the vaudeville houses integrated films under more or less fancy designations, some of them with a genre-specific slant, like The Laugho-scope at the Los Angeles Theater. Earlier on the Unique offered the Uniquescope and Walker the Walkerscope.

Venues on the Move

Newspapers often displayed highbrow disdain for what were considered cheap amusements. The short-lived *Evening News*, for example, in the fall of 1906 dubbed Los Angeles "the home of fine theaters," and listed the Belasco, Burbank, Orpheum, Grand Opera House, Hotchkiss (formerly the Casino), and the Mason (the latter soon to face competition for patrons seeking musical attractions at the Temple Auditorium), but found it superfluous to "speak at length" about "the cheaper places," namely Fischer's, Unique, Empire, Cineograph, Lyric, and Broadway.[16] So, let us fill in some gaps in order to illustrate the extreme fluidity of the small-time theatrical market. Among the minor houses, the Novelty, which had opened at 523 South Main in October 1905, is conspicuously absent from the list. It was probably dark at this particular point after being renamed People's Theater, and had not yet been reopened as the New People's by Sullivan & Considine; it later became the Olympic and, in 1912, the Century. The Unique, a small-time vaudeville house managed by Flora E. Hentz and John U. Zallee, opened at 456 South Spring in 1901. The bill at the Unique catered to the family audience, and according to the *Times'* theater page, "[t]here is no place in the city where women and children can more safely go. [...] All low allusions in any act placed on the bill are cut out by the management," and it was reassuringly pledged, "the women on the stage are there to perform, and not to flirt with men in the audience."[17] The Unique moved to 629 South Broadway in 1902 and remained there until the fall of 1909, when Hentz and Zallee relocated to the Empire Theater at 128 East Third Street for a short stint. The house on Broadway was torn down and replaced by the Co-Tenant Building in 1910 as part of the business center's migration. On May 10, 1910, the small-time house the Cineograph Theater, which had opened early September 1902 as a sister to the Cineograph in San Francisco, closed down, only to reopen as the Court Street Theater a few months later. Before closing, the Cineograph, named after a film projector manufactured by Lubin, had passed through several program models, trying first to substitute unsuccessful vaudeville for drama, and finally opting for pictures only before calling quits.[18] The establishment shared fate, time frame, and billing concept with the Unique. When the Cineograph opened, it was described as "a new moving-picture theater" mixing pictures with vaudeville; the house seated 1,200 and did not sell drinks or allow smoking.[19]

The volatility of the small-time vaudeville market offered a backdrop for the first film venues, such as Tally's The Lyric, which had opened as the Electric Theater, programming pictures only in April 1902 before turning to a combination program under the new name. Tally dropped the house for other ventures, but returned as an exhibitor in late 1905 when he acquired the Broadway, which had been one of A.J. Morganstern's venues. Morganstern, a lawyer trying to build up a chain of theater houses in California with the Broadway Theater, which opened in December 1903, as his flagship, had also acquired the Casino. In the turmoil following Waldeck's death the Casino took on a hoodoo reputation, a fate experienced by both Morosco and Wyatt before Morganstern acquired the lease in February 1905—with little success, which forced him to curb his theatrical ambitions later that year.

Overall, the competition for attractions had escalated among the small houses in both San Francisco and Los Angeles, and acts priced at $75 in the middle of 1905 could bring in as much as $125 in 1907; costs hard to bear for the small-time houses, which the multitude of management changes shows. After the nickel houses began to enter the market, most small-time venues dropped out or settled for mixed bills under a steady stream of intrepid managements.

When the Orpheum moved again in 1911, at a time when film and theater venues were flocking to the new business center, the abandoned building on Spring Street was turned into the Lyceum. On June 30, 1912, Morosco and Cort turned the Lyceum into a house for high-class pictures, but already in November, J.A. Quinn added the lease to his many other film ventures under the incorporated Q Amusement Co.

Apart from its discussion of the theatrical scene—breathtakingly mercurial as the run-through above evidences—the *Evening News* observed a shift in city gravity underway already in 1906 when the key developments still were at the planning stage.[20] A migration south of the business center was thus in the works when the nickel proprietors started scouting for locations. It was therefore no accident that their venues formed another cluster further north at less expensive addresses, but still along the busy streets running north to south: primarily on South Main and South Spring. Already in 1895, at a critical phase of the city's development, the *Times*, in a remarkably prescient piece, had speculated on the future of South Main Street, foreseeing a trajectory in the making that eventually transformed the street into an ideal avenue for nickel culture.

This is just now a critical time for the Main-street property-owners. As The Times has frequently pointed out, it rests largely with them to say whether the business section shall keep on in a southerly direction and work into Main street again after passing the junction of Broadway, or whether it shall turn westward on Hill street and cluster around Central Park, in which case the probability is that Main-street property will not be much more sought after than property on North Main is today.[21]

The staff writer proposes three initiatives to prevent the slump: paving the street, electrifying the car line, and building a much-needed hotel on South Main near 10th Street. According to the *Times'* ever-optimistic assessment of business prospects, a syndicate formed around such a plan would double their investment in twelve months. The hotel was not built and paving and electrifying was not enough to turn South Main into a prominent part of the business center. An editorial in the *Los Angeles Express* from 1903, titled "Financial Center of the City," prophesized a concentration of banks and financial institutions in one block. "Fourth street from Main to Broadway seems destined to become to Los Angeles what Wall Street is to New York, the financial center of the city, where the great majority if not all the banks will have their headquarters."[22]

A magazine writer in 1907 bemoaned the dispersal of the former business center around Third and Spring Street claiming, "To-day there is no center."[23] The shopper who could once find everything in the old intersection now has to explore Broadway, Spring, Main, and Hill between Fifth and Seventh to pick up all items; a predicament remedied when Hamburger's Department Store opened on Broadway and Eighth. The *Times*, proudly reporting on the business and construction developments, claimed to have scooped all the new ventures on South Broadway early in 1910, which solidified the shift of metropolitan gravity. The total cost of projects to be finished within 1910 was estimated at $2,000,000, among the building projects were three theatrical enterprises: the Pantages in the Garland Building (534 South Broadway), the Tally Theater Block, starting with two floors but designed for eight, and the new Orpheum.[24] Not yet reported on was William H. Clune's new theater, for which the *Times* could publish architectural sketches in July.[25] Thus, the closer to the emerging business center the more prestigious the venue, as defined by land prices.

In June 1910 Tally had moved his New Broadway from 554 to 833 South Broadway, which confirmed the gradual shift of prestige venues further south on Broadway signaled by the building of the Majestic in 1908. The Hyman Theater, which opened late in 1910, was located at 804 South Broadway, opposite Hamburger's Department Store. On June 26, 1911, the Orpheum had relocated to a new, purpose-built house at 624 South Broadway. The most symbolic shift took place in January 1913 when Morosco moved one of his stock companies away from the Belasco to a new house, the Morosco Theater at 744 South Broadway, while the old venue switched to small-time vaudeville as the Republic Theater, better suited to the location. Thus, all the new ritzy showplaces were located in the 5–800 blocks on South Broadway, the main artery and white way in the new amusement and business district. The older theaters resided further north, in the old business district, on Broadway, Spring or Main, which evidences the observation concerning a migration a few crucial blocks south: Belasco (Republic from 1913) at 337 South Main; Burbank, 546-48 South Main; Grand Opera House, 108 South Main; Mason Opera House, 127 South Broadway; and Los Angeles Theater, 340 South Spring (this was the old Hotchkiss/Casino, which later turned into the Empress). Nearby, the Temple Auditorium on Fifth and Olive had since 1906 been the home for musical attractions of the highest class. The cheaper film theaters and small-time vaudeville houses lined the busy 100-500 blocks on South Main and South Spring. On North Main, close to the Plaza, the oldest nickel house and a few newer ones still catered to the ethnic patrons in the vicinity, predominantly of Mexican, Japanese, and Chinese descent. In 1912 Broadway came across as the prestige street in respect to amusement venues, which mirrored the business center's migration south. Add to this the branching out of film exhibition to the suburban districts in the early 1910s. We will return to the breakthrough of features at the Majestic, Mason, and the Auditorium in conjunction with the discussion of the Mozart Theater.

Tricky Traffic and Cinematic Vehicles

Prior to the opening of nickel houses, the *Times* occasionally reported on some particularly noteworthy aspect of a film, most often Biograph material at the Orpheum, but silence was otherwise the default mode in the columns. On June 7, 1899, a hitherto unknown film venue, the Los Angeles Theater, advertised mutoscope pictures of Pope Leo XII "taken at the Vatican by the American Biograph Co."[26] Biograph pictures at the Orpheum received attention due to the technology involved when shooting films depicting "persons in epileptic fits," as well as "the movements of all kinds of microbes," and "the growth and flowering of plants." The latter type of films presupposed single-frame exposures at regular intervals, in this instance every half hour.[27] Later, the use of "machine evidence" in divorce cases was discussed. The writer was however not fully convinced concerning the proposal's practicality: "This has often been done in theaters where such things can be easily arranged, but there would appear to be difficulties in the way of its being attempted in actual life."[28]

The nature of the representations and the intricate ways of capturing new types of content provided the focal points for reporters rather than the machine per se. In 1901 an article provided an in-depth account of how biograph tricks were perpetrated, a discursive genre that gained ubiquity five to six years later and experienced a renaissance after the publication of Frederick A. Talbot's *Moving Pictures. How They Are Made and Worked.* One particular trick effect seemingly never ceased to stir popular imagination: body parts, especially legs, severed from the body in automobile accidents.[29] Such shocking images of gore and carnage placed cinema as an integral part of modernity's perceptual fabric and at times deadly physicality.

It has turned into a scholarly staple to discuss the alleged shock aesthetic of early cinema in relation to means of transportation—both the mindset adopted when people were packed with others on the crammed streetcars as well as the carnage wrought by the metropolitan traffic on rails. Numerous contemporary commentators sported reflections in a similar register. An automotive sketch of Los Angeles can illustrate a shift of focus from early cinema's association with trains, or trams in Simmel's case, to an alliance between automobiles and feature films. The latter format's success was often evidenced by the capacity to attract automobile patrons. The risk for shocking carnage did not disappear in the era of automobiles. An accident killed fewer for sure, but the grand total of casualties escalated. Also, in a comparatively small town like Los Angeles the streets were perceived as "deadly," according to an early 1908 editorial in the *Times.* Even in the face of a "sizeable death toll inflicted by automobiles, streetcars, and objects falling from sky-reaching structures," commentators claimed this was a "price necessary to pay." Attempts at far-reaching corrections would namely serve as "a deathblow to progress, the decay of empire, the stifling of the grand ambitions of a wonder-making era." Therefore, the only available cure is for everyone to develop a "habit of alertness," a perception echoing the Saunterer's ambivalent stance concerning progress. Thus, nobody should walk the streets of the "roaring town without concentrating his or her undivided attention on the business in hand, which business is to keep out of danger."[30]

As early as 1905 the *Los Angeles Times*' Lancer, Harry C. Carr, had noted that "almost every other entry in the Coroner's book of records reads: 'Killed by street car' or 'struck by automobile.' "[31] Local lore has it that the first known automobile to appear on Los Angeles' streets was built by S.D. Sturgis in a downtown Los Angeles shop for one J. Philip Erie in 1897. In 1900 driving was common enough for the establishment of The Automobile Club of Southern California. Four thousand automobiles traversed Los Angeles' streets in 1908, a year when the first taxi service went into business. In 1911 about 21,000 automobiles were registered. So important was the automobile market that the Goodrich Company elected to rent the Auditorium for an hour-long advertising film on the rubber industry. "The films will be shown free to all automobile dealers, dealers in rubber goods, and autoists, and other people interested in the rubber industry." The film was accompanied by a lecture.[32] A month later Studebaker hosted a screening at the Gamut Club for automobile dealers.[33] At the end of 1913 150 automobile accidents were recorded daily. Among remedies proposed for making the streets safer was taking advantage of motion pictures and showing correct and incorrect driving behavior at all the city's theaters, a proposal that never came to fruition.[34]

For a time, the intense traffic made Los Angeles a city predicated on both mass-transit and automobiles. Pacific Electric, Huntington's corporation, offered extensive opportunities for convenient rail travel across the region, and trams lined the downtown area. Huntington was also involved in the Los Angeles Railway Corporation, which operated 761 passenger cars carrying 125,000,000 passengers in 1911. A total of 1494 injuries were reported during the year, 31 of them fatalities. In evaluating these dismal figures, the Board of Utilities predictably expressed concerns about the number of injuries, but reassured passengers that the percentage was lower when compared to similar systems of metropolitan transportation in the nation, this in spite of the higher level of congestion in busy downtown Los Angeles.[35] Among future transportation projects, Harry H. Culver advertised a subway between downtown and Culver City. The Pacific

Electric Railway, he claimed in his ad, "has bought and paid for a right-of-way for this eight million dollar project," which would cut the time for traveling from Sixth and Hill Street to Culver City from 25 to nine minutes, a grandiose idea never realized and still sorely missed.[36]

FIGURE 8: Advertisement for planned subway between downtown Los Angeles and Culver City. *Los Angeles Tribune*, November 2, 1913, VII:5.

Fads, Figures, and Recreation Patterns

If the bicycle craze and vaudeville mania putatively combined for the sorry state of American stage in New York City in 1896, a quartet of "theatrical evils" loomed large in 1911: automobiles, moving pictures, free passes and tickets, and "the theatrical civil war."[37] By then the interest in biking as a pastime diversion had lost its momentum. For society people, if one can trust the *Moving Picture World*, "the bicycle [was] dead as a doornail."[38] The strict divide formerly separating the precincts of vaudeville and the legitimate stage had become increasingly muddled in the 1900s. And in 1911, it was opined, the gallery was no longer considered the "final arbiter" to be played to in the vaudeville houses, which attests to a partial eclipse of the frivolous and the risqué—as well as the dominance of new audience groups. At this juncture, legitimate actors oftentimes found themselves doing turns, dramatic sketches or playlets, while "vaudevillians" moved into musical comedy; a castling responsible for higher prices for first-rate attractions. Seemingly unencumbered by the theatrical evils listed by the *Venice Vanguard*—in a syndicated piece penned on the East Coast—Los Angeles presented itself as a vibrant theater city in the early 1910s with a strong and variegated vaudeville scene and several first-rate, legitimate stages under the management of theatrical tycoon Oliver Morosco and his business associate John Blackwood. Meanwhile, struggling small-time vaudeville houses, in the wake of a craze for popular vaudeville peaking in 1910, were the causalities when the leading circuits upped the ante by moving into new lavish houses and offering attractions matching the ambience of the venues.[39] As part of the crossover of the formerly ironclad division between vaudeville and legit, feature films made conspicuous inroads in legitimate houses from 1911, as will be shown. While film exhibitors were on the verge of lining the scintillating theater district with palace-like structures alongside vaudeville houses and legitimate theaters, the old nickel culture still lingered in venues catering to the diverse ethnicities in the former business center in Los Angeles, along the low-digit blocks of South Main and South Spring, and further north around the Plaza. These geographical fault lines between venues were clearly mirrored in the levels of runs carried by exhibitors, which in turn were reflected in the ticket prices. And the admission charged translated into patterns of attendance in terms of class and ethnicities.

112

A statistical exercise from 1910, in its headline proclaiming the picture show "omnipotent," counted 60 shows and 400 patrons in attendance at each house on average per night, adding up to between 30,000 to 40,000 tickets per week. Thomas L. Tally and William H. Clune stand out from the overall exhibition fabric; Tally's Broadway house was dubbed the finest in town, perhaps in the country, and Clune's popular venue could allegedly seldom accommodate all would-be patrons.[40] The number of houses represented a substantial increase in venues, in fact doubling between the spring of 1909 and the summer of 1910.[41] In August 1911 local exhibitor Arthur S. Hyman presented statistics he had compiled on behalf of the Southern California Motion Picture Men's Association (SCMP) which documented yet another sharp expansion. According to Hyman, 96 moving picture houses resided in the city, 84 of them members of the SCMP. Patrons numbering 60,000 attended the shows each weekday, while 100,000 lined up in front of the box offices on Sundays, which translated to $52,000 in weekly receipts.[42]

The newspapers continued to offer a slew of statistical accounts, particularly in early 1913, when the *Times* provided its readers with a condensed recreational survey, as it were, by riveting its attention to a run-of-the-mill Saturday afternoon when pleasure seekers gallivanted about the city. Two hundred six thousand were said to be on the move. What were people up to, then? Streets and stores attracted 100,000, 15,000 visited parks, 20,000 were enjoying excursions on the beaches or in the suburbs, and the same number of people was out motoring, readers were told. The regular theaters sold 5,600 tickets, while the movie houses catered to 25,000 patrons. As the reporter puts it, and note the focus on sound, or, rather, noise, "[s]eventy motion-picture theaters made their noisy bid for the restless nickel, and at practically every one of them it was impossible to find sufficient chairs to supply the demand. The seating capacity of these twentieth-century attractions varies from 100 to 1,800 and the crowd shifts constantly."[43] Four months earlier, the *Los Angeles Examiner* had provided its readership with statistical data concerning film culture in Los Angeles. The material was based on a report submitted by director Hobart Bosworth to the local censorship board. According to his estimates, 90,000 tickets were sold every day by the film theaters, 550 reels were used every week, 40 of these were first-run items, and 25 produced by the Edison trust. The bills offered 50 % drama, and 25 melodrama, the remainder consisting of educational films and comedies. A few years ago, he claims, 75 % of the program was made up of melodramas. In the East melodramas still enjoyed currency, especially Western material, he maintains. Los Angeles boasted 90 theaters, and six to eight of them showed first-run films.[44] Figures in the *Los Angeles Herald* corroborate Bosworth's material: Of the 87 theaters in Los Angeles, 75 to 80 were movie theaters.[45] Estelle Lawton Lindsey, a pioneer contributor on film matters in the *Los Angeles Record*, interviewed a General Film executive who also confirmed the figures in an article published between the interventions in the *Times* and the *Examiner*.[46] An article on the trust phenomenon, by and large from the heyday of General Film, estimated daily attendance of 95,000 at the 110 theaters—the latter figure seems exaggerated, however.[47] If nothing else, these numerical exercises underwrite film culture's firm grip on local audiences during the first half of the 1910s. Thus, moving pictures played a crucial role in most peoples' everyday lives at time when exhibition practices and modes of production were in obvious transition and the overall amusement market in a state of flux.

A report on Los Angeles in *Billboard* highlighted the city's financial straits; cold spells in 1911 and 1912 had allegedly hurt the economically important citrus markets. While legit and big-time vaudeville were doing well, small-time houses and nickel theaters were said to be in a state of disarray, "particularly on Main Street, which happens to be the Bowery of Los Angeles." The number of low-priced houses was estimated at around 120 to 142, though 80 was more accurate. "Furthermore," the correspondent claims, "many of these nickelodeons are frail rattletraps, such as mar and sear the cheaper section of New York City." The writer predicts that this over-saturation of exhibition venues will result in closedowns until a reasonable market level is in place. The article then shifts focus: "Luckily, Los Angeles is busy manufacturing films, or else it would not rank high right now as a film business center. But the manufacturing of films has no relation to the present dull spell."[48] The gradual emergence of "Hollywood," initially scattered throughout the area, gave the exhibition market a unique sense of local grounding.

Data gleaned by a reporter from the recently published 1913 edition of the local City Directory bespeaks the overall business structure in Los Angeles: The city was home to 2408 realty dealers occupying more offices than any other line of business, 1507 building contractors came in second, which underpinned a city rapidly expanding to accommodate newcomers. Further down the list, one finds 194 saloons, 108 automobile dealers, and 90 garages, while livery stables were pressed down to 54 by the onslaught of motorized horsepower. Finally, 77 picture theaters were listed, considerable less than estimated by *Billboard*, but close to the rest of the estimates.[49] Film theaters were however not only to be found along the white way of Broadway and around the Plaza—the nodes for high and low, respectively—the suburban districts were in the process of being dotted with houses. As a reporter put it, "the calico drama [is] trespassing upon" the residential districts, a point illustrated by a house planned for the corner of Moneta Avenue and 50th Street to be leased by H.H. Knapp and F.W. Stewell and scheduled to open in October 1911.[50] The suburban boom took off in 1909 when 25 permits for "the maintenance of moving picture exhibitions" were approved, gaining additional momentum in the spring of 1910, when its trajectory can be followed in the weekly reports on building permits in *Southwest Contractor and Manufacturer*. For a year, there seemed to be a new picture theater in the works every week, both along and parallel to the main thoroughfares.[51] In assessing the market, a correspondent for the *Times* talked about "a moving picture craze in Los Angeles" when theaters opened "faster than they can be counted."[52]

Prior to the real-estate boom that shaped the new, affluent suburbs, exhibition on the fringe had primarily been temporary and conducted in airdomes operating during the summer season, which is documented by the surviving license records. A survey of the picture market in the *Los Angeles Times* describes in passing the suburban market conditions on the verge of the upheaval from temporary to permanent exhibition. "In the suburban districts the little airdomes flourisheth like the scriptural green bay tree, and young men and maids, and old men and old maids, also infants and motherlings, flock there rather than go downtown of a summer evening," a demand soon to be capitalized on year round.[53] When standing film theaters opened in the suburbs, the airdomes came to represent a concern for the permanent exhibitors. The competition was unfair, they argued, since airdomes were not compelled to operate under the costly regulatory framework adopted for the standing film theaters, for example concerning fire protection. Suburban exhibitors even organized themselves in the Suburban Moving Picture Men's Association, a body that complained to the City Council in April 1912 about this particular state of affairs.

In 1910, when film culture reached suburbia and film production gradually turned into a fixture of life in Southern California, the city of Los Angeles, with about 320,000 inhabitants, was by no means a major metropolis. The city and its commercial brass were entertainment-oriented and business-shrewd enough however not to ignore the impact of the new phenomenon and its potential for tying in with the boosterist discourse unflinchingly trumpeting the boons of the area to prospective colonists from near and far.

The year 1911 was when both *Moving Picture World* and *Moving Picture News* for a time published weekly reports from Los Angeles, initially including observations on exhibition also; soon enough, however, only the production angle merited coverage in the letters from the West Coast. *Film Index*, which occasionally devoted attention to Southern California, ceased publication in June 1911 when *Moving Picture World* absorbed it. The *Index* provided some bits and pieces of information from Los Angeles in early 1911, and so did *Nickelodeon*, which became *Motography* in April 1911.[54]

Theatrical trade papers addressing the broader amusement field provide only scant information on film exhibition in Los Angeles. *Billboard, Variety, Show World*, the *New York Dramatic Mirror*, and the *New York Clipper* are however still part of the backdrop for this chapter. The Los Angeles-based theatrical trade weekly, the *Rounder*, gradually opened its columns to film matters in 1909. Its initial position vis-à-vis film culture was clarified in one of its earliest editorials from November 1908:

> The moving picture show in some instances needs a moral disinfectant and in others encouragement. We lament the prevalence of these institutions, not because we fear any serious moral plague, so much as because we think they in some degree affect the patronage of the regular high-class theaters, where the drama not merely amuses, but uplifts.[55]

Thus, for the *Rounder*, theater proper was in the limelight, and cinema still mainly a distracting nuisance diverting patrons from drama's higher mission of uplift. Film culture hovered between being perceived as a distraction vis-à-vis the nobler forms of entertainment, or an outright moral plague, to pick up the term dismissed as inadequate by the editorial due to the medium's future potential. The use of moving images for purposes other than mere entertainment turned into a set of diverse practices for cultural uplift around 1910; church screenings in Los Angeles and screenings for the poor at the Bethlehem Institute were part of such a movement. Nationwide, legions of editors had taken it upon themselves to expose cinema as a "moral plague," particularly in 1907, in contrast to the stance in the *Rounder*. Irrespective of its early misgivings, the *Rounder* elected to cover local film issues in late 1909, albeit in a highly condensed fashion at a time when exhibition had moved up a notch on the cultural ladder.[56]

In 1911 vaudeville was ubiquitous in Los Angeles, and both big-time and small-time houses offered films and live turns in various combinations. Arthur S. Hyman presented roughly the same number of live attractions as pictures, first-run independent films in his case. He operated five houses in downtown Los Angeles, the Luna Theater in the amusement park, and a new, elegant theater on the beach in Venice. His bankruptcy in 1912 after a meteoric career marks the end of an exhibition chapter characterized by extreme instability which took on new forms as feature films began to emerge, and big-time vaudeville houses upgrading the overall theatrical scene in Los Angeles.

The geographical coordinates for amusements in Los Angeles prior to the breakthrough for moving pictures outlined above set the stage for the nickelodeon era and its entrepreneurs, foremost Thomas L. Tally and William H. Clune. 1909 was the year when local film exhibitors in Los Angeles began building plush "film palaces," a term used by a trade commentator in 1911. Tally and Clune spearheaded this shift and their efforts attracted attention in the national trade press.[57] They were, however, not the only Los Angeles exhibitors with track records from the early days and stretching well into the 1920s, but no other exhibitors managed to successfully take the step from no-frill places to palaces. Tally in particular was in the forefront at all exhibition phases. In addition, Clune and Tally operated licensed exchanges and later invested in production ventures. Somebody like R.W. Woodley represented the middle ground in the upgrading process when he inaugurated his New Optic at 533 South Main, with 800 seats, on March 26, 1911. The old Optic was located at 460 South Broadway and torn down when the business center pressed south and land prices soared.[58] Woodley thus moved to the less ritzy Main Street and soon enough delved into the small-time vaudeville void after the closedown of the Unique and Cineograph, and similar casualties. He thus "added a flasher electric sign with the word 'Vaudeville' visible to all parts of South Main Street within a block of the theatre."[59] A few years later, the Woodley Theater opened on Broadway, between Eighth and Ninth Streets. The house was perceived to "mark another southward advance in substantial and sightly structures of the business district."[60]

FIGURE 9: Woodley's New Optic (Courtesy of the Los Angeles Public Library)

H.W. Nixon built a string of Globe Theaters—the first one at 202 East Fifth Street in 1908—outside the traditional theater district. Another of Nixon's modest first efforts was the Nickelodeon at 527 South Spring, which in 1909 became the Odeon. In 1911 it was reported that Nixon entertained ambitions of acquiring the leases for a bevy of first-class houses along the West Coast from San Diego to Seattle within the framework of the Consolidated Security Company, a business backed by local banking interests. The underlying assumption of the scheme was that, as the "individual has reached the zenith of his financial possibilities in this enterprise," it was time for consolidation in order to rationalize the exhibition business and put it on an industrial scale.[61] Big-time exhibition without a doubt needed a solid financial base, which marked a gradual dependency on banks and financial institutions writ large. The other side of the spectrum, pegged by *Billboard* as Bowery-like, advertised its final throes in small-print classified ads in the for-sale and wanted sections of the Sunday papers, which provides a revealing indication of how fast film exhibition changed hands in 1911. The typical ads painted highly lucrative business outlooks for prospective investors.[62] This ad market evidences the claim made in *Billboard* of an overabundance of small, fly-by-night houses.

From Dreamer to Capitalist—Thomas L. Tally

Thomas Lincoln Tally (1861–1945) is the most renowned film exhibitor in Los Angeles with a historiographic stature and prominence harking back to a modest phonograph parlor on Spring Street which, in a subsequent incarnation, became the home of the Vitascope after its two-week debut at Los Angeles' Orpheum in the summer of 1896. For a boy born in Rockport on southwest Texas' Gulf coast in the momentous year of 1861, the parental choice of naming him Thomas Lincoln has the ring of a political statement. Thomas was otherwise named after his father, Thomas J. Tally, a carpenter. The family was big and Thomas had several brothers and two sisters. Thanks to Terry Ramsaye, a pregnant moment of epiphany shaped and sealed Thomas L. Tally's destiny after an alleged first encounter with the kinetoscope in his native state in 1896, shaping part of Tally's biographical legend.[63] The tale is apocryphal—or at best slightly misdated—since the Tallys were already offering the kinetoscope and the famous James Corbett-Peter Courtney prizefight film to paying customers, in a phonograph parlor at 248 South Spring Street, in October 1895.[64] This might have been a temporary venture at a makeshift location, since the next trace of the Tally business displayed a new address, 311 South Spring.

On April 16, 1902, Tally opened the Electric Theater at 262 South Main. The Electric Theater changed programs around once a month and advertised irregularly; its last ad was placed on March 11, 1903. As Musser speculates, Tally might have toured with his films after wearing out his local audiences and before transforming his movie theater into a small-time vaudeville house.[65] After changing the venue's name to the Lyric on July 18, 1903, Tally opted to show films as part of a vaudeville program, which attests to the vicissitudes of offering films exclusively prior to an industrial production structure. Moreover, there was com-

119

FIGURE 10: Tally's Phonograph and
Vitascope Parlor (Courtesy of Marc Wanamaker)

petition to reckon with, not only from films at the Orpheum, but from combination programs at the Cineograph, which opened in September 1902, and the Hentz and Salle's the Unique as well; in addition, Chutes Park regularly screened Vitascope films. The pitch in the *Times* for the Lyric locates the business in the "old" Electric Theater, which perhaps alludes to a temporary closedown prior to the shift to vaudeville, a shift that emulated the Cineograph's billing concept. Exactly how long Tally held on to the Lyric we do not know; the city directories for 1904 to 1906 listed Harry W. Oviatt as its manager.[66]

Tally sold the Lyric to become a traveling exhibitor in late 1903 or 1904 and made handsome profits by showing Porter's *The Great Train Robbery* on the road.[67] Thomas Tally reemerged as a film exhibitor in Los Angeles in 1905, but only for a few days. A *Los Angeles Times* report tells of a fire in the Hotel Nadeau building, located at the corner of First Street and Spring, where Tally had opened a picture business a few days ago. The room had for some time been occupied by The Merchants' Bank, and a tailor was a tenant shortly before Tally moved in. The blaze was fed by "80,000 feet of the celluloid film containing the moving-picture negatives."[68]

On March 3, 1906, he opened Tally's New Broadway Theater at 554 South Broadway. His son Seymour was part of the business, initially a bookkeeper, but soon promoted to the New Broadway's assistant manager. Tally seems to have acquired the place in January 1906, in the wake of Morganstern's unsuccessful tenure, a couple of months before the re-opening. When the nickel era was ushered in in Los Angeles, Tally offered films and illustrated songs, but no vaudeville acts, in a venue on par with the small-time vaudeville houses. In 1909 Seymour Tally was listed as the theater's proprietor, while Thomas Tally officially confined his activities to his exchange business. Tally's next venture was reported on in the *Examiner* on November 28, 1909: Tally had acquired the lease for a lot intended to be the new site of his theater. Several of Seymour's cousins had been working in the business, but when Tally built his new theater and later sold his exchange, the cousins moved into real estate, a business of industrial proportions in Los Angeles.

FIGURE 11: Patrons lining up outside Tally's New Broadway
at 554 S. Broadway (Courtesy of Marc Wanamaker)

When the New Broadway Theater opened in its upgraded incarnation at 833 South Broadway, the business-friendly *Los Angeles Times* opined that the enterprising Tally's career was a "testimonial as to what it is possible for a moneyless but energetic man to accomplish here in Los Angeles in a few years time. With nothing but his energy and direct application business, Tally has raised himself, in half a dozen seasons, from the position of dreamer to capitalist," as the *Times* phrased it.[69] Four years later a theater critic, taking stock off the theatrical situation, bestowed unparalleled praise on Tally in an article containing both a succinct career outline and extolling D.W. Griffith: "Locally we have in T. L. Tally a man who began in 1896 with the Kinetoscope where you paid a nickel, pushed a button and saw pictures; in 1897 [should be 1896] he put on the first life-sized pictures; in 1902 he opened the first moving picture theater here and in 1906 on Broadway and Sixth street, where Mr. Silverwood now advertises his conscience, he had the first real picture house in the country and people blocked the street trying to get in. Now he has his own theater on Broadway and three others where he releases his Paramount Pictures, and he is a very rich man."[70]

Apart from exhibiting, Tally was also engaged in the exchange business until General Film bought him out on March 6, 1911; he was paid $47,193.30 in addition to stock worth $14,000.[71] In December of that year he sublet his lease for the New Broadway to the Kinemacolor enterprise, but the lack of success enjoyed by the manager W.A. Kramer soon put the theater back in Tally's lap in May 1912. Tally subleased the house to the Quinn Brothers under the Q Amusement Co., and they switched the name from Tally's to the Colonial Theater in July 1912.[72] Prior to this, the Q Company had instituted a new program at its other houses, one quite similar to Clune's: high-class pictures together with seven vaudeville acts.[73] Tally still consistently avoided vaudeville. When Tally built his theater, he had a permit for building six additional stories. Quinn planned to build the additional stories for a hotel when he acquired the lease, for which Tally was to be paid $2,400 a month for forty-seven years. Tally, in his turn, paid $1,000 for the lease to the land.[74] The hotel was however never built.

In 1914 *Motion Picture News* offered a biographical overview of Tally's career. Just like the 1909 portrait in the *Times* and the *Examiner*'s in 1914, it portrayed him as enjoying exemplary financial success: His assets were valued at a grand total of $500,000. The value of the theater on Broadway was estimated at $100,000, evidence that land was the prime source of value in Los Angeles; the property on which the theater stood was considered to be worth $400,000. By then, Tally had acquired the lot from the

Lang estate.[75] The secret behind his successful ventures, readers were told, was his dedication to studying his audiences and their preferences, which translated into shows devoid of vaudeville turns, but with first-rate music, sumptuous ambience, and personal attention to the patrons.[76]

Towards the end of the decade Tally was one of the leading exhibitors in the First National Exhibitor's Circuit and instrumental in signing both Charlie Chaplin and Mary Pickford with United Artists. In the early feature days he was closely affiliated with Paramount. Tally retired in the early 1920s, only to return to exhibition by acquiring the Criterion Theater, located on Grand Avenue just a block away from what was once the Mozart Theater. When Tally died in 1945, the Criterion site was "occupied by a parking station," showing once again that if it is not motion pictures, it is automobiles.[77] Tally's New Broadway was by then long gone, albeit not replaced by a garage, but a department store under the management of the May Company.

William H. Clune—From the Nickel to the Auditorium

Most nickel texts in the local press, which will be discussed in a later chapter, described conditions in a house at 349 North Main in the Baker block. The Nickel Theater was opened by William H. Clune and Charles Bockover late in 1906; the building permit was dated November 1. This was their second storefront theater. The Nickle, as it was called in *Billboard*'s list of electric theaters, was the first nickelodeon in Los Angeles and opened sometime late in the summer of 1906. The building permit for the house at 255 South Main was signed by Bockover only, but Clune co-owned the theater. The permit was dated July 13, 1906, and the costs for the unspecified improvements were estimated at $300.

When Bockover and Clune branched out in the course of 1907, it was as the Southwest Amusement Company; the business was incorporated on February 11, 1907. Bockover was however neither among the three directors nor its four share subscribers. The capital stock was $25,000, and $7,502 was subscribed, 7,498 shares by W.H. Clune.[78] The Southwest opened a third nickel theater in Los Angeles late in 1907, La Petite Theater at 508 South Broadway. Bockover and Clune broke up in 1908 around the time the theaters on South and North Main changed names.

The Nickel on South Main was still in full swing in 1907, as was Tally's house on Broadway. The Scenic Theater at 522 South Spring was a new venture operated by Southwest; it seated 300. The company also managed the Family Theater at Ocean Park, the Empire in San Diego— opened on March 23, 1907—and the Pavilion Theater on Coronado.[79] In late October 1907 the Southwest Amusement Co. opened the Unique in San Bernardino. It was reported that the company controlled theaters in seven cities, in "Los Angeles, Long Beach, San Diego, and elsewhere."[80]

Early in 1909 Robert Brackett was hired as manager for the Clune Vodville Circuit, and when Clune opened his new theater in May 1909, Brackett was its manager.[81] When dismantling Southwest, Clune at some point placed his theatrical assets in the Clune Amusement Company, which might have occurred in conjunction with his split with Bockover. In the spring of 1912 the subsequent incorporation of The Clune Theaters Co., with capital of $2,000,000, absorbed the holdings in the Clune Amusement Co., which comprised houses in a bigger league than Southwest's venues. Clune's new company offered stocks at par value, $1, for the general market. The prospect explained the business strategy and emphasized the difference in exhibition practice vis-à-vis the cheap theaters, which was evidenced by Clune charging from 10 to 30 cents. Vaudeville was an integral part of the program, but instead of the few shows a day presented at the Orpheum, for example, Clune ran multiple shows. The turns were on a higher plane than the cheap vaudeville offered in small-time houses, and the films were of course from the trust's producers, high-class and first-run. The prospect promised generous dividends of at least one percent to be paid every other month, beginning immediately. When new theaters were added to the company, dividends were expected to rise.[82]

Bockover was a front man for Clune's discreet expansion during 1906. Clune soon moved on to the big league and respectability, which was quite unexpected given his early notoriety as a union activist in league with the political machine. Meanwhile, Bockover's career petered out into obscurity at the heel of the nickelodeon era, before his carpentry talents took him to Hollywood as stage builder.

Tally was an unfailing supporter of the trust and operated one of two licensed exchanges in Los Angeles; the other was in the hands William H. Clune.[83] Clune's early days were as spectacular as Tally's, but he apparently preferred a shroud of silence to be draped over his youthful escapades. As for Tally, Clune's business acumen illustrates the importance of real-estate investments and owning land as a prime success factor. Even more

124

so than Tally, Clune was involved in real-estate ventures and mining projects, dying a very wealthy man on the verge of the sound-film era.

William H. Clune was born in Hannibal, Missouri, in 1862, and came to California in 1887 during the boom years when the railroad's cutthroat competition fueled unprecedented expansion in Los Angeles. In the early 1890s he was secretary of the American Railroad Union's local branch there, and for a while the branch manager also. In 1894, when one strike after another paralyzed the U.S. railroads, conductor Clune, employed by Southern Pacific, also owned a cigar store opposite the River station, which served as the strikers' headquarters. He was eventually convicted of conspiracy together with other local union officials for having obstructed delivery of the U.S. mail and lost his business in the process. Furthermore, he was fired from his job as a conductor for Southern Pacific in the aftermath of the strike and was soon affiliated predominantly with liquor and cigar interests in the notorious Eighth Ward. Clune was politically active and nominated as a Democratic Party candidate for council seats in the Eighth Ward run by boss Tom Savage, a notorious player in the local machine and involved in an array of obscure schemes in Los Angeles' vice and liquor districts. In 1895 Clune was featured in a much-publicized shooting brawl. The account in the *Times* described Clune as having "acquired more or less unenviable notoriety," and later articles evidence the claim by recounting several instances when he had assaulted police officers and, on one occasion, a streetcar conductor. He was convicted in one of the cases. Clune was then still under $10,000 bond in the strike matter, for which he had been sentenced for conspiracy to eighteen months in prison in December 1894. After serving nine months he and his fellow strike leaders were however granted pardons by President Cleveland in November 1896. Cleveland stated that he was convinced of the prisoners' guilt, but they were to his mind no ordinary criminals, instead "laboring men swept into the violation of the law by first listening to the counsel of disorder."[84] Clune was hence not around when the Vitascope premiered in Los Angeles.

After a short run in 1904 Clune disappeared from the license records, only to resurface five years later in a grander exhibition league with a house at 453 South Main, opened in May 1909 under the management of Robert A. Brackett. In the absence of records, virtually nothing is known about the day-to-day operation of his busy activities in 1905-1908, when he branched out in several directions in addition to his music boxes: the exchange business, the Southwest Amusement Company, and Clune's Vodville Circuit. Shortly before the opening of his theater on Fifth and Main, an initial career sketch was ventured in a trade organ's piece covering the local exhibition scene:

> There are between twenty-six and thirty moving picture theaters in Los Angeles, Cal., all more or less elaborately appointed, and doing a thriving business; several introduce orchestral accompaniment and there is one house which uses the talking machine in conjunction with certain of its films [Fischer's Chronophone Theater]. There is in course of construction one of the best equipped moving picture and vaudeville theaters in the states, which when completed will seat 1000 persons and besides having a full orchestra, there will be operated from an electric keyboard a set of chimes. This house is being built on the corner of Main and Fifth streets, and is one of the many owned in southern California by the Southwest Amusement Company, of which W. H. Clune is president. Los Angeles can brag of one of the largest film exchanges in the country, the Clune Film Exchange, which buys the entire output of all combined film manufacturers licensed by the Motion Picture Patents Company. This film exchange has been in existence for the past three years, supplying practically all of Southern California, Arizona and New Mexico.[85]

Clune's new theater had 900 seats, including six loges seating twelve persons each. The program, which played twice in the afternoon, offered a show combining pictures and vaudeville. The house became the starting point for an array of large-scale theatrical developments in the era post-Southwest Co. Apart from building yet another house in Los Angeles—on Broadway—and leasing the Walker, Clune was operating first-class venues in both San Diego and Pasadena.[86] The latter, which seated 1,400, opened on March 1, 1911, with alternating films, vaudeville, and legitimate theater—the attractions were furnished by Klaw & Erlanger in the same way as for the Mason and the Majestic.[87] In addition, Clune was building a house on the new amusement pier at Ocean Park. Reporting on his success, trade sources estimated "that the present seating capacity of 900 should be 9,000" at his theater at Main and Fifth, which at the time was showing "the pictures of Colonel Roosevelt in Africa."[88]

Clune's second purpose-built theatre in Los Angeles, located at 528 South Broadway close to the center of the business and theater district, opened on October 10, 1910. Architect A.F. Rosenheim's building plans were published in the press.[89] The house was run under the auspices of the Clune's Amusement Company, which had been incorporated for $500,000.[90] The subsequent incorporation in May 1912 of the Clune Theaters Company for $2,000,000 in authorized capital came about partly in preparation for Clune's takeover of the Grand Opera House in September that year.[91]

FIGURE 12: Clune's Broadway; the advertised film was released in April 1910 (Courtesy of Marc Wanamaker)

FIGURE 13: Interior of Clune's Broadway
(Courtesy of Brent C. Dickerson)

The expansion of his theatrical business coincided with the sale of Clune's exchange to General Film on March 27, 1911, which released a substantial amount of capital. He accepted stocks in General Film (seven percent preferred) for $20,000; the rest, $48,996.40, was paid in cash.[92]

In July 1914 Clune added a new house to his chain of theaters when Clune's Exclusive opened at 547 South Broadway in the former Shell Theater. The house catered exclusively to women and their children, and men were not welcome unless in the company of a female. The house offered retiring rooms for mothers as well as nurseries. The bill was adapted to the sought-after audience, female shoppers and their children, previously catered to by the Arrow Theater in Hamburger's Department Store, and also by the Mozart Theater. The Exclusive's program ran from 10 a.m. to 11 p.m., charging 5 cents for children and 10 for adults. Clune's initiative was applauded by the Parent-Teachers' Federation, but did not last long for reasons not accounted for.

The Exclusive was a small venture targeting a niche market, as the name evidenced. On May 4, 1914, Clune took film exhibition to a realm of quite a different magnitude by converting the Auditorium into Clune's Auditorium, marketed as the largest film theater in the world. At the verge of the era of the "monster films," multi-reel feature films, Clune considered his new house to be the only appropriate viewing context for theatrical features in longer format then on the brink of, if not taking over the market, at least recasting the exhibition realm.[93] The Auditorium was outfitted with a pipe organ, allegedly "the largest west

128

of New York," and Clune also employed a twenty-piece orchestra. The trade press heaped accolades on Clune for taking film exhibition to an unprecedented cultural level: "Probably the greatest success in the motion picture field of the greatest motion picture city in the country—greatest because of the many studios, film manufacturing plants, and general interest in the film industry—is that of W.H. Clune, who recently leased the Auditorium, the former home of all grand opera, musical recitals, etc., with a seating capacity of more than 2,500."[94]

Clune's opening program featured Griffith's *Home, Sweet Home*, the director's first release for Majestic/Reliance after leaving Biograph. The absence of a steady flow of "monster films" with strong audience appeal prompted Clune to financially back such big-scale epics as *The Clansman* and *Intolerance*, as well as embarking on film production himself in order to secure attractive vehicles for his colossal theater. The programming at Clune's Auditorium during 1914, up until Clune contracted *The Clansman* early in 1915 for a record-breaking run lasting months, attests to the difficulties exhibitors had acquiring popular feature subjects on a weekly basis in the early years. Clune hence programmed films from several different exchange services besides screening state-right titles, some of them international features like *Anthony and Cleopatra* and *Julius Caesar*, both Cines productions distributed by Kleine, as well as the Danish film *Sealed Orders* directed by Benjamin Christensen. Lack of suitable long features at times necessitated double bills featuring shorter subjects, for example Dr. Leonard Sugden's exploration documentary *The Lure of Alaska* together with *The Hoosier Schoolmaster*, as well as Selig's *In the Days of the Thundering Herd* with the same studio's *The Story of the Blood Red Rose*. Most films programmed during 1914 remained on the bill for a week, but a few titles were popular enough to merit a second one: Vitagraph's *The Christian*, Ince's *The Wrath of God*, Griffith's *The Escape*, Pathé's *Les Miserables*—all these titles were shown between July and September. In the following months no film stayed on the bill for longer than a week, and Clune even offered return engagements for some of his previously screened successes, for example *The Escape*, which returned for a third week on November 16th.[95] The most successful title prior to *The Clansman* was the Selig production of Rex Beach's *The Spoilers*, which premiered on May 25th and was given a two-week run and two return engagements.

1914 was a year when the industry increasingly became part of the social and cultural scene in Los Angeles, not least by way of the numerous new associations like the Photoplayers' League, which organized parades, pageants, and dances. This was partly an effect of the status accorded actors thanks to the star system and reinforced by visibility in the community. Furthermore, scores of big theatrical names had recently joined the ranks of photoplay actors. Their conspicuous presence outside the frame encouraged live appearances in various promotional contexts, for instance in conjunction with screenings. When *The Spoilers* was on the bill, Clune, as an extra enticement, managed to present the leading cast members live prior to a June 4th show. According to a news item this was "the first time any of the Selig performers have consented to appear in public."[96] The initiative bespeaks new opportunities for marketing afforded by the features' programming format, which coincided with the serial films' protracted exhibition span. Both formats encouraged film companies to expand their publicity departments so as to find new ways of capitalizing on the medium's cultural leverage. Exhibitors even adopted novel ways of marketing their business: Clune, for example, launched Clune's Amusement Newspaper to promote his ventures—this in addition to a spin on a well-known gimmick advertised as "Walk in front of the camera and see yourself at Clune's Broadway."[97]

Actors appearing live and taking bows prior to the film incurred a theatrical aura eagerly sought after by the feature format. This vein of theatricality additionally motivated adjuncts to the narrative proper, integrated in the form of prologs, epilogs, and an emphasis on acting and creative agency in the story, aspects of filmmaking we will return to in another chapter. *The Spoilers*, in fact, opened with a sequence introducing the leading players, made even more poignant and vivid by the actors' live appearance in Clune's theater prior to the film's opening prolog. In a slightly different register Charles Chaplin, Roscoe Arbuckle, and Charles Murray made a guest appearance at the Morosco Theater in a musical farce, *Let's Get Married*, which included a "pretended filming of a picture." The three Keystone comedians "volunteered to enact a moving picture comedy on the stage to show the patrons of the Morosco how it is really done."[98] Vitagraph on a regular basis had its leading players doing cameo appearances or acting in short plays in conjunction with film exhibitions at the Vitagraph Theater in New York City.[99] Overall, such appearances blurred the border between stage and screen by highlighting the actors' role and capitalizing on their star status in the production process.

The Spoilers returned to Clune's Auditorium for a third week on August 17th, and again on October 5th for a fourth week. This attests to the film's enormous popularity, noticeable elsewhere also, but the return engagements are testimony to the difficulties of finding "monster films" with unequivocal blockbuster appeal. Clune's investment in Griffith's *The Clansman* proved to be a highly lucrative and shrewd move due to the controversial film's unprecedented success and drawing power. Clune's previous experiences billing Griffith titles, from the house's opening feature *Home, Sweet Home* to *The Avenging Conscience* and the three weeks devoted to *The Escape*, was part of the investment equation. Clune's willingness to gamble on big spectacles might also have been prompted by the success of *Cabiria* (Itala Film, 1914), which impresario L.E. Behymer offered for three weeks in the newly refurbished Trinity Auditorium. Joseph Carl Breil conducted a score compiled by Manlio Mazza; a large choir further added to the effect.[100] Behymer waxed eloquent on the spectacle of *Cabiria*, which the *Times*' interviewer perceived as being indicative of the medium's maturity.[101]

Overall, the competition for the new feature format was fierce, and Clune's old rival Tally had already scooped up all the Paramount organization's features. It thus made sense to embark on the production of films, which so many besides Clune had elected to do in the mid-1910s.

In 1916 Clune produced *Ramona* and *Eyes of the World*—both state-right pictures—in a studio at the corner of Melrose and Bronson bought from Famous Players in 1915. Famous Players had picked the studio up a couple of month's earlier when the Fiction Company, headed by novelist Louis Joseph Vance, went out of business. Clune needed big productions to fill the nearly 3,000 seats at the Auditorium, which his partial financing of Griffith's *The Clansman* and *Intolerance* achieved during their respective opening rounds.[102] Clune's studio, later known as Tec-Art, was one of the major rental studios for productions during the 1920s, at a time when Clune had relinquished his exhibition interests for real-estate ventures.

Just like Tally, Clune was praised for his amazing career leap from modest circumstances to full-fledged capitalist. When Clune opened his Pasadena theater in 1911, one of the local newspapers outlined the trajectory of his success, perhaps somewhat papered over and not quite accurate concerning chronology: "From railway passenger conductor to owner of a string of motion picture and vaudeville theatres in several of the principle cities of Southern California is the jump that W. H. Clune, proprietor of Clune's new theatre in this city, made in the short space of three years. He wasn't a capitalist when he quit the railroad, but he is now."[103] In addition, his career is perhaps the most distinctive illustration of the new film culture's place within the dominant culture, while the film culture of old still resided in a different realm in other parts of town.

Jinxed Exhibition: Grand Avenue and the Mozart Theater

After outlining the careers of the two exhibition pioneers in Los Angeles, both prominent figures within the licensed faction, we will now turn the attention to an independent venture and its overall exhibition context. Even more important here is the attempt at providing an example of film exhibition's vicissitudes during the period we are investigating by following the fate of a particular house across a series of management changes.

The highfalutin exhibition of film at the Mozart Theater in Los Angeles represented yet another effort to dispel the dismal history of a house at a precarious location: 730 South Grand Avenue. From its inauguration as the Walker Theater in December 1908, a select series of managements with shifting billing policies had marched past. The reasons for the lack of éclat irrespective of ambitious offerings and a sumptuous theatrical space might be explained by exploring downtown Los Angeles' exhibition map around 1910. When the Mozart Theater opened in August 1912, it was not only against the backdrop of the Walker's austere reputation, but also in the face of a multitude of upheavals that had an effect on Los Angeles' amusement scene overall in 1911 and the following year. To be sure, the Mozarts were no novices, but seasoned theatrical veterans with long résumés. Still, they faced an uphill struggle, further complicated by personal matters, both expected and unexpected. Before we approach the Mozart Theater, here is a historical, although cursory, run-through of previous managements at Grand Avenue, and some sketchy coordinates of the early phases of feature exhibition in Los Angeles.

In December 1908 the Walker Theater opened at a purpose-built venue for vaudeville and moving pictures with a seating capacity of 900; parquet and balcony were outfitted with opera chairs. Housed in the six-story Walker Auditorium, the theater shared space with assembly and lodge halls besides a few studios. The main lobby, decorated in green, occupied the entire frontage, which measured sixty feet, including a pa-

goda-shaped box office. The range of colors inside for parquet and balcony was dominated by "quiet tints in the art nouveau manner [...]
in green and gold-brown, touched with gold." J. Harry Pieper, the first
manager and lessee, had secured vaudeville attractions from Sullivan &
Considine and promised a bill mixing the live acts with first-run films
and illustrated songs.[104] The house labeled its film slots on the bill the
Walkerscope for regular first-run releases, while the Travellette showed
"scenes in other lands."

The house became Clune's Grand Avenue Theater in June 1910 after
two unsuccessful attempts at billing comedy theater. The theater opened
under Clune's management on June 18th, promising to be the "home
of refined pictures and song," which meant travel, scientific, and educational films "interspersed with clean dramatic and comedy pictures,"
supplied of course by the licensed producers, given the owner's affilia-
tions and exchange business.[105] Tickets prices were 10, 15, and 20 cents.
Irrespective of Clune's successful history as an exhibitor on Fifth and
Main, the house turned dark after only a few months. In early 1911 the
ubiquitous Arthur S. Hyman expanded in all directions in downtown
Los Angeles and acquired the lease for the Walker in February. Little
is known concerning the mix of pictures and acts Hyman billed at the
Walker, supposedly a similar string of vaudeville acts and three or four
independent films, as he presented at his other houses. In a final, desperate attempt to revitalize the Walker, Hyman assembled a stock company offering comedy built around Eugene B. Gear. In all likelihood, only
Gear's own three-act piece "Kate" reached the stage.[106] According to the
license records, Hyman's sojourn at Grand Avenue lasted from February
to June, followed by a few dark months.

An enigmatic news item in a late May issue of the *New York Clipper*
furnished the earliest trace of that an initiative was underway. Scheduled for reopening on September 1st, the former Walker was to "be re-
christened with a magic name," and the new management planned to
offer only the best feature and state-right films. Furthermore, the enterprise was part of a new chain of first-class theaters in major western cities that belonged to a syndicate represented by Harry M. Scott.[107] *Motography* provided more details in its June issue. The Mozart circuit was
named and apart from Scott, formerly with Drew & Campbell of Cleveland, Harry Davis' name came up. Davis was an amusement veteran in
Pittsburgh and more recently the New York representative of the Mo-

FIGURE 14: Hollywood's assets. Cartoon from *Los Angeles Herald*,
23 January 1910, 6.

zart circuit. The Mozart Theater planned to change programs every second week, a decidedly high-class arrangement matching the longer exhibition spans for the feature material shown at leading theater houses.[108] At this time, there was however no mention of Mrs. Mozart's role in the endeavor. In the same issue of *Motography* a short notice mentions plans for a Los Angeles Women's Photo-Play Theater to be "built, owned, and managed entirely by women and for women," a venture attributed to a Mrs. Hester Grant Giles. This playhouse never left the blueprint stage, but it is not unlikely that the Mozart people picked up the idea on the fly when reading the clippings and decided to configure their own establishment in a more or less similar fashion. The Grand Avenue house did not however become a theater for women only; such an initiative was sponsored by Clune for the short-lived Exclusive later on, but the women-only-management-and-work-force concept became a trademark for the Mozart Theater which exercised an irresistible pull on the press when it opened in August with Anna Mozart at the helm.

Evidently, Anna Mozart was not the only American woman in charge of film exhibition, not even in Los Angeles. The local pioneer in this respect seems to have been a Miss F.T. Emery, "who enjoys the distinction of being the city's first woman exhibitor." Her El Rodeo at 807 East Fifth opened in 1911.[109] Actually, the most prominent woman in charge of a major American theater was Josephine Clement, manager of the prestigious Bijou Dream in Boston from 1909 to 1913 and a prolific spokesperson for carefully planned quality programming mixing one-act plays, films, and lectures with or without slides.[110] A potential rival for prominence was Anna H. Gill of Cleveland, Ohio, a pioneering traveling exhibitor in addition to building three picture houses in Cleveland; Gill was affiliated with the Lyman Howe Circuit. The Gill Travel Tours visited Los Angeles' Temple Auditorium in late April 1913 with a show featuring talking motion pictures with sound effects and a group of seven invisible actors delivering the dialog from behind the screen by way of the Humanovo system.[111] The travelogues were presented under the slogan "We Bring the World to You" and interspersed with comedies in the manner of the old split reels.[112] While bringing the world to Grand Avenue proved to be a trickier proposition, the Mozarts, after testing other billing concepts, eventually settled for a bill of travel films exclusively.

Grand Avenue ran a couple of blocks away from the theater-and-film district dominated by houses on Main Street, Broadway, and Spring Street. The location away from these three busy thoroughfares proved to be a liability at a time when the business center was gravitating toward Spring and Seventh Streets and the elegant new theater venues gradually clustered on Broadway. When the Mozarts arrived in the early 1910s, it was apparently a tough proposition to lure patrons away from the glittering theater district proper that had mushroomed around the new business center. If the bills were similar to the offerings on Main, Spring, and Broadway, patrons resisted the darker Grand Avenue, located opposite the quiet Postal Office—which in the mid-1910s was converted into a department store—and in the vicinity of the Normal School at the current site of the Los Angeles Public Library. Further north, the hilly section of Grand Avenue was lined with private mansions. In 1912 suburbanites deliberating how to spend an evening could view moving pictures at neighborhood houses, or if lured downtown, they apparently preferred the offerings in the livelier theater district, which was also more conveniently located in relation to the transportation nexuses.

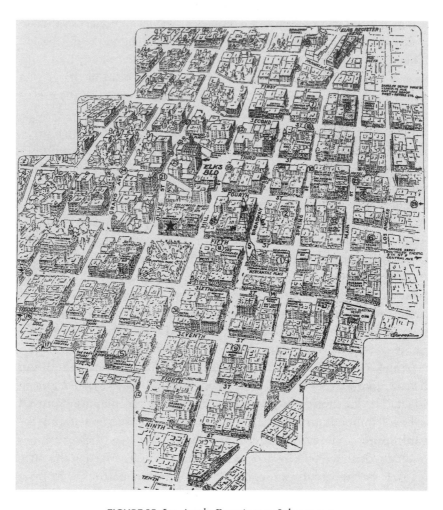

FIGURE 15: *Los Angeles Examiner*, 13 July 1909, 9.

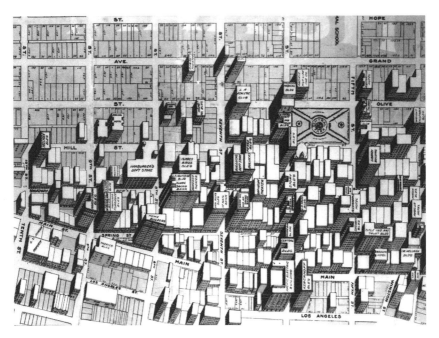

FIGURE 16: Bird's-eye map showing Los Angeles business properties, published in 1913 (Courtesy of Seaver Center for Western History Research)

Hence, something spectacular was required for creating lasting patronage at Grand Avenue, a fatal couple of blocks west of the ritzy and glittering Broadway, albeit at an excellent east-west street. It was not only a sign of class that automobiles lined up outside the Mozart in the early days; the location was not within convenient walking distance. Moreover, the Mozart Theater encouraged this type of exclusive patronage that arrived in private cars.

When the Mozarts tried to turn the tide at the Grand Avenue house, Los Angeles had experienced an amazingly rapid transformation of its amusements. Offering patrons program bills distinctly different from those of the competition was crucial for the Mozarts, and they opted for high-class features from the independent exchanges, which indeed was something of a novelty. Arthur Hyman was the leading independent exhibitor in 1911, but his bills had offered only single-reel films between the vaudeville acts; he was however history when the Mozarts arrived. Tally and Clune showed material from the trust companies, which meant primarily a steady menu of one-reel subjects along with an occasional

137

longer film released in separate installments, for instance by Vitagraph, or a rare two- or three-reel title. Prior to the Mozarts' arrival, the legitimate theaters began booking high-class films in feature format. *Dante's Inferno*, produced by the Italian company Helios, broke the ice and was chiefly followed by longer, educational subjects depicting adventurous explorations of remote terrains shown at the Majestic, Auditorium, or Mason. Eventually, in July 1913, Morosco took over the Lyceum's lease and turned it into a house for regular presentation of features.

In 1911 film shows sometimes found their way to venues uninvolved with regular theatrical exhibition. In an interview Reverend Reutepohler colorfully elaborated on the motivation for screening films in his church: "In the past we have sent out our people to be amused by the devil. The direct cause for such a large percentage of the people seeking amusements in places of ill-repute, is that a large portion of them have at least eight hours each day in which to be amused. As nearly all amusements have been commercialized, the keen minds at the heads of them have resorted to the practice of giving the public shows of a sensational and suggestive nature, instead of furnishing them with places where good, uplifting pleasure can be had."[113] Screenings in churches as part of sermons or as independent entertainment became a hot topic after Rev. Reutepohler's plans for the Salem Congregational Church reached the newspapers. After a series of conflicts with licensing authorities the shows were able start off to the accompaniment of *Los Angeles Times'* editorial misgivings concerning "vaudeville in church," while Hearst's *Examiner* applauded the initiative.[114] Around the same time, the Bethlehem Institute, a charitable institution, began to show film as part of its "juvenile work among the foreigners"; the initiative was reported to be highly popular among the poor.[115]

Against this background of emerging alternatives to theatrical exhibition, the fall of 1911, and especially September, proved to be *the* time for the introduction of feature films in Los Angeles. On September 2nd *Dante's Inferno* opened at Oliver Morosco's prestigious Majestic, and Los Angeles was reported to be the third city to show the film after Baltimore and Washington, D.C.; screenings in New York City at the Herald Square Theater and one August screening in Cincinnati, where the film caught fire, were conveniently forgotten in the promotional hype. The matinee screening at the Majestic at 2:30 was universally priced at 25 cents, while the evening show at 8:30 ranged from 25 and 35 to 50 cents.

The film, marketed as "a sort of motion picture de luxe," was shown for two weeks and lavishly promoted in the press. Julian Johnson, drama critic in the *Times*, attended a sneak preview on August 31st and was highly impressed by the cinematic rendering of Doré's famous illustrations of Dante's work, the selection of locations, and the lighting and mechanical effects, that is the animation work.[116]

During the second week of *Inferno* at the Majestic, on September 9th, the Kinemacolor Company took over the Grand Opera House for a presentation of its 11,000-foot film of George V's coronation in London. The show lasted two and a half hours, and a lecturer interspersed the musical accompaniment with commentary. The amount of patronage was overwhelming, and the film remained on the bill for four weeks. When the third week commenced, Julian Johnson penned a detailed account of the shooting of some of the film's more spectacular scenes.[117] The success at the Grand Opera House inspired the hiring of Tally's New Broadway Theater for regular color exhibition, and Tally's formally changed its name to the Kinemacolor Theatre on December 4th. The initial interest for this two-color additive system slowly waned in the absence of a regular output of new titles however, and after relinquishing the lease for the Tally's Broadway, the Kinemacolor Company put on shows at other local venues for limited engagements. The famous film of the Delhi Durbar, the most spectacular of the Kinemacolor films, chronicled George and Mary's coronation as emperor and empress of India. The film of the pageant was screened for three weeks at the Auditorium starting March 18, 1912, with two shows per day; all in all, 60,000 spectators bought tickets. The *Delhi Durbar* returned to the Auditorium for two more weeks starting July 15th. Parallel to the first Durbar screening, the Majestic double-billed two French stage titans on its screen: Sarah Bernhardt in *Camille* and Gabrielle Réjane in *Madame Sans-Gêne*.

The Mason was the next legitimate venue to take on film by introducing the *Alaska-Siberian Motion Pictures* about Captain F.E. Kleinschmidt's expedition, sponsored by the Carnegie Museum in Pittsburgh; the film opened on July 29, 1912. Julian Johnson's witty review titled "His Bruinship" was based on a viewing of the film and not only press releases.[118] The film was exceedingly popular and remained on the bill for six weeks; it returned to the Mason in December and had a final one-week engagement at the Majestic in August 1913. This exceedingly popular Carnegie film is not to be confused with one about another Arctic expedition,

139

Beverly C. Dobb's *Atop of the World in Motion*, billed at the Auditorium on May 12, 1913. Interestingly, this film was also billed at the Mozart Theater for a week, starting on June 2nd.

Meanwhile, the Majestic offered an expedition film from warmer latitudes: *Paul J. Rainey's Jungle Pictures*, also known as *African Hunt*, which opened on September 6, 1912, and drew crowds for four weeks. Morosco hosted a one-week return engagement for the film at the Lyceum late in March 1913. The choice of the Lyceum as the venue was partially motivated by Majestic being booked for another film, namely Ambrosio's *Satan*. In February the Majestic screened *One Hundred Years of Mormonism* at the same time the Orpheum offered their patrons a sound film in the form of Edison's Kinetophone. This epic history of Mormonism stimulated reflections on film formats, if not much critical attention otherwise: "[T]here is a rapidly growing tendency to discard the short, unimportant film plays, produced only for the purpose of amusement, and to turn to the larger photo-plays of a more educational nature."[119] Simultaneously, the Auditorium hosted Kalem's biblical spectacle *From the Manger to the Cross*, a film distributed by William H. Clune on a state-right basis for California as well as Arizona. The promotion for this production was unprecedented, and the *Los Angeles Record*, for example, published stills from an array of scenes on an installment basis, encouraging readers to hold on to them: "[T]he editor suggests that these pictures will prove of permanent interest, especially to children, CUT THEM OUT and SAVE THEM."[120] Kalem's ambitious production failed to attract the expected following, however, allegedly being controversial for Roman Catholics as well as "Israelites," and as Hector Alliot put it: "We want to be cheerfully entertained in this superficial age of ours: a sermon even in beautiful pictures is no longer appealing to the vast majority of those who, suffering from the disease of religious and ethical unrest, float aimlessly, seeking amusements in rapid entertainment."[121]

The leading film theaters affiliated with the licensed companies and General Film tried to meet the competition from the feature attractions at the legitimate houses by occasionally showing multi-reel titles. Before Tally elected to lease his theater to the Kinemacolor group, he offered Selig's three-reeler, *The Two Orphans*, on September 24, 1911, "not to be outdone by the larger theaters in the production of feature motion pictures." The program played for four days at a time when the Grand Opera House was running the coronation film for the third week.[122] In 1912 the enterprising William H. Clune took over the Grand Opera House, two years before he acquired the Auditorium on May 4, 1914.

Summing up the initial feature frenzy, drama critic Otheman Stevens concluded: "A couple of years ago we were somewhat startled here by having moving pictures billed at the Majestic; since then the Mason and the Auditorium have frequently presented the movies and often to more money than they could have expected from even a two-dollar production."[123] The following week yet another ethnographic spectacle opened at Mason, the 6,000-foot *Picturesque Hawaii*, and as Hector Alliot poignantly phrased it: "Without the fear of sea sickness and without inconvenience one can learn, from an opera chair, more of the picturesque features of the fifteen islands than would be possible to obtain in two month's journey."[124]

So, while Mr. and Mrs. Mozart designed their plans for taking over the Walker, they later faced a highly competitive market for feature material, at both the leading film theaters and the legitimate houses. *Dante's Inferno* opened up the market, here as elsewhere, but in Los Angeles it was predominantly the expedition films that attracted the most patrons, and some of them enjoyed four to six weeks of successive billing plus return engagements. In addition, the leading vaudeville houses were still showing films, though of course they shied away from longer subjects, instead opting for newsreels or the Kinetophone, Edison's system for sound films, in the same way as the Orpheum, while the Empress specialized in Keystone comedies.

When Anna and Edward Mozart arrived in Los Angeles, they could draw on a great amount of distinguished experience managing a vaudeville circuit based in Lancaster, Pennsylvania, and a couple of picture houses in addition. For a time, Edward Mozart had merged his interest with the White Rats Actors Union of America, throwing in the Independent Booking Agency as well as his remaining two houses, the Family Theatre in Lancaster and the Mozart in Elmira, New York. The Rats formed a separate unit, The Associated Artists, when teaming up with Mozart. In February 1912 Feiber & Shea acquired Mozart's former houses at a time when the Rats failed in their attempts to challenge the big centralized booking agencies.[125] The Mozart Theater in Elmira had opened as a joint venture between Mozart and his partners, Mrs. Mozart and Ralph V. Alexander, on one side, and the White Rats on the other. The house in Elmira opened in November 1909 and replaced

Mozart's old venue, the Family Theater, which had opened in 1907. The Mozart Theater offered vaudeville in 1909 and 1910, then switched to stock in 1911. Local sources speculated that the price for the Lancaster house amounted to about $50,000 and that the theater in Elmira went for $65,000. Edward Mozart had however already relinquished management of the Family Theater in February 1911 and moved to Springfield, Massachusetts, from there relocating to Los Angeles in 1912.[126]

In a 1909 book Robert Grau in passing mentions Edward Mozart and describes his early days as being similar to those of a magician or necromancer, or as a "customary career of one pursuing such a vocation in the distant past" of the 1880s. "In the evening of his life," as Grau phrases it, Mozart build up an impressive booking agency for vaudeville acts from 1903 onwards, encompassing about 20 houses, two of them directly controlled by Mozart, one in his hometown of Lancaster, Pennsylvania, and the Mozart Theater in Elmira, New York.[127] Edward Kuttner was born in 1857 and died in October 1937 at age 80 in Los Angeles. He apparently started his career as the driver of P.T. Barnum's famous Tom Thumb; the Lilliputian performer died in 1883. Edward Kuttner's tenure as driver took place during his boyhood, and when a young man he teamed up with Georgia Kane for a vaudeville routine and adopted his new name, Mozart, as an advertising gimmick. The couple had a son out of wedlock, which became an issue when the Pennsylvania court system summoned Mozart after his relocation to Los Angeles. Whether Georgia Kane's activities prompted Mozart to move to Springfield and a new state remains an open question.

The press in Los Angeles had whipped up considerable anticipation for the opening of the Mozart Theater as an out-of-the-ordinary film venue. By putting independent feature films on the bill—mainly historical spectacles produced by Eclair and Thanhouser plus European features at first—the new management embarked on a decidedly ambitious undertaking, hoping to attract audiences willing to be entertained away from the offerings along the main thoroughfares. Unlike most other houses, the Mozart Theater offered neither vaudeville acts nor illustrated songs as adjuncts to the films. If spending a nickel or a dime on film shows was considered an unpretentious aspect of everyday life, a visit to the Mozart catered to an entirely different type of upscale sensibility. The reports from the gala opening underscored the exclusive, high-class nature of the house: "The character of the patronage was indicated by the private automobiles lined in front of the brilliant lighted house," wrote the progressive *Los Angeles Express* when the Mozart opened in August 1912.[128] A few days later the *Express* revisited the theater and noticed a similarly moneyed and celebrity-dense audience: "Several box parties of prominent personages witnessed the initial performance, and a number of well-known persons had orchestra seats. Every night there has been an automobile patronage."[129] The *Times* further elaborated on the automobile patrons and even provided a list of prominent personalities in attendance. Apart from the *Times* own publisher, General Otis, Prince and Princess Lazarovich, Mrs. Charles Wellington Rand, and Count Stephen Szymanowski were listed among the luminaries.[130] Given the house's location, it took a conscious effort to visit. The casual pleasure-seekers found their fare elsewhere, along the traditional theater streets where houses managed by Tally, Clune, and Quinn dominated. Given the initial reports, a place otherwise considered a hoodoo was on the verge of being successfully transformed into a decidedly high-class venue by the industrious Mrs. Mozart and her all-female staff.

Anna Mozart's exhibition policy was explicitly based on the principle of targeting "the best theatergoing clientele in the city." Running only the highest class of picture initially translated into bills consisting of domestic and some Italian features, predominantly historical spectacles, rounded off by educational, historical, industrial, scientific, and scenic material.[131] Contemporary melodramas were conspicuously absent from the olio. The exhibition policy promised subjects "absolutely clean and free of sensational features"; this in order to make children and their guardians feel welcome.[132] Due to their billing practices, the Mozarts placed themselves in the upper bracket of the entertainment offerings, thus hoping to cater to patrons more likely to otherwise visit stock houses and theatrical venues proper rather than drop in at other film theaters. High-class exhibition was predominantly associated with white middle-class women as bearers of genteel culture. Discourses targeting women and children as preferred patrons had, as we noticed throughout this chapter, circulated from the earliest days of exhibition in Los Angeles. In 1902, when Thomas Tally opened his Electric Theater at 262 South Main, the *Times* ad (April 16, 1902) described this new place of amusement as "up-to-date, high class moving picture entertainment, especially for ladies and children." And in 1910 the leading vaudeville house, the Orpheum, confirmed that it was "[p]aying particular attention to entertaining Ladies and Children." The Mozart Theater tapped into this sensibility with its clean bills and all-female staff.

Apart from the high-class bill and the theater's opulent ambience, the much-heralded Foto Player was heavily promoted as an additional attraction that embellished the visual display with musical accompaniment and sound effects.[133] After a couple of weeks of films only, recorded music by way of the Auxterrephone was advertised as a program attraction. Live music and illustrated songs reeked of nickel exhibition and were hence unsuited to a high-class house. The Auxterrephone, in contrast, presented classical renderings recorded by top performers, while illustrated songs predominantly featured local talents of questionable merit. The screen arrangements were another feature indicative of quality. The house had a so-called "bright light" screen enclosed in a shadow box, an arrangement endorsed as ideal by trade authority Epes Winthrop Sargent in a series on projection and screens.[134]

The Mozart Theater commanded yet another attraction that exercised irresistible drawing power on the press, which helped launch the theater: the women-only staff. The all-female concept was marketed as an indicator of a responsible manner of conducting a business associated with an educational approach to exhibition. The *Tribune* published an illustrated advance article portraying Mrs. Mozart and her female staff.[135] "Man is conspicuous by his absence," the *Record* summed up in another notice.[136] The *Record* returned to this topic several times over the next few days: "girls to take your money at the box office; girls to usher you to your seat; girls to manipulate the moving picture machines, play the musical invention, the photoplayer, and last but not least, a young woman to pinch you and take you to the city bastile if you're not good!"[137] A photograph of Mrs. Mozart and her employees evidenced the list of female responsibilities. Instead of having a police officer in the vicinity of the house, the theater would have one positioned inside, a policewoman to boot. The *Times* provided a detailed chronicle of the difficulties involved with swearing the lady in as a special deputy.[138] In the *Herald*, after the fact, Miss Ellen Coglin was described as an "officer of the fair sex who will squelch all mashers."[139] The *Tribune* continued to demonstrate interest in the Mozart enterprise by presenting Nellie Lee, the only woman projectionist in Los Angeles. She had picked up her expertise from her husband, a manufacturer of film equipment.[140] The trade press somewhat modified the portrayal of the all-female business concept by focusing on Mr. Mozart and his role as advisor. *Variety* even referred to Mrs. Mozart as only "nominally the manageress of the house."[141]

The Mozart Theater in Los Angeles ran continuous shows between 1 and 5 and from 7 to 11, charging 10 or 15 cents in admission, 10 cents uniformly during matinees. According to the *Times*, the opening feature, *St. George and the Dragon*, proved "perhaps a little more finished than the films that are 'homemade.' " This film in three art-colored reels was produced by Milano Film in the spring of 1912 under the direction of Giuseppe De Liguoro and sold on state-right basis by Crown Feature Films Co. of New York City.[142] It was emphasized in the trade ad that the film was a "romantic, historical drama" and "not a religious picture." The film, its original Italian title *San Giorgio cavaliere*, was not devoid of sensational features, however, offering Roman orgies, human sacrifices, a mad king, and heavenly messengers, and several of the more than 50 scenes showed interiors of the dragon's lair. Anna Mozart's exhibition concept was that the films should be as exceptional as the patrons, and the opening feature flamboyantly illustrated the point. The program bills mainly headlined quality features—the manageress claimed in a *Tribune* interview that she had acquired exclusive films from abroad not previously shown in the U.S., which was a slight exaggeration, of course.[143] *Variety* reported that Mr. Mozart traveled to both New York and Europe to acquire feature subjects.

Apart from features, travelogues turned into a house trademark, and later the Gaumont newsreel was added to the program. Newsreels carried a distinct quality aura, and the Orpheum a couple of blocks away offered Pathé's pioneering run as their only pictures on the bill. In early January 1913 admission prices at the Mozart Theater were changed to 10 cents for all seats except boxes—children still paid a nickel only. The lowering of the entrance price was not indicative of a slacking quality standard, as Mrs. Mozart assured the press. It was however obvious that the business needed a makeover to attract patrons to Grand Avenue. Donating proceeds for equipping a school at the George Junior Republic underscored the theater's reform spirit, an effort confirming its allegiance with progressive forces in the city. The change of prices was part of an overall shift in billing policy. Films from the studios that had dominated the bills during 1912—Thanhouser, Gaumont, Milano, and Eclair—were less visible if not totally weeded out in the case of Gaumont and Eclair, but the policies employed were broader, and occasionally, the bill even headlined a sensational melodrama like Swedish Biograph's *Saved in Mid-Air* (originally *De svarta maskerna*, literally "The Black Masks," directed by Mauritz Stiller), which was however advertised without clear studio attribution. Female stars like Asta Nielsen and Helen Gardner were featured at the Mozart during this period, as well as Sarah Bernhardt in *Adrienne Lecouvreur*.

In a sense, the two-week stint for Thanhouser's *The Star of Bethlehem*, which opened on December 30, 1912, terminated the initial exhibition concept at the Mozart Theater. The slashing of admission price in January ushered in the second phase, more diverse in terms of its programming policy. The second phase lasted until late in June 1913, when travel films alone made up the bill. The only film awarded a two-week run during the second phase was Helen Gardner's *Cleopatra*. The last feature film shown before travel films took over was Eclair's three-reeler *Why?*, which features a scientist devoting all his energy to the betterment of mankind. His high-rolling son eventually joins him in the cause after suffering an Armageddon-like nightmare, an attraction that encompasses most of the film, which otherwise ends with revolutionary scenes in a ravaged New York City. As an extra incentive, the theater ran a voting contest during its run—"The Old Maid's Contest for a Husband," destined to lead up to a wedding ceremony performed on stage by Judge Summerfield on June 21st. Women were apparently to explain on the stage *why* patrons should vote for them as the ideal candidate for the eligible bachelor, thus tying in with the feature. The contest terminated the second exhibition phase; after that, the Mozarts divorced themselves from features while settling for travel films only.

The third exhibition phase, which started in late June 1913, was devoted to travel films from all over the world, not least from Europe. It lasted until J.W. Ross took over the lease in September 1913 in the wake of Edward Mozart's legal shambles in Pennsylvania. Travel films had emerged as a fixture on the repertory more or less from the outset. In June they turned into the sole element of programming, in all likelihood an afterthought inspired by the success of feature-format travel and expedition films at the legitimate houses.

In an interview for the *Tribune* by Florence Lillian Pierce, in conjunction with its first anniversary—ironically just a month before the lease changed hands—the Mozart enterprise was described as "the theater with a conscience."[144] Female prowess and competence provided the background for the interview. An article in the *Times* published the same day applauded Mrs. Mozart's achievements and underscored the fact that "[s]ex has little to do with success nowadays; results only are taken into account."[145]

Pierce's interview in the *Tribune* was part of her series of feature articles about prominent women. She later devoted considerable attention to moving pictures. One of her earliest film-related pieces was the second installment in this series, entitled "Live Talks With Live Women of Los Angeles" and featuring Anna Mozart. Mrs. Mozart was headlined as a woman pioneer in movies and said to have managed 14 theaters, and was further characterized as an "amazon of the motion picture world." The ambition, Mrs. Mozart claimed, is to show clean material only, which necessitated her inspecting film titles herself in addition to the local censorship body, thereby supplementing the first round of inspection by the National Board of Film Review in New York City. The thrice-inspected films on the Mozart bill, it was said, were primarily supposed to please women and their children, and local women demanded a high standard. "A character-building resort," a place for "education in motion pictures," "cultivation of our taste for the beautiful," "the softening of harsh temperaments by awakening tender sympathy": These were guiding mottoes for the theater's management. The success was attested to by the fact that "[m]any parents cross the entire length of the city to take their children within the influence of the Grand avenue movies." Los Angeles was indeed a both progressive and puritan city due to the mindset of its particular mix of inhabitants. Discounting those amusement seekers singled out in what is termed the Main Street discourse in a following chapter, clean high-class bills were otherwise carefully planned to suit the ideal audience, to wit women with or without children in tow. Mozart's high-class concept catered to this prospective audience segment, initially by way of arty features, finally by specializing in educational travel films.

Anna Mozart's curriculum vitae went all the way back to 1898 when she married Edward Mozart and the couple acquired what sounded like a Lumière projector, their intention being to travel the state of Washington as itinerant exhibitors of films. Reminiscing about her early days in the interview, Anna Mozart recalls having screened films for Native Americans. "The French cinematograph was the original machine. It came to this country in company of a Frenchman who found a venture-

147

some purchaser." Adding to the anecdotes or perhaps underpinning a salient aspect of early film reception, she recalled that "[t]he pictures were of Paris trains and locomotives bore directly towards the great audience. The first time they were shown the audience ran from the building and leaped through the windows, fearing to be pursued by the monster that was bearing down the curtain toward them." Mrs. Mozart's success, Pierce explained, was the result of her ability to deal with the business big wigs on an equal footing, which was partly attributed to her upbringing in a military family with a lineage reaching back to General Stonebreaker "of revolutionary fame." Anna's own father had, in fact, fought in the Civil War.[146]

Shortly after celebrating their first anniversary in August, and simultaneously announcing plans to expand the business by opening several houses along the California coast that specialized in travel pictures, Mr. Mozart was convicted of bigamy. He had apparently not realized the legal repercussions of his antediluvian past when marrying Anna May Kennedy in 1898, unless the move to California via Massachusetts was triggered by this discernment. Mozart had previously lived together with a fellow vaudevillian, a certain Georgia Kane, for seven or eight years, allegedly without having been married to her. The crucial matter was that the couple had a son, and in Pennsylvania such a liaison equaled marriage under common law. The White Rats' trade paper reported on the brewing situation early in 1911 when Judge Magill in Philadelphia's Common Pleas Court No. 1 ordered Edward to pay weekly support to Georgia Kane. This coincided with the Mozarts' move from Lancaster to Springfield, Massachusetts. Kane upped the ante by claiming that she and Edward Mozart had in fact married in Louisville, Kentucky, in 1882.[147] The *Los Angeles Times* elaborated at length on Edward Mozart's confusing arrest and subsequent transport to Pennsylvania for trial two years after the first report.[148] In the first round Judge P.J. Landis acquitted Mozart of charges of adultery. Should Georgia Kane indeed be Edward Mozart's wife, he concluded, she has no legal right to make a complaint against her husband, since man and wife cannot witness against each other. If she is not his wife, she has no right to claim adultery. The proceeding was therefore declared null and void and Edward Mozart was free to go.[149] In September 1913 Edward Mozart was back in Lancaster, and this time he was convicted. Georgia Kane and her son were recognized under the inheritance laws, which left his second wife, Anna, out in the cold. The court annulled the

1898 marriage in the state of Washington, and Mr. Mozart had to spend six months in prison.[150] Eventually, a divorce from Georgia Kane was followed by a remarriage uniting Anna and Edward for good.

As a result of the family crisis, the lease for the theater on Grand Avenue was sold to veteran exhibitor J.W. Ross in mid-September 1913. He announced that he would combine the travel pictures, which by then was the Mozart's exhibition trademark, with state-right features. Ross' tenure at the Mozart did not last long; he apparently faced the old hoo-doo from the pre-Mozart days. In 1914 the trade press was able to report that the house had changed hands again after being dark for a couple of weeks and was now under the management of C.H. Harris—he had formerly managed the Isis at 542 South Spring—and a Mr. Goldfield from Nevada.[151] At the Mozart, the duo exhibited Famous Players features during their short-lived tenure.

On September 20, 1914, the Mozart reopened under the management of Anna M. Mozart. The ad for the opening program in the *Tribune* offered ladies a coupon for *Uncle Tom's Cabin* (World, 1914) "in five big acts." Five shows were presented daily; tickets were priced at 10 and 15 cents.[152] After being reinstated as an exhibitor, Mrs. Mozart hosted special events as side attractions to broaden the audience base. In March 1915 she screened infants filmed at the Better Babies Congress. "Babies are judged like little animals for development, mental and physical, and general conditions, not looks," reported the *Examiner*.[153] The children, over 1,000 of whom entered the contest, "will be placed in separate booths, where they will be on exhibition to the public." According to one authority, the contest offered a rare opportunity "to judge children from different races, classes and home surroundings."[154]

The following week, a horticultural exhibit was part of the screening of the seven-reel film *California*, a depiction of the Golden State's many scenic attractions, harking back to the old travel-film concept.[155] In addition to the seven reels, Anna Mozart added a Vitagraph one-reeler to the show, *The Making of Newspaper*, which was produced at the *Los Angeles Examiner*'s new headquarters, an initiative appreciated by the paper. The showcasing of its new home had originally premiered on November 18, 1914, at the Arrow Theater inside Hamburger's Department Store.

The second time around as exhibitor at the ill-fated address 730 South Grand Avenue, not even the energetic Mrs. Mozart could attract enough patrons to get the business going, and in February 1916 the Mozart turned into the Strand Theater, then Woodley's Strand in October. The mercurial pattern for the venue continued in the years to come. In 1923 the Fine Arts Theater resided in the Walker building, offering legitimate drama; later, in 1924, it became the Grand Avenue Theater under Arthur Freed, but turned into the Orange Grove Theater for musical revue in September of the same year. In May 1935 the rebuilt house opened as the Grand International Theater, specializing in foreign features; the opening film was a Swedish production, *The Song to Her* (*Sången till henne*), with Martin Öhman as the male lead. Professor Emory S. Bogardus, no less, mentioned this incarnation in a 1938 booklet detailing the cultural and scholarly resources in Southern California. It seems however that the Grand International Theater had closed down in August 1937, in fact prior to the booklet's publication. The house became the Grand Avenue Theater once more and ended its career by showing "old movies advertised for their spiciness." The building was wrecked in July 1946 and turned into—a parking lot, of course.

George W. Walker, who owned the Walker building, home to the Mozart Theater and all the other previous and subsequent theatrical endeavors, had made his fortune by speculating in land and stocks in the 1890s before turning banker and simultaneously investing heavily in downtown real estate as well as oil properties. Walker was one of the principal owners of the Broadway Bank and Trust Company, which in that momentous year of 1911 merged with the Citizens National Bank to form the Citizens Trust and Savings Bank. Walker was a director for over twenty years before becoming chairman in 1935. Apart from his interest in numerous corporations, Walker was a trustee at the University of Southern California.

The amusement geography regulated patterns of attendance by creating zones and gateways with a more or less built-in hit-or-flop factor depending on location—an elegant venue and ambitious billing were not enough to counteract a bad location, which the myriad regimes at Grand Avenue clearly evidence. Add to this the precariousness of a stratified exhibition philosophy primarily targeting only one audience segment, the middleclass, and foremost white middleclass women and their children. The automobiles symbolize this notion of well-heeled patrons pulled in from all over town. The Mozarts' business idea, high-class exhibition rooted in a genteel conceptualization of culture, automatically relegated certain types of films and their audience to other, less highfalutin venues. This was a high-risk gamble in an overheated market, when le-git houses were clamoring for longer features and successfully managed to attract the same audience segment between regular theatrical attrac-tions. Mixing up the bill with sensational material after rethinking the billing practices and lowering the admission prices—let alone running a gimmick like the Old Maid's Contest—spelled desperation at Grand Av-enue before the bills were given over to travel films exclusively. The big-amy case cut short the experiment with the travel concept, so the billing leverage was not tested on its own merits when aborted along with the lease, due to the family misfortunes. For the same reason, the advertised plans for expanding to other cities never got underway.

Conservative investments in real estate was a recipe for weathering the volatile exhibition market inherited by the surviving exhibition pi-oneers, unlike Bockover, Clune's partner, whose exhibition career was over when the palace era gained traction in the business center. Clune and Tally, the palatial czars, literally built their respective businesses from the ground up over several years and diversified the risks by man-aging successful exchanges. By leasing their own premises, the money stayed in the business and could later be reinvested in other types of film-related affairs, for instance distribution and production, which ad-ditionally secured attractive material for their screens in advance of the competition. In the mid-1910s Clune bought studio space and invested in Griffith's films, while Tally was a prime mover behind First National and initially controlled the local distribution of Paramount's features.

Mozart's exhibition concept was trapped between not being elitist enough to lure the automobile patrons to the theater on a regular basis, but too highbrow to divert film patrons away from Broadway, Spring, and Main to Grand Avenue. The films on the bill did not have enough draw-ing power to command regular attendance of patrons choosing between attractions at stock houses, musical offerings at the Auditorium, and high-class vaudeville. As a novelty, the all-female-staff-and-management con-cept had created headlines and attracted first-night patrons, but in the brutal competition the Mozart Theater never found an audience segment large enough to sustain its exhibition practice over the long haul. Further-more, the location was far from the depots, transportation nodes, and the white way, as well as the undesirable patrons that kept the cheaper house going by way of a more casual type of attendance. In the end, the Mozart Theater was cornered by its own exhibition practice.

The 1883 call for permanent stages formulated by the Saunterer had for sure been answered thirty years down the road. In 1913 Los Angeles came across as a city of palatial theaters, primarily thanks to Oliver Morosco's untiring initiatives as an impresario. Parallel to Morosco's multiple endeavors, the City of Angels spearheaded the era of movie palaces. Thus, colonists from Iowa and elsewhere had an array of amusement alternatives to choose from.

Nickel culture in Los Angeles, on the brink of being phased out in 1914, according to trade sources, finally heeded, as it were, the strategy outlined by General Film and the local trade organization as well in 1911. "During the past week three five-cent houses have closed, and two suburban theaters have changed their programs and stepped into the ten-cent class. Of the number of five-cent houses now in this city where there are more than one hundred motion picture theaters, there are less than twenty that charge less than ten cents admission, and of the twenty a majority of the managers argue that the bottom has fallen out, as compared to business of one year ago." The nickel houses commanded a small, residual market segment for single-reel films "in the shopping districts, where people may rest for half an hour or an hour during the day." For evening entertainment, however, "it is generally conceded Los Angeles picture fans want the feature programs with good music." The article otherwise extols Clune in his early days at the Auditorium, appreciating his use of newspaper columns for advertising as being indicative of a shift in exhibition practice which necessitated lavish marketing efforts, in Clune's case "twenty inches of space daily in the five leading newspapers, and 24-sheet stands on the most conspicuous boards." If newspaper advertising signifies the ushering in of a new multi-tiered exhibition era built around serial films and features, with a niche market for more casual viewing of single-reel films, Los Angeles in this respect was at the forefront. Here, "[a]ll of the larger theaters are free users of newspaper space and very frequently the space occupied in the local newspapers by the motion picture theaters is twice as great as that of any other theater."[156] Such an advertising practice, combined with the relocation to the business center, which we have outlined in great detail, aligned high-class film exhibition with the dominant culture. Still, film culture was complex enough to cater to other audience segments in other parts of town by offering variety programs, if not predominantly for nickels, at least for dimes.

CHAPTER 4

STREETS, SCREENS, AND SCRIBES

"The idle youth gaping and ogling; the bullet-headed,
unwashed roustabout; the rich and poor. The old and young,
the dumb Chinese, the laborer, the ignorant, the cultured, the deaf,
the indigent, the dumb—all the world but the blind."[1]

AT THE ONSET of the nickelodeon era film culture took on a new prominence as a visible (audible at times) aspect of street culture commanding
and attracting attention in a multitude of ways, as the previous discussion of Simon N. Patten's 1909 pamphlet shows. Newsprint turned into
the obvious clearinghouse for the whole gamut of reactions and observations triggered by the mushrooming street/screen phenomenon. The
intricacies of coming to terms with the nickel shows and their audiences
inspired scores of witty first-hand accounts of the sometimes puzzling
modes of interaction between screen and patrons. The rhetoric was tantamount to a form of "alien perception" with a racist slant underscoring the inability to navigate screen space and the demarcations between
screen and auditorium, and at times even between screen and street. We
will predominantly move along Main Street in Los Angeles.

From Pennies to Nickels

While Mexicans made up around one percent of the population in 1900 in
Los Angeles, their relative importance in terms of sheer numbers increased
gradually and conspicuously. Hence, Mexicans were one of the more
prominent groups of the foreign-born in Los Angeles when the nickelodeon culture took off, but a constituency that displayed limited permanence

as citizens on an individual level and therefore tricky to frame in a community perspective. Most Mexicans were not immigrants coming to Los Angeles and staying on as colonists; instead, they were part of a constant flow of temporary dwellers in search of employment, stints temporary and seasonal in nature, rootless in the new city, and ideally suited to the nickel shows' restless variety format and daily program changes. The available types of manual labor in Southern California were primarily agriculturally based or related to construction, in addition to the mainstay occupation for Mexicans: employment in so-called railroad gangs, as members of maintenance crews. Since the railroads often owned their employees' living quarters in the depot area, the gangs could be shipped elsewhere at virtually no notice. The Los Angeles Housing Commission reported that Mexicans living in the slum areas in Sonoratown performed "the hardest manual labor," earning $1.25 to $1.75 per day. According to Mitchell Brian Gelfand, "Mexicans came to Los Angeles to earn higher wages than available in their native land, although in Los Angeles Mexicans worked for less than any other group."[2] A significant aspect about Mexicans in Los Angeles is that those living around the Plaza consisted overwhelmingly of young men, with or without family responsibilities across the border. Consequently, the Plaza was a haven for employment agencies that took advantage of a circumscribed and mobile ethnic group—and after hours, a group easy to mobilize for the cheap amusement places. Crossing the border between the U.S. and Mexico was an unproblematic affair in those years, which facilitated temporary working sojourns in the U.S. George J. Sánchez's research on Mexican-Americans in Los Angeles provides ample documentation of employers' racist handling of allegedly docile Mexicans, the only group perceived to be able to endure the hard working conditions imposed by the railroads and contractors.[3] In terms of ethnic film spectators, the Plaza area housed an abundance of prospective male patrons that were rooted in the area to a limited extent only and consequently not part of a community in the traditional sense.

As we have shown, the geographical drift of film culture in Los Angeles gradually shied away from the immigrant areas around the Plaza to the affluent business district, and hence moved from nickels to dimes, even dollars when it climbed the cultural ladder. This process can symbolically be localized as a transfer from Main Street to Broadway, a shift preceded by the relocation from Spring Street to Main Street. Spring Street had more or less housed all the phonograph parlors and most of the arcades.

In mid-1907 journalists discovered the pull from the emerging nickel-odeons and audiences willing to part with nickels if the experience was rewarding enough, a mindset signaling the gradual demise of the penny arcades. The novelty of nickel shows triggered several reports from curious journalists attracted by the spiel on the sidewalks. "The frantic efforts of a spieler drew me into a 5-cent show, which equipped with a small stage, a moving picture apparatus and an electric machine furnished more amusement for the money than I have ever accepted before." In this pioneering, anonymous account from inside a nickel show in Los Angeles, the reporter noted that "[t]he crowd about me was composed principally of laborers and young fellows wearing dirty soft shirts," no added specificity by way of ethnicity was offered.[4] This early foray takes off from the penny arcades. The man-about-town concludes after having spent twenty coppers, "I had not seen anything wicked." Via the moving picture show, he enters a glaring establishment with free admission. In glass cases in a "Gallery of Science" waxworks depicting body parts are on display as an enticement to X-ray examination, free in name only. Customers believing themselves afflicted by some of the ailments depicted in wax were the hoped-for victims of this medical hoax.

In order to better understand the city fabric into which the nickel-odeons were inserted, we will discuss a series of discursive interventions elaborating on the street culture on Main Street and its exotic demographics as perceived by the chroniclers walking the beat for color from 1907 to 1913. Harry C. Carr (1877–1936), legendary reporter for the *Times*, is one of the most distinct voices in this street discourses and one example of his reportage takes center stage in that context. Carr's interventions straddle the period under investigation. Initially, Carr discussed nickel exhibition in relation to the general production history of the medium, but when the Los Angeles area gradually emerged as production hub, Carr reported on the early stages of local film production. His pen will guide us through the mercurial amusement scene in an uninterrupted initial stretch lifted from the street discourse to give a sense of film culture's manifestation as observed by an inveterate film enthusiast. After 1910 Carr rarely wrote on film matters in the *Times*, a responsibility gradually transferred to Grace Kingsley or Julian Johnson for film attractions programmed in legitimate theaters. When we subsequently embrace the larger body of street/screen writing, Carr will be represented by a single report only.

Harry C. Carr—Flaneur for the *Times*

The Saunterer's brand of journalism reluctantly embraced the modern Los Angeles against the backdrop of excursions to the literally receding aspects of the city fabric. A decade later Harry C. Carr took in occurrences in the city from the sidewalks, and relishing the new urban spectacles and vivid amusement scene. His writing exudes a sense of witnessing an emergent cultural form rapidly transforming city life. He and his fellow city chroniclers were observers of novel forms of popular amusements as well as agents underwriting their emergent character in a pact with an overall cultural trajectory.

A text deliberating on a monetary shift from amusement pennies to nickels bears Carr's imprint, even if unsigned. A bacteriological observation—microbes eat other microbes—sets the stage, leading to the witty conclusion that nickels eat pennies, that is projected moving images destroy spectators' appetite for looking into slot machines. The text's flippant analysis, Carr's trademark, merits quotation more or less in full.

A canvass of the nickel theaters in Los Angeles last night revealed a very large percentage of foreign patronage in the plain wooden chairs. The Mexican, especially, is an enthusiastic devotee. As far as education concerned, the peon, of whatever age, is not on par with the American newsboy, and to his simple mind the unfolding of the kinetoscope drama is a wonderful and thrilling event.

You can find the nickel theater with its familiar price sign and flaring advertisement, as far north as the Plaza, and as far south as Sixth and Broadway. There is one near the Baker block—adjoining an undertaking room—which has scores of Mexican patrons each day. And yet a cheap theater right in Sonoratown has failed twice this year. Strange anomaly!

The nickel theater and the penny arcade furnish most of the distinctive features connected with the mechanical side of theater development. They came into being about the same time, and have grown, mushroom-like, into a noisy popularity.

In the midst of a campaign against these establishments Carr elaborated on the penny arcades' history and widespread popularity prior to the establishment of nickel houses. Initially, the cheapness of arcade entertainment worked to its advantage, but when the five-cent shows arrived, he claims, the arcades

> dropped with a bump. Peons, bums, drunks and naughty little boys who had been dropping their pennies down a slot, to see all manner of horrid happenings, began to realize that there was a great deal more joy in depositing a whole nickel, and then sitting easily in a real chair for a half-hour or so, while a large, life-sized picture of the same melodrama danced before one's vision.
>
> The basis of the 5-cent theater show is always the moving-picture exhibit. Excitement, of a dangerous sort, is mainly the subject of all these whirring illustrations. These pictures are mainly 'Dick, the Daring' stories done into things for the vision, just as the Kremers and Davises do them into stunts for ears and sight together.
>
> The establishment of the 5-cent theater is sometimes even a cheaper matter than the penny arcade–in fact, as it is conducted in Los Angeles, on a sort of fly-by-night basis, it may be said to be pretty regularly so. In the parlance this is called the 'store show.' The 'store show' is supremely simple in its equipment. An ordinary, small store, provided with a sheet for a curtain, a cheap moving-picture machine, a few rented films, as many old chairs as the place will hold, a ticket-seller, a machine operator, perhaps a heavy-fingered pianist, and rarely a sad-voiced 'singer,' and you have the equipment. A few electrical connections and a barker in front—may be the ticket-seller will do that, too—and you have the outfit.
>
> The arcade on the other hand, must be equipped with rather expensive machines, and its profits, on the investment, are probably smaller.
>
> Moving picture nowadays come in reels from 1000 to 3000 feet, instead of by separate scenes, and each reel may include from one to four subjects. Two or three subjects constitute a performance—and at the end, a turning-up of the lights tells that public that's time to go.[5]

The text sets a discourse in motion predicated on a peripatetic framing of the early nickel culture a year or so after the first two shows had opened. The breakthrough in Los Angeles is here outlined in a historical trajectory, a parallel track where projected moving images eventually get the upper hand over the residual slot-machine exhibition. Observations on the no-frills architecture and outfit of the cheap theaters are effortlessly combined with characterizations of audience groups. Overall, Carr's pen displays an unflattering penchant for racist slighting of the Mexican patrons which runs through several of his texts. The rationale for this piece is the canvass, the resolute rounds among places of amusements for purposes of investigative mapping. At times, such discourses spring from slumming, or emanate from a chance encounter with new phenomena along the streets. The stylistic flavor at times brims with charmed excitement, at times displays clinical observation, but often dismay, moral outrage, and calls for action, or only blazing boredom. Carr was an informed chronicler and up to speed on film history, in contrast to most other writers in the daily press. Several of his pieces were consequently reprinted in the trade press, and later he became a regular contributor to *Photoplay*.

The nickelodeon was new enough to attract curiosity and a sense of discovery among street reporters in 1905-1907 as well as outrage and crusades from other observers. These types of text were all predicated on highlighting the relationship between the representations on display and the audience groups flocking before the screens; Carr's journalism is indicative of precisely such a negotiation. "Cheap" was a favored term, whether referring to pennies or nickels, and with more or less of an edge. The nickel discourse seems to have been a global undertaking resulting from more or less similar shifts caused by the well-oiled distribution machinery, which initially carried foremost Pathé titles to patrons everywhere. Carr was however a staunch champion of Pathé. To his mind, Pathé, more or less alone, produced screen enchantment, while domestic producers delivered mindless films.

Carr's knack for witty pen points served him well as he turned into an ardent film buff. On several occasions he took it upon himself to outline playfully condensed yet perceptively clever film-historical sketches. By comparing French and American pictures genre by genre, he rubbed in the inept shortcomings of domestic production and extolled the superior elegance of the Gallic works. In his first essay he reluctantly had to conclude that the crowd "seems every whit as entertained by the good French melodramas as the bad American ones." A couple of years later, as it was felicitously phrased in the *New York Times* apropos "critical 'movie' audiences" and their sharp eyes, patrons were less forgiving: "In short, the moving-picture enthusiast is no longer a 'fan,' willing to accept whatever may be handed to him, but is a connoisseur as critical as the most blasé of Broadway's first-nighters."[6] For Carr in 1907, the nickelodeons, much to their credit, afforded "the poorer and uneducated American people [...] a peep at real French art". However, the putative sorry state of affairs of domestic production represented a source of much humiliation to everyone born in America. He explains:

> [O]ur humiliation lies in seeing our raw, cheap, vulgar, aimless pictured melodramas displayed alongside the swift artfulness and grace of the French melodrama.
>
> In short, we come to the conclusion that we Americans may be great for designing trashing machines and devising get-rich-quick schemes, but that art was left out of us.

His long article leads up to a discussion of a new trend in motion-picture production relating to what film historians label pre-features, story films in short format set in scenic backgrounds outside studios, in the manner of *Escape from Sing Sing*. This observation prompts a sketch for perspective:

> [The medium] began with mere scenes that were not prearranged—such as marching regiments, panoramas from moving railroad trains, Emperor William reviewing his guards, President McKinley at Canton, hurdle races.
>
> The next step was the little prearranged dramas, that began with crude ideas, such as a supposed quarrel between a man and his wife, and developed to these little pictures playlets—which are legitimate children of the pantomime.
>
> Lately, a combination of the two ideas seems to have come in. They are using the old panoramas of the first stage of the picture business, combined with the play idea. The 'Revenge of the Sicilian' was set in surroundings of surpassing beauty and picturesqueness.[7]

The film alluded to is Pathé's *La Fille du Corse* (1907). The changes in narrative structure noted by Carr prefigure shifts in formats, representations, acting style—and perhaps audience composition. When, in May 1909, William H. Clune opened his high-class house at Fifth Street and Main, seating 900 and featuring a six-piece orchestra, Carr mocked the attempt at taking leave of the five-cent audience in a column notice:

> An experiment is being tried in this city of producing what might be called expensive moving pictures.

That is to say pictures from which the taste and demands of the 5-cent public are to be eliminated.

What a beautiful world this would be were the 5-cent public wafted out of it! How pleasant the world would be if there were no girls who scream or men who slick their hair down. [...] The purpose of this new picture show is educational and delightful. One of the most charming theatrical entertainments is the really good picture show.

In the French film, you see a type of acting—a delicacy of art—that cannot be even approached by any of our best actors.

I am sorry to say that the foreign films are the only ones worth while. The moving picture business in this country seem to have fallen into the hands of imbeciles.

I am in hopes this picture show will cut out the 'comics' and confine itself to little French playlets and travel scenes and, oh yes, plenty of army pictures.[8]

Carr's propensity for characterizing audience groups in broad strokes and incorporating domestic producers into the same category as unsophisticated operators ("imbeciles" in the glib vernacular of his Lancer column) is here married to a desire for an audience smart enough to match and appreciate the artful elegance of the French actors. Racial stereotypes and witticisms aside, his observations are riveted to critical exhibition junctures—here 1909—which in Los Angeles were closely tied to the breakthrough for new, purpose-built, and elegant venues, of which Clune's house was the first. Such houses were decidedly unfit for the nickel audiences of old. Carr's interventions are all predicated on the fluid nip and tuck between the exigencies of viewing contexts—spectators as well venues—and stylistic qualities of the film eventually meriting a new designation. For a few crucial years the preferred term was photoplay, but soon running in tandem with the slightly frivolous movie.

The year 1909 presented further unexpected developments for film culture. An unsigned article from March headlined "Moving Picture Theaters Popular" outlines the medium's following as an affirmation which "prove[s] beyond a question of doubt that the shows are highly moral, educational, amusing, and instructive," thus members of the "best families" regularly visit them. An important shift of focus can be teased out between the production structure discussed in this piece—films "exhibited in Los Angeles" are produced in Chicago, New York, Paris, and Berlin—and the headline in the next feature article in the *Times*, "New Plays Without Words Are Put On Films Here."[9]

The March text, which was not written by Carr, is one of the last to zoom in on audiences. The burgeoning—soon booming—production realm henceforth took center stage in the columns, a process also detectable in the reporting from Los Angeles in the trade press. The October article, unsigned but clearly written by Carr, signals this shift in emphasis by returning to the discovery mode and giving colorful details, not from inside theaters but outdoor shooting of moving pictures. The article offers a general account of the surroundings of Selig's new studio at Edendale before providing a meticulous description of the shooting of one particular film and its storyline. By chance, Carr's piece was published the same day as the *New York Times* ran a story on Griffith's *Pippa Passes* (Biograph, 1909), presented within the production context provided by the Board of Censorship's dialog with the industry. Here we have yet another type of discovery: a reformed industry, hence "[t]he clergyman who denounced the cheap moving picture of the past would be surprised and enlightened to find the Biblical teaching, eliminated from the public schools, being taken up in motion pictures."[10] From the opposite coasts, these two articles clearly belong to the fourth movement in my boxing in of the interaction between the press and film culture.

Carr was not the only journalist to visit Edendale. A couple of 1909 texts on film matters in the *Los Angeles Record*, written at long intervals by Katherine M. Zengerle, were highly local in their approach. In November, shortly after Carr's piece, she signed a lengthy report from Selig's plant out in Edendale chronicling a film shoot by Francis Boggs. Just like Carr she refrained from naming actors in her piece, which is telling.[11] Her text moves away from exhibition and toward production at a time when film culture in Los Angeles was taking on new meaning due to the proliferating studio context, the initial stage of which was described in the two pieces by Carr and Zengerle. Actors were however not yet part of the picture, so to speak.

Carr seems to have monopolized the film field in the *Los Angeles Times* during 1910, a year characterized by studio migration on a grand scale, which turned Southern California into one of the nation's prominent film hubs, particularly during the winter season. In a winter article Carr anonymously takes stock of the industry from a perspective dear to the *Times*' publisher, namely the commercial value of the unintentional marketing of the area's splendor by means of the films' scenic backgrounds. In a comment on acting, inserted as an afterthought concerning the medium's obsession with realism and accuracy, Carr detects a domestic "school of pantomimists" in the making. A harmless enough observation, but there is an unexpected punch line, namely that this school has "already outdistanced the French, who held undisputed possession of this class of entertainment until the advent of the motion picture."[12]

Yet another long unsigned piece from late 1910 sports the Carrian discourse's hobbyhorses when tracking the development of the medium and the handicapped domestic production, not yet fully redeemed by the quality of the acting. Carr writes:

> The picture drama is still in a raw, crude state.
>
> When they first began taking pictures, they were nearly all of dancers, military parades and the like. The first attempts of play were those technically known as 'chase films.' They were without plot. The villain committed some offense and a comic hue-and-cry with women and children and dogs and men and things, strung out along the road after him. The drama mainly consisted in falling over things.
>
> The picture play then developed to the short crude melodrama. In France, they were not crude. The little playlets put forth by the Pathe Brothers were charming and of the most subtle art. It must be confessed that those put out by the Americans companies were something fierce.
>
> Americans are not natural pantomimists. French are. French actors turned easily to the moving picture drama. Our actors had a hard time. Some of them never could learn. Some of the best actors were impossible for this work. Among the best people in the stock companies that all picture firms now maintain are those who came into the work as amateur 'supes.'[13]

Hence the natural American school of film acting, unencumbered by stage training, was on the verge of catching up with the best of French cinema. Two weeks later Carr returned to the state of film production after having run into Hobart Bosworth on the street and apparently received an earful for his recent piece. Bosworth was to lecture at the Friday Morning Club on the educational value of film, and as a warm-up exercise Carr visited a film theater to take in a recent production from the studio for which Bosworth worked, Selig, based in Edendale. The title neatly sums up Carr's opinion: "Educational Values—Huh!" Interestingly, Carr felt no need this time around to embellish his piece with audience observations. The film described was an army drama featuring period uniforms and real-enough Indians. However:

> Then they made the whole thing ridiculous by showing an officer playing cards with enlisted men. To which they added the spectacle of the villain called before the court-martial and grabbing his guilty heart as they READ HIM THE VERDICT! Wow! Wouldn't that give you ptomaines?
>
> Any child ought to know that men of the members of a military court take an oath not to reveal the verdict of the court to any one except the 'reviewing authorities.'
>
> What a shame that men of the high ability of Hobart Bosworth should be obliged to waste their fine and artistic productions such crude, silly stories.[14]

Carr refrains from invoking French eminence here, but foresees a future when stories for the screen will be written by the likes of Augustus Thomas and produced by David Belasco. Shortly afterwards, Carr, in another unsigned article, interviewed William Wright at the Alexandria Hotel; Wright was new in town and had been hired to oversee Kalem's studio construction "near Verdugo Park." Talking about realism by and large, Wright comes close to Carr's pet subject, but from a different direction: "There is a tendency to be as nearly true as possible and work out really accurate incidents of life. Formerly the French film makers were the premiers. Today one American film company is selling more pictures in Europe than all of the European makers combined."[15]

Carr was decidedly unimpressed by the many melodramas produced by local studios. A Lancer column, nostalgically bemoaning cinema's lost future, poignantly illustrates his dismay:

> Once upon a time I thought the moving picture had a great future. Some of the films they used to exhibit were fascinating.
>
> Now they show nothing but a collection of ham actors doing plays about the naughty man with a black mustache from the heartless city who corrupted the farmer's daughter and sent her home with her child.
>
> About twenty-five minutes at a picture show would make the average citizen choke the family dog to death from sheer exasperation.[16]

If such misgivings prompted Carr to hand over the sorry state of cinema to his colleagues is hard to tell, but the fact remains that he seemingly more or less gave up on film matters for a time before starting to write feature articles for *Photoplay*, for instance on D.W. Griffith. His assignment as his paper's Washington correspondent no doubt played into the equation also. Apart from a report from the shooting of a big explosion scene in Selig's *The Spoilers*, with the actors named in contrast to his Selig piece from 1909, his few-and-far-between interventions held on to the lost-future stance, until he was ready to predict a redemption for the movies, which we will return to.[17]

Street Talk—The Main Street Discourse

Egged on by the claptrap of clappers and brash noisiness on the street, intrepid flaneurian journalists crossed the threshold to the nickelodeons. In the passage from sounds to sights, from the realm of street excitements to those on the screen, the peripatetic scribes, Carr and others, discovered a new type of public space peopled by an odd assortment of audience members in establishments far from luxurious. Besides children gloating over the films with wide eyes and open mouths, a mainstay in the accounts, the chroniclers oftentimes encountered bizarre modes of engagement and spectatorship, frequently ethnically inflected. Troubled civic activists, when looking into the matter from different vantage points, replicated these insights, but in another register. Initially, the enveloping soundscape was perceived as a more problematic feature of the new establishments than the screen content and the audiences frequenting the nickel shows. As mentioned, the magistrate in Harlem could not contain the racket from the Nicolet from enveloping the area on 125th street in 1906 when a coalition of businessmen and neighbors asked for relief, and in several other cities businessmen complained that the noise drove away their customers. In Atlanta merchants on Whitehall Street fretted "that the stentorian tones of the phonograph" outside a new moving-picture theater "clogged the wheels of commerce," and after hearing witnesses and experts Judge Broyles ordered the "phonograph muzzled."[18] On Market Street in Philadelphia the clash between business interests and picture amounted to a "war."[19] In Los Angeles in 1911 a group of businessman on Main Street petitioned the City Council, asking for regulation of ballyhoo, spiel, and musical contraptions via an ordinance which was adopted on August 2nd. On December 21st it was applied to two theaters: Banner, located between Fourth and Fifth, and Clune's Fifth and Main.[20] After complaints were leveled at eight houses a couple of months later, a police judge decided to summon the proprietors; all promised to tone down machine sounds from horns outside their establishments as well as dampen the barkers' spiel.[21]

After critical overtures ranging from discovery to dismay, the press came to embrace the new phenomenon of film culture in its cloak of everyday life. In Los Angeles this process of reporting, monitoring, and policing prior to embracing literally takes us from Main Street to the mainstream, from exhibition in the old city center to elegant Broadway on the cusp of the Hollywood era. Irrespective of newspaper morgues providing convenient access to previously published material, the fourth estate oftentimes displayed acute amnesia concerning its own print history and contradictory responses when effortlessly moving from disgust to delight.

The newspapers in Los Angeles never mounted a sustained crusade on moving pictures, partly due to the success of the campaign flurry in late 1906 and early 1907 in the *Times*. Misgivings were indeed voiced later on, albeit in a more general fashion, for instance as a desire for blue laws curtailing amusements on Sunday, the Lord's day, a top priority for the *Los Angeles Express*, which led to an ad boycott by the theaters. The matter was however buried by the City Council and a vote on this issue deferred for a period of two years.[22] A campaign for censorship, which will be discussed in another chapter, emerged from the murky political situation in Los Angeles prior to the move to recall Mayor Harper, followed by a progressive regime. The City Council created a Board of Film Censors in 1912, more as an afterthought than the result of fierce campaigning. All newspapers displayed vigilance in regard to safety measures and the houses' readiness to deal with fire hazards: aisles that were wide enough, a sufficient number of exits, etc. The disaster at Rhoades Opera House in Boyertown in January 1908, where over a hundred people were killed in a stampede after a gas tank attached to a lantern projector exploded, prompted nationwide attention to fire regulations. Authorities in Los Angeles had however been on their toes in this respect well in advance of the Boyertown disaster. The late 1903 conflagration at the Iroquois Theater in Chicago, which left over 600 dead, was a wake-up call in regard to fire risks, spawning stricter regulations nationwide.[23]

Progressive reformers, many of them women, were active in the regulation of film culture in Los Angeles, and also in mobilizing resources for playgrounds. From the breakthrough of nickel culture to the gradual establishment of standing press genres for more or less daily reporting on film matters, women played decisive roles, here as elsewhere. In this chapter we will approach film culture in another register—regulatory discourses will be the next chapter's focus—by zooming in on Main Street and the discursive frames employed for popular culture. Albeit centrally located as a lively midway-like street culture, bisected by the Plaza and catering to the neighborhood's rich ethnic mix, a series of textual interventions in flaneurian fashion pinpointed emerging film exhibition at the outskirts of the city's fabric, irrespective of its location along a busy thoroughfare, which here oscillates between historical and symbolic functions: Main Street. This artery turned into an entertainment street, after the era of parlors and arcades, when Spring Street was unrivaled.

From 1907 until 1913 reporters repeatedly returned to a cultural scene little affected by the changes normally associated with spectatorship during the transitional era; this scene is here metonymically referred to as Main Street. By 1913 film shows proliferated in all parts of town, and the finest had found elegant homes on Broadway. Patterns of spectatorship were then as diverse as the neighborhoods, and shaped by location, level of run, exhibition practices, theater architecture, influences from other types of entertainment outlets, and proximity to nexuses of transportation. Everyday life around the Plaza and on North Main Street, however, seemed unperturbed as far as a certain aspect of its film culture is concerned. Novelistic snapshots and peripatetic journalism taking in street life and popular entertainment venues there consistently discovered a plethora of attractions patronized by scores of immigrant groups and day laborers living on top of one another in squalid tenement ghettos with precious few playgrounds for the children. The exotic differences merited venturesome explorations from inquisitive journalists, like Carr's exposé below from the Baker block on North Main. In the main, and on Main Street especially, journalists ended up inside movie theaters, taking in patrons and the moving-image fare bestowed upon these predominantly non-white audiences. Street life there and everywhere was regulated by the city; an ordinance had, for example, by then been adopted to prohibit solicitation of trade by "sidewalk cappers." An editorial singling out Main Street urges authorities to enforce this particular ordinance, since the capper system is said to be of "foreign importation and has become an intolerable public infliction and nuisance."[24]

Film culture and spectatorship have consistently been associated with modes of visuality outlined in a limited body of literary texts, most prominently Edgar Allan Poe's short story "The Man of the Crowd," which formed the basis for Walter Benjamin's discussion of features indicative of modernity. Tom Gunning's analysis, for example, which is underpinned by an array of studies, is built around three visual regimes embodied by the flaneur, the gawker, and the detective. Detached observance, absorbed gawking, and instrumental surveillance, respectively, characterize these three modes of vision. As Alison Griffiths reminds us, gawking is closely related to gaping, the latter a bad word for museum curators in the latter half of the 1800s who were eager to avoid "gapers" and their shortsighted absorption and attention span. To stare wonderingly with open mouth, one aspect of the term's lexical definition, is a key aspect of numerous descriptions of film audiences alluding to a similar combination of curiosity and lack of sophistication as displayed by the undesirable "holiday people" with time to kill in the museum context.[25] The discourses brought to the fore in this inquiry are predicated on metaspectatorship, that is observation of audiences in front of the screen and their mode of attention.

The mode described as flaneurian represents a holdover from a time when the street and the *interieur* merged under the roofs of the more sedate arcades. In a small city with a perpetually mild climate peripatetic journalism takes on different frames, as is evidenced by the Saunterer's brand of writing. When the literary market changed and aspiring writers found themselves working for newspapers, new genres emerged, upgrading the pace at which impressions were taken in while preserving a detached mode and adopting a window-like perspective, as it were. True to form, Carr wittily titled one of his standing columns "From a Carr Window."

At the nickel shows flaneurs discovered gawkers totally absorbed by the spectacle on the screen, which oftentimes was evidenced by accounts of misreading and patrons forgetting themselves prior to the active type of spectator Simon N. Patten describes as a "watcher [that] thinks with purpose," which conforms to the detective's instrumental mode of vision as described by Poe. The shift from flaneurian accounts to crusades genders vision differently, since women took the lead in Los Angeles in late

1906 as well as in New York City in 1913. The latter mode of vision was far from detached and had nothing to do with gawking, rather a mode of surveillance associated with the detective's comprehensive mode of vision and critical processing of insights. Removing the element of alarm, the crusaders' discourse often rested on investigations, which were further promulgated by the crusades' subsequent gelling into the genre of the recreational survey with its systematic approach. The gender shift has however nothing to do with replacing flaneurs with flaneuses, which in the context of modernity are mainly pegged as streetwalkers prior to walking the safer aisles of the department stores. In this context the Saunterer in Los Angeles, Mrs. Otis, might represent an exception confirming the rule of female absence on the sidewalks. Her safe sauntering in 1880s and 1890s is indicative of the slow rhythm of a small-town prior to the proliferation of automobiles and other gadgets transforming the city's fabric.

Leaving behind the crusade mode for now, we will focus on Main Street and its diverse crowds, cheap attractions, and lively excitements as observed in a series of textual interventions from 1907 to 1913. In 1914 a local reporter concluded: "Los Angeles has a 'Bowery,' it is in the vicinity of the Plaza. Strange people inhabit this district," which is exemplified by prostitutes and dope fiends.[26] Main Street's daily display of carnivalesque business hoaxes and cheap entertainment outlets attracted audience groups framed by the city reporters as primitive and child-like in their responses. A novel published in 1910, which was set in 1902, offers a prototypical street tapestry of everyday life along Main Street prior to the presence of nickel shows. The observant mode, the crowd-gazing, and the barrage of impressions work in tandem as motivational devices for the text passage below. The protagonists walk along the "principal streets, watching the crowd."

> Electric signs blazed everywhere. Bob was struck by the numbers of clairvoyants, palm readers, Hindu frauds, crazy cults, fake healers, Chinese doctors, and the like thus lavishly advertised. The class that elsewhere is pressed by necessity to the inexpensive dinginess of back streets, here blossomed forth in truly tropical luxuriance. Street vendors with all sorts of things, from mechanical toys to spot eradicators, spread their portable lay-outs at every corner. Vacant lots were crowded with spielers of all sorts—religious or political fanatics, vendors of cureall, of universal tools,

of marvelous axle grease, of anything and everything to catch the idle dollar. Brilliantly lighted shops called the passer-by to contemplate the latest wavemotor, flying machine, door check, or what-not. Stock in these enterprises was for sale—and was being sold! Other sidewalk booths, like those ordinarily used as dispensaries of hot doughnuts and coffee, offered wildcat mining shares, oil stock and real estate in some highly speculative suburb. Great stores of curios lay open to the tourist trade. Here one could buy sheepskin Indian moccasins made in Massachusetts, abalone shells, or burnt-leather pillows, or a whole collection of photographic views so minute that they could all be packed in a single walnut shell. Next door were shops of Japanese and Chinese goods presided over by suave, sleepy-eyed Orientals, in wonderful brocade, wearing the close cap with the red coral button atop. Shooting galleries spit spitefully, Gasolene torches flared.[27]

Eventually, the hero ended up in an open-air theater, an airdome, with a bill offering no moving images. The attractions, business schemes, and trinkets for sale on the street were laid out for a tourist's eye as well as for folks from the ethnic neighborhoods and the local transients in an area offering temporary tenement quarters for scores of day laborers, mainly from south of the border. White's novel is a travelogue, and while brushing Los Angeles only in passing, it bisects and reframes the Main Street discourse from the salient years 1907 and 1913, respectively. The fact that the text is set in 1902 is of little consequence, apart from explaining the absence of nickelodeons. It otherwise harks back to a long tradition of 18th century travel accounts from Los Angeles. Later narratives from Main Street otherwise inevitably end up inside film shows. The lively street panorama seems, in fact, to rehearse scenes of attraction which automatically led to those on the screen. The noisy capper culture—tuned by an ensemble of spielers and blaring horns—performs on this liminal threshold of attractions by staging "the noisy bid for the nickels," as the amusement report in the *Times* phrased it, on the street for the benefit of the screen. It is not by chance that film scholars are debating whether the Janus-faced cinematic soundscape was directed solely toward the street or predominantly had its place inside the theaters.[28] Accounts from inside such venues emerged as the most significant aspects of what Main Street was about. Cinema thus comes across as a ragtag rialto with blurred borders between street and screen. The dingy sideshows on the street effortlessly blend with the auditorium. Street life itself takes on a cinematic

169

quality here in its effervescence and constantly shifting overflow of impressions. In White's text the peripatetic and panoramic mode of impression when walking along the sidewalk elicits a mobilized glance unable to freeze the flow of impressions. The walk along the Midway-inflected street is thus wrapped in a decentered, centrifugal attraction sphere predestined, almost, to discover the nickel venues. White's timeframe however takes us elsewhere, to an airdome featuring a flimsy vaudeville show leading up to a marketing hoax for dental anesthetics. The main impression is of hoaxes, fakes, and unauthentic offerings lacking real substance, ending in a marketing show. It takes a detective's skill to see through the dragnet of illusory offerings intended to rope in the money of the gullible.

Before the nickelodeons turned from novelties to fixtures of everyday life on Main Street, Spring Street, and Broadway, two fine-grained depictions of film audiences—brimming with ethnic stereotypes and the sometimes bizarre practices of spectatorship—emerged. The first article was published unsigned in the working-class newspaper the *Record*, the second a couple of months later in the *Times* by Harry C. Carr. The timeframe between flaneurian interventions and crusade pieces is only seemingly reversed: The earlier texts, which will be discussed later, hit the columns prior to the onset of the nickelodeon's proliferation in Los Angeles and were textually confined to the nature of representation in relation to young audiences in upscale venues. The anonymous reporter in the *Record* instead focuses on the three streets where a handful of nickel houses were located in 1907, characteristically describing their patrons as "characters worth watching."

> Have you ever been in one of the 5-cent moving picture shows in this city, of which there are half a dozen on three of the principal street of this city?
> [---]
> The audience is made up of interesting characters worth watching also. The bulk of the nickels received in each show—and their quantity would amaze the license collector—comes from cholos and Japanese, who have a perfect passion for moving pictures. The former believe that they are portrayal of things that have actually happened in real life, not knowing that most of the playlets are the work of syndicates in Paris, London and New York, which employ good actors, acrobats and variety show performers and have on hand all the accessories of real theaters, besides availing themselves of streets and parks for the production of their episodes.

The writer then offers an account of the Mexican patrons' engagement with the screen:

> The cholos groan with the victim, hiss the villain, approve such acts as in their philosophy seem right, have the goose flesh when something in which red fire and demons, fairies and gnomes is dished up and many of them make rapid signs with their thumbs on their forehead and lips when they suspect that Satan conjured up the marvels they see but do not understand.
>
> 'Que lastima!' 'mira, no mas!' and 'Adios!' are the expressions beside other unprintable, which surprise, admiration or strong feeling draws from them as the show goes on.

The Japanese audience watches differently:

> The Jap sits wide eyed, open mouthed and silent but with fully the same apparent enjoyment. Recently one watching a Main st. show nearly fell of his chair when he saw himself in his national costume, with a paper umbrella over his head and his feet splashing in the mud, trotting down a Tokio street on a rainy day in a crowd. He stayed three hours to make sure that it was no other than his honorable self. He came back the next and every day thereafter until the pictures were transferred to another 5-cent show, whither he followed. He thus made in a month the rounds of each one of the shows, day in and day out, and as he brought with him every Jap of his acquaintance to look upon this miracle there was quite an influx of Japs and nickels which the managers were unable to account for by ordinary explanation.[29]

A journalistic trajectory, spanning six years or so, spun off from this mode of early portraiture of audiences' allegedly "primitive" behavior and reading practices. Convivial interaction between expressive patrons versus audience members categorized as "mute receptors" are established criteria bearing on changes in spectatorship that are affected by shifts in filmic address, programming practices, theatrical architecture, and modes of presentation in a broad sense, as well as location and the neighborhood's characteristics. Lawrence W. Levine has outlined a general cultural perspective on this process, while Miriam Hansen, in an influential study, discusses cinematic spectatorship in such terms.[30] In the

Record article above modes of spectatorship are unequivocally bound to ethnicity: on the one hand boisterous "cholos," on the other mute Japanese. The two groups otherwise display "fully the same enjoyment," irrespective of differences in how they engage with the screen. Thus, the theaters along the three streets in this respect—and at this time—simultaneously housed at least two distinct modes of spectatorship inflected by ethnicity, but both in the register of gawking. This first round of Main Street discourse was grafted onto an exotic street panorama localizing and enclosing early film culture within patterns of everyday amusement life far from the mainstream.

A few months after the July 1907 report in the *Record*, a mapping of the smaller venues presented in a long piece, signed by Harry C. Carr, emerged. This is the most ambitious individual piece on film exhibition in the Los Angeles press during this period. Carr addresses reform issues in a playful manner, and the tone is couched in the peripatetic mode. Given its scope, it is not surprising to find it reprinted in *Moving Picture World*. Carr takes off from an intervention by the Associated Charities in Sonoratown and devotes several lengthy passages to metaspectatorial observations apart from touting French cinema's superiority vis-à-vis American. After noting that the theaters are scattered along Broadway and Main Streets (he could have added Spring Street to the list), he surmises: "The people who patronize them are of such varied quality that you could tell at once, if brought in blindfolded, in just which particular film show you were enjoying life. One finds Chinese and Mexican audiences at the Plaza, they progress to crowds where the women wear new hipless corsets and get up in the middle of it and walk out, if bored." We are then invited to what Carr calls the quaintest of them all, a place on Main Street near the old Pico House (at 349 North Main Street in the Baker block), in a neighborhood richly saturated with tenement houses peopled by Asians and Mexicans. Carr's observation that the Nickel Theater projected images on a wall shared with an undertaker gives a new twist to the metaphors on liveness. Carr notes: "Hidden back of the white screen upon which the pictures of dancing ballet girls, and wedding festivities are flashed, is the horrible room where the dead are 'laid out.' " It is a narrow hall and "squalid," and "[a]long the wall, at mathematically regular intervals, are grease spots where the delighted spectators have leaned their enraptured heads." There is never-ending piano music and signs on the walls in Spanish asking patrons to refrain from smoking, to remove hats, and not talk during the show. "Nearly all the spectators are Mexicans, Chinese or Japs," and by way of further characterization, Carr writes:

> The peons come in from the cheap lodging-houses nearby. They are of the lowest type. They have heads that rise to a peak in the middle and foreheads about an inch broad. They laugh prodigiously when some is [sic] pictured as doing some simple and childish thing like falling into a wash tub, or when some one is stabbed or a horse falls in a bullfight and gored to death, their thick lips almost seem to make the sipping noise of a man drinking a luscious draught.

Framed in highly racist terms, Carr outlines an active engagement with certain types of representations; the transfixed silence noted in many contemporary reports applies to other ethnic groups. The involvement however, described as primitive and childlike, and conditioned by race, is thus implicitly deviant. Furthermore, if the audience is grown-up, it still behaves in a childish way. Next the Chinese, who are

> different, dignified, self-contained men with slender graceful hands. John comes shuffling with two or three Chinese girls paddling along in his wake—a great family treat. Chinese are devoted to picture shows. They have a quick intelligence that the pictures appeal to. They would probably be as fond of other theaters if they understood the language. The Chink girls giggle and are much ashamed when the ballet girls come onto the screen in tights.
>
> Americans, who have been, from childhood, going to theaters and seeing half-clad women, little imagine the shock an oriental woman must feel at such an exhibition.[31]

Besides these two dominant groups of patrons, there are "Japs, occasionally with women and more often without" who are said to be "frequent visitors." Finally, "newsboys used to haunt the places until the City Council, at the request of the Juvenile Court Committee, drove them out."

FIGURE 17: A cross section of nickel audiences. Cartoon from
Los Angeles Times, 13 October 1907, III:1.

Harry C. Carr's topical report offered views from inside the Nickel Theater on North Main, described as "[p]erhaps the quaintest" of them all. The discourse on race in both Carr's article and the account in the *Record* accede to a pronounced anti-Japanese stance, which relegated the Japanese together with the Mexicans to the bottom of the demographic hierarchy. The influx of cheap labor was an important strand of the campaigns besides the highly volatile issue of whether to keep Los Angeles an open shop or not. The ethnic workforce made up a substantial part of the inhabitants in the cheap lodging houses scattered around the Plaza.

The interactive aspect of audiences negotiating screen content is here framed from a perspective of primitive and childlike delight at putting down authorities or glorying in criminal activity. The noise level even called for signs putting a damper on the volume. In both outlines the house takes on a den-like atmosphere far removed from the clubhouse mentality for interaction hinted at by Jane Addams' classic description.[32] In Carr's rhetorical spin the ethnic patrons are invoked from one end of the spectrum to be set against the blasé "hipless corsets" on the other. As the cartoon spells it out: "It is different Up Town." The patrons discovered by progressive ladies late in 1906—see the next chapter—were girls on the verge of the hipless corset stage—to use Carr's phrase—and their suitors, while the boys and nondescript younger men peopled the balcony, or "Nigger Heaven" in the racial vernacular used in the article.

Five years later the *Times*, apparently in response to a derogatory article about Los Angeles in a New York paper, sent Grace Kingsley and a sketch artist to retort with an account from the Ballyhoo circuit or the Rag-Tag Rialto, aka Main Street. After a vivid report from an amateur afternoon on stage, Kingsley devotes the bulk of her text to the picture shows. And she finds "every kind of moving picture show, too—from the nifty ones—to penny arcades where you can be shocked out of your senses." The misspelling she notices on posters and billboards confirms the ethnic spread among exhibitors. On the screens she finds color films, operatic titles synchronized with sound, Indian reels, and "sacred pictures." And there are "light and frivolous theaters" offering comedies. Uptown, the audiences seem to be even more diverse and varied than the bills:

> [W]hat a queer lot of human junk they are—the banker from the big money palace nearly sitting cheek by jowl with the flotsam and jetsam that drifts up from of Main; pretty, innocent little girls side by side with un-ladies; old graybeards next to impish youth; people from Van Nuys jostling the sort that believe vaguely a bath tablet is something you take internally in place of a bath. We are all film-fighters, and the moving picture makes brothers of us all.[33]

If the theaters around the Plaza and North Main once upon a time catered to all the readily identifiable others—the Mexicans, Japanese, and Chinese—the exhibition scene was now both more and less inclusive: One could thus find a Japanese theater on First Street, the International, while the place at 349 North Main had turned decidedly Mexican. Kingsley dropped in during her tour and noticed:

It has atmosphere, it has setting, it even has a palely imitative Moorish architecture. And a pretty little senorita in a black lace mantilla, with a red rose over her ear, sells the tickets behind the wicket. Here the scenes are of Mexicans senors and senoritas, dancing the dreamy jota, bull fights and bits from old Seville. Here the dark-eyed Mexicans throng the seats, doffing sombreros, an occasional bright serape glancing in the darkness, and the women wearing shawls over heads. It is all as distinctive as the Moorish architecture, and is the nickel-snatcher of Sonora-town.[34]

Kingsley's account underscores the democratic aspect of the medium and its ability to attract—at least for certain venues—spectators from almost all walks of life. That the description of the patrons as "flotsam and jetsam" should be translated as "nondescript transients" is, if not obvious, at least probable.

The next report from Main Street represented the opposite ideological camp. Emanuel Julius, editor of the Labor Council's weekly, the *Citizen*, penned an account of street life along Main framed from the irked perspective of an imaginary visitor arriving by train. The travelogue mode harks back to the textual strategies in White's novel and its manner of street observations and crowd watching. If Kinglsey recently, and to some extent Carr years earlier, discovered a certain diversity impacting all aspects of spectatorship, the *Citizen*, by way of broad strokes, instead associated cinema with the general unpleasantness of Los Angeles' version of the Bowery, Main Street.

When the stranger first arrives in Los Angeles, when he strolls from the station, looking to the right and left for the much-heralded sights fertile-imaginationed pen-pushers have told him Southern California affords, his first impression is not pleasant.

Instead of seeing palms and rose bushes, poppies and banana trees, sward and bubbling brooks, instead of seeing beautiful things, the stranger beholds a sense that gives him a dark-brown taste.

And if that stranger happens to hail from New York, he is almost certain to exclaim: 'Why, bless me, this looks just like the Bowery!'

And then, he glances up to see the name of the street, wondering if, by chance, its name is similar to New York's topsy-turvy street, and learns it is called 'Main Street.'

Main street is the 'pleasure' street of the migratory workers of Southern

California. It is the club-house of all the day laborers, the orange grove hands, the fellows who keep Southern California in repairs and who help make it rich.

Main street is crowded with 'movies'—five cent 'movies' that display lurid pictures of Handsome Harry rescuing fair damsel from the cruel hands of Desperate Desmond, of masked train robbers engaged in the gentle task of holding up a flyer, or of a tawny haired heroine tied to the well-known saw mill.

And from early morning until midnight, a motley crowd of Mexicans, 'rag-head,' ranch hands, and the like, make a noise like a nickel and seat themselves before the living screen.

If this is the people's Main street there's another that has art, music, the stage, magnificent restaurants, high-speeding automobiles and beautiful homes.

The writer from the *Citizen* rounds off and concludes his report with a pointed class polarization, his last paragraph's version of genteel life contrasting with the rest of the depiction: "That is the fairy Main street given those who reap what is made by the ill-clothed, poorly fed denizens of the real Main street—sordid Main street."[35] Here the film patrons are again unified in terms of race. Color is advertised early in the text via the bad taste in the mouth, designated as "dark-brown," functioning as a synesthetic harbinger of the later tag "a motley crowd of Mexicans." The clubhouse mentality characterizing the street interaction presumably corresponds to a kindred code of conduct in front of the screen, albeit the phrase "noise like a nickel" is nebulous and positioned on the threshold between the street and the auditorium.

Six months later a feature article in the *Tribune*, the morning paper published by Edwin T. Earl of the *Express*, slightly reversed the "sordid" perspective by paying tribute to Main Street's multitude of noisy and colorful attractions, or the side show, as the headline has it. The lively commercial panorama is contrasted with Broadway's more refined manners of doing business. Main Street's ebullient and noisy style is set off as distinct from the rest of the city's street life. We are however not invited inside the film shows; it is apparently enough to characterize them as a group by way of the ballyhoo racket out on the street.

In practically every section of Los Angeles there are moving picture theaters, some as magnificent and as expensively appointed as the largest playhouses. In Main street they have nickelodeons. You can hear these nickelodeons before you can see them. About three blocks before. Some are a trifle less loud than others, but on the general run there isn't much difference between them.

Adjoining the nickelodeon you'll find the penny arcade. The arcade is, if anything, more boisterous than the nickelodeon. That is, the musical contraptions aren't any louder than those of the nickelodeon, but there are more of them.[36]

In yet another article from 1913 Estelle Lawton Lindsey took leave of the civilized part of town and ventured into Main Street and the Plaza area one Saturday evening to observe the ethnic throng and the array of attractions and amusements on display. This intervention is a companion piece to the *Times*' amusement report, offering a closer look at one specific part of town and its entertainment outlets. The abundance of happy faces surprised Lindsey, and she wondered where these hardworking folks otherwise dwelled. After visiting a French restaurant and passing a rescue mission and a drink emporium, she hazarded a visit to a film show; again the noise is a salient aspect of the street culture. She is however willing to be enticed by the ballyhoo, and steps inside.

The picture shows invited patronage with music and cries and we passed in with the crowd.

The films run at the plaza houses are good and they are doubly beautiful because of the spirit of the audience. A big Chinaman in front of us held a diminutive replica of himself on his shoulder and talked to it in his native tongue. A peddler passed holding aloft ice cream cones, at which the baby reached, gurgling infantile persuasion. The horny-handed men around laughed in sympathy and spoke kindly to the little child.

Just here six 'broilers,' pink-clad, danced across the stage singing a Mexican song. It is safe to say the elite will greet Mary Carden with no more enthusiasm. The dancers finished their turn and the screen showed a little lad's dream. The youngster in the dream became a great Indian slayer, and his feats of valor were cheered by hundreds sympathetic voices.

'Go it, kid. That's right, kill him again. Good boy. Gee, ain't the kid all right?' I suppose the pandemonium all about was the same thing in a dozen or more languages. Every face that passed out of that house passed out smiling. There were gnarled truck gardeners, ancient women dried like desert-exposed beef, mothers burdened with many children and horny-handed fathers.

All that joy for five cents! The flaming posters seemed less exaggerated since the show produced such results.

Lightly we walked back toward the city watching the happy crowds.

This world and its inhabitants are not only totally different from the rest of the city and its folks; it is out of time. This is confirmed by an encounter with a young girl "in a white satin skirt that showed every curve of her figure, hugged an enormous pillow muff to her bosom. Her painted face beneath her plume-shaded hat showed weariness and discontent. We were back in the twentieth century."[37] Amusingly, this sketch harks back to the Saunterer's 1887 description of made-up faces. The bill reported on in 1913 mixed screen and stage entertainment in the manner of small-time vaudeville—the live act obviously created quite a stir. The running commentary accompanying the film attests to a lively, interactive clubhouse type of exhibition, yet ethnically diverse to the extreme. Irrespective of nationality and race, it seems as if everybody, "in a dozen or more languages," were vocally responding to the representations, creating an audio kaleidoscope characterized as pandemonium. The isolated voice reported by Mary Heaton Vorse in her much-discussed sketch on spectatorship from the Lower East Side in New York City here takes on a chorus-like quality, when patrons turn into a unified viewing body, discounting ethnicity and language. The sole German voice, characterized by Vorse as "a little unconscious and lilting *obbligato*," was also cued by an Indian picture, which the young woman engaged with as if it were a communicable "reality."[38] Lindsey's account is more compressed, but highlights a similar type of engagement with a reality of sorts. The vocal panorama she mentions is, however, not severed from the audience members' linguistic specificity, hence the pandemonium. Content-wise, the choir gives voice to a polyglot universalism transcending and dislodging the spectators' cultural anchors. The story's interpolating power apparently triggers the unified response. Still, the choir displays a similar cine-naïveté as Vorse's lone German voice. According to the reporter's interpretation, all patrons are sharing the same set of cued emotions and articulate them in so few words and as one universal body and one voice, irrespective of the dozen languages used.

By discursively divorcing Main Street and the Plaza area from the rest of the city—physically, culturally, and even historically—this pocket of spectatorship, in the two reports from the *Record*, from 1907 and 1913 respectively, stands out as being unaffected by the changes in film culture reported elsewhere. And likewise, street life, in its Midway-like stability, comes across as radically different from the urban panorama uptown. A cartoon accompanying Lindsey's text with a concise caption claims that "mission workers are about the only white people in evidence."

Thus, judging from these journalistic interventions, everyday life and spectatorship on parts of Main Street remained surprisingly intact, irrespective of changes in film style and program formats. Regulating the ethnic fabric of spectatorship in this part of town did not command the same level of urgency as coming to terms with the moral contamination allegedly threatening the primarily young white girls inside and in the vicinity of places of amusement, particularly film shows. Instituting a system of prevention and protection shouldered by a new category of enforcers, policewomen, was one response to the problem. Not only the noise, but also the overall loudness of cheap amusements represented a problem vis-à-vis the community at large, especially in 1911 when exhibition was on the verge of leaping to a new level of ambition a few blocks away. It is therefore not surprising that the new trade organization wanted to discontinue "the practice of issuing souvenirs, prizes, coupons and other 'ballyhoo' business enticers."[39]

A typical Los Angeles solution to problems was to tear down and rebuild. The *Times* ventured the following observation: "In Los Angeles just now popular speculation on each new excavation is that it is either for a skyscraper, a garage or a moving picture show. In any event, building operations were never so brisk."[40] This activity was however confined to the new theater district, the erstwhile business district and the Plaza area operated according to a different logic.

The Main Street discourse was by no means confined to this particular Los Angeles street. As mentioned, it was predicated on a specific type of peripatetic journalism grounded in and reporting from metropolitan amusement districts. In the eyes of the writer in the *Citizen*, Main Street blended with the Bowery; in the article they are unified in sordidness and their equally unappealing foreignness. Estelle Lindsey, however, read the happy faces crowding the Plaza area in much more benign terms. A comparable account of Rivington Street on the Lower East Side from 1910 paints a street panorama where the exoticness and differences are again assets rather than drawbacks, leading to eulogizing about feminine charm and loveliness compared to the girls on Fifth Avenue or elsewhere in New York City. "Whatever the reason might be, there is no getting around the fact there is an astonishing number of beautiful women in Rivington Street. Girls who haven't at least passably good looks are the exception. There is an exotic quality about the most of them—with their dark hair and eyes, their full, lithe figures and easy, careless demeanor. [...] And they apparently get more real enjoyment out of Rivington street than the average woman does with the whole of uptown to play in."[41] As for film shows, they are commented on in passing only. For those that "desire to be amused," there is no shortage of cheap theaters and arcades. An interesting observation rounds off the article, namely why these "foreign citizens," who are "generally prosperous, healthy, and happy," as a visiting Westerner asks, should "go West and work our farms when they may have this sort of life by staying in the city." Government efforts to lure people from the inner cities to the farm states consequently went unheeded. A companion article on the same page is devoted to moving pictures exclusively, and if the first article mirrored Estelle Lindsey's intervention, this one harks back to the *Record*'s July 1907 report by focusing on screen illiteracy, as it were, wrapped in ethnic terms. The author, F.C. Taylor, as did virtually all writers reporting on flaneurian escapades, offers a sketch of spectatorship gone awry, a case of misreading, dressed down as primitive or alien—perhaps the former due to the latter. Such snapshots are in the main evidenced by the writer as an eyewitness, simultaneously reporting on what is on the screen and how it is perceived. Here, Taylor removes himself from the scene via a bird's-eye view, thereby giving the account more of an anecdotal flavor. Interestingly, the spectator singled out is an elderly man, a Russian Jew; the scene here is Manhattan Street, "in the Jewish section of Williamsburg," Brooklyn.

One day there was a picture being shown called 'Exiled to Siberia.' Outside of the theatre a man was placed as an advertisement, dressed in the uniform of a Russian soldier, such as guards the Siberian convicts. The poor fellow at once became the target for the people of the neighborhood, some of them

181

spat at him as they passed and others throw things. One old Russian Jew, who went in to see the performance was very much affected. He became excited and wept and cried out that the pictures were true to life in Siberian convict camps. He even recognized the scene where the pictures were taken, and some of his fellow countrymen, victims of the Russian cruelty. So wrapped up was he in the subject that he refused to go out with the rest when the show was over, and insisted on remaining to see the pictures again. At last, when the attendants were about to remove him by force, the old fellow exclaimed: 'Meester, meester, please don't put me out. I must see the pictures again.' And then, sublime sacrifice for one so poor, he added: 'See, meester, if you let me stay I give you another nickel.' Which showed that one man, at least, appreciated the pictures the operator in that house was showing. As the old man had never been further West than New York after coming from Russia, it is not likely, however, he recognized the scenes he thought he did, because the Siberian horrors the pictures showed were, as it happened, photographed by a Chicago concern that never had been nearer Russia, or Siberia either, than the Windy City.[42]

This brings us, more or less accidentally, to Chicago. An article in the *Chicago Tribune* zooms in on Halsted—the Windy City's counterpart to the Bowery in New York and Main Street in Los Angeles—and its many nickelodeons. The readers are treated to observations on both the exteriors of the establishments and their posters and spielers, and also what is on display inside, for instance pictures with actors supplying a soundtrack, the popular Indian pictures, and "Halsted nickelodeons are strong on the labor question." To be sure, the most colorful spectacle is provided on the sidewalk and by the variety of the street's make-up, which is read in moving-picture terms evidencing the liminality between street and screen:

But Halsted street itself is its greatest moving picture show. For blocks and blocks in ceaseless perambulation pass the crowning medley of humankind.

The 'bruiser' with the 'bun' gazes with leering indecision at the slogans booming the 'redhot' and the massive 'schooner of suds' side by side in the windows before him. The svelt courtesan arrogantly tosses her dearly purchased plumes in the face of the mother of the slums, tottering along under the burden of years.

The children of the ghetto mingle with the 'childer' of the transplanted Irishman on rollers upon the pavements. Half a dozen boys roll a barrel of whisky from the curb to the tavern door, exchanging doubtful humor with undersized girls who venture observations anent the action.

Every other store is a clothing store and the next is a saloon. Every other place is a restaurant or a playhouse, if it isn't a shoe shop, a 'cafe,' a billiard hall, an undertaker's, or a lawyer's. Turkish coffee rooms vie with the Greek eating houses. The Acropolis is there. The daughters of Ruth rub elbows with the son of Siberia. The Lithuanian links arm with the Lowlander.

And up and down the dirt laden thoroughfare clang the trolleys—now modern!—ever crowded with toilers to the south and toilers to the north, from Dan to Beersheba and back again.[43]

It is obvious that the street culture along Halsted in Chicago spawned a similar type of reporting as generated by Main Street, and that the variety on display, as it were, on the sidewalks offered a cross section of ethnic backgrounds reflecting the influx of immigration to the respective city. The diversity is read in terms of motion pictures, which are the prime focus of this journalistic genre, the flaneurian fact-fiction accounts of metaspectatorship. Thus, the elements mobilized in the *Tribune* piece play out along predictable lines.

As the interventions discussed here show, myriads of peripatetic accounts resulted from either casual flaneur reports or more systematic attempts at shedding light on what went on inside the storefront houses. John Collier was appointed field officer for an ambitious survey to be undertaken on behalf of a large coalition of organizations, which gradually led up to the formation of the National Board of Review headed by the People's Institute in New York City. Collier's April 1908 report, published in *Charities and the Common*, is well known.[44] His more detailed piece in the *New York Press* published two months earlier attracted little attention. The fieldwork lasted four months, and the *Press* article was the first result from the investigation. Some facts are reported in both texts, but the *Press* article includes a long section reporting from a specific screening, in the vein of the flaneur accounts. Much to the surprise of social reformers, a popular, downmarket institution, a veritable people's theater, has emerged from the people's need for entertainment as a strictly commercial venture, an observation foreshadowing Simon

N. Patten's booklet from the following year if not his 1905 analysis of amusements. The phenomenon's magnitude is underpinned with statistics, a staple of the transitional discourse, which coalesced in the recreation surveys mainly conducted by field investigators from the Playground Association. The centerpiece of the article in the *Press* is a full account of a visit, described as a slumming party to an East Side nickelodeon on the Bowery, but one of the "better sort." It is just after suppertime and "children were clamoring at the door, fathers and mothers, sisters and brothers, infants in arms, were pouring in." The show is situated between a beauty parlor and a penny arcade "whose pictures are vile and which is a loafing ground for Bowery 'floaters.'" The district has only one settlement house and no place for children to go, the "only ameliorating influence" after school is offered by the nickel show.

The seats were packed, the aisle was already half full. Forward against the curtain were fully a hundred children, with no single adult chaperoning them. There were Chinese, absorbed, taciturn and eager. There were Italians—mothers, often with sleeping bambinos in their laps. Fully a third of the audience was Yiddish—Russian and Austrian Jews. Order was perfect. Only the phonograph sent a muffled chatter over its shoulder into the hall, the pianist drummed, the picture machine whizzed.

And the play? There was a foreign quality about it but which went well with the foreignness of the motley immigrant audience. A Gothic castle, stately, with wide arches, washed with sunlight, but with ominous shadows in the background and sinister doors with immense padlocks—Bluebeard's own castle—was the scene. So Bluebeard wedded him an eighth fair wife and went on a journey, and the story which all children know unrolled. It was a French production, with perfect pantomime, which told all that words could have said. The secret closet with its horrors, the bloody key, the return of Bluebeard, thrills upon thrills in the closet-tower, when Bluebeard toyed with his wife's delicate head and swung his broadsword— all, till the brothers arrived on champing steeds and Bluebeard was no more. By this time the interest of the audience had reached the gasping point, and with a royal banquet, in which all the land celebrated the finish of Bluebeard, the drama closed.

Then came a minstrel, and his singing was only half bad. It was the sorrow of Red Wing:

Now the moon shines bright on pretty Red Wing,
The breeze is sighing,
The night bird's crying,
For afar 'neath his star her brave is sleeping,
While Red Wing's weeping
Her heart away!

Colored stereopticon illustrated the sentiments, and the audience, not there for the first or second time, joined in the chorus with a will. Then came a geographical scene—the growing of coffee in Java. Then a rough-and-tumble tableaux, with an innocent countryman tied by mistake in a clothes bag, and his awakening in a Chinese laundry, whereupon the Celestials, whose routine was understood never to vary whatever task might be set them, proceeded to launder the countryman. The audience laughed and kept on laughing, and suddenly Paul Revere made his bow.

Here all was wide-open country, and the spire of Boston-town. Longfellow's poem outlined the plot and was shadowed on to the curtain between the incidents. The children knew it by heart, and shouted the lines in unison, though their accent was varied. This feature lasted nearly twenty minutes; it seemed an hour. Colonial house and stone wall in eastern Massachusetts seemed to have been photographed for scenery. At the end, the Battle of Lexington, accompanied with patriotic music. Then the audience joined in the 'Star-Spangled Banner,' and the programme was ended.[45]

Given the genre, this in-depth report from a world presumed unknown to the readers leads up to a discussion in sociological terms—it was after all a "problem" that had motivated the field investigation. The tone is however sober, no dismay here, and the control measures proposed are ventured in the spirit of turning the nickelodeon into "an instrument for lasting good." The multiple aspects of foreignness emphasized in the article leads up to a moment of cultural cohesiveness in the collective rendering of the national anthem, while the children's shared knowledge of Longfellow's poem is "shouted [...] in unison," but with varied accents. We will return to a discussion of cinema's role in Americanization in the concluding chapter.

By way of reform, a coalition of progressive organizations sought to re-tailor a mushrooming cultural arena for educational purposes, at least partly, by recognizing that its unprecedented popularity reflected real-enough social needs. Collier's report is benign in tone, in contrast to the harsh article comparing Main Street to the Bowery. "A Suburban Exhibitor" ventured a more sinister portrayal of East Side audiences in a letter to *Moving Picture World* at a time when Collier was trumpeting the progress made in the wake of voluntary inspection of films by the National Board of Film Censorship. The anonymous exhibitor complained that the might of the East Side exhibitors dictated what the film exchanges offered, a point underpinned by a sketch of the audiences these exhibitors allegedly catered to. The theater visited was located at the intersection of Essex and Rivington Streets. After commenting on the films screened, the letter writer rounded his report off with an acerbic metaspectatorial reflection:

> I would have been more comfortable on board a cattle train than where I sat. There were five hundred smells combined in one. One young lady fainted and had to be carried out of the theater. I can forgive that, all right, as people with sensitive noses should not go slumming. But what is hardest to swallow is that the tastes of this seething mass of human cattle are the tastes that have dominated, or at least set, the standard of American moving pictures.[46]

This niggardly note does not reflect the overall impression conveyed in the newspaper discourse, which painted a much more fine-grained picture concerning the diversity of audiences as well as what was offered on the screens. In a *New York Herald* article, published five months earlier, J.A. Fitzgerald surmises: "At the start this form of entertainment was patronized almost exclusively by youngsters, but now the audiences entertained at the better picture houses are on par with those which can be found in any of the high class vaudeville theatres," a point underscored in a cartoon of "The Moving Picture Audience of Today."[47] Audiences here wear evening clothes and approach the films with an attention level worthy of Broadway productions, and on their way out "discuss the merits of the actors."

The standing columns devoted to film topics, which emerged in the mid-1910s, were penned against a distinctly different backdrop than the first wave of ethnographic accounts from inside nickel venues. The early accounts hoped to convince authorities to come to grips with the vexing

FIGURE 18: High-class audiences in New York in 1910.
Cartoon from *New York Herald*, 17 April 1910, III:14.

aspects of film culture, primarily its obvious appeal for children. Young
girls' and women's places in the public sphere were discursively related
to the magnetic pull from amusements, attracting the girls and in turn
scores of male predators—mashers of all stripes—lurking inside theaters
and out, around dance halls, and on the streets. For reformers, the surrounding street culture represented a greater problem than the representations on screen. The white-slave discourse, which overall was related
to commercialized amusements, in its multiple facets elicited a regulatory agenda for obviating joy rides and other schemes and scams for
framing girls. Appointing policewomen was one of several responses to
the girl problem. The women on the beat were supposed to regulate and
police the girls' access to amusements, monitor their behavior on the
streets, crack down on mashers, and educate irresponsible parents. A tall
order. At a time associated with the beginning of high-class exhibition
and a film culture in rapid transition, it was apparent that not everybody
focused on the screen in awesome silence. Some preferred to take in attractive partners in viewing. The masher in his many guises was the focus of attention for a multitude of measures aimed at protecting suscep-

tible girls and young women. In a series of alarmist articles from 1914 about the shady sides of Los Angeles, written by John Danger for the *Record*, one installment focused on male predators hunting young girls in the dusk of the movie houses. Danger followed three such creatures and their methods of preying, offering little new information besides a detailed description of the tactics of moving close to objects of desire. With his alarmist account, this type of discourse culminates and thereafter gradually petered out.[48]

FIGURE 19: Mashers and their alleged tactics.
Cartoon from *Los Angeles Record*, 23 July 1914, 1.

CHAPTER 5

REGULATORY DISCOURSES

"To estimate the social effect of motion pictures
is as difficult as to estimate that of the modern newspaper."[1]

FROM THE INCEPTION of the nickelodeon boom to the emerging feature market, the press recurrently staged tribunals in the columns directed at the allegedly detrimental influence of film culture. In the process audiences were monitored, mapped, and discursively policed, places of exhibition singled out as health hazards or firetraps and regulated to offset such risks, suggestive representation condemned as instructive and glorifying crime. For many reformers, instruction was perceived as the medium's true mission and foremost rationale, but the curriculum implemented by local exhibitors was putatively confined to nefarious realms and thereby counter-productive for the susceptible students. Appropriating cinema for purposes of salutary instruction, propitious education, and cross-cultural awareness bolstered film-campaign efforts outside commercial exhibition, but even within the sphere of regular theatrical exhibition certain distributors carved out a niche market on the variety bill, most prominently George Kleine for the titles in his massive educational catalog. In a market operating on protocols of variety, film companies diversified and, due to their product differentiation, released titles at times singled out by critics as truly educational, while other films were flogged as examples of malicious instruction. Certain formats on the bills were predicated on balancing education and entertainment, not least the numerous split reels from 1907–10 featuring two short subjects, one with an educational slant, the other often a comedy.[2] Gradually, so-called high-class exhibition upgraded the cultural as well as educational aspirations of programming and presentation, while levels of run still upheld a hierarchy within the release circuit.

In Los Angeles, as in most other cities, women affiliated with clubs, civic organizations or municipal bodies sounded most of the warning calls for regulation of film culture under the banner of extended motherhood. Later appropriated by an organization like the Practical Mothers' Association and applied to the film field in New York City, this body of initiative has been discussed by Elizabeth J. Clapp among others as a touchstone of the progressive discourse.[3] Bliss Perry approached the sacralization of mothers from a slightly different perspective in a discussion of sentimental impulses animating American literature as well as the yellow press and the illustrated magazines. All gravitate around "the home" and "the child," and "without that appealing word 'mother' the American melodrama would be robbed of its fifth act," Bliss opines.[4] Concerns about the exploitation of children in relation to moving images were voiced well in advance of the nickelodeon. A couple of interventions in the *Los Angeles Times* surveying the slot-machine market in the picture arcades are indicative of moral outrage in the face of children being catered to.

Thomas W. Johns—"Picture Skunk"

In the pre-nickelodeon era Thomas W. Johns was unflatteringly branded a "picture skunk" when the *Times* exposed the seedy offerings at the Penny Arcade, Johns' place, as well as the similarly sleazy views on display at the Automatic Vaudeville managed by Harry Temperly. The Arcade, located at 431 South Spring Street, opened in September 1904; the Automatic at 340 South Spring had already begun exhibiting in 1903. Spring Street was the artery for popular attractions harking back to the phonograph parlors of the 1890s. The text in the *Times* is a prototypical specimen indicative of a genre of reportage on visual attractions which takes unscrupulous exhibitors to task for indiscriminately offering all types of views without any precautions for preventing children from being exposed to adult material.[5] Johns and Temperly earned their skunk label by displaying material appropriate for smoking rooms to all patrons and facilitating children's access to such illicit views by providing stools high enough for short-legged patrons eager to use the peep machines. The reporter had visited the two establishments several times and explored the material in virtually all the machines there. Furthermore, he had checked the license records to be able to publicly denounce the two managers, and he was also aware of a state law banning exhibition of "obscene or indecent pictures"; this was investigative journalism on a moral mission. Already in the heading, the tone is sharp and high-pitched: "Vice Swamps for Children." According to the reporter, the pull of the scurrilous images threatened to land the children in a moral quagmire. An alarmist tone permeates the text, and its verbal imagery imparts an acute urgency calling for immediate intervention from authorities. Detailed accounts of the images on display are offered to show a blatant mismatch in relation to the young patrons frequenting the establishments. The arrangement for facilitating children's access is particularly unsettling. The arcades operated under the guise of phonograph parlors, but visual material dominated the offerings. As in numerous later crusade pieces, the metaphors revolve around pedagogy, here termed "lessons." Thus, "[u]nder this cloak hundreds of boys and girls are weekly learning lessons that in all likelihood will go far—already have gone far—toward breaking down their physical powers, undermining their moral conscience, and preparing misery and wretchedness for all the years of their maturity." With pennies to spare, children could, for example, watch views of "women and girls in various stages of undress." For the reporter, the females come across as prostitutes or the "cheapest of cheap actresses," and their posing is designed for the arousal of "bestial pleasure" in mature men. The text singles out two young patrons, a girl around seven and boy circa ten "doing the machines together."

The girl had no pennies, but the boy held some in his hand. The girl, standing on one of the foot stools, was gazing wide-eyed into one of the several decent machines; the boy had dropped a penny for her, and the pictures happened to be photographs of the streets of Washington City during the funeral procession of the late President McKinley. Presently the child cried out, excitedly; 'Oh, Cliff! Cliff! You ought to see this one; it's perfectly beautiful.'

The boy, his eyed glued to the glass sights of a machine close by, made no answer; he was utterly absorbed by what was passing before his vision. When his last picture had dropped and his machine gone dark, he turned to the girl: his boyish cheeks were flushed, his lips were parted loosely, and there was a look in his young eyes that was not good to see.

'Gee,' he said slowly, 'I bet it wasn't as good as mine. Mine was a p-e-a-c-h.'

This dramatization of spectatorship, without specifying what the young boy took in from the peep machine, includes detailed observations of the viewing experience's physical manifestations. Accounts of enrapt absorption, as always, center on physiological symptoms—wide eyes, open mouths, and flushed cheeks. This interfacial portraiture is a recurrent feature of the metaspectatorial discourse. Thus, the sketch of the boy being deaf to the world when viewing, as it were, resonates with modes of absorption that often inspired involuntary comments, advice or suggestions to players or addresses to the fictional world in later nickel accounts.

The following day the proprietors were promptly brought to court. Johns pleaded guilty, claiming however to be unaware that his manager had acted against his order concerning the type of images in the machines. Temperly pleaded not guilty, but the court's assessment of the evidence collected from machines at both places was that the images were "lewd and obscene." The court sentenced the promoters to a sixty-dollar fine or sixty days in jail. In this case, one alarmist article was enough to alert the police and place the alleged perpetrators in front of the bench.

A little more than a year later the *Times* opened a second round of investigation, again targeting T.W. John's place though without specifying name and address this time around, as one of many "iniquitous dens." The patrons—men, women, and numerous children according to the reporter—were treated to suggestive titles like "Three in the Bath," "She Served the Tomatoes Undressed," and "The Sultan's Favorite." Women of the street are shown in "disrobing acts; actresses, ballet girls, intrigues of various kinds, are portrayed, all more or less suggestive." Again, the reporter had provided the police authorities with evidence and immediate action was expected. No scene of actual spectatorship is recounted this time around; instead, a textual snapshot featuring two little schoolgirls provides a more general depiction of the atmosphere and modes of interaction with a racist slant:

The little girls went to a machine marked 'smutty,' and each deposited a coin. The little ones passed from one machine to another. A burly negro followed the little girls closely and twice endeavored to engage them in conversation. The children seemed frightened as the man followed them to the rear of the place, but the attraction was great and they continued the round.

Persisting in his attention, the negro followed the girls around the back room, making remark about the pictures, and once directing their attention to a particularly 'desirable' subject. The intention of the 'coon' became so evident that a stranger interfered and the man hurried away.[6]

The encounter took place at "the joint on South Spring Street, near Fourth," T.W. John's place, apparently still offering the same repertory as in 1904.

Arcade proprietor Thomas W. Johns later turned film exhibitor without making it to the big league when exhibition moved from nickel shows to palace-like venues in the business district. His career represents a case in point on the fringe of the exhibition map, moving from arcades and slot machines to nickel shows. In 1909 his Edison Theater at 436 South Spring, across the street from his old arcade, was less impressive than its stellar name. The targeting of his arcade by an investigative *Times* reporter clearly evidences that activist journalism predicated on safeguarding children from risqué visual material had already adopted the discursive frames indicative of phase III interventions prior to the nickel era and its crusades. Key metaphors and dramatization of spectatorship were thus readily available when young patrons gathered in front of allegedly corrupting film screens.

The Playground Movement and the Practical Mothers' Association

Vitriolic campaigns in the *Chicago Tribune* and the *New York Evening World* disparaging film culture bookend regulatory efforts during the tempestuous days of nickel culture. The *Evening World*'s campaign ended with a seal of approval for the film shows in New York City. The *Tribune*'s crusade in the spring of 1907 paved the way for stringent police censorship of films in Chicago (an ordinance concerning obscene and immoral pictures was passed by the City Council on November 4, 1907). In Los Angeles reformers noticed a putative mismatch between audiences and film content late in 1906 and persuaded the City Council to take action in May 1907. Schools of crime emerged as a singularly widespread metaphor for nickelodeons straddling virtually all the regulatory efforts. Before returning to this proliferating metaphor, we will look at the relationships between campaigns for wholesome recreations for children and how commercial amusements were negotiated within the playground movement.

Recreational initiatives were intertwined with the efforts at regulating the market for popular amusements, especially the nickel shows. The movement's objective was to open up society's institutions for after-hour activities for youngsters and children otherwise deprived of arenas for play and education outside the streets and what the commercialized amusements had in store. The movement's ambitious program would, if implemented, illuminate the dark side of the street in Simon N. Patten's sense and offer recreations and educational activities competing with the commercial attractions on the bright side of the street. Initiatives to build playgrounds and recreation centers topped the agenda. Such venues were home to a wide assortment of outdoor and indoor activities: sports, games, drills, folk dance, storytelling, gardening, fishing, and other local offerings, depending on the locale. In the progressive analysis play and recreation were central elements of children's development and often pitted against the purportedly detrimental and passive nature of the commercial amusements widely patronized by children.

The playground movement was given momentum by a $75,000 grant Congress awarded the District of Columbia in 1907, and the Playground Association of America recruited President Roosevelt, himself an avid sportsman, hunter, and outdoor enthusiast, as its honorary president next to an impressive roster of officers, among them Jane Addams and Jacob A. Riis. In 1907 the monthly magazine *Playground* commenced publication as a forum for debate and update on all matters bearing on recreation in general and playgrounds in particular.

Even if supported by Congress and awarded local grants in numerous cities, for instance Los Angeles, where a Playground Commission had already been appointed in 1904, acquiring grounds generally proved to be a taxing matter. Grants or allotments seldom translated into anything but locations unattractive for other purposes or discarded lots. Morbidly enough, several playgrounds were built on abandoned cemeteries, for instance in New York City and the District of Columbia. As Jacob A. Riis put it in a lecture, "[T]he dead rest better because of the patter of the feet of little children over their resting place."[7] The idea of using old cemeteries was apparently pioneered in London on a grand scale. In Los Angeles children's feet did not however patter on formerly sacred ground, albeit some of the grounds were built on decidedly unattractive land. Bessie D. Stoddard describes the second playground in the city as originally "a miserable hole in the ground, a detriment to the neighborhood."[8] The tract was donated by the Park Department, filled and handed over to the Playground Department. Bessie D. Stoddard was one of the five members of Los Angeles' Playground Commission appointed by the mayor in September 1904. She and her sister Evelyn had been active in an array of civic organizations since the mid-1890s, the Settlement Association, the Civic League, the Juvenile Court Association, and more. Within the framework of the Civic League's Child Study Circle, the sisters delivered a joint speech in March 1905 on the urgent need for playgrounds. When the first playground on Violet Street in Los Angeles opened in May 1905, on a lot bought by the city for $11,000, Bessie D. Stoddard and her colleague, Mrs. Willoughby Rodman, were described as "most zealous in originating and promoting the scheme for the children of the city."[9] Bessie D. Stoddard also played a role on a national level, giving speeches all over the country and publishing interventions in *Playground*.

FIGURE 20: Bessie D. Stoddard, *Playground*, Vol. 4, No. 4 (July 1910): 135.

The playground movement gained momentum more or less at the same time as the breakthrough of the nickelodeon era. The numerous civic organizations supporting the playgrounds were involved in an array of ventures for civic betterments ranging from garbage collection to campaigns against billboards and "offensive signboards." It was thus self-evident that the nickel culture would be scrutinized under the progressive lens as previously the penny arcades. Evelyn Stoddard became one of the first progressive activists to report on film audiences in the nickelodeon era, even if the report was made at a vaudeville-like theater.

John Collier, a key figure in the process leading up to formation of the New York Board of Censorship for Motion Picture Shows (soon the National Board of Censorship and from 1913 the National Board of Review), was actively involved with the playground movement and delivered several addresses in conjunction with the Association's congresses. Moreover, the meetings preceding formation of the Board of Censorship clearly connected the commercial and non-commercial fields.[10] The broad scope of Collier's numerous essays and articles engages with film issues in fashions attuned with the playground movement's recreational agenda. Prior to becoming the Board of Censorship's secretary, he was the field investigator for the Committee on Cheap Amusements formed by the People's Institute and the Woman's Municipal League in 1908. The paramount text, however, was a report, virtually a recreational survey, undertaken in the wake of the clampdown on nickelodeons in New York City at Christmas 1908 by a handful of social organizations under the umbrella of the Ethical Social League's Cheap Amusement Committee: the Neighborhood Workers' Association, the Parks and Playground Association, the People's Institute, and the Committee on Amusement and Recreation Resources for Working Girls. A meeting at Hotel Astor on February 23, 1909, devoted to "the Amusements of the People," adopted a resolution to organize a committee of "100 prominent men to formulate a constructive plan to proper recreations and to co-operate with the city authorities in the censorship of theaters and dance halls." During the meeting John Collier, one of those responsible for the report, informed that he had attended a meeting of the Association of Moving Picture Show Investigators, where a resolution had been passed "asking for censorship to protect exhibitors from the film manufacturers [that] foisted improper pictures on them."[11] The Cheap Amusement Committee's comprehensive report focused on parks, playgrounds, moving pictures, theaters, and dance halls. True to form, the report differentiates between commercial and non-commercial recreations and amusements; together, they form "the single, large proposition of public recreation." Commercial culture was said to be aggressive and making inroads everywhere, while authorities were berated for having missed opportunities for a full-fledged development of playgrounds and parks. The numerous outcries against the nickelodeons are described as shortsighted in their ambition to institute policies of repression bordering on extermination; instead, the report advocates a constructive approach since "no agency in New York at this moment draws as the motion picture show draws. It reaches a broad stratum of the people not reached by the recreations centers or the social settlements. Moving pictures, because of their cheapness and often their real excellence, represent the theater itself to the great majority, the wage earners. They are a social force of commanding importance whether for good or ill,—a force which must be used and developed."[12] According to the report, the way to go was to work with the film manufacturers, since producers decide what is available on the market. The report is circumspect in holding on to a wholesale approach to recreations, not just targeting commercial amusements, but critically assessing the curtailment of what the city provides via its "free agencies." It still argues that some restrictions regarding moving pictures are called for in addition to a need for "regulation of the dance hall," which echoes the contentions in Chicago both before and during the campaign in April and May 1907.

The report outlined a constructive program summed up in five axioms: "[H]uman beings have an instinct for play; in the young this instinct is especially strong; it is not in itself bad; it will seek gratification; where proper means of gratification are not provided, improper ones are more apt to be enjoyed."[13] The amusement report, penned by John Collier and Michael Davis Jr. among others, outlined a veritable blueprint for the so-called constructive approach to recreation to which the film manufacturers subscribed by supporting the Board of Censorship and its work. As will be shown, the measures instituted did not satisfy the whole gamut of reformers. For some, the Board was far too lax in its censorship practices. From a broader perspective, Michael Davis Jr. would in 1911 undertake an ambitious amusement survey on behalf of the Russell Sage Foundation.

In an address delivered at the fourth annual congress of the American Playground Association, held in Rochester in 1910, John Collier, after a year as secretary of the Board for Censorship, concisely formulates the cultural connection between playgrounds and moving pictures: "The desire of the playground movement is that children shall have life in greater abundance; and the motion picture is a movement toward the enjoyment of larger life among the people." The theaters are peopled by the leisured classes, he claims, while the "audience of a motion picture show is the immigrant, the wage-earner, and the child, the formative and impressionable elements of our people." The motion picture audience is described as "a family audience," a sociological claim reiterated in all Collier's texts from 1908-12.[14] Collier's ordering of the audience composition reflects a New York sensibility; it was otherwise children that were most frequently focused on by the various reform interventions, not least in Los Angeles and Chicago. In conjunction with the Playground Convention, the Rochester school district opened a moving-picture theater at one of its schools as an adjunct to the educational curriculum.[15]

Just like Simon N. Patten, Collier considered the church to be a virtual non-factor in contemporary social life in America and fundamentally out of touch with the organization of leisure time for productive purposes; productive for him means educational. Transforming commercialized amusements—the main vessel for spiritual ministering to the masses—into educational institutions, or at least minimizing their unchecked impact, motivated his involvement with the National Board of Censorship of Motion Pictures.[16] Hands-on policing is presented as only a partial remedy for saloons and dance halls as well as the movies. "Not for a moment would I claim that the motion picture is not doing a great good. It is a vast educational force in this country—even in New York. What one cries out against is rather the neglect of community duty, and the consequent waste of opportunity through failing to recognize that our police functions reach out over the places of public amusement."[17] Collier considered himself a socialist in the sense that he wanted film theaters to operate under the auspices of society, as a moral agent.

In line with the Board of Censors' agenda, Edison's film company produced a wide variety of films with moral lessons in the early 1910s as joint ventures with or commissioned by business and social organizations. *Charlie's Reform* from 1912, for example, was built around an adage: "The girl without a social center is mother to the woman without a home." The film, supported and probably also sponsored by the Russell Sage Foundation, features a young man "won back to sobriety from the dance hall and the saloon by finding the girl he used to court at one of the social centers." It was part of a campaign intended to promote "the idea of having the school buildings in the evenings turned into social centers to compete with the dance halls as places of recreation."[18] The film medium was thus enlisted as a representational force in the recreational competition by taking the message concerning the desirable non-commercial alternatives to the patrons at the commercial venues.

Discounting such efforts, the *New York Evening World* in 1910 and 1912 indicted the medium, as it were, before eventually giving it a clean bill of health.[19] Prior to this turnabout, film representations were pegged as suggestive, coarse, and incitements for the young patrons to commit crimes. Judging from the *Evening World*'s columns, exhibition practices in New York City seemed beyond redemption, a state of affairs documented in the investigation conducted by Commissioner Raymond Fosdick, which was eventually remedied by the so-called Folks ordinance.[20] In an address delivered at the annual meeting of the Playground and Recreation Association of America in May 1913, Alderman Ralph Folks outlined the background for motion picture legislation. Siding with Fosdick's report, that the theatrical conditions in New York City were the worst in the country, Folks attributes the sorry state of affairs to the absence of a coherent legal framework for regulations. Under the current conditions, proprietors had held on to the store shows due to the low cost of a common-show license, $25 per year versus $500 for a theatrical license, and also due to the high costs of building theaters under section 109 of the Building Code. "While the provisions of this law are satisfactory for theaters they are necessarily very drastic and building under it is very expensive, in fact so expensive that 800 proprietors have elected to operate places of amusement, known as assembly rooms, having less than 300 seats." Just like the reformers, Folks valorized the educational potential of the medium and wanted to transform the schools to alternative, high-class venues for educational moving pictures in the evenings. Sketching a trajectory for the medium and the reactions it had encountered over the years, he claimed that films initially met with "toleration with an inclination toward suppression." In an accurate description of what has been outlined above as phase III, Folks told his listeners that "[i]nfluential and high-minded citizens have believed that motion pictures are bad, that the shows are immoral and that the legislative policy should be one of suppression." Apropos this mindset he concludes that:

The press has been an influential factor in this situation. Public opinion has now changed, however. The doctrine of extermination has ceased and the best elements of the community, including clergymen, lawyers, educators, social workers and public officials have come to realize that motion picture may and does serve a great public need in the field of education and amusement; that it is unparalleled in its possibilities for the masses of the people and that it has become a worthy substitute for many lower and frequently harmful amusements.

Folks, like many other reformers, entertained high hopes for a future film culture where education had the upper hand over the amusement aspect, if one can separate the one from the other. The school-of-crime discourse served as a headline for the crusade efforts, and "the masses" were still perceived in terms of students by Folks. Overall, he underwrote the alliance between the popular press and the movies in his hope that the "masses may be educated through the motion pictures as well as through the columns of the newspaper."[21]

Folks' redrafted model ordinance was adopted after initially being vetoed by Mayor William J. Gaynor. The shift described by Folks after the passing of his ordinance coincided with the last hurrah in the *Evening World* after a campaign that had run since December 2, 1912, and was kept going until mid-January 1913 in more or less daily installments. Eventually, the paper virtually recanted from its longstanding position by enlisting a civic organization, the Practical Mothers' Association, to perform a thorough independent audit of the medium's books, as it were. This coincided with the reintroduction of the Folks ordinance. The Practical Mothers took stock of the figures in a survey that delivered a tally distinctly in the black. Film culture was finally a winning enterprise, in the *Evening World*'s columns also, which praised itself for bringing about the regulations and better conditions for film culture overall: "[T]he results [of the Practical Mothers' Association's inspection] plainly show what has been accomplished by the vigorous hammering for better moving pictures and better conditions in the moving picture houses." Mrs. Harry C. Arthur, one of the many women involved in civic work under her husband's name, headed the Practical Mothers' Association of Greater New York, and she seconded the paper's role in bringing about changes: "While 90 per cent shows are safe and well managed, The Evening World has done splendid work in attacking the films and houses which deserve reprobation and which are now being forced to reform themselves." The leading Practical Mothers had visited most of the picture theaters in Manhattan, Brooklyn, and the Bronx, and they had found very little to criticize; instead, they heaped praise on the establishments and lauded their beneficial social role. The Practical Mothers in the field all had large families: Mrs. Harper, for example, was a mother of ten and the organization's secretary, Mrs. Elisabeth K. Thompson a mother of eight. Their report focused on the place of children in film culture, which was on the sidewalks outside the theaters, given the framework of the Folks ordinance, according to which unaccompanied children under 16 were banned from entering the shows. Hence, children were mobbing grown-ups to buy their tickets, with or without success. The Practical Mothers' prime objective was to aid a bill in Albany, sponsored by Senator Griffin, which would support matinees for children and a system of supervision by matrons offering unaccompanied children a safe environment for their viewing enjoyment. The Practical Mothers dismissed the medium's critics and described them as animated by the "prejudice of fanatics who allow their theoretical notions to prevent the practical care of children." The lengthy report, purportedly unedited by the paper, practically without exception awards seals of approval to all the theaters from Park Row to the Bronx, from Second Avenue to Tenth Avenue and in Brooklyn as well.[22] After the Practical Mothers' intervention, the last stronghold of press opposition to movie culture caved in for good. The unequivocal endorsement of a coalition of mothers represented the strongest advocacy imaginable. The Griffin Bill finally instituted a system for providing safe access to film culture for children under matronly supervision. Still, it took private initiative to further implement screenings for children, namely under the auspices of the Children's Motion Picture League of Greater New York, founded by Mrs. Laura Cogswell and featuring a singularly impressive roster of honorary vice presidents: President Wilson, Governor Sulzer, and Mayor Gaynor. The initiative was outlined in an interview in the *New York Times*. The League organized screenings specially adapted for children and free of charge, held throughout the New York area on Saturday afternoons. A matron approved by the League was in attendance, segregating children from the adult patrons, and the buildings were inspected in advance. In each participating theater, the first three rows were reserved for crippled children. In June 1913 thirty-three theaters were enrolled in the initiative, which evidences a form of extended motherhood underpinning the bulk of the progressive mode of reform.[23]

From Schools of Crime to "The Moving Picture University"

In the course of 1907, shortly after the *Times'* second survey of the arcade market, nickelodeons turned into a conspicuous aspect of city life in Los Angeles. It was however film shows in vaudeville houses that first triggered civic groups to take action; this already took place in late 1906. A coalition of progressive activists representing the Pasadena Shakespeare Club, the Juvenile Court Commission, the Los Angeles Humane Society, and the Los Angeles District of the California Federation of Women's Clubs petitioned City Council on May 20, 1907, asking for an ordinance prohibiting children under fourteen from visiting places of public amusement if unaccompanied by a parent or guardian.[24]

Paving the way for this intervention, the *Los Angeles Times* published an article based on an investigation by two "prominent women," Mrs. Mary Coman, president of the Pasadena Shakespeare Club, and Miss Evelyn Stoddard of the Juvenile Court Commission.[25] Observations related to audience composition and modes of spectatorship provided the rationale for the field trip. A plot synopsis for a film called *A Marriage in Hell* (*Le Fils du diable à Paris*, Pathé, 1906), playing in one of the "cheap moving-picture vaudevilles," offers the point of departure. This investigational foray precedes the discovery of nickel shows, apart from Harry C. Carr's prediction in May, which is couched in bacteriological lingo. The ladies visited a vaudeville house, in all likelihood the Hotchkiss (formerly the Casino), which explains their findings concerning audience composition and observations on dress code. Unaccompanied by parents and guardians, "a number of respectably dressed children, in the plastic stages of development, have been viewing this film. Young eyes have stretched and young cheeks grown hot with excitement at the first appearance of hell with its lurid lights"—the copy seems to have been tinted red. Satan's son falls in love with a country girl who later commits suicide on his account. "Gee, said a small boy who was seeing the show, you just watch for the next, it's a peach. The next is the region of Satan where the girl has gone." The "two prominent women" are said to "make a round of the cheap amusements of Los Angeles to see what harm was coming to the children watching them. These two good women, accustomed to investigating depravity for the sake of correcting the conditions that bring it about, felt that a week's purification would not serve to remove the unsavory taste left by that series of visits." The regime of metaspectatorship is clearly defined in the text: The women were out "to see [. . .] children watching." The next section of the article focuses on the spectators in alignment with the women's instrumental gazing. The ladies asked for seats "in the highest gallery."

'Why, that is Nigger Heaven, ladies, you don't want to go up there,' said the ticket man. 'Yes, that is just where we are going,' said Miss Stoddart,' [sic] and that is where they went. On the way up they passed a poolroom, and a bar where drinks were sold. When they entered this 'Nigger Heaven,' an approximate count of the men and boys showed that there were 700 there, of whom one-third were boys under the age of thirteen, many of them in white blouses and ties. Needless to say, these boys were deeply interested in the blood-thirsty performance that was going on. Scarcely a man over twenty-three years of age could be seen by the two investigators.

Descending to the second gallery, the ladies' girl count amounted to

about 400 of them, nearly all in groups of three and four, and unattended by any grown person, but in most cases, in the company of boys a little older than themselves, laughing and behaving in a most objectionable way.

And they were boys and girls of fairly good appearance. [---] Much better dressed and looking far more prosperous than I had thought possible for people who frequented, or allow their children to frequent such places.

The two field workers observed a more vocal response from the girls than from the boys. The text reinforces the impression that moving pictures primarily belonged to children and adolescents in the early nickel phase, a hypothesis that animated the investigation and was confirmed by the visit, albeit not to a nickel show proper. Charles M. Bockover and William H. Clune had opened Los Angeles' first nickelodeon at 255 South Main in the summer of 1906, and their second storefront show was soon to begin operations at 349 North Main.[26] The inquiry is outlined as an exploration of an unknown province. The investigators even ventured into galleries demarcated by a racial slur, but populated by a crowd of seemingly all-white youngsters. One should doubtless be cautious when making inferences from individual reports, but the bulk of such texts from both the U.S. and several European countries underpin the conclusion that the audience was predominantly very young. Regarding class: The ties and dress code commented upon by the ladies several times might be a good indicator for the fault line between vaudeville houses and nickelodeons. The Hotchkiss billed pictures together with vaudeville acts. The context was a vaudeville-like picture theater and much bigger than the storefront places. The piece was published on December 6, 1906, and after the May 1907 petition initiated by the groups the investigators represented, City Council was convinced that regulations were required imminently. Afterward, the reports in the press focused on the emerging storefront shows, and one of them became a synecdoche for the nickel culture, the aptly named Nickel Theater at 349 North Main Street.

A couple of weeks after the vaudeville account, Chief of Police Edward Kern seconded the reformers' concerns. In a signed statement Kern claimed, "I do not propose to allow the moving picture theaters to conduct schools of crime. That is what picture films showing robberies, theft, and diamond nipping amount to. On account of the low price of admission, these shows are attended by young boys of an impressionable age. Some sort of city ordinance must be found to stop these exhibitions of crime."[27] Later, we will take a closer look at the ubiquitous school-of-crime discourse, which in interesting ways rubbed shoulders with a more benevolent appreciation of the film medium's educational clout highlighted in industry responses to criticism from reformers.

Two articles accompanying the chief's statement in the *Los Angeles Times* reinforced the analysis. The first offered a mix of metaspectatorial impressions and plot synopses, indicative of both flaneur reports and crusade interventions. The Nickel Theater on North Main, recently opened by Bockover and Clune, was the focus of virtually all pieces on the early nickel shows; the building permit for the new front was issued on November 1st. Given the location close to the ethnic hubs around the Plaza, the place was said to be "crowded every night with the lowest class of cholos and white boys and intermingled with Japs and a few Chinese," which is a radically different patron profile than the one ventured by the two women visiting a vaudeville venue closer to the business center. At the Nickel Theater the audience is virtually outside the precincts of language, "no words could describe some of the repulsive,

brutish 'low brows' who bubble with applause to see pictures of policemen being slugged and killed, diamonds stolen, automobiles held up and
robbed, and houses entered by ladder thieves." By way of sampling, two
lengthy plot synopses are offered, and the report concludes:

> There are scores more. Nearly all the recent films relate to crime. There are
> many pictures of safe-cracking. There are even train robberies. The most
> famous picture ever taken was a big train robbery.
>
> Most of them were taken in Philadelphia. A moving picture company
> [Lubin] of that city maintains a big company of actors with horses, au-
> tomobiles, special scenery and costumes. The films are leased to theaters
> throughout the country.[28]

In a signed piece on the same page Fred R. Bechdolt, perhaps best
known for his 1908 book on juvenile delinquency, *9009*, further elaborates the chief's conception of theaters as schools of crime. Perhaps pioneering the catchphrase "school of crime" in relation to film exhibition,
Bechdolt writes:

> As a school of crime the penny arcades and 5-cent theater educates two
> classes of pupils. These are boys and ignorant men. Its curriculum includes
> highway robbery, thuggery and murder. Its graduates, if given freedom in
> exercising their acquired talents, swell the ranks of a peculiar class of reckless
> crooks very similar to yeggmen. Notable among these crooks are such men
> as the Chicago car-barn bandits and the San Francisco gas-pipe thugs.[29]

Here, dime novels and the yellow press, in cahoots with penny arcades
and nickelodeons, are perceived to "breed in these young hoodlums a
desire for fame and a spirit of adventure. The films are especially conducive due the vividness of the moving images, and the criminal deeds have
a heroic slant." The article is illustrated with mug shots of two named
young boys to drive home the point; both "admit being driven to crime
by dime novels and picture machines," which prefigures hosts of con-
fessions to crimes allegedly inspired by films. Simultaneously, the penny arcades were again in focus. Amidst a reform wave targeting the unchecked sale of liquor and banning boxing bouts, eliminating children's
access to "moral plague spots," that is the penny arcade, was also on the
agenda. The city attorney, together with Judge Wilbur of the Juvenile

Court, were said to be busy drafting an ordinance.[30] According to a separate news item, policemen were visiting the penny arcades and picture houses on the lookout for indecent material, but managers had apparently removed the objectionable images. While the criticism leveled at the arcades predominantly focused on sexually suggestive representations, the nickel shows in the early days were berated solely for showing crime films. This changed in the spring of 1907 when the discourse was split into a double focus.

The concentrated campaign in the *Los Angeles Times* paid off when the newspaper alert was followed by a direct intervention to the City Council. The petition from civic organizations resulted in a hearing, and council members listened to statements from Evelyn Stoddard, representing the Los Angeles District of the Federation of Women's Clubs, Judge Curtis D. Wilbur of the Juvenile Court, and Professor E.J. Lickley, special school supervisor. In the spring of 1907 nickel houses and penny arcades rather than vaudeville theaters took center stage in the eyes of the reformers; the arcades had long been monitored and railed against in the columns of the *Times*. Professor Lickley had recently conducted an investigation, which he presented to the council members. The *Express* had reported on his findings a few weeks earlier. Lickley focused on the streets and the lax enforcement of the curfew ordinance, which was however difficult to uphold in downtown due to the lack of backyards and playgrounds. The brunt of his criticism was leveled at the "five-cent picture theaters," and many of the films presented were

> nothing but reproductions of murder stories found in 'Nick Carter' and 'Diamond Dick' literature. Frequently the culprit is made to triumph over justice, which is a poor moral lesson for the youthful mind. In some of the theaters, which have been under the surveillance of the investigators for some time, pictures have been found containing almost depraved suggestions. Cheap ballet pictures, life-like reproduction of dances, etc., which should be prohibited, are frequent features of the 'entertainment' provided for the youthful mind. Murder has been mixed with depravity.[31]

After the council hearing, City Attorney Hewitt was instructed to prepare a penal ordinance regarding minors in amusement places, which was approved by City Council in late May 1907.[32] Under the ordinance it was unlawful "for any person, either as a proprietor, manager, keeper, agent, employe [sic] or otherwise, to admit any minor, under the age of fourteen years."[33] The swift adoption of the ordinance coincided with the much longer crusade in the *Chicago Tribune*, which eventually led to local police censorship.

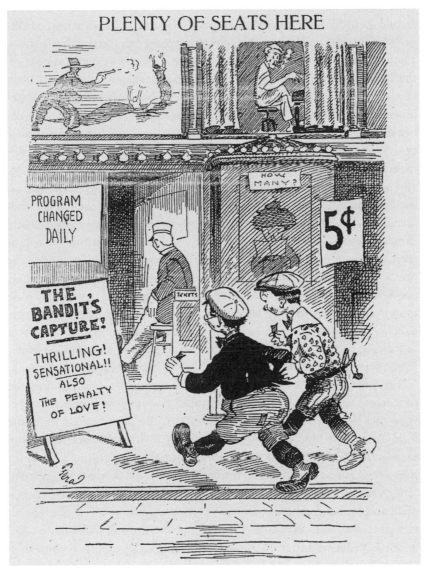

FIGURE 21: Young film enthusiasts. Cartoon from *Los Angeles Examiner*, 17 September 1909, ed. page.

In contrast to New York's Penal Code relating to amusements, the Los Angeles ordinance was strictly enforced, not least by way of civic interventions alerting the police. In fact, the first two perpetrators were managers of theaters that did not show films, the Burbank Theater, a legitimate theater, and the Grand Opera House, which offered musical comedy and melodrama. The houses' respective managers were arrested: Oliver Morosco of the Burbank for allowing young boys to watch the show, Thomas G. Baker of the Grand for having a twelve year old appear on the stage; the latter offense was not unique—managers had earlier been taken to court under the child-labor laws.[34] The *Los Angeles Express* later reported that warrants had been issued for the arrest of a Mrs. M. Norton and a Mrs. O. Andros, owners of a short-lived moving picture house at 618 San Fernando Street in Sonoratown, primarily a Mexican tenement area close to the Plaza. The two ladies had just opened their house and paid for their first license in September.[35] Another warrant was issued for the arrest of Charles M. Bockover, co-owner of the Nickel Theater at 349 North Main Street, the popular venue close to the Plaza and earlier targeted in the *Los Angeles Times*. At both establishments volunteers from the Associated Charities had discovered children under the prescribed age of fourteen: nineteen youngsters at the house on San Fernando Street, five on North Main. Vigilant progressives apparently took it upon themselves to assist the police in upholding the legal framework. And on January 2, 1909, *Show World* could report that "two proprietors of moving picture theaters in this city were arrested and pleaded guilty to allowing children under 14 years of age to enter their theatoriums."

The *Los Angeles Express* for several years argued for expanding the framework of control by giving the police commission authority to revoke nickelodeon licenses, and in addition, the paper called for some form of censorship. Throughout, it was the schools-of-crime analysis that lurked behind the recurrent proposals, underpinned by blunt characterizations of audiences, implicitly perceived as hyper-suggestive: "[m]oving picture theaters that feature films calculated to instruct children, and Japs and cholos in ingenious forms of crime."[36] The *Express* returned to this issue, claiming, by way of plot synopses, that such studies in crime "educate lower classes to whom such scenes largely appeal."[37] Otherwise, the big issue in the autumn of 1907 was the proposal by a coalition of civic and clerical groups to get City Council to adopt Sunday closure for amusements. The *Express*, the prime voice for charter reform and progressive reforms in all respects of city life, had taken on a leading role in the blue-law movement and in the aftermath lost the theaters' advertisements. The boycott that continued well after the proposal had been buried by City Council.

Parallel to the constant repositioning on the theatrical market, Los Angeles' nickelodeon culture took off from the epicenter of the Eighth Ward and later found its way into the residential areas in the form of neighborhood theaters. When the storefronts had played out their role as key venues for moving pictures, forerunners of the movie palaces were built in the midst of the new business center. This shift was prefigured in October 1907 when local newspapers reported that the new building for Hamburger's Department Store at Eighth Street and Broadway would include a major theater, the Majestic under Oliver Morosco's management, as well as a smaller theater for the department store's patrons and, especially, their children. The Arrow Theater was planned to be an "advanced form of the moving picture entertainment" featuring fairy tales, topicals, and travelogues, and a "wee orchestra, or perhaps an enlarged phonographic device" will provide incidental entertainment.[38] This double relocalization was indicative of changes in audience composition, where the ethnic others and children were no longer dominating the patronage, unless exclusively catered to.

In Los Angeles calls for censorship, in addition to the 1907 ordinance barring unaccompanied children from places of amusement, were championed by the Police Department and supported in the columns of the *Express*. In the fall of 1908 leading police officials asked the mayor to sponsor a proposal for an ordinance making it possible to remove film scenes depicting crimes and immorality. Furthermore, the *Los Angeles Express* wanted the Police Department to exercise jurisdiction over theatrical licenses so that violation of an ordinance could lead to the license being revoked, a proposal that the *Express* first introduced in its columns in 1907. On February 24, 1909, the *Herald* reported that the moving-picture interests apparently had managed to convince City Council that no new ordinance for film exhibition was required. City Council had referred a proposal from the mayor to a committee on legislation, which, according to the *Herald*, meant a "quiet burial."[39] The *Times'* succinct headline "In the Pit?" supported the *Herald*'s reading by explaining that "the Legislative Committee is frequently a bottomless pit into which undesirable ordinances are dropped."[40]

The politics around this attempt to implement film censorship and its burial are highly instructive and part of a bigger picture. Chief Kern himself initiated the move by urging Mayor Harper to ask City Council for a censorship ordinance. In an article in the *Los Angeles Express* Kern reported that the police had recently arrested a dozen young boys who had stolen bicycles and sold them to junk dealers to get money for tickets to film shows, which he reiterated were schools of crime.[41] When the draft for an ordinance was referred to the Committee of Legislation two months later, the disappointed *Express* advised the committee's members to take a look at what was being shown at a theater in "the shadow of the City Hall [the house at 349 North Main in the Baker block]," explaining that three out of six films dealt with murder, one containing "a particularly revolting scene in which a jealous lover strangles a woman to death in a brutal and hideously realistic manner. Almost every moving picture show in the city has at least one picture showing the killing of a human being or the commission of some lesser crime."[42]

The *Express* and the police brass were otherwise strange bedfellows, but had joined forces around the schools-of-crime discourse. The campaign emerged after a previous proposal for censorship concerning "schools of vice" had been dismissed by the city attorney as unconstitutional.[43] Yet another crusade in the *Express* focused on the billboards, both the sheer number of them blanketing the city and the nature of their representations, a cause championed by the Billboard Committee of the Civic Association. In February 1908 the *Express*, relying on police sources, elaborated on the crime curriculum offered by the nickel shows as a series of instructive lessons. For just a nickel, pupils were offered something tantamount to a crash course in criminality during the half hour the show lasts.

'How to Commit Murder' is alleged by some to be the course now being taught under the title, 'For Hate of the Miller,' in one theater. Incidentally, conspiracy and domestic infidelity are offered as branch courses in this curriculum. The technique of splitting open a man's head with a hatchet and throwing his body down a well is outlined. The advantages of throwing a living man into a flour mill and grinding up his body are set forth as another ingenious manner of making away with him. Two thoroughly modern methods of committing burglary are explained in detailed pictures at another theater. Practical direction for the handling of a jimmy are included as well as directions for outwitting the police after being cap-tured in the act.[44]

An editorial in the *Los Angeles Herald*, "Suggestive Pictures," provided a similar type of account when talking about pupils and proprietors of the "academy of crime." Moving pictures were considered more danger-ous to society than "even the billboard atrocities" by depicting "high-way robbery, burglary, murder, arson and all kinds of crimes of violence in which the spectators can follow the actions of the criminals." Still, the editorial observes, the medium is unequaled as an educator when showing travel films, "actual scenes," pictures of historical occurrences, and harmless comedies.[45] The *Times* offered its editorial account a cou-ple of months later, entitled "Schools for Crime." After a discussion of stage offerings, the focus shifts to moving pictures, which "attract a large number of children." After having previously depicted "real events," films now feature "made-up scenes," readers were informed. The magni-tude of the industry is illustrated by the example of France, and after in passing mentioning pictures that make heroes of villains, implying the risk of impressionable youngsters emulating the example, the attention turned to a couple of French films featuring brutality towards animals. No specific claim for censorship was however put forward.[46]

In a subsequent editorial in the *Express*, commenting on the highly publicized murder of Police Captain Walter H. Auble, a veteran on the force, the *Express* posited a causal connection, not without some caveats however, between representations on billboards, stage, and screen, and criminal activities: "We venture the assertion that some luckless day or fateful night, some faithful officer shall go down to death as Auble did, before the pistol of criminal, and were it possible to trace the chain of events in all their lengthened sequence, precisely such billboard glori-fications of crime as those that now offend the public sight would be found to constitute a link."[47] Auble's killer, a white man in his late 20s, committed suicide, leaving behind an autobiographical sketch painting a decidedly grim life story, albeit without describing any links between his criminal escapades and fictional representations.

When the city prosecutor, Thomas Woolwine, stepped forward to ac-cuse the mayor and the police commissioners of protecting vice, the *Ex-press* and its progressive publisher and owner, Edwin T. Earl, immediate-ly sided with him, which lead to the most polarized situation in the city's

FIGURE 22: Cartoon from *Los Angeles Express*, 26 February 1908, 10.

political history. When the *Express* expanded on Woolwine's accusation, the mayor sued its publisher, a case he eventually dropped when resigning. In the midst of this political crisis the Police Department decided to display resourcefulness in dealing with vice by raiding the red-light houses and, additionally, expanding its vigilance to moving pictures, one of the *Express*' pet concerns. Predictably, both measures won the paper's support. Thus, the censorship initiative put forward by the police authorities in the fall of 1908 and later endorsed by the mayor formed part of an explosive political situation in Los Angeles, which added to longstanding conflicts between the *Times*' publisher and the unions. Police officials and the mayor retaliated against Woolwine, which started a protracted political process that eventually turned into a formal recall, in the face of which the mayor elected to step down, thereby paving the way for progressive leadership in the city and charter reform.

In the conflict's initial stage the Police Department demonstrated its resolve to clean up the tenderloin. A raid in early October 1908 led to the arrest of twenty-two women working in houses on Commercial, San Pedro, and Alameda Streets. A debate followed on whether the authorities had promised some of the notorious landlords protection from legal interference, foremost Tom Savage, who paid bail for several of the arrested women. The initiative from the chief bearing on the "schools of crime" can be seen in the same light as the crackdown on the red-light business, an exhibition of purposeful resoluteness in order to fend off allegations from political reformers and critical forces inside the administration. Recent killings of police officers—Auble was the third victim in the previous two years—played into the fracas when attributed to criminal gangs allegedly inspired by representations of crime. According to police sources, such representations had instigated the murders, and particularly the "posters of melodramatic scenes are said by police officials to have furnished the suggestions for more crimes in Los Angeles than the dime novels. [. . .] The boy doesn't see the hero triumph. He sees only the desperado."[48] The connection was made explicit in the *Express*, and the line of reasoning played into the paper's longstanding campaign against billboards. A month later the editorial in the *Times*, entitled "Schools for Crime," echoed the *Express*' concern over the many children attracted to the nickelodeons, and especially the "large amount of evil that may easily be done if the pictures displayed make heroes of villains."[49] Captain Flammer—chief of detectives and long-time friend of Auble, and at the scene when the

FIGURE 23: Political entertainment. Cartoon from
Los Angeles Examiner, 15 October 1908, 1.

214

latter was gunned down at the intersection of Grand Avenue and Ninth Street—entered the discussion a week later. He was particularly worried by films about Jesse James shown at two houses on Main Street, saying: "Main Street is a bad thoroughfare for such pictures. The young fellows who loaf at that street are inclined to be a little wild and the pictures suggest methods of perpetrating crime which they would never think of." Given this, a censorship ordinance was called for, he maintained. Two months later the chief urged the mayor to ask City Council for an ordinance, which he did early in 1909, though after considerable maneuvering, and the proposal ended up in the bottomless pit.

FIGURE 24: When the proposal for film censorship was presented, the *Times* illustrated its playful account with a cartoon. *Los Angeles Times*, 27 January 1909, II:2.

The *Express* ventured yet another editorial piece late in 1909, again elaborating on the school metaphoric, this time around having no qualms concerning the cause-and-effect patterns "directly" linking crime melodramas on stage and screen to crime.

> Many a theft, many an embezzlement, many a hold-up, many a murder is directly attributable to the lessons inculcated by displays wherein crime is invested with attraction and the criminal's head surrounded with a halo. In play and picture his meanness is represented as skill, his resistance to the officers of the law as courage and all his actions as admirable.
>
> Policemen of Los Angeles walk their beats today who shall yet be placed in coffins and carried to their graves, victims of the bullet or the knife of some murderer educated to the work in the crime academies that eulogizes the criminal.[50]

The sweeping indictment targeted primarily crime melodramas on the stage, a genre that had lost something of its screen momentum in the interstice between the French Grand Guignol and the onset of the crime serials. The impact of the pressure put on manufacturers by the voluntary inspection of films in New York City was not yet obvious to editorial crusaders at a time when the paper was still pursuing its billboard campaign. For many, billboards and posters were worse in their concentrated display than the actual offerings on stage and screen. In the midst of a crime wave, which officials blamed on the crime pictures, the editorial in the *Express* ran in tandem with police initiatives. For a time, police officers were stationed outside moving picture shows, and one manager, J.A. Brown at the Cineograph, was arrested for selling tickets to children under 14, still unlawful under the ordinance. The *Examiner*'s source assured that "by and by we shall have an ordinance prohibiting crime pictures."[51]

In 1910, when a bevy of new, elegant theaters was built and planned, such as Pantages, Clune's Broadway, and College, the *Express* refrained from commenting on film culture until November, when it proclaimed the "picture theater standard raised," again relying primarily on police sources.[52] This assessment marks the end of the editorial vigilance concerning film theaters as schools of crimes in spite of the paradoxical fact that local film censorship was not instituted until August 1911. It was, however, no longer possible to police film culture uniformly in the era of movie palaces located in the business district and catering to an audience no longer dominated by children and ethnic others. The industry supported national inspection, and leading local exhibitors were eager to win community support for their business. The appointment of a police-woman, Alice Stebbins Wells, marked a novel approach and an emphasis on prevention focused on young girls.

The playground movement, which has been used here as part of the sober side of amusement offerings, in contrast to the brightly lit commercial attractions described by Simon N. Patten, accepted film culture as a given when discovering its unprecedented inroads in the early days. The momentum of the nickel culture was unstoppable, the only plausible strategy was to check its negative aspect and reform the medium by developing its educative potentials and weeding out its blatant transgressions. The editorial appreciation in the *Express* confirms the success of this strategy, even if dissenting voices continued to be heard for years to come.

William A. McKeever, professor of Philosophy at Kansas State Agricultural College, formulated one of the harshest broadsides against film culture in terms of schools of crime; his piece in *Good Housekeeping Magazine* singled out the moving picture as "a primary school for criminals" which undid the work of schools proper due to its suggestive curriculum teaching criminality and depravity. The shows seemingly operated under the motto "A red-light district in easy reach of every home. See the murderers and the debauchery while you wait. It is only a nickel." In McKeever's opinion the medium was not inherently bad, on the contrary, but it was conducted as a business without concerns other than the maximization of profit. The professor did however recommend measures for rectifying the alleged sorry state of film culture and gradually turn it into an "instructive and moralizing agency." If such a transformation were profitable, exhibitors would reform their bills, he claimed. What can bring about such a change, then? Writing "strong" articles in the local press, supporting clean managements, securing a censorship ordinance, finding in the juvenile courts connections between criminality and depictions of criminal acts in the picture shows, gathering data for reform by mapping the bills offered by exhibitors. In combination this will lend specificity to the campaigns for "purification of the moving picture business." The rationale for such efforts was the conviction that moving pictures could potentially be made into one of the most "powerful agencies for the moral and spiritual uplift of any community."[53]

In June 1911 Reverend Herbert A. Jump laid the schools-of-crime discourse to rest in *Playground*. His essay was initially delivered as an address
to the People's Institute in March. Jump, minister of the South Congregational Church in New Britain, Connecticut, had in December 1910 published a pamphlet titled "The Religious Possibilities of the Motion Picture," not least emphasizing that many films provide ideal points of departure for sermons. His overall perception was that the movies popu-
larized drama and brought to the people "that which hitherto had been
a monopoly for the well-to-do," thus, our "age is the age of 'canned drama,' " providing endless opportunities for an extended democracy. If the
"full purport of this new movement" were completely grasped, the picture
should have new signs over their entrances, reading " 'The Nickel College,' or 'The Dime Civilizer,' or 'The Moving Picture University.' "[54]

Students eager to learn a trade, profession or skill cleverly seek out
the best available information. In a surprising spin on the "schools for
crime" rhetoric the *Chicago Chronicle* ventured an in-depth piece on the
criminal courts. Here, Judge Kersten of the Superior Court told the reporter, "boys get pointers from trials for vicious careers." The judge had
therefore cleared the courtroom of persons under 18 years of age for the
trial of police killer Charles Hansen. Judge Kersten's bailiff, previously
employed in the county jail, provided additional details concerning the
fascination concerning crime narratives, which prefigures television's
obsession with gory court cases. The bailiff's account neatly sums up the
underlying assumptions of the school discourse and the teaching process
from which students/apprentices putatively graduate into a professional
mastery of the "art":

> The boys sit and drink in the testimony of a murder trial with the greatest
> eagerness. They dwell on the exciting details and they go out and discuss
> the cases among themselves. Murder and burglary are trades the same as
> anything else. Novices in the business learn how to become profession-
> als in the courtrooms. They listen and learn how this man and that man
> committed murder, and they go out and try a holdup trick themselves.
> Familiarity with the details of murder and robbery suggests to these boys
> the possibility of trying the same desperate methods.[55]

This lengthy piece was published toward the end of the crusade against
nickel culture in Chicago, without however making any references to

the suggestiveness of crime depictions on nickelodeon screens. The article does not mention the boys having any kind of ethnic or foreign background, and the figures in the accompanying cartoon sport decidedly Anglo-Saxon features. In 1912 Edison waxed eloquently on a professed long-term commitment by his company to produce educational films, which would provide schools with welcome adjuncts to instruction by books. His plans for spending $3,000,000 over eight years attracted much attention and garnered praise in the press and the trade organs. An editorial in the *New York World* made a playful inference which takes the discourse we been charting full circle: "School as moving picture shows?" The question mark registered grave doubts concerning this short-cut scheme to learning and the appropriateness of turning schools into "amusement resorts for boys too lazy to study."[56]

From Censor Board to Film Commissioner

In March 1911 civic organizations in Los Angeles, silent for more than a year, petitioned City Council to appoint a censorship committee under a proposed new ordinance with a relevant provision, which it eventually adopted. Among the petitioners were some familiar names: Ernest J. Lickley and Evelyn Stoddard. A prelude to the intervention was published in an editorial in the *Herald* headlined "Censorship Needed," claiming that, "[n]o one who has investigated the matter will venture to say it is not an evil." The only remedy possible for saving plastic young minds from the devastating influence of this alleged evil is censorship in the hands of a "committee of sensible women, preferably mothers"; the latter point latches onto a well-established discourse.[57]

The exhibitors, organized within the Southern California Motion Picture Men's Association, were not totally averse to local censorship in addition to the national inspection, but successfully remonstrated against a key element of the proposed ordinance, the transferal of licensing responsibility from the Board of Public Works to the Police Commission and giving the latter authority to revoke licenses in cases of ordinance violation. A censorship ordinance came into effect in August 1911 in an amicable atmosphere, but the licensing process was not transferred to the Police Commission. A board of five, later expanded to seven, was to be nominated by civic activists and trade interests—the five members were to be appointed by the mayor, the Police Commission, the Board Of Education, the Los Angeles Civic Association, and the Southern California Motion Picture Men's Association. This proved to be a complicated matter: It took more than six months until the formal overtures were over with and operations could commence. Finding a venue for inspection also proved to be a problem, which remained unresolved until the Board got a theater of its own on Franklin Street in November 1913.[58] Board members came and went, and with a new mayor who was bent on trimming the administration in office, the Board of Film Censors came under fire. Mayor Henry Rose tried to dismantle the board by stalling appointments, which further crippled the operations.[59] Even after this conflict was resolved, the committee continued to face problems and disrespect and overall had little impact on local film culture. The few times the Board tried to put down its collective foot, the courts overruled its decisions. A new ordinance was proposed in 1914 by one of the Board's members, creating a major controversy. The draft proposed replacing the old Board with a new one. Nobody affiliated with the industry would be allowed to serve as board member, and all theaters and exchanges had to secure a revocable permit from the new Board, which was to have wide-ranging jurisdiction concerning the regulation of exhibition. The only specified requirement in the ordinance regulated lighting in the theaters.[60] Furthermore, dissatisfied civic activists leveled complaints concerning the ineffectiveness of the local censorship. The chair of the Board, Mrs. E.K. Foster, sought to counteract this perception by issuing a list of what reformers should not expect, formulated as a set of don'ts: don't expect only high-brow films, or demand perfection, or that holy days are now holidays, don't forget that films are the workingman's sole amusement outlet—and cooperate with the Board in its mission to uplift artistic standards.[61] Mrs. Foster returned to this topic when addressing a club in Pasadena, again emphasizing "a practical view" besides urging clubwomen "not to expect more of a motion picture play than [...] of a book, a lecture, or a real play," and overall appraising the value of the medium as "enormous." In this respect it was important "not to nullify the good by making the shows so deadly educational that the people will not attend them." As part of the effort she urged clubwomen to help develop the community's taste by patronizing the film shows.[62] This call was already heeded by the P.T.A. Federation, which, as mentioned, had appointed a censorship committee of its own aiming at getting all film theaters on a "white list," which amounted to a clean bill of health.

Meanwhile, the proposal for a new ordinance stirred considerable controversy and did not manage to receive City Council's approval until the spring of 1915, so things remained the same for one more year. In an ironic report on the Board the *Times* revealed that some members never attended meetings, and that the secretary had hired a clerk to perform her duties. Even worse, exhibitors seemed to have submitted film copies after rather than before screening them and had little respect for the Board, which was characterized as a dainty tea party holding viewing sessions primarily for the benefit of the Board members' friends.[63] In addition, the Budget Committee demanded a new ordinance to clarify the Board's responsibilities before approving further appropriations, which exerted pressure on City Council to take action. From the point of view of the trade, the Board served no purpose, given the inspection conducted by the National Board. The new ordinance gave the Board considerably more clout and backed it up by the possibility of using police force if necessary. In fact, one theater was shut down for showing a film banned by the board, *The Nigger* (Fox, 1915). Still, the Board's authority was not absolute; the mayor overruled its position regarding *The Clansman*, for example. The beginning of the end for the new Board was the controversy over *Damaged Goods* (American, 1915) in November 1915.[64] The question of the appropriateness of depicting issues of venereal disease on screen shattered an already infighting Board. The minority in favor of allowing the film to be screened resigned in protest while the court promptly reversed the majority's decision. The subsequent dismantling of the Board was a process over several innings, which ended when a film commissioner replaced the Board by authority of an ordinance passed on March 29, 1916. While the commissioner was primarily perceived as a facilitator for the industry and was not to inspect films, s/he still had the authority to prohibit the exhibition of films, even if approved by the National Board, that overstepped the decency clause or represented criminal activities too graphically. The film industry in Hollywood by then had global reach. For a business-friendly city it made more sense to facilitate Hollywood's operations than regulate local exhibition on top of the work performed by the National Board.

The potential for more than just mere entertainment by way of policing underpinned the crusades against the nickel culture, which was fueled by misgivings voiced by clerics, educators, and civic organizations before turning into editorial matters in the columns. The responses from local exhibitors as well as the licensed companies created multi-tiered exhibition practices reflecting class divisions, ethnic fault lines, and the diverse cultural geographies of city life. When the manufacturers realized that self-imposed regulations best served the industry's interest, novel exhibition practices literally turned into the clearinghouse for societal support of film culture.

CHAPTER 6

UPLIFTING INITIATIVES: COUPONS, DAYLIGHT SCREENS, AND POLICEWOMEN

"Great newspapers will be run in connection with auditoriums where great events will be seen in their actual occurrences."[1]

THREE INITIATIVES FROM phase IV in my crude typology of press/ cinema interaction are indicative of a period of negotiations and reform enterprises. Issuing coupons for film shows can be seen as shrewd business tactics on the part of a press engineered to sell newspaper copies and in the process perhaps pick up advertising clients also. Irrespective of such murky strategies, the press' attention bestowed legitimizing recognition on local film culture. The push for daylight screenings was an effort from within the industry to preempt a recurrent complaint from the medium's critics—that the dark exhibition halls offered a haven for untoward activities. Eliminating the darkness by way of new types of screens turned into an important concern for trade papers affiliated with the trust. Appointing policewomen to monitor the amusements habits of young women and safe management of the relevant venues was an initiative pioneered in Los Angeles. The system attracted considerable interest and was emulated by many cities after the first woman appointed for this purpose became a national spokesperson for the model. Together, the three case studies highlight film culture's internal and external alliances during a time of repositioning in response to the regulatory campaigns.

Coupons

Late in 1908 the *Los Angeles Herald* sponsored a motion-picture campaign under the management of Robert A. Brackett. Brackett had worked for Lyman H. Howe before embarking on a road show in his own name in 1906. Charles Musser and Carol Nelson found Brackett's show in Wichita in the spring of 1907, then lost track of him.[2] Late in 1908 Brackett started a longer Los Angeles engagement, initially playing at two venues—423 South Spring Street and 246 South Broadway. He later downsized to South Spring Street only, previously the venue for Gaumont's chronophone films under E.A. Fischer's management. Brackett's show was marketed as a reform undertaking by the *Herald*, which offered free coupons to its readers. Brackett presented an hour-and-a-half program with instructional lectures; the show played twice in the afternoon and twice in the evening, with illustrated songs rounding off the bill.[3]

The *Herald* launched the coupon initiative on November 7th with much fanfare. According to the promotional text, Burton Holmes, "the world's greatest exponent of educational moving pictures and stereopticon enterprises," endorsed Brackett's show. The opening program included *The Wright Aeroplane in Action in France*, *Water Play at Versailles*, *Steeplechaising at Burlingham* [sic]. Block letters informed readers that sensational and melodramatic pictures would be barred, and parents were assured that nothing objectionable would be screened. The coupon printed in the paper admitted one person free of charge. The following day's newspaper offered a new coupon and reported on the success of the initiative, that "scores of people seized the opportunity to see both shows." Underscoring the educational aspect of the show, the ad informed that "the Herald is a home paper and these are HOME ENTERTAINMENTS. Take the children." On November 9th the *Herald* reported that the free tickets proved a "delight to children" and that hundreds of fortunate persons had taken advantage of "[t]he Herald's generosity." The bill for the following week included: *Thou Shalt Not Love*, beautifully hand colored; *Elixir of Strength*, comedy; *Young Lady's Telephone Message*, comedy; *Concealing a Burglar*, dramatic; *Bear Pits of Berne*, educational.[4] Additionally, J.P. Wilde delivered "his famous stereopticon monologue entitled 'People We Meet.'" Three more films followed, and the program closed with illustrated songs performed by Marion Thompkins, billed as a "prima donna."

The following week, the show on Broadway was cancelled, while the program at the Spring Street venue offered moving pictures only, five titles. In early December the *Herald* reported that there were twenty-four moving-picture entertainments in Los Angeles, but the Brackett theater still drew afternoon crowds steadily. The show was described as ideal for women and children, since all "cheap sensationalism has been carefully eliminated." The following week, the *Herald* noted that the coupon system had been adopted by a number of California newspapers. The free coupons discreetly stopped in February, however, even if an ad published on February 1st informed that the management had "decided to continue its Los Angeles engagement indefinitely." Why, then, was the initiative terminated? In a sense it was not because William H. Clune opened a regular high-class theater under Brackett's management a couple of months later, creating a long-standing venue emulating Brackett's exhibition concept. Clune was himself by then a veteran, but had hitherto remained in the background.

In the light of the debate targeting moving pictures accompanying a larger offensive by the Police Department, the *Los Angeles Herald*'s initiative for uplift featuring the Brackett show makes sense. Clean, safe, and de-sensationalized moving pictures, offered for the two cents the paper cost, provided a way to attract audiences with prices even lower than what the nickel houses charged. High-class pictures were framed from an educational perspective, thus enabling the screen to become a force for good and thereby dodge the accusations of sensationalism. At this time both the *Los Angeles Times* and the *Express*, which differed in terms of political persuasion, supported proposals to transfer the jurisdiction for licensing film shows to the police, while the *Herald* refrained from taking advantage of its own exhibition initiative during the campaign and maintained a low profile.

In the midst of the political commotion characterizing this period William Randolph Hearst's newspaper, the *Los Angeles Examiner*, embarked on a much bolder course of action than the *Herald*. The *Examiner* gave away coupons to fourteen regular nickelodeons, primarily located on busy commercial streets—Broadway, South Main Street, and South Spring Street, and one each on East Fifth Street (very close to South Main) and West Seventh, a block south of today's Pershing Square. Later, a few more theaters were included—including two in Long Beach, both on the Pike. The theaters on South Main Street, previously singled out by the chief of detectives, were part of the *Examiner*'s giveaway. The coupons were not offered daily as those offered by the *Herald*, but weekly and were published in the Sunday paper. As for the *Herald* coupons, these applied to afternoon shows only.

The *Examiner*'s coupon scheme was introduced on November 22nd, a couple of weeks after the *Herald* started promoting the Brackett Show with free coupons. For both papers, the initiatives were calculated to boost circulation. For the nickelodeons, the *Examiner*'s scheme offered a welcome endorsement and a stepping stone on the way to respectability. In the face of fierce accusations from the *Express* this initiative provided a valuable counter-discourse from the exhibitors' perspective. The promotional advertisement in the *Examiner* painted the local exhibition situation in a flattering light; in fact, it even tried to cash in on the high-class designation. The *Examiner*'s venture was an intrepid one, launched at a time when leading police officials singled out some of these nickelodeons as "schools for crime." Not so according to the *Examiner*:

> No other city offers a wider variety of really high-class moving pictures entertainments than Los Angeles. Their proprietors have been leaders in the movement to put them on the highest possible plane, and how well they have succeeded is shown by the excellent characters of the entertainments they are presenting today. Everything that might tend in any way to offend the morals of the spectators has been removed, the halls where the pictures are shown have been more carefully ventilated and protected against fire, and no effort has been spared to make them worthy in every way of the liberal patronage they are receiving.
>
> All these entertainments have been selected with the greatest care. They are clean in every sense, and nothing will be found in any of them which could possibly injure the morals of any man, woman or child. Whatever one you choose to visit with the 'Examiner's' free ticket you will find wholesome and enjoyable.[5]

Each theater was given space for self-promotion. Predictably, most of them claimed to cater especially to women and children, and all of them allegedly offered good, clean programs. Some listed their bills, and in most places there were two to three program changes each week. The overwhelming majority were regular nickelodeons presenting only films and illustrated songs, but the roster included one small-time vaudeville house, The Regal, with a second added later, The Lyric. On November 25th, the following Wednesday, the *Examiner* reported that thousands had used the coupons during the week, and the paper encouraged readers to buy the upcoming Sunday edition and hence a new coupon. Interestingly, the bill for the Optic Theater offers more or less the same titles as the Brackett Show previously: *Elixir of Strength*, *A Young Lady's Telephone Communication*, and *Water Play at Versailles*, which blurs the boundaries between self-proclaimed high-class initiatives and the regular nickel shows.

FIGURE 25: Picture Theater (545 S. Main Street); the advertised film was released on September 24, 1910 (B'hend and Kaufmann Theater Collection, Courtesy of the Academy of Motion Picture Arts and Sciences)

227

FIGURE 26: Unidentified nickelodeon, downtown Los Angeles; the advertised picture was released on July 15, 1911 (Courtesy of Marc Wanamaker)

FIGURE 27: California Theater (238 S. Spring) in 1910, (B'hend and Kaufmann Theater Collection, Courtesy of the Academy of Motion Picture Arts and Sciences)

228

Exhibition during this period was generally in a state of flux. Many houses were undercapitalized and, consequently, vulnerable, which is illustrated by two suits filed against the manager of one of the theaters included in the *Examiner*'s coupon system, the Duchess. Construction workers had apparently not been paid in full, and a woman who had invested in the house claimed that she had been "induced by fraudulent representations to invest $1,300 in the business." Both the Duchess and the Princess were temporarily closed, but furnishings and machines were leased and thus exempt; somehow, the conflict was eventually resolved.[6]

The *Examiner*'s coupon system ended quietly in early January 1909 without explanation. The complex web of press interventions and various initiatives related to film culture in Los Angeles, at a time when the police actively sought a legal framework for controlling screen representations, underscore a shift in perspective. It is tempting to read the police push primarily as a showy demonstration of resourcefulness in the face of allegations from progressive forces within the city administration, severe allegations albeit totally unrelated to film exhibition, namely concerning graft and protection of gambling, liquor, and vice interests. The absence of civic groups during the coupon campaigns and the push for censorship as well is telling, and in the end, the business-friendly City Council sided with the exhibitors rather than the police.

The *Examiner* returned to film culture in Los Angeles in a long write-up published in March 1909, proclaiming in the headline that the pictures offered high-class entertainment. If this was a pitch for advertising the scheme worked, since several of the small film theaters advertised in the *Examiner* over the next few months. The article was flattering in the extreme to the theaters and described them as "excellently managed." Moreover, "[t]he service is polite and dignified. The audiences comprise as many women as men. The houses' attaches are painstaking and thoughtful." All in all: "[T]he price is low, bringing moral, high-class and generally uplifting amusement within the reach of all."[7] This wholesale championing of film culture presumably originated from within the trade and was probably paid for as an ad even if it looked like editorial material. The reason for this presumption is a reprint of the same text in the *Los Angeles Record* ten days later, and the *Times* published a variation, which in interesting ways shows the complex interaction between the fourth estate and the film business.

229

The dismantling of the *Examiner*'s coupon initiative coincided with the beginning of a crusade against the cheap theaters in San Francisco led by the managers of vaudeville houses and legitimate theaters: Orpheum, Van Ness, Columbia, Tivoli, Valencia, Princess, and American. The managers petitioned the Board of Supervisors, protesting the fire protection at the cheap theaters. The *San Francisco Examiner* addressed the issue in an editorial under the ominous headline "Protect Life Even in the Cheap Theater," which accused authorities of neglecting the safety of people who only can afford the nickel admission. "Scores of five-cent and ten-cent theaters have been established with no more precautions than are taken in opening or running a grocery store." Irrespective of this, the stance in Hearst's San Francisco paper mirrors the contention underlying the coupon venture in Los Angeles: "The five-cent theater is all right, but it is not privileged to risk the lives of those who attend it."[8]

Daylight Screening and Spectatorship

Edison habitually speculated on the future of electrical entertainment, and so did his legal right-hand man, Frank L. Dyer, a leading force and lightning rod within the Motion Picture Patents Company. Interviewed in August 1909, Dyer anticipated a new rung on the ladder of film culture offering long, talking films in color to be shown in "lighted rooms."[9] The latter point was no pipe dream, but already more or less on the verge of being implemented by model theaters affiliated with the Patents Company. For the licensed combine, daylight projection turned into a touchstone for the desired vanquishing of the nickel culture, most adamantly advocated by the trade organ representing trust interests, the *Film Index*. In the spring of 1909 it was reported that a device had been "invented by Frank Oliver, chief of the License Bureau, New York City, by which moving pictures can be shown without darkening the auditorium. The plan has been submitted to Mayor McClellan, and will probably be made compulsory as a condition to the issuance of licenses. It will effectually answer the criticisms of many clergymen."[10] The method, readers were told, was to use "a few shaded reflectors for the ordinary incandescent lights."[11] In Europe a similar method was tested at Paris' Cinéma Palace in February 1909; for how long this type of light arrangement was used in France and how widespread it was is unclear.[12] In England two systems for daylight screenings were reported early in 1910 as being "on the market or shortly to be introduced."[13]

In an invitation to Mayor McClellan to attend an exhibition in the wake of the picture shows' closedown for Christmas 1908, the Patents Company further elaborated on the lighting arrangement as a crucial aspect of film exhibition for insuring moral safety and uplift in combination with the inspection of films by the Board of Censorship. The shutdown of the nickel shows formed part of a campaign for stricter adherence to blue laws. Clerics were key moral arbiters concerning the nature of New York City's film exhibition prior to the mayor's clampdown—just like in Chicago—thus the reference above to "clergymen." As the mention of the clergy makes clear, the dark auditorium and the opportunities it afforded for presumed untoward activities had troubled authorities, moral guardians, and reformers since the inception of the nickelodeons. Progressive activists were particularly distressed concerning what young girls and women were exposed to in several dimensions of the word, as the dark exhibition spaces were perceived as encouraging mashing and immoral behavior.[14] The wording in the invitation clearly reflects the film manufacturers' willingness to address and resolve these "criticisms" by convincing exhibitors to invest in lighting and screen arrangements making the premises unsuitable for the solicitudes:

> The exhibition of our new lighting system marks a revolution in the motion picture business. The nature of these shows has heretofore required a dark theater, with all its attendant evils. By the use of this device, theaters now can be kept brightly lighted with only the stage in semi-darkness. Not only do we intend that all our licensees shall use this device, but we would cheerfully acquiesce if your Honor made it a condition in the granting of every motion picture license in this city, that the theaters be kept lighted during all the performances.
>
> And in this respect we would like to lay emphasis on the fact that this new lighting device is not a patent controlled by this Company, but free to all, and can be installed at very slight expense. Our object in perfecting it was to better the condition of the motion picture business and to co-operate with you in your effort to rid it of abuses that merited criticism.[15]

This model screening took place on May 15th at a regular theater, the Nicoland at 162nd and Third Avenue. Apart from outlining the plotlines of the films, the accounts elaborated on the mode of projection:

The theater instead of being dark as formerly was light enough for the reading of a newspaper. This change, the Board of censors believes, does away with one of the criticisms of the old theaters. In place of the cloth screen of which the pictures were reproduced an aluminum sheet was used which allowed pictures to be shown in a lighted room.[16]

The Patents Company continued to take an active interest in lighting arrangements and had prior to the model show circulated a sketch from their projection room in New York City.

On either side of the screen the lights are green, while along the sides amber lights are used. These colors were found to be the best for the purpose, as the rays were not sufficiently strong to neutralize the light on the screen, or to intercept the reflected rays from the screen to the eye of the observer. At the same time sufficient light was diffused in the room to render legible ordinary print, and faces and objects were perfectly distinguishable.[17]

In Chicago, where light regulation was already in place in 1910, "A Picture Lover" offered highly discerning criticism of theater lighting sometimes leaking over to the screen with disastrous results. "The result of this brilliant lighting is that all detail is lost in the shadows of the pictures, halftones lose their value and the picture has a tendency to become merely a white silhouette. The delicate shading of a Biograph or Pathé becomes flat, and the rich soft darks of a sepia-toned Vitagraph become dull, uninteresting patches of a nondescript yellow-brown."[18] The manager of the Orpheum in Chicago took exception to the criticism, which in turn prompted a second intervention by Picture Lover elaborating on the light quality and color from incandescent lamps, mainly yellow or brownish, which drives the blackness out of the black parts of the picture if light hits the screen, particularly "in a blue-tinted or blue-printed scene such as are so well done by the Edison Company." The article lists a handful of "well-arranged" theaters and especially extols "the little Theatorium at 44 State Street "in which the lamps, located on the ceiling, are enclosed in deep cone shades, which confine the light to the place where it is needed, and protect the screen at the same time."[19]

In late 1910 and the first half of 1911 ordinances regulating light were adopted in numerous cities and the licensed companies pushed the envelope. According to one of the more comprehensive articles on the Board of Censorship, "the makers [...] are refusing to do business with places which are too dark, which harbor objectionable characters, or which display unlicensed films."[20]

Instrumental in stirring lawmakers was a much-noted article in the October 1910 issue of *Pictorial Review*. Although the *Film Index* and the Patents Company had repeatedly advocated daylight projection and urged exhibitors to adopt it, the question took on an acute level of urgency after Anna S. Richardson's hardnosed intervention "The Menace of the Moving Picture Theater."[21] Richardson's point of departure aligned her with the progressive conviction concerning the medium's suitability as an educational tool and as a "tabloid drama" for "the individual with a limited income." Furthermore, for "detached men" it is "a successful rival to the saloon." Richardson, however, in a diatribe-like fashion elaborates on how the moving pictures' value hinges on the vicissitudes of dark theaters:

[T]here was just one factor in which these men [inventors and manufacturers] did not count, and that was the dark auditorium, affording opportunity to the moral degenerate and the 'cadet' to seek their victim and ply their trade.

Recently, she claims, a coalition of organizations spearheaded by the Children's Society "united to make war on the dark auditorium." There is a solution to the moral umbrage, however, namely:

It is—Light! The dark auditorium is not a necessity, it is an economy.

The pictures are now projected through darkened space to a huge canvas screen. That screen can be coated with a newly patented material of which aluminum forms the basis, and the picture can then be seen in a house as light or lighter than the ordinary theater. Pictures shown on this screen are free from the annoying flicker, but more importantly those who prey upon youth will find it impossible to carry out their vile designs in an auditorium where the safe and blessed light reaches every bench and corner of the room.

A portion of Richardson's article was reprinted in the *Film Index* in a defensive Chicago Letter, in which James S. McQuade at length reminded readers of the paper's track record concerning daylight propaganda. *Film Index* had moved from cajoling to indicting negligent exhibitors as the

233

light issue spread and spawned regulations, for instance in Indianapolis, which provoked the headline "Light Up the Picture Theater." The next city reported on was Detroit, and the headline read "More Light Wanted," which was followed by Buffalo.[22] The *Index* repeatedly lauded A.L. Simpson's Solar Screen, the first time on June 25, 1910, after a demonstration in Cleveland. Yet another showcasing of daylight projection was held at Joseph Driscoll's Nicoland in conjunction with a meeting hosted by the New York Picture Theater Men's Association. Driscoll had perfected his lighting arrangements for the demonstration in 1909 by investing in a Simpson Solar Screen. In addition, the light from his lamps were directed towards the ceiling and reflected back to the auditorium. "Entering the auditorium we stepped into an almost brilliantly lighted room from which one might easily see a pin on the floor."[23] The indictment of exhibitors came after Anna S. Richardson's article, "when the cause of lighted auditoriums for picture theaters had received a big boost."[24] Thus, Richardson's strong words reflected a longstanding concern on the part of the manufacturers in regard to exhibition which was repeatedly argued in their own organ after Dyer had initially set the tone. At the Patents Company changes in production practices and voluntary submission to film inspection by the Board of Censors together with daylight projection were perceived as cure-alls for disarming critics of all stripes.

FIGURE 28: Daylight screening in progress (Courtesy of Marc Wanamaker)

The daylight stance has been too gingerly formulated as helpful advice and a warning to exhibitors in lieu of a requirement from the manufacturers, as James S. McQuade lamented when discussing Richardson's piece. The producers' untiring efforts and "lavish expenditures" in raising the quality and "moral standard" of each individual film, he maintained, and in addition submitting them to the National Board of Censors for inspection, obligated the exhibitors to create a safe environment, "a fitting and decent home for the presentation," for their audiences on par with the value of the product. Before returning to the Richardson piece, McQuade rhetorically upped the ante by unequivocally—and in block letters for effect—defining the trust's position, as it were, thereby partly undermining Richardson's criticism from outside the industry:

> There can be no mincing the matter, DARK PICTURE THEATERS MUST GO.
> The exhibitor who persists in ignoring intelligent and moral opinion in this matter, will find himself placed on the shelf in company with wooden ploughs and other relics of semi-barbarism. He is a real menace to the moving picture business and, if he persists, the law will compel him to do what he should gladly do voluntarily.[25]

As daylight exhibition was voluntarily adopted as a keystone for responsible house management—or by legal requirement—dark auditoriums became associated with the primitiveness of the storefront shows as a remnant lingering only in metropolitan nickel vestiges. As the editor of *Moving Picture World* put it in 1913 in an article for another magazine: "[T]he disreputable 'store show' is to be found only in our largest cities."[26]

The discourse on daylight screens gained momentum after Anna S. Richardson's article. The technical authority in *Moving Picture World*, F.V. Richardson, addressed the various methods of projecting in lighted halls on several occasions when the licensed companies began pushing for daylight exhibition through its model theater in 1909. Half a year after the model theater was opened, he discussed auditorium light in a detailed "chapter," and returned to the matter by referencing his text when an exhibitor asked about a light problem.[27] In addition to his columns Richardson also published several handbooks. His final stance was that there should be enough light during projection so that one could see "dimly all over the house, clearly for some 20 feet." This recommendation from his 1912 handbook reflects ordinance requirements—the 1910 edition does not address this particular issue, which underpins the conclusion that 1911 was the year when daylight projection attracted attention on a grand scale. Richardson explains the background for his advice: "The principal objection to the dark theater lies in the opportunity afforded for improper acts, verging on immoral, or at least tending in that direction. The above-mentioned illumination fills every need in the prevention of such acts and more light is unnecessary from any point of view. It also helps the usher, and empty seats are easier found." According to Richardson, his recommendation afforded enough visibility in the auditorium to offset illicit activities. Many theaters were not content with that level of auditorium lighting however and adopted higher levels of lighting by taking advantage of the brilliance of new types of screens that did not require darkness. Richardson's recommendation corresponded to the amount of light in the regular dramatic theaters, and he adamantly dismissed "most of the talk about daylight theaters [as] pure buncombe."

In New York City, as the trust had hoped, illuminated auditoriums became a requirement starting November 20, 1910, shortly after Anna S. Richardson's charge. This regulation was apparently not very strictly enforced, however, and it was not part of a formal ordinance until 1913.[28] In a retort to an editorial in *The Sun*, which pronounced cinema a fad, W.H. Kitchell noted: "Each municipality has its own method of regulating the picture shows, and conditions vary. In New York the authorities are going after the dark houses. [...] There is no excuse for a dark house where unmentionable evils may flourish."[29] Rhetoric apart, film exhibitors in New York City did not universally turn on the auditorium lights until required by an ordinance passed early in 1913.

The fledgling screen industry hoped to capitalize on New York City's 1910 light regulations and the overall clamor for pellucid exhibition practices in the wake of the commotion caused by Richardson. The marketing for Simpson Solar Screen, embraced by the *Film Index*, underlined the fact that "Mayor Gaynor has ordered that your motion picture theater must be light. Get a Simpson Solar Screen and comply with the law. The only screen upon which pictures can be shown in light."[30] The Solar Screen was not alone on the market, which is evident from the advertising for Herbst's Bright Light Motion Pictures, a company based in Chicago.[31] Mirror Screen Co., a manufacturer of glass screens in Shelbyville, Indiana, was one of the pioneers on the market and still doing business in 1914.[32] In the mid-1910s, exhibitors wanting to screen films in illuminated auditoriums had several options: besides installing a Mirror Screen, exhibitors could procure a Radium Gold Fibre Screen from the American Theater Curtain & Supply Co in St. Louis, or a Mirroroide Screen from J.H. Genter Co., Newburgh, N.Y.[33] Lighted auditoriums hence turned into a slowly implemented aspect of film exhibition from 1909 and remained in place, enjoying discursive heed, well past the mid-1910s. In an article on film-theater architecture, Charles A. Whittemore recommended glass screens over other available types, and while describing exhibition practices claimed, "many theaters are so well illuminated throughout the entire performance that, without diminishing the effect of the picture, one can read at any time in any part of the house. So long as no direct light from the fixtures shine on the screen or in the eyes of the audience, the picture may be seen to as good advantage as if the house was completely dark."[34] The possibility to effortlessly read a newspaper during projection turned into a key criterion for ordinances in many cities.

In New York City the Society for Prevention of Cruelty to Children campaigned for an ordinance changing current projection practices—namely "presenting pictures in a darkened place"—evidence that the License Bureau's 1910 requirements had been disregarded by exhibitors, apparently without repercussions. The Society proposed the use of glass screens, which obviated the need for darkness.[35] Exhibition practices did not change in this respect until the adoption of the previously mentioned Folks ordinance in 1913, even if numerous theaters projected in daylight conditions to be able to market their theaters as safe environments for their patrons. One of the crusade installments in the *Evening World* in December 1912 attest to the current diversity in exhibition practices by making the far-from-novel claim that darkness offered incentives for accosting both girls and boys: "This is a situation the better class of 'movies' does not have to contend with. Where the best films are shown it is no longer necessary to keep the theater in absolute darkness."[36] During a very comprehensive inspection in New York in 1913 by the Practical Mothers' Association most of the problems reported on were localized outside the theaters, where swarms of children accosted grownups to help them get inside; unaccompanied children under 16 years were banned from the shows under the Folks ordinance. Inside, the level of light during exhibition was an important aspect commented on by the inspectors. At this juncture, after the adoption of the Folks ordinance, more or less all exhibitors projected in accordance with the new requirements. The passing of the ordinance was a key aspect of the *Evening World*'s crusade, and the initiative to enlist the Practical Mothers' Association signaled "mission accomplished" and passed the baton over to the Children's League.

When the Folks ordinance came into effect in New York City early in 1913, the lighting requirements were defined by reference to the Snellen Eye Chart, developed by Dr. Hermann Snellen in the 1860s for measuring visual acuity:

> Every portion of the motion-picture theater, including exits, courts, and corridors, devoted to the uses or accommodation of the public, shall be so lighted by electric light during all exhibitions and until the entire audience has left the premises, that a person with normal eyesight should be able to read the Snellen standard test type 40 at a distance of twenty feet and type 30 at a distance of ten feet; normal eyesight meaning ability to read type 20 at a distance of twenty feet in daylight. Cards showing type 20, 30, and 40 shall be displayed on the side walls together with a copy of this paragraph of the ordinance.[37]

The so-called Griffin Bill, which was adopted by the state of New York on July 1, 1913, included provisions regarding lighting similar to the Folks ordinance. For some, however, such specificity was "simply absurd, referring to a standard test for reading type of a certain size at a certain distance. Nothing of this kind is ever dreamed of in a regular theater."[38] The New York bill did not cover houses licensed as theaters, only venues operating as common shows with a seating capacity below 300 patrons.

In 1911 Los Angeles' City Council adopted an ordinance with very precise lighting strictures "requiring a sufficient number of white lights in the room to enable a person to distinguish the face of another ten feet away." Local exhibitor Arthur S. Hyman guided a reporter through a substantial amount of film venues, and according to the journalist "a number [of theaters] were so illuminated that there was no difficulty in recognizing the face of a friend 40 or 50 feet away."[39]

In March 1911, prior to the adoption of the ordinance, the Orpheum in Los Angeles began showing and marketing their films as "daylight pictures."[40] The novelty was announced as "Moving pictures shown in the full glare of the illuminated theater, with every light on. No flicker, no darkness, no danger. [...] The most remarkable development in theatricals in a decade."[41] The method used was devised by S.L. Rothapfel and consisted of a special lens projecting onto a coated screen. Exactly which mix of fluorescent chemicals was applied to the screen remained a secret.[42] When the Orpheum gave over its screening section to newsreels only, the daylight aspect was still underscored in the explanatory outline of the novel newsreel phenomenon:

> The Orpheum has arranged through Pathé Frères for a series of daylight pictures for exclusive showing there this series to portray the most unusual events now taking place anywhere in the world. Operators will cover these just as newspaper reporters do, taking pictures instead of notes and the views will be rushed to this city to be shown at the earliest possible moment after they happen.[43]

By chance or design, the inception of daylight screenings at the Orpheum coincided with the passing of a comprehensive regulatory bill regarding moving pictures, known as the Strobridge Bill after its sponsoring senator, in the California Assembly in Sacramento. The bill included provisions concerning light in the auditorium, namely: "[E]nough light shall be maintained while the show is running so that the face of everyone in the audience can be plainly seen."[44] Even if passed by the Assembly, bill no. 964 never came into effect due to a veto by Governor Hiram Johnson after numerous interventions from the Golden State's film exhibitors, which did not preclude lighting regulations at the local level. California exhibitors were not troubled by the lighting requirements, but feared stringent censorship provisions. The wording concerning light was more precise in the city ordinance adopted for Los Angeles shortly afterwards and published in August 1911: "[...] light sufficient in quantity so that the features of any person in such place may be distinguished at a distance of not more than ten feet from such person."[45] This requirement was upheld in all modifications of the ordinance well beyond 1916.[46]

Numerous cities outside the states of New York and California had adopted similar regulations. Elsewhere, many exhibitors had voluntarily invested in the daylight screens. In Pittsburgh in 1911 the Light Motion Picture Co. used the Casino Theater as a showplace for their daylight technology developed by Thomas McWatters.[47] A Pittsburgh newspaper, commenting favorably on various facets of film culture less than a year later, noted that the masher had been weeded out by daylight projection. "Every 'little manager' has long since recognized the responsibility of having personal direction, and be it only by the addition of a 16-candlepower light, they have made every presumably dark corner as bright as the daylight outside for, motography has reached the zenith in the projection of its film subjects, and no longer requires darkness, excepting within a radius of feet too infinitesimal to be of any consequence, and the 'masher' of today is an obsolete and unknown factor and has been for some time back."[48] In a 1912 recreation survey on Milwaukee Rowland Haynes noted, "Milwaukee moving picture houses are superior to those of most cities at present in the lighting of the audience halls, an important safeguard to the morals of those who attend."[49] In Grand Rapids the Drama League closely monitored local film culture in the spirit of betterment rather than censorship and reported in 1915 that all but one out of twenty-six theaters "are lighted so that every person is distinguishable." The female informant concluded, "I want to say right here that the danger that used to surround girls and boys through darkened theaters has chiefly been done away with."[50] So important and ubiquitous was daylight projection that Epes Winthrop Sargent in a book review expressed outrage against Frederick A. Talbot's assessment in his *Moving Pictures. How They Are Made and Worked*, "that Moving pictures without darkness have been exploited in the United States upon a small scale, and on one or two occasions in this country [England]." Sargent dismisses Talbot's preference for the dark house and his contention that "daylight projection is no more popular today than it was in 1897" as absurd. In the face of such ignorance concerning contemporary American exhibition practices Sargent does not even bother to marshal evidence, merely noting with a disdainful exclamation mark: "This in a book just off the press and with the 1912 imprint!"[51]

Talbot was however not alone in his predilection for darkness during film projection. In the *Los Angeles Times* Harry C. Carr repeatedly voiced misgivings concerning the zeal of reformers in policing the movies; one of his Lancer columns at length addressed the issue of darkness in his trademark jocular fashion.

It was a great thing for the reformers when the moving-picture business started. They had reformed everything else that was possible to reform.

They had stuck their noses in everyone's affairs, regulated their neighbor's habits, and made a mess of things generally. They were about to throw up the sponge because there was nothing left for them to meddle in, when—lo, and behold!—here came the moving-picture boom.

O joy unconfined! Here was something else they could tackle.

They did the job up brown, and when they had finished it they were filled with gloom.

But no! Ha, ha! It required darkness to show moving pictures. And as everyone knows, the dark is very immoral. To sit in a theater full of people in the dark is an awful thing.

Personally, I can't see exactly what could happen, inasmuch as the lights were turned on between each picture. But the reformers decided that it was very naughty to sit in the dark. I suppose they thought you might hold hands with the woman next you, or stroke the back of the neck of the lady in front of you, or something equally impure.

But there really isn't much danger of these things, for no woman is going to let a strange man stroke the back of her neck, or even hold her hand. And no man wishes to hold a woman's hand when he doesn't know what she looks like.

Of course, you might hold the hand of the lady you escort to the moving-picture show, but I don't see that that's any of the reformer's business. And you certainly wouldn't go to a moving-picture show so that you could hold hands, for there are plenty of dark places where this indelicate pastime might be indulged in—provided the party of the first part was open to argument.

Anyhow, we now have to attend moving-picture shows with electric lights glaring in our eyes.

There is only one thing left, now, for the reformers to do with moving-picture shows, and that is not to let them run the films fast.

If the pictures moved quickly, the rising young voters in the audience might immediately think of the word 'fast.' And, as the word 'fast' is very often applied to persons of irregular habits, it might put improper ideas into their heads.

And that would never do.[52]

Projecting practices and the undoing, at least temporarily and in most upscale theaters and areas, of the darkness by way of so-called daylight screens, mirror screens, or screens with different types of reflective surface coating remain a seldom discussed aspect of the progressives' many reform initiatives, this one implemented in close alliance with the industry. As is evidenced from the discursive run-through, daylight or mirror screens were very much on the agenda in the 1910s, and widely adopted more or less at a time when spectatorship came to the fore, in contrast to and gradually supplanting earlier convivial modes of audience engagement with moving pictures, according to Miriam Hansen's analysis. A core requirement for turning audience members into spectators—apart from the narrative configuration of the filmic address—was not to feel observed from the screen, hence the ban on actors looking into the camera. The dark auditorium seems to have been perceived as a given in the analysis, so self-evident that the issue remained unaddressed. Apart from sparing spectators from characters' gazes, which apparently penetrated the dark and thus were banned in shooting practice, dark halls furthermore isolated, segregated, and privatized spectators from each other, thereby heightening the psychic engagement with the unfolding story world. Thus, darkness was almost a sine qua non and defining factor for a sense of obliviousness vis-à-vis the exhibition space and the concomitant and non-distracted projection of mental energy into the diegetic world. For latter-day theorists, describing the cinematic apparatus as a version of Plato's cave, where darkness enveloped the bodies in front of the screen, this was a prerequisite for unleashing the conscious and unconscious processes defining cinematic metapsychology.

The classical style elicits a mode of spectatorship designated by Ben Brewster, with a felicitous phrase borrowed from a passage in Olivy Prouty Higgins' novel *Stella Dallas*, as "a scene at the movies."[53] This classical mode is grounded in an estranged impression of proximity and—at the same time—distance vis-à-vis the story world. Unseen in the darkness and from a vantage point on the threshold to the story world, the spectator, more or less absorbed, observes the unfolding of events. The analysis is seconded—but with a reversal of terms—by a trade-paper commentary signed "One of the Multitude." Under the heading "What the Public Want," s/he writes: "[W]hat we *do* like are the sorts of stories which make you feel you are peeping unseen though not indelicately into a neighbor's lighted window—the home of some commonplace family that might be yours or mine."[54] In the novel *Stella Dallas*, as Brewster reminds us, the young girl in a key scene lurks unseen in the dark, watching her father and his new family. By translating her experience into a "scene at the movies," she negotiates the feeling of being positioned in the dark outside "the picture," contiguous yet removed. The viewing positions, irrespective of whether framed as a scene at the movies or in front of neighborly curtains, are virtually equivalent, a detached peeping into strangely familiar territories where the gazing body is enveloped by darkness.

But how was the conversion to this brand of spectatorship affected in the 1910s if the darkness was partly dispelled and exhibition practices instead favored illuminated halls and an upgraded visibility in the theaters? Did heightened visibility in the auditorium militate against an absorbed, classical attitude, which putatively required a privatized and dually unobserved mindset (due to the auditorium's darkness with regard to other audience members, and from the story world by way of the ban on gazes, which in combination encouraged a state of willing suspension of disbelief)? It seems as if the conversion to spectatorship was a highly ambiguous and intricate process and that exhibition practices did not seamlessly work in concert with the shifts in filmic addresses and modes of storytelling. Projection under daylight conditions made audiences more visible than ever in the early 1910s, both from the screen and by other patrons, which fostered a heightened awareness of the public nature of the viewing experience. Reflected light from the screen had always provided some level of visibility in the auditorium, but daylight projection took visibility to unprecedented levels. The more or less distinct visibility of other patrons offered opportunities for distractions and shifts of attention between story world and auditorium attractions, which in all likelihood encouraged a less absorbed engagement than posited by the received theories of spectatorship. Daylight projection seems to at least partly undermine and somewhat offset the absorption required for a sense of private connection with and privileged relation to the story world. As important, audiences must have experienced an unprecedented level of surveillance from ushers and management staff as well as fellow patrons under daylight conditions, which was the rationale for adopting the novel lighting regime: to facilitate policing of the audience and thus discourage improper behavior. Only a panoptic-like regime could fend off the concerns associated with the nickel shows' moral contamination by ushering in an illuminated environment for film culture. Thus, light defined audience members per se as controlled and observed, which was supposed to influence behavior in all kinds of respects, most likely affecting the psychic relation to the screen also.

Given daylight projection—even if it is hard to tell how widespread and lasting such projection was—the viewing situation in the auditorium was all but private. In a rare comment on the effects of daylight projection from inside a house, W.F. Wallace noted that at the Queen Theater at the intersection of Jefferson and Vermont in Los Angeles, the "pictures are shown with the house fully lighted so that newspapers can be read with ease and the picture is bright, clear, and sharp and free from the flicker so noticeable in dark houses."[55]

Walter Prichard Eaton's cinematic misgivings might have had something to do with pre-classical film culture's inability to bring the spectator mentally close enough to feel absorbed. Comparing the theater to cinema, as Hartt already did in 1909 as we have shown, Eaton discounts the free play between audience and actor, which "baffles analysis, perhaps, but is too real to question," since the experience seems to touch the soul and affect a change in both parties. Such a change is not possible in film theaters, he maintains; it is as if the audience "viewed some far-off action of strangers in a dumb show through a window. The soul is not reached."[56] It is evident that the mechanisms for forging an alliance between screen actor and spectator is very much dependent on the figuration of the diegesis in all dimensions, especially the shot scale and the proximity vis-à-vis the story and the actor, who is in a strict sense intangible in the absence of real actors. Illumination allowing reading, distracting awareness of other audience members, and surveillance from ushers in the auditorium no doubt impacted the psychic mechanism mobilized by audience members in relation to the screen and might have made it even more difficult to reach the spectators' soul.

Eaton had delivered criticism along similar lines in 1913, in one of his first essays on "the menace of the movies," which echoes Richardson's 1910 intervention. Eaton formulates a key point as a metaspectatorial enigma, perhaps due to the darkness in some New York City theaters: "That the emotional appeal is negligible is attested by the fact that motion picture audiences sit hour after hour without smiling, without weeping, without applauding. They sit in solemn silence in a dim dark room, like certain gentlemen of Japan. Yet they keep on coming back for more; so something must please them."[57] This silence and lack of reactions from audiences were often commented upon prior to 1910. Paradoxically perhaps, the old dark theaters provided the prerequisites for privatized, silent, and absorbed viewing to a higher degree than was the case after the breakthrough of daylight screenings.

In March 1909, prior to the onset of daylight projection, Garnet Warren penned an ambitious survey from New York City, offering snapshots of all forms of popular entertainments: the melodrama, the burlesque, the penny arcade, the dime museum—and the dark nickelodeons. Against the backdrop of a loose sociological framing of the patrons frequenting the various types of establishments, Warren's metaspectatorial intervention displays a pronounced interest in how audiences engage with material on the screen and the galvanizing power of the cinematic apparatus. His text seems to evidence that conditions for transfixed absorption and undistracted, silent engagement with the screen were in fact more favorable in nickel shows—due to the darkness—than when audiences had a choice between watching the film or reading a newspaper in an auditorium.

The city streets are littered with nickelodeons, writes Warren, ironically dubbing them "the reigning sovereign of cheap amusement." Outside a "hoarse voiced man, with tapping cane, invites the populace to enter." The style sets up a strict demarcation between the slumming observer and the patrons as if to emphasize the detached observation motivating his field trip. Thus, his intervention carries a phase IV sensibility, as outlined in Chapter 2. We are further informed that:

As with the slot machine patrons, the audiences vary with the location. Swarms of children constitute a great part of the patronage in Grand street: young men with shaven necks and well oiled hair, whose young women friends publicly display their appreciation of them, appear prominently in Eighth avenue. But whatever the audience, it appears to be affected by the machines as with a species of hypnotism. Incident after incident, sensational or grotesque, shadows itself bewilderingly upon the screen and moves in front of audiences transfixed—audiences with staring eyes, who sit in a kind of waking stupor. No comment is ever heard, and hardly any sound of life. Indeed, a species of atrophy seems to affect the mind of the constant attendant at these places. Women sit there for hours each day watching the same representations again and again with a satisfaction which has in it something of torpor. Many of them pass all their afternoon there. It seems to suggest the generation of some new disease akin in its way to the speed mania. The moving pictures, for these persons, have the obscure fascination of some serpent.

Warren notices the diversity of the bill and the combination format including vaudeville acts, ironically described as "ladies with harsh, tired voice, who mechanically grate songs," while the picture in the main depicts "robberies and the tracking of criminals." Chases seem to end all films, he quips. "There are, however, at exceptional moments other pieces of vague historical interest. The assassination of the Duke of Guise is one of this class." These performances are better than the old melodrama, "but the desperate rush of each succeeding thrill sends one out with a dizzy head." The ten-cent places offer more elaborate vaudeville attractions, "singing and dancing specialties enliven the deadly monotony of the pictures." Some places have voices behind the screen, "which speak words to fit the action of the moving shadows." Concerning the houses on 14th Street, we are told that, "quite a middle class crowd assembles. Shopping women come and render homage to the reigning sovereign." Summing up, Warren writes:

> One closes one's eyes; the soft whirring of the machine relentlessly strikes upon the ear; one opens them; pale faces look through the gloom with looks of enspelled bewitchment. One is in the presence of a very great God indeed, the God of Cheapness. He is the sovereign of the present day amusement, and the moving of his wheels is thinning the ranks of his human competitors every day.[58]

A long article in *The Sun*, published later in 1909, is another flaneurian intervention resulting from visits to theaters all over town (reprinted in *Film Index*, 25 December 1909). Here, too, silence and rapt attention seems to prevail except at the highbrow theaters on Grand Street, while audiences on 14th Street, Broadway, and Rivington Street on the East Side refrain from boisterous interaction. A trade paper ventured an explanation for silence, lack of applause, and general reticence from the perspective of the legitimate theater and their audiences' audible enthusiasm. "The stranger within the photoplayhouse gates takes the surrounding silence to be an expression of cold and blighting disapproval. [---] Of course, there is good reason why photoplay audiences hold their silence. Applause is not so much a demonstration of approval as a tribute to the performers, a sign of admiration and encouragement; consequently when one knows that the actors of the photoplay are not within a thousand miles of hearing, there is small reason for applauding. The performers seen by the audience have no more reality than a mirage."[59] All this changed when studios gradually began billing actors already recognizable to audiences, whilst a system of storytelling was teased out, awarding characters a psychological dimension in which audiences could invest. And as important, daylight modes of presentations framed the viewing experience differently. Paradoxically, the first shards of a "classical attitude" might have emerged in the dark nickel venues rather than the upscale ones where audiences enjoyed less privacy in viewing due to the lighting and projecting arrangements in the auditorium, and in spite of unnamed actors and only a shallow level of character psychology.

Warren's 1909 observations above were replicated by Olivia Howard Dunbar in 1913, in a piece predicated on the same type of detached slumming for the purpose of witnessing the "riotous joy of the multitude, however grimly unmoved his own less facile springs of mirth." The text was published prior to the adoption of the Folks ordinance, so it is unclear whether the theater was lighted or not. Dunbar reports on audience members devoid of all signs of appreciation, animation, boredom, or excitement; a state of torpor seems to prevail in front of the screen. Warren associated this with hypnotism, Dunbar with "semi-somnolence," which suggests darkness. Dunbar is puzzled by the hold the films exercise on the patrons, given the paradigm of non-responses scattered in her text: phlegmatic, apathetic, emotionless. Her concluding explanation for this state of affairs, accurately observed or not, highlights the limited demands the medium makes: cinema "requiring neither punctuation—for it has no beginning—nor patience—for it has no end—nor attention—for it has no sequence. No degree of intelligence is necessary, no knowledge of our language, nor convictions nor attitude of any kind, reasonably good eyesight being indeed the only requisite."[60] Her comments seemingly refer to a continuous show, which indeed moved in a form of loop while the individual films were very much organized according to narrative patterns with beginning, middle, and end in 1913.

A short story from early 1910 set in the kind of inconspicuous nickel theaters visited by Warren, James Oppenheim's *Saturday Night*, toys with light in multiple dimensions and creeps inside a film patron, albeit a fictional one. The text foregrounds musical accompaniment as the key avenue for turning a woman into an absorbed spectatrix who forgets herself while watching and rediscovers aspects of the girl she once was. On a Saturday evening Oppenheim brings his protagonist out of a gloomy and dark little apartment on Third Avenue in Yorkville to the street, where faces are "bathed in gold and blue and orange." The avenue is described as a lover's lane peopled by washwomen, factory girls, salon dwellers, and workers, among others. The old dressmaker Mrs. Breitmann and her forty-year-old "maiden daughter" live on 83rd street, and on this particular Saturday Lilith cannot help herself and is about to step out for the first time ever, which freezes her mother "with terror." Someone had whispered to Lilith that her high-school love, Henry Lutz, was back in town after being expelled from Harvard, having squandered family money and moved progressively deeper into the underworld and alcoholism over the years. He was now playing the piano at the local Nicoland, not to be confused with the Patents Company's model theater on 162nd Street. Lilith moves away from the dark and drab 83rd Street out to the Elysian, enchanted Third Avenue bathing in a "golden glow." And the "lights, the tides of men and women, the sights, the lustrous leather of shoes in the brilliant show window, the glamour of high-heaped fruit on the stands, the keen air, the buoyancy and sparkle of Holiday—all these flooded through her, until she was transfigured." In this state of revived excitement, Lilith enters the darkness of Nicoland to listen to Henry playing after glancing at the posters for *The Actor's Wife* and *Lost in the Desert*. Due to the transformation, she now enters a "Dream-World" as a "Dream-Person," and in this overwhelmed state she seemingly reacts with one sense at a time: "The first sensation was weird, uncanny, unreal. The room was in blackness and warm with dense humanity—a smell of people." After the olfactory impression comes sight: "Above her from a little aperture in the street-wall, a beam of white light penciled through the air, widening out as it went, until it splashed the white framed plaster of the rear. Far away she saw the gray-white-black kaleidoscope-effect of the cinematograph pictures." Then the prime draw—sound, or rather music: "sweet, penetrating, weird and wild," and perfectly suited to the flow of the pictures and their emotional rhythm. The music translated the characters' "feeling and thinking. It gave them the last touch of life; they became living human beings," and tears "rolled down" Lilith's checks. The illusion was ripped asunder when lights "came sprouting out of the walls" to reveal an auditorium "commonplace enough." As the audience files out and new patrons enter, the

248

narrator takes a few moments to philosophize on film culture and its ability to swing the "fat washwoman" into the "Heroic and Romantic." Furthermore, the narrator waxes in the spirit of Patten's analysis by singling out a washwoman as indicative of the patronage:

> This was truly the Theater of the People—the Theater of Democracy—come of itself—not born of statesmanship or university. Here it was, a part of the daily lives of the unlearned and the unmoneyed. This washwoman had neither time nor money for the real theater. But here—tales of love, scenes of far land, romances of heroism became part of her heart and soul. She struggled—laughed, cried, felt and thought—with these strange heroes and heroines! She forgot her own life; she entered the common life of the race—she expanded her soul over earth and through human hearts. This was the release, the glorification of the day's work.

The light comes down again and the focus returns to Lilith, who sits through the show five times. Now, her attention is riveted to the pictures, not only the music, which however still steers her emotions. As evidenced by the posters outside, the variety program opens with a melodrama, which absorbs Lilith. She thus

> forgot all else; so did these laborers, these clerks, these shopgirls and tenementwomen. Truly Lilith was not herself. She was in the pictures there; she was that beautiful, unfaithful wife; she ran away from her child and her actor-husband; she kidnapped her child; there was fire in the house; there was a wild drive to a deserted barn; there was ultimate disgrace. What a wonderful way to live! Carriages, a rich mansion, wine, fire, ruin! And all so much more real than reality! She did not know that it was the music that made the illusion perfect—that made her feel and see so intensely. The audience was breathless when the series stopped, and a new drama—a drama of the Western desert, the trail-lost man, wife and child, unfolded its grim tragedy. The women—Lilith, too—sobbed as if their hearts were broken. Whereupon a topsy-turvy picture followed, full of laughter—and then a plaintive song sung by a girl and illustrated by brilliantly colored slides—and then—the lights went up, and the audience trooped out.[61]

Seeing her present self mirrored in Henry's face, described as "cynical, hard, blotched with pimples," Lilith is thrown back to her real identity as a "poor shriveled thing—not a Girl of Lover's Lane." Love is still there in both their hearts, but only for their respective memory of a person from long-gone days severed from their present physical incarnations. Henry even professed to being married to the immortal Lilith of old, who now lives in his music. Lilith staggers out into the cold night to Third Avenue, which after the show is "dark, vast, deserted" and again back to being "a sordid, a squalid market street" devoid of romance. She returns to her mother, but Lilith is changed and both women's faces "shone with strange light." After having touched her mother's hand for the first time in years, she eventually falls asleep, happy that her soul henceforth is married to Henry's and alive in his music.

The account of Lilith's viewing experiences, certainly deeply permeated by her love for Henry, still foregrounds an absolute absorption in the story world cued by the music and triggered by the enveloping darkness which blocked out all distracting influences from other audience members, a regime dismantled by daylight exhibition.

In November 1913, when testifying in conjunction with the antitrust suit leveled against the Motion Picture Patents Company, Frank L. Dyer had the opportunity to address multiple issues bearing on film exhibition. He thus presented a condensed overview concerning the trust's attempts at eliminating the dark theaters harking back to his efforts in 1909.

> The Patents Company also were the first, or, at least, one of the first, to realize the necessity of doing away with the showing of pictures in absolutely dark theaters, and it maintained an exhibit at the Patents Company for a long time demonstrating how pictures could be shown in lighted auditoriums, and this work was taken up by the trade papers, and the theaters throughout the country were convinced of the advisability of this reform, so that at the present time, I think, that all, without exception, of the motion picture theaters of the country are now showing pictures under reasonable good conditions of light.[62]

The lighting of the auditorium was still very much an issue even towards the end of the silent era. Projection authority James R. Cameron discussed the matter in detail in his comprehensive 1928 handbook. Relying on researchers at Eastman Kodak's laboratory, Cameron stated that the illumination "should vary 1/10 ft. candle at the front of the theater to 2/10 ft. candle at the rear while the pictures are being exhibited." The benchmark was still the ability to read a newspaper: "With the intensity graduated as mentioned ordinary newspaper print can be read with ease by an observer." Furthermore, Cameron recommended that illumination throughout the projection of the film should be correlated by the nature of the light and emotional tone in each scene.[63]

Light inside the theaters was however not enough to fully silence the worries concerning film culture. Literal policing in the theaters' environs by women in uniform to regulate amusement traffic began in Los Angeles not long after the light ordinance was adopted. Los Angeles' example was soon copied by numerous American cities, so let us begin in Chicago.

Policewomen

In July 1913, when 10 policewomen were appointed in Chicago, a group of suffragists protested against the very appellation "policewoman," claiming it was "highly improper because the duties are on a higher plane than those of a mere policeman." Furthermore, the designation "is not suggestive of refinement, [and] does not support the dignity of the office."[64] Less than a year later, the hiring system's pros and cons were scientifically evaluated from a psychological standpoint. Refinement, it seems, was a less than appropriate description of the rugged day-to-day practice on the streets experienced by some of these brawny policewomen, according to the report card.

In a 1914 Sunday article syndicated by the Hearst press Columbia professor David Edgar Rice thus attempted to explain why "women would rather be arrested by men," that is instead of by policewomen.[65] Proffering a scientific explanation for the "failure of Chicago's policewomen," Rice reported that the excessive force allegedly used by policewomen when arresting female felons was grounded in a sex-specific excitability. "When woman occupies the place of physical force she is naturally apt to be more violent and cruel than men." In addition, and from the victims' perspective, women allegedly accustomed to seeing men in positions of public power therefore "resent seeing a woman in such a place." According to Rice, women "are more likely than men to act hastily, to form snap judgments, to confuse means and ends, and resort to tears when logic fails." Since women in general are physically weaker, the police departments apparently tend to overcompensate by appointing exceptionally strong women, Rice claimed. One of the policewomen in

251

Chicago was, for example, an "accomplished heavy-weight lifter." Since superior physical strength is perceived culturally as a male prerogative, Rice argued, the strong, husky policewomen are inclined to act extremely forcefully in the line of duty, given their psychological makeup and susceptibility. Hence, policewomen were said to invest all their power in the first round, while their male colleagues are confident enough in their strength and physical superiority to show restraint and patience.[66]

Rice's worries appear unfounded, since the policewomen's prime responsibility in Chicago up until April 1914 was juvenile protective work, continuing the civic monitoring carried out by the Juvenile Protective Association around dance halls and five-cent theaters. The civic vigilance had helped reduce liquor sales to minors in dance halls and, with policewomen in charge, it was now possible to step up the surveillance and arrest perpetrators. In addition to watching dance halls and cheap theaters, amusement parks were surveyed by the ten policewomen. It was hoped that their jurisdiction would later be extended to the public parks. Initially, there were concerns that policewomen would be "overzealous, injudicious, and meddlesome [. . .] but they have not been, so far."[67] In April 1914 Chief Gleason decided to remove the policewomen from the "moral section of the department" and instead assign them to patrol work in the "outlying districts," measures against which the Woman's Athletic Club filed a protest.[68] Rice's contention concerning excessive violence goes against the grain of the numerous facetious reports underlining the timidity of the female law enforcers and seems to be part of the chief's backlash. One unflattering report from a crime scene of sorts, featuring the Chicago policewomen, reversed the perspective by framing policewomen as clueless movie cops and failures akin to the incompetent Keystone brand. "The lady cop seems to be a failure" since the policewomen this time around were too reticent regarding striking waitresses at a downtown restaurant, hence "the higher-ups called off the women and sent a gang of roughnecks down to the restaurant to crack heads in the good, oldfashioned way," while the policewomen "tried hard to make themselves feel they were not acting for the benefit of the movies."[69] Thus, the policewomen in Chicago occupied a highly ambiguous discursive terrain, too forceful according to Rice, too meek according to other reports, and relegated to patrol work by the chief instead of continuing their work in the "moral section." Perhaps the lady cops had been too efficient and annoyed the liquor interests, which were well connected to the Police Department for a long time. Their preventive line of work in

Chicago was inspired by the pioneering efforts of Alice Stebbins Wells in Los Angeles, the first American policewoman.

Alice Stebbins Wells and her fellow policewomen in Los Angeles were not out there to "crack heads," instead performing a different, perhaps more refined brand of police work clamored for in Chicago, and hence never encountered discursive resistance in the press, though at times a measure of glee. The focus of attention for Mrs. Wells and her colleagues in Los Angeles was primarily preventive, namely steering young girls and women away from bad influences by an extended form of mothering. In the role of municipal chaperons, policewomen should institute codes of conduct impeding moral corruption, which was mirrored in their erstwhile responsibility in Chicago. Places of amusements were perceived to represent a high level of risk, and therefore significant arenas to monitor for the policewomen in both cities.

In September 1910 a slot in Pathé's American newsreel featured Alice Stebbins Wells, the newly appointed policewoman in Los Angeles. She was depicted as a gender pioneer in her profession, as the very first woman on any American police force. In the newsreel she was seen on the streets and "descending the Court House steps."[70] The decision to appoint a policewoman was made by City Council on August 12th, and the ordinance became effective a month later. The appointment of Mrs. Wells marked a new phase in the supervision of young girls' amusement habits and their access to a heterosocial public sphere replete with exciting allures, sensual temptations, and numerous unspecified risks. Anna Shaw's well-known adage-like description of movie theaters as "recruiting stations of vice" succinctly associated moral turpitude with film exhibition and the amusement space by and large. Shaw's proposal for purifying New York City and halting the alleged white-slave traffic was to appoint one thousand policewomen.[71] In the press' coverage of the nickelodeon culture several groups were indirectly singled out as urgently deserving observation in terms of movie-going habits, auditorium etiquette, and susceptibility. Young girls emerged as the core group receiving attention, thus substituting a first wave of interest focused primarily on the ethnic other; apparently, the fact that these groups shared amusement space was particularly unsettling to some. The ethnic others' fascination with and reputed proneness to misread screen content, and their more or less bizarre patterns of spectatorship, offered ethnographic excitement to readers rather than alarmist fuel exacerbating an imminent need to regulate this sealed-off exhibition culture in the early period. Boys soon emerged as especially risk-prone, although in a different register. If they were seduced, it was primarily by example, by representations open to emulation—in particular portrayals of crimes and the methods of perpetrating them, at times glorifying the outlaws in the process, even if they were punished in the end as a matter of course. The perception that the exhibition space and its environs threatened to deprave girls and suggestive representations on the screen could corrupt their moral compass and lead them astray provided motivations for appointing a policewoman.

FIGURE 29: Aspiring policewomen take aim (From the author's collection)

This alleged detrimental influence of moving pictures on young girls inspired the superintendent of schools in Los Angeles, John H. Francis, to establish a special grammar school for girls out of tune with their studies. The school was said to be the first of its kind in the country, modeled on a similar type of school for truant and unruly boys. The girls eligible for enrollment were singled out as "confirmed picture-show patrons, to the peril of their morals and the destruction of their education," alternatively as "chronic patrons of the moving-picture shows." The hope was to steer the afflicted girls via special training back into "normal channels and to rob the juvenile court of many of its wards," a pedagogical initiative tying in with the policewomen's responsibilities and program of preventive measures.[72]

Mrs. Wells had a background as a graduate theology student and had been employed as a pastor's assistant on the East Coast besides being active in the Prison Reform League. She promulgated progressive ideas, but with a twist. In an interview she analyzed the "alarming increase in the delinquency of girls" as conditioned by economic factors—they were underpaid and overworked, she explained, as previously argued by Simon N. Patten. The solution she proposed was an upgrading or "dignifying of domestic service to a profession." By removing women from offices and shops—workplaces apparently tending to corrupt young women—for positions in democratic homes run by way of domestic science, these women would thereby place themselves in line for "homes of their own." This scheme answered a vocation of sorts, according to Mrs. Wells, since many girls were said to be "domestic at heart."[73] On a similar note, apropos the proposed breakup of the red-light district in Chicago, Wells believed that all Christian women would gladly take in reformed prostitutes to work in their homes.[74]

Not being formally appointed during her initial time in the force, but merely included on the emergency list pending a civil-service examination, Mrs. Wells eventually had to endure competition for the job she had already performed for a year. This meant that she was up against a bunch of other ladies applying for the title of policewoman; for the time being, the police commission had decided to appoint only one woman. Wells emerged from the examination with fanfare, however, and was formally appointed and attached to the juvenile bureau. Henceforth, Policewoman Stebbins Wells consolidated Los Angeles' reputation as a city bent on reform.

Her responsibilities comprised preventive measures intended to steer young girls and women away from situations and places that could lead them morally astray. Wells' speaking engagements were supposed to build an awareness of threats and risks in these respects by inspiring a multitude of preventive initiatives for negotiating a young woman's daily urban life. Prevention rather than cure turned into a mantra for her work. After being appointed, she outlined her upcoming responsibilities in an interview: "My field of work will be chiefly wherever young people gather for entertainment in parks, penny arcades, moving picture shows, and dance halls," she said. "I will deal chiefly with the proprietors of such places seeing that all laws are obeyed and that the places are kept clean and moral. In the dance halls I may find it necessary to talk to some of the young people personally."[75] After policing the streets for around a year, Mrs. Wells took to the road for motivational tours across the U.S. relating to her line of work. The *Examiner* headlined one of her speaking tours as a success when she returned after six months.[76] Wells was, however, no friend of moving pictures and at times the take on film culture in her speeches was challenged.

Her opinions have little in common with the progressives' hopes for pushing the envelope of film culture in an educative direction. Late in 1912 Wells was headlined after a speech in Philadelphia and quoted as saying: "We are going at too fast a pace in the matter of amusements, and the feverish form of pleasure found in the moving picture shows is not for the best interests of the rising generation and is not helping to build lives that will stand the test. We are being consumed by a thirst for amusement, and the thirst is not being quenched in a healthy manner. We are feeding the children of our city into a great devouring hopper so long as we allow this neglect and these questionable forms of amusement to go on."[77] This was welcome news for the *New York Evening World*, as it played into its ongoing crusade against the local film shows. Wells' later appearance in Boston and her misgivings about film culture provoked a retort from William C. Franke, who was affiliated with the Moving Picture Operators Union:

> Every moving picture house in Boston is licensed and fitted up as a public theater, and is under direct supervision of the mayor's office, the inspectors of the State police, and in some instances under the supervision of the clergy. They are owned and operated by conservative business men, who have invested thousands of dollars in their respective theaters, and are daily under an enormous expense, and it does not stand to reason that a good business man is going to jeopardize his business for the sake of running objectionable pictures or of allowing a child under age to enter the theater.
>
> I do not understand what Mrs. Wells means by 'amusement parlors.' Presumably she refers to the antiquated 'store show.' A man may rent an empty store or two, install a cheap and out-of-date machine, and proceed to get the nickels and dimes, regardless of the quality of his pictures or the

moral atmosphere of the house. There is not such a parlor in Boston. I am in a better position to understand conditions than any investigator, and I want to say that the moving picture show is a legitimate business enterprise, and as such will flourish under the laws of the State.[78]

This clash between perspectives neatly illustrates film culture's diversity a couple of years before the breakthrough of features. Franke downplays what he considers to be residual aspects of film exhibition indicative of an early phase of emergence. Contemporary film culture, he maintains, is highly regulated and closely aligned with high-class theatrical venues in tune with dominant culture. According to Franke, Wells' terminology describes a receding form of film culture far removed from recent developments.

Wells continued to address conferences and congresses on the topic of crime prevention in relation to young women. She gave a talk at the International Purity Congress in Minneapolis in October 1913 among dozens of other engagements. In March 1914 she embarked on a new trip, this time touring the Midwest and East Coast.

The appointment of Alice Stebbins Wells as a policewoman attracted the attention of suffrage groups and legislators all over the country. When appointed, Mrs. Wells expressed her hope in an interview that the "newspapers would not make fun" of her "serious work."[79] Reporting to the police commission after a year of service, Wells could boast 17 arrests under her belt, in addition to her 13 speaking engagements. A couple of her arrests elicited reports in the press. For example, when she was guiding a woman legislator from Colorado, Helen Robinson, through the commercial district, Wells arrested two Japanese film exhibitors, Mr. Oku and Mr. Hamada, on the fly. Outside their film theater alluring posters depicting sword duels caught the ladies' attention; the perpetrators were taken to the police judge and arraigned on charges of violating the city's advertising ordinance.[80]

In her annual report to the police commission she proposed the institution of new body, a Public Morals Commission responsible for, among other things, education in "social hygiene," securing "safe boarding houses for working girls," having hotels "ask questions," and conducting "a campaign for clean amusements." Her recommendations went unheeded, but a related system later emerged when so-called City Mothers were appointed.[81] The same day that Wells' first annual report was featured in the *Examiner*, a news item on the same page chronicled her latest arrest. Yet another poster depicting swords and firearms led to the arrest of the two proprietors of the Plaza Theater, Sigmund Stern and Mike Gore. Thus—by chance, it seems—Wells arrested proprietors of Japanese and Mexican screen venues, that is exhibitors running theaters catering to the core groups singled out in "the Main Street discourse." A more amusing case reported by the *Los Angeles Herald* was transformed by the cartoonist into "moving pictures," just like the previously discussed report on Ida Appelgate's suicide.[82] The six panels depict a situation developing outside a movie theater and ending in front of the police judge. Two days later the *Herald* reported that the court had released the accused, James Gibbon, a night watchman. The judge had to rule on the meaning of a complicated scene set outside the Electric Theater at 215 North Main Street. The key issue was whether Mrs. Wells had flirted with Gibbon or he had flirted with her, thus being a masher of sorts. The decisive matter was the tone used by Mrs. Wells when she approached Gibbon and asked if he had winked at her. A mocking or inviting gesture? According to Gibbon, Wells was standing outside the theater blocking traffic—embodying Anna Shaw's idea of having a policewoman outside every theater. Wells was however masquerading in plainclothes, which set the scene in motion. Did she ask, in a friendly manner, if he had winked at her? Or did he propose a drink? Anyway, they walked away from the scene together—and to the police judge. The reporting here is not openly sardonic, but the subtext most certainly operates in that register. According to the trade press, this theater catered primarily to Latin audiences, screening Pathé titles produced by their branch in Mexico City.

A similar predicament affected "city coppess" Alice Clement in Chicago, prompting inventive press coverage there. The *Tribune* literally split the column for the two conflicting testimonies, and in the end the jury, after pondering for only three minutes, released the alleged masher Clement had arrested. Apparently, they were unable to ascertain who had pressed knees against whom. " 'What should you expect from a jury of men?' quipped Policewoman Clement, with resignation."[83]

Minor mishaps or misfortunes affecting Alice Stebbins Wells did not escape the city editors in Los Angeles. In July 1912 the *Examiner* reported that Policewoman Wells had been robbed in her home. The stolen satchel contained her badge and revolver in addition to personal items.

It was later recovered, its contents intact apart from a small amount of money. Thus, the press was apparently on high alert in its reporting on Policewoman Wells, both on and off duty.[84] An additional indication of this interest is evidenced by a Selig film documenting the annual inspection of the police force by the mayor and the police brass on May 1st. In the film Mrs. Wells and her new colleague, Mrs. Shatto, were awarded special attention in a scene documenting their "answering a fast call, the first scene of its kind ever registered on film."[85] The scene was of course staged for the benefit of the camera. The Selig Polyscope Company later donated a print to the police chief.

By 1914 women were carrying badges in the police departments of cities all over the U.S. The practice of hiring policewomen was established and widespread enough to inspire Alice Stebbins Wells, the American pioneer in the field, to organize an association for her female partners in crime prevention. The International Association of Policewomen came into being in 1915, and for five years Mrs. Wells was at its helm. The organization survived until 1932 when lack of funding temporarily curtailed this line of preventive police work.

In the mid-1910s Wells was a renowned spokesperson for a form of police work she herself had campaigned for and managed to pilot through Los Angeles' City Council in 1910 with the support of several women clubs. At that time, proposals for hiring policewomen had been on the agenda for some time outside Los Angeles. In Europe policewomen had been hired well in advance of Mrs. Wells, in Stockholm, for example, as early as 1908. On December 1, 1908, the *Evening Sun* reported that the Board of Aldermen in Bayonne, N.J., were to review a proposal for appointing policewomen. No measures were taken, however. This was the belated result of Julia Goldzier's campaign for a salaried position that had been ongoing since 1906. She envisioned monitoring children on the streets as her prime line of responsibility in the service of better citizenship, and her proposal mirrored the work entrusted policewomen when finally appointed. The *New York World* ridiculed the idea in a featured article, listing a string of petty offences considered appropriate for women to go after.[86] Sprinkled with cartoons, the text presented a costume for policewomen by theatrical designer Caroline Siedle. When Julia Goldzier was featured in 1907, the press report again focused on the costume and elected to doll up a slightly younger version of the matron in dominatrix fashion. Mrs. Wells, on the other hand, designed her own uniform when embarking on one of her numerous speaking tours, a dress more in tune with the role of municipal chaperone.

FIGURE 30: Dress code for police-women. Cartoon from *Chicago American*, 24 April 1907, 2.

FIGURE 31: Alice Stebbins Wells in uniform, *Los Angeles Examiner*, 15 September 1912, I:2.

In April 1913 the policewomen in Los Angeles—Mrs. Wells and her colleague Mrs. Rachel Shatto—were awarded a new type of assignment somewhat in the line of Anna Shaw's proposal, albeit on a miniscule scale. The background was a perception that white slaves were recruited on the streets and in places of amusements—dance halls, skating rinks, motion-picture theaters, cafes, and penny arcades. In addition, evening amusements were considered prone to elicit "delinquency among young women." By having the policewomen work in the manner of detectives and plainclothes officers, and between four in the afternoon and midnight, authorities hoped that young girls roaming the streets and "conducting themselves in an improper manner" would be escorted home by the officer. Furthermore, the policewomen were to oversee compliance with ordinances affecting places of amusement, something Wells had already taken upon herself during her first year in service.[87] So problematic was the white-slave situation in Los Angeles, according to the police leadership, that the police commission urged City Council to pass an emergency ordinance appointing 30 policewomen destined to participate in a planned vice crusade. The mayor spoke in favor of the police commission's proposal. Parallel to police efforts, the local Parent-Teacher Federation launched a campaign for inspection of all film theaters. Two women from each of the 118 circles were appointed for the job.[88] The Federation's vigilance lasted well into 1914, resulting in a white list of theaters with a clean record. The *Express* published the very short list: Tally's, Garrick, Jefferson, the Globe at Sunset and Echo Park Avenue, the Globe at Arlington and 24th, and the Woodley.[89] Somewhat earlier, Dr. Jessie Russel of the Juvenile Court confirmed from her experience that a "large number of delinquent children are recruited from the ranks of those allowed to roam the streets at will, especially at night, attending moving-picture shows without a chaperone and strolling through the parks."[90] In May 1914 the chief had nine women on the force, and wanted to hire still more. The policewomen described their line of work in a programmatic outline:

> Preventing girls and young women from entering lives of shame and rescue others who are not hardened. Bring parents into closer touch with their daughters. Show girls the folly of flirting with strangers and the danger of occasional 'joy rides.' Emphasize the joy of right living and right thinking, and explain away the folly of the so called grand time that girls seek in the cafés and the dance hall.[91]

Estelle Lawson Lindsey interviewed one of the policewomen, Mrs. Aletha Gilbert, to assess the situation. Supervising girls, educating parents, punishing men who take advantage of the innocent ones, and having schools adopt codes of decorum forbidding makeup and conspicuous accessories were the most urgent remedies, according to Gilbert. Parents' laxity was illustrated by a story about a girl of 15 who made $45 a week working in a movie theater. The family lived from her wages and was therefore reluctant to curb her nightly excursions. The damage was done when the policewomen picked her up, claimed Mrs. Gilbert. Vigilant attention concerning movie theaters and girls working in them, patronizing them, or hanging around in their vicinity was still on the policewomen's agenda.[92] And makeup was still as problematic as in 1887 when the Saunterer reviewed female patrons outside Mott Hall.

Late in 1914 movie theaters and places of amusements seemed to impose less of threat than before. When Althea Gilbert was appointed City Mother-in-Chief, she and her squad of ten City Mothers were awarded a new type of badge for those serving in the novel Mother's Bureau. In the program outlined by Gilbert nothing was said about places of amusements, however.[93] It might be that film culture and the values associated with its representations and exhibition contexts had turned as chemically pure as the rest of amusement life in Los Angeles was said to be (see Chapter 10).

When appraising the situation in the interview by the *New York Times* late in 1912, Wells painted a very optimistic picture of the ordinances pertaining to dance halls and picture theaters in Los Angeles, particularly compared to the situation in New York City. Holding theater proprietors to the letter of the ordinance "will do much to develop moving pictures as an educative force." Elaborating on which types of scenes needed to be cut out, Wells further opined, "There is no need, of course, for the completely darkened hall any more than for the dangerous 'moonlight dance,' which I believe you have been quite successfully fighting here in the East."[94] Daylight projection and the manufacturers' push for safe exhibition contexts, in combination with the preventive measures policewomen so successfully embodied, seemingly changed the public perception of film culture. And the products and programs offered in the gradually more lavish theaters bore little resemblance to the films of the early nickelodeon days, to which Hearst's *Los Angeles Examiner* issued free coupons for a time. The film studios simultaneously interfaced with the community in unprecedented ways, especially on Universal's studio lot located on the old Lankershim ranch in the foothills beyond Cahuenga Pass.

FIGURE 32: In an illustrated magazine interview from March 1911, Alice Stebbins Wells is seen talking to a young boy outside Horne's Big Show (423 South Spring Street). Tellingly, from the perspective of 1911, the only point in the interview bearing on film exhibition is her appreciation of the fact that "there is no longer need for a completely dark auditorium." *Good Housekeeping Magazine*, Vol. 52, No. 3 (March 1911); photograph on p. 296, quotation from p. 298.

While Alice Stebbins Wells was the first American policewoman, Laura Oakley was the first woman in the U.S. to be elected chief of police. A municipal election was held at the Universal plant as a precursor to the incorporation of Universal City. The company actively cultivated a frontier spirit by operating as a city, thus not only seeking incorporation for the ranch locally, but also promoting an idea about film culture with hoped-for universal appeal. And what could be more appealing than building a town, a real place for workers turning space into screen magic? In the municipal election three tickets competed for the film folks' votes: the Democrats, the Progressives, and the Suffragettes. The campaign started on May 11, 1913, when all candidates for office were awarded three minutes to present their respective platform. The Suffragette candidate for chief of police, actress Laura Oakley, in her playful campaign promised to hire only policewomen for the force—and they would not be allowed to flirt with unmarried men. Furthermore, the city would remain an open town, and "the patrol wagon can not be used for 'joy rides.' "[95] Oakley's victory was overwhelming, 305 votes versus 140 for her closest contender; all in all 588 votes were cast. The manager of the studio, A.M. Kennedy, a Democrat, won the mayoral race by a slim margin over the Suffragette candidate, director Lois Weber—219 versus 204 votes; the progressive William Foster received 165. When Kennedy stepped down from office, Weber replaced him. The determination to build a real, incorporated city was attested to by the election of a Board of Film Censors, a prime fixture of responsible towns. Oakley stepped down from her office in March 1914 and was then succeeded by Stella Adams. Before leaving office, Oakley received formal recognition from her fellow chief of police in Los Angeles, was sworn in as a policewoman on the Los Angeles force, and even awarded a regular badge.[96] The honor bestowed upon her by the chief of police did however not spill over to actors performing as police officers—on the contrary. When the International Association of Police Chiefs gathered in Grand Rapids, they unanimously supported a resolution recommending that all films caricaturing or burlesquing the police should be "forbidden by law."[97]

As the number of policewomen on duty increased across the U.S., film comedies could not resist addressing the phenomenon; one of several such spoofs was Lubin's *The Lady Police* (1912). A town has elected a female town council, who appoint a law enforcer of the fair sex. Enamored by the lady in uniform, the men are only too eager to be arrested and put in jail. The wives storm the jail, take their husbands away, and leave the police in tears. Kalem released a comedy burlesque on a similar note in 1913, *When Women Are Police*. In 1914, this time on a serious note, the Balboa Company in Long Beach announced production plans for a four-reel docu-feature, *The Policewoman*, starring Alice Stebbins Wells, no less; F.M. Wiltermood wrote the scenario. Even if the film is listed in the *American Film Institute Catalog*, it was in all likelihood never produced. Apart from advance notices in the Long Beach and Los Angeles press that spilled over to the trade weeklies, there is no indication that the film went beyond the scenario stage.[98] This would otherwise have been a key document in film form of the regulatory struggles highlighting preventive measures according to the Los Angeles model, which was embodied and disseminated by Alice Stebbins Wells, running in tandem with daylight screening and numerous other practices that transformed amusement geography overall in the 1910s.

CHAPTER 7

"WHIZZ! BANG! SMASH!"—HEARST, GIRLS, AND FORMATS

"The closing words of the last chapter lead naturally
to the commencement of this, its successor..."[1]

ECLECTIC CONTENT, INNOVATIVE format, and hard-nosed promotion stand out as key aspects of the newsreel's operational strategy. The
selective discussion of the newsreel and its relation to modernity in this
chapter concerns primarily the promotional overlap between newsreels,
series, and serials on the American market in the mid-1910s, and their
shared strategy of putting forward girls as the center of attention in order to connect with young female patrons.[2] The discussion of the *Hearst-
Selig News Pictorial* is confined to a string of slots featuring roving reporter Grace Darling and the celebrity status conferred on her during
a protracted trip in early 1915 which was designed to boost California
on behalf of the *News Pictorial*. According to her biography, Darling had
previously appeared in uncredited bit parts in *Our Mutual Girl* and *Perils of Pauline*, but returned to modeling before being cast as a girl reporter, sponsored by Mary Pickford no less.[3] In this chapter, Grace Darling
furnishes the link between the newsreel and the serials—cliffhanging or
not—while Reliance's series in 52 installments, *Our Mutual Girl* starring
Norma Phillips, provides food for thought concerning the intermediary series format, which for Reliance led to production of a serial proper
with Phillips as the lead.

A conspicuous feature of the newsreel and related genres and formats
is the function of women as centers of attention—and particularly note-

worthy are the dynamics between these types of films. By focusing on the casting of women, the crossover between the newsreel, series, and serial becomes obvious when looking at the promotional contexts, that is the mutually reinforcing alliance between the press and film industry. Talking about casting in relation to newsreels might sound misguided at a time prior to the visible presence on the news scene of star reporters on CNN and other globally operating news organizations. Then again, the early newsreel emerged as a less pure genre than what one might perceive in hindsight and the division of labor between series and serials and newsreels proper was far from strict. The casting of Grace Darling represented a strategy for creating news and scoops exclusive to the *News Pictorial*, a wished-for effect reinforced by the intense promotional buildup in the Hearst press. The slots featuring Darling were interspersed with the sensational material advertised as the prime focus of newsreel reporting, much in the vein of the sensational events affecting young women in serial films.

Our Mutual Girl and its series format ran parallel to the early serials and functioned as the precursor to a later format, the cinemagazine, which additionally came across as human-interest oriented spin-offs from the newsreels with a decidedly female slant and targeting a sought-after audience base.[4] The Mutual series' final couple of episodes innovatively blended with Reliance's subsequent serial, *Runaway June*, thus opening a porous demarcation line between the formats. The Darling slots in the *Hearst-Selig News Pictorial*, and Mutual's series format as well, were highly transitory efforts, both leading up the more lasting serial format. Darling was thus featured in *Beatrice Fairfax*, and Norma Phillips moved from series Margaret to serial Jane.

The serious marketing endeavors for the Mutual series and Darling's segments in the *Hearst-Selig News Pictorial* both had in-house character. Mutual refrained from teaming up with a daily newspaper or magazine, instead opting to launch its own tie-in publication, *Our Mutual Girl Weekly*, after initially having showcased the series in its regular in-house publication, *Reel Life*. Hearst used his newspaper chain to propel the slots featuring Grace Darling in the newsreel, which were designed to advertise California's scenic assets, cultural heritage, and business opportunities after the opening of the Panama Canal and during the expositions in San Diego and San Francisco. Sending Darling through the Canal Zone via water highlighted the shifting geopolitical parameters

in the canal era, also signaling increased prosperity and immense opportunities for California and its economy at a time when the Golden
State and especially Southern California was already a powerful magnet
for tourists, entrepreneurs, and colonists from the Midwest. Transportation was crucial for California's prospects and access to markets, and
the near-seamless connection of various means of transportation figured
prominently during Darling's trip: Boats, airplanes, automobiles, and
trains interlocked Darling's journey to and excursions within California. The Panama Canal thus comes across chiefly as yet another gateway to California and a parallel track to the railroads, which had initially
opened up the area for incoming tourists and colonists, and for outgoing
goods, not least fruit and produce. The teeming business and construction boom in Southern California was thus expected to gain additional
momentum in the wake of the Panama Canal's opening, which prompted one financial institution to paint Los Angeles' glowing prospects in a
crossover ad made up as "a Moving Picture Show."

Representatives from the film industry, and particularly the trade
press, repeatedly tried to switch focus and downplay newspaper criticism
of the medium by highlighting the so-called yellow press' penchant for
sensationalist accounts as being even more instructive and gore-orient-
ed than what the screens offered their audiences. Crimes, accidents, and
disasters seemingly provided almost welcome pretexts for loud, in-your-
face print reporting predicated on a form of shock aesthetics. Reinforced
by innovative visual layout, such articles underpinned a sense of acute
crisis displayed by attention-grabbing typeface and the overall makeup of the page. Hearst's *New York Evening Journal* and Pulitzer's *Evening
World* were the unrivaled masters of the yellow sheets thriving on this
mode of reporting. Visual frenzy propelled the yellow reporting in alignment with the overall privileging of vision ushered in by metropolitan
modernity. The press, moving pictures, vehicular speed, and tourism are
key aspects of this visual upgrading, and cinema gradually replaced electricity as the prime metaphor for the invention of modern life.[5]

For many contemporary commentators, film culture in its effervescent guises emblematically embodied salient signs of an era associated
with modernity and its machines for an increasingly global flow of capital, labor, products, and representations. Stars turned into ideal commodities for global traffic in lifestyles and ideals fueling imaginaries and
fantasies, which were additionally underpinned by an industrialized fan

Los Angeles—"a Moving Picture Show—in 3 Reels"

The prime object of these "Moving" Pictures *is to set people thinking.* When people don't *think* they can't be reached—and they won't *act.* If people don't do any *thinking,* they are not to be reached even with "Moving" Pictures. But when they *do* get to thinking they are apt to act.

So many things are happening these days, and so many other things are about to happen, that we feel as if we were not doing our duty unless we posted these happenings, present and to come, in large pictures, before your eyes, and said: "There, now, is proof of what we have been contending. Will you believe it now, and, believing, will you follow instructions?"

THE THREE YEARS OF PLENTY

As this Company has repeatedly said before in its ads, there are three years of plenty before us—'13, '14, '15. Great things are to be done in these three years. The greatest feat of engineering of 1913, almost, if not quite, equal to the digging of the Canal, is that of the Aqueduct, where, at a cost of millions, this city is bringing water overland, through tunnels, over hills and valleys, hundreds of miles, into its own reservoirs, a priceless gift for those here now and for the generations who will follow them. Wonderful —but we are getting so used to wonderful things that we miss seeing some of them.

The pictures move fast before the visions of the citizens of Los Angeles, like a three-ring circus, where there is so much going on one can only catch a glimpse here and there as they unfold before our eyes.

ARE YOU READY FOR OPPORTUNITY?

The vital question before you is, What will you do with your opportunities in the three years before you?

Here stands a new Company, alive to what's going on, which says, "Climb aboard and ride to the front with us." Will you do it? We can't *make* you.

To our intense gratification, an army of men and women *have* already responded to our call, with the result that we have broken all records for *stock selling during a three weeks' period!*

MAKING PEOPLE THINK

So, you see, these sermonettes we have been preaching each Sunday morning must have been reaching some people and making them think.

If we can only get people to *think,* then they will come up here and *argue,* and if they will *argue,* then they will *join* us, for none can argue *against* us.

We are simply taking the tide at its flood, and that sort of work leads on to fortune. They can see it as well as we can.

CO-OPERATION IS THE THING

We were saying that if we could get people to come and talk over the situation with us, we could convince them of what is before them and us, and how easy and thoroughly practical it is, to *co-operate,* so all can share according to our holdings.

"MOVING" PICTURES

Picture No. 1 shows the opening of the great Canal. The first boat through will be headed, we believe, for the "First Port of Entry"—Los Angeles, Queen of the Pacific.

The opening of that Canal, the sailing of the first boat, the completion of the waterway, marks the beginning of a new epoch in the history of Los Angeles.

Picture No. 2—Ships of all nations in the harbor and flags of all nations waving and snapping in the breeze.

This picture is to prove to you that picture No. 3 must come true within the time set, five years later—Los Angeles, a million in 1920, built solid from the foothills to the sea—A WORLD CITY.

All three pictures are meant to stimulate your powers of imagination. Without imagination man would be rooting in the ditches, and even if we all are blessed with it, we need something to stimulate it every so often, so we can take in a wider perspective than usual.

WHAT IT MEANS TO YOU

If you have any interests in this city, the opening of that waterway in 1915 will make those interests more valuable. If you have *no* interests, then come and *join us,* and get some, at once. We have a place for you, but we are throwing you a line, *right now,* and beg you to reach out for it, haul it in and make fast, now, so *you* can be, not merely an *interested* spectator, but an interested stock owner, a co-operator, with an axe to grind in future events.

Come and join *our* army.

We will make you pay 12 cents a share for your stock today, but that is nothing to what you will have to pay sixty days from now.

A BOOM AT LAUREL CANYON HEIGHTS

Our big subdivision at Laurel Canyon Heights, near Hollywood, over 750 lots, is attracting the attention of buyers, and each day sees greater activities out there.

Each day our Autos are busy taking people out to this beauty spot, people who demand something else besides a house and lot on a side street. *That's not typical of California.*

They want a Vista of Mountain, Valley and Sea, and still they can't go into the wilds to get the combination. That's not practical. But Laurel Canyon Heights offers the solution of their problem, as it lies *within 30 minutes of Broadway, and every lot has a beauty of its own.* And so, Laurel Canyon Heights is enjoying a season of great activity. Lots are being purchased, and directly we shall see a number of artistic bungalows and chalets dotting the sides of these romantic homesites.

But lots at $200 will no longer be available when that day comes. They should be selling at double today's prices.

HOW CAN WE PROFIT BY THE PICTURES?

"MOVING" PICTURES are mostly thrown on the screen of memory— they are fleeting. Some of us profit by them, some not.

It is a little thing to ask—that you come and say "Howdy-do!" Come and look into our faces, see what we look like, talk to us, see what we are aiming at and striving for, and why we are so anxious to get going in the shortest possible time.

We are all traveling along the same road—with the same goal in sight—the goal of Success, and in our opinion we can reach it better by working together.

A RAISE IN PRICE OF STOCK IS NEAR

The shares of stock in *First National Securities Company* are now 12 cents, *but only for a short time. The activities of our Laurel Canyon Heights properties demand a higher price. We advise the purchase of stock now before the entire 12c allotment is taken.*

Meanwhile, shall we send you our book, "The Greatest Investment"?

ANNOUNCEMENT: *Owing to the enormous response to our advertising and the consequent crowding of our offices daily by the buyers interested in the FIRST NATIONAL SECURITIES COMPANY'S stock, we have found it necessary to SEEK LARGER QUARTERS, and have secured the entire building at 645 South Spring Street. Temporary offices will be maintained at the new address while the extensive work of remodeling and refinishing of the offices is going forward. WATCH US EXPAND. LOOK FOR THE BIG EAGLE. The Spring Street offices will be open evenings.*

FIRST NATIONAL SECURITIES COMPANY, Inc.

Home Builders—Subdividers

314-317 Story Building

Phone Home F4531

Phone Main 3338

Sixth and Broadway, Los Angeles

Cut this out and mail at once to First National Securities Co. 314-317 Story Building.

I hereby subscribe for and agree to purchase ....shares of your stock at 12 cents per share, payable $........cash, and balance in nineteen installments of $........ per month.

Signed ....
Address ....

Schedule of 20 Monthly Payments At 12 Cents per Share		
$ 1.20 Monthly pays for	200 shares, total	$ 24
1.80 Monthly pays for	300 shares, total	36
2.40 Monthly pays for	400 shares, total	48
3.00 Monthly pays for	500 shares, total	60
6.00 Monthly pays for	1000 shares, total	120
12.00 Monthly pays for	2000 shares, total	240
30.00 Monthly pays for	5000 shares, total	600
120.00 Monthly pays for	20,000 shares, total	$2400

FIGURE 33: The city in three reels, *Los Angeles Tribune,* 9 February 1913, 7.

culture spawned by fan magazines and the coverage of film matters in newspapers—and by having newsreel slots built around a star reporter, or a star playing a reporter.

In the early 1910s the newsreels positioned themselves on the journalistic entertainment market by implementing modes of address designed to corral a broad cross-section of film publics. When domestic newsreels had established a foothold on the news market in 1914, after Pathé's pioneering efforts from 1911 onwards, the U.S. trade press could not resist scoffing at the yellow press at a time when film censorship was on the agenda in many states. In January 1915 *Moving Picture World* wrote:

> For a clean record of the news, omitting all tales of crimes, we have to turn to the motion picture weeklies. We have seen scores of these weeklies and they have all been singularly and gratifyingly free from the portrayal of contemporaneous crime. They have amply demonstrated that it is possible to inform the public of all important current events without specializing in crime stories. [---] We ask the heroes of yellow journalism all and singular to watch the motion picture weeklies and take their cue of what is fit to print from the news-screen.[6]

Equating clean reporting with suppression of crime reporting, which is only one facet of sensationalism, provides a somewhat narrow model for adjudicating both print and cinematic newscasters.

On February 28, 1914, a novel American newsreel hit the screen, a cine-publication with one leg firmly rooted in William Randolph Hearst's press empire, a newsgroup unafraid of unconventional and pugnacious publishing practices. A promotional notice for the upcoming newsreel marked the day in stalwart and almost threatening terms by announcing that "the first big gun will be fired."[7] In true yellow fashion, and contrary to the assessment quoted from the *Moving Picture World* regarding the sobriety of newsreel reporting, the trade-press ad in large, bold typeface offered a set of sound cues promising colorful stuff in an informative headline reading "Whizz! Bang! Smash!" The wording, more visceral than cerebral, alludes to speed and crashes, and in an all but celebratory manner rivets its attention to the exigencies of modernity to be scooped up from the metropolitan fabric and briskly disseminated to screens everywhere. Fast-paced mobility, earsplitting energy, and urban disarray bolster this far from unsophisticated promotional set of threats, not to mention shock-oriented exclamations framing the news-reel scene. The headlines seem to cater to those savvy straphangers and street-smart urbanites with a selectively insulated mindset that populated and traversed the modern urban landscape, according to Georg Simmel's influential analysis of turn-of-the-century metropolitan mental life. For Simmel, a proper balance between sensory attention and selective intake of impressions was critical for the subject's equilibrium. The stakes were high—miss a beat and you risk ending up in the papers as a victim of an urban accident. Contemporary accounts of the metropolitan terrain in many respects depicted a form of war zone replete with sensational occurrences readily available for newspeople to scoop.

In terms of subject matter, it thus sounded as if the *Hearst-Selig News Pictorial*, under Edward A. McManus' stewardship, was embarking on decidedly yellow course (sensations minus crime reporting)—the whizz-bang-smash model. According to a press release, one could hence expect "battles, riots, wrecks, massacres, holocausts,—in fact, sensational happenings all over the world."[8] The emphasis on the sensational sounded very much like a Hearstian recipe for news coverage, and far removed from the role-model impression conveyed by the *Moving Picture World* when reproving the yellow press for its predilection for sensationalist reporting.

The *Hearst-Selig News Pictorial* emanated as a joint venture between a major press organization and one of the leading film companies. The Hearst conglomerate housed sensational sheets and more sober papers in addition to several magazines and special-interest publications. Gradually, the organization began to publish film-related material in its dailies, for instance lengthy plot lines for Pathé releases, later storylines for serial films, for instance *Perils of Pauline* and *Exploits of Elaine*, and long feature articles in the Sunday supplements on educational films. Eventually, the Hearst organization distributed both fiction films and news-reels by way of a subsidiary company, International Film Service. One of its own productions, *Beatrice Fairfax*, a serial featuring Grace Darling, in clever ways harked back to the *Hearst-Selig News Pictorial*, though even more so to the daily operations at the *New York Evening Journal* and an advice column for the lovelorn published under the name of Beatrice Fairfax. Selig Polyscope, Hearst's partner for the newsreel, was among the pioneers in the film field and also an intrepid innovator in respect to using newspapers for marketing purposes.[9] Scores of newspapers printed fictionalized accounts of the installments for the Selig serial *The Adventures of Kathlyn*, written by Harold McGrath, which commenced publication just before New Year's Eve, 1913; its success inspired multiple promotional alliances for serials. A.P. Robyn, Sunday editor and syndication manager for the *Chicago Tribune*, orchestrated the publishing feat for Kathlyn.[10] He later established his own organization and continued to connect serial films with the press, for instance *Lucille Love: The Girl of Mystery* produced by Universal, and Reliance's *Runaway June* distributed by Mutual.

Thus, 1914 was a pregnant year in terms of cross-fertilizing alliances between the film industry and the press after an initial promotional flurry in magazines in 1912 for the Edison/McClure series *What Happened to Mary?*, which was published in *Ladies' World* from August 1912.[11] The installments were released once each month, matching the pace of the magazine's publication. Publishing storylines seems however to have been pioneered by the *Chicago Tribune* late in 1911 and continuing into early 1912 in alliance with Chicago-based film companies: Essanay, Selig, and American Film Manufacturing Co. Hearst's *New York American* elected however on two occasions in April 1910 to publish elaborate storylines illustrated with cartoons from Kalem's *The Gypsy Girl's Love* and an unnamed Pathé film.[12]

Before actively entering the film field, the Hearst press had led the way in instituting unconventional methods for handling film matters, particularly in New York during the year 1913. *Variety* characterized the policy at the *Evening Journal* as a trading of film write-ups for liberal advertising, a claim approached from a less critical perspective by Robert Grau in his early 1914 *Theater of Science* and previously by Will Irwing. According to *Variety*, other evening papers emulated the *Evening Journal*'s practice and replaced critics with movie editors expected to solicit advertisements. This good-notices-for-ads policy was discernible at the *Sun*, *World*, and *Globe*.[13] In some of the sheets this state of affairs represented a drastic turnabout after years of recurring crusades against both film representations and exhibition practices. The Hearst organization had a less inflammatory track record in this respect, even if the *Evening Journal* had staged a campaign as early as 1899 against indecent film representations in penny-in-the-slot machines.[14] Hearst was no stranger to film, however. He had himself used sync-sound film technology for reaching voters in upstate New York during the gubernatorial election in 1906, which he lost.[15] Moreover, his paper in Los Angeles had actively promoted the local nickelodeon culture by offering coupons to its Sunday readers late in 1908, as previously discussed. "The newspapers have awakened to the fact that there is circulation in motion picture news, and their coming to the field is the proverbial 'bow to the inevitable,'" wrote the *New York Dramatic Mirror*, providing examples such as Hearst's promotion of Pathé, the stories of Kathlyn in scores of papers, the storylines in the *Chicago Tribune*, and the film-news column in *New York Herald*.[16]

Hearst's alliance with Selig to make newsreels came to the fore as somewhat of a surprise in early 1914, but it was no secret that Hearst and his people had for some time entertained plans of entering the film field. A more likely partner had no doubt been Pathé, given that Hearst, in February 1914, began syndicating stories of Pathé films under the heading "Read play, then enjoy movies" and started to promoting *Perils of Pauline* in March, a serial more or less produced by Hearst but released via Pathé and General Film.[17]

Pathé had been the dominating force on the American newsreel market since 1911 when its American newsreel edition, *Pathé Weekly*, was first released.[18] This was a highly successful endeavor, but Pathé was apparently unwilling to share the glory let alone profit with Hearst on the newsreel front—thus Hearst's partnership with Selig. The Pathé newsreel moved from weekly to biweekly and later even daily service to compete with the *Hearst-Selig News Pictorial*. A joint venture with the Associated Press for newsgathering paved the way for Pathé's daily edition, which was soon scaled back, mainly due to a war-related lack of the type of film stock used for the *Pathé Daily*. Effective distribution required the non-inflammable stock produced in France only. Regular nitrate stock could not be shipped in the mail, and hence the daily service had to be discontinued, with the daily edition reemerging as a weekly release labeled *Pathé News*. Pathé's publicity manager, Herbert Case Hoagland, underscored the importance of shipping via "Uncle Sam's mail" when the daily service was launched.[19]

At a time when Pathé was rethinking its place on the American market and particularly its relationships with the licensed companies and their distribution network, General Film, the news service was a vital component of the operations along with the new serial format released under the Eclectic brand. Apart from *Perils of Pauline*, the serial films produced in cooperation with Hearst were predominantly shot in an Ithaca studio owned by the Wharton Brothers.[20] After Charles Pathé's visit to the United States rumors abounded, for example that Fox was going to take over the studio complex in Jersey City. This did not happen, but Pathé adopted a new business strategy tailored after the publishing industry: packaging and distributing finished products instead of producing films themselves. Charles Pathé arrived in the U.S. on December 27, 1913, and stayed for a couple of months; this was his first visit since 1908, when the alliance with the licensed companies had necessitated his presence. His lengthy stay attests to the gravity of the situation in early 1914; in fact, his two visits bookend Pathé's involvement with the licensed companies.[21]

When the *Hearst-Selig News Pictorial* premiered in late February 1914, which just like the *Pathé Weekly* was distributed via General Film, the already tense relations between General Film and Pathé turned even worse. The leading vaudeville chain, United Booking Office, replaced the Pathé service with the *Hearst-Selig News Pictorial* at some of the flagship houses, which coincided with a general drop-off in demand as the result of strategies orchestrated within General Film in relation to the licensed exchanges that supplied exhibitors nationwide. Pathé took legal action and published an open letter in the trade press in May 1914, some three months after the Hearst-Selig newsreel had premiered.[22] It seems as if the conflict regarding the newsreel was the last straw for Pathé. Eventually, the company left General Film at a time when the organization was under severe pressure for business practices allegedly violating the antitrust laws and a court investigation was in its final phase. As worrisome for the trust was the progressively increasing strength and might of the independent organizations, now posing real threats on the market. When Pathé left General Film, the company began to distribute temporarily under the Eclectic organization, before teaming up with Mutual. Eventually, Pathé launched a new company of its own for distribution, the longstanding Pathé Exchange.

The year 1913, and 1914 even more so, marked several important changes in the American film industry, as indicated by the fledgling columns devoted to film matters. Besides a slow shift to feature production triggered by the success of the European titles and their stars on the American market, the mushrooming serial format provided vehicles for new marketing strategies and product differentiation. The protracted release span for the serials and the longevity of their theatrical presence inspired promotional initiatives to capitalize on this new type of commodity. Previously, the mostly daily program changes and its variety format had more or less precluded newspaper advertising due to the model's brisk exhibition clip. This was a time when several studios and exchanges upgraded their publicity departments and staffed them with experienced marketers, agents, and newspaper journalists. Overall, the focus on features and serials provided a rationale for marketing efforts on the local exhibition scene, but also beyond it. A first national ad campaign was in fact placed for *Our Mutual Girl* in the *Saturday Evening Post* in late 1913, in addition to general ads for the exchange brand in Sunday newspapers.[23] Mutual's visibility in the press coincided with the first round of shooting at the new Reliance studio in Yonkers in early December. Janet Staiger, Jane Gaines, and Moya Luckett have, in important essays and from different perspectives, analyzed the new marketing approaches and their scope, modes of address, and relations to reception and gendered spectatorship.[24]

The newsreel proper, which for a long time coexisted on the bill together with other short subjects, leading to the feature, and which also found a place on the vaudeville bills, displayed a variety format within its own reel in addition to being a component of variety programs. In the main, features did not kill off the variety model; the true culprit was the strict regulation of format in terms of feet per unit, namely a full program comprised of a diverse set of single-reel films—all of them 1000 feet long if not split reels—and in its early stages perhaps an illustrated song thrown in for good measure. *Our Mutual Girl* displayed an unprecedented level of heterogeneity and variety within its 1000-foot format offered free of charge to subscribers of the Mutual service, which was evidenced by an early outline in the trade press.

> These films will show a young country girl in her simple home, and taken in the midst of fashionable New York, whither her wealthy aunt has taken her to make of her a society belle. She will be shown with the most prominent people in New York, socially, financially, artistically, musically and politically, in the great show places of the great metropolis, in the smartest shops, hotels and theaters, at the horse show, the opera, and in the stock exchange, meeting the biggest steamship in the world, the massive *Imperator*, at her dock.
>
> Her gowns, her hats, her furs, her hose, her boots, her gloves, her lingerie, her jewels, all will be the most beautiful, the smartest up-to-the-minute equipment which the fashion experts can supply.[25]

Eileen Bowser, in a passing comment, perceptively discerns the series' hybridism and adequately characterizes it as "somewhere between a newsreel and a serial."[26] A closer look at the early newsreel genre reveals a hybridism focusing predominantly on hard news and sensations—mixed with lighter items at times delivered in a playful fashion—and fashion proper turned into a mainstay of the newsreels. Newsreels were on the bill primarily for entertainment purposes and can therefore hardly be described as journalism proper, though the Sales Co.'s *Animated Weekly*, for instance, was marketed as "A Visualized Newspaper" in 1912.[27] The newsreel in addition covered an array of scheduled events besides what we now call breaking news, the sensations. The latter category was for obvious reasons presented well after the fact, with some notable exceptions. Then again by, for instance, placing cameras close to the line of fire during WWI, footage hovering between the scheduled and the breaking was captured. By chance or accident, tragic news sometimes took place in front of the camera, for example when the aviation show in conjunction with the opening of Universal Studios in March 1915 ended in disaster. Staging events was sometimes an irresistible temptation—hence, faked news was a more or less regular component of the newsreel; Raymond Fielding accounts for scores of examples in his pioneering survey of the American newsreel.[28] An analysis of the makeup of these reels reveals a highly mixed format balancing its core slots: scheduled events and the sensational type of material advertised for the Hearst-Selig run, the whizz-bang-smash model, interspersed with lighter material, for instance the slots featuring Grace Darling.

Before focusing on the Hearst-Selig newsreel and Grace Darling, let us take a brief look at Mutual's series experiment inaugurated in early 1914, *Our Mutual Girl*, starring Norma Phillips, which ran for a year in weekly releases.[29] No copies of the 52 episodes seem to have survived, so the outlines are based on paper sources: promotional material from Mutual's in-house publications—*Reel Life* and *Our Mutual Girl Weekly*—in addition to information gleaned from the trade press. As a protracted advertising gimmick, the series was designed to draw attention to the Mutual network of distribution. By offering both the series itself and the promotional magazine, *Our Mutual Girl Weekly*, free of charge to service subscribers, Mutual tried to orchestrate product differentiation by highlighting the brand and the logo, thus hoping to set them apart from the competition.

The series format offers more or less standalone, self-contained units—and in this case highly eclectic content—while the serials, in terms of content, display a higher degree of homogeneity in an open-ended, if not always cliffhanging structure. Both formats call for visit after visit to the theater: the serial for resolution or closure, the series for vicariously following the enterprising girl's various endeavors week after week, eventually leading up to marriage. *Our Mutual Girl* sported an innovative format in its crossover between serial-like strings of suspense running across several segments of the series before climaxing or at times only petering out without a proper resolution, and regular standalone slots. The series was written and directed by different authors and directors in a relay, which further added to the heterogeneity. The overarching elements were combined with commercial-like display and instruction, besides featuring appearances by well-known personalities at times bordering on newsreel slots. The series was predicated upon placing the girl, Margaret, in situations featuring celebrities and allowing her to hobnob with a wide gamut of famous people from sportsmen to newspaper cartoonists, from capitalist/philanthropists like Andrew Carnegie to actors, for instance a young Douglas Fairbanks. The situations Margaret encountered were framed by the series' premise—a young (she turns 18 in one installment), inexperienced country girl coming to New York City, but not meeting the fate indicative of the white-slave films à la *Traffic in Souls*. Instead, the audience was invited to experience the wonders of the metropolitan world together with someone not at home in this epitome of modernity with all its landmarks, celebrities, opportunities, temptations, and risks. And a girl could shop—assuming access to money was no issue—meet fascinating people, make a difference through charitable and resourceful initiatives in the progressive vein, and also face plotting akin to the crime serials, which occasionally provided a suspenseful backdrop for Margaret's navigation of the metropolis. This literal navigating by way of limousine was a staple of the series harking back to the well-established phantom-ride format for taking in metropolitan space, landmarks, and lively street panoramas. A couple of episodes featured automobile scenes so risky that a stand-in for Norma Phillips was summoned, namely Jean De Kay.[30]

Margaret's guardian, Aunt Knickerbocker, lived in a palatial mansion on Fifth Avenue, which turned into the main transportation artery for automotive excursions in the series, up until Margaret relocates to the Westchester area to stay with another aunt after a clash with Aunt Knickerbocker. Romantic interests permeated the series. Margaret's own preferences in this respect seldom sit well with her "patrician" Aunt Knickerbocker until the final episode, when the liaison with Jack Stuyvesant offers closure by seemingly ending the girlish phase of Margaret's life. Jack was introduced in episode 28, when Margaret and her entourage look for a mysterious woman along the Jersey coast.

The series started off with the Girl receiving an invitation from her aunt to come to New York City to visit. Margaret arrives at New York's Pennsylvania Station and was whisked in a limousine to Aunt Knickerbocker's posh residence on Fifth Avenue. The latter part of the first installment shows Margaret looking at gowns at a renowned fashion boutique as part of a makeover directed by the aunt. "Little mannerisms and personalities—not objectionable in her country home—go through a modifying process resembling the polishing of a diamond."[31] The italicized text in the promotion for the series assured readers that "[i]n no single instance has any portion of her wardrobe been loaned as a model." The producer of the series paid for "frocks and frills," which is an interesting aspect of the series' promotion of New York's most exclusive shopping venues—if accurate.[32]

In the second episode, the plot already began to thicken with the introduction of a melodramatic component spilling over to the next few installments and running in tandem with Margaret's progressively busier social calendar, thrilling tourism, and voracious shopping. John Storm, a sweetheart from Margaret's hometown, has followed her to New York City and secured a job at the Cunard Steamship pier. John notices a suspicious-looking character—a foreign count tailored from stock melodrama fabric—and trails him to Margaret's new domicile. At this point, the mode abruptly relays from melodrama to shopping, but instead of gowns, hats were featured in episode two. Margaret also finds time for a sporting event—a football game between Yale and Princeton in New Haven; this latter segment could very well have been part of a regular newsreel. The installment closes with a celebrity slot when Margaret meets with the only woman senator in the U.S., Mrs. Helen Robinson, who represents Colorado. Encounters with successful women—at times worked into the plot line, at times by sheer happenstance—became a fixture of the series.

The storyline involving John Storm continues through episode six; thereafter, both he and the count fade from the series seemingly without explanation, at least judging from the printed synopses. A climax for this arc connects installment five and six. In episode five, Margaret meets Andrew Carnegie while en route to a shopping spree at Jaeckel & Sons' fur house, spotting Mr. Carnegie, in his garden at Fifth Avenue and 19th Street, from the car. The shoppers make a stop and are introduced by a mutual friend of the business tycoon/philanthropist and Aunt Knicker-bocker.[33] The series offers several close encounters with the fourth es-tate, at times generating cross-coverage in the columns. In episode 16, Margaret, after giggling over a funny cartoon in the *New York Tribune*, visits the newspaper's offices and is sketched by cartoonist Clare Briggs. In other episodes, she meets with celebrities well known from the col-umns, for instance Dorothy Dix and Irving S. Cobb. In due course, the latter emerged as the author of a few episodes.[34] And one night Margaret sneaks into the offices of the *New York Times* to hinder publication of an unfavorable article.

The most appreciated stretch of the series from the perspective of nar-rative coherence opens in semi-documentary or topical fashion when Margaret meets New York's commissioner of corrections, Katherine B. Davis, before visiting Blackwell's Island, which housed New York's facil-ities for delinquents.[35] A victim of vicious scheming, Ada had ended up at Randall's Island, but through Margaret's intervention and by way of legal assistance provided by Inez Milholland Boisevain, she is released. Milholland Boisevain had been introduced in episode seven as a mem-ber of an exclusive group of suffragists. Ada's release leads to a criminal plot in which Margaret appears to be kidnapped and is, in fact, totally absent from an entire installment. Eventually, it turns out that a reck-less autoist, whom nurses Margaret back to health at his mother's house, had hit her. This story development was applauded by the critics in *Mov-ing Picture World*: "The story, now that it has got started on the right track, keeps up well—frocks and frills have given place to melodrama. [---] Plain clothes men and gangsters look like the real thing."[36] The follow-ing week, a critic from *Moving Picture World* was even more enthusiastic: "This installment has some of the best city street work we have seen any-where. The very slums of the city, not a catch of them, but the whole tan-gle, seem to be laid before us."[37] Then the series shifted tone once more and returned to "frocks and frills," which represented the outset, provid-ed the selling points in the ads. For the opening episode, the Broadway Theater promised "a fashion story told in motion pictures" showing off "the very latest smartest things in gowns & hats & furs."[38] Obviously, the heterogeneous format troubled critics looking for straightforward narrative momentum unhampered by the series' standing sidebars devoted to consumerism, sightseeing, and social functions.

When the storyline turns serial, Margaret is initially not as resourceful as some of her more daring sisters in the serial films proper—say a Helen or Kathlyn—but in between trying on garments at "a well-known sporting house," she also conducts a fingerprint test in the same installment.[39] Moreover, she proves to be both brave and highly resourceful in episode 46 when single-handedly rounding up a couple of thieves. In installment number 43, with a new author and producer in charge, John W. Grey, Norma Phillips got to play two roles in an episode apparently replete with double exposures and camera tricks and featuring Margaret in a more active mode than usual. Special effects also ended episode seven when Margaret, after a strenuous day, dreamt that she was dancing with the city and its landmark buildings.

The last few episodes were built around well-known authors telling Margaret their favorite stories, and visits to artists in their studios. In the concluding episode Margaret reviews her experiences and finds a new lover and, as *Moving Picture World* describes it, "she finds promise of future happiness. In the closing scenes she bids good-bye to the observer."[40] The ending of the series spans two episodes with partly metafilmic character besides functioning as launching pads for Reliance's new serial *Runaway June*, which transformed the former Mutual Girl to serial queen proper. In episode 51, James Montgomery Flagg arrives for a meeting with Margaret at the Union Square film studio, but Our Mutual Girl is late. Flagg had already drawn Margaret's portrait in episode 32. He manages to steal inside and pokes around in the busy studio, and when Margaret arrives, they shoot some scenes. Later on Oscar Eagle, the director of *Runaway June*, mistakes Flagg for an extra, and Flagg is cast for a bit part and paid as an extra without revealing his identity. The promotion for the final episode explicitly steered audiences to the upcoming serial written by George Randolph Chester. "In this serial your favorite actress will appear weekly," spectators were informed.

Our Mutual Girl was not promoted by way of a coalition with the daily press in the same way as Kathlyn and most other serials, but it was prepromoted by advertising in the *Saturday Evening Post*. *Our Mutual Girl's* numerous links to advertising practices is excellently covered in Moya

Luckett's essay on the series. The production company, Reliance, instituted a new weekly magazine within the Mutual organization, aptly named *Our Mutual Girl Weekly* and explicitly catering to a feminine readership, a couple of months into the series. The publicity department at Mutual was one of the best in the business and extensive enough to produce three publications: *Mutual Movie Fillers*, *Reel Life*, and "a new woman's publication of sixteen pages, entitled *Our Mutual Girl Weekly*."[41] It was headed by Philip Mindil, brought in from *Vanity Fair*, and staffed by a select group of newspaper veterans: Arthur James, former editor of the *New York Sunday Telegraph*; W. Bob Holland, formerly assistant manager of the American Press Association's news service; Helen Starr of *Vogue* and the *New York Herald*; Robert S. Doman of the *Evening Sun*; Frank J. Wilstach, a former theatrical press agent, and Albert S. Le Vine, formerly of the *New York Times* and *New York American*.[42]

The multiplicity of topics embraced by *Our Mutual Girl*, evident from my cursory run-through, partly overlapped with the newsreel's heterogeneity, and some of the featured events could easily have been slotted into newsreels. The format seems to have been too disparate and eclectic to be really successful, however. When the series came to a close in late 1914, it was unsurprisingly supplanted by a regular serial, *Runaway June*, featuring the former Our Mutual Girl Margaret, Norma Phillips, as the lead. During the series' run during 1914, the serial format had proved to be highly successful and was consequently adopted by virtually all studios, and the most appreciated episodes in *Our Mutual Girl* were in the serial vein, hence the conversion.

The newsreels adopted elements from *Our Mutual Girl*—if not the other way around, which seems likely, considering early Pathé and Gaumont newsreels featuring fashion. Fashion turned into a regular aspect of the *Hearst-Selig News Pictorial* when Lucille, that is Lady Duff-Gordon, showed the latest fashion every other week or so; she was also awarded space in the Sunday Supplements of the Hearst papers. In addition, Lucille was responsible for Pearl White's outfits in the serial films. Later, fashion was a prime focus for a serial produced by Hearst's International, *The Adventures of Dorothy Dare*. Sports events fitted comfortably into both *Our Mutual Girl* and the *Hearst-Selig News Pictorial* and so did celebrities; Andrew Carnegie, for instance, cameoed in both formats. Otherwise, the main topic for the newsreels in 1914 was of course the war in Europe. Eventually, in the early sound era, cinemagazines like *Eve's*

Film Review played down the serial elements, turning to a playful format that worked in the blurred area between the series à la *Our Mutual Girl* and the newsreel, at least in England. But the newsreels, too, were increasingly prone to incorporate human-interest slots, and even camera tricks—at times even resorting to faking news.[43]

Coinciding with the wrap-up of *Our Mutual Girl*, the *Hearst-Selig News Pictorial* introduced a novelty by putting a female reporter on the screen.[44] There was no promotional fanfare initially, but after a few weeks she was advertised as a major star and surrounded by unprecedented levels of media hype and promotional brouhaha. Grace Darling was however a non-entity when hired. A who's who section in *Moving Picture World* listed bit appearances in both *Perils of Pauline* and *Our Mutual Girl*, but for all practical purposes she was a film ingénue when allegedly moved from the newspaper ranks to the *News Pictorial*. She was born November 20, 1893, in New York City as Elsie with an unknown surname. On May 29, 1913, the *New York Telegraph* notified its readers that she had divorced a Harry Turek. She died on October 7, 1963, though in 1918 a few papers prematurely announced her death in an automobile crash; the deceased turned out to be another Darling, namely Ruth.

Grace Darling's first four slots for the *News Pictorial* were pretty inconspicuous. In *News Pictorial No. 6*, issued on January 21, 1915, she "visits the foreigners who sought to enter the United States; were denied admittance and have been held since the beginning of the war." At this time the *News Pictorial* was biweekly, but Miss Darling appeared as reporter only once a week. In *No. 8*, January 28th, she "goes down to New York Bay on a revenue cutter, boards incoming liner Lapland with other ship news reporters, interviews Edna May and pays a visit to the steerage." After interviewing a film actress, her next victim was the secretary of state, William Jennings Bryan, which entailed traveling to Washington, D.C. This section was part of issue *No. 10*, released February 4th. A week later, she visited a home for abandoned animals in New York City, which in a sense put an end to Grace Darling's stint as a rookie cine-reporter. From then on she was promoted as a star and an undisputed attraction. Her status and fame were in fact more or less non-existent, but the efforts put into the promotional process were tremendous due to the might of Hearst's newspaper empire. A couple of years after the build-up during her tour from New York City to California via Panama and then back via Chicago, one of the trade papers described her meteoric flight from scratch to alleged world-wide fame: "Upon her was bestowed the biggest campaign of publicity ever delivered by the most powerful chain of daily newspapers in the United States when Miss Darling made a continental trip from New York to California. [---] As the star of the *Hearst-Selig News Pictorial* she was photographed more actual times than any individual in the world. Stops were made in every important city, the leading officials visited and celebration held in honor of Miss Darling's arrival. An ovation was accorded her at every station, and she met innumerable celebrities of every station in life."[45] According to Selig's ads in the trade press, Darling was "the most popular young lady in the whole wide world." The massive publicity promised to "drive people" to the theaters.[46]

The profuse tie-ins for the serial films during 1914 had prepared for this unprecedented campaign, simultaneously turning the roving reporter into a celebrity. Her fame was non-existent beforehand, the result of a promotion that ushered in and confirmed her status in a form of shrewd spin-doctoring *avant la lettre*. The marketing of her slots rested on the practices tested out in the serial format, viz. advance coverage of screen content by way of stories in the press. The scripted nature of her slots in the newsreel made it possible to announce upcoming installments weeks in advance.[47]

A news item in the trade press noted that Miss Darling was engaged for a "series of special interviews with public personages for reproduction in motion pictures" and that on January 20th she had sailed from New York City for Colon, Panama, aboard the steamship Almirante. From there, the Great Northern was to take her to San Francisco via stops in San Diego and Los Angeles.[48] The Hearst press had introduced Grace Darling on January 20th. The *New York American* printed a letter dated January 19th, which she was to take from Governor Whitman to Governor Johnson in Sacramento, and an illustration from Albany showed Whitman handing the missive to Miss Darling. She was to chronicle her trip in the newspaper, and her article in the *American* further states that her name was "registered [by the] U. S. Patent Office."[49] A witty article in *Photoplay* toys with the scenario of a visit to the Patent Office to register far more than the name. The future scientist envisioned in the piece had not been able to uncover any trace of the patented model, a commodity worthy of protection in 1915. In a further spin on controlling the circulation of commodities, the Hearst press gleefully reported on Grace

Darling's attempt at patenting her face in 1916, during the release period for the *Beatrice Fairfax* serial. In contrast to the insurance of Pavlova's toes, Paderewski's hand, and all of Charlie Chaplin, which seemed fair enough to the anonymous writer, Darling's endeavor is described as a "stunt," which is somewhat surprising to read in the Hearst press, perhaps signaling a strained relationship; the Fairfax series turned out to be Darling's last assignment for the Hearst corporation. The reason for the patent application was that "Grace Darling has for some time had cause for worry because other screen players have made themselves up to resemble her. [...] In case the application is granted the files of the patent office will be the richer by one marble replica of Miss Darling's face, carved by a competent sculptor."[50]

Whether Hearst's young maiden, divorcee Elsie Turek—before becoming, in addition to her name, a household face to allegedly appropriate—was named after the original Grace Darling in the first round before being patented by the corporation is unclear but highly probable. The "original" Grace Darling's bravery when rescuing survivors from a ship wrecked in the unforgiving North Sea is commemorated by a museum bearing her name in Bamburgh, England. Verbal accounts and visual depictions of her audacious feat proliferated, and as Elinor DeWire aptly put it: "She became the model for Victorian girls, her story of feminine courage repeated so often in magazines of the day that her name was absorbed into everyday English as a term meaning 'brave woman.' " Her perilous exploits that morning in 1838 resonated with the latter-day cinematic bravadoes performed by the intrepid heroines of serials in the mid-1910s.[51]

Besides writing about her experiences, Darling was to be featured in the *Hearst-Selig News Pictorial*. Her primary goal was visiting the Panama-Pacific Exhibition in San Francisco and traveling via waterways, making several stops along the way. The tone in her texts is excited, invoking fairy tales and explorations of old as a frame of reference for eager expectations. Her putative ordinariness and girlishness aligns her with a young female readership without extensive traveling experience, akin to the strategy adopted for *Our Mutual Girl*.

How'd You Like to Be the Patent Man?

How'd You like to work in the Patent Office?

Especially, the Model Department?

Perhaps it's going to be very interesting soon—highly interesting, in fact.

You see, something *alive* has just been patented.

It isn't guinea pig, or trained horse, or champion cow, or—performing chimpanzee.

It's a girl.

Its name is Grace Darling.

The Patent is held by the International News Service.

Now the government rules, like time, tide and Western Union clocks, admit no change. Rule A No. 1 special, Extra and Important, says that model *must* be filed.

Models, furthermore, must be exact.

Now, where can you find an e x a c t model of this Darling mechanism?

Remember—if it's not absolutely like the machinery it's supposed to represent it isn't a model. If there's any other hair in its eyebrow, or if its small shoe is a quarter size bigger—or even if there's an unclassified mole missed somewhere, it isn't right, and therefore it isn't a model as defined by the Patent Office.

It isn't probable, you see, that they can find a Darling model.

So, according to the present outlook, there's nothing for the Hearst-Selig newsmaker to do but to go to Washington, abandon all hope as she enters the Patent Office, and stand in a glass case not only for the rest of her natural life, but forever!

You see, they keep models very carefully preserved, so she couldn't grow old, but can you imagine what might happen about the year 2000 in that Patent Office?

Imagine day after tomorrow's scientist, in queer clothes and crystal spectacles and wearing antiseptic gloves, opening It's glass door, and taking It down—carefully—and blowing the dust from the nape of Its neck, and polishing up Its fluffy skirts with trembling hands, and showing It off to a new wondering century.

It is quite probable that this custodian of the live model would have to take It to keep It from getting rusty. How dreadful when Its small slippers couldn't tango, or if Its fingers lost their suppleness, or Its eyes some of their brightness!

How terrible it would be if a cold blast from the north should chap Its perfect hands, cause It to catch cold in Its beautiful throat, or to have to resort to cold cream for Its red and curving lips! Then i n d e e d would the owner of this patent fall upon the custodian in wrath—wouldn't you?

Grace Darling is a patented entity and a patented name.

Specifications, as viz., namely, to-wit and the following:

Size, petite.

Eyes, dark blue; have distracting effect.

Mouth, rose; can work at high speed; for effect, see eyes.

All attachments movable and highly practical except financial sense; this is said to be impractical, but is being treated with a gold process.

Detailed measurements and specifications—what they ought to be.

Photo in profile with hat. Caption: U.S. Patent No 9,999,999

Grace Darling's departure for California via Panama coincided with the release of the first rookie slot for the *News Pictorial*. The *American* printed her interview with "$100,000,000 Baby" Vinson Walsh McLean in Washington, D.C., illustrating the piece with a photo courtesy of the *News Pictorial*.[52] This particular assignment was however not outlined in the story section in *Moving Picture World*.[53] The *American* continued to publish stories involving her early newsreel slots the following Sundays. On the 31st her interview with Edna May was featured—it appeared in *News Pictorial No. 6*. On February 7th she interviewed an assortment of politicians in Washington, D.C., for *News Pictorial No. 8*: the Speaker Champ Clark, Secretaries Bryan and Daniels, among others. No print promotion seems to have been awarded her report on foreigners denied admittance to the U.S.; that slot appeared in *News Pictorial No. 6*. These articles, credited to Grace Darling, kept her in the pages between her departure from New York and publication of material from her trip. One can follow the promotion of Grace Darling's triumphant tour in the Hearst papers as a relay from New York via Los Angeles and San Francisco to Chicago, when the emphasis shifted between respective regions. The missives Miss Darling was taking from the mayor of New York City to the mayor of San Francisco, and from the governor of the State of New York to his California counterpart, functioned as relay batons.

Both the *New York Evening Journal* and the *New York American* carried her departing epistle on January 21st, but their illustrations differed. The *Evening Journal* showed her saying farewell to Fire Commissioner Robert Adamson, while the *American* had a photograph of her receiving the letter from Mayor Mitchel to be delivered to Mayor Rolph in San Francisco. On February 14th the *American* reported from her short stop in Los Angeles. Darling did not sign this article, but midway into it, the text is given over to her poetic waxing on California's beauty witnessed as she motored from San Pedro to downtown for a meeting with the brass at Hearst's *Los Angeles Examiner* before having lunch at the elegant Hotel Alexandria. The following day the *New York American*'s Sunday edition began publishing "The Dance Songs of Grace Darling," a series running up until number eight, published on March 28th. The first song was published on February 7th, though mistakenly labeled "The Dance Songs of Dorothy Darling." The series showcased different lyricists and composers, presenting new dance styles every week. Darling got to practice one of them during her visit to Chicago.

The chronology of the journey was not strictly preserved given the report from Los Angeles. The accounts from the sailing and the stops were put on hold to function as enticers to be published just prior to the release of the slots covering that segment of the trip in the *Hearst-Selig News Pictorial*, a pattern emulating the strategy for the serial films. *News Pictorial No. 16*, released on February 25th, depicted her "on board the Almirante, owned by United Fruit, en route to Panama."[54] The *American* offered its readership an account in her own words, which gave extra background for the upcoming newsreel slot. Darling's girlish prose bubbles with excitement, anticipation, and wide-eyed amazement. During the first phase of the trip she watches onboard drills and is brought up to speed concerning the functioning of the navigation instruments. The sighting of a drifting ship provided extra narrative embellishment.[55]

News Pictorial No. 18 featured her stop at Kingston, Jamaica, and a text in the *American* the Sunday before the Thursday release offered the backdrop. After chronicling the protracted landing at Kingston, Jamaica, Darling notices "colored people swarming over each other" at the docks, selling beads and fruit. Miss Darling is however whisked away by automobile from this colorful scene to the safe haven of her comfortable hotel. When the ship leaves the following day, hundreds of "deckers" were onboard. The exotic spectacle of this poor class of passengers was both astounding and "interesting [to] watch," particularly a vaccination process conducted by the ship's surgeon. "They were lying all over the deck, the mothers with their children in their arms and baskets of eatables beside them. They never moved from their position until we reached Colon, two days later. It seemed astonishing to think of people living that way."[56] The deck passengers furnish a poignant contrast to the elegance and upscale environments, otherwise providing a very different kind of backdrop for Grace Darling's travel adventures.

A week later, in *Hearst-Selig News Pictorial No. 24*, Grace Darling was seen leaving Panama to continue her trip to San Francisco. This newsreel slot was the last one promoted by the *New York American*. The young traveler wakes up when the ship arrives in Colon and dresses in a hurry, eager to observe the bustling activities. After passing through customs she is taken to a palace-like hotel. Along the way "the colored people sat along the streets with their children in their arms." The headline is blunter in the *New York Evening Journal*: "Panama a City of Darkies and Beautiful Cocoanut Palms."[57] The following day, Miss Darling took the Pull-

288

man to Panama City and the Canal Zone with its impressive locks and spillways. Her enraptured description evokes the technological sublime, and most fascinating to her was the small locomotives called electrical mules, which she associates with the "thrillers" at Coney Island. As if by chance, an engineer stops his mule and treats her to a ride down the incline. The mules' role was to pull big ships through the canal. Afterwards, she was invited to afternoon tea by the captain of the regiment stationed in the Zone. The account ends with the information that "[m]otion pictures showing events of Miss Darling's trip will be shown in the *Hearst-Selig News Pictorial* on Thursday, March 11th."[58] That very day, the *Evening Journal* published a second report by Darling from the Canal Zone in which she recounted her encounter with the acting governor, Col. Harding. The text ventures a slightly different account of the "deckers," this time Darling focuses on the "pretty little children." In Panama City "darkies," though now lumped together with "hackers," who were in charge of transporting tourists in their cabs, again dominate her narrative. A meeting with a local woman adds color to the Zone sojourn in several different senses.[59] The *Evening Journal* offered several shorter items to the newsreel releases penned by Darling, which were sandwiched between the companion pieces. Her short stop in San Diego, on the Panama City-to-San Francisco leg, merited an installment centered on her brief visit to the Panama-California Exposition, a tour guided by President Davidson himself after Darling met with the reception committee. Besides the exotic displays, foremost the Japanese and Indian villages, Darling admired the beautiful California scenery along Coronado Beach before re-boarding the Great Northern to sail onwards via Los Angeles.[60]

In episode number 26, released April 1st, Darling finally arrives in San Francisco, "receives an unusual reception, and visits the exposition." The account of her arrival was however published far ahead of the newsreel release. On February 16th the *Evening Journal* covered aspects of the entire trip from New York City to San Francisco; Darling's text is illustrated with photographs of a New York skyscraper on the left and a tall tower on the Exposition grounds on the right, connected by a photograph from one of the Panama Canal locks; the montage provides a neat emblematic, photographic concatenation of the water link between the East and West Coasts.[61] The smart Miss Darling, holding a suitcase and dressed in furs aplenty, is placed in the foreground of the photomontage, which symbolically bridges her physical travel between the photographed points. Apart from delivering the missives from New York City and Albany she was carrying, her mission, she claimed, was to describe the wonders of the Panama Canal and the Panama-Pacific International Exposition for readers. Contending with the limitation of language, she is grateful that the film camera is able to capture the indescribable marvels. "In fact I feel, when I hear the whirr of the camera every time I go any place, that you are all here, and while I know that you are not, I feel that you will feel as if you were when you see the pictures." The passage is indicative of the tone in Darling's texts and the constant attempts made at creating an allegiance with readers/spectators, an allegiance targeting predominantly young women. By focusing on the dream-and-fairy-tale-like aspects of the trip, the marvels, wonders, and the multitude of amazing encounters as discursive strategies for framing her experiences, Darling upgrades her girlish gaze and simultaneously downplays the exclusive slant of the trip and her own star status, hovering between vicarious reporting and scripted tourism. She looks far from girlish, however, when arriving in San Francisco garbed in smart furs. Overall, the voyage, and her encounters and impressions, invoke the exotic, the picturesque, and spectacle redolent of the technologically sublime within a discursive frame predicated on boosterism. From a putative girlish perspective, "the wonders and beauties of California" overwhelm her while the Golden State's two exhibitions signal glorious prospects after the opening of the Panama Canal.

The particular brand of feminine cine-journalism instituted by the *News Pictorial* was elaborated upon in a condensed introduction to a chronicle of Darling's trip in her own words:

The American newspaper reporter leads the vanguard for emancipated woman—a position attained not through any gallantry toward the sex or catering to feminine weakness; for she has survived the 'double-ci' and the 'scribe' in earning a place among the 'top-notchers' for pen cleverness— since the days Nelly Bly circumnavigated the globe with a small hand-bag, the news-seeking sisterhood has been persistent and progressive in chronicling the day's doings.

The latest type news-notcher is the moving picture reporter, originated and invented by Grace Darling, who is making the rounds of the continent as the representative of the Hearst-Selig News Pictorial. From the standpoint of enthusiastic and unprejudiced youth, she is looking over the ways of the world news and the works of man. From locations that may have grown monotonous and creations that may appear commonplace—vital interpretative sense given them a new and vivacious interest in delightful affiliation with the new art-form—moving pictures.[62]

Darling's youthful accounts were reinforced by a second part of the article as well as in an article published in the *Evening Journal*, both offering a much-needed outside perspective on Miss Darling's personality and experiences. Grace and gentle courtesy are keywords, in addition to her impressionable temperament. The texts further navigates gender stereotypes: "Miss Darling took almost a man's interest in the mechanism of the Panama Canal, but the woman's instinct showed plainly when she expressed delight at the little town of Gatun, with its picturesque surroundings." Her kitten-like qualities are emphasized by epithets like "girl tourist," "relish of schoolgirl," and "girl of spirit." She was however also a star, evidenced by the reception she was accorded in San Francisco, and she dressed the part: "Seldom has even the richest girl in the world had so many privileges and so wonderful a series of experiences, and seldom has San Francisco showered so many honors on any woman, splendid as is the attitude of Californians towards womankind," and San Francisco's mayor chimed in by endorsing Grace Darling's beauty. Adding an extra touch of modern adventure to her arrival, she was treated to a spin in a hydro-aeroplane before being automobiled over to the St. Francis Hotel for a lunch reception courtesy of Hearst's *San Francisco Examiner*.[63] *Movie Pictorial* "found Grace Darling as befitting her name, a blonde type, with clear cut features, svelte-lissome figure—a regular Nell Brinkley girl—pictorially impressive." She "unconsciously" carried her Cornell fraternity ring, and her innocence was further underscored by never having traveled west of Albany before.[64]

After her arrival in San Francisco, the principal coverage of the trip was turned over to Hearst's newspapers in San Francisco and Los Angeles. The *Los Angeles Examiner* liberally covered her days in California from her arrival in San Francisco to her departure from Los Angeles to return to New York City via Chicago. In a lengthy article the *Los Angeles Examiner* of February 15th primarily reported on a train trip along the "crookedest railroad in the world," from Mill Valley to the summit of Mount Tamalpais, featuring Grace Darling as engineer by special appointment. The bulk of the article recapitulated Darling's arrival in San

Francisco, when the steamship Great Northern was escorted into the harbor by an airplane circling above. Two photographs on the front page of section II depicted the plane circling and the second Darling stepped down the gangplank to be greeted by Mayor James Rolph. The *Los Angeles Examiner* described Grace Darling as a "winsome, lissome—ingenue and impressionable girl-child," adding "she has had all San Francisco at her feet since her arrival." Moreover, the text states explicitly that Darling was "scheduled to write her impressions for other girls all over the world to read." On her first full day in town Darling visited the Exposition and its host of halls and attractions during the opening days.[65] Overall, Darling had a very busy schedule in the Bay Area, so strenuous, in fact, that she suffered a small breakdown.[66] After acting as an engineer, she visited an Indian reservation, hobnobbing with Earl Cooper, the racer hoping to win the Vanderbilt Cup. In the depths of Sutro Forest she had an encounter with Ishi, "the wild man, the primitive being who was captured in the remote wilderness of the Sierras by the scientific experts." The *Los Angeles Examiner* again depicted Darling's activities in registers embracing the wonders of modernity, giving her report on the alleged primitive a racist slant by treating Ishi as an exhibit. "From the last word in twentieth century mechanism to the crude beginnings of primitive life went Grace Darling today." The reporter from the *Examiner* vicariously translated Ishi's emotions: "All the gallantry that slumbers in the breast of the cave man awakened in Ishi when he met his fair visitor."[67] Darling's stop at Stanford University did not however merit coverage in the *Los Angeles Examiner*, but was featured as a slot in the *News Pictorial No. 32*, released April 22nd, "Grace Darling at Palo Alto touring Stanford University."

Even if Darling was a celebrity in the making, she still enjoyed anonymity in San Francisco, while she later was mobbed in Chicago. The *San Francisco Examiner* even ventured an account with metafilmic implication when Darling took in herself on screen:

> During the afternoon Miss Darling's attention was attracted by a big sign announcing herself outside the Market Street Theater.
>
> So, in she went, paying her money and all unrecognized by ticket seller and collector alike, took a seat and watched herself go through several reels of film taken in New York before she left for her voyage of discovery to California.[68]

Thereafter, Darling traveled south, to Los Angeles, which she had already visited in passing during a stopover in San Pedro on her way north. The first time she was received at the *Examiner*, the second time around Hearst's partner, Selig, provided a spectacular background, the Selig Zoo, which was to formally open its gates on June 20th. The illustrations in the *Examiner* show her petting a leopard and, mounted on a ladder, feeding giraffes. The text describes her guided tour and her excitement in front of and inside the cages. The zoo provided the Selig studio with ample opportunities for staging pictures in exotic vistas filled with the kind of animals Darling faced: camels, zebras, lions and other big felines, an assortment of monkeys, and elephants. Darling's unfazed attitude vis-à-vis Bonita, the leopardess, matches another Selig star's affection for big cats, namely the serial queen Kathlyn Williams.[69] Grace Darling's visit to the Selig Zoo was featured in *News Pictorial No. 34*, released April 29, 1915.

From her base in Los Angeles Darling and the Hearst-Selig photographer visited San Gabriel and the old mission. The author of *The Mission Play*, John S. McGroarty, and the actor playing the part of Father Junipero Serra, George Ousborne, escorted her. She was treated to a history lesson and even got a chance to chime the historic bell from 1769. Darling's alleged unwillingness to leave and her hope to come back and spend more time was a fixture of her accounts, irrespective of where she visiting. She was however invariably whisked away to the next dot on her travel map, in this case a return visit to San Diego and the Exposition. The automobile taking her away from the Mission again bridges the gap between her own time and days of old, or so-called primitive cultures. As always, the young traveler assures her readers that she is fascinated and overwhelmed by all her "wonderful" experiences.[70] It does not seem as if this particular field trip was used in the *News Pictorial*.

In addition, the account from San Diego offered another summary of her trip from New York to Panama, material partly new to the readers in Los Angeles. The chronicling was in a sense local: The New York press followed the first leg of the trip before the California papers took over. On the way back, Hearst's Chicago newspaper covered her days in the Windy City, while her return to Gotham went unnoticed overall. The final slot from the journey ended up in *Hearst-Selig News Pictorial No. 36*, and showed Grace Darling at the California Panama Fair at San Diego.

Grace Darling Makes Beasts of Prey Her Pets

Hearst-Selig Star Discovers Friends in Zoo

'LOS ANGELES IS GLORIOUS'

By Grace Darling
Famous Hearst-Selig Moving Picture Star.

BACK again in Los Angeles, the glorious! I love this city and my regret at leaving wonderful San Francisco was forgotten only in the pleasure of coming back here.

When I first touched foot on Los Angeles streets I had only four hours, as I had to go on with the steamship Great Northern to San Francisco, but those four hours, brief as they were, were long enough to give me an inkling—just a tiny inkling, at least—of what living here all the time must mean.

All of this has already been proved again to me since my second arrival here. My ride through the downtown section showed me what a busy city Los Angeles is and the trip out to the Selig zoo and the lovely time I had with the animals there showed me another possibility in the combination of climate and moving pictures.

I had one of the most delightful times of my life at the Selig zoo, not only with the beasties, but in seeing the hills all covered with green—so much quicker than we would see the grass in the East. And the fine air and the beautiful flowers and the semi-tropical trees—oh, they are all just perfect!

The more I see of this city—and I want to see more of it, until there isn't a square foot of it that I have missed—I believe more and more that Heaven must be very, very near to Los Angeles.

HERE Are Snapshots of Grace Darling, Famous Hearst-Selig Motion Picture Actress, Taken During Her Visit Yesterday to the Selig Zoo. They Show Miss Darling Playing With a Leopard and Also, Mounted on a Ladder, Feeding a Pair of Giant Giraffes.

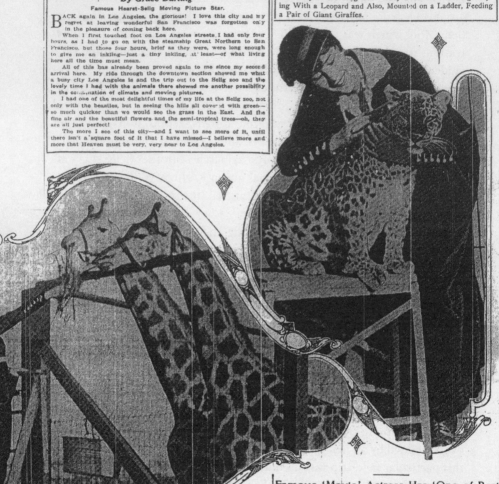

FIGURE 34: Playing with the beasts, *Los Angeles Examiner*, 26 February 1915, II:1.

Famous 'Movie' Actress Has 'One of Best Times of Her Life' Among Animals

"I DON'T see why they made such a fuss over Daniel."

With that exclamation, Miss Grace Darling, the Hearst-Selig moving picture star, emerged yesterday afternoon from a leopard's den at the Selig zoo, near Eastlake Park, after fondling and actually hugging one of the wildest of the spotted creatures.

Miss Darling, accompanied by her friend and traveling companion, Miss Hazel Deyo, returned yesterday morning from San Francisco, where the star was feted lavishly during the opening days of the exposition. On the way South she had her first experience in a sleeping car, which she liked much better than the Great Northern steamship, upon which she arrived in California because, she said, "the sleeping car had a motion without a roll."

"Every time I fell asleep," she said, "the rumbling of the train woke me. But I didn't mind, at all. It was such an odd, new experience."

Calls Lion 'Darling'

was evidently wash day at the zoo."

And the zebras and the camels, and Anna May, the baby elephant, and the giraffes, Fritz and Lena, which she fed, and the monkeys, especially "Noisy," which chattered away at her in a manner to make her wish she had an interpreter—they all caused her great pleasure for she has an intense love for animals.

Perhaps that love was what made "Bonita," a leopardess, sit calmly through a visit to her cage of the svelte young moving picture star, who patted her and cuddled her and hugged her, while she murmured pet names into the feline ear.

"Well, if lions are no worse than this dandy 'Bonita,' she said, as she left its den, "I don't see why they made such a fuss over Daniel!"

Then she went to the home of the giraffes and climbed up on a ladder to feed them.

"Oh, you old dears!" she called them, as she alternately gave a nibble of sweet grass to Fritz and then to Lena. "You sweet things, are you glad to see me?"

Mutt and Jeff Visited

In a hackneyed farewell notice when leaving Los Angeles, Darling invoked her mother, "who is waiting for me and longing to see me as much as I long to see her. There is only one mother, of course, but only one Southern California. The next time I come here, I shall bring my mother with me, then life will be perfect."[71]

Grace Darling then left California for Chicago, a visit covered profusely in Hearst's local newspaper, the *Chicago American*, and the trade papers reported on her meeting with Colonel Selig during a visit to his studios. Concerning the Chicago part of the tour, thousands of people were said to have "followed the charming lady through the streets and she was escorted by policemen, who were obliged to clear a path for her."[72] Grace Darling's triumphant days in Chicago were not included in the *News Pictorial* however, corroboration of the fact that her tour was intended solely to showcase California. The stops along the way to the Golden State functioned as enticements advertising the link between the Panama Canal and California. Her absence in the *News Pictorial* after the slot from San Diego was as complete as the buildup had been intense. It seems as if the slots conducted by Lady Duff-Gordon supplanted Grace Darling by addressing women, and not only girls, from the perspective of fashion.

When Darling arrived in Chicago, the story highlighted her modest desire to ride a jitney bus instead of a taxi to her hotel. She provided some shorthand impressions of her six-week trip for local readers, summed up as stupendous, wonderful, marvelous. The readers were offered a description of the star in the veneer of the patent spoof in *Photoplay*: "slim and petite, with wonderful golden hair, clear blue eyes and a cherry red mouth that smiles and smiles." She planned to see everything during her days in Chicago, and her schedule was busy indeed.[73] Miss Darling sat as judge in the new Court of Domestic Relations and suggested a sentence in a domestic dispute between two small-time film actors. The husband who had deserted his wife was to pay her half his salary even if she made more money than he did. She visited the Selig Studios and cranked the camera when a scene was shot for a film featuring Grace Darmond, *The Quarry*. Darling passed on the stockyards, but enjoyed motoring along Lake Shore Drive, visited a life-saving station, and relished the shopping district and the courtesy shown to women by the salespersons. She also met with the famous diet expert Martin A. Delaney and coaxed him into joining her in one of her dances, the Grace

Darling Foxtrot, previously described in the *New York American* as one of the "Grace Darling" dances. In addition to advice on exercising and fox-trotting, she received Delaney's suggestions for diets. In Chicago Darling spent her days in the fashion of Our Mutual Girl, meeting colorful personalities and interacting with important progressive aspects of society in a more informal manner besides embarking on shopping and motoring excursions. Pressed by the interviewer in *Movie Pictorial*, Darling ranked her aeroplane spin over San Francisco Bay and the encounter with felines at the Selig Zoo as the highlights of her trip.[74]

The tradition of boosterism is a mainstay of Californian politics, particularly in Southern California, and perhaps most conspicuously in Los Angeles, no doubt most vocally in the *Los Angeles Times*. Tapping into this prevalent discursive mode, the Hearst organization framed Grace Darling's visit to the region as a gigantic advertising campaign—beneficial for all parties concerned. An editorial in the *Los Angeles Examiner* calculated the promotional gift bestowed upon the State by the campaign in hard currency—the grand total was estimated at $100,000.[75]

Grace Darling arrived in California in the spring of 1915, a momentous period full of initiatives in a Golden State that entertained high hopes in the wake of the Panama Canal's opening. Apart from hosting two major exhibitions, in San Francisco and San Diego, this was the time when Griffith's *The Clansman* ran at Clune's Auditorium in Los Angeles week after week in a theater described as the largest in the country. Los Angeles had experienced phenomenal growth, and the future looked bright while Hollywood gradually turned into the center of the nation's film industry. When Grace Darling left for Chicago, a special train from New York was on its way to the opening festivities for Universal's new studio grounds, and later Selig chartered a train for a trip to California and his studio and new zoo. The Darling slot from his zoo functioned as an advertisement for Selig's newest venture, which eventually came to house his studio and in fact outlast his film company.

After Los Angeles had been linked with the East by way of railroads, Southern California proved to be a magnet attracting a gushing flow of tourists, particularly during the winter season. Initially, the film industry tapped into this mode of winter tourism before a gradual relocation spearheaded by Selig placed the industry in and around Los Angeles. Movies set in the Los Angeles area advertised the region's cornucopia of scenic attractions around the world, which further fueled interest. As the editorial in the *Los Angeles Examiner* put it when analyzing the impact of the Grace Darling campaign:

> Grace Darling as an individual is only an attractive and pretty girl who photographs well. Grace Darling as the representative of the Hearst-Selig Pictorial is an institution of importance to the entire region. As the interest in her personality increases throughout the country through publicity in the Hearst and allied newspapers, the interest in the places she visited and admired increases. She is the focal point around which the splendid beauties of California, the marvelous expositions, the State's natural wonders are grouped in a mammoth campaign.[76]

After further elaborating on this theme, one branch of the Hearst empire, the *Examiner*, graciously acknowledged the accomplishments of another, the *Hearst-Selig News Pictorial*, and particularly its management for successfully conducting the campaign. Hearst's alliance with Selig was not to outlast 1915 however. Hearst then teamed up with another newsreel partner, Vitagraph, for an even briefer collaboration. In 1916 Hearst issued his own newsreel before cooperating with Pathé for a period until launching the longstanding *International News*.

When Miss Darling reemerged on the screen in 1916 after her inconspicuous return to New York City, it was as Beatrice Fairfax, a signature used in Hearst's *New York Evening Journal* for a longstanding column in which letters from the lovelorn were answered. Marie Manning inaugurated the column in 1898 and was in charge for several years with assistance from Bettina (aka The Fearless Child) and Alice O'Hogan. After marrying, Manning moved to Washington, D.C., and did not return to the column until the 1920s. She was thus not affiliated with the paper when Beatrice Fairfax became the topic of a serial film featuring Grace Darling.[77] *Beatrice Fairfax* was however not the first film serial featuring a female reporter, an honor accorded Mary Fuller in *The Active Life of Dolly of the Dailies*, produced by Edison in 1914.[78]

Prior to taking on the role as Beatrice Fairfax, Miss Darling returned to the *Evening Journal* on February 24, 1916, for a column called "Grace Darling's Talks to Girls," which was published on the Women's page, sharing space, in fact, with Beatrice Fairfax. Darling penned a series of fourteen cautionary talks, the last one published on April 15th. "Girls" is a somewhat tricky category to play with. At times, Darling distinguishes girls from women predominantly on the basis of age, it seems, although un-married status appears to be the truly salient quality for being addressed as a girl. The very aim of the talks is to eliminate girls, as it were, by con-verting them into married young women. Read in that spirit, Darling's discourse offers staunch makeover advice and roadmaps for reaching this goal. The target group comes across as avid theatergoers and patrons of the moving-picture shows, even if pictures are described as a budget alter-native to opera. Darling is defined as a film celebrity and the bylines sport alternating characterizations in this vein: "the charming young American moving picture star," "Grace Darling, whose talent and beauty have won for her an enviable place in the moving picture world," or, more modestly, "wide reputation," or "nation-wide following." The last three articles in the series draw on aspects from the stage and screen for exemplary advice; the stage gives a clear indication of how a character is defined by proper selection of costumes and skillfulness in playing the part, while examples from the world of moving pictures underscore the importance of back-ground in a wider sense for defining character. In the latter case Darling's point is that girls should stay home to be associated with a more attractive background than the "free and easy Bohemianism" defining the bachelor girl's pad. Largely, the overt assumption in the talks is predicated upon the idea that girls must please men, and that marriage is the desired "ca-reer outcome" for a girl. Being charming and attractive is hence impera-tive, but an even more winning concept is cultivating a desirable persona in a general sense. The most beautiful girl apparently does not always land the catch of the season; men allegedly prefer more homey qualities. While girls are supposed to be agreeable, likeable, and adaptable, men and their predilections seem to be static factors in the marriage equation.

The prerequisite for the discourse is mulled over in the opening piece: "How can a girl tell when she is really in love, forever and ever, with a man, or whether she has merely a passing fancy for him?" A couple of sug-gestions are ventured: when listening to a man is more exciting than go-ing to the theater. Another sign is when a girl wants him to economize in his efforts to amuse her: going to moving pictures rather than the op-era, having sandwiches at home instead of dinner at a restaurant. Also when she "grows domestic" and cares about cocking and recipes. The fi-nal test: if she does not find him boring when exposed to "unlimited doz-es of his society." Holding onto and further cultivating one's proper iden-tity is tantamount for girls: "Don't pretend to be what you are not"; instead, "sincerity, genuineness and simplicity are three of the most charming qualities a woman can possess." Again, men are the arbiters and they appreciate unsophisticated manners, so airs, affectations, fibs, and bluffs must be avoided. Just as important, men abhor the prospect of supporting an overspending woman, a girl should therefore not scorn the domestic. "No man knowingly marriages a woman who loathes children and can't keep house." The ability to find friends is important. Apparently, a girl who is alone has only herself to blame: thus, be friendly, agreeable, cherry, and companionable. Girls with a stiletto tongue are unattractive to men, as are those that are selfish, spoiled, or finicky.

Men used to appreciate female fragility of body and weakness of mind, Darling informs her readers, and the Victorian ideals and sensibilities when girls fainted by the slightest shock. The young men of the 1910s, on the other hand, prefer robust outdoor girls able to walk, golf, and row a boat, besides being good chums. In addition, girls are supposed to have good sense and independent views, and be capable of intelligent conversation, a capable ideal far removed from Victorian fragility. Beauty is not of paramount importance, Darling repeatedly emphasizes; instead, it is imperative to learn how to do things liked by men: Gauging one's talents properly in these respects is essential. Thus, girls should not pursue endeavors for which they have only a bit of talent. "Don't let your vanity mislead you into thinking you can do things that you never can do." The ideal girl to marry seems to be a working girl, particularly an office worker, which probably mirrors the occupations of a sizeable portion of the readership. Office training corrects "many of the essentially feminine faults" and makes a girl prompt, orderly, and decisive. Such a girl is the ideal wife because she understands her husband and his problems, can exert self-control and knows how to handle money, a veritable Cinderella. Many girls have a very limited vocabulary, readers are told, and their conversation is infested with colloquialisms like fierce and swell. Another type of coarseness has to do with boasting conquests of men, which is vulgar, silly, and in bad taste, since matters of the heart are sacred, Darling admonishes. Girls should avoid having an intimate friend, even if previously advised to cultivate acquaintanceships. Women talk too much and pass on confidences that become public after being told to an intimate friend, who tells her intimate friend, and so on.

A key section in one of Grace Darling's talks is an answer to a letter from "an ugly duckling," which functions as a blueprint for the upcoming Fairfax genre, invariably predicated on distressed letters. This particular "duckling" is consoled with the reminder that beauty fades and is further counseled to cultivate agreeable qualities and to try to master as many accomplishments as possible, which, one assumes, will award swan-like qualities in the eye of the beholder. Men, Darling tells her readers, "rave over beauty, but pick out for wives plain-faced women who are willing to burn incense before a husband instead of expecting to be worshipped as goddesses themselves." On such a tenor, mothers are scorned for overprotecting and spoiling their girls. A girl must be able to cook and manage domestic affairs to be a contender in the marriage game; mothers are responsible for cultivating such skills in their daughters. Finally, Darling turns to stage and screen to disclose the importance of dressing your part and learning lessons relating to manners, deportment, and expressing personality by way of clothes. Knowing one's own personality facilitates playing the right role, a point further elaborated on in the piece devoted to proper background.[79]

This is straight talk indeed, and Darling reverted to the columns with another round of cautionary talks to drive the points home while simultaneously plugging the upcoming serial film. Darling's new column commenced publication on July 21st, and she again shared space with the Beatrice Fairfax column. The last installment, No. 9, was published on August 18th, shortly before the synopses' run began on the 21st in preparation for the debut of episode one of *Beatrice Fairfax* on the 28th. The second string of articles was labeled "Roads to Somewhere"; the tone was again scolding, didactical, and Darling talks down to her audience when duplicating the analysis and reiterating the points from the girl talks. The "somewhere-pieces" are broken down into a set of designated routes to travel, some highly desirable, others only mirage-like dead ends. The final destination is invariably matrimony, and proper guidance and direction are paramount in order to avoid pitfalls along the way. The byline introduces Grace Darling as a newspaper writer and actress soon to appear in the film version of Beatrice Fairfax, and she is said to have occasionally edited the column in the absence of Miss Fairfax.

The complex program, outlined by Darling as a road map, targets in looping variations a readership implicitly eager to move up from a humble station in life, predominantly working-class girls that have to earn their own living, which is a prerequisite for finding a more secure position through attachment to a man. Little is said about these men apart from which qualities they are likely to find attractive in a girl, namely: prudence, realistic aspirations, a puritan work ethic, good-natured appearance, neat dress, chumminess, and a modern sensibility expressed as an interest in physical activities and sports. The tone is harsh at times, and girls as a group are scolded for seldom being able to map the terrain. Roadblocks can be dealt with productively; girls do have options, choices, and opportunities, and there are desirable goals to pursue if a Protestant work ethic is combined with Catholic capacities for pleasing. Success is however never described as an end in itself; the good life presupposes matrimony and friendship with a male partner. The program spelled out is highly disciplinarian in its emphasis on hard work and self-control, thrift and moderation, and restrained desires and aspirations. As in the girl talks, readers were asked to analyze themselves in order to play the right role, and cultivate talents within reach to travel well on the roads to somewhere, which eventually might take them to the coveted station.

Grace Darling's road maps were interspersed with articles promoting the upcoming *Beatrice Fairfax* serial. Actor Harry Fox, who played reporter Jimmy Barton in the film, told anecdotes from shooting at the Wharton Studios at Ithaca and especially how Italian gangsters in episode two had maltreated him; the extras were recruited from the sports team at Cornell University and hence tough customers. A second piece on Fox discussed his interest in aviation and his enrollment in a class at an airfield outside Ithaca. Overall, Fox was undergoing a makeover, since his role as intrepid newspaperman was far removed from the persona he had successfully trademarked in the musical comedies.[80] In addition, extracts from a letter written by publisher/film magnate William Randolph Hearst outlined the impetus for the serial's production in terms of audience:

> Miss Fairfax's writings are wonderfully vivid, but it occurs to me that their value and power could be greatly increased by adapting Miss Fairfax's work and ideas to the most modern form of presentation, the moving picture. That which is shown in moving pictures impresses itself upon the mind with a force not equaled in any other way. I'm aware that Miss Fairfax personally has avoided publicity and shuns it. But I believe that she will do whatever she can to increase the usefulness of her work. And I should like to have an experiment made, with the best of moving pictures that can be had and with the collaboration with the best dramatic writers, to give the suggestion a complete test.[81]

The first two episodes were screened for an invited audience of 1,500—500 of them exhibitors—at the Criterion Theatre on August 8th. The guests greeted Darling and especially Fox warmly, reported the *Evening Journal*.[82]

On the 21st the first novelized text from the initial episode of the serial appeared; this episode is the only film installment that has not survived. The promotional format was different than for previous serials, however. Instead of publishing one long account in the Sunday Magazine section for the upcoming film episode—which was impossible for the simple reason that the *Evening Journal* was published only weekdays—each film episode was broken down into six segments. These were published daily the week before the episode in question was released, which forced everyone interested to purchase the paper for months. On the other hand, this promotional method made it possible for fans to read first and then take in the actual film episode. The alliance between text and film was more than tight, given that the film picked up an imaginary character from the *Evening Journal* and in the prolog even featured the legendary editor Arthur Brisbane as well as Tad (Thomas Aloysious Dorgan), the famous cartoonist at the *Evening Journal*. Beatrice Fairfax's sidekick in the serial, exuberant reporter Jimmy Barton, played by Harry Fox, had only a fictive connection to the paper. Since all this was published in the *Evening Journal*, one could hardly ask for a more natural venue for publishing the storylines. In a sense, this serial took the Grace Darling story full circle. Pretty much all imaginable bases were covered by featuring Grace Darling in a serial produced for Hearst and distributed by Hearst, and by featuring Darling as a reporter in one of Hearst's own newspapers, thus taking advantage of her stardom built-up by the Hearst newspapers for a campaign featuring Darling as a reporter, character, and celebrity in Hearst's *News Pictorial*. True to this mutually reinforcing publishing style, Hearst's current newsreel included a slot showing a scene from shooting of one of the *Beatrice Fairfax* episodes. Topping this, Beatrice Fairfax even reviewed the serial in a piece brimming with excitement over the wonders of filmland.[83] And prior to the serial, Grace Darling had shared space with Beatrice Fairfax on the human-interest page of the *Evening Journal*; according to the promotional spin, Miss Fairfax herself was responsible for casting Grace Darling in the role.[84]

The prolog to the serial in episode one offers a historical background, a frame story, presented as a flashback, which harks back to the topics

Grace Darling had discussed in her columns, the "Talks to Girls" and the "Road to Somewhere." In the opening of the first installment, Beatrice's grandmother states: "Beatrice, you ought to get married," then outlines a road to somewhere for Beatrice which leads to the universal goal of marriage as defined in the columns. Beatrice considers herself too busy, and besides, there is no likely candidate at the paper, she quips. We learn that she is in charge of a column giving advice to the lovelorn as a response to a keystone letter of advice she herself received from her deceased father: "[F]ind some means of helping girls less fortunate than yourself." This solemn entreaty prompted her to pitch the advice column to the *Evening Journal*'s editor, and the flashback shows her meeting with newspaper legend Arthur Brisbane. The paper and its editor are described in glowing terms. Brisbane is "America's greatest editor," and "the man that stands for all that is most progressive in modern journalism." This alleged champion of humanity and brotherhood in the tabloid camp gives Beatrice a chance to implement her father's program. Thus, the column was born and she had found a mission in life. Pondering her own life situation, she wonders: "Was it every woman's duty to fulfill her destiny by love and marriage?" Her chance for service seems to be to help others, at least for the time being. Arriving at the office, she runs into energetic reporter Jimmy Barton, and soon, he is very much infatuated with Beatrice. Even if the serial refrains from spelling it out, there seems to be an amorous future in store for them.

The episodes are standalones featuring the recurrent newspaper team Barton & Fairfax dealing with dire straits, and in the process unabashedly marketing Hearst's paper, the *Evening Journal*. Each of the fifteen episodes in the serial is set off by an imploring letter sent to Fairfax, beseeching her for help and advice, thereby lending an urgency to her work and prompting her to declare: "I don't pretend to be a newspaper woman. I'm just a 'big sister to troubled hearts.' "[85] The troubles are however invariably part of a bigger picture. The missives to Beatrice jump-start the narrative engine, but the amorous vicissitudes regularly shift the story into a different gear due to misperceptions of the situations at hand. Beatrice and her colleague Jimmy therefore end up in the midst of criminal onslaughts. Jimmy, city reporter on the *Evening Journal*, amateur sleuth, and Beatrice's untiring suitor, resourcefully untangles these fiendish plots by mobilizing his network of law-enforcement contacts and resorting to an array of unconventional methods, not to mention disguising his identity. Initially, there was however some uncertainty concerning which direction the serial was to take. As *Moving Picture World* put it indirectly in an unflattering comparison of the opening episodes of *Beatrice Fairfax* and the "pilot" for *The Mysteries of Myra*, the troubled heart mainly belonged to girls "on First, Second and Third avenues, in the Bronx and other strongholds of Hearst journalism."[86] A Mary Ryan from the Bronx indeed penned the epistle in the first episode, thus underwriting—or perhaps prompting—the analysis. The story emphasis gradually shifted however, and the narrative picked up momentum when crime-busting took center stage. *Moving Picture World* partly reassessed its stance further along in the serial when it became clear that the crime plots had the upper hand and that the love affairs were mere adjuncts to suspense stories. "The idea of the serial is novel: if the successors to the two under discussion [episodes three and four] match with them, the group should be successful. The field is of the widest and practically unlimited."[87] *Variety* also noted an ascending quality—"it is manifest that serial will improve as it goes along. No. 3 is better than 1 or 2 and No. 4 is superior to the first three"—but refrained from reviewing later installments.[88]

The first episodes all display a xenophobic slant by showcasing crooks tailored from melodramatic stock conceptions of foreigners. Doctor Schultze, for example, is the loosely defined brain behind the heist in the first episode. His professional status is questioned by quotation marks around "Doctor" throughout the outlines in the *Evening Journal*. No specific information is imparted concerning his background, and the nondescript underlings named Defarge are equally indistinct besides the foreign connotations implied by their family name. The Black Hand, the Italian gang in episode two, is distinct enough in terms of ethnicity. In episode three a French-named governess in drag is in league with a crook named Pete Raven and abducts the young girl "she" is responsible for. The Indian story in episode four is more complex. The Indian prince and his entourage are as exotic as can be, but they are on a mission to avenge the theft of a holy Buddha statue, a robbery and desecration with colonial overtones perpetrated by Christopher McRay, a "sometime officer in the English army," according to the intertitles. In the end McRay and an Indian priest are both killed, which prepares the scene for a marriage and the episode's denouement when Dorothy's father, the robber, ceases blocking her road to wedded bliss. In episode six Madame Gaillard belongs to a group of counterfeiters, while episode ten introduces an Irish gambler who resorts to kidnapping to achieve his goals, and in episode eleven a man named Sverdrup leads a gang of bearded anarchists. All in all, the serial musters up a remarkably diverse gallery of foreign-born or immigrant criminals.

Episode five may serve as a demonstration of the narrative structure of the serial's episodes, all written by Bruce Dickey. A Japanese secret agent, in league with a Spanish woman, is out to steal the blueprints for a new weapon, which prompts his jealous girlfriend, Mimosa San, to write to Beatrice Fairfax. Obliquely, Jimmy gets involved in the story due to his journalistic assignment; he is to interview the inventor of the new rifle for the *Evening Journal*. The inventor, however, declines to be interviewed. Jimmy and Beatrice visit the teahouse where Mimosa San works, but after being called on the telephone by the agent, Satsu, the girl refuses to talk. Jimmy decides to return to the inventor to try to get an interview after all. When driving there he notices a fast-moving automobile with the Japanese agent and his Spanish partner in crime speeding in the opposite direction. The inventor's home is in a state of disarray when Jimmy arrives—and the plans have been stolen. Hence, Jimmy returns with a story to write, but in a different vein than expected. Later on, Beatrice spies on Mimosa San, who leads her to the agent's quarters. Jimmy is working on the theft story together with a detective and the inventor when Beatrice calls to reveal Satsu's whereabouts. The rifle plans are eventually recovered, and Beatrice persuades Jimmy not to fire at Mimosa San and her lover as they escape in a boat, according to the outline in *Evening Journal*. Crime is thus not punished and in a paradoxical fashion love is restored even in this case, which gives this prototypical storyline an unusual twist. The preserved copy at the Library of Congress closes differently however: An automobile chase involving the escaping couple ends in a crash. Satsu dies and Mimosa San is injured, but her status is not revealed in the scene's final shot. Why crime had to be punished to the full in the actual film—if the Library of Congress copy is identical with the release version—while not so in the printed version remains unclear.

Not only girls in dire straits penned the letters to Beatrice; several men, and even a lovesick boy, were among the lovelorn correspondents, and to broaden the palette with something out of the ordinary, a missive from a circus sideshow provides the impetus for one episode. The letter writer, the sideshow's fat lady, loves a faithless dwarf and implores Beatrice for help. The short man is mixed up with crooks and, due to his miniscule size, is able to tamper with racehorses inside seemingly sealed stables, a scheme unraveled with alacrity by the ever-enterprising Jimmy.

Harry Fox plays the dynamic and resourceful Jimmy with infectious tongue-in-cheek, bravado, and good humor, and he outshines the more timid Grace Darling with his energy. Jimmy proves to be a master of disguise and relishes the game when outsmarting the bad guys that invariably appear in gangs, his all-American brain and good cheer winning the day. Making reporter Jimmy the active force and prime mover in the serial expanded the prospective audience base, moving it away from the girls-only address in the promotional buzz. The crossover between amorous and criminal stories was designed to appeal to serial fans with a fancy for intrigues featuring infernal machines, poisonous devices, mysterious documents, fistfights, weapons, smuggling, secret rooms and passages, and suspenseful chases. These fans were predominantly if not exclusively men. The resolutions disentangle the dual registers of the intrigues, uniting troubled lovers by apprehending or eliminating the criminal elements. At the same time, the resolutions of criminal plots function as prerequisites for the resolutions of amorous vicissitudes, while the anthologized love stories, by their sheer number, gradually seem to break down Beatrice's resistance to the road to wedlock.

The promotional discourse penned by Grace Darling targeted malleable girls willing to prepare themselves by means of a character makeover for successfully traveling the roads to that coveted somewhere called marriage. If the reviewer in *Moving Picture World* had it right in singling out girls along First, Second and Third Avenues as well as young women in the Bronx as a metonymy for Hearst readership, it should be translated as young working-class women, many of them immigrants or the children of immigrants. The talking cure in the girl columns condemns deviant behavior that risks obviation of the marriage goal by providing instructions to emulate. In a sense, Darling, in her stern talks and straight road maps, doles out cultural instruction for girls addressed as lacking an in-depth familiarity with dominant views, and not only due to their young age.

In the serial Beatrice is totally dependent on Jimmy to straighten out the plots initiated by the letters. In their teamwork the division of labor is highly conventional from a gender perspective, in contrast to several other serials sporting more independently resourceful serial queens. Beatrice certainly offers some important intelligence, but is often literally tied up with the victims and released only due to Jimmy's sly outfoxing of the crooks. Beatrice is allied with the letter writer because of their spatial proximity, and they are often joint victims of the gang's machinations, while Jimmy pursues the crooks on his own or together with the police or other authorities. The law enforcers are however brought in only at the final stage of the wrap-up.

The missives set in motion standalone picture stories in terms of character, which in a sense would hark back to the series format had it not been for the preponderance of criminal suspense over amorous exigencies—and Beatrice is never seen shopping, which does not preclude her wearing nice outfits. The final episode is still open-ended in respect to marriage between the protagonists, which might have reflected the producer's uncertainty concerning whether to return with additional episodes.

In this chapter we have tried at length to highlight the dynamic exchange between series, serials, and newsreels by initially looking at *Our Mutual Girl*, the *Hearst-Selig News Pictorial*, and their rich promotional contexts. Both formats—the series and a stretch of a newsreel—lead to serials featuring their respective leading ladies: Norma Phillips and Grace Darling. One can read this development as a purifying of eclectic formats—that the newsreel had no place for featured players of Grace Darling's ilk, and that heterogeneity à la *Our Mutual Girl* presented an unattractive grab bag stuffed with too many items. This type of series thus provided an example of excessive variety. The solution to both dilemmas was transferring the respective star to the serial format, by then an established and thriving platform, and one with more potential for cross-fertilizing promotion and dynamic storyline variety than any other type of film. Thus, the Beatrice Fairfax serial combines thrilling suspense with romance in its standalone episodes.

From the very outset of the serial, Beatrice is encouraged to find someone to marry and is hence placed on the matrimonial track. Beatrice and Jimmy are seemingly on the cusp of a formal relationship outside the paper after having worked in tandem to untangle the intertwined plots. The introductory mulling of Beatrice' grandmother over the young woman's amorous future is however never quite resolved. Romance is budding and Jimmy openly shows his infatuation, but the serial quietly peters out, leaving grandmother's hope for a match hanging in the air. In this respect, the serial deconstructs its own underlying object lessons so unfalteringly administered to other girls as gospel in Darling's print discourse. Beatrice Fairfax, as a professional woman, stakes out her own roads, apparently enjoying leeway in terms of the marriage doctrine. The draconian makeover proposed as a panacea for girls in the Bronx and along Manhattan's low-number avenues was perhaps not the right model for Beatrice to emulate when embodied by a girl patented as one of her kind. To be sure, she has more options to pursue due to class background and cultural wherewithal, and a professional career defined as a mission to boot, and therefore has no reason to rush to the altar.

The society depicted by Darling's texts comes across as decidedly patriarchal, given that women's happiness is predicated on finding a husband. In this equation, young women must tailor themselves to appeal to men or risk being left behind in the apparently dismal abyss outside wedlock. At a time when young women were part of the workforce, therefore enjoying a broader range of opportunities in the public sphere, a young working-class woman's life was still outlined as a prelude to marriage—and preferably sooner rather than later. Beatrice, however, is the exception to the rule, or, rather, class factors reframe the equation.[89] A decade later, Hearst's Cosmopolitan Productions resurrected Beatrice Fairfax in a feature film called *The Lovelorn*; Grace Darling was substituted for Dorothy Cumming in a lost film with limited following.

CHAPTER 8

DOUBLE SHOOTING, DIGNIFIED TERMS, AND FEATURED PROLOGS

"... in movies, or in films if we want to call them by a more dignified name, or motion pictures to go a little further..."[1]

THIS CHAPTER WILL begin with one item of testimony to the cultural wherewithal of film culture, the appropriation of film matters in short stories and novels. This line of publishing turned into a literary sub-genre in the 1910s at a time when publishers began to put out editions of novels adapted for the screen in volumes illustrated with publicity stills from the films. From a discussion of some pioneering literary endeavors in this field, a conceptual detour leads to an analysis of the prevalent practice of appending prologs to numerous early feature films in 1914 and 1915.

The First Film Novelists

The first film novels were published by the Stratemeyer Syndicate as juvenile series, the authors unnamed: Victor Appleton for "The Motion Picture Chums" (seven volumes, 1913-1916), the prolific Appleton signature was used also for "The Moving Picture Boys" (ten volumes, 1913-1919), Laura Lee Hope was on the cover of "The Moving Picture Girls" (seven volumes, 1914-1916), while other publishers were responsible for Alice B. Emerson's "Ruth Fielding" series (30 volumes, 1913-1934; film related starting with volume nine, which was published in 1916), and Elmer Tracey Barnes' "The Motion Picture Comrades" (nine titles during 1917).

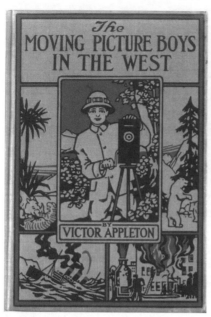

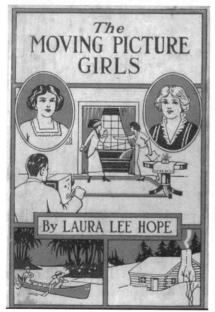

FIGURE 35: The first film novels: book covers for juvenile series.

Outside the juvenile field, authors began to explore film topics in short stories in the early 1910s and in novels from the middle of the decade. This film fiction in print form runs parallel with numerous films addressing film matters. Together, print fiction and metafilms provide a popular repository for negotiating and disseminating various facets of film culture.[2]

Throughout film history, movie theaters have been favored settings for metafilms and cinematic reflexivity, oftentimes with a comedic touch. The critical discussion of the phenomena routinely backtracks to the turn of the century and Uncle Josh's alarmed reactions—migrating from Robert Paul's 1901 version to Edison's spin-off from 1902—when Josh, among other things, faces an early train film and is attracted by a desirable woman on screen. Josh's fazing partly represents a spoof of one of the foundational myths of early film reception: that hicks, other others, and perhaps even non-others, were initially prone to misread screen content and its interfaces.[3] By 1901, the medium had been around long enough to dramatize and poke fun at antediluvian modes of spectatorship with a wink to contemporary audiences in the know. For patrons well aware of the screen's nature of representation, Josh's unseasoned manners of processing screen matters offered reflexive amusement. Stories of cine-illiteracy—often ethnically inflected—again proliferated during the first nickelodeon years when these new venues and their audiences where reported on by the local press, as previous chapters show.

Thus, self-reflexive metafilms—numerous and eclectic as they are—depicted screen realities and indirectly historiographic and mythological re-readings of reception patterns, genre conventions, and shooting parameters. For example, the pistol aimed at the audience in *The Great Train Robbery* (Edison, 1903), irrespective of whether the shot opens or closes the film, is a complex and compelling gesture of address couched in the cinema of attractions style. Mack Sennett reversed the direction a decade later when his character tries to interact with the projected film world by desperately firing at the screen in *Mabel's Dramatic Career* (Keystone, 1913). Sennett's character, yet another specimen in the hick roster, is unable to fully fathom the absolute divide between reality and screen reality. Film comedies routinely parade spatial mix-ups, though mostly shifting the location from theatrical to studio space. *Merton of the Movies*, for example—shot in 1924, 1932 (*Make Me a Star*), and 1947—provides a paradigmatic, but highly intriguing example. Merton, a not-too-bright aspiring screen star, believes he is acting in a high-art context, but is doubly framed by the company during the protracted shooting period and unaware that he will come across as the ultimate burlesquer of a popular Western character. Eventually, the truth dawns on him, but not until the opening of the film when he sees himself on screen. *Show People* (Cosmopolitan/MGM, 1928), featuring Marion Davies, displays a series of spatial mishaps by way of literal walk-throughs straight into sets during shooting, a prevalent form of clueless accident in films about filmmaking. These late works are classical versions of genre elements established in the mid-1910s.

The classical metascenes, and their far from clear-cut meanings and implications as well, inhabit the same cinematic borderland as the twice-screened events in the Tom Mix vehicle *The Moving Picture Cowboy* (Selig, 1914). Here, mythic heroism and Western dexterity are flaunted in reel one, only to be ruthlessly deconstructed as inept foible in reel two. It seems as if this lost film somewhat earnestly—and convincingly for the diegetic audience—depicts Western prowess in a series of scenes visualized for the "real" spectators from the Luke character's (played by Tom Mix) narrative. When the series of scenes is repeated, both dexterity and veracity are tested. Retrospectively, the first round of scenes is mercilessly deconstructed and turns out to be empty bragging. As the printed program has it: "All of the scenes shown in the first reel, are reproduced, only the climax of each scene is entirely different. The boastful Luke has a most comical mishap at each attempted 'stunt.' "[4] Thus, the audience has been treated to a series of misleading flashes (whether back or forward is not clear) in the vein of the famous flashback scene in Hitchcock's *Stage Fright* (Warner Bros., 1950).[5] Then again, the title and the mise-en-scène might have given the game away by way of winks to the audience advertising the character's inadequacy. The stagy costume, for example, offered one such clue.

Several metafilms, as well as literary texts representing film matters, describe the film camera as a lethal weapon, taking the metaphor of shooting almost literally. In the case of *The Movie Cowboy* the narrating instance unsentimentally opens up a gap between the two terms "movie" and "cowboy" by showing that the combination is oxymoronic, a contradiction in terms. The narrator's shots at the character—and incompetence in Western ways—are by no means blanks. Oxymoronic genre variations, hence, make up a prominent strand of metafiction (irrespective of whether shot or penned) dealing with studios shooting Westerns. The frictions between Western studio culture and "the real thing," or "the genuine article," are mockingly fleshed out in terms of character when capable bit players critically observe ridiculous stars and their blatant shortcomings.

Maurice Tourneur's *A Girl's Folly* (Paragon, 1917) is, perhaps, the best depiction from the 1910s of an actual studio busy at work. The studio lot's bewildering geography—with back-to-back stages juxtaposing biblical vistas with saloons and salons—are in certain respects instances of what Michel Foucault in a preliminary text characterized as heterotopias, transitory, stand-in places.[6] Such places offer gateways or thresholds to other places, real or imagined, thus functioning as vehicles or platforms for communication and transportation, both literally and symbolically. Heterotopias are spatial anthologies framing malleable places or plastic grounds for culturally homeless or imaginary practices; they connect and organize access by offering transitions between times, spaces, states, and contested or semi-secretive practices. Hotel lobbies, railroad stations, airports, fairgrounds, zoological gardens, theaters, and movie studios fall into this category, which Foucault frames in his paper in theoretical form, evocatively but far from conclusively. For the purpose of this chapter, however, his tentative set of demarcations provides direction enough. In turn, the natives inhabiting the plastic studio spaces, players/actors, carry identities as malleable as the places invoked. They are anybodies and everybodies—heterocorpora, to coin a phrase. The early term for film people, "movies," alludes to this hetero-quality, a vicarious moving in and out of characters by migrating between traits, identities, cultures, and experiences. Add to this a rootlessness and otherness vis-à-vis the place where the studios were housed—this was at least the impression in Los Angeles when the film colony began to form.

In dealing with dangerous scenes or those demanding skills, however, heterocorpora had to yield to the real article, stand-ins with specific competencies and corporeal stability. The restricted cinematic range embodied by the stand-ins, in turn, was pointedly evident when such non-players were inserted into film types out of touch with or out of reach of their personality's limited range of competence: Cowpunchers do, for example, not excel in polo movies. They are therefore not "movies." In an interesting spin prior to conceptions of stardom from later eras, actors were perceived as mannequins, statues, or models, which prompted Chicago film producers in the early years "to change their models frequently so as to prevent the same faces to appear too often in the pictures." Even if the shooting process had been facilitated by holding onto the seasoned models, "the requirement of the business, according to those who are engaged in it, make it necessary to introduce new faces and figures into the picture constantly."[7] Given the quality of heterocorporeal malleability for "movies," it made sense to suppress players' name from the bill as the Biograph Company insisted on doing longer than other studios. Faces and bodies could thereby circulate freely from film to film, until worn out, as studio property without being tied to a proper name. The excitement of recognition soon turned picture personalities into stars, which recast industry and billing practices and was further fueled by proliferating fan magazines and Sunday supplements in the press.

If a first strand of metawesterns disrupted the concept movie cowboy, a second wave of such films and texts strove to close the gap—momentarily at least, and as a paramount achievement—between the terms "movies" and "cowboys." The strategy here was abandoning the heterotopical lot and its fictions, instead tracking locations, realities, and persons standing up to an allegedly truer, celebratory vision of the lost West. Thereby, the space between the terms is pulled together in a suturing operation through the cleansing and healing impact of the vestiges of real places and real Westerners. In the process, heterocorpora were upgraded from stand-ins to uncontested, skilled, although uncomfortable centers of attention. Thus, a real enough Western girl like Jean of the Lazy A (more about her later) unwillingly surrendered to the camera, but without accepting the role of movie star. Her eagerness to take leave of the movie world—and even its celebratory docu-fictions—underwrites the precarious and uncomfortable framing of the West and the overall brittleness of the genre when stripped of studio pretense. To be sure, genuine Westerns can be made and released according to fictional logic, but only as a paradoxical overcoming of a double set of constraints defining the old West as already dispersed and thus out of commission, in addition to the further constraints imposed by a film industry recycling stagy models. The ruthless flogging of Jersey Westerns in the critical discourse, especially in the *New York Dramatic Mirror*, prior to shooting in "real" western settings encouraged this sensibility. The genre's popularity and complex cultural status sparked numerous debates in the trade press as well as probing in films, short stories, and novels.[8]

The quest for true Westerns—even after the studio relocation out west—instituted a prelapsarian reenactment, which in several senses relied on heterotopian amalgamation. Real characters had to be unearthed, proper settings found, the hardships of bygone days unleashed as a string of obligatory scenes functioning as a condensed metonymy for what the West was once about, while stagy plot lines were discounted. For the toiling heroes out in the unforgiving wilderness of the cattleland, the shooting process, which occupied the bulk of such texts, offered rites of passage, a cleansing process removing corrupt representations by overwriting. Still, the fragments of a lost culture were too precarious to furnish heterotopical ground for regular cinematic dissemination outside the chronicled exemplary efforts. A prolific genre devoted to life once upon a time in the West therefore represented a contradiction in terms. The genre could not be reinvented as genre; the process of making just one such a film, we are shown, was too complex and cumbersome to be readily emulated. Instead, the texts offered a production process with highly existential overtones, a pilgrimage paying tribute to quintessential American moments harking back to the days prior to the official closing of the frontier.[9]

The thriving metacinematic spins of the mid-1910s, invading a multitude of genres and semiotic carriers, corroborates the transformations of the film industry toward the integrated system we now label classic Hollywood cinema. Both classic and post-classic meta-activity has been promptly summed up under genre headings such as "Hollywood novels," "Hollywood Fiction," "metafilm," "film within film," "self-reflexive film," and "self-conscious film," just to mention some of the current headings. Hardcore definitions of the genre variations at stake are beyond the scope of this chapter: We are primarily dealing here with a reframed appropriation of genres or genre elements—formulas, settings, and characters—from a skewed viewpoint: displaced in order to either belittle stagy Westerns, or to purge Western historiography from celluloid corruption by reinventing, if not the genre, at least an exemplary feature of it.

The novels/short stories' and films' overt genre aspirations or designations, fictions about film Westerns, are taken at face value here. The reflexive quality is paramount and the topic primarily double fictions negotiating film culture, a film culture pronounced by the texts themselves as preoccupied with Western material. As overt intertexts, the exchanges

315

with the rich history of Western representations are openly acknowledged as points of departure. The overarching plot conflict is outlined as stage Western versus realistic depiction—or usurpation of the Western heritage versus being true to the lost life and lifestyle of the West; middle terms are unheard of. To further complicate matters, this discourse of the real is embedded in a complex process of recognitions à la melodrama, encompassing both the negotiated genre—film Westerns—and the chain of story events running parallel to the fictional shooting process.

Many such films were spoofs filtered through a set of hybrid genre aspirations, for instance the series *Buck Parvin and the Movies* based on Charles E. Van Loan's collection of short stories, which burlesque the film world in general and in particular the celluloid Westerns' appropriation of stagy intertexts. In contrast to this mode, a second strand displays romances directed at depicting the true West and a vanishing culture's hardships to dazzling life on the screen. We will discuss novelist B.M Bower's work as a shining example of this latter sentiment.

In a letter from Bliss, Idaho, dated June 8, 1912, Bertha M. Sinclair responds to a query from The Selig Polyscope Co.: "Replying to your letter of June 6th, I will let you have the moving picture rights of my stories at the same rate which you made with Mr. Sinclair [her brother, Bertrand], i.e. $75 each for short stories, $100 for novels." The correspondence—a few scattered letters have been preserved in the Selig Collection at the Academy of Motion Picture Arts and Sciences—led to the filming of several stories and novels in the mid-1910s from the extensive oeuvre of "B.M. Bower" (her penname).

Bower's early writing was confined to *Popular Magazine* before she reached the book market via Dillinghams in 1906 with *Chip of the Flying U*, illustrated by the famous Charles Russell. Most of her numerous books from the early 1910s until her death in 1940 were published by Brown, Little and Co. in Boston, and reprinted several times by dime presses like A.L. Burt and Grosset & Dunlap. New editions emerged in the 1940s, and reprints appeared well into the 1970s—as late as 1995 in the case of *Chip of the Flying U*. Douglas Brunch, in his 1926 book *The Cowboy and His Interpreters*, includes B.M. Bower among a quartet, along with William McLeod Raine, Charles Alden Seltzer, and Clarence Edward Mulford, he labeled the aristocracy of Western novelists, above whom only Zane Grey had secured a place. In a 1913 manual, *Writing the Photoplay*, J. Berg Esenwein and Arthur Leeds note "that the Selig Company is regularly producing photoplays written by Randall Parish, Molly Elliot Seawell, Albert Bigelow Paine, Bertrand W. Sinclair, B.M. Bower," and a handful other authors who are now not very well-known.[10]

In her reply to Selig Bower mentioned a story called "Like A Knight of Old," which was her first shot at a film motif; this story appeared in *Popular Magazine* in August 1910. In it the setup leads up to a classic misreading, the shooting of a film scene taken for reality. In this case, what later developed into a stock situation is given a twist in that the footage depicting the uncalled-for chivalry actually could be used to improve the planned scene. That is, if and only if our valiant, albeit misguided knight agreed to continue working for the company. Normally, such an intrusion kills off otherwise good footage; *A Girl's Folly* is a prototypical film example in this respect. Mustang filmed Bower's 1910 story in 1916 as *A Modern Knight*, more or less in the wake of the Buck Parvin films.

The sale of stories to Selig, and Bower's subsequent move to California, provided her with insights into the nuts and bolts of film production. Nancy Brooker-Bowers, in her bibliography, dubs Bower's 1916 novel *The Phantom Herd* as the first such work set in Hollywood. Credit for the initial mapping of Hollywood undoubtedly belongs to Bower—but for another novel: *Jean of the Lazy A* from 1915.[11]

The latter book is set in Montana, but introduces a set of characters different than Bower's usual crowd, the Happy Family at The Flying U Ranch, of which the knight of old is also a member. Instead, we encounter the brothers Carl and Aleck Douglas and their respective ranches, Bar Nothing and Lazy A. The story intertwines two threads: the murder of a troublemaker, a deed for which Aleck is sentenced and put behind bars, and a film company busy shooting Western films in the vicinity of the two ranches. Jean and her fiancé and temporary guardian, Lite Avery, a cowboy of the right sort, both try to clear the innocent Aleck's name. In the meantime the Lazy A is in the hands of brother Carl. Jean encounters the film crew, and in the conventional manner intrudes upon the scene being shot by apprehending three men—film actors, as it turns out—tampering with Lazy A cattle. Director Burns of the Great Western Film Company is however highly impressed by the unimpressed girl's talents. Gradually, Jean becomes involved with the crew and the production, first as an extra, then doubling for the leading lady; the latter is unable to deliver stunts with punch. Soon, Jean emerges as a star in her own right in a serial she authored by and large herself, and simply called

Jean of the Lazy A, just like Bower's novel. Jean's reasons for participating are chiefly financial. She wants to clear her father's name by hiring a lawyer and reopening the case. More importantly, she hopes to settle the debts to her uncle and regain possession and control of the Lazy A. In the background, Lite Avery entertains similar ambitions on her behalf.

Jean signs a contract with the Great Western for one year and accompanies the troop back to Los Angeles in the fall together with Lite, whom she has brought into the company to spice up the stunts with down-to-earth Western know-how. The backdrop for Jean's success is her natural Western skills and the gradual elimination of hokum scenarios and stunts alien to the line of work. When Jean arrives in Los Angeles as a star, her films are lavishly advertised and screened in one of the leading theaters downtown. The president of the company welcomes her at the railway station and chauffeurs her in his limousine to the Hollywood studio via the theater exhibiting her film. Predictably, she is unimpressed by the film world and more concerned about the well-being of her horse and Lite's whereabouts than the president's ramblings.

The two lines of action eventually merge during Jean's viewing of her own film. Of course, while she is not interested in the film per se, she longs for the range, and the imagery temporarily transports her back. Jean's pursuit of the murderer boils down to finding a man called Art Osgood. Osgood once worked for Carl Douglas, then left Montana in conjunction with the killing. Narrative stumbling blocks are often bypassed thanks to more or less elegantly motivated coincidences. The cinematic detour "by chance" provides Jean with the crucial clue. When she steps into the theater to watch her own film, both her concern about her father and the unpleasantness of Los Angeles mysteriously vanish in the soothing atmosphere:

> A huge pipe organ was filling the theater with a vast undertone that was like the whispering surge of a great wind. Jean went into the soft twilight and sat down, feeling that she had shut herself away from the harsh, horrible world that held so much of suffering. She sighed and leaned her head back against the enclosure of the loges, and closed her eyes and listened to the big, sweeping harmonies that were yet so subdued (256).

The pleasant feeling and the lure of this picture palace, underscored by the organ music, prepare her for the imaginary return home, initially as a pure fantasy by way of the recreated sounds, then via an imaginary flight triggered by the moving pictures:

> Down next the river, in a sheltered little coulee, there was a group of great bull pines. Sometimes she had gone there and leaned against a tree trunk, and had shut her eyes and listened to the vast symphony which the wind and water played together (256).

The illusion is so strong that she forgets about her own role in creating the film. She watches the screen and herself up there as an ordinary spectator. "Involuntarily she smiled back at her pictured self, just as everyone else was smiling back" (258). Given her mindset, the scenes take her home to Montana, as it were: "Presently she was back at the Lazy A, living again the scenes which she herself had created."

Throughout the screening, her mode of spectatorship oscillates between Jean being aware of watching screen Jean, and Jean seeing a character entirely detached from herself. The novel's explicit address to the readers heightens the impression of representation, distance, and doubling in reminding us of previous story moments now fixed in fictive, celluloid form: "You will remember that Robert Grant Burns had told Pete to take all of that encounter, and he had later told Jean to write her scenario so as to include that incident." The text repeatedly recalls such traces of unexposed chunks of text, giving them a definite fixation through a retelling as screen practice in what narratologists call exphrasis, a framing of a description and transfer of an artifact from one realm of discourse into another art form via a semiotic transposition. The process is quite intricate in this case since the whole loop is devised by way of words, as the paraphrased "film" exists as text only.

Before the feature commences Jean dozes off, then wakes up during the final, flickering frames of a topical film from the Mexican border town of Nogales. Her semi-conscious impression of something familiar, but critically important, escaping her is quite enigmatic until the topical returns after a second screening of her own feature. For conclusive confirmation, Jean later watches the film again, this time in Lite Avery's company, not telling him in advance what to expect, namely Art Osgood on the screen among the Mexican revolutionary soldiers. This coincidental clue paves the way for resolution and closure.

Screenings are often kernels in the narrative fabric of films about films and novels about films, dense moments either triggering salient aspects of the storyline or climactically preparing for closure. Such highly condensed narrative moments are usually filtered and focalized through the protagonist's mind—or mindscreen[12] (to borrow a phrase)—and sometimes offer an apotheosis over an undisputed success, sometimes a bittersweet achievement. In *Merton of the Movies* said Merton faces a shocking recognition in the auditorium. He is an undisputed hit on screen, but until this moment he had entertained career ambitions diametrically opposed to his actual screen persona. Henceforth, he is forever fixed as a star in a genre he despises.

Jean is an atypical character in this respect in that she does not seek screen fame in the first place. Consequently, she returns home after Art Osgood is rounded up and willing to testify that the killer in fact was Carl Douglas, whose subsequent suicide note proves the innocence of Jean's father. "Some things are greater even than the needs of a motion-picture company," the president philosophically muses when releasing Jean from her contractual obligations (321).

Bower's narrator and characters are lovers of the wilderness of the open range, the prairie, prior to the fencing in of farmland. The cowpunchers of the lost cattle era, when the herds were driven north from Texas and transported to the beef trains, are the so-called "real boys." Gradually, settlers turned the cowpuncher into an obsolete figure. The Flying U Ranch in Montana is Bower's fictive haven, where, in spite of current conditions, a group of 15–20 punchers and their women still lurk, providing her with a pool of characters for most of her stories. In her 1916 novel *The Phantom Herd* director Luck Lindsay's goal is to produce The Big Picture, a realistic depiction of the West, when the West was cattleland and the cowpunchers reigned unrivaled. Luck's quest takes him to the Flying U, and with this bunch of real boys he produces the true masterpiece with their own meager funds after an abundance of sacrifices are made. The only audience that the director respects, the assembled members of the Texas Cattle Convention, endorses the final result, and their accolades are reprinted in the trade press for a film titled *The Phantom Herd*. This seal of approval opens the market for the selling of state rights, and eventually a contract between the whole bunch and the leading studio, by chance the one that Jean of the Lazy A left, is signed. The president, in fact, entertains hopes that she will be tempted to return to the screen together with his new, first-rate stock company.

In a paradoxical move the lost West and its laid-off punchers are moved from the ranch to Hollywood to represent bygone days in Montana on the screen. The cinematic backdrop for Luck's uncompromising efforts is furnished by the stories his former studio boss initially wanted him to direct, based on synopses written by a pompous author in the despised tradition of the stage Western. When Luck and his real boys burlesque the stories, the author threatens to sue and, to Luck's dismay, the hack author is backed by the studio head. This provides the incentive for Luck to sever his ties with the studio and produce from scratch a true Western in the best of company. Prior to that, he is however offered a position by Great Western, but the president refuses to hire Luck's cowboys and is therefore turned down.

The screening of the attempt at burlesque inspired Luck's exodus from Hollywood, while the screening of *The Phantom Herd* for the Texan convention opens all doors for a triumphant return. This time the real boys are invited as an undisputed part of the Western package. Luck has proved that the market appreciates Western stories without phony melodramatic intrigues and trigger-happy characters. The screening of the film in Texas is filtered through Luck's nervous anticipation. Just like for Jean of the Lazy A, screen instances recall shooting situations. Luck is on high alert for the reactions from his ideal audience and thrilled when they respond favorably. Rugged cowboys are humming to well-known lyrics quoted in the intertitles. Overall, their comments are in tune with the film's realistic rendering of the merciless hardships the cowpunchers face, which were mirrored by severities during the shooting process. Overcome by pent-up emotions, Luck sneaks out before the screening is over, unable to share his moment of triumphant success with anybody.[13] The loss propelling the narrative desires in Bower's novels and the ensuing quest for screen realism lacks, by definition, a basis in reality—the good old West is gone for good. The boys from the Flying U are relics from a bygone era that which can be restored as fiction only, at best informed by historical and documentary authenticity. The fictive celluloid aspires to a melancholy fixation of times lost, space transformed, and characters out of place—a heterotopia peopled by heterocorpora.

When cinema turned predominantly narrative, writers of popular fiction encountered yet another potential outlet for stories and novels as well as a bustling job market at the scenario departments in Hollywood where Bower worked. A market for a new genre of original writing dawned, the peculiarities of which were outlined in an abundance of screenwriting manuals from the first half of the 1910s. The interaction, story flow, and migration of pens between the popular press in its many guises—pulp magazines, story papers, yellow-press books—and screen fiction proper still await in-depth mapping, likewise the implication of the influx of popular writers to the payrolls of the film company's emerging scenario departments. Both Charles Van Loan and B.M. Bower evidence this shift, which is only one aspect of the cornucopia of changes that repositioned film culture in the mid-1910s. In the early feature days a few authors, Rex Beach among them after the success of *The Spoilers*, even started short-lived studios of their own. The avalanche of film motifs in short stories and novels from the 1910s attests to the ascending leverage of film culture in the world of publishing. In the main, these texts and the new genre of film fiction still await their interpreters.

Nomenclature

The term "photoplay" was the winning result of a prize contest in 1910 for a new word to describe "the entertainment given in motion picture theaters."[14] In a temperamental discussion of the term "movies" the *Moving Picture World* noted with alacrity that the word nickelodeon "is dead," while " 'Photoplay' is being so seldom used that it may soon be forgotten, especially so now that the abominable 'movies' has risen. [---] What an excruciating sound this has!—at once vulgar and repulsive." True to the paper's name, the writer preferred "moving pictures" and "cinematography" when referring to individual films and the art form.[15] The term "photoplay," cushioned in the uplift initiatives from the trade and its press during phase IV, bisects the period discussed in this study in a number of different ways.

So widespread was the medium's cultural clout in everyday vernacular in 1914 that the *New York Times* saw fit to expound on the linguistic aspects of its processes: "The verb 'to film' having gained currency, it must be graciously admitted to the language. It will soon be in the 'advanced' dictionaries and it must be recognized. The old idea of protecting the English language from invasion is extinct. To 'film' means to make a picture for a 'movie' show. 'Movie' is a tolerably new word, too, but all the elite use it."[16] *Photoplay*, the magazine named after the winning term in the nomenclature contest, considered itself to have settled the linguistic quarrel in April 1915, when a questionnaire sent to 733 editors confirmed that the word "movie" was indeed a word in good standing. 511 editors were in favor of "movies" as the designation for moving pictures, while 222 voted nay. The magazine thus urged the nation's editors to adopt the term movies, claming "the question is now settled."[17] Even if the term movies, according to William Lord Wright in a comment from the same month, "does not well represent the value and educational importance of the Motion Picture art," he still considered "the violent agitation against it [...] 'much ado about nothing.' " The term, he explains, is widely embraced by the public and "can never be supplanted." More importantly, the expression is ideal for newspaper use. The six-letter term "fits easily into the single column width of great daily newspapers; the expression is greatly desired by writers of headlines." Summing up the debate, Wright also claims that " 'movies' will soon appear within the pages of standard dictionaries. Like [...] many other expressions that were primarily considered as slang expressions. 'Movies' is not undignified any more. It is a vital expression used everywhere by those who love Motion Pictures."[18]

As early as February 1913 the editor of *Motography* made it clear that he preferred moving pictures over movies.[19] This periodical was an upgraded incarnation from the unassuming days when it was called *Nickelodeon*. The name change and the switch from weekly to monthly publication began with the April issue of 1911, at a time when the nickel phase was a liability commonly dispensed with in the interests of uplift during phase IV. In the wake of the film business' unionization not all were pleased by the vernacular term movies in its different derivations. The Photoplay Authors League, for example, embarked on a campaign to abolish the word as undignified. The *Los Angeles Tribune* provided some of the background:

'De Movies' was first used to describe pictures by eastsiders in New York in the early days of photoplays. There is nothing cultured about these audiences and they seized on the expression that was easy to remember and that described, in a word, the shows that were beginning to interest them.

'The Movies,' however, seems scarcely the correct expression to apply to such elaborate productions as The Greyhound, My Friend from India, The Spoilers, and The Man on the Box, all filmatized plays which are to be

323

seen in Los Angeles this week. It sounds flippant and familiar to allude to works of art in such a careless way, and the public no doubt would obligingly adopt a more dignified designation for the pictures, if some intelligent photoplaywright would come to the front with a suggestion for a short, terse and descriptive substitute for 'movies.'

The only ban on the part of the public to relegating 'movies' to the dead languages is the lack of a dignified word that is just as expressive. Time is fleeting, even if art is long, and people have not leisure in this hustling young country to talk of the cinematograph or any of the foreign variations of that jaw-splitting word.[20]

Local exhibitors sided with the drift in the photoplaywrights' sensibility, and in September 1914 the trade press reported that the word was boycotted in Los Angeles.[21] When the smoke had cleared on the linguistic battlefield, Gene Morgan in the *Chicago Herald* redressed the clash between dignified appellation and popular idiom:

Poor 'movies'! On that day the word was torpedoed, annihilated, sunk, banished, exiled, proscribed and panned. Everything that could be done was done to chuck it out of the American vocabulary. Magazines and newspapers were beseeched to thrust it from their columns.

Motion picture firms were begged to eliminate it from their press sheets and posters. Dictionary builders were asked to blackball the word, at least to call it an obsolete vulgarism, a word fit only for the hoi polloi and others who eat hash with a bowie.

Alas, poor 'movies.' Did it stagger back to the word hospital, while a scornful nation brushed it off the vocal calling list?

Of course, it didn't.[22]

Another trade paper joined the linguistic fray late in 1915. In an editorial the *Exhibitors Herald* suggested use of the term "film play." Running through the expressions currently in use, movies is pronounced as "a legitimate offspring of 'Nickel Show,' and it is this latter term, which W. W. Hodkinson, president of the Paramount Pictures Corporation, says has been the greatest single retarding influence in the history of the motion picture industry." For different reasons, picture show (lack of dignity), motion picture (technical connotations), photoplay (no popular ring and not "suggestive of screen production from the spectators' point of view"), and cinema (foreign connotations) are all undesirable. Film play, the editor hopes, is dignified enough, lip friendly, potentially popular, and could be "a big factor in driving home the gospel of the constantly improving art of the screen."[23] Kitty Kelly commented upon the semantic suggestion from *Exhibitors Herald* in one of her columns, "Flickerings from Film Land." Siding with the editorial's line of reasoning, she still found it unlikely that headline writers and fans "can be induced to relinquish their beloved 'movies.' " Kelly simultaneously launched her own semantic protest against the phrase "film manufacturing company." She found it demeaning to term film plays "manufactured," but refrained from suggesting an alternative term. Taking stock of the situation in late 1915, Kelly neatly sums up the drift underlying the discursive processes we have been tracing in the preceding chapters by observing: " 'Movies' and 'dignity' aren't so far asunder as they used to be, and the distance is narrowing all of the time."[24] Her contention was foreshadowed a year before when the *Evening Sun* published a comprehensive list of technical film terms as "The 'Movie' Dictionary."[25]

The terminological debate surrounding the term "movies" attests to more general cultural anxieties concerning the language of cinema, which according to a British newspaperman, W.G. Faulkner, threatened to "corrupt the English language."[26] Faulkner's observation from 1913, that American English—its slang and otherwise—exerted a profound cultural influence, was prescient. In his influential essay from 1941, "The American Century," Henry R. Luce could thus wax poetic on Americana as the sole common currency across the globe: "American jazz, Hollywood movies, American slang, American machines and patented products, are in fact the only things that every community in the world, from Zanzibar to Hamburg, recognizes in common."[27] Luce's observation is as true of the current era of globalization as it was in the 1940s, not least due to the ubiquity of American television. In 1913, Faulkner noticed that the film trade overall operated on American slang: "[I]t is adopted by all English and Continental firms in describing their goods, and to-day it takes the place in the moving-picture business that French words and phrases held in the novels thirty and forty years ago." Picture patrons were in addition, he maintained, offered a crash course in American English as the alleged slang terms "are taught nightly on the screen." The patron learns "to think of his railway station as a 'depot'; he has alternatives to one of our newest words, 'hooligan,' in 'hoodlum' and 'tough'; he watches a 'dive,' which is a thieves' kitchen or a room in which bad characters meet, and whether the villain talks of 'dough' or 'sugar' he knows it is money to which he is referring." Thus in the most literal sense film language affected the use of English across the globe and while simultaneously invading other languages by way of Americanisms. Most alarming, however, is that American slang has invaded the "conversation of English people who have not been affected by the avalanche of Americanisms which has come upon us through the picture palace." For example, "peach" for pretty girl, "scab" for strikers, "fall" for autumn, and words like junk, stunt, boss, crook, elevator, janitor, buggy, dope, etc. Well in advance of American English dominance as the idiom of global culture, Faulkner's somewhat alarmist article caught the drift in the process of emergence.

Prologs

Time now to address the gradual increase in the production of multireel films, albeit in light of one particular feature of the early feature films, namely the opening sequences and their rhetorical manners of preparing the spectators for the story by ushering in readings of features in terms allied with other arts or as a specific form of film art. By way of filmic strategies, numerous features stake claims in the realm of art by means of rhetorical stances predicated on balancing a multiplicity of voices with different types of artistic leverage and authority. The feature films pitched their newfangled format, highlighted their artistic ambitions, and underscored their differences from run-of-the-mill productions. During a brief introductory phase, features were often adorned with scripted prologs and epilogs commenting upon and enveloping the story proper by way of narrative framing.

The emergence of features did not set in motion an orderly wholesale shift from shorter to longer subjects. Still, when William A. Brady's formation of the World Film Corporation was announced, an editorial in the *New York Review* quipped that the "mediocre, ordinary photo play, which sufficed for several years, has about had its day." The writer further noted that feature films currently were as important as new plays and that the "moving picture devotee looks forward to next week's film feature as ardently as ever play patrons do the coming of a new production in which their favorite star is to appear."[28] The variety model still reigned supreme even if the once ironclad practice of billing, consisting of a sequence of one-reel films of mixed genre, was gradually being replaced by programs offering a feature film together with a few shorts and newsreels for variety. And parallel to features, series and serials, the latter, predominantly two reels per episode, enjoyed a strong following at American theaters in the mid-1910s.

Some of the early American features were perceived as padded narratives with stories not deserving several reels of screen time.[29] Soon, however, the format displayed a series of concomitant shifts which redefined the new vehicles in several dimensions, most of them grounded in a form of amplifying recognition bearing on spectatorship and suggesting reading protocols aligned with other arts. The fields of recognition were related to actors and stage practices, authors, brand or studio names, and eventually acceptance of claims to cinematic authorship. Copyright issues were crucial aspects when publishers began to include film rights in the standard contracts for literary properties.

The strategies employed for early multi-reel films—labeled monster films in the previous discussion of Clune's Auditorium—intertwined both filmic and extra-filmic devices. The mix of devices sought to fashion a conceptual identity for the features based on human agency and creativity by singling out individual preeminence against the backdrop of collective efforts channeled via the studio under a recognizable brand, for instance Famous Players. The very fame of the players, earned largely on the stage in the early days of the feature, provided a focus on acting, which forged a link to the theatrical arts embodied by luminaries such as the legendary Sarah Bernhardt and the charismatic opera star Geraldine Farrar. Since features were often based on well-known texts, the screen adaptations guaranteed fame by association, and therefore, in a sense, heralded the feature format as a quasi-literary vernacular. Finally, by transcending the longstanding emphasis on the cinematic apparatus as a mere mechanical contraption, geniuses in the system emerged, namely producers, which was an early term for what we now call directors. So, three dominating, at times overlapping strands or registers suggested that the features were akin to artworks on account of creative impetus from authors, actors, and directors. Signatures on screen at times reinforced this claim, for example the autographed intertitles in D.W. Griffith's films. Brand recognition and studio identity took on extra significance in the feature era. Each film, due to the greater investments and downscaling of the number of titles produced, relied on a perception of exceptional merit, which encouraged flaunting of brands. *Patchwork Girl of Oz*, for example, opens with the girl in closeup wearing a diadem sporting the studio logo. Lasky's 1914 *Ready Money* was based on a Broadway success about mining speculation penned by James Montgomery. In the opening sequence's playful billing concept the actors are framed within the presidential oval of a $1,000 bill. After the actor takes a bow, George Washington is reinserted into his rightful place on the bill while the surrounding text banners right and left shift to "Lasky Features," which vouched for the currency, as it were.

When film performers emerged as actors and not mere mannequins subordinated to the machine, the talent they brought to the characterization underscored the fact that there was more to the medium than only grinding machines and models who could be substituted when worn out. Achievements before and also behind the camera mattered, and perceived differences perhaps even had a bearing that could be gauged in terms of art or degrees of artfulness. Hence, discourses began to crop up, and not only about actors and acting; the general term producer also took on a previously unknown precision, and the new entity of director emerged in the process. By literally introducing named persons as actors, or, for a time, amplifying various aspects of acting in opening sequences, or showcasing authors and eventually directors, the fecundity of the machine was downplayed to the status of a supplement, as it were. These strategies impacted the product and its brand name as well as the institution showing the material. Consequently, machine names gradually lost currency and fancy technical terms like motography vanished, while the term photoplay, coined in order to underwrite the putative theatrical nature of moving images, competed with the irreverent term movie before it became ubiquitous, though not without debates and misgivings, as we have shown.

In yet another reflection upon "The Actorless Theatre," this one published in the momentous year of 1909, a literary journal identifies cinema as a sign of the time, and, as was often the case, in the form of a catalog: "The age that has give us horseless carriages, smokeless powder and noiseless guns, has, in other words, also developed the actorless theatre."[30] The putative supremacy of the machine represented an important strand in the earliest response to film technology, outlined most distinctly by O. Winter in his attempt at placing the medium within a broader aesthetic precinct.[31] A decade later, the fledgling star system was about to fundamentally change the perception of the medium by upgrading the impact of human agency, processes analyzed by Richard DeCordova in his important study of picture personalities, a term picked up from the vernacular back in the day.[32] Parallel to the human agency in front of the camera, David Horsley offered unique specificity when hailing creativity behind the camera also in a 1911 list of distinguished "producers"; the latter concept makes most sense for modern readers when read as "directors." This list is indicative of changing perceptions from within the industry as the result of a breakthrough for short-story films, meriting a transition to credits and face, name, and brand recognition before and behind the camera for purposes of differentiation. Previously, studio branding was the product's most salient distinguishing feature. Here, the brands are connected to names and creative individuals. This sensibility found a new outlet a few years later in the prologs to feature films. According to Horsley in 1911:

> When one considers the wonderful work of men as Griffith, of the Biograph; Taylor, formerly of the Reliance; [Thomas] Ricketts, of the Nestor, formerly Essanay; Porter, of Rex, formerly with Edison; [Harry] Salter, now with Lubin, and Milton H. Fahrney, of the Nestor Western Company, in the producing line, the average old time director becomes a joke."[33]

One of these directors, D.W. Griffith, was not averse to shouldering the brunt of creative responsibility himself when talking about actors: "These people are merely automatons to me," he maintained. "I act out the whole thing for them, and imagining myself each individual character." Moreover, Griffith claimed in an aside, "I find I get much better results from the people that have never been on the stage." The interviewer, Louella Parsons, full of enthusiasm for the director, later compared his stature to a group of select cultural titans when describing him as the Shakespeare of Moving Pictures, the Edison of the Cinema, and the Marconi of the Screen.[34] This flamboyant characterization signals cinema's cultural command in the mid-1910s. When Griffith directed his landmark film *A Corner in Wheat* in 1909, nobody outside the industry took notice—except audiences perhaps.

Irrespective of this trade recognition, Griffith had never received any credit on screen due to company policy before leaving Biograph in the fall of 1913. To remedy the lack of recognition, as previously mentioned, Griffith had an ad published in the trade press in which he claimed responsibility for an extensive roster of films as well as for having introduced scores of stylistic novelties, among them the closeup, long shot, switchback, fade out, etc.[35] After making a handful of films at Reliance, he was ready for a bold move. Hence, in the opening credits for *The Birth of a Nation* we read a signed statement: "This is the trade mark of the Griffith feature films. All pictures made under the personal direction of D. W. Griffith have the name 'Griffith' in the border line, with the initials 'DG' at bottom of captions. There is <u>no exception</u> to this rule."

Not only directors went unrecognized, so did actors, even if audiences spotted recurring picture personalities, at times identifying them by way of gender and studio, such as the Vitagraph Girl, the Biograph Girl, etc. At American studios a shooting style that depersonalized players, not least by way of impersonal long shots in uncredited performances, eventually gave way to screen billing and more flexible thinking concerning spatial parameters for shooting and camera distance. A realm of subjectivity emerged when characters took on a dimension of actual personhood due to a shooting style that gradually redefined acting. Ghosts, shadows, models, and mannequins were thus turned into characters. This sea change in the public's perception of actors is concisely outlined in an article published in 1912:

> A few years ago the moving-picture actor wasn't given any consideration by his audience. He was merely a part of the mechanism at least in the public's opinion. With the advancement of the work this has been changed; regular 'movie patrons' have grown accustomed to seeing the same face week after week in the most varied actions.
>
> Favorites have grown up in their minds, and they look forward eagerly for their parts. It is possible to see them in at least one new role a week and become acquainted to a certain extent with their personalities as reflected by the film. The manufacturers and moving picture theater owners have recognized this growth to such extent that in many cases players are being featured almost as prominently as the reels.[36]

Discussions on spectatorship are intimately correlated with the interface between screen and the spectators' minds, beliefs, and emotions. By mentally isolating real audience members from the auditorium context and privatizing him/her qua spectator/spectatrix, the viewing position tended to favor a narrative mode rather than a dramatic one. In the early feature era filmmakers apparently still felt unease and misgivings concerning the threshold from which spectatorship was launched, namely the film's opening, which inspired a set of core approaches for channeling proper audience responses and suggestions for spectatorship balancing between the narrative, the dramatic, and the cinematic. These intertwined modes are radicalized here for the sake of argument concerning strategies for setting the features apart from the conventional crop of films. Irrespective of how one decides to label the type of opening sequences we are about to discuss—prologs, avant-propos, pre-diegetic sequences, expository sequences, pre-credit sequences, preliminary scenes, emblematic shots, cameo introductions, etc.—such story framing was in vogue during the mid-1910s. In passing Barry Salt mentions several striking examples from the past in films produced by Biograph, Vitagraph, and Ambrosio.[37]

The opening sequences invariably impinge upon three, sometimes overlapping, levels of creativity in order to anchor the artistic process behind the features and thus offer suggestions for modes of spectatorship: These levels involve the author behind the text, the actors performing on screen—defined in stage-like terms or not—or the director as the grandmaster of the artistic machinery as the Griffith signature boldly suggests. A few rare films operate on all three levels. We will move from authors to actors and finally discuss pitches for cinematic authorship by directors.

The Authors' League of America was in an awkward position vis-à-vis the movies in 1914. In an effort to seek better recognition for their work—not only on the screen—the League produced a film program together with Vitagraph, which was shown at a League function held at New York City's Plaza Hotel on February 19, 1914. A select group of writers had chosen a favorite scene from their literary corpus for shooting and, in addition, they appeared on screen as an adjunct to the story, either seated at a desk writing or at ease in a library, reading their own books. An impressive roster of authors was on display: Ida Tarbell, Princess Troubetzkoy, Booth Tarkington, Ellis Parker Butler, George Ade, Rex Beach, George Barr McCutcheon, and Louis Joseph Vance.[38] This playful event soon turned into a standard practice for placing an authorial imprint on feature films.

Putting authors on screen in a signature-like fashion, as a quality seal to bridge the transposition from text to film text—the latter's prestige was underwritten in the (para-)textual process—ostensibly warranted a hoped-for seamless transposition from novel or play to screen. The practice originated in Europe, where the longer film format was pioneered. In *Ingeborg Holm* (Swedish Biograph, 1913), for example, three introductory shots open the film: a still portrait of the play's author, by no means a household name, followed by a shot of the well-known leading lady walking through a door, and a child in bed hugging a teddy bear. The last two shots were hijacked and repositioned from ensuing sequences. The first two, displaying Krook and Borgström, played with recognition and naming, while the young boy was introduced as a nameless character. The claim is here dual, and in this respect the film rests on two pillars: as based on a play authored by Krook and with the title role acted by a renowned actress from the Royal Dramatic Theater in Stockholm. A similar strategy was outlined in the script for *Terje Vigen* produced two years later by the same company, but the scene featuring Henrik Ibsen ended up on the cutting-room floor or was lifted prior to shooting.

The literary anchoring is even more explicit in the opening of Hobart Bosworth's 1914 film *Martin Eden*, based on Jack London's novel and part of a series of London adaptations.[39] The film opens with a photograph of Jack London in a circular frame, followed by the cast list. The first moving images treat the audience to a shot of a relaxed Jack London seated in a reclining chair, a subsequent edit moves in to a very close shot of his face. The film chronicles an autobiographical story about a sailor struggling to become a writer, a process personalized by putting London on the screen.

The opening of *The Italian* (New York Motion Picture Co., 1915) is even more elaborate, resorting to a dual strategy: Besides the theatrical frame, the prolog toys with conventionalized representations of literary prestige, though in a purely virtual register in this case. Curtain-like drapery opens to reveal a room. In the prolog lead actor George Beban picks up a book and starts to read; we are privy to his view of the first page, which takes us into the diegesis. Prior to this we get to see the cover of what looks like a novel; one could easily be mislead into believing that there actually was a novel called *The Italian* on which the film is based, as the cover lists two "authors": Thomas H. Ince and C. Gardner Sullivan. That was, however, not the case: Sullivan was the principal scriptwriter and shares credit with studio head Ince for the doubly fictional novel. The non-existent novel provided grounding for the film text even in this imaginary case: The film is defined as being based on a novel.

The Danish film *Ned med Vaabnene* ("Down With Weapons," Nordisk Films Kompagni, 1914) opens with Nobel prizewinner Bertha von Suttner at her desk, possibly where she penned the pacifist novel from which the film was adapted. A similar method was devised in a serial context for introducing the prolific Charles Van Loan, author of the collection of short stories filmed as *Buck Parvin and the Movies* (American, 1915-16). The author was featured in a concentrated opening scene showing him being inspired to write the stories on which the film installments are based. A trade paper provides shorthand for this lost first episode in the serial: "From the time that Charles E. Van Loan, the author of these stories, is seen in the act of conceiving the idea of their being put on the screen, the action does not lag for one moment during the three reels."[40] Here, we are presented with a pilot introducing a string of independent serial installments all related to the character Buck Parvin and set in a studio context—and the stories were all penned by Charles Van Loan, whose presence on screen, however, was restricted to the pilot. Even after the feature format reigned supreme, well-known authors at times were introduced in advance of the story proper. In F.W. Murnau's *Phantom* (1922), for example, Gerhard Hauptmann is showcased in a prolog.

Biopics are special cases, but at times tie in with the strategies for prologs. Essanay's 1915 production of *The Raven* offers a complex introduction of Edgar Allan Poe in a prolog featuring several generations of ancestors. First, we witness John Poe's arrival in America in 1745, while the next sequence shows Daniel Poe as a revolutionary patriot in 1776. Next, David Poe, Jr. marries a Mrs. Hopkins in 1805; they are introduced in their profession, as actors. Finally, Edgar, or, rather, a photo of him, dissolves into the actor playing Edgar, Henry B. Walthall, who acknowledges an imaginary audience in closeup. This complex introduction combines two strands of authority related to both acting and the stature commanded by a canonical literary figure in a film named after one of his most famous poems. Biopics might be a special case, but putting bard figures on screen for purposes of story framing at times inspired revival of even the most prototypical of authors. In Milano Film's *Una Tragedia alla corte di Sicilia* (1914) the two leading characters are introduced in costume before a prolog presents William Shakespeare, reading his *A Winter Tale* to a group of people seated around a table no less. His reading opens up the fictional world, and after the story comes to a close we return to Shakespeare and his audience for a concluding epilog. Here, the film comes across as a hybrid between the text as read and listened to by the vicarious audience around Shakespeare's table and unfolding on the screen; the film is thus more or less analog to Shakespeare's reading. This is a plea for the film's integrity in terms of a posited non-infringing identity between the dramatic text and the film text, mediated by a reading. Scores of films adopted similar strategies, using however simpler means by focusing on a copy of the text, a strategy appropriated by Sullivan and Ince for *The Italian*. The cover or a page transports us into the fiction as if it were a literary one, while other films resorted to intertitles to ensure the authenticity of their respective narrational processes. An early American feature like Kalem's *From the Manger to the Cross* offers precise quotations of verses from the gospels, while *Terje Vigen* gives us Ibsen's poem in the intertitles, canceling however the script's introduction and refraining from showing an actor play the playwright in the prolog. The move from the author to the book, or to text quotations, is somewhat akin to the even more common device of defining a feature presentation as a theatrical event by invoking the stage or introducing actors as acclaimed stage stars, a strategy to which we now turn our attention.

In *The Bargain* (New York, 1914) the leading actors, starting with William S. Hart, acknowledge the audience as from within an auditorium by nodding right and left before ceremoniously bowing deep to the middle, and when rising they are in character. In this case the stars do not draw upon previous stage fame. Prologs featuring actors often playfully orchestrate the shift from actor to character, simultaneously highlighting the actors behind the characters and the acting dimension overall. *The Typhoon* (New York, 1914) opens with curtains parting and a traditionally dressed Japanese boy nodding left and right before taking a deep bow; when he rises, a dissolve leaves him in Western street clothes. He is close to the camera before the curtain closes. The leading player, Sessue Hayakawa, is then introduced via a credit text and by way of the same procedure stripped of Japanese clothes and turned into an actor in Parisian costume. The leading ladies are then introduced and transferred from street clothes to character costume. After the dissolve they all act in their respective parts, which means that the cultural background is defined by their garb when out of character. After the presentation of the leading players the curtain parts to open up the entire visual field before vanishing in a decidedly theatrical masking of the full film frame. The direction of the process of transformation was far from unilateral. Instead of actors turning into characters via a simple film trick, many films reversed the order, some in a highly elaborate fashion, for instance by lap-dissolving from actors out of character to characters in costume and makeup, thereby underscoring the dimension of acting. The move is primarily from street clothes to costume, but *The Royal Pauper* (Edison, 1917), rather late in this context, reverses the order by showing Francine Larrimore transformed from the character of a poor girl to an expensively gowned star off-screen, thereby having her step out of character rather than step in.

Curtains are key indicators of theatricality and stage anchoring. Maurice Tourneur used a quartet of dancers on a shallow stage to open one of his filmic fictions. The players and story seemingly reside behind a curtain, which closes after the denouement in *The Wishing Ring* (World, 1914). A very elaborate address to the audience as if from a stage can be found in the recently restored *Tillie's Punctured Romance* (Keystone, 1914), which opens and closes on such notes featuring Marie Dressler. The move is highly unusual, as this is a comedy, which, apart from the longer format, carries genre connotations steering clear of the feature's otherwise loftier artistic aspirations. The leading actress, dressed in street clothes, is introduced in front of a curtain; her clothing then transforms into her costume, and in a final transformation she is propelled by an edit from her position in front of the curtain into the fictional world. As the film ends, she and her fellow players step in front of the curtain, emerging from the fictional world more or less ruffled as if from a theatrical performance to take applause from an imaginary audience. In *Tess of the Storm Country* (Famous Players, 1914) Mary Pickford enters from behind a curtain and puts flowers in a gigantic vase. She is elegantly attired and does not acknowledge the camera. In this case there is no smooth dissolve to her ragged and folksy film character. In more tongue-in-cheek play with both star and character status Max Figman is introduced as the last leading character in the prolog to *The Man on the Box* (Lasky, 1915): He is literally seated while the other leading players are summoned by a coachman calling out their names via megaphone, after which each actor emerges from the carriage before taking bows right and left. Eventually, Figman steps down from the box, grabs the megaphone and calls out his own name, which just like the others emerges as letters scrambling from it. The bulk of the story is predicated on Figman assuming a coachman's identity, far below his natural station. In the end he is recognized and rightfully upgraded to his proper place in preparation for getting his dream girl.

The many bows to the camera in the prologs mapped out a putative theatrical terrain by scattering gazes around a virtual auditorium. The prologs thereby established an imaginary threshold, allowing a form of direct address otherwise prohibited en route to classicism; this address, with its obvious attraction status, in numerous ways negotiated a plastic film culture while simultaneously teasing out the nuts and bolts of the format.

Numerous introductions discounted a stage frame. In the opening of Selig's 1914 film *The Spoilers*, based on Rex Beach's novel, the leading players, beginning with Dustin Farnum, are framed in a kind of glassless French window. Beneath the opening, the characters' names are noted as an inscription or caption, and the transition from one character to the next is effected by way of dissolves. Overall, film effects are commonly used in these opening sequences to facilitate a smooth billing process, and when actors play multiple roles, such effects abound. In Lasky's 1915 film *The Secret Sin* Blanche Sweet plays a pair of twins. In the opening Sweet walks toward the camera, dressed in black against a black background. To her left one of the twins, in costume, is matted in; Sweet then greets herself. When she turns to the right, the other twin is matted in and again greetings are exchanged. The twins then disappear, and thereafter Sweet herself. In this social melodrama focusing on unemployment and the temptations of drugs all scenes with the twins are shot in split screen, many of them featuring witty solutions for crossing the frame for the two versions of the actress.

Our final theatrical example offers a highly elaborate introduction, but is totally devoid of tricks; instead, we are back to stage frames and curtains. Jacob P. Adler, the famous Jewish actor, appeared in only one film, *Michael Strogoff*, produced by Popular Plays and Players in 1914. The film opens with an intertitle promising "Mr. Jacob P. Adler in some of his famous characterizations." Adler enters in tailcoat, and takes off his top hat as if to greet the audience. After a fadeout he returns in four different costumes from some of his trademark theatrical roles, and after doing a bit of business in each part, he acknowledges the audience's presence, as it were. Prior to the film, we are thus treated to Adler as "Shylock," "Uriel Acosta," "Solomon De Kaus," and finally "The Wild Man" before the curtain closes, signaling the opening of the Strogoff story. Here, a theatrical career crossing over to film is outlined by anthologizing of his legendary stage roles as a kind of résumé for his showcase in the title role of *Michael Strogoff*.

Other films offered prologs as complex as the Adler film, but from different vantage points. D.W. Griffith's lost film *The Escape* (Majestic, 1914) came with a lengthy, allegorical prolog which positioned the ensuing story on human hardships on the Lower East Side in relation to breeding patterns of and natural selection in primordial life forms. From there the prolog moved on to frogs and sheep before introducing a laborer with three children, a girl plagued by consumption and a boy criminally insane after being brutally assaulted by his father; while the third child manages to escape, the moral is fairly obvious.[41]

Our final example takes us to Denmark and a film with an impressive critical following in the U.S. *Blind Justice* (*Hævnens Nat*, Dansk Biograf Kompagni, 1916) takes cinematic authorship to a paramount level by means of Benjamin Christensen's multitasking, the foregrounding strategies, and the marketing; in fact, the prolog was part of the marketing and exhibition, at least when the film opened in Copenhagen.

The opening of Christensen's film is spectacularly succinct, yet rich in revealing salient information. Still, we are literally left in the dark and forced to ponder the meanings of this enigmatic pretext, which also proves to set the visual tone for the entire film. The stylistically charged opening is centered on a model of one of the prime locations in the film. An intertitle identifying Benjamin Christensen (1879-1959) as the producer, scenarist, and male lead against the backdrop of his previous success with *Sealed Orders*—Christensen's first foray into filmmaking in 1913—is followed by a second intertitle introducing the model. At the outset only a few windows on the model's first floor are lit. After an invisible cut all windows are suddenly blazing and the model starts rotating counterclockwise while the background remains black and opaque. When the rotation comes full circle, an intertitle furnishes a bridge to the next shot, in the process shedding light on the prosaic meaning of the sequence if not the intricate manner of conveying the information: "[P]roducer Christie explains to Miss Katherine Sanders the location of the rooms in the doctor's villa."

The advertised shot initially shows the model up close, and when the camera tracks back, the characters become semi-visible in the darkness. Christensen removes the roof of the model and uses a tightly rolled architectural blueprint of the house as a pointer to explain and demonstrate the location's outlay to his leading lady as the camera retreats further. When the roof is removed, the sparse and dramatic light from inside the model visibly sculptures the characters standing in profile. Christensen moves around in the dark area frame right when fidgeting with the roof, therefore moving in and out of the light and semi-visibility; Karen Sandberg is more or less stationary frame left. Both protagonists wear dark clothes, so only skin—their hands and faces—offers sufficient contrast to be visible, apart from Christensen's white collar and cuffs. The three-dimensionality of the model, in combination with natural light, conveys a flair for realism, though simultaneously a penchant for propelling diegetic motivation to symbolic levels. Moreover, Christensen apparently took the sequence one step further by converting the model to a display item in the lobby at the Palads-Theater when the film opened in Copenhagen. A reviewer noted in passing that "people flocked around the model of the villa in the lobby."[42] Thus, for the first audience, the meaning of the film's opening carried different connotations than for later audiences not treated to this type of lobby display.

The two named figures presented in dramatic low-key lighting are the leading characters in the film. Christensen is further singled out as its veritable auteur: director, screenwriter, male lead, and in control and command of virtually all aspects of the production process, which is underscored by his demonstration. His name is also inscribed in the main title. We are, of course, not encountering real persons positioned outside the story who are destined to turn into characters just a few shots ahead, but liminal figures, in several respects, hovering between blurred diegetic spheres. Films offer no unscripted spaces of fictional innocence unaffected by storytelling; instead, we are offered a rhetorical gesture highlighting a threshold of performance putatively framed as an aspect of total authorial command, a substitute for a run-of-the-mill credits sequence splitting the laurels. All credit due, it seems, is wrapped around Christensen's persona. The sequence thus mounts an unequivocal case for authorship by reminding us of Christensen's first film and its success in addition to the full panoply of roles in front of and behind the camera in the production being shown. Defined as auteur via the information in the main title and intertitles, we are invited to watch him share information from this position with his fellow featured player. After the demonstration Christensen switches on the light in the room while he and Karen Sandberg continue to make small talk in an apparently upbeat mood. According to Christensen's will, one lighting protocol is substituted for another; such shifts in lighting and visibility permeate *Blind Justice*. The film is replete with trick-like invisible cuts, and it is invariably the two characters introduced here that regulate these shifts. Authorial intervention, visible as elements of style or "trickality," defines the story as told rather than shown.

Blind Justice was received very favorably on the American film market after the trade show in mid-September. Not only the style and narrative were praised, but foremost the acting, particularly Christensen's. The reviewer in *Variety* was typical in this respect: "But it is not the play, the fine scenic detail or anything else—it is the remarkable acting of Benjamin Christie that makes *Blind Justice* a masterpiece of motion photography."[43] Adam Hull Shirk expressed a similar assessment in the *New York Morning Telegraph*: "Two things stand out pre-eminently in this picture—the acting of Mr. Christie and the photography. Coupled with the latter is the remarkably fine lighting." Shirk was, however, displeased with the opening: "The details of the direction are finely carried out, though the preliminary scenes showing the model of the house, etc., might be eliminated without loss to the story."[44]

Vitagraph put the film on the market as a Blue Ribbon Feature distributed by the new VLSE exchange. A second series of trade publicity was accorded the film when officially released on January 22, 1917. The reviewer in the *New York Dramatic Mirror* neatly summed up the excessive claim to authorship the film makes: "To prove that one is thoroughly proficient in not only one but practically all the departments that are combined under the general head of film production is no mean feat. Benjamin Christie, a remarkably versatile Dane, has done just this. His first picture shown in this country, 'Sealed Orders,' generated the idea, and the second, 'Blind Justice,' surely cements it. One learns that he wrote the story and scenario, directed the production and then sees him further gather in honors by giving a performance in the star part that is in the highest artistic attitude. If a choice had to be made regarding which branch he was most proficient in, it could be truthfully said that he is a better actor than anything else, but at that it is pretty close judgment."[45]

In the case of Christensen, one can tease out authorship as a result of omnipresence across the board and total command of all aspects of a leisurely production process. Style, trickality, and excess function as elements of a signature underwriting a conscious manipulation of devices, which can be summed up as expressivity. The narration thereby becomes less transparent, the fictional world less independent, and the story more openly narrated by someone shouldering active responsibility for the process. Works by Christensen, DeMille, and Tourneur offer stark instances of such a cinema of expressivity, which gradually shifted the emphasis away from prologs to the overall narrational process for which directors gradually assumed responsibility. Few directors were marketed as heavily as Christensen for *Blind Justice*, not even Griffith for *The Clansman/The Birth of a Nation*; the latter was of course still the prototypical director in the American trade discourse, which we will return to.

When features became the prime product in Hollywood, the format needed no caveats and little extra backup from stage titans. Authors still could impart added marketing value, but overall, the film industry and its own people in front and behind the camera provided excitement enough to disseminate the classically told features. Moreover, these films found audiences all over the world ready to embrace Hollywood products and idolize American screen stars.

CHAPTER 9

PIONEERING PENS:
KITTY KELLY, MAE TINEE,
AND GERTRUDE PRICE

"Even the sophisticated early morning audiences gasped at certain
suggestive scenes which out-keystoned the limit of Keystonism."[1]

IN HER IMPORTANT book on movie-struck girls, vice films, and serial queens, Shelley Stamp meticulously discusses ambiguities concerning
female spectatorship.[2] Women patrons apparently exhibited auditorium
behavior at odds with the silent, privatized, and absorbed mode considered indicative of the burgeoning classic style. Narrational address
from within the films has often been perceived as powerful enough to
coerce boisterous interaction in the auditorium and in the process engineer a privatized mode of absorption, a theoretical framework Stamp
calls into question. Stamp's material indeed evidences a preoccupation
with problematic female spectatorship in both the trade press and general-interest magazines. The rich materials Stamp has unearthed carry
little specificity regarding actual transgressions, however. The string of
caricatures, poems, etiquette rules, etc. policing alleged deviations often
seems to sport prejudiced anecdotal flavor rather than describing a dominant mode of historical spectatorship. Hats blocking views were most
certainly a much-noticed problem, overdressing perhaps likewise, and
also the distracting presence of cute usherettes and pianists. And wom-
en apparently conversed and commented on screen content. Newspaper material rarely underwrites such a reading as dominant gender practices, apart from the avalanche of cartoons devoted to the alleged hat
problem. If this discourse is only substantiated infrequently by reports

341

on spectatorship and fueled by other concerns instead, at the same time it no doubt evidences a running anxiety regarding women's new role in the public sphere at large, which is Stamp's point. On the other hand, reporters were fascinated by women's presence and roles in all forms of contexts, from policewomen to all-female film shows and all-female staffs, and soon enough women were penning film columns and reviewing films besides "chatting" with fans.

When James Keeley left the *Chicago Tribune* early in May 1914 for other newspaper ventures, the ensuing revamp of the Sunday edition included "the latest movie news and gossip."[3] According to a Web site, "the first newspaper to introduce regular film reviews was the *Chicago Tribune* which appointed Jack Lawson as film critic." Lawson had the misfortune of falling into an elevator shaft at the Chicago Press Club and dying on March 19, 1914, so literally by accident Miss Audrie Alspaugh stepped into his shoes and after a few months sported the byline "Kittie Kelly" the first few days in late June, after which she was "Kitty Kelly." Her column proved to be a huge success, and she became "the best disliked name in the world of film studios and it was said that 'Kitty Kelly' could make or break a picture in the Middle West."[4] Audrie Alspaugh entered film journalism by way of the *Tribune*'s literary page after academic studies at the University of Iowa. She married the *Tribune*'s real-estate editor, Al Chase, in October 1915, an occurrence that was turned into a "Reel Romance" in four reels by blithe colleagues at the paper who were taken by surprise when the news came in over the wires.

Later in this chapter Kelly's writing, and that of her colleague Mae Tinee, will serve as indicators for film culture's breakthrough in the daily press during phase V of my roster of press-cinema interaction. In the scholarly discourse the *Tribune* figures primarily in accounts of the 1907 crusade against the nickel shows and the publishing of serial tie-ins in 1914. As a leading daily newspaper, the *Tribune* continued to publish film material in the gap between the 1907 campaign and the column headed by Lawson.

Late in 1911 the *Tribune* offered readers illustrated accounts of films produced by local film companies; the first film accorded attention was Essanay's *The Wife's Story*. Here and for some of subsequent "photo play[s] in story form," the original film title was modified.[5] The following week a column on "Moving Pictures and Makers" appeared. Penned by Gene Morgan, it treated readers to tidbits of information on film matters, for example the fact that California was on the verge of becoming a film center, that Kalem had commissioned a musical score for the studio's film *Arrah-Na-Pouge*, and that the National Association for Study and Prevention of Tuberculosis had sponsored a film.[6] The week after that, the column had acquired a new title, "In the Moving Picture World"; henceforth, it was edited by "Reel Observer" but still reported on a wide variety of film matters in weekly installments until mid-September 1912, when it petered out. Reel Observer did not purvey the gossipy fare later trademarked as a preferred genre for fans; this was trade paper-like reporting with a Chicago slant and provided only a limited amount of personal information on actors and actresses.

The story focus returned in the *Tribune*'s revamped department, "Today's Best Moving Picture," which was inaugurated on February 5, 1914, and introduced in the following manner: "To more than half a million Chicagoans moving picture plays present the drama of daily life. A newspaper man has been assigned by The Tribune to view the films in advance of their release, and to write for Tribune readers a daily short story of what he considers the best film to be shown each day. The story may be read in the morning. The picture play may be seen in the afternoon or night." This unsigned column, in the hands of Jack Lawson, was launched around a month after the *Tribune* had began publishing story accounts of Selig's serial film *The Adventures of Kathlyn*.

The inaugural title presented as "Today's Best Moving Picture" was Biograph's *The Dilemma* starring Louise Vale. The text was arranged in six chapters and, true to the headline, strictly focused on the story outline. The *Tribune* diligently spread its graces among the producers: The next day an Edison title followed, thereafter stories based on titles from Pathé, Kleine-Cines, Selig, etc. The stories were often introduced by a credit list more or less fully accounting for the roster of players. The outlines were all unsigned and published six days a week. Its format changed on February 16th: Instead of endorsing one film with a longish story, several films were encapsulated under a new headline, "Today's Best Photo Play Stories." The first day showcased titles produced by Selig, Biograph, Kalem, and Keystone, still without a signature.

On February 29th a Sunday department devoted to "the silent drama and the silent players" was launched in addition to the stories; Mae Tinee conducted this "Film and Screen Department." The advance notice concerning the department promised: "It will be different. It will be dignified. It will abound in color and pictures, humor and romance. It will give you local, national and international news of your favorite players. It will give you intimate and personal gossip of your favorite players. It will show you the latest pictures and poses of your favorite player. It will print the principal scenes in which your favorite players are playing." But this was not all: "It will take you into its confidence, ask your wishes about what you want to read and see in it, and give you any and all information you desire concerning moving pictures and their people. It will take you into the home and depict the comedies and tragedies therein."[7] The *Tribune* kept this format—stories Monday through Saturday and a more personalized department on Sundays together with serial fictionalization—until June 30th, when the story section was suddenly signed—by Kitty Kelly. Under Kelly, the column gradually expanded and on July 7th a new headline emerged: "Photoplay Stories and News," which in turn was changed to the longstanding "Flickerings from Film Land" on September 25th. While this column promised broader optics apart from story accounts and reports on censorship excisions, the latter still remained a regular subject. The shift of headline—which however alternated with the old one for a time, for no discernible reason in terms of content—reflected Kelly's writing, which over the summer had turned into reviewing proper. The first film under the new heading was Great Northern's *Lay Down Your Arms*, based on Bertha von Suttner's pacifist novel. According to Kelly, "the picture is a fine achievement, continuing Baroness von Suttner's propaganda in spirited fashion and purveying much pictorial beauty along with its didactic purpose."[8]

Frances Peck Grover, Kelly's colleague, was visible in the *Tribune* well into the 1960s, "adopting a chatty persona" and shrouding the lady under the pseudonym Mae Tinee. The address and interactive ambition in her columns most certainly tried to forge a gender bond to the readers and elicit responses based on the assumption that film fans were predominantly women, perhaps even young women. Grover retired in 1945 and died in May 1961, but the *Tribune* kept her pseudonym going long after her retirement as a *nom de plume* for various contributors writing on film matters. She also published a couple of booklets on film stars, a slim brochure in 1916 and a second volume in the 1930s. Initially, she sometimes appeared under her own maiden name, Frances Peck Barnes, when writing on matters outside stage and screen. Miss Barnes debuted as Mae Tinee on October 31, 1909, and the first piece was consequently headlined: "Her First Assignment: Interviewing Maxine," that is Maxine Elliott. The aspiring young woman of journalism came across as enchanted with her new line of work, and she was as intrigued by Maxine as with her brand-new profession. Tinee continued to rack up assignments: James K. Hackett was number two, Billy Burke number five, etc. Even after she abandoned the number crunching, stage-related journalism remained her prime focus.

In her very first film column Mae Tinee paid a visit to the Essanay studio and was so bitten by the film bug that on the following Sunday she reported, "I was a movie actress for two days."[9] As an extra, she tangoed with a policeman the first afternoon, and the next day she was awarded a small part in a Francis X. Bushman film, in a courtroom scene. This experience led to a more comprehensive piece when Tinee was sent to New York City to visit the studios there. On April 12, 1914, the *Chicago Tribune* inaugurated a weekly, unsigned column called "Gossip of the Movie Plays and Players" on the page edited by Mae Tinee. The format expanded on June 14th, but was still unsigned. Credit was however given Tinee from August 2nd and onwards.

In 1911 Mary Heaton Vorse published an account from a nickel theater on New York City's East Side focusing on an immigrant woman in the audience who was both entranced by the film and unaware of commenting on it "in a lilting *obbligato*."[10] This is a moment in film reception which has been discussed extensively by theorists of spectatorship, Miriam Hansen most prominently, focusing on a juncture when individual absorption allegedly supplanted a previous mode of lively engagement with the screen. Mae Tinee takes us back to the same show, as it were, but three years later, and paradoxically reports on modes of spectatorship far from silent and privatized. A male friend escorted her to a couple of shows on the East Side one Saturday evening. One of the films was an Essanay title, which harks back to Tinee's days as an extra in that particular studio. Writes our metaspectatrix:

If I tried all night I never could make you understand the enthusiasm of that audience.

There were sobs for Bushman and Miss Stonehouse—hisses for the other girl; and when Miss Dunbar, taking the part of the hero's mother, knelt by his side endeavoring to comfort him in his vicissitudes, one woman said right out loud:

345

'That's right young feller, you let yer mother make ye feel better. Forget the good for nothin' huzzy!' And there came a chorus of approval from the other women in the house and several acquiescent grunts from the men.

'Isn't this perfectly lovely,' I murmured. 'Isn't it great to be able to live things the way these people do? They just keep on being children for all of their lives, don't they?'

He nodded. 'Yes,' he said, 'and because they have the hearts of children I believe they're the happiest people on earth in spite of the poverty.'[11]

Much could be said about this unsettling observation and cinema's role as an escapist haven for those that had entered through the golden door as well as poor people by and large. After this excursion Tinee devoted the rest of her attention to the studios in Gotham and its environs. At a time when the *Tribune*, during a short overlap, serialized both *The Adventures of Kathlyn* and *The Million-Dollar Mystery*, both by McGrath, Mae Tinee still was in New York City and particularly close to the Thanhouser studio, the producer of the latter serial. She thus published several long pieces related to *The Million-Dollar Mystery* and its cast and production crew. Tinee even secured parts as an extra in some Thanhouser titles. This interactive approach takes the tie-in genre to a new level of proximity, foreshadowing even closer collaboration like the alliance between Hearst and Selig for a newsreel and its aftermath featuring Grace Darling, but the most obvious example is Gertrude M. Price, another pioneering film pen who eventually landed a bit part in a studio.

Price made her debut as "The Record's Moving Picture Expert" in the *Los Angeles Record* on April 21, 1913, with a featured article about actor King Baggot. Nothing else was heard from Moving Picture Expert Price until September 30th, five months after the first piece, when she signed a featured article on Lois Weber. Her third signed piece was published nine months later, on June 20, 1914. Because of the syndication within the Scripps-McRae League, it is difficult to ascertain where material originated; at least some writers visible in the *Record*'s columns were most certainly based elsewhere before ending up in Los Angeles. A couple of texts on film matters from 1909, published in the *Los Angeles Record* at long intervals by Katherine M. Zengerle, were however highly local in their approach. In March she visited the projection booth at the American Moving Picture Theater on South Broadway, in November she returned to the columns with a lengthy report from Selig's plant out in Edendale. After these two pioneering articles Zengerle disappeared, unless two unsigned film pieces from 1910 emanated from her pen. One printed in February dealt at length with film and eye strains, and an interview with Hobart Bosworth was published in March.[12]

It seems as if Gertrude M. Price was based in Chicago in 1912–1914, from where she published regularly on film matters, or rather film personalities. Exactly when the Scripps-McRae League hired her remains unclear, though it was probably during 1911. In the Chicago City Directories for 1912 and 1913 she was listed as a reporter, in 1914 as an editor. From 1915 she can be found in the directory for Los Angeles. It does not seem as if she was transferred to Los Angeles to write on film only. In fact, a colleague took over her title on August 1, 1914, when Ester Hoffmann emerged as "The Record's Picture Play Reporter," writing about "the shyest man in the movies," namely Francis X. Bushman. Hoffmann was writing from Chicago, often reporting on recent openings at the Studebaker Theater. On November 5th, featured with a byline portrait, Hoffmann wrote about a visit to the Essanay studio in Chicago. That particular studio turned into a fixture of reporting in the *Record*—the company's scenario editor even published screenplay advice which was probably syndicated in other Scripps papers. Hoffmann returned on November 17th to introduce a contest for a part as a telephone girl in an Essanay film to be awarded to the most beautiful professional operator in the country. In between the feature articles Hoffmann signed numerous biographical sketches of film personalities, focusing on actresses mostly. Many if not more film stars were presented in unsigned articles.

After having been invisible for some time, Price returned with a signed piece on December 28, 1914. In January 1915 she introduced herself as an aspiring movie actress—and she had indeed spent a day in front of the camera at Universal, a scoop outlined in detail over three days. Unfortunately, the film Price graced with her acting, *Smouldering Fires*, is lost. Egged on by colleagues who dissuaded her from an allegedly futile attempt at landing a part, she took the streetcar to Hollywood, "the mecca of the movies," and entered the Universal lot at Gower Street. She applied for a job as an extra without flaunting her newspaper affiliation—and promptly landed a bit part in a film, under director Jacques Jaccard and starring J. Warren Kerrigan, to be shot the following day by the Victor Co. The second installment elaborated on her visit to the studio the following day, the drive out to Universal City, and the costume and makeup process prior to shooting. Price was assigned a part as a "Spanish Girl." After the makeover, the reporter felt like a "Christmas tree," but was assured she looked just fine. On the set Price had a long talk with Kerrigan prior to shooting, and before the camera was cranked, she was instructed to "BE NATURAL" and "DON'T LOOK INTO THE CAMERA." Price was to sit at a table in a saloon somewhere out west and casually smile and make small talk before hiding under the table during a shoot-out in the following scene. The experience earned her studio insights and five dollars.[13]

Price's presence in Los Angeles did not preclude Ester Hoffmann from reporting on film issues occasionally. Price, however, covered the major local film events—the opening of *The Clansman* at Clune's Auditorium, the inauguration of the Universal Studios, a piece on Mae Marsh and her family, Geraldine Farrar's arrival in Hollywood, etc. In fact, for the opening of Universal Studios, Price might have rubbed shoulders with Kitty Kelly, who came in on the celebrity train from Chicago.

If Price was the League's film expert for a time, this specialization did not prevent her from writing on an array of other matters. Soon enough she was in charge of the Woman's page and answering inquiries as Cynthia, and from there she was put in charge of the Club page. In this latter capacity she became an institution in Los Angeles for decades. As we know, women's clubs played an important role as arenas for civic initiatives, cultural activities, and political missions. In a sense, Price's career as Cynthia in important respects mirrors the Beatrice Fairfax column in the *New York Evening Journal*.

While Mae Tinee befriended the studios on the East Coast, Kitty Kelly joined the entourage for the opening of the Universal plant outside Hollywood in 1915. And she stayed on for a couple of weeks, reporting back to the *Tribune* from studio activities on the West Coast. The inauguration of the new Universal Studios was a major news event in mid-March 1915, and not only in the film columns. On March 7th Kelly joined the party leaving Chicago on the Santa Fe, bound for Los Angeles. Her first report, published on March 6th, reported on the planned activities during the inauguration on the 15th, featuring the formal opening, scores of parades, and shooting in progress to amuse and educate the visitors. Studio head Carl Laemmle and his crowd had reached Chicago from New York City in a "brand new style in social functions." Kelly provided her readers with a long list of people arriving from New York; apart from Laemmle and his family, P.A Powers, representatives from the *New York Dramatic Mirror* and *Motion Picture News*, Homer Croy—known for his 1918 volume *How Motion Pictures Are Made*—and Hy Mayer of *Puck*, who also did cartoons for Universal, turned up. Robert Grau was also part of the entourage as a prominent and highly prolific writer for stage and screen, particularly after his recent *Theater of Science* and scores of articles in general-interest magazines and trade papers. Numerous travelers joined the party in Chicago. Besides a phalanx of exhibitors from all over the country, trade journalists from *Billboard* and *Motography* boarded the Universal Special, which was chartered for the occasion and scheduled to make only three stops before Los Angeles: Kansas City, Denver, and the Grand Canyon.

Kelly's first report provided an in-depth account of Carl Laemmle's success story, from his days as manager of an emporium in Oshkosh to his first theater, which opened in Milwaukee in February 1906, to his Chicago activities as exhibitor and exchange man turned producer on a miniscule scale, and lastly to his subsequent glory at the helm of Universal, an organization run from New York City. Universal City was the crowning triumph at this stage of his career.[14] In Denver the Universal Special was greeted by a host of dignitaries led by the governor of Colorado and Denver's mayor. Parades, a reception, and a lunch banquet were part of the festivities Kelly reported on.[15] On the 13th the Special reached "Film Land," according to Kelly's report from Hollywood dated that day. Los Angeles reporters had boarded the train in San Bernardino together with the local management of Universal Studios, headed by Isidore Bernstein.[16] Throughout the trip U.K. Whipple shot footage destined for newsreel coverage.

Cameras ground throughout the day of the inauguration, March 15th, when invited guests were treated to a showy display of festivities while films were shot on many different stages for the visitors' benefit. One directed by Al Christie included the Universal brass and such featured players as Eddie Lyons, Lee Moran, and Victoria Forde. Wrote Kelly: "The day ended with a festive ball at the interior studio and Universal city was counted on the map with emphasis that it will be kept there permanently and the camera kept on grinding."[17] Kelly stayed on in California for more than a month, reporting on all kinds of film activities from the studios around Los Angeles, while Mae Tinee occasionally filled in between Kelly's letters. Rain or shine, the column "Flickerings from Film Land" still ran every weekday.

An exchange of blows between columns at the *Tribune* in the fall of 1915 featured Kelly in a prominent role. The debate sheds an interesting light on the complexities of film culture when features competed with serials and shorter subjects, not least comedies. While women had championed uplifting causes throughout the nickelodeon era and motherhood had offered pivoting core values for their vigilance, the gender balance concerning film culture then took on new overtones. At a time when Keystone films were part of the new Triangle organization, Kelly voiced misgivings about the billing value of the studio's output. Apropos one program, comprising two reels of the four-reel show, she claimed, "[W]hat fun Keystones can be"; the companion titles on the other hand "evidence without pessimism how vulgar and pointless Keystones can be." As part of the opening program for Triangle, she concludes that the films she considers vulgar are not for the people "Triangle aspires to reach," and on a more general tenor: "Slapstick comes in for a good many brickbats from good taste, but there is an instinctive reaction to slapstick planted in almost every normal person, if it be clean. If it be coarse, it is outrageous, and invites an increased shower of cultural brickbats."[18] The discussion of the value of the Keystone films was not new in the *Tribune*'s columns. In her "The Voice of the Movie Fans" Mae Tinee had printed scores of interventions from readers triggered by a letter penned by a R.S. Travers, a self-professed movie lover with one exception: when Keystone titles were part of the bill.

> There is one thing in life I resent, and that is the attitude of the Keystone company toward the American sense of humor. What do they think we are, a lot of vulgarians? Where do they get the slapstick stuff they garnish with drunkenness and serve up to us as comedy? If they think there is anything funny about a delicate little scene where a big fat man puts his foot into the lap of a slender girl or where a doting husband steals the money out of his wife's purse in order to go out and get pickled they are surely mistaking the bump of viciousness for the bump of humor.[19]

For Mr. Travers, the Keystone title *Mr. Full and Mr. Fuller*, which is not to be found in the filmographies, represented the acme of bad taste. A first rebuff of Kelly's stance was published two weeks later, claiming that while audiences roar with laughter at slapstick, they seem "much displeased" by light comedy. Refinement is not relevant, since "managers cannot get enough Keystones" to supply the people in "the higher class districts," according to Fred T. Lexin, Jr.[20]

In the second round of skirmishes concerning the value of the Keystone brand of humor, Kelly added new fuel by berating the Chicago censor for leniency vis-à-vis a couple of Keystone films at the Studebaker. Her quoting of and siding with an audience member's commentary concerning what Kelly characterized as the bill's "so-called comedy" irked her editorial colleague. I quote Kelly quoting:

'If only they would arrange this bill with these outrages at the beginning and the end so decent folks might come late and leave early and so avoid the Keystones it would be a big improvement.'[21]

The titles in question, *His Father's Footsteps* (1915) and *Fickle Fatty's Fall* (1915), deal with infidelity and, in Kelly's terse dismissal, sport all of the "standard Keystonisms, such as throwing pie and paste and falling into rain barrels, and so on through the well known list, offering neither novelty nor cleverness." Two days later an unsigned editorial in her own paper took Kelly to task for feminine squeamishness: "Being a lady, her natural impulse was, of course, to remain oblivious to the robustious antics of Messrs. [Roscoe 'Fatty'] Arbuckle and [Ford] Sterling. Being a critic, it was her duty to enlighten the public concerning them." The conclusion clings to the gender polarization, proffering a symptomatic reading reminiscent of Roosevelt's strenuous version of masculinity: "Nevertheless something within us rebels against the elimination by lady censors and lady critics of all the crude gusto of abounding animal nature. Are we all to shudder at the name of Rabelais and take to smelling salts? Are we to be a wholly ladylike nation?"[22] Keystone comedies and their place on the bill, off-color or not, had thus emerged as a litmus test for deep-seated cultural concerns defined in terms of gender, with a touch of class thrown in for good measure.

A couple of days later the editorial page returned to the topic with a more philosophical and circumspect piece called "Making Them Laugh," pronouncing all modes of expression wholesome except suggestiveness regarding sex, which provokes "moral nausea" but is more likely, however, to be found in picture postcards and on the stage than on screen, as we are told. Moreover, the writer opines, the movies do not attract a "sophisticated crowd," but rather give something of an Elizabethan freshness to the masses. "The movies are doors into a world of fancy imagination, emotion, and sentiment." The door metaphor mirrors Vorse's imagery in her piece from New York City's East Side, by the way. In conclusion, the editorial claims that there is "nothing for refinement to fear in the corporeal punishment form of humor." And in addition, "[t]rue culture does not subject the uncloistered world to contemptuous or even pained criticism. That happens about the samovar when life presents itself to a little group by candle light in the afternoon."[23] By situating cinema as a mass phenomenon of popular or even "true culture" with roots in Shakespearean comedy far removed from Philistine, stifling refinement, the writer tries to further underpin the gender polarity set up in the first editorial. Feminine culture is described as insipid and detached, and, even worse, antithetical to popular sentiment, the latter construed in terms of unladylike masculinity: the salon's vapid tea versus the saloon's slugs of whiskey, as it were. To boot, Kelly, in her capacity of critic, is labeled a "recording angel." We are hence witnessing a contest bearing on the very definition of the public sphere, which moves from salon culture outlined in feminine terms to venues where popular spectacles are presented and their class- and gender-defined audiences can be found. Movie theaters are not framed as a predominantly male affair, which would be an unsubstantiated claim, but a concept like the masses most certainly bears predominantly masculine connotations.[24]

The following day Kitty Kelly elected to praise two Keystone titles, but only to confront her detractors in a pointed analysis.

> But here one must pause. This comment is made merely from the viewpoint of the feminine recorder. Judging from recent remarks, the gentleman on the editorial page will find no joy in them. For there is nothing suggestive, nothing of infidelity, no pie throwing or rain barrel ducking. Altogether too unendurably dull for one self-confessed 'deplorable masculinity.' He shouldn't go there this week; the chairs ought to be saved for folk who like clean fun.
>
> These two Keystones have actual plot to them—yokels have a way sometimes of being surprisingly intelligent—nor below the intellectual grasp and the risible appreciation of the normally refined who fill our homes and business offices and, be it said, a good many seats in our movies.
>
> Beside plot, there is much originality of acting and many unique devices for extracting the laugh, with little of old Keystoneism apparent except

the silhouette chasing and the skidding automobiles, which never cease to
be funny.

There is the customary Keystone incredible speed of action and the un-
customary Keystone freedom from suggestiveness.[25]

The editorial attempt to frame the controversy in terms of gender did
not pay off when the female film critic pitched a curveball. Kelly opted for detailing her misgivings as clean fun versus suggestiveness, the
weak spot in the editorial armature. Given that women had dominated
the regulatory discourse on cinema, the attempt at carving out space for
male spectatorship with the Keystone films as touchstones represents a
truly fascinating backlash. The editorial tries to put the record straight
by distancing male spectatorship from infatuation with suggestiveness,
but Kelly decides to nail the gentleman on the editorial page by framing
his criticism as a desire for precisely that. This entrenched controversy
marks a rift in the regulatory machinery which had been fueled by progressive activism for a decade almost. It is not by chance that Kelly ap-
pealed to the rigid Chicago censor to clean up the bill.

The exchange of blows coincided with Miss Alspaugh's (Kitty Kelly)
marriage to Al Chase, which might have shortened the debate; Mae Tinee penned the column a few times during this period. The editorial was
however attacked in a letter published in the column "Voice of the People." Ida Ferguson sided with Kelly by accusing the editor of "slipshod
thinking," opining that "radical platitudes are no better than the prudish variety." Ferguson additionally addressed the gender polarization:

> The captious play on your film critic's sex is a cheap artifice to cover the
> old, old insinuation that masculinity, as opposed to femininity, demands
> a wider field of animal expression. You argue either that Kitty Kelly is a
> prude, or that man being as he is and woman as she is, we ought to censor
> film humor on a double basis. I suspect that Kitty Kelly is not a prude, and
> I am certain that 'tremendous jokes about infidelity' are condemnable on
> other than prudish basis.[26]

Kelly returned to Keystone material on November 16th, when Syd Chaplin sparkled in the Keystone four-reeler *A Submarine Pirate* (1915) while
brother Charlie made a less spectacular impression in an Essanay two-
reeler. Syd's film was the funnier on a day heralded as a "great day in

cinematic comedy land." The film was replete with "originality and action, so exceedingly interesting in mechanics, so amazingly funny in situations, that it carries the audience along on a thirty-one knot burst of laughter and its four reels seem about like four minutes." Kelly took cues from the debate when framing her appreciation by noting that the film was not suggestive, "and only one thing at which good taste may cringe. That doesn't mean it is a ladylike picture. Bless you, no, the bumps are large, the blows a-fly are of Keystonely frequency and punch."[27] The review was published the same day as the newly appointed censor board in Evanston scissored its first film, Charlie Chaplin's *A Night in the Show* (Essanay, 1915). An Evanston spokesperson, Mrs. Rose, informed Kelly that her colleague Miss Juul had cut out a scene "where a fat woman falls on Charlie." The reason: "It wasn't proper."

Film culture seems to have reached a crossroads where a leading editorial department could question the process of regulation, and where film regulation could be framed as part of a broader cultural palette spelled out in gender terms. In this sense the conflict over the Keystone films is a much more important clash than many similar altercations featuring female film critics versus male writers, the latter primarily dismissive of the cultural cachet of movies. This happened for instance in Sweden when Asta Nielsen took on the critical establishment after one of her films was banned in late 1911. The debate in the end focused on whether film was a potential art form or not.[28]

Louella O. Parsons was on the barricades in 1915 when her paper's dramatic critic, Richard Henry Little, pronounced cinema a fad. The silence of the silents, the human voice substituted by intertitles, and the lack of audience interaction during shooting to his mind forever removed cinema from art, which was a rehash of timeworn complaints. Parsons retorted with a scathing dismissal of drama and its future prospects.[29] It seems as if the respective gender of the defender and her accuser tied in with issues of class just like the debate between Kelly and the anonymous editor in the *Tribune*.

Kitty Kelly was one of the pioneering film-critical pens at a time when film reviewing was still a contested genre on the lookout for a format. Kelly's background was in literary criticism and at times she divided her graces between Chaplin and Lady Gregory—as Kitty Kelly and Audrie Alspaugh respectively. She was in charge of the film column until mid-October 1916, when taking responsibility for her family became her prime focus. Her last column, published on October 14th, reviewed Lasky's feature *Anton the Terrible*, and in addition presented *Motion Picture News Studio Directory*, one of the first attempts at providing biographical and filmographical information about some 200 screen players. Here, she mockingly observes, Mr. C. Spencer Chaplin is introduced. Kelly's colleague Mae Tinee published a booklet of her own around this time with succinct information concerning a more modest roster of players—sixty-four all in all—*Life Stories of the Movie Stars*.[30] This was a genre that trade papers also cultivated on an installment basis, for instance *Moving Picture World*'s section "Popular Picture Personalities. Who's Who in the Moving Picture World." Charles Spencer Chaplin, for example, was featured on the same page as Grace Darling in April 1917. As a further evidence of authenticity, the bios here were autographed by the respective star.[31]

When Kelly stepped down after less than one and a half years as film columnist, Mae Tinee replaced her. The latter had since the spring of 1914 supervised the Sunday page on moving pictures, answered letters from fans, and provided "Gossip of the Movie Plays and Players" in addition to featured articles. A one-day hiatus followed Kelly's uncommented retirement, but on the October 16th, Tinee penned "Flickerings from Film Land" as she had done before when filling in for Kelly. Kelly continued to write for the *Tribune* on and off, but now as Audrie Alspaugh Chase and on more general topics such as vice issues.

Kitty Kelly's month-long visit to Los Angeles in the aftermath of the opening of Universal clearly showed where film land and its flickering could be found in 1915. When features began to dominate the market, the controversy over the Keystone titles evidenced the continuing clout and popularity of short subjects. Refined and uplifting pleasures resonated with the puritan mindset carried from the Midwest by the colonists and tourists. For some, Los Angeles had in the process moved away from the rambunctious days of the 49ers to the bland, salubrious, and spiceless—though Hollywood was of course soon to overturn that perception.

CHAPTER 10

AMERICANIZATION AND IOWANIZATION—SPEED CULTURE AND LEISURELY FILMMAKING

"In some parts of England Red Indians are supposed to walk up and down Broadway, and [...] the enterprising American sportsmen shoot buffalos around Forty-second Street and Seventh Avenue."[1]

"You must be English.
No, native Californian.
You don't see many of them.
Most Californians were born in Iowa."[2]

ON THE THRESHOLD of the 20th century H.G. Wells had set the tone for what to expect: "After telephone, kinematograph and phonograph had replaced newspaper, book, schoolmaster, and letter, to live outside the range of the electric cables was to live as an isolated savage."[3] Electricity turned into a sparkling banner concept for a new century on the verge of being ever more connected, interlocked, and positioned by systems, machines, and media indicative of modernity. In the process, time and space took on new dimensions in contemporary discourse—simultaneously more pliant and rigid—in the face of speedier modes of transportation and brisker informational flows. As is often the case with elements of culture, outright replacement is rare, and contrary to Wells' expectations, newspapers, books, and schoolmasters are still prominent aspects of dominant culture in the digital 21st century.

The *New York Herald* expanded Wells' roster when short-listing a parade of marvels worthy of jumping century, not all of them however propelled by electricity directly: the locomotive, the dining car, the automobile, the bicycle and the pneumatic tired sulky, Roentgen rays, the sulfur match, the sewing and knitting machines, the typewriter and the fountain pen, the steam fire engine and water tower—and the snapshot camera and moving pictures.[4] Serializing modernity in fashions akin to these long and short lists formed part of a turn-of-the-century discourse lining up the past as a set of archaic technologies overwritten by triumphant new systems and media predominantly fed by "electric cables." This was the basis for serving up the world on the breakfast tray as proclaimed by the behemoth Sunday issue of the *Los Angeles Times*, which we will return to below. In negotiating the modern condition and its technological scaffoldings, commentators recurrently lined up chains of linked items. For such open-ended catalogs of inventions, technologies, and machines, electricity, or the dynamo, to use Henry Adams' terms, provided the main current.[5]

When the second Motion Picture Exposition opened in New York City's Grand Central Palace on June 8, 1914, the general audience was invited to a display of all aspects of film culture. The advertisement showcased four elements, priced at 50 cents: how pictures are made, a popularity contest, the photoplayers' tango contest, and film shows in model theaters. As a headline in the *New York Herald* phrased it, "Advance of the 'Movies' To Be Illustrated at This Week's Show."[6] The very word "the movies" was magical, and the exposition was to "reveal" some of the industry's "mysteries." Much was made of one feature of modernity—electricity. At 2 p.m. President Wilson pressed a button in Washington, D.C., to "electrically open" the exposition. When the signal came through and the bell chimed at the Grand Central Palace, the assembled throng was to partake in opera star Alma Gluck's rendering of the national anthem.[7] Thus, the event was steeped in a decidedly nationalistic veneer by electrically interlocking the president in the White House and the singing representatives of the people under the sign of the movies, most of which were shot in California in 1914.

In this closing chapter we will revisit and elaborate more fully on some tenets previously touched upon, namely: cinema as a cultural mediator for processes of Americanization; the commingling of cinema and technologies of transportation; and the marketing of Los Angeles and the clashes over the city's cultural ethos. Furthermore, we will look at the introduction of film pages in the New York City press during 1914 and their assessments of American features' shortcomings prior to the opening of Griffith's *The Birth of a Nation*. The attention paid Griffith's controversial screen epic motivates a return to Harry C. Carr and his racial pigeonholing of nickel audiences in Los Angeles. In 1907, when Carr took in the racially mixed patronage of storefront theaters, the vaudeville houses segregated their audiences. Walter Chatham, for example, sued the Southwest Amusement Co.—owned by Clune—on November 6, 1907, for having relegated "negroes, Indians, and Mexicans to sit apart from whites" at the Unique in San Bernardino. As the notice in the *Los Angeles Times* succinctly phrased it, the "negro wants to sit among whites."[8] Racial segregation was still a standard practice in Los Angeles theaters in the mid-1910s, as we will show, which forges a dark connection between Carr's flippant discursive racism and Griffith's full-fledged racist screen historiography. To boot, Carr ventured a piece for *Photoplay* which added to the glowing body of appreciation of Griffith's filmmaking inside the trade press and out.[9]

Griffith's work at Biograph, and especially one film, *A Corner in Wheat*, has served as a linchpin for pre-classical cinema by its testing of devices, sophisticated intertextual play, and editing protocols. As a spectacular allegorical project, *A Corner in Wheat* offers an exercise in screen modernity by taking advantage of the cinematic mechanism's capacity to bring together on the screen strands separated in space. The temporal dimension induces causality, albeit without clearly marking time outside a cyclical conceptualization of the agricultural processes: sowing preceding harvesting, commodity speculation before flour and bread shortages and higher prices. In retrospect, Griffith's film stands out as an unrivaled narrative feat due to its method of correlating dispersed scenes by way of an abstraction of editing. Griffith's experiments were part of the medium's cultural strides further marked by a theoretical interest in cinema outside the precincts of the trade.

Griffith's universally acclaimed masterpiece has been praised for its innovative style and for taking on controversial subject matter.[10] James A. Patten's spectacular corner on the wheat market at the Chicago Board of Trade in May was one of the major news stories of 1909 and drew attention throughout the year. The ubiquitous wheat and bread discourse resulting from the speculation directly inspired *A Corner in Wheat*, shot in November. The film was marketed and read as an editorial, to employ the oft-quoted phrasing from the *New York Dramatic Mirror* when the film opened in December, a mature designation for voicing opinions in print, but, at least for the film industry and its nascent trade press, applicable to the screen as well.[11]

Newspapers had yet to discover individual film titles outside campaign pieces disparaging cinema's overall tendency through exemplary accounts of representational transgressions, a mode that still flared up occasionally. The daily press otherwise housed a wide assortment of responses to film culture around 1910. We will thus turn our attention to a highly circumspect editorial piece published in New York's *Sun* on December 1909, a negotiation indicative of the open-mindedness previously labeled phase IV. In *The Sun*'s editorial, penned around the time when Griffith's film opened, cinema is viewed as an instrument for teaching modernity lessons to immigrants, clearly in line with the stance underlying the progressives' hopes for an educative film culture. Late 1909 and early 1910 was a pregnant time for the film industry when the medium not only was considered an educational force *in spe*, but when such initiatives came to fruition.

As the film industry's relocation out west gained momentum, producers, depending on genre requirements, could pick and choose locations from a veritable anthology of landscapes around Los Angeles. The popular Western films in particular benefited from genuine western environs when produced at ranch studios, after having previously been scorned for their inauthentic backgrounds in New Jersey's hinterland. If Westerns for a time represented the quintessential American film genre, as Richard Abel convincingly maintains, the genre was also an obvious choice for authors like B.M. Bower to address and capitalize on due to its cultural clout in the early days of the film novel.

In a discussion of American film exports an anonymous writer in *Motography* provides a somewhat oblique perspective on the popularity of Western films as embodiments of the picturesque, which allegedly resonates with preconceived notions prevalent outside the U.S. as well as among immigrants residing in American metropolises in the East.[12] This contention from 1911, in turn, mirrors Hobart Bosworth's claim from late 1912 regarding the lingering appreciation in the East of Western melodramas as well as the musings of Kalem's William Wright two years earlier when interviewed by Harry C. Carr: "You know, it's a funny thing, this moving picture business. It has revivified the decadent cowboy of the frontier and made him live again in the eyes of the people."[13] In terms of exports, the writer in *Motography* reflects, "it does not seem as if too many of these Indian and cowboy films could be fed to the moving picture goers of the rest of the world." Western films apparently struck a global chord by matching ideas of "the America that they have long imagined and heard about." The core conception of this imagined America, apart from big cities "teeming with gold for the worker," is grounded in a national iconography of endless vistas "just beyond the skyscrapers" where "there is a great, open wild-land, filled with almost savage beings." Films matching such ideas enjoyed a domestic following also, the writer observes offhand and with a caveat concerning reception: "perhaps because of the many foreigners that crowd the moving picture theaters." If notions about an imagined geography and its ethnographic spectacles reverberate both inside the U.S. and outside, it made good business sense to cater to the "foreign" mindset and thereby reverse the direction of film imports, which in some quarters had spawn anti-Gallic sensibilities when Pathé's red rooster crowed from screens everywhere. In Richard Abel's analysis the Westerns negotiated this French dominance by launching a rugged, red-blooded, black-and-white, all-American iconography—imagined or not, stagy or not, regardless of whether produced mainly for export and "foreign" audiences in the East or for incurring a sense of the national in domestic audiences. A couple of years down the trail the international market was less keen on Westerns and Indian pictures. According to a report from Vice Consul Rice K. Evans in Sheffield, American cinema was losing market shares partly due to "the decline in popularity of the erstwhile film hero, the American cowboy. [---] The public is getting overfed with them. Too often have they seen the same old cowboy ride madly down the same old trail."[14]

As reformers repeatedly contended, going to the movies was a learning process, a form of schooling. At the cusp of the 1910s, an editorial in the *Evening Sun* maintained that films teach modernity lessons for immigrants eager to escape from the traditions of their home countries, which ties in with the Western's popularity in an interesting way. Allegedly, the new Americans were willing—even eager—to embrace the culture and emblematic vistas indicative of their new country as represented by an imaginary amalgamation of industrial Chicago, Coney Island, and the Wild West. From such a concept of cultural variety, readily available through nickelodeon programming, cinema offered illuminating dynamite in Walter Benjamin's sense for those that had fled unforgiving conditions in Europe and wanted to branch out from the cultural confines of the ethnic colonies in American metropolises. This environment was poignantly depicted a handful of years later by Thomas Ince's bleak feature *The Italian* (New York Motion Picture Corporation, 1915). In the film an infant born to Italian immigrants succumbs in the tenement ghetto for lack of money to buy milk.

The editorial in the *Evening Sun* cuts to the chase regarding processes of Americanization by addressing the migratory amusement preferences of Italian immigrants in New York City. If we are to trust the account, uprooting and transplanting apparently could not only change the skies but also habits. The point of departure for the editorialist was that the marionette theater on 11th Street had lost its Italian audience and closed down. Once, readers were told, "[i]t was the most 'distinctive' place of amusement in New York (so the overeducated will tell you); far more so than the Chinese theatre, or any of the *cafés chantants* of the various 'quarters,' Russian, Syrian, Greek or what-you-like. And sure enough, for a time, the place was packed with the sons and daughters of the Sicilians, comforting their homesick eyes with the play of the old puppets, nursing their nostalgia."

But then things changed and "somehow the spell broke and pouf! Away went the audience." For awhile, American children carried the show, but now both Italian immigrants and American children "all like the moving picture shows better." The new Americans do not look back "to the land which bore them and starved their souls and bodies." And therefore, "away with the foolish old puppets, and the old tales, and the old order. Moving pictures of steel bridges with express trains crossing them, of new scenes, of the new life [. . .] and never mind about Firenze or Napoli or Amalfi—talk about Coney Island and Chicago; they are all Americans now."[15] Still, it seems as if the eagerness to adapt to the new skies and turn into real Americans applied primarily to the young ones, those born in the new country or who arrived with their families at a tender age. The analysis might be over-optimistic in its assessment of film culture's potential for transforming the mindset of immigrants. More important, however, is the fact that an editorialist in a leading metropolitan newspaper elected to address the educative potential of cinema as part of culturally integrative processes, and in a manner underpinning the explosiveness of a new medium that blows away the cultural debris of the old order described as an unforgiving prison-world. For many, no doubt, the ethnic enclaves in the tenement districts offered few opportunities for "betterment."According to Howard B. Grose, the newcomers seem destined to end up in "the colonies which tend to perpetuate race customs and prejudices, and to prevent assimilation. Worse yet, these colonies are in the tenement and slum district, the last environment of all conceivable in which this raw material of American citizenship should be placed." Given the horrendous conditions in the colonies, "the immigrant is likely to deteriorate in the process of Americanization, instead of becoming better in this world," Grose concludes pessimistically.[16]

In the editorial written around four years later America, in its multiple facets, as an industrial powerhouse represented by Chicago, and as a provider of popular amusements inflected by modernity, Coney Island, together with the perceptions embodied by the landscape itself, predominantly the spirit of the Wild West, came together on the screen to instill a liberating sense of belonging with opportunities richer than what the old country had allegedly offered its sons and daughters. Immigrant audiences had to grapple with these ideas of imagined communities and their own place and belonging in a novel cultural context, and position themselves in relation to the roar of modernity with cinematic trains crossing symbolic bridges.

The *Evening Sun* editorial ventured a utopian blueprint for the role of film culture in relation to the transformation of immigrant experiences in American metropolises. In addition, the text offers an optimistic antidote to previous sinister newspaper accounts of the medium's penchant for teaching criminality and loose sexual mores. The latter type of discourse, as we have seen, riveted its attention predominantly to adolescents, often those with an immigrant background. This editorial instead positions the new Americans outside the ethnic colonies and places them in the heterotopical context of cinematic modernity. Simultaneously, it relegates the old country, here Italy, and its old order to a series of picturesque vistas, sights, or places—often familiar from travelogues in nickel shows—albeit with little to offer native-born working men and women. The twice-emphasized newness in the editorial, in a pact with progress, singles out film representations, express trains on steel bridges, in pointed contrast to the thrice reiterated oldness of the cultural scene removed as far as possible from the fast-paced thrills of Coney Island. Chicago, home to the 1893 exhibition and a magnet for European immigrants, just like New York City, seems to represent a metropolitan experience running in tandem with this newness as a city of the future. The metropolitan experience, the amusement park, and the movies harnessed together, as it were, teach the immigrants modernity lessons, severing the ties to the old skies for good. Thus, the editorial triumphantly proclaims, "[T]hey are all Americans now." Albeit a lone voice, the 1909 editorial in the *Evening Sun* epitomizes a salient shift in the perception of film culture's role within the larger fabric of modernity.

At the end of the 1910s, to continue with our examination of the Americanization debate, Emory S. Bogardus framed his critical take on modernity in terms of speed, restlessness, and an onslaught of intense distractions while bemoaning the loss of a more contemplative era free from the racket of amusement parks and automobiles. Bogardus' 1920 volume, *Americanization*, provides a concentrated appraisal summing up a decade of American values and sensibilities to be negotiated by native- and foreign-born alike. In the book, published by his university, Bogardus expresses hopes for an extended form of democracy buttressed by a cluster of progressive social values. Against the backdrop of an analytical outline of republican ideals, Bogardus voices misgivings and grievances concerning numerous aspects of contemporary American society in a negative Decalogue. This set of proclivities risks undermining the inherent idealism of the average American, whose character, he claims, at best strikes a productive balance between self-serving utilitarian crassness and idealistic sentiments with loftier aspirations. The potentially vitiating perils listed by Bogardus are still under intense debate in the American political landscape. According to Bogardus, the sanctity of marriage is threatened by a perception that the institution represents a mere civil contract to be terminated at will; he stresses the importance of good homes and homeownership—apartment houses, he quips, are conducive to "a maximum of indulgent pleasures," and lack of homeownership equals homelessness; disregard for religious life runs rampant; extravagance and recklessness are prevalent, exemplified by excessive spending habits and a foolhardy depleting of natural resources in disregard of future needs; he further perceives a lack of cultural cohesion which leads to race prejudice, distressing differences in world outlook, and an uneven distribution of wealth perpetuated by the inheritance laws; he notices a lukewarm interest in political life and public welfare, and, lastly, he detects a lack of courtesy coupled with exploitation of the weak, and a snobbish attitude towards foreigners.

But this is not enough: In addition to his slightly overlapping qualms, Bogardus remonstrates most vehemently against the increasingly voracious speed culture. In his analysis, dispatch is correlated with a "deification of bigness," and the fast and the big are ushered in by "strident noise." The adage "time is money" is pronounced a meretricious slogan for the foreigner, instead Bogardus argues for "pristine emphasis upon quality and quietness." Speed infests not only production, sometimes for the good, and transportation, mostly for the bad, but also how Americans engage with recreations and amusements. Coney Island stands as the negative beacon for the brand of brash amusement culture Bogardus takes aim at. The description he musters up indeed reeks of such contexts, for instance in the breathtaking characterizing of the "unfortunate habit of rushing at thirty miles an hour to places of amusement and recreation, trying one artificial and excitement dealing device after another in rapid succession, and then dashing for home at forty miles an hour, arriving there more tired than when they started."[17] In pointed contrast to Simon N. Patten's 1909 analysis, popular culture, in the opinion of Bogardus, offers neither climax nor regeneration, only tiring over-excitement for toilers and others. His critical stance mirrors previously discussed misgivings concerning modernity's visual frenzy and claims about tired optic nerves and restless eyes, where one impression after the next was wiped off the retina before having time to sink in, as it were.

In a physical sense, structures used for purposes of film exhibition mushroomed and dissolved in Los Angeles, where Bogardus was teaching, in the overall construction frenzy that took off after the turn of the century. Moving pictures and automobiles are often grouped together to describe a mindset or state of affairs indicative of the era, for instance as an explanation for the construction boom in downtown Los Angeles in the early 1910s.[18] Bogardus refrains from such specificity; as a sociologist he operates with more general categories, not surprisingly the same as those mapped by his students in 1911: commercialized amusements and recreations. After underwriting the "raped-fire production" of Ford automobiles in his 1919 volume, he shifts gear to examples of "unworthy forms of speed [...] illustrated by get-rich-schemes of the hour, by the neurasthenic chase after new fashions, by curricula for giving students superficial knowledge in several fields simultaneously, by the kaleidoscopic dash by automobile to snatch a few hours of nerve-wrecking amusements at a pleasure resort."[19]

Los Angeles was a city that moved away from the era of horses at lightning speed. Automobiles and moving pictures propelled people along the routes of modernity, and the city could also boast an excellent system of public transportation. At the verge of the Jazz Age Bogardus paints an entrenched picture of American values and mentalities echoing a by then well-established tradition of critiquing modernity and a conspicuous leisure culture discussed by Thorstein Veblen in terms of excessive spending on more levels than just monetary, further underpinned by Georg Simmel in his book on the philosophy of money, and from a different perspective in his famous essay on metropolitan mental life.[20] Bogardus frames his review from the perspective of cultural differences vis-à-vis the experiences of the immigrants and as an unfortunate model for Americanization post-WW1. He would for sure side with the analysis ventured by an anonymous reviewer of Jane Addams' book *The Spirit of Youth and the City Streets* rather than the optimistic assessment in the *Evening Sun* editorial, both from 1909. Writes the reviewer: "The modern city, the factory, and the modern farm have sprung upon us as thieves in the night. They have swept away old conventions which, growing for centuries, have been our guides and safeguards. We are in a great unknown forest of social conditions, new powers, new dangers."[21] Intertwined with cities, factories, and industrialized agriculture, the moving picture show, according to numerous reformers, spearheaded this rush into the "great unknown."

In the early 1910s successful boosterism continued to attract hordes of permanent or temporary citizens—colonists and tourists—to the Golden State, and particularly Southern California and Los Angeles and its nearby beach resorts. As a headline had it in 1911, "beach glory shifts from Atlantic to the Pacific."[22] Praising the prospects for the beaches ranging from Santa Monica to Venice and Playa del Rey, and the two private amusement piers on the way, the reporter foresaw world fame for the local beaches. Fraser's Million Dollar Pier at Ocean Park opened on June 17, 1911, only to be more or less totally obliterated in a disastrous conflagration on September 4, 1912. In an attempt at defining the differences between the respective pleasure cultures on the Atlantic and Pacific, a grid of salient differences bearing on modernity is laid out, featuring an intricate brew of science, thrills, dispatch, and nerves. A key section in the text on "beach glory" quotes Guy Wetmore Carryl's famous analysis of Coney Island, published in September 1901, but without giving away the source:

> This fame will not be the fame of Coney Island with its crazy tumult, or the more quiet fame of Atlantic City, the pride of which is the splendid steel esplanade. Science almost had nervous prostration when it gave

Coney Island its thrillers. Science will not in the future pander to deliri-um-producing constructions.

Los Angeles does not want a Coney Island, which as it has been depicted 'leaps with a shout upon the casual visitor as he steps from a 5-cent trolley into the seething heart of her 10-cent chasm and pours out, as it were, the whole contents of her horn of plenty in a trice before his astounded eyes.' Babel and Bedlam have had their day. The amusements of the future will be allegorical, not phantasmagorical, educational rather than titillating.[23]

The polarization between the phantasmagorical and the allegorical sepa-rates physical attractions and thrills from more classical and contempla-tive approaches to pleasures and amusements. The relocation of filmmak-ing from the bustling urban metropolises of the East, New York City in particular, to the wholesome, picturesque, and more laid-back West Coast mirrored this separation. Edendale, home to some of the first studios in the Los Angeles area, for sure sounded more paradise-like than Flatbush Avenue in Brooklyn. Thus, the phantasmagorical and titillating attraction era can be associated with Coney Island, while the gradual dominance for cinematic storytelling on the Pacific shores enlisted the educational and allegorical. The beach developments in Southern California are indicative of the overall migratory patterns alluded to above.

The establishment of a film industry on the West Coast coincided with massive population growth in Los Angeles. Census figures for Los Angeles County underwrite an enormous swelling of the ranks: from 170,298 inhabitants in 1900 to 504,131 in 1910. The city of Los Ange-les alone could boast 300,000 inhabitants in the early 1910s, plus about 150,000 tourists wintering in the area. As part of the Chamber of Com-merce and the Merchants' and Manufacturers' Association's untiring campaigns to lure colonists to Los Angeles, the railroad companies were enlisted to show films onboard trains.[24] Besides recruiting new citizens, both the Chamber and the Association hoped to attract entrepreneurs to Los Angeles and its business-friendly infrastructure. After having an-nexed parts of the San Fernando Valley and Palms, the city's population amounted to 528,817 in 1915.

As film producers began to build studios in the area after 1910, pag-eant-like shooting spectacles were offered as attractions and film compa-nies invited visitors to witness movies in the making as an amusing out-ing. As evidenced by the accidentally formed audience for the shooting of *Escape from Sing Sing* on a rooftop in 1905, film work was an appealing form of romance. Selig seems to have pioneered the idea of marketing film work when advertising two days of shooting of a film called *Blackbeard* at Redondo Beach on September 9 and 10, 1911. The initiative was not replicated until Universal placed an ad in the papers in 1913 under the heading "See Movies in the Making"[25]—later the same year Vitagraph staged a public shooting event.[26] Thus, well in advance of the opening of the new Universal plant and the incorporation of the 456-acre Universal City, studios had on rare occasions invited people to watch film production. When Universal City opened, the slogan read "See How the Movies Are Made."[27] Insiders, little thrilled by the spectacle, complained that "curiosity seekers" swarmed the studios on various pretexts to watch films in the making.[28]

When shooting turned into an everyday event on the streets in Los Angeles—remember the conflicted editorial praising screen advertisements for the city while at the same time considering the ubiquitous film crews shooting in the cityscape something of a plague—the local amusement scene slowly began to change. Simultaneously, a narcissistic explanation for the popularity of movie-going in Los Angeles was ventured—the theaters were constantly crowded since so many of the new players were checking themselves out on the screen with their friends.[29] This practice inspired scenes featuring players watching their own screen appearance, from Jean of the Lazy A to Merton of the Movies a decade later. Such scenes of (mis-)recognition turned into moments of epiphany in an avalanche of short stories, novels, and films depicting a film world progressively synonymous with Hollywood.

The notion of Hollywood was built around a community blessed with a superior locale, a place unrivaled in scenic opulence, and a region endowed with both natural and industrial resources. Some, however, wrote Los Angeles off as the epitome of boredom, much to the dismay of the local press. *Smart Set*, the sophisticated New York-based magazine, published a scathing overview of the unentertaining nightlife in Los Angeles from a pronouncedly modish perspective, and when talking about theaters bypassed film shows, however palatial, for vaudeville and legit. In Willard Huntington Wright's acerbic March 1913 sketch Los Angeles comes across as a provincial, non-cosmopolitan, and prudish city devoid of nightlife, excitement, and allure. According to the headline's hard-to-shake characterization, it was chemically pure. The boring homogeneity painted by Wright was far removed from the impressions imparted by the recurring reports from the exotically vibrant area around the Plaza and the blocks immediately north and south on Spring, Main, and Broadway. The elitist *Smart Set* looked elsewhere and for other types of pleasure and did not even notice the popular offerings.

FIGURE 36: Street life, "The Post Cards of a Tourist—No. 1."
Cartoon from *Los Angeles Herald*, 9 February 1910, 1.

FIGURE 37: Corporeal ideals, "The Post Cards of a Tourist—No. 2."
Cartoon from *Los Angeles Herald*, 10 February 1910, 1.

Predictably, touchy editorialists in the local newspapers took Wright to task. The *Los Angeles Express*, without even mentioning Wright's name, time and again rubbed in the fact that he was a former member of the *Times*' editorial staff. Overall, Wright's article hit a nerve by questioning the deep-seated conviction that Los Angeles was in all respects an earthly paradise, an ultimate destination, and of late politically cleansed and ruled by a progressive mayor and administration. Wright, apparently, missed the snake and the apple. The *Express* considered the article "defamatory" and characterized it as a "public plea in behalf of prostitution and gambling." By attributing Wright's piece to the *Times*, the *Express* found a pretext for a local political gambit. The publisher of the *Express*, Edwin T. Earl, represented progressive interests and had successfully campaigned for a new, pure administration and a recall of Mayor Harper. In the process Earl confronted the *Times* and its publisher, Harrison Gray Otis, a staunch defender of the machine.[30] Wright's slur regarding the proliferation of Midwestern sensibilities and puritan ideals in Los Angeles played into the political fracas between the publishers. Wrote the *Express*: "If the machine that formerly ruled Los Angeles to the satisfaction of this critic [Wright]—the machine that is misrepresenting and vilifying the present administration—if that machine is returned to power, then Los Angeles again may be able to offer 'racy and satisfying entertainment for the traveling Don Juans.' But will it be with your help, despised men and women of the Middle West?"[31] Alma Whitaker of the *Times* resorted to glee and irony in her rebuke of Wright's article. By dismissing his disparaging diatribe as the result of unworldly lack of experience and youngish hubris, she made him out as a vain, shallow, and unseasoned traveler.[32] This trenchant rebuke of a former colleague—Wright had however not been attached to the editorial staff at the *Times*, he was the literary editor for almost five years and it continued to publish his book reviews—discounted his Harvard education, his critical affiliation with the flamboyant "Town Topics," and his travel experiences. Wright later published a volume on nightlife in a handful of European cities, *Europe after 8:15*, together with his fellow editors at *Smart Set*—H.L. Mencken and George Jean Nathan. Apart from books on modern art and a volume on Nietzsche's philosophy, Wright is however mostly remembered for his detective stories under the pen name S.S. Van Dine, many of them adapted for the screen.

After completing the fieldwork for *Europe after 8:15*, he passed through Los Angeles and was interviewed by the *Herald*. Wright here partly reappraised the city's nightlife. He had come to believe that it had the upper hand on any American city; it was both "more cosmopolitan and more entertaining." In fact, Los Angeles was the only city that could match the European capitals in this respect. "You know you have New York in the infant class when it comes to startling stage developments." In conclusion, he still maintained that the city was as chemically pure as ever, exemplified by the current "wave of reformatory plays." And he asked: "Don't any of you violently progressive Angelenos fear too much knowledge?"[33] According to a playful notice, this alleged purity caused problems for film companies. Selig's producer was, for example, unable to find a joint resembling a dive. "There was such a place on Alameda street, a relic from the pre-pure days, but when it was found, it was being wrecked and the Selig company set to work to build their own 'joint.' "[34]

The widespread perception that Los Angeles was dominated by prudish Midwestern sensibilities turned Iowa into an imaginary stomping ground for defining a demographic mindset. Wright's designation lingered well into the 1920s, for example in the characterization of the city as permeated by a "sluggish sort of idealism, common to our older American stock, [which] vents itself under new skies in home building, theosophizing, keeping Los Angeles chemically pure, and adding new amendments to the State Constitution."[35]

Harry C. Carr, always quick on the trigger with colloquialisms, flaunted the phrase in his 1935 book on Los Angeles. Our perennial guide throughout all previous chapters here recounts his family story as prototypical for the migration from the Midwestern states, in popular vernacular subsumed as an Iowa exodus. Carr, in fact, was one of those sons of Iowa proper who was brought to Los Angeles by his parents in 1887, the same year the Saunterer scolded the city's women for excesses in the makeup department. Carr poignantly sums up the unique aspects of the exodus from the Midwestern states in that well-off farmers transplanted themselves to a new environment without having a pressing need to do so. In Carr's words:

The Iowans [a generic term for immigrants from the Midwest] left one of the richest agricultural communities on the face of the earth [...] one of the areas most assured in its prosperity. Those who trekked were not those who had, in some manner, failed in Iowa. They were almost invariably successful people with money in their pockets—the pick of the prairie. They did not come to loot; they came to pay. Hundreds of millions of dollars have come into Los Angeles from the richness of Iowa farms. [...] But not even the Normans, over-running England, or the Spanish conquest of Mexico, made a more profound change in the psychology of an invaded land than did the Iowans make in Los Angeles.[36]

John O'Hara, a handful of years after Carr's book was published, characterized Los Angeles and Hollywood—the place and the mindset—in a manner reminiscent of Huntington Wright and clearly catching Carr's drift:

‘It's a fantastic place, you know, Malloy. Fantastic. You know why? Because it's so incredibly ordinary.’ [...] ‘Consider this: the really fantastic thing about it is that it's the crystallization of the ordinary, cheap ordinary American. The people. The politics. These Iowa people that come here and really assert themselves.’[37]

Ideologically, centuries after the Midwestern colonization, the city was still permeated with a Protestant ethos brought from the Midwest by the first wave of new Angelenos in 1880s and constantly replenished after then. The folks that had moved there from other parts of the U.S. drastically outnumbered the immigrants and dominated all aspects of city affairs. Overall, only a fraction of Los Angeles' population was born in California, in contrast to comparable cities. The influx from other countries as well as from other parts of the U.S. represented a dominant demographic current. The majority the colonists from other parts of the U.S. were middle-aged, Protestant, well-to-do, and white, and for Wright and later generations of critics, the very incarnation of philistinism. In an acerbic offhand characterization from the pens of Willard Huntington Wright's co-editors at the *Smart Set* these folks were pegged as "retired Iowa steer stuffers and grain sharks who pollute Los Angeles."[38]

The tasteless gaudiness Eliza Wetherby Otis criticized in 1880s also lingered, according to observers, and was apparently even more conspicuous in the 1920s: "Young women are unspeakably tawdry; their diaphanous gowns and gilt slippers are those of the ballroom, their hats are of lace, they are loaded with artificial flowers in a land famous for its natural ones, and their countenances convince you that the cosmetic industry in Southern California must be second to none but that of the movies."[39] This late 1920s appraisal from a popular-magazine essay by Sarah Comstock offers a concentrated appraisal of the dominating strands of the Los Angeles/Hollywood discourse. Comstock encountered a city sporting the whole gamut of modernity traits, many of them still evident in 21st century Los Angeles. She highlights an "incongruous" impression to European eyes due to the city's "mushroom growth, its sprawling hugeness, its madcap speed, its splurge of lights and noise and color and money; and against all this boisterous crudity, the amazing contrast of its cultured charm, its mature discrimination, its intellectual activities—this is sprung from American soil, and could come from no other. If we are a nation of extremes, Los Angeles is an extreme among us" (715). Appropriately, her piece is titled "The Great American Mirror," thus Los Angeles "becomes the portrait of ourselves as others see us" (723). Mirrors are of course not to be trusted, and what the movies themselves mirror merits a discussion too complex to be addressed here. In Comstock's mirror Los Angeles, "The Paradise of the Cornbelt," razzle-dazzles as "a country fair or a carnival." And her sketchy impressions from the sidewalk—"a strange street rabble, yokels rubbing elbows with cheap sophistication" (716)—replicate the numerous accounts from Main Street discussed previously.

Comstock maps a decidedly Eastern mental landscape in the first wave of "immigration." "Los Angeles, coupled with Pasadena, at the turn of the century was," she writes, "the least 'Western' community in the United States. 'It out-Easts the East' " (717). Parallel to the buildup of Hollywood, Comstock argues, Los Angeles was the recipient of the "exodus from the Midwest" after "a series of bumper crops. Superficially seen, Los Angeles seems to consist chiefly of these 'Iowans,' as they are called (although other states contribute) and the swarms of busy traffickers who cater to their needs, their vanity, their sex, their eager childishness" (717–718).

If modernity, among other designations, can be described as an era of electricity, speed, commodity flow, and cinema, Los Angeles is made to order in terms of mentality. As outlined by Comstock, Los Angeles represents a mental affliction of sorts due to its "[p]ower-madness, speed-madness, the selling mania, which may be summed up as our Fourth-of-July-complex—our insane lust for hurry, noise, and glare" (723). Demographically, she maintains, as "New York is the melting-pot for the peoples of Europe, so Los Angeles is the melting pot for the peoples of the

United States." The city's "juxtaposition of unlikes" echoes Hutchins Hapgood's definition of vaudeville, and Paul Starr's of newspapers, while Carr compares Los Angeles' many makeovers to a "vaudeville actor putting on a new costume for every act."[40]

At the end of silent-film era Los Angeles was "a completely motorized civilization," according to Bruce Bliven, editor of the *New Republic*. In his analysis, "an Angeleno without his automobile is marooned, like a cowboy without his horse, and cannot stir from the spot until it has been restored to him." Bliven did not mobilize Wright's pervasive term, instead titling his piece "Los Angeles. The City That Is Bacchanalian—in a Nice Way." His pointed description of the city as a "middle-class heaven," but less pleasant for the wage earner, still rings true. Furthermore, Bliven's unscientific reception study seems to mirror a still dominating perception:

Nearly everyone I know who comes from the East, or from Europe, to visit Los Angeles, goes away declaring that it is embodied nightmare; but I can only say that those who hold this view seem to me amazingly short-sighted. For this city is a social laboratory *in excelsis*. It offers a melting-pot in which the civilization of the future may be seen, bubbling darkly up in a foreshadowing brew. Besides, it is gorgeously amusing. Anything may happen in Los Angeles in the next quarter-century, and nearly everything did in the one just gone.[41]

As results of the sought-after influx of colonists and businesses to Los Angeles, land values shot up, the network of public transportation expanded, the number of automobiles multiplied, and amusement offerings exploded. The paradise-like qualities already renegotiated in the Saunterer's accounts gradually gave way to metropolitan frenzy and an increasingly large fleet of automobiles. So intertwined were the industries in 1915 that an editorial in *Motion Picture News* perceived "many points of similarities between the two industries of automobiles and motion pictures." Both had experienced "swift, amazing growth, unparalleled in recent years." At that time, the motion picture industry was up against "the very same menace that all but disintegrated the business of automobiles," the editor quipped. For the film industry, the "menace is *inflation*. I mean overproduction, which means wild-cat production." By way of further explanation:

375

Wild-cat production means wildly extravagant production, production so *needlessly expensive* that it cannot possibly pay; and *faulty production*; and production without hope of adequate distribution. Generally all three go together.

Every picture put under such circumstances makes a sore spot in a healthy industry.

It isn't healthy competition.

It is, merely, wild, illogical activity. [---]

These pictures cut prices and thereby disorganize and destroy established and logical methods of distribution.

They are most to blame for the chaotic market conditions that disturb the industry right now.[42]

The editorial fears were voiced as the feature film was making noticeable inroads and a multitude of new producers hoped to seize a moment of change and establish themselves on a market in flux. Los Angeles on the verge of turning into Hollywood was the place for launching such efforts, whether modest endeavors built around an individual author's work, for example Louis Joseph Vance's unsuccessful attempt and Rex Beach's more felicitous, or gigantic, city-like enterprises (Universal), or a zoo cum studio (Selig).

The Selig Zoo and Universal City were both adjuncts to film studios. In 1915 their respective studio heads, Laemmle and Selig, organized two highly publicized train journeys to Los Angeles with multiple stops, events, and receptions. Tellingly, both trains published their own newspapers. Showcasing filmmaking as a spectacle as Universal did and assembling a menagerie for the purpose of producing animal films presupposed a seasoned film culture mature and surreal enough to find fertile ground in a region henceforth read through the lens of moving pictures.

Los Angeles could also offer its movie patrons—many of them colonists from elsewhere—palace-like venues for an evening's film entertainment along its white way, and legitimate venues competed to add the new feature films to their bills. By and by, new genres, like newsreels and serial films, took part in an ongoing transformation of formats, which for a time were also negotiated by the prologs to the many feature films produced by American film companies from 1914 onward. By then, the newspapers had begun to take notice of the movies as a cultural phenomenon on the verge of transforming the American way of life in numerous respects, while film culture itself was under constant repositioning in relation to the larger sociopolitical shifts in American society.

Exhibitors surviving and making leaps along the timeframe discussed here were championed in the local press as Horatio Alger-like heroes due to exemplary careers taking them from dreams of success to full-fledged capitalist realities. A Tally and a Clune were cases in point, shrewdly navigating the frenzy of transformations which brought moving images to the feature era—in which they were important players for a time. Clune clamored for "monster films" at the Auditorium in 1914 and, in order to secure such items for one of the U.S.'s most upscale film venues, he invested in the production of Griffith's *The Clansman*, which enjoyed an unprecedented exhibition run at the Auditorium in 1915. During the initial throes, the industry negotiated the burgeoning format in prologs and otherwise, a process only alluded to in this inquiry; this is still visible in numerous national cinemas, a visibility defining new parameters for script prestige, acting, and directing on the verge of Hollywood's global dissemination. Hollywood's success enveloped the City of Angels and widened the dragnet for prospective colonists hoping to turn dreams into screen realities. The breakthrough for the film novels coincided with a many-sided migration for film culture spearheaded by the serial films and features when the emergent era of film palaces ushered in a repositioning of audiences by way of filmic address, programming, and modes of exhibition, for example by screening in "daylight." Marketing turned into a key aspect of this newfangled film culture, demonstrated by the hiring of seasoned journalists at Mutual, for example, as well as other studios. The publicity departments operated via numerous channels, but in addition to their own trade organs, the daily press became a leading forum for marketing at a time when the newspapers instituted standing columns for criticism, succinct trade information, and dialog with fans.

Three "players" featured in previous chapters embody different aspects of the overall shifts in film culture in the mid-1910s: Kitty Kelly, Grace Darling, and B.M. Bower. On a symbolic level, they discursively moved film culture away from the regulatory phase, here metonymically initiated by the Stoddard sisters in Los Angeles and later acquiring a preventive realm practiced and advocated by Alice Stebbins Wells. Consequently, when the first exposition devoted to moving pictures opened at New York City's Grand Central Palace in July 1913, "Miss Lillian Terry, age 20, the Englishwoman who went to the Mayor's office to ask him to make her the first policewoman, was on duty. [. . .] Her task was to take care of the children."[43]

The new cultural purchase of the movies in the mid-1910s garnered a wide variety of cultural imprints and responses. When the war erupted in Europe, the scales on the global film market tipped for good, it seems, after which Hollywood formed part of a global imaginary. In 1914, during the first American feature phase, domestic films still played second fiddle to the European titles. The "complete superiority of European feature films over those made in this country" is explained by an unwillingness to spend enough dollars on the productions, besides the fact that the "American manufacturer is always in a hurry." An analysis ventured by the *New York Tribune* unfavorably compares *Judith of Bethulia* (Biograph, 1914) to the best foreign imports, *Cabiria* (Itali Film, 1914), *The Last Days of Pompeii* (Ambrosio, 1913), and *Quo Vadis?* (Cines, 1912). Griffith's film, still considered the unrivaled American feature to date, did not match the epic scope, numbers of extras, spectacular trick effects, and mise-en-scène displayed by *Cabiria*. With similar resources at hand, however, and the same "leisurely methods" of production, American directors would be able to contest the European mastery, the anonymous writer maintains.[44] According to this cross-cultural reading, the brisk American tempo permeating all aspects of society, as Bogardus later claimed, was considered a drawback for work in the film factories. Leisurely methods are represented as the sole avenue for feature success. The backbone of American film production, advocated and practiced by the trust—the hurried, regulated, and machine-like grinding out of single-reel titles—streamlined the output of genre items. According to the *New York Tribune*'s comparative analysis, leisurely methods spelled heavier investments per title, product differentiation, and a focus on historical spectacle in multi-reel titles replete with narrativized attractions.

The burgeoning critical institution, gradually established in American newspapers from the spring of 1914, exerted discursive pressure on domestic film producers to challenge the feature competition from abroad. In New York City the leading dailies focused on two aspects of the film medium: serial films and features, both important vehicles for advertising and promotion. The one-reel films had little clout in this respect. In his overview of the publishing field for film culture Robert

Grau noticed that regular film columns had recently emerged in the *New York Herald* and *Evening Globe*. The *Herald* inaugurated its unsigned column on February 17, 1914, remarking that, at the time, many films were enjoying long runs; the observation was exemplified by a handful of a titles currently playing. *The Globe and Commercial Advertiser* inaugurated its moving-picture department on February 21st, publishing a rationale for the endeavor which was filled with statistics compiled by the man in charge, George Henry Smith. Readers were invited to participate in a review contest. "Cash prizes [will be] awarded each week for the best criticism of motion picture plays." The *New York Tribune* followed suit on March 15th, promising readers "items of general interest concerning motion pictures, and motion picture players with special attention to productions which stand for the better things in the cinematographic art."[45] Parallel to the New York dailies' embrace of cinema, the entertainment magazine the *New York Review* launched a standing film column, "Flashes from Filmdom," which was first published on March 7th.

Already in late July 1913 the *Los Angeles Tribune* had inaugurated a film column appearing on a more or less daily basis, "Lights and Shades of the Movies." Although *Moving Picture World* lauded the initiative, the column soon petered out. The compliments in *Moving Picture World* included an appreciative stance on a film-friendly editorial published in the *Tribune*, which might have been unwelcome kudos for the progressive management to digest. Film coverage thus for a time was cut short, and on October 3rd the editorial page sported a cartoon labeled "Ad Nauseam" which seems to be targeting the recent conversion of the Lyceum to a house for feature films under the management of Morosco and Cort. The opening feature at the Lyceum was *The Battle of Gettysburg* (New York Motion Picture Corporation, 1913) on July 4th.[46]

When the *New York Tribune* began publishing a Sunday page devoted to motion pictures, a year or so before *The Birth of a Nation* premiered in New York City, domestic producers were chastised for rushing productions. Local producers turn out films more speedily than others, which however "is not always conducive to quality," readers were told apropos Benjamin Christensen's *Sealed Orders* (Dansk Biograf Kompagni, 1913), whose unhurried production process was lauded as exemplary.[47] As if responding to such charges, Kitty Kelly, in a review of Griffith's *The Escape*, noted with regard to the director's working methods that "time is

379

FIGURE 38: Disgusted by the movies. Cartoon from
Los Angeles Tribune, 3 October 1913, 16.

regarded by this master as essential to adequate picture production as is money."[48] Interestingly, half of this allegorical film was shot at the Atlantic shores (New York City), half at those of the Pacific (Los Angeles). The critic's contention that foreign productions had the upper hand mirrors Harry C. Carr's protracted extolling of French films over American in the early days.

FIGURE 39: Two postcards from South Broadway in Los Angeles,
circa 1910 (Courtesy of Brent C. Dickerson)

A year later, in March 1915, the tables had turned. Griffith now incarnated the clout and preeminence of Hollywood cinema and was hailed as the "revolutionist of the photo play."[49] The same month, Grace Darling, after traveling from New York City to California via the Panama Canal, held court at the San Francisco Exposition, the center of which was the Column of Progress. Among the multiple events hosted by the exposition was the second conference devoted to race betterment and eugenics, a topic Griffith had touted in his lost film *The Escape* and its full-reel prolog. It was thus no authorial accident that the theme of the film that propelled Hollywood to putative feature dominance read American history through the lens of race.[50]

When speculating on the future of the movies in May 1914, at a time when Griffith was busy shooting *The Clansman*, an editorial in the *New York Review* ventured an analysis from the perspective of domestic ingenuity and practical determination. The writer foresaw a "field for inventive genius" to tackle. Thus, "when the resourceful American mind gets to working on the problems involved it is almost a certainty that they will be solved sooner or later."[51] As Sime in *Variety* cautioned producers apropos *The Escape*, in the same way that thrilling "mellers" had been able to find an audience two years before, there was also an audience for a new type of film.[52] From a different perspective, Daniel Carson Goodman, responsible for *The Escape*'s prolog, analyzed such films and their audience in evolutionary terms by resorting to good old metaspectatorial methodology:

> To my mind the flowering of the evolutionary process in motion pictures has brought about a change, so far as the manufacturing end is concerned, in the usual order of stunt pictures and dramatic climaxes. Today we find audiences tired of the physical stunts, jumping over cliffs, hair-breadth escapes from moving trains, etc. I have watched faces in a moving picture audience and note the fact that a face will depict surprise, or horror, or emotional tenseness in direct proportion to the emotional value contained within the picture. I will illustrate what I mean by saying, whereas an auditor is held spell-bound for from three to five seconds by a plunging automobile, which fact only surprises him and is not emotional, he is held for an indefinite period by the working out of a dramatic situation which catches his heart-strings and his mind.[53]

The "new order" he foresees in the immediate future will dispense with the stunts, most prominent in the serial films, and

> within one year not a picture over one reel in length will have a stunt of the physical kind in it. This means better stories on the part of the manufacturing concerns to meet the higher and more intelligent demands of the moving picture audiences.

Goodman's analysis positions itself at a critical juncture in the medium's short history and takes stock of formats, contents, audiences and their emotional engagement with films. Accurate or not, his text is only one of numerous testimonies from contemporary observers inside the industry and out claiming that a new era was dawning if not already in place—and American cinema would lead the way. This putative dominance confirmed a sweeping analysis of American wherewithal ventured from a British perspective concerning the press in 1901. W.T. Stead's analysis mentioned in passing the "mission of the cinematograph" and its educative potential by predicting a coming visual turn under the rubric "Eye-gate." Fifteen years or so later, Hollywood emerged along the more general path delineated by Stead, namely as yet another aspect of "the advent of the United States of America as the greatest of world-powers [which] is the greatest political, social, and commercial phenomenon of our times."[54]

Early in 1915 Griffith had answered the call for leisurely produced domestic features when a film of unprecedented scale, epic scope, and production costs opened: *The Clansman*, soon to be *The Birth of a Nation*. Albeit inflammatory and highly controversial due to its racist historiography, Griffith convinced virtually all critics, irrespective of persuasion, of his and Hollywood's leading positing in the feature field. Louis Sherwin's enthusiastic review evidenced the fact that the tables had indeed turned and American features now ruled. In Sherwin's account all the shortcomings listed by the *New York Tribune* in the summer of 1914 apropos American features were laid to rest. Moreover, Griffith's film impressed a critic—Sherwin was a drama critic and did not normally write on cinema—who responded with a lukewarm appreciation of the movies in general.

> Here is beyond question the most extraordinary picture that has been made—or seen—in America so far. In perfection of detail, in the care and time that have been expended on it, and the huge scope of the tremendous drama it depicts. 'The Birth of a Nation' is far and away above everything that has been attempted hitherto. In fact, I seriously doubt whether it does not excel even the most pretentions [sic] of the European feature films like 'Quo Vadis.' [---]
>
> At first thought it may seem an exaggeration to talk so enthusiastically about a picture. Personally, I do not happen to be a lover of the ubiquitous movie. Nearly all the so-called feature 'fillums' I have seen heretofore have turned out to be a bit of a bore. All the more surprising was it to see anything so interesting, so intensely absorbing, as this one.[55]

Irrespective of the drama critic's enthusiasm, the *Globe*'s editorialist elected to address the film's blatant racism head-on a month later, much in the spirit of Francis Hackett's review in the *New Republic*. "If history bore no relation to life," writes Hackett, "this motion picture drama could well be reviewed and applauded as a spectacle. As a spectacle it is stupendous." But, Hackett continues, "since history does bear on social behavior, *The Birth of a Nation* cannot be reviewed simply as a spectacle."[56] The editorial in the *Globe*, titled "Capitalizing Race Hatred," thus discounts the spectacle and sees only an attempt to "pander to depraved taste and to foment race antipathy" for the purpose of making "a few dirty dollars."[57]

Conflicts abounded wherever the film was shown, which has been analyzed in-depth, particularly in Janet Staiger's ambitious reception study.[58] In Los Angeles several organizations petitioned the City Council asking for a ban on Griffith's film. After a hearing the Council unanimously supported a ban and referred the matter to the Board of Censors to expedite. The Board's ban was however overturned in the court and by the mayor, thus affecting only one show. Clune, in more senses than one, had thus shored up a veritable monster film to fill up one of the largest theaters in the U.S. for months.

During its process of deliberation, the City Council solicited opinions on the film from, amongst others, Emma L. Reed. Her report strikes a balance between the dramatic achievements and the racially degrading theme, as did the majority of commentators in the following months. Permitting the film's exhibition, she concludes, would be a "a gratuitous insult to the larger number of colored people who are good and worthy citizens of Los Angeles."[59]

Whether African-American patrons were relegated to unattractive balcony rows at Clune's Auditorium we do not know. Segregation practices in theaters, restaurants, bar, drugstores, soda parlors, and department stores otherwise represented a daily insult for African-Americans and other others in Los Angeles. When Georgia A. Robinson and her husband and daughter were overcharged for entering the Victoria Theater at 2570 West Pico Street, a moving-picture show run by Sigmund Stern, she took the matter to the City Council, which led to a hearing hosted by the Council's Public Welfare Committee on November 3, 1913.[60] Stern's ticket seller had demanded a quarter instead of the advertised dime for the adults and a dime instead of nickel for the child. Adding insult to injury, Stern had informed them that this was his way of doing business. Colored people, he explained, had at times created disturbances and "this is the best way of keeping them out: by charging them more" (3).

In her petition, Robinson urged that Stern's license to run his theater should be revoked, as his discriminatory practice violated city regulations, state laws, and federal statues. The city of Los Angeles had however not adopted an ordinance explicitly defining discrimination against a particular class of citizens as a misdemeanor. Besides Robinson, thirteen witnesses, all African-American professionals, gave testimony attesting to widespread discrimination in all walks of life. Many restaurants and bars displayed signs noting that they reserved the right to change their prices without notice. Prices could thus, on the spur of the moment, jump from a quarter for a meal or drink to five or six dollars, depending on the customers' skin color, while other places had signs informing potential patrons outright that they "draw the color line." In addition, many others ignored colored patrons or refused to serve them—and Bullock's department store refused to fit gloves to colored customers and was said to be highly discriminatory overall. According to one witness, a previous investigation had shown that "102 saloons [...] absolutely refused to serve any Negro. I found out that there were sixty-eight restaurants in the city where a Colored person could not get accommodation, for love or for money" (15).

Many theaters and picture shows relegated African-American patrons to unattractive sections of the house, raised prices, or flat-out denied access. Pantages had apparently been taken to the Superior Court and convicted for such practices. Among picture theaters, one witness named "[t]he Optic, Isis, Banner, and various other places which are too numerous to mention" (5). Several witnesses had been forced to the Orpheum's balcony after having reserved tickets for other seats in the house via the color-neutral telephone; the Burbank and Century entertained a similar policy. One witness recounted his experience when buying tickets at the Regal and was forced by ushers to a dingy corner in an otherwise sparsely attended house. "As I sat there, I noted what occurred at the door. All Negroes, Japanese, Chinese, and Mexicans, were seated on the dark dingy side where I was, while all others where given the best seats available" (24). Summing up the sentiments, one witness concluded that "as American citizens we intend to preserve our rights and not be treated as animals" (27). Several months later, the Public Welfare Committee reached the conclusion that an ordinance making discrimination in public places a misdemeanor was uncalled-for, given the existence of a "state law by which the aggrieved person may recover damages to the extent of $100 for each discrimination." According to the city attorney, revoking a license because of segregation was unconstitutional. Thus, the *Record*'s headline—"Protest by Negroes Gets Them Nothing."[61]

The petition, without alluding to it, indirectly challenged the Supreme Court's ruling in Plessy vs. Ferguson from 1896. In it, the Supreme

Court legalized the doctrine of separate but equal, as Homer Plessy lost the case against East Louisiana Railway and learned that he had indeed committed a crime when refusing to move to a car designated for colored passengers. As long as racially segregated facilities were equal, the segregation did not violate the Fourteenth Amendment's guarantees of equal protection under the law. The theaters in Los Angeles were not formally segregated, but African-American patrons and other non-whites were unofficially relegated to seats and sections in the houses not considered equally good as those available for white patrons.[62] It was against this background of systematic discrimination and Jim Crow practices that the protests against Griffith's *The Clansman* were voiced in Los Angeles.

Throughout this book we have repeatedly turned to offhand audience observations with a racist slant from the pen of Harry C. Carr. African-Americans were however not part of his portraits of nickel patrons in the early days. He could not however resist weighing in on the intense debate and protests that preceded the screening of *The Clansman* at Clune's Auditorium. From his detached vantage point the ever-jesting Carr elected to frame the conflict over the film's racist historiography as the best marketing imaginable—and free of charge. In his account he thus foregrounds the film's press agent and his celebration of the proceedings leading up to the screening. His playful outline shows little sympathy for the issue at stake. Not that Carr drew the cartoon, but his jocular retelling of the story lends itself to a depiction on par with the film's racism even if he, in a postscript-like musing, concedes that the film is "rather rough—decidedly rough, in fact, on the colored people." The cartoon takes blackface to a whole new level, with the celebratory dancing featuring director and press agent as all-out black caricatures.

From recounts of his boyhood in Los Angeles it is obvious that white people shied away from ethnic mixing. As Carr formulates it, the Iowan colonization "had completely wiped out the Spanish atmosphere" and the white invaders stayed apart from the non-white aspects of city life. The three civilizations Robert Grau placed around the old Plaza—Chinese and Japanese, the Spanish and Mexican, and the 'Gringos,' or Americans—did not meet on equal terms, if at all.

> I do not remember as a little boy to have heard a word of Spanish spoken; to have known any Spanish or Mexican boy, or to have seen more than one Spanish house; that was an adobe on Main Street just south of Pico.

Keefe, the sagacious press agent of "The Clansman," sits and sobs alone.

Judge Jackson yesterday made permanent the injunction to prevent the Chief of Police from interfering with the production of the much-agitated play.

Unless some other City Council now bobs up and offers to lend him the whole machinery of another city, it looks as though Keefe would have to be content with a miserable million dollars or so of free advertising.

I will not go so far as to say that the promoters of this moving-picture play actually brought about all this stew; sundry excited ministers and certain Councilmen with an almost inhuman ability to get agitated, saved them the trouble. But when the trouble did come up, "The Clansman" promoters and Keefe, the press representative, endured all the incidental free advertising with Christian fortitude and resignation.

What the Judge Said.

In deciding the injunction case yesterday, Judge Jackson addressed a few words to the colored people who half-filled the courtroom.

He told them that, while he did not approve of the play himself, he advised them to stop talking about it and to calm their stormy agitation. "There is a certain feeling between the races and there always will be as long as both live in this country," said the court. "But the production of this play will neither make the position of the colored people better nor worse and it will have no effect whatever upon the standing of the colored citizens of this community."

Everybody Helps.

"The Clansman" people fired another battle bulletin through to the papers last night to the effect that the Merchants' and Manufacturers' Association has adopted resolutions denouncing the interference of the City Council with the production of the play.

We have ceased investigating these rumors; we believe it all on sight. Everybody with strength enough to resolute has resoluted. The only thing that could happen now would be for the fire department to cut in somewhere and help advertise the show. The police and the City Council and the courts and the commercial bodies and the parsons have been willing if unwitting volunteers.

Dream Come True.

Hereafter press agents will sigh and sigh in the effort to think of some way to libel the colored race. But alas! It is doubtful if any other City Council will ever be found easy enough to fall as this one did.

Sensible Deacon.

In the midst of all the excitement, the only sensible remark I have heard made about the "race feeling" roused by "The Clansman" was made by my old friend Deacon Anderson, the giant colored brother, who runs the Courthouse elevator.

I asked him yesterday if he had been to see "The Clansman."

"No, sir," he said, "I don't think I'll go around and pay my good money to see something that I don't think I'm going to like."

I have thought about the deacon's remark all day long. It impressed me so much that I will now rise and take off my hat to the deacon. Oh, for more deacons and fewer City Councilmen.

Terrible Thought.

Keefe, the press agent of the show, probably does not join me in this prayer. Were all the public as cool and full of sense as the deacon, the press agents would starve to death. Press agents thrive and grow fat on agitations that fan to flame in the breasts of City Councilmen and such.

Well, Now, Why?

We will kiss all this rather ridiculous affair a fond good-by with this sage remark:

One of the mysteries of modern American life is the alarmed solicitude that the public has over the morals of the movies. Cheap plays, cheap magazines, cheap books, cheap orators are allowed to publish and expound all manner of dreadful things every day without the slightest comment—things that would drive a moving picture censorship board into hysterics.

Oh, You Suckers!

The agreement was that we would pass this thing by, but I can't resist adding this:

That I think "The Clansman" is rather rough—decidedly rough, in fact, upon the colored people, and is a glorification of mob law that is not approved of; but no one can help feeling contempt for an agitation that chases itself around in circles like a cat in a fit, an intolerable and meaningless agitation—a legislative body that creates a board of censors without power; then tries to go behind its own agents; issues racous orders without authority to a Chief of Police who is told by the courts not to obey them and finally falls with one wild yell into the bag held open by an astute press agent.

The King of France who drew his sword and put it up again, was a prodigy of efficiency and achievement compared with Press Agent Keefe's faithful band of excited, blundering volunteer assistants.

Grief displayed

By the sorrow-stricken director and the press agent of "The Clansman" over the hullabaloo caused by the attempt to stop the showing of the film.

FIGURE 40: Harry C. Carr on the attempts to ban the screening of *The Clansman. Los Angeles Times*, 11 February 1915, III:1.

We played a game of leap-frog that we called 'Spaniola," and I dare say we were trying to say Espanol. The nearest that we came to the atmosphere of the old pueblo were the water ditches—the *zanjas*—whose names we twisted into sankey. Iowa couldn't see any sense in calling *zanja* sahn-ha.

From these zanjas the inhabitants got their irrigating water. They ran down Figueroa to Jefferson and along West Adams Street until a comparatively recent time.[63]

Carr's flippant analysis of city life in the *Times*' columns relayed the Saunterer's vacillating stance vis-à-vis modernity and the makeover of the old adobe and garden city. Carr celebrated city attractions and closely monitored a mass culture built around movies and sport. His rambling writing style mirrors the hectic urban perception and its numerous speed phenomena. When seriously speculating on the future of the movies, but only for a minute, the "inevitable conclusion" he arrives at is that, since their invention, moving pictures have failed to move beyond the building-block stage. "The films await their Shakespeare."[64]

Carr's colleague, theater critic Julian Johnson, in another register reflected on why Shakespeare is irrelevant to modern man. He attributed this sorry state of affairs to modernity's rush and speed culture in an age progressively more artificial. Technological conveniences, writes Johnson, now shield people from pre-industrial hands-on processes in the manner analyzed by observers from Wells to Bogardus.

While the predictions of certain alienists that we will be a nation of nervous wrecks in another quarter-century hardly need to be taken seriously, it is still tremendously true that at no period of history has life been lived with such speed and intensity. The conveniences of the age of invention have brought resultant tragedies, and behind the smiling sunshine of a rushing world hangs a veil of tears. The age has, to a certain extent, grown artificial, and as his daily surroundings are forced away from simple fidelity, man longs for unwavering truth in the arts.[65]

Two years before the opening of *The Birth of a Nation*, Harry C. Carr hastily speculated about cinema's future. He vouched for spectacle and films catering solely to the eye, and since the minute he had awarded himself for pondering this matter was running out, he only reeled off a couple of recent examples: the original settings for Kalem's Christ film shot in Palestine, a film on the history of steam moving from Watt watching a tea kettle to the latest engines, and the film depicting the history of Mormonism, *One Hundred Years of Mormonism* (Utah Moving Picture Co., 1913). From these crude beginnings he predicted a "future so big that it almost scares you."[66]

A month later Carr returned to the future of moving pictures after theatrical tycoons Klaw and Erlanger had announced plans to enter the film field. Up to that point, Carr maintains, films have been written by "street car conductors, office boys, even café waiters," but with high-class promoters coming in, "the bell-hop playwright" will sooner or later vanish.[67] Two years later Carr finally discovered two pictures meeting his scriptwriting standard: *The Captive* (1915), written by Jeanie Macpherson for Lasky and directed by Cecil B. DeMille, and *Two-Gun Hicks* (1914), written by C. Gardner Sullivan for Broncho Film Co. and directed by William S. Hart. Carr praises these films for their "atmosphere and charm and real characters," while "all other picture plays I have seen consisted simply of plots laid on its slabs." Alluding to his old piece, Carr considers it unthinkable that "the photodrama should continue to be written by unsuccessful newspaper reporters out of a job and by office boys and street-car conductors." For the director of the future "the plot will not matter so much: it will be all in the way the plot is told." Thus, "the cheap trash of the photoplay world is nearing the end. The villain who ties young ladies to railroad tracks, and the wicked city man with patent-leather shoes who leads the simple country maid into a pretended marriage are about ready for the final curtain."[68] Such plots hark back to the inception of story films in the manner of *Escape from Sing Sing*. As it turned out, the future had an endeavor in store for Carr by offering him an opportunity to influence promotion and scenario work at a film studio. From 1919 to late 1921 Carr worked as publicity representative, scenarist, and head of the scenario department at Griffith's Mamaroneck studio.[69]

Carr's jesting stances from 1913 and 1915 mirror the hopes for a different type of cinema voiced by virtually all critics of the medium during the period under discussion. In an era of reform and progressive initiatives, boosters and hecklers alike entertained utopian aspirations for the medium's future. As is evident from previous chapters, nickel shows emerged as a contested cultural phenomenon challenged by reformers and often flogged in newspaper campaigns. According to Raymond Williams, cultural forms harbor a perpetual struggle between three strands or layers—the dominant, the residual, and the emergent. Throughout this book we have engaged with complex processes of repositioning of cinema in a dialog with culture at large via newspaper discourses. William's concepts have functioned as a theoretical framework for analyzing processes involving film culture and, in turn, film culture's place vis-à-vis the culture at large. In its discursive framing, which has been the focus here, cinema has served as a clearinghouse for compounded processes of cultural transformation in a consumerist society. Initially criticized for its unchecked commercial brashness, but too popular to be shut down, negotiations across a wider precinct of culture remained as the sole options for addressing the emerging nickel phenomenon. Policing and progressive reform worked in tandem with the industry in regulating exhibition and representation practices. As a vehicle for education, instruction, and betterment in schools, churches, and many other institutions, the film medium as a whole commanded cultural clout far beyond that of theatrical exhibition. The valorization of non-theatrical screenings did not curb the prospects for education and instruction inside theaters. In combination, the many parallel tracks of film culture discussed in this book from the perspective of Los Angeles illustrate a jagged trajectory from contested nickel culture around the ethnic Plaza and its many "civilizations" to the upscale business center and dominant culture.

In the mid-1910s it was however still business as usual for cheap shows and small-time vaudeville houses parallel to the dominance of feature films at prestige venues. In a market divided by distribution practices and levels of runs, screen entertainment on the fringe survived as a residual practice. Meanwhile, film culture that pivoted on feature films dominated the advertising accounts and coverage in the press. Within dominant culture—and in the form of feature films—such programs were advertised as theatrical attractions for predominantly white, middleclass audiences on white ways across metropolitan America.

The Progressive Era, the general historical term for the period of 1890–1920, suggests processes of cultural change and progress at work in dialog with social science and scientific management. The perceived rationality of such changes no doubt depended on a vantage point inflected by class, race, and gender. Economists like Simon N. Patten sought to place their discipline in the midst of the social conversation by influencing journalists and eventually lawmakers to change society for the better, a salient term circulating across many realms of society.

On the streets an array of groups came together, some enjoying themselves on the bright side of the street, others educating themselves when the various institutions such as libraries, museums, etc. were open. Other groups—journalists, economists, and a wide assortment of reformers—studied street life with different emphases and balances concerning Patten's light and dark sides, and between commercial amusements and recreations. Reform and uplift were crucial terms for social activists. For a cultural analysis pivoting on negotiations between emergent, residual, and dominant strands, the contemporary terms reform and uplift cannot be discounted. The changes we have examined did not come about by happenstance or teleology, but as the result of rational negotiations. The determinants of the changes operated on multiple levels. Reform and uplift, the key progressive terms, span an array of initiatives and discourses, obviously influencing film culture's shaky route from emergent to dominant. Or, in tune with Lee Grieveson's analysis, one can subsume reform and uplift under policing. Business and market logics and processes of self-regulation balanced outside pressure from reform groups and lawmakers. At the end of the period the government deregulated the industry by way of the antitrust laws at a time when the independents had undermined the trust's dominance from within.

In the mid-1910s cinema was a medium with a scary future due to its opportunities, according to Harry C. Carr. The linguistic struggles around the term "the movies" were part of a process of negotiation concerning film culture, as were the allegories in the prologs of the feature format. According to the new film pages in newspapers, the birth of an American film nation happened around the time Griffith's *The Clansman* premiered. In the process, cinema had broadened its class base and established a foothold along the best amusement streets, where non-white patrons, however, still were treated as second-class citizens.

In 1915 Guy Price appraised the ascendancy of film advertising as the result of a deeper understanding of the importance of showmanship for the business. This type of showmanship was, however, not to be confused with the ballyhoo of the attraction days:

Now enters the 'the showman.'
The cord pulled so tight that it choked the rapidly-swelling pocketbook is unloosened. A little money drops out and falls into the channels of advertising. People sit up and take notice. Theaters are drawing larger audi-

ences. The string is again unraveled—more money is carried away by the advertising current and pretty soon the cord is thrown away and the film makers, exchange men and the many other branches of the tremendous industry are 'spreading themselves'—with remarkable profit to their respective business line.[70]

Returning to the *Los Angeles Times'* massive Sunday edition on January 10th as a final exercise, we will take a closer look at Price's "now." On that day the *Times* consisted of eight sections and a Sunday Magazine, in all amounting to 136 pages comprising 466 columns of advertising and 389 of text. The Mexican War dominated the front page, and elsewhere Harry C. Carr discussed the war between the two European super armies, the French and the German. Classified ads filled several sections, some of them for makeshift film theaters. The large-scale advertisers were the department stores: Bullock's had three full pages, Hamburger's and Broadway no less, apart from countless ads for ladies' fashions. Automobile news and advertising commanded a separate section.

Few movie theaters advertised their programs, and the ones that did were the big palaces in the business center. In January 1915 most of them offered domestic features: Tally's showed *The Girl of the Golden West* (Lasky, 1915), Auditorium billed *Mrs. Wiggs of the Cabbage Patch* (California Motion Picture Corporation, 1914), Quinn's Superba offered Ince's *The Italian*, Quinn's Garrick a second week of *The Naked Truth* (*La Donna nuda*, Cines, 1914) featuring Lyda Borelli, while Woodley advertised *A Florida Enchantment* (Vitagraph, 1914) in five reels. Miller's Theater presented the second installment of *The Exploits of Elaine* (Wharton for Pathé, 1914) together with *Samson* (Box Office Attraction Co., 1915) featuring William Farnum; the ad assured prospective patrons that this was not a biblical story. The *Los Angeles Examiner* published a photograph of the audience lining up for *The Exploits of Elaine* outside Miller's; surprisingly, the crowd was dominated by older folks, some of them perhaps of Iowa descent.[71] Simultaneously, Clune's Broadway offered a parody of the serial films—the second installment of *The Ten Billion Dollar Vitagraph Mystery* featuring Clara Kimball Young as Flora Flourflush. The episode was billed together with a variety program consisting of Edison's *The Girl at the Key* with Gertrude McKey; Norma Talmadge in *A Daughter of Israel* (two reels, Vitagraph, 1915); a comedy featuring Elsie Greerson and Lillian Leighton, *The Strenuous Life* (Selig, 1915); and *Hearst-*

Selig's News Pictorial. Two vaudeville houses screened films that particular week: Alhambra featured Chaplin's six-reel comedy *Tillie's Punctured Romance* (Keystone, 1914), while Republic presented *After the Ball* (Photo Drama Co., 1914) plus six high-class live acts.

As all these films opened on January 11th, the *Los Angeles Express* published a piece by the president of the Merchants' and Manufacturers' Association waxing eloquently on why "Los Angeles is a Wonder City." President Geissler's piece rehashed the familiar gamut of local attractions: unrivaled climate; scenic splendor; unsurpassed harbor; excellent railroad facilities; ideal circumstances for manufacturing; the best labor relations in America, with "union and non-union men working side by side"; clean business conditions, and "wealth and culture giving opportunity for civic betterment." Adjacent to this article, a piece on one particular industry seemingly drove Geissler's point home—according to the headline "Movie Actors are Paid $7,000,000 Every Year."[72] The facts and figures mirror the fuller account in the *Times*' "Annual mid-Winter Issue."[73] This appraisal genre harks back to 1911 when the *Examiner*, in its annual anniversary edition, for the first time included the film industry among local resources under the rubric "Southland Is A Moving Picture Eden."[74] This Eden discourse in turn harks back to the 1870s and was later negotiated by both Mrs. Otis and Charles Fletcher Lummis, colleagues at the *Times*.

Gertrude M. Price's paper, the *Record*, began publishing a series of installments on Marie Walcamp, "Dare-Devil Girl of the Movies," the week the *Times* published its mammoth Sunday edition. The stories from shooting at 101-Bison Company relate attacks by lions and tigers, dives into shark-filled water, and describes how to throw horses and work with elephants, all in the line of duty for the undaunted Walcamp. The most visible star in January 1915 was otherwise Mary Pickford. After arriving at the Santa Fe station on the ninth, she was busy "holding court" at the Alexandria Hotel the following day. Pickford had recently renewed her contract with Famous Players, worth $200,000 according to the press, and was to star in *Rags* next. Working in California was ideal, she claimed, "[t]here is something subtle, something vaguely powerful in the very air that brings out all one's latent faculties."[75] The next few weeks she busied herself with social functions. Little Mary participated in the Photoplayers Club's parade, seated in a canoe with Seymour Tally at the wheel, and the following evening she was crowned queen of the ball hosted by the Southern California Motion Picture Exhibitors' Association at the Shrine. And just like today, the Academy Awards having relocated from the Shrine to the Kodak Theater in Hollywood, "several hundred persons were waiting outside the building, eager for even a sight of their picture favorite."[76]

Mary Pickford's remarkable story from rags to *Rags*, as it were, was presented to the *Times*' readers in a featured article signed Grace Kingsley, the prime chronicler of motion-picture matters in the paper's columns for years to come.[77] On the East Coast some took a more somber view of screen fame. When William Fox hoped to acquire storage space for films in New York City's Central Park, the idea was ridiculed in the press, not least in a *New York Times* editorial, dripping with irony, about plans for what the paper elected to call a film mausoleum: "It would be disheartening to think after all the scientific progress of this age Mr. Chaplin was writing his name in water as Kean and Kemble wrote theirs, or that future generations would have only a vague idea, derived from the chronicler, of the charms of Miss Pickford and Miss Theda Bara."[78] Fierce opposition killed off the idea. The charms of Misses Pickford and Bara have however not been lost on future generations, partly due to "the chronicler." To be sure, we can bemoan the loss of this and other film mausoleums, still it is somewhat consoling that the newspaper morgues remain for chroniclers' use.

NOTES

Introduction

1. Will Irwin, "The American Newspaper," *Collier's*, Vol. 46, No. 18 (21 January 1911). The quotation is from the opening article, "The Power of the Press." The series was reprinted in 1969 as *The American Newspaper* with comments by Clifford F. Weigle and David C. Clark for the Iowa State University Press (Ames, Iowa); the quotation is from this edition, p. 15.

2. Wolfgang Schivelbusch, *The Railway Journey: Trains and Travel in the 19th Century* (New York: Urizen Books, 1979). Publication of his book in English came shortly after the legendary FIAF conference in Brighton, which marked new alliances betweens scholars and archives concerning early cinema. Among a host of investigations concerning panoramic perception and cinema, the most ambitious is Lynne Kirby, *Parallel Tracks: The Railroad and Silent Cinema* (Durham, N.C.: Duke University Press, 1997).

3. For an account of the automotive scene in Los Angeles, see Scott L. Bottles, *Los Angeles and the Automobile: The Making of the Modern City* (Berkeley: University of California Press, 1987).

4. The research process for this study started at what was then the School of Cinema-Television (now the School of Cinematic Arts) at the University of Southern California as a seminar series entitled "Silent Discourses," which was predicated on metaphorically mapping early screen cultures from a variety of reception perspectives. A few semesters later, a seminar series on pre-classical American cinema, held at UCLA on the west side, provided a wel-

come opportunity for more specifically and concretely addressing the intricacies of film exhibition with a manifestly Los Angeles slant. A subsequent seminar at USC in 2004 on D.W. Griffith and Cecil B. DeMille focused on the emerging production realm in the Southland, but also prompting a challenging look at received histories and their historiographic underpinnings.

5. The most well-known crusade against the nickel shows was published in the columns of the *Chicago Tribune* in April-May 1907, the fullest account of the campaign is found in Lee Grieveson, *Policing Cinema: Movies and Censorship in Early-Twentieth-Century America* (Berkeley: University of California Press, 2004). See also Kathleen D. McCarthy, "Nickel Vice and Virtue: Movie Censorship in Chicago, 1907–1915," *Journal of Popular Film*, Vol. 5, No. 1 (1976): 37–55; Mary Carbine, " 'The Finest outside the Loop': Motion Picture Exhibition in Chicago's Black Metropolis, 1905–1928," *Camera Obscura* 23 (May, 1990): 9–41; Moya Luckett, "Cities and Spectators: A Historical Analysis of Film Audiences in Chicago, 1910-1915," diss., University of Wisconsin-Madison, 1995); Julie Ann Lindstrom, " 'Getting a Hold Deeper in the Life of the City': Chicago Nickelodeons, 1905–1914," diss., Northwestern University, 1998; and her essay " 'Almost worse than the restrictive measures is our apparent belief that the city itself has no obligation in the matter': Chicago Reformers and the Nickelodeons," *Cinema Journal*, Vol. 39. No. 1 (Fall 1999): 90–112; Lauren Rabinovitz, *For the Love of Pleasure. Women, Movies, and Culture in Turn-of-the Century Chicago* (New Brunswick, N.J.: Rutgers University Press, 1998); Jacqueline Najuma Stewart, *Migrating to the Movies: Cinema and Black Urban Modernity* (Berkeley: University of California Press, 2005).

6. Paul Starr, *The Creation of the Media: Political Origins of Modern Communications* (New York: Basic Books, 2004), 250–260; the quotation is from p. 251.

7. Maps proper have however been less useful for such mobilization than hoped. *The Sanborn Fire Insurance Maps*, for example, unfortunately cover Los Angeles in 1906 only, which was shortly before the era of nickel madness reached the City of Angels, and thus before the phenomenon was readable as a constellation of potentially hazardous fire dots in the cityscape. The 1909 aerial map of Los Angeles is not detailed enough to zoom in on the nickel houses—the big theaters are of course marked; this is also the case for the bird's-eye map published by the *Los Angeles Examiner* on July 13, 1909 as well as another bird's-eye map from 1913. *The Rand-McNally Indexed County and Township Pocket Map and Shippers' Guide of California* from 1911 and *Baist's Real Estate Map* from 1912, while admirably precise and highly meticulous for their respective purpose, offer precious little information bearing on the amusement geography in Los Angeles. *The Standard Guide Book to Southern California*, published in 1910, listed only two "moving picture shows":

Clune's and Tally's New Broadway. The yearly theatrical directory *Julius Cahn's Official Theatrical Guide* offered no information on film venues during its publication span from the late 1890s to 1913/1914. The follow-up publication, *Gus Hill's National Theatrical Directory*, which commenced publication for the 1914/15 season, listed only three movie theaters in Los Angeles: Clune's, Tally's New Broadway, and the Mozart. The lists of nickelodeons periodically published by *Billboard* in the early years are far from comprehensive; a first list of "Electric Theaters and Nickelodeons" was published on December 15, 1906, *Billboard*, Vol. 18, No. 50 (15 December 1906): 32. Subsequent attempts at comprehensive lists were published in Ibid., Vol. 19, No. 1 (16 March 1907): 113; Vol. 19. No. 49 (7 December 1907): 52; Vol. 20, No. 11 (21 March 1908): 95. These lists are the only sources in which pioneering exhibitor Mark Hanna can be found; apart from the information on his handful of La Petite Theaters scattered in towns around Los Angeles and one in the downtown proper, which in all likelihood never opened, few traces of his activities have emerged.

8. There is no distinction between the various types of theatrical exhibition in the license material, and the indications provided by licensees are not always consistent: Sometimes the name of the venue is given, sometimes only the licensee's name. In the fatal gap between surviving license ledgers, the years 1908–1910, film exhibition took off at lightning speed, and houses and managements relieved each other at a frantic pace. The houses defining the palatial breakthrough in 1910 and 1911 were in the main stricken from the exhibition map a decade or two later to yield space for even more lucrative ventures.

9. The best monographic account of the *Los Angeles Times* is Robert Gottlieb and Irene Wolt, *Thinking Big: The Story of the Los Angeles Times, Its Publishers and Their Influence on Southern California* (New York: Putnam, 1977). See also Jerome Wolf, "The Los Angeles Times, Labor, and the Open Shop, 1890–1910," diss., University of Southern California, 1961.

10. David Nasaw, *The Chief: The Life of William Randolph Hearst* (Boston: Houghton Mifflin, 2000). Concerning Hearst's use of film during his campaign in the 1906 gubernatorial election in New York, see Jan Olsson, "Sound Aspirations: The Two Dimensions of Synchronicity," in Didier Huvelle and Dominique Nasta, eds., *Le son en perspective: nouvelles recherches/New Perspectives in Sound Study* (Brussels: P.I. E.-Peter Lang, 2004), 99–114.

11. For an analysis of the league's press politics, see Gerald J. Baldasty, *E.W. Scripps and the Business of Newspapers* (Urbana: University of Illinois Press, 1999).

12. The papers consulted are: the *Evening News* from October 1905–1907, *Los Angeles Examiner*, *Los Angeles Express*, *Los Angeles Herald*, *Los Angeles Record*, *Los Angeles Times*, and *Los Angeles Tribune* (which began publication on July 4, 1911). In addition, the *Los Angeles Municipal News*, April 17, 1912–April 9,

1913, *Los Angeles Citizen*, March 1, 1907–March, 1915 (weekly); *Common Sense* April 1, 1905–Aug 7, 1909, and *California Social-Democrat*, 1911–March 1915. Circulation figures as reported in *N.W. Ayer & Son's American Newspaper Annual*, after 1910 *N.W. Ayer & Son's American Newspaper Annual and Directory* (Philadelphia: N.W. Ayer & Son): for 1907: *Evening News* (Republican, commenced publication in 1905) 20,736; *Examiner* (Democratic, commenced publication in 1903) 35,000; *Express* (Republican, commenced publication in 1871) 26,791; *Herald* (Democratic, commenced publication in 1873) 25,170 on weekdays and 31,435 Sundays; *Record* (Independent, commenced publication in 1895) 24,697; *Times* (Independent Republican, commenced publication in 1881) 46,250 on weekdays and 68,875 on Sundays; for 1909: *Examiner* 40,000 and 70,000 on Sundays; *Express* 39,580; *Herald* 22,000 and 30,000 on Sundays; *Record* 29,710; *Times* 53,792 and 76,741 on Sundays; for 1913: *Examiner* 54,593 and 107, 660 on Sundays; *Express* 47,030; *Herald* 65,000; *Record* 47,470; *Times* 57,614 and 85,000 on Sundays; *Tribune* 55,500.

13. For discussions of Wolfe's lost film, see David E. James, *The Most Typical Avant-Garde: History and Geography of Minor Cinemas in Los Angeles* (Berkeley: University of California Press, 2005), 97–104; Steven J. Ross, *Working-Class Hollywood: Silent Film and the Shaping of Class in America* (Princeton, N.J.: Princeton University Press, 1998), 95–98.

14. Raymond Williams, *Marxism and Literature* (New York: Oxford University Press, 1977), Chapter entitled "Dominant, Residual and Emergent."

15. The concept has been discussed in several texts, for example "The Cinema of Attraction: Early Film, its Spectator and the Avant-Garde," *Wide Angle*, Vol. 8, No. 3/4 (1986): 63–67. For a recent reassessment from multiple perspectives, see Wanda Strauven, ed., *The Cinema of Attractions Reloaded* (Amsterdam: Amsterdam University Press, 2006).

16. Tom Gunning, *D.W. Griffith and the Origins of American Narrative film: The Early Years at Biograph* (Urbana/Chicago: University of Illinois Press, 1991).

17. Ben Singer, *Melodrama and Modernity: Early Sensational Cinema and Its Contexts* (New York: Columbia University Press, 2001), Chapter 4.

18. Kristin Thompson, "The Concept of Cinematic Excess," in Philip Rosen, ed., *Narrative, Apparatus, Ideology* (New York: Columbia University Press, 1986), 130–142. Thompson's later use of "expressivity" is closely linked to her previous discussion of excess; see her essay "The International Exploration of Cinematic Expressivity," in Karel Dibbets and Bert Hogenkamp, eds., *Film and the First World War* (Amsterdam: Amsterdam University Press, 1995), 65–85.

19. Charles Musser, *The Emergence of Cinema: The American Screen to 1907* (New York: Scribner, 1990).

20. Eileen Bowser, *The Transformation of Cinema, 1907-1915* (New York: Scribner, 1990).

21. Richard Koszarski, *An Evening's Entertainment: The Age of the Silent Feature Picture, 1915–1928* (New York: Scribner, 1990).

22. Miriam Hansen, *Babel and Babylon. Spectatorship in American Silent Film* (Cambridge, Mass.: Harvard University Press, 1991).

23. The star phenomenon and film acting during the period have been diligently discussed in a series of studies, for example, Richard DeCordova, *Picture Personalities: The Emergence of the Star System in America* (Urbana: University of Illinois Press, 1990); Roberta E. Pearson, *Eloquent Gestures: The Transformation of Performance Style in the Griffith Biograph Films* (Berkeley: University of California Press, 1992); Ben Brewster and Lea Jacobs, *Theatre to Cinema: Stage Pictorialism and the Early Feature Film* (Oxford and New York: Oxford University Press, 1997); Richard Abel, *Americanizing the Movies and 'Movie-Mad' Audiences, 1910–1914* (Berkeley: University of California Press, 2006).

24. An "ultimatum" was delivered by Universal to Los Angeles along with a sixty-day deadline for meeting a series of demands, otherwise the studio would move to Albuquerque; *Los Angeles Express*, 7 February 1914, 1. The *Los Angeles Examiner*, 17 February 1914, 7, included a Universal ad seeking an alternative location for the studio. The purchase of its new tract across the Cahuenga Pass was announced in the *Examiner*, 15 March 1914, I:4. See also *Los Angeles Times*, 11 February 1915, II:1.

25. The still unrivaled discussion of these processes can be found in Gunning (1991).

26. The most recent debate on film exhibition in New York City was published in *Cinema Journal* in several installments, but harked back to a previous round of discussion. The first debate was inaugurated by Robert C. Allen, "Motion Picture Exhibition in Manhattan, 1906–1912: Beyond the Nickelodeon," *Cinema Journal*, Vol. 18, No. 2 (Spring 1979): 2–15; for a response, see Robert Sklar, "*Oh! Althusser!:* Historiography and the Rise of Cinema Studies," in Robert Sklar and Charles Musser, eds., *Resisting Images: Essays on Cinema and History* (Philadelphia: Temple University Press, 1990), 12–35. Later, Ben Singer addressed Allen's piece in "Manhattan Nickelodeons: New Data on Audiences and Exhibitors," *Cinema Journal*, Vol. 34, No. 4 (Spring 1995): 5–35; a riposte from Allen appeared as "Manhattan Myopia; or, Oh! Iowa!", *Cinema Journal*, Vol. 35, No. 3 (Spring 1996): 73–103; and was commented on by Singer in "New York, Just Like I Pictured It," *Cinema Journal*, Vol. 35, No. 5 (Spring 1996): 104–128. William Uricchio and Roberta E. Pearson coauthored an essay, "Manhattan's Nickelodeons: New York? New York!", which appeared in *Cinema Journal*, Vol. 36, No. 4 (Summer 1997): 98–102; along with further contributions in the same issue by Judith Thissen, "Oy, Myopia!", 102–107; and Ben Singer, "Manhattan Melodrama," 107–112.

27. David Bordwell, *On the History of Film Style* (Cambridge, Mass.: Harvard Uni-

versity Press, 1997), 139–149; Charlie Keil, " 'To Here from Modernity': Style, Historiography, and Transitional Cinema," in Charlie Keil and Shelley Stamp, eds., *American Cinema's Transitional Era: Audiences, Institutions, Practices*, (Berkeley: University of California Press, 2004), 51–65.

28. Richard Abel, *The Ciné Goes to Town: French Cinema, 1896–1914* (Berkeley: University of California Press, 1994).

29. Tom Gunning, "Modernity and Cinema: A Culture of Shocks and Flow," in Murray Pomerance, ed., *Cinema and Modernity* (New Brunswick, N.J.: Rutgers University Press, 2006), 297–315.

30. The term "erudite histories" comes from Francesco Casetti's research, particularly his *The Theories of Cinema 1945–1995* (Austin: University of Texas Press, 1999), 309.

31. Richard Abel, ed., *Encyclopedia of Early Cinema* (London and New York: Routledge, 2005).

32. David Bordwell, Kristin Thompson and Janet Staiger, *The Classical Hollywood Cinema: Film Style & Mode of Production to 1960* (New York: Columbia University Press, 1985).

33. Charlie Keil, *Early American Cinema in Transition: Story, Style, and Filmmaking, 1907–1913* (Madison, Wis.: University of Wisconsin Press, 2001); Keil and Stamp (2004).

34. Jane Gaines, *Fire and Desire: Mixed-Race Movies in the Silent Era* (Chicago: University of Chicago Press, 2001); Stewart (2005). See also Thomas Cripps, *Slow Fade to Black: The Negro in American Film, 1900–1942* (Oxford and New York: Oxford University Press, 1977), especially Chapters 1 and 2; Daniel J. Leab, *From Sambo to Superspade: The Black Experience in Motion Pictures* (Boston: Houghton Mifflin, 1975).

35. William Uricchio and Roberta E. Pearson, *Reframing Culture: The Case of the Vitagraph Quality Film* (Princeton, N.J.: Princeton University Press, 1993).

36. Shelley Stamp, *Movie-Struck Girls: Women and Motion Picture Culture after the Nickelodeon*, (Princeton, N.J.: Princeton University Press, 2000); Rabinovitz (1998).

37. Gregory Waller, *Main Street Amusements. Movies and Commercial Entertainment in a Southern City, 1896-1930* (Washington, D.C.: Smithsonian Institution Press, 1995); Kathryn H. Fuller, *At the Picture Show. Small-Town Audiences and the Creation of Movie Fan Culture* (Washington, D.C.: Smithsonian Institution Press, 1996).

38. Robert C. Allen, "Relocating American Film History: The 'Problem' of the Empirical," *Cultural Studies*, Vol. 20, No. 1 (January 2006): 48–88.

39. Richard Abel, *The Red Rooster Scare: Making Cinema American, 1900–1910* (Berkeley: University of California Press, 1999); Abel (2006).

40. Grieveson (2004).

41. Stamp (2000).

42. Singer (2001); Linda Williams, *Playing the Race Card: Melodramas of Black and White from Uncle Tom to O.J. Simpson* (Princeton, N.J.: Princeton University Press, 2001); Gaines (2001).

43. *Los Angeles Times*, 17 January 1911, II:4.

44. Among a host of such pieces, many of them penned in the wake of the opening of Universal City and Selig's Zoo, include "Film-making Means Millions to Los Angeles," *Los Angeles Times*, 1 January 1916, III:66; "Los Angeles the Film Capital of the World," ibid., III:70.

45. The department was awarded formal status in 1915.

46. *Los Angeles Examiner*, 12 December 1911, 8. The students' maps have not resurfaced in spite of searches at various USC depositories. Walter E. Lagerquist, Professor of Economics at Cornell University, had already undertaken a similar attempt at mapping, but more limited in scope. Lagerquist focused on New York City's Lower East Side, still the prime research scene for scholars mapping popular amusements in the early 20th century; his map was published in the *New York Times*, 3 April 1910, Magazine Section, 1–2. Lagerquist's map marks saloons, cafes, billiards, five-cent vaudevilles, theaters, clubs, Protestant churches, charity institutions, synagogues, settlement houses (the name for community centers at the time), public schools, kindergartens, hospitals and dispensaries, cheap and institutional lodging houses, public baths, Catholic churches, missions, and YMCAs and YWCAs. For comments, see *Moving Picture World*, Vol. 6, No. 15 (16 April 1910): 591.

47. Among a dearth of in-depth studies of social life in American cities around 1910, the six volumes comprising the *Pittsburgh Survey* represent the most thoroughgoing and grandiose effort. Scholarly wherewithal aside, minimal attention was paid to Pittsburgh amusements in the survey in spite of the fact that the city was one of the pioneering places for nickel houses. Several minor studies, however, among them a 1913 recreation survey devoted to Pittsburgh, specifically analyzed the local amusement scene and its film culture. *The Pittsburgh Survey*, vols. 1–6 (New York: Russell Sage Foundation, 1909-1914); *Report and Recommendations of the Morals Efficiency Commission* (Pittsburgh: The Morals Efficiency Commission, 1913). Other cities examined in such surveys were for example Chicago (1909 and 1911), Boston (1910), New York City (1911), Cleveland (1913), Milwaukee (1911 and 1914), Indianapolis (1914), Portland (1914), Madison (1915), and the famed amusement city of Peoria in 1916: Louise de Koven Bowen, *Five and Ten Cent Theaters. Two Investigations* (Chicago: Juvenile Protective Association of Chicago, 1909 and 1911); *The Amusement Situation in Boston* (Boston: The Drama Committee of the Twentieth Century Club, 1910); Michael M. Davis, Jr., *The Exploitation of Pleasure* (New York City: Russell Sage Foundation, 1911); Robt. O. Bartholomew, *Report of*

Censorship of Motion Pictures and of Investigation of Motion Picture Theaters of Cleveland (Cleveland: Council of City of Cleveland, 1913); "Recreation Survey. Milwaukee," *Playground*, May 1912, Vol. 6 No. 2; *Amusements and Recreation in Milwaukee: A Bulletin of the City Club, 1914* (Milwaukee, Wis.: The Club, 1914); *Indianapolis Recreation Survey* (Indianapolis: General Civic Improvements Committee of the Indianapolis Chamber of Commerce, 1914); William Trufant Foster, *Vaudeville and Motion Picture Shows: A Study of Theaters in Portland, Oregon* (Reed College: Social Services Series 2, 1914); *Madison, "the Four Lake City," Recreational Survey Prepared by a Special Committee of the Madison Board of Commerce* (Madison, Wis.: Tracy & Kilgore, printers, 1915); *Report of the Recreation Conditions and Problems of Peoria, with Recommendations and Suggested System* (Peoria: Peoria Association of Commerce, 1916). Rowland Haynes conducted many of these surveys; he shared his expertise in "Making a Recreation Survey," *Playground*, Vol. 7, No. 1 (April 1913): 19–25.

48. Richard Henry Edwards, *Popular Amusements* (New York and London: Association Press, 1915).

49. For example in Singer (2001); and Constance Balides, "Cinema under the Sign of Money: Commercialized Leisure, Economies of Abundance, and Pecuniary Madness, 1905–1915," Keil and Stamp (2004), 285–314.

50. For speculation regarding women's role in the election's outcome see Peter Clark MacFarlane, "What is the Matter with Los Angeles?", *Collier's*, Vol. 48, No. 11 (2 December 1911): 28, 30. It was widely agreed that the recently adopted suffrage laws made women the decisive force. In the days leading up to the voting the local newspapers rallied around their opposition to Job Harriman, the socialist candidate, which helped secure progressive Mayor George Alexander's reelection.

51. *Views and Film Index*, Vol. 2, No. 9 (2 March 1907): 6.

52. Daniel Carson Goodman, *Hagar Revelly* (New York: M. Kennerley, 1913), 262.

53. *Los Angeles Herald*, 8 January 1915, 14.

54. Mary Heaton Vorse, "Some Picture Show Audiences," *The Outlook*, Vol. 98, No. 8 (June 24, 1911): 441–447; reprinted in Gregory A. Waller, ed., *Moviegoing in America* (Malden, Mass.: Blackwell Publishers Inc., 2002), 50–53, and most recently in Antonia Lant, ed., *Red Velvet Seat: Women's Writing of the First Fifty Years of Cinema* (London and New York: Verso, 2006), 68–75. The most detailed discussion of Vorse's essay comprises part of Chapter 3 in Hansen (1991).

55. Janet Staiger, "The Future of the Past," *Cinema Journal*, Vol. 44, No. 1 (Fall 2004): 126–129. Her discussion is part of a dossier comprised of several interventions edited by Sumiko Higashi under the rubric "In Focus: Film History, or a Baedeker Guide to the Historical Turn." For an excellent analysis of the African-American experience at the movies see Stewart (2005).

56. For monographs built around lost films see Jan Olsson, *Sensationer från en bakgård: Frans Lundberg som biografägare och filmproducent i Malmö och Köpenhamn* ["Sensations from a Backyard: Frans Lundberg as Exhibitor and Film Producer in Malmö and Copenhagen"] (Stockholm and Lund: Symposion, 1989); Giuliana Bruno, *Streetwalking on a Ruined Map: Cultural Theory and the City Films of Elvira Notari* (Princeton, N.J.: Princeton University Press, 1993).

57. "Moving Pictures: Their Function and Proper Regulation," *Playground*, Vol. 4, No. 7 (October 1910): 232-240; quotations from p. 235.

Chapter 1

1. *Los Angeles Herald*, 18 October 1911, 4.

2. A detailed the description of magician The Great Herrmann's routine was ventured by the *New York Times*, 10 May 1893, 11. "Escape from Sing Sing" was performed at the Los Angeles Theater in September 1901; *Los Angeles Times*, 22 September 1901, III:2. Hermann died in 1896, but family members carried on the act under his name.

3. *Moving Picture World*, Vol. 18, No. 9 (29 November 1913): 1004-05.

4. An eventful shooting of a fire-rescue film was published in a magazine late in 1903, "How a Unique Moving-Picture Was Made," *World's Works*, Vol. 7, No. 1 (November 1903): 4153; and in 1904 a production account of one of the train-robbery films was ventured, "Train Robberies Now Made to Order," *Philadelphia Inquirer*, 26 June 1904, Comic Section:3.

5. Michael Paul Rogin, *"Ronald Reagan," the Movie: and Other Episodes in Political Demonology* (Berkeley: University of California Press, 1987), 191.

6. For analyses of feature distribution prior to when the trust was dissolved in 1915 see Janet Staiger, "Combination and Litigation: Structures of U.S. Film Distribution, 1896–1917," *Cinema Journal*, Vol. 23, No. 2 (Winter 1984): 41-72; Michael Quinn, "Distribution, the Transient Audience, and the Transition to the Feature Film," ibid., Vol. 40, No. 2 (Winter 2001): 35-56; as well as Abel (2006), Chapter 1.

7. Waters worked for several of the major dailies in New York City as well as magazines and wrote primarily on technological developments. Scores of his featured articles were syndicated and can be found for example in the *Los Angeles Times*. Among the topics covered were X-rays, skyscrapers, pneumatic postal systems, air conditioning, railway systems, electricity, tropical medicine, and ice plants. He was also part of the muck-racking movement and, for example, exposed "the beggar syndicate in *Everybody's Magazine* in 1905."

8. The pinnacle piece in this tradition is the account of another Vitagraph film,

The Smoke Fairy of 1909, appropriately published in *Scientific American* and widely reprinted; L. Gardette, "Some Tricks of the Moving Picture Maker," Vol. 100, No. 26 (26 June 1909): 476–477, 487; reprinted in *Nickelodeon*, Vol. 2, No. 2 (August 1909): 53–57. See also Frederic Colburn Clarke, "Moving Picture Tricks," *Vanity Fair*, Vol. 3, No. 1 (September 1914): 63.

9. Interestingly, his piece was re-published in a Swedish newspaper with an introduction and epilog that shifted focus by sounding a warning concerning the effects of the representations of and lively cultural scene for moving images in Stockholm. *Cosmopolitan*, Vol. 40, No. 3 (January 1906): 251–259; reprinted in *Film History*, Vol. 15, No. 4 (2003): 396–402. The Swedish translation was published in *Vårt Land*, 20 January 1906, B:1. For appreciative comments on the film, see also an article on film production from the *Kansas City Star*, reprinted in the *Washington Post*, 9 January 1907, 6.

10. *New York World*, 27 April 1906, 1.

11. Simon N. Patten, *The New Basis of Civilization* (New York: The Macmillan Company, 1907).

12. For a fuller discussion of the struggle for leisure time see Roy Rosenzweig, *Eight Hours for What We Will: Workers and Leisure in an Industrial City, 1870–1920* (Cambridge and New York: Cambridge University Press, 1983).

13. Simon N. Patten, *Product and Climax* (New York: B. W. Huebsch, 1909), 15.

14. Patten's debate with Mary Richmond, a leading spokesperson for the charity approach, is analyzed in Daniel M. Fox, *The Discovery of Abundance: Simon N. Patten and the Transformation of Social Theory* (Ithaca: Cornell University Press, 1967), Chapter 6. See also William Leach, *Land of Desire. Merchants, Power, and the Rise of New American Culture* (New York: Pantheon Books, 1993), 231-244. For a discussion of the concept of progressivism see Daniel T. Rodgers, "In Search of Progressivism," *Reviews in American History*, Vol. 10, No. 4 (December 1982): 113–132.

15. Simon N. Patten, "The Making of Economic Literature: Annual Address of the President," *American Economic Association. Publications (1886–1911)*, Vol. 10, No. 1 (April 1909): 1–14; passim.

16. "The World in Motion," *Survey*, Vol. 22, No. 10 (5 June 1909): 355–365; quotation from p. 365.

17. Sherman C. Kingsley, "The Penny Arcade and the Cheap Theatre," *Charities and the Common*, Vol. 18, No. 10 (8 June 1907): 295–297; quotation from p. 297.

18. For a fuller analysis of the context for Griffith's films, see my essay "Trading Places: Griffith, Patten and Agricultural Modernity," *Film History*, Vol. 17, No. 1 (2005): 39–65.

19. Luigi Pirandello, *Shoot! (Si gira) the Notebooks of Serafino Gubbio, Cinematograph Operator*, authorized translation from the Italian by C.K. Scott Moncrieff, (New York: E. P. Dutton & Company, 1926 [1914]).

20. *New York Evening Post*, 14 June 1909, 6.
21. *Chicago Tribune*, 18 December 1910, E:3.
22. *Moving Picture World*, Vol. 13, No. 6 (10 August 1912): 542.

Chapter 2

1. P.T. Barnum, *The Life of Barnum, the World-Renowned Showman* (Buffalo, N.Y.: Callahan & Connealy, 1899 [1855]): 506.
2. For perspectives on advertising's role relating to the burgeoning consumerism see for example Stuart Ewen, *Captains of Consciousness: Advertising and the Roots of the Consumer Culture* (New York: McGraw-Hill, 1976); and Stephen Fox, *The Mirror Makers: A History of American Advertising and Its Creators* (New York: William Morrow and Company, Inc., 1984).
3. *Los Angeles Times*, 24 September 1909, II:4.
4. "Newspapers as Historical Sources," *Atlantic Monthly*, Vol. 103, No. 5 (May 1909): 650–657. Rhodes' discussion stems from his own work on American history in the decade leading up to the Civil War. For comments see for instance *The Sun*, 5 May 1909, 8.
5. *Moving Picture World*, Vol. 6, No. 14 (9 April 1910): 552.
6. *Motography*, Vol. 6, No. 1 (July 1911): 20.
7. The widely syndicated article, "Edison's Latest Marvel," was published for instance in *Los Angeles Times*, 14 April 1895, 17.
8. Ibid., 16 June 1896, 22. His speculation was probably triggered by the publication of Octave Uzanne's short story "The End of Books," lavishly illustrated by Albert Robida. *Scribner's Magazine*, Vol. 16, No. 2 (August 1894): 221–232.
9. *New American Standard Bible* (1995).
10. Paul S. Moore, "Everybody's Going: City Newspapers and the Early Mass Market for Movies," *City & Community*, Vol. 4, No. 4 (December 2005): 339–357; quotation from p. 343. See also Gunther Barth, *City People: The Rise of Modern City Culture in Nineteenth-Century America* (Oxford and New York: Oxford University Press, 1982 [1980]): especially Chapter 3.
11. *Chicago Herald*, 5 July 1914, V:1.
12. *Motion Picture Magazine*, Vol. 7, No. 6 (July 1914): 36.
13. For general perspectives on the press scene around 1900, see George Juergens, *Joseph Pulitzer and the New York World* (Princeton, N.J.: Princeton University Press, 1966); Nasaw (2000); Gottlieb and Wolt, (1977); Baldatsy (1999); Don C. Seitz, *The James Gordon Bennetts, Father and Son: Proprietors of the New York Herald* (Indianapolis: Bobbs-Merrill, 1928); Richard O'Connor, *The Scandalous Mr. Bennett* (Garden City, N.Y.: Doubleday & Company, Inc., 1962); Charles Rosebault, *When Dana Was The Sun* (New York: Robert M. McBride & Co.,

1931); John L. Heaton, *The Story of a Page: Thirty Years of Public Service and Public Discussion in the Editorial Columns of the New York World* (New York: Harper & Brothers, 1913); Frank M. O'Brien, *The Story of The Sun: New York 1833–1928* (New York: Greenwood Press, 1968 [1928]); Harry W. Baehr, Jr., *The New York Tribune Since the Civil War* (New York: Dodd, Mead & Co., 1936); Willard Grosvenor Bleyer, *Main Currents in the History of American Journalism* (Boston: Houghton Mifflin Co., 1927); and Helen MacGill Hughes, *News and the Human Interest Story* (Chicago: The University of Chicago Press, 1940).

14. For an analysis, see Gerald J. Baldasty, *The Commercialization of News in the Nineteenth Century* (Madison, Wis.: University of Wisconsin Press, 1992).

15. Will Irwin, "The American Newspaper, Part II: The Dim Beginnings", *Collier's Magazine*, Vol. 46, No. 19 (28 January 1911): 17.

16. Daniel F. Kellogg, "The Changed American," *North American Review*, Vol. 200, No. 704 (July 1914): 59–70; quotation from p. 63.

17. Irwin (1911): "Part X: The Unhealthy Alliance," *Collier's* Vol. 45, No. 10 (10 June 1911): 17–19, 28–29, 31–32.

18. Ibid., "Part VI: The Editor and the News," (1 April 1911).

19. Crane however came up with a film simile in "The Blue Hotel" (1898) comparing the mind to a film, which records "lasting impressions." Thomas A. Gullason, ed., *The Complete Short Stories and Sketches of Stephen Crane* (Garden City, N.Y.: Doubleday & Company, Inc., 1963): 498.

20. The term was introduced by Lennard Davis in his *Factual Fictions: The Origins of the English Novel* (New York: Columbia University Press, 1983) and later adopted in relation to Crane by Michael Robertson in *Stephen Crane, Journalism and the Making of Modern American Literature* (New York: Columbia University Press, 1983). For a selection of Cahan's early journalism, see Moses Rischin, ed., *Grandma Never Lived in America: The New Journalism of Abraham Cahan* (Bloomington: Indiana University Press, 1985).

21. Lincoln Steffens, *The Autobiography of Lincoln Steffens* (New York: Literary Guild, 1931), 312. Concerning his experience at the *Post* and its gospel riveted to facts, Steffens writes: "Reporters were to report the news as it happened, like machines, without prejudice, color, and without style; all alike. Humor or any sign of personality in our reporters was caught, rebuked, and, in time, suppressed," 179.

22. Michael Scudson, *Discovering the News: A Social History of American Newspapers* (New York: Basic Books, Inc. 1978), 105.

23. *Los Angeles Times*, 23 January 1887, 4.

24. Gottlieb and Wolt (1977), 25. When Eliza A. Otis died late in 1904, her husband edited and published a representative selection of her writings; Harrison Gray Otis, ed., *California "Where Sets the Sun": The Writings of Eliza A. Otis in Poetry and Prose* (Los Angeles: Times-Mirror Co., 1905).

25. *Los Angeles Times*, 22 July 1894, 15.

26. Ibid., 29 March 1885, 2.

27. Ibid., 20 June 1897, 21.

28. Ibid., 24 January 1892, 10.

29. Ibid., 19 September 1897, 18.

30. Ibid., June 20 1897, 21.

31. Ibid., February 2 1896, 15.

32. Terry Ramsaye, *A Million and One Nights: A History of the Motion Picture* (New York: Simon & Schuster, Inc., 1926), especially Chapter 10.

33. For a general discussion of the Vitascope, see Charles Musser's well-researched Chapter 4 in Musser (1990). For a later overview, see Charles Musser, "Introducing Cinema to the American Public: The Vitascope in the United States, 1896–7," in Waller (2002), 13-26.

34. An account of screenings at Tally's can be found in Ramsaye (1926), 277–78. See Musser (1990), 506, note 11, for additional information on Tally's attempt at acquiring a Vitascope projector from Raff & Gammon early in April 1896.

35. *Los Angeles Times*, 5 July 1896, 8. The *Times'* readers were however already partially up to speed concerning the Vitascope. Immediately after the first press showing in West Orange, when Edison himself, in company with a select group of newspapermen, was treated to a screening, the *Times*, the same day and in a slightly edited format, dispatched the report from the *New York Herald*, 4 April 1896, 2.

36. The most thorough study of the travel genre and its metapsychology can be found in Jennifer Peterson, *World Pictures: Travelogue Films and the Lure of the Exotic, 1890–1920* (Ph.D. diss., University of Chicago, 1999).

37. *Los Angeles Herald*, 5 July 1896, 14.

38. *New York Times*, 26 April 1896, 10.

39. *Los Angeles Times*, 6 July 1896, 6.

40. *Los Angeles Herald*, 7 July 1896, 4.

41. *Los Angeles Express*, 7 July 1896, 4.

42. *Los Angeles Herald*, 12 July 1896, 14.

43. *Los Angeles Times*, 5 February 1911, III:1.

44. "The Vaudeville Theater," *Scribner's Magazine*. Vol. 26, No. 4 (October 1899): 485–495; quotation from p. 495. Alan Dale took up the lunch-counter metaphor when trying to understand vaudeville's popularity with those that "clamor for quick results." Furthermore, he writes, "[t]hese people are, of course, imbued with the fever of the city life. They are, moreover, the people who make the 'quick lunches' popular." And, "[i]t is these people with the tabloid mind and the condensed appreciation, who patronize that form of entertainment which has assumed such gigantic proportions today." *Los Angeles Examiner*, 12 February 1911, IX:7.

45. *Variety*, Vol. 1, No. 1 (16 December 1905): 2.

46. William Dean Howells, "Editor's Easy Chair," *Harper's Monthly Magazine*, Vol. 106, No. 5 (April 1903): 811–815; quotation from p. 815.

47. Hutchins Hapgood, *Types from City Streets* (New York: Funk & Wagnalls, 1910), 86.

48. Some of the early comments seemingly underpinning the so-called chaser theory were however quite lenient: "Whatever shortcomings there may be in the early part of the programme is fully made up before the biograph brings the evenings entertainment to a close with a series of moving pictures which are growing just a trifle stale." *Los Angeles Times*, 21 May 1901, 8. Years later, in 1907, the *Times* stage reporter noted little if any enthusiasm for the moving fare, at this time more or less exclusively produced by Pathé: "The Orpheum circuit has advanced a standard of high art in motion pictures. As is evidenced by the total lack of applause, and even of attention on the part of the audience, the pictures are seldom appreciated. They are regarded possibly as a small piece of amusement goods 'thrown in for the money'. Most of the pictures that the Orpheum has used lately seem to be of European make." *Los Angeles Times*, 9 October 1907, II:5. In Chicot's (Epes Winthrop Sargent) review of the program at the Fifty-Eight Street Theater, the pictures are positioned outside the program, which indeed conveys a chaser perception: "... the Florenz troupe closed the show with a whoop and there were pictures *afterward*" [italics added]. *Variety*, Vol. 1, No. 12 (3 March 1906): 9. For the polemics directed at the chaser theory, see Robert C. Allen, "Contra the Chaser Theory," *Wide Angle*, Vol. 3, No. 1 (1979): 4–11; Charles Musser, "Another Look at the 'Chaser Theory,'" *Studies in Visual Communication*, Vol. 10, No. 4 (1984): 24–44, 51; Robert C. Allen, "Looking at 'Another Look at the Chaser Theory,'" *Studies in Visual Communication*, Vol. 10, No. 4 (1984): 45–50.

49. For a discussion of the vaudeville context, see Robert C. Allen, *Vaudeville and Film, 1895–1915: A Study in Media Interaction* (New York: Arno Press, 1980 [1977]).

50. *New York Tribune*, 10 May 1896, 6. "It consists of a series of views, of exquisite design and execution, in which the objects that naturally afford the materials for making up a picture are rendered animate thus, the sun rises and sets; the moon silvers the landscape, and retiring, leaves darkness as her successor; the waters ebb and flow, and the various actors in the scene meet and join in mutual greeting."

51. Ibid., 26 April 1896, 32.

52. *Chicago Tribune*, 4 November 1896, 10, 11.

53. *Harper's Weekly*, Vol. 40, No. 2082 (14 November 1896): 1122.

54. *New York Herald*, 4 November 1896, 8. According to Dan Streible, Hearst's

New York Evening Journal also offered some form of moving images in between projecting slides on its walls, Dan Streible, "Children at the Mutoscope," *CINéMAS*, Vol. 14, No. 1 (2003): 91-116. See also Streible's, *Fight Pictures: A History of Boxing and Early Cinema*. Berkeley: University of California Press, 2008.

55. *New York World*, 5 April 1896, Colored Supplement. The microfilm edition of the paper is however in black and white.

56. *The Chap-Book*, Vol. 5, No. 6 (15 July 1896): 239–240. Previously quoted by Ramsaye (1926) and Gunning in Keil and Stamp (2004).

57. Hjalmar Söderberg, "En barnföreställning" ["A Matinee for Children"], *Svenska Dagbladet*, 27 April 1904, 8. For a discussion of Söderberg's text, see my "Pressing Inroads: Metaspectators and the Nickelodeon Culture," in John Fullerton, ed., *Screen Culture: History and Textuality* (Eastleigh: John Libbey Publishing, 2004): 113–135.

58. *New York Evening World*, 26 September 1910, 5.

59. *New York World*, 12 April 1906, 20.

60. Petition 505, 1907. *The City Council of the City of Los Angeles*, Vol. 74 (20 May 1907–27 November 1907), Records Management Division.

61. From New York's *The Sun*, December 1909; reprinted in *Film Index*, Vol. 4, No. 2 (25 December 1909): 3.

62. For a detailed account of the expedition films, see Alison Griffiths, *Wondrous Difference: Cinema, Anthropology, and Turn-of-the-Century Visual Culture* (New York: Columbia University Press, 2002), especially Chapter 7.

63. *Editor and Publisher and Journalist*, Vol. 13, No. 29 (4 January 1914): 560. The film page was launched in November 1912. For an appreciation of the daily newspapers' attitude vis-à-vis film culture in early 1913, see W. Stephen Bush's address before the Woman's Press Club of New York, *Moving Picture World*, Vol. 15, No. 10 (8 March 1913): 975.

64. See Richard Abel, "The Passing (Picture) Show in the Industrial Heartland: The Early 1910s," in John Fullerton and Jan Olsson, eds., *Allegories of Communication. Intermedial Concerns from Cinema to the Digital*, (Rome: John Libbey, 2004), 321–332.

65. *U. S. Supreme Court Mutual Film Corporation v. Industrial Commission of Ohio*, 236 *U.S. 230 (1915)*, 244. See Grieveson (2004) for an in-depth discussion of the policing of cinema.

66. *Woman's Home Companion*, Vol. 42, No. 4 (April 1915): 16.

67. *Independent*, Vol. 78, No. 3409 (6 April 1914): 8.

68. For instance ads in the *Atlanta Constitution* in 1906 and 1907.

69. The material in the *Los Angeles Examiner* provides the following pattern of program changes in late 1908: American Theater (452 South Broadway): new program every Thursday; Globe Theater (202 East Fifth): new program every

Monday and Friday; Odeon Theater (527 South Spring Street): new program every other day; Union Theater (255 South Main Street): new program every Monday; Regal Theater (323 South Main Street): new program every Monday and Thursday; Picture Theater (545 South Main Street): unclear how often, but programs last at least two days; Hermann Theater (456 South Spring Street): new program every other day; La Petite (508 South Broadway): new program every Monday, Thursday, and Saturday; Lyric Theater (262 South Main Street): weekly program changes; Crystal Theater (211 South Main Street): new program every Tuesday, Friday, and Sunday; Edison Theater (436 South Spring Street): new program every Monday, Wednesday, and Saturday; Arcade Theater (125 South Main Street): new program every Monday and Thursday; Duchess Theater (408 W. Seventh Street): new program every Sunday and Thursday; Optic Theater (446 South Broadway): new program every Monday and Friday. On July 9, 1910, the *Los Angeles Record* opened an advertisement section called "Moving Picture Theaters", featuring a small group of the minor houses. The section did not survive long, but some patterns of program changes can be teased out: Bijou Theater (553 South Main Street): program changes three times per week; Horne's Big Show (423 South Spring Street): program changes twice per week; California Theater (238 South Spring Street): program changes three times per week; Union Theater (255 South Main Street): program changes three times per week; Picture Theater (545 South Main Street): program changes three times per week.

70. *New York Clipper*, Vol. 59, No. 37 (28 October 1911): 9.

71. *Film Index*, Vol. 4, No. 27 (3 July 1909): 3.

72. Ibid., Vol. 5, No. 2 (8 January 1910): 2.

73. For example, ibid., Vol. 5, No. 3 (15 January 1910): 19, on *St. Louis Times*; *Moving Picture World*, Vol. 7, No. 7 (26 February 1910): 295, on *St. Louis Republic*.

74. *Moving Picture World*, Vol. 14, No. 11 (14 December 1912): 1056.

75. *Billboard*, Vol. 23, No. 46 (18 November 1911): 15; the film was released the same day.

76. The editorial entitled "Film Criticism in the Lay Press," *Moving Picture World*, offered general reflections on the topic, Vol. 8. No. 20 (20 May 1911): 1114.

77. See Anna Brady et al., *Union List of Film Periodicals: Holdings of Selected American Collections* (Westport, Connecticut and London: Greenwood Press, 1984).

78. *New York Dramatic Mirror*, Vol. 59, No. 1537 (6 June 1908): 6.

79. Ibid., Vol. 59, No. 1538 (13 June 1908): 10.

80. *Film Index*, Vol. 4, No. 34 (21 August 1907): 2.

81. *New York Dramatic Mirror*, Vol. 62, No. 1601 (28 August 1909): 15.

82. *Moving Picture World*, Vol. 3, No. 15 (10 October 1908): 279.

83. *Moving Picture News*, Vol. 2, No. 46 (13 November 1909): 3.

84. Ibid., Vol. 2, No. 51 (18 December 1909): 9.

85. *New York Dramatic Mirror*, Vol. 69, No. 1778 (15 January 1913): 45.

Chapter 3

1. John Ferguson in Alfred Hitchcock's *Vertigo* (Paramount Pictures, 1958).

2. Robert Grau, *The Business Man in the Amusement World: A Volume of Progress in the Field of the Theater* (New York: Broadway Publishing Co., 1910), 213–14.

3. *Los Angeles Times*, 18 March 1883, 2.

4. Robert M. Fogelson, *The Fragmented City: Los Angeles, 1850-1930*, (Berkeley: University of California Press, 1993 [1967]).

5. In *Forty Years Observation of the Music and the Drama* (New York and Baltimore: The Broadway Publishing Company, 1909). Robert Grau here offers a glowing outline of Behymer's career as impresario and manager.

6. An interview with proprietor Jew Ah Mow has been preserved as congressional testimony in conjunction with an investigation of Chinese immigration to the U.S.; see "The Chinese Theater, Law and Order in Los Angeles; Jew Ah Mow and His Congressional Testimony," *Chinese Historical Society of Southern California*, Vol. 7, No. 2 (December 1984): 1–4.

7. *Los Angeles Times*, 28 August 1910, III:1.

8. Ibid., 30 December 1909, III:4. See also *Los Angeles Herald*, 27 August 1910, 5.

9. *Los Angeles Times*, 23 September 1894, 17.

10. Ibid., 19 April 1936, H:8.

11. The German-born Waldeck's sad fate was commented on in the *Los Angeles Times*, 7 May 1904, 6.

12. *Los Angeles Daily Journal*, 24 July 1896, 1.

13. For a chronicle of Morosco's career, see Oliver Morosco, *Life of Oliver Morosco: The Oracle of Broadway Written from His Own Notes and Comments by Helen M. Morosco and Leonard Paul Dugger* (Caldwell, Id.: Caxton Printers, 1944).

14. For a concise history of the Orpheum up until it was closed in December 1929, see Stan Singer, "The Orpheum Theater of Los Angeles: A Chronology," *Southern California Quarterly*, Vol. 72, No. 4 (Winter 1990): 339–372.

15. "The greatest departure in motion-pictures since the Orpheum inaugurated its daylight showing of them, will be put into operation at that theater this afternoon, when it will begin a weekly interchange series of 'motion views of the world's news.' In other words, it will show a lengthy set of reels portraying actual happenings of world-importance. The Pathe Freres have operators who cover these events now just as do newspaper correspondents and the resulting films are sent by fast express to the Orpheum, there to be shown on the screen." *Los Angeles Times*, 14 August 1911, I:7.

16. *Evening News*, 24 October 1906. Special section called "Made-in-Los-Angeles," II.

17. *Los Angeles Times*, 16 March 1902, III:2.

18. *Film Index*, Vol. 7, No. 9 (4 March 1911): 10.

19. *Los Angeles Times*, 31 August 1902, III:2.

20. *Evening News*, 19 February 1906, 7.

21. *Los Angeles Times*, 3 May 1895, 8.

22. *Los Angeles Express*, 25 July 1903, 6.

23. Bertha H. Smith, "The Making of Los Angeles," *Sunset Magazine*, Vol. 19, No. 3 (July 1907): 237–254; quotation from p. 253. For a general perspective of the development, see "Is Los Angeles the New York of the Pacific Coast?" *Leslie's Weekly*, Vol. 102, No. 2637 (22 March 1906): 282–283.

24. *Los Angeles Times*, 13 March 1910, VI:1, 6.

25. Ibid., 17 July 1910, VI:18.

26. Ibid., 7 June 1899, 1.

27. Ibid., 19 November 1899, II:6.

28. Ibid., 6 March 1900, I:7.

29. Accounts again flourished in the wake of Frederick A Talbot's book, *Moving Pictures. How They Are Made and Worked* (Philadelphia: J.B. Lippincott Company, 1912), for instance "Drama and Playlet Views Crowd Out the 'Trick' Motion Picture," *Christian Science Monitor*, 25 January 1913, 27. *Washington Post*, 2 August 1914, Evening Supplement:11; comments on the article can be found in July's *Green Book Magazine*, which harks back to Talbot. This ur-scene for explaining animation movies is predictably recounted in the opening chapter of Victor Appleton's first volume of the juvenile series, featuring the Moving Picture Boys. "Why, one man was run over by an auto, and his legs were taken off, and a minute later a doctor stuck them on, and the man got up and danced as well as ever." *The Motion Picture Boys* (New York: Grosset & Dunlap, 1913), 6. An early account of this scene with drawings was published in *Stockholms-Tidningen*, 3 April 1908, B:2, and retold in *Dagens Nyheter*, 19 April 1908, B:2. Rollin Lynde Hartt offered an account plus sketches in his *The People at Play* (Boston and New York: Houghton Mifflin, Co., 1909), 136–138. A shorter account was published in *Literary Digest*, 21 March 1914, 615–616, based on an article in the March issue of *Popular Electricity*. Speculating on the effects of such scenes, the *Rounder* opined: "The curious tricks of the camera, by which legs are removed from the body or heads are taken from the shoulders and similar horrors are mirrored forth cannot fail to produce a deleterious result upon the childish fancy." *Rounder*, Vol. 2, No. 9 (27 February 1909): 1.

30. *Los Angeles Times*, 7 February 1908, II:4.

31. Ibid., 5 March 1905, II:5.

32. *Moving Picture World*, Vol. 8, No. 19 (13 May 1911): 1068.

33. Ibid., Vol. 8, No. 22 (3 June 1911): 1245.

34. *Los Angeles Tribune*, 17 December 1913, 16.

35. *Los Angeles Examiner*, 20 October 1912, 7.

36. Ibid., 2 November 1913, VII:5.

37. *Venice Vanguard*, 22 June 1911, 2.

38. *Moving Picture World*, Vol. 6, No. 15 (16 April 1910): 591.

39. Ibid., Vol. 8, No. 19 (13 May 1911): 1068, commented on the "craze for 'pop' vaudeville in Los Angeles."

40. *Los Angeles Times*, 17 July 1910, II:1

41. *New York Dramatic Mirror*, Vol. 61, No. 1584 (1 May 1909): 40, reported that Los Angeles could boast 26–30 film shows; figures corroborated by the license records as well as by an article in the *Los Angeles Record*, 1 March 1909, 2, mentioning 27 moving-picture theaters.

42. *Los Angeles Tribune*, 30 July 1911, 2. In September 1911 Arthur S. Hyman ventured the figure 85 picture theaters within the city limits when interviewed by the *Times*' Julian Johnson, 15 September 1911, II:5, 10.

43. Ibid., 9 March 1913, II:1, 7.

44. *Los Angeles Examiner*, 5 November 1912, I:1.

45. *Los Angeles Herald*, 13 January 1912, 11.

46. *Los Angeles Record*, 29 January 1913, 4.

47. *California Social-Democrat*, 19 August 1911, 1. Judge Tugwell, the head of the local exhibitors association, complains about too many theaters: 104 paid licenses at this time, *Motion Picture News*, Vol. 9, No. 25 (27 June 1914): 26.

48. *Billboard*, Vol. 25, No. 50 (13 December 1913): 18.

49. *Los Angeles Record*, 26 June 1913, 2.

50. *Los Angeles Times*, 28 August 1910, V:20.

51. Some of these houses were described in *Nickelodeon*, Vol. 5, No. 2 (14 January 1911): 63–65.

52. Ibid., Vol. 4, No. 5 (1 September 1910): 138.

53. *Los Angeles Times*, 17 July 1910, III:1.

54. Richard V. Spencer penned the "Los Angeles Notes" in *Moving Picture World* of February 25, 1911 (Vol. 8, No. 8); his last report was published on August 19ᵗʰ. *Moving Picture News* commenced publishing reports from Los Angeles on June 3, 1911. The first were unsigned, but soon Leo Feinstein emerged as the correspondent, after a few weeks the column was signed Alex. Feinstein—unclear if a typo or a different person. After a couple of unsigned interventions, Phil Whitman shouldered the responsibility for the reports from Los Angeles; after February 17, 1912, the column disappeared and the attention to the West Coast was henceforth geared to production only.

55. *Rounder*, Vol. 1, No. 2 (7 November 1908): 3.

56. Unfortunately, the complete run of the *Rounder* has not survived; there is an unfortunate gap from August 1910 to July 1911 during a period when local film matters were part of the magazine's agenda. Two surviving issues available at the Margaret Herrick Library from the period evidence the magazine's interest in local film culture. The complete run at Los Angeles Public Library was destroyed during a fire in 1986, which wiped out a sizeable portion of its collections. The run consulted, with gaps, is available at the Seaver Center for Western History Research.

57. *Moving Picture News*, Vol. 4, No. 22 (3 June 1911): 12.

58. A Mrs. Neanette G. Donovan of St. Louis purchased the lot on which the new Optic was erected for $135,000. The building was said to have cost $30,000. *Moving Picture World*, Vol. 8, No. 14 (8 April 1911): 767.

59. Ibid., Vol. 8, No. 17 (29 April 1911): 944.

60. *Los Angeles Tribune*, 13 July 1913, VII:4.

61. *Moving Picture News*, Vol. 4, No. 41 (14 October 1911): 28.

62. For example: "Want partner for moving picture theater and film exchange. Best theaters now in operation all making big profits. Will start the largest in the West February 1. The best chance ever offered. Nothing less than $10,000 considered. All money secure. Investigate. Sunday only." Or: "For sale–Moving Picture show. Proven money maker; no swaps: a small place, but a dandy." Some days later: "For sale – a splendid moving picture theater, in heart of city. If sold immediately, $2,500. Other shows $500; $650, and up. See Up-To-Date Film Exchange, 438 San Fernando Bldg." On February 12, 1911, this particular section in the *Los Angeles Times* carried fifteen ads for picture shows.

63. Ramsaye (1926), 276–277.

64. *Los Angeles Times*, 10 October 1895, 12. For accounts of the shooting and distribution of the film, see Ramsaye (1926), 100, and Musser (1990), 83–84.

65. See Musser (1990), 296, for the traveling hypothesis. An opening ad was placed in the *Los Angeles Herald*, 18 July 1903, 2; advance announcement of the program, still under the name the Electric, was carried by the *Herald*, 12 July 1903, IV:1; and by the *Times* under the new name, 19 July 1903, III:2.

66. Oviatt was fined for having allowed a girl under 16 years of age perform during an amateur night in September 1906. Reports in *Los Angeles Times*, 5 September 1906, II:2; and 7 September 1906, II:2, and on the conviction 20 January 1907, II:6.

67. Ramsaye (1926), 426.

68. *Los Angeles Times*, 23 January 1905, I:4. See also fire accounts in *Los Angeles Examiner*, 23 January 1905, 1, *Los Angeles Express*, 23 January 1905, 8, and *Los Angeles Herald*, 23 January 1905, 3.

69. *Los Angeles Times*, 2 June 1910, II:5. The *New York Dramatic Mirror* ventured an account of Tally's activities in progress for its readers: "At Los Angeles,

Cal. T. L. Tally has secured a ground lease on 60 feet of property on Broadway, north of the Majestic Theater, for a term of fifty years, at a total rental of $600,000, and on which his syndicate will commence the erection of a large building. The ground floor of which will be given over to his moving picture theater which is at present running on the same street, between Fifth and Sixth Streets." Vol. 62, No. 1616 (11 December 1909): 27. Tally's old house was torn down to make way for expansion of the neighboring clothing store, Silverwoods; see the account of this wittily advertised "New Show" in the *Los Angeles Herald*, 4 May 1910, 5.

70. *Los Angeles Examiner*, 13 September 1914, American Magazine Section:5.

71. *Transcript of Record. Supreme Court of the United States, October term, 1917, No. 155. Motion Picture Patents Company, General Film Company, Biograph Company, et al., Appellants, vs. the United States. Appeal from the District Court of the United States for the Eastern District of Pennsylvania. Filed April 22, 1916* (New York: Appeal Printing Co., 1916)

72. "Q" Amusement was absorbed by "Q" Investment & Security in August 1912. The theatrical branch consisted of Colonial, Garrick, and Banner. *Los Angeles Express*, 3 August 1912, 9.

73. *Los Angeles Record*, 3 June 1912, 8.

74. *Los Angeles Examiner*, 1 June 1912, 4.

75. The lot was bought by John Lang prior to the real-estate boom for "a few hundred dollars" and was estimated to be worth $240,000 when Tally signed the lease for the lot at $1,000 a month for fifty years. Ibid., 28 November 1909, 6.

76. *Motion Picture News*, Vol. 10, No. 11 (19 September 1914): 51–52.

77. *Los Angeles Examiner*, 24 November 1945, II:6.

78. *Articles of Incorporation of the Southwest Amusement Company* (#8223), Seaver Center for Western History Research.

79. The only name mentioned in conjunction with Southwest opening the Empire in San Diego, which had been dark for a month, was "manager Bochoven [sic]." *San Diego Union*, 9 March 1907, 16. The Coronado house opened late in the summer; plans that were already underway were mentioned in the *San Diego News*, 18 July 1907, 4.

80. Ibid., 19 September 1907, 8.

81. *Rounder*, Vol. 2, No. 17 (24 April 1909): 15.

82. *Los Angeles Tribune*, 5 May 1912, VI:3.

83. For a time, Los Angeles had three licensed exchanges; the Kay-Tee Exchange, managed by W.E Kreiter, soon went bankrupt. A letter from the three exchanges to General Film, dated November 22, 1909, complains about tight market conditions due to the presence of independents, among other grievances, see *Transcript of Record. Supreme Court of the United States.*

84. *Los Angeles Times*, 10 November 1896, 7.

85. *New York Dramatic Mirror*, Vol. 61, No. 1584 (1 May 1909): 40.

86. *Film Index* offered an exhibition report from Los Angeles focusing on Tally and Clune's many ventures at a time when the Southwest Co. was on the verge of being dismantled; Vol. 5, No. 24 (11 June 1910): 11.

87. The *Pasadena Star* published several reports on progress of the theater's construction as well as its opening and the bill featuring fifteen numbers; 2 March 1911, 5.

88. *New York Dramatic Mirror*, Vol. 63, No. 1635 (23 April 1910): 17.

89. *Los Angeles Times*, 17 July 1910, V:18. The fullest local account of the opening was published in the *Los Angeles Express*, 10 October 1910, 18. The *New York Dramatic Mirror*, Vol. 64, No. 5174 (9 November 1910): 31, offered the following report: "Clune's new picture house, Los Angeles, Cal., seating 900 people and coasting over $50,000, was opened to the public at 10, 15, 20 cent prices October 10. Mr. Clune runs two shows in the afternoons and two in the evenings; five films and four singers, together with a ten-piece orchestra, furnish the balance of the programme. Around the walls of this spacious theatre are electric chimes and bells, and the decorations are dainty and tastefully carried out. The immense electric sign on the roof outside cost $3,500 and is conceded to be the largest and most beautiful west of New York. The completion of this house gives the Clune Amusement Company two large houses in this city, one in San Diego, and a house seating 1,400 people being erected in Pasadena, and which will be thrown open about the middle of November. Negotiations are being entered into for houses for this company in both Phoenix, Aris. [sic], and Salt Lake City, U." Photographs from the well-equipped operating room can be found in *Moving Picture World*, Vol. 10, No. 12 (23 December 1911): 985, while the auditorium and exterior were documented in a previous article, Vol. 8, No. 6 (11 February 1911): 296–297.

90. *Los Angeles Times*, 17 July 1910, V:18.

91. Ibid., 2 September 1912, II:5. The opening bill included Clune's mascot film, a picture of Niagara Falls, which he apparently always screened when opening a new house.

92. *Transcript of Record. Supreme Court of the United States.*

93. *Los Angeles Record*, 24 April 1914, 6.

94. *Motion Picture News*, Vol. 10, No. 1 (11 July 1914): 63.

95. *The Escape* returned one last time on October 3, 1915.

96. *Los Angeles Record*, 4 June 1914, 6.

97. *Los Angeles Herald*, 8 August 1914, 18; *Moving Picture World*, Vol. 22, No. 2 (10 October 1914): 198.

98. *Los Angeles Record*, 10 October 1914, 3.

99. See for example *New York Times*, 24 May 1914, C:8; and 3 January 1915, C:6.

100. *Los Angeles Times*, 30 September 1914, II:6.
101. Ibid., 14 September 1914, II:6; 29 September 1914, II:8; *Los Angeles Record*, 1 October 1914, 7. For a discussion of the score, see Martin Miller Marks, *Music and the Silent Film: Contexts and Case Studies, 1895-1924* (New York: Oxford University Press, 1997), 103–108.
102. *Moving Picture World*, Vol. 25, No. 1 (3 July 1915): 42.
103. *Pasadena Daily News*, 4 March 1911, 12.
104. *Los Angeles Times*, 18 December 1908, II:5.
105. *Los Angeles Examiner*, 17 June 1910, 6.
106. The play featured Gear, Doris Wentworth, O. B. Nair, Walli Hobart, Teddie La Due, Frank Williams, and William Bertram; the latter joined IMP as an actor in 1912 and started directing in the mid-1910s, mainly Westerns; *Los Angeles Times*, 1 May 1911, II:5.
107. *New York Clipper*, Vol. 60, No. 15 (25 May 1912): 4.
108. *Motography*, Vol. 6, No. 6 (June 1912): 284.
109. Ibid., Vol. 6, No. 1 (July 1911): 47.
110. Clement's address at the state educational conference at Haverhill, Massachusetts was published in *Motography* as "Standardizing the Picture Theater," Vol. 8, No. 13 (21 December 1912): 457–460. See also Mabel B. Ury, "The Evolution of a Moving-Picture Show: An Interview with Josephine Clement," *Twentieth Century Magazine*, Vol. 5, No. 2 (December 1911): 135-141. In addition, Clement's programming philosophy for the "ideal amusement center" was published as "What the Public Wants," *Playground*, Vol. 7, No. 1 (April 1913): 60–66.
111. In an interview for the *Los Angeles Herald*, Gill adamantly outlines the excellent business prospects for women in contemporary society, 25 April 1913, 1.
112. In *Billboard*'s film number, Vol. 20, No. 26 (27 June 1908): 19, Sarah West, co-owner of Jewel Theater, Waterloo, Iowa, was the only woman in the roster. According to the *Los Angeles Herald* in 1910 there was "in Connecticut [...] at least one female moving picture operator, a young Italian girl, who not only runs the machine, but is manager of the place as well." (*Los Angeles Herald*, 25 September 1910, IV:4): In November 1912 *Moving Picture World*, Vol. 13, No. 7 (16 November 1912): 671, featured Miss Flo Peddycord, manager and projectionist of the Bell Theatre, Buchanan, Michigan, apparently a veteran with seven or eight years in the business. In its report, *Motion Picture World* claims that a man is operating the projector in an interview with the female projectionist, Nellie Lee, in the *Los Angeles Tribune*, 23 August 1912, 7. Bowser (1990), 46–47 offers a short list of women exhibitors.
113. *Los Angeles Express*, 31 March 1911, 1. In a sermon extolling moving pictures as a splendid aid to religious instruction, Rev. Brougher of Temple Baptist

Church, owner of the auditorium complex, made a similar point about the importance of "surrender to the devil all the bright and happy things of life." *Los Angeles Times*, 13 November 1911, II:2.

114. *Los Angeles Times*, 20 July 1911, II:4; *Los Angeles Examiner*, 3 April 1911, 18; *Los Angeles Times*, 19 June 1911, II:8. All three elaborated on the newly adopted license requirements permitting frame buildings exclusively for screening films at church services; see also *Moving Picture World*, Vol. 8, No. 16 (22 April 1911): 890. For yet another clerical endorsement of the religious possibilities of the film medium, see Rev. J.W. Coontz signed statement in *Film Index*, Vol. 6, No. 17 (22 October 1910): 3.

115. *Moving Picture World*, Vol. 8, No. 16 (22 April 1911): 890.

116. *Los Angeles Times*, 1 September 1911, II:5. Julian Johnson became the *Times* drama critic in 1911 after having studied at USC. Virtually all the early high-class features were given space in his columns. After a short stint at Hearst's *Cosmopolitan* Johnson was recruited as the editor of *Photoplay*, published in his native Chicago. Scores of pens from the *Times* were frequent contributors to the magazine during Johnson's tenure, among them Harry C. Carr and Grace Kingsley. Johnson moved back to Los Angeles in the 1920s for a career in screenwriting. He was head of the story department at 20th Century from 1932 to 1957, and at his death in 1965 Johnson was considered the dean of the story editors in Hollywood.

117. *Los Angeles Times*, 25 September 1911, II:5.

118. Ibid., 30 July 1912, III:4.

119. *Los Angeles Tribune*, 9 February 1913, VII:15.

120. *Los Angeles Record* published the pictures from December 10, 1912 to January 1, 1913, when number 20 appeared. The quotation is from 10 December 1912, 3.

121. *Los Angeles Times*, 13 February 1913, II:7.

122. Ibid., 24 September 1911, III:1.

123. *Los Angeles Examiner*, 1 June 1913, IX:5.

124. *Los Angeles Times*, 4 June 1913, III:4.

125. *Variety*, Vol. 25, No. 13 (2 March 1912): 5.

126. *Lancaster Daily Intelligencer*, 16 February 1912, 4.

127. Grau (1909), 19–20.

128. *Los Angeles Express*, 6 August 1912, 8.

129. Ibid., 10 August 1912, 9.

130. *Los Angeles Times*, 7 August 1912, II:5.

131. *Los Angeles Herald*, 31 July 1913, 8.

132. *Los Angeles Tribune*, 4 August 1912, IV:3.

133. The music column in the *Los Angeles Municipal News* had praised three local theaters for offering arrangements of classical music to accompany the pic-

tures only a few weeks before the opening of the Mozart Theater: Liberty, College, and Garrick; the latter was formerly the Hyman. For information on the Liberty Theater, see *Moving Picture World*, Vol. 8, No. 13 (1 April 1911): 701; on the College, ibid., Vol. 8, No. 21 (27 May 1911): 1184. Elaborating on "Beethoven and the Box Office," the music critic in *Municipal News* appraised the arrangement of classical music as "pioneering uplift measures" (24 July 1912, 3). The following week, the music critic reported enthusiastically on plans for the Mozart, a theater predicated on showing films of "an educational, informative or artistic nature," and, equally as important, "the accompanying music will be, not alone appropriate to the pictures, but predominantly of a sort seldom heard outside the concert hall" (31 July 1912, 3). Two weeks later, the columnist described the function of the Foto Player and the musical accompaniment for a recent film at the Mozart, *The Crusaders* (14 August 1912, 3).

134. *Film Index*, Vol. 7, No. 18 (6 May 1911): 2; and Vol. 7, No. 19 (13 May 1911): 6.
135. *Los Angeles Tribune*, 30 July 1912, 9.
136. *Los Angeles Record*, 26 July 1912, 3.
137. Ibid., 10 August 1912, 3.
138. *Los Angeles Times*, 2 August 1912, II:5.
139. *Los Angeles Herald*, 8 August 1912, 5.
140. *Los Angeles Tribune*, 23 August 1912, 7.
141. *Variety*, Vol. 27, No. 10 (9 August 1912): 6.
142. Advertisement in *Billboard*, Vol. 24, No. 25 (22 June 1912): 52.
143. *Los Angeles Tribune*, 4 August 1912, IV:3.
144. Ibid., 2 August 1913, 13.
145. *Los Angeles Times*, 2 August 1913, III:1.
146. Ibid.
147. *Player*, Vol. 3, No. 6 (13 January 1911): 1. A week later *Player* reported that Mr. Mozart planned to appeal the decision.
148. *Los Angeles Times*, 5 January 1913, II:1, 2.
149. "Commonwealth vs. Edward K. Mozart," *Lancaster Law Review*, Vol. 30 (Lancaster, Pa.: Wickersham Printing Co., 1913), 147–148.
150. *Los Angeles Times*, 13 September 1913, II:1, 5.
151. *Billboard*, Vol. 26, No. 4 (24 January 1914): 15.
152. *Los Angeles Tribune*, 20 September 1914, IV:1.
153. *Los Angeles Examiner*, 9 March 1915, I:5.
154. *Los Angeles Times*, 7 March 1915, II:7. Photographs of the perfect boy and girl, both white, were published on 13 March 1915, II:1.
155. *Los Angeles Tribune*, 15 March 1915, 4.
156. *Motion Picture News*, Vol. 10, No. 1 (11 July 1914): 63–64.

Chapter 4

1. *Los Angeles Herald*, 19 June 1910, 6; reprinted from the *Detroit News*.
2. Mitchell Brian Gelfand, *Chutzpah in El Dorado. Social Mobility of Jews in Los Angeles, 1900-1920* (Ph.D. diss., Carnegie-Mellon University, 1981), 66.
3. George J. Sánchez, *Becoming Mexican American: Ethnicity, Culture and Identity in Chicano Los Angeles, 1900–1945* (New York and Oxford: Oxford University Press, 1993).
4. *Los Angeles Times*, 28 October 1906, II:16.
5. Ibid., 31 May 1907, II:8.
6. *New York Times*, 3 August 1913, Sunday Magazine:4.
7. *Los Angeles Times*, 13 October 1907, III:1.
8. Ibid., 30 May 1909, II:5.
9. Ibid., 19 March 1909, III:2; 10 October 1909, II:16.
10. *New York Times*, 10 October 1909, 8.
11. *Los Angeles Record*, 11 November 1909, 4.
12. *Los Angeles Times*, 1 February 1910, II:14.
13. Ibid., 16 October 1910, II:1, 9. Reprinted in *Moving Picture World*, Vol. 7, No. 19 (5 November 1910): 1044.
14. *Los Angeles Times*, 30 October 1910, II:5.
15. Ibid., 2 December 1910, II:5.
16. Ibid., 17 July 1910, II:5.
17. The report from the shooting of *The Spoilers* was published in ibid., 18 July 1913, III:1.
18. *Atlanta Constitution*, 1 March 1907, 7.
19. *Billboard*, Vol. 19, No. 45 (2 November 1907): 28; a first report was published in Vol. 19, No. 44 (26 October 1907): 13, 46.
20. *Moving Picture News*, Vol. 5, No. 1 (6 January 1912): 24.
21. *Rounder*, Vol. 5, No. 10 (9 March 1912): 24. The eight proprietors operated theaters on South Main, but also on South Spring: J. Rose, J. Roos, G. Steets, J.W. Northery, G.M. McLain, [T.] W. Johns, A.M. Allen, and B. Tani. *Moving Picture News*, Vol. 4, No. 41 (14 October 1911): 28.
22. *Los Angeles Times*, 8 October 1907, II:2. The Los Angeles Fire Department's Annual Reports—Collection 1170 at the Seaver Center for Western History Research—list causes of alarms by year; multiple categories were used for cinema-related fires. "Moving Picture Machines" caused one alarm in 1905, two in 1906, five in 1907, three in 1908, records are missing for 1909, one in 1910, one in 1911, four in 1912, one in 1913; the category was abandoned after that. New categories emerged starting in 1908, namely "Moving Picture Shows"—four alarms, in 1910 the category was "Moving Picture"—three alarms, in 1911 "Moving Picture Theater"—two alarms, in 1912 eight alarms,

in 1913 five alarms, in 1914 six alarms, plus two alarms that year in "Moving Picture Studios." In 1915 nine alarms in "Moving Picture Theaters." Finally, "Films"—one alarm in 1910, five in 1914, and four in 1915.

23. The most far-reaching follow-up of the Boyertown disaster was printed in the columns of the *New York Herald*, 20 January 1908, 1, 6; and 21 January, 1, 5. Pennsylvania was hit again in late August 1911 when twenty-five persons were killed in the panic caused by a booth fire in the Canonsburg Opera House. One of many reports in the press can be found in *Los Angeles Times*, 27 August 1911, I:1–2.

24. *Los Angeles Express*, 31 March 1913, 14.

25. Alison Griffths, "'THEY GO TO SEE A SHOW': Vicissitudes of spectating and the anxiety over the machine in the nineteenth century science museum," *Early Popular Visual Culture*, Vol. 4, No. 3 (November 2006): 245–271, especially 249–251.

26. *Los Angeles Record*, 8 July 1914, 1.

27. Stewart Edward White, *The Rules of the Game* (New York: Doubleday, Page & Co., 1910), 137–138.

28. See Rick Altman, "The Silence of the Silents," *Musical Quarterly*, Vol. 80, No. 4 (1996): 648–718.

29. *Los Angeles Record*, July 1, 1907, 2.

30. Lawrence W. Levine, *Highbrow/Lowbrow: The Emergence of Cultural Hierarchy in America* (Cambridge, Mass.: Harvard University Press, 1988); Hansen (1991).

31. *Los Angeles Times*, 13 October 1907, III:1.

32. Jane Addams, *Spirit of Youth and the City Streets* (New York: Macmillan, 1909), Chapter 4, "The House of Dreams," especially 85–88.

33. *Los Angeles Times*, 12 May 1912, II:1, 15.

34. Ibid., II:15.

35. *Los Angeles Citizen*, 31 January 1913, 1.

36. *Los Angeles Tribune*, 13 July 1913, Magazine Section:1.

37. *Los Angeles Record*, 25 February 1913, 4.

38. Vorse (1911).

39. *Moving Picture World*, Vol. 8, No. 26 (1 July 1911): 1536.

40. *Los Angeles Times*, 13 December 1913, II:6.

41. *New York Press*, 22 May 1910, 8.

42. Ibid.

43. *Chicago Tribune*, 28 March 1909, B:4.

44. "Cheap Amusements," *Charities and the Common*, Vol. 20, No. 2 (11 April 1908): 73–76.

45. *New York Press*, 23 February 1908, III:1.

46. *Moving Picture World*, Vol. 7, No. 13 (23 September 1910): 698.

47. J.A. Fitzgerald, "The Lure of the Moving Picture Show," *New York Herald*, 17 April 1910, III:14.
48. *Los Angeles Record*, 23 July 1914, 1, 6.

Chapter 5

1. *Indianapolis Recreation Survey*, 41.
2. The Lubin catalogs from 1905 to 1909 at the Margaret Herrick Library advertise scores of such split reels. In an accurate assessment from 1913 *Motography* observed that "while split reels, as an American institution, have not entirely disappeared, lingering still in the old combination of comedy and scenic, they have lost their importance to the manufacturer." Vol. 10, No. 6 (20 September 1913): 191.
3. Elizabeth J. Clapp, *Mothers of All Children: Women Reformers and the Rise of the Juvenile Courts in Progressive America* (University Park, Pa.: Pennsylvania State University Press, 1998).
4. Bliss Perry, *The American Mind* (Boston and New York: Houghton Mifflin Company, 1912), 112.
5. *Los Angeles Times*, 13 December 1904, I:1.
6. Ibid., 22 February 1906, I:15.
7. Ibid., 4 January 1905, II:1. A successful transformation of a former cemetery into a playground in Washington, D.C., was illustrated by photographs in *Playground*, Vol. 4, No. 1 (April 1910): 34.
8. "Recreative Centers of Los Angeles, California," *The Annals of the American Academy of Political and Social Science*, Vol. 35, No. 2 (March 1910): 426-435; quotation from p. 427.
9. *Los Angeles Times*, 19 May 1905, II:6.
10. For accounts of the preambles to the formation of the New York Board of Censorship for Motion Picture Shows and its later incarnations, see Daniel Czitrom, "The Redemption of Leisure: The National Board of Censorship and the Rise of Motion Picture in New York City, 1900–1920," *Studies in Visual Communication*, Vol. 10, No. 4 (1984): 2–6; Nancy J. Rosenblom, "Between Reform and Regulation: The Struggle over Film Censorship in Progressive America, 1909–1922," *Film History* Vol. 1, No. 4, (1987): 307–325; and Uricchio and Pearson (1993), Chapter 1. See also Robert Sklar, *Movie-MadeAmerica: A Cultural History of American Movies* (New York: Random House, 1975), Chapter 3; Garth Jowett, *Film: The Democratic Art* (Boston: Little, Brown, and Co., 1976), 52–58.
11. See the article "Committee to Censor Cheap Amusements," *New York Times*, 24 February 1909, 6.

12. Extracts from the report were quoted in an account of the Hotel Astor meeting in "Recreation Program For a Million Children," *Charities and the Commons*, Vol. 21, No. 23 (6 March 1909): 1037–1039; quotation from p. 1038.

13. Ibid., p. 1039.

14. John Collier, "Moving Pictures: Their Function and Proper Regulation," *Playground*, Vol. 4, No. 7 (1910): 232–240; quotations from p. 232 and 233.

15. Reports from the opening were published in the Rochester papers on June 9; one of the accounts was reprinted in *Film Index*, Vol. 6, No. 1 (2 July 1910): 28.

16. Concerning the formation of the Board of Censors, see for example Uricchio and Pearson (1993); and Grieveson (2004).

17. John Collier, "Leisure Time, the Last Problem of Conservation," *Playground*, Vol. 6, No. 1 (June 1912): 93–106; quotation from p.103.

18. *New York Times*, 3 April 1912, 4.

19. *Film Index* claimed that the crusade in 1910 was staged by independent interests trying to discredit the licensed companies' efforts and especially their cooperation with the Board of Censors, while a subsequent editorial dismissed the crusade as merely a dishonest circulation stunt; Vol. 6, No. 15 (8 October 1910): 2; Vol. 6, No. 16 (15 October 1910): 1; see also *Moving Picture World*, Vol. 7, No. 15 (8 October 1910): 797.

20. Raymond B. Fosdick, "Report on New York Picture Theaters," *Motography*, Vol. 5, No. 4 (April 1911): 27–31. *Suggestions for a Model Ordinance for Regulating Motion Picture Theaters* (New York: National Board of Censorship of Motion Pictures, 1913).

21. "Motion Picture Legislation," *Playground*, Vol. 7, No. 5 (September 1913): 227–234.

22. *New York Evening World*, 17 January 1913, 4–5. In a previous article, Mrs. Arthur defended the moving-picture shows at length, *New York Tribune*, 4 May 1910, 10. Shortly afterwards the Practical Mothers' Association was formed. In her capacity as president Mrs. Arthur addressed the newly organized New York State Motion Picture Exhibitors' League on June 19; *New York Times*, 20 June 1912, 10.

23. *New York Times*, 8 July 1913, 7.

24. City of Los Angeles, Records and Management Division, *City Council*, Vol. 74 (20 May 1907–27 November 1907): Petition 505.

25. "Horrid Scenes for a Penny," *Los Angeles Times*, 6 December 1906, II:22.

26. The nickelodeon at 255 South Main was damaged by fire in 1913 and accurately described as the "first picture theater to be established in Los Angeles" in the notice published by the *Los Angeles Record*, November 19, 1913, 1. The house, then called the Arcade, was gutted by fire, thereby closing an exhibition era. The building permit for the house at 349 North Main was listed in *Los Angeles Builder and Contractor*, Vol. 14, No. 715 (8 November 1906): 2.

27. "Five-Cent Theaters Schools of Crime," *Los Angeles Times*, 21 December 1906, II:1.
28. Ibid.
29. Ibid.
30. Ibid., 22 May 1907, II:2. See also *Los Angeles Record*, 23 April 1907, 2.
31. *Los Angeles Express*, 29 April 1907, 7.
32. For an account of the hearing, see *Los Angeles Times*, 21 May 1907, II:2.
33. Ordinance No. 14, 865, New Series.
34. In 1906 Hentz and Zallee at the Unique were fined $50 for having a twelve-year-old girl do a "song-and-dance-stunt." The arrest was prompted by a report from the Humane Society. *Los Angeles Times*, 31 July 1906, II:2. Regarding Morosco and Baker, it was again civic groups that alerted the police concerning violations of the ordinance.
35. *Los Angeles Express*, 7 October 1907, 1.
36. Ibid., 26 July 1907, 1.
37. Ibid., 19 February 1908, 9.
38. *Los Angeles Times*, 4 October 1907, III:1.
39. *Los Angeles Herald*, 24 February 1909, 12. For the mayor's missive dated January 26, 1909, see *Los Angeles City Council*, Vol. 77 (2 November 1908–30 March 1909): 341.
40. *Los Angeles Times*, 24 February 1909, II:2.
41. *Los Angeles Express*, 23 December 1908, 6.
42. Ibid., 24 February 1909, 10.
43. Ibid., 26 July 1907, 1.
44. Ibid., 19 February 1908, 9.
45. *Los Angeles Herald*, 29 August 1908, II:4.
46. *Los Angeles Times*, 13 October 1908, II:4.
47. *Los Angeles Express*, 10 September 1908, 10.
48. *Los Angeles Times*, 13 September 1908, II:1, 11.
49. Ibid., 13 October 1908, II:4.
50. *Los Angeles Express*, 18 November 1909, 14.
51. *Los Angeles Examiner*, 16 November 1909, 8.
52. *Los Angeles Express*, 4 November 1910, 22.
53. "A Primary School for Criminals," *Good Housekeeping Magazine*, Vol. 51, No. 2 (August 1910): 184–186.
54. "The Social Influence of the Moving Picture," *Playground*, Vol. 5, No. 3 (June 1911): 74–84; quotations from p. 78. Jump had made "a thorough investigation of the moving picture problem for the purpose of ascertaining the advisability of introducing Sunday evening moving picture service at the South Church during the winter." An account of Reverend Jump's visit to New York City, hosted by fellow clergy affiliated with the censorship board, was reprin-

ted by the *Film Index*, Vol. 6, No. 6 (6 August 1910): 24; from *New Britain Record*. By 1914 film screenings in churches were so widespread that an exchange was established to cater to 400 of them, *Evening Sun*, 6 June 1914, 5.

55. *Chicago Chronicle*, 28 April 1907, 3.

56. *New York World*, 7 May 1912, 8; see also, for example, *Motography*, Vol. 6, No. 2 (August 1911): 67.

57. *Los Angeles Herald*, 26 June 1910, 6.

58. *Los Angeles Times*, 8 November 1913, II:6.

59. Ibid., 7 October 1913, II:12.

60. Ibid., 22 January 1914, II:12.

61. *Los Angeles Express*, 12 January 1914, 4.

62. Ibid., 16 January 1914, 9; *Los Angeles Examiner*, 1 March 1914, X:5.

63. *Los Angeles Times*, 25 May 1914, II:2.

64. For a detailed account of the clashes involving *Damaged Goods* and the dismantling of the Board of Censors, see *Exhibitors Herald*, Vol. 1, No. 24 (4 December 1915): 3–4.

Chapter 6

1. Jacques Lavosier, quoted in the *Los Angeles Herald*, 20 May 1908, 18.

2. Brackett, a former druggist and traveling salesman, had signed a two-year contract with Howe in August 1906. It is unclear if Brackett served the entire contractual period or severed his association with Howe earlier. *Billboard*, Vol. 18, No. 34 (25 August 1906): 7. Charles Musser and Carol Nelson, *High-Class Moving Pictures: Lyman H. Howe and the Forgotten Era of Traveling Exhibition, 1880–1920* (Princeton, N.J.: Princeton University Press, 1991), 180.

3. *Los Angeles Herald,* 20 May 1909, 18.

4. Ibid.

5. *Los Angeles Examiner*, 22 November 1908, 9.

6. *Los Angeles Herald*, 11 November 1908, 12.

7. *Los Angeles Examiner*, 14 March 1909, II:4.

8. *San Francisco Examiner*, 14 January 1909; the managers' protest is on p. 9, the editorial on p. 20. The protest inspired a campaign which the nickelodeon proprietors responded to in a leaflet signed by the Moving Picture Exhibitors' Association of San Francisco, "Facts all should know and consider regarding Nickelodeons and Moving Picture Exhibitions." [June, 1909] Huntington Library [Call No. 406442 (Rare)]. At that time, 63 nickelodeons operated in San Francisco. In support of their businesses the exhibitors quoted an assessment from the Superintendent of the Boys' Institute, in New York: "I have personally made a canvass of the East Side, among the professional men,

who are in a position to know whether these theaters are a menace or not, and find that the unanimous opinion is that if we do away with moving pictures we are depriving the poor of their greatest source of recreation and education, and driving the boys back to where temptation assails them on all sides, the cheap theaters, the gambling dens and the streets."

9. *Munsey's Magazine*, Vol. 41, No. 5 (August 1909): 638.

10. *New York Clipper*, Vol. 57, No. 6 (27 March 1909): 178.

11. *Billboard*, Vol. 21, No. 18 (1 May 1909): 14.

12. *New York Herald*, 28 February 1909, Magazine Section:4. Judging from a report after John Collier's visit to Europe in 1910, it seems as if film theaters in London were lighted during projection: "The houses were generally well lighted and ventilated." *Film Index*, Vol. 6, No. 13 (24 September 1910): 2.

13. Article from the *Kinematograph and Lantern Weekly*, reprinted in *Moving Picture World*, Vol. 6, No. 9 (5 March 1910): 331.

14. One of numerous cases was reported from Philadelphia in an account indicative of the *Philadelphia Press*' sober attitude vis-à-vis film culture devoid of condemnations and caveats. The premise for the mashing was afforded by the darkness enveloping the patrons: "Florence Summers, a child of seven years, has saved up her pennies to go to the 'shows' and shortly after eight o'clock paid her way into the place of amusement. It was noted by one of the attendants that soon after the child entered she was followed by Antinio Bells, an Italian about fifty years old. He took a seat next to the child and when he believed he was completely covered by the darkness attacked her. In a moment the child was screaming with pain and fright." The incident interrupted the projection of *Lynching a Horse Thief*, and the police had to fight of patrons attempting to lynch Mr. Bells. *Philadelphia Press*, 23 July 1908, 3.

15. *Moving Picture World*, Vol. 4, No. 20 (15 May 1909): 630.

16. *New York Times*, 16 May 1909, 7. See also *Film Index*, Vol. 4, No. 22 (29 May 1909): 3 as well as *Moving Picture World*, Vol. 4, No. 12 (20 March 1909): 331. The comments in the *World* by "Our Own Critic" indeed address the Solar screen, but the critic does not comment upon the lighting arrangements at the Nicoland.

17. *Film Index*, Vol. 4, No. 18 (1 May 1909): 11.

18. *Moving Picture World*, Vol. 6, No. 13 (2 April 1910): 507.

19. The Orpheum manager's retort was published in ibid., Vol. 6, No. 18 (16 April 1910): 603; "Picture Lover" returned on 7 May 1910, 741–742.

20. "The Only Censorship of Plays in America," *North American, Philadelphia*, 25 September 1910, Sunday Magazine.

21. Anna S. Richardson, "The Menace of the Moving Picture Theater," *Pictorial Review*, Vol. 12, No. 1 (October 1910): 9, 67.

22. *Film Index*, Vol. 5, No. 7 (12 February 1910): 2; Vol. 5, No. 10 (5 March 1910): 3; Vol. 5, No. 20 (14 May 1910): 8.

23. Ibid., Vol. 6, No. 3 (16 July 1910): 2, 30.

24. Ibid., Vol. 6, No. 14 (1 October 1910): 2.

25. Ibid., Vol. 6, No. 16 (15 October 1910): 8. McQuade returned to the dark theaters in a letter two weeks later, Vol. 6, No. 18 (29 October 1910): 5.

26. James L. Hoff, "The Era of the Motion Picture," *The Chautauquan*, Vol. 71, No. 1 (7 June 1913): 1–10; quotation from p. 7.

27. *Moving Picture World*, Vol. 5, No. 15 (9 October 1909): 484; Vol. 6, No. 8 (26 February 1910): 297.

28. *New York Clipper*, Vol. 58, No. 39 (12 November 1910): 974.

29. From New York's *The Sun*; reprinted in *Film Index*, Vol. 6, No. 27 (31 December 1910): 4–5.

30. *Film Index*, Vol. 6, No. 20 (12 November 1910): 31. The *Index* had previously recommended this particular screen and urged exhibitors to "Turn on the Light." Vol. 6, No. 16 (15 October 1910): 2.

31. *New York Clipper*, Vol. 59, No. 2 (25 February 1911): 27.

32. *Moving Picture World*, Vol. 5, No. 1 (3 July 1909): 116, announced that the company was ready to debut its plate-glass "curtain."

33. See ads in *Moving Picture World*, Vol. 17, No. 3 (19 July 1913): 374.

34. *Brickbuilder*. Supplement to Vol. 23, No. 3 (February 1914): 42. For a comprehensive discussion of the advantage in adopting indirect light fixtures, see "The Lightning of Moving Picture Theaters," *Billboard*, Vol. 24, No. 5 (3 February 1912): 24.

35. *Los Angeles Herald*, 14 March 1911, 3.

36. *Evening World*, 6 December 1912, 12.

37. John Collier, "'Movies' and the Law," *Survey*, Vol. 27, No. 16 (20 January 1912): 1628–29, reprinted in *Moving Picture News*, Vol. 5, No. 8 (24 February 1912): 13–14.

38. C.H. Blackall, "New York Moving Picture Theater Law," *Brickbuilder*, supplement to Vol. 23, No. 3 (February 1914): 47. The ordinance is reprinted on pp. 48–50

39. *Los Angeles Tribune*, 30 July 1911, 2.

40. The *Los Angeles Express* reported on a screen experiment at the Orpheum vaudeville house on 4 March 1911, 3.

41. For instance in *Los Angeles Herald*, 7 March 1911, 11.

42. *Moving Picture World*, Vol. 8, No. 12 (25 March 1911): 645.

43. *Los Angeles Times*, 11 August 1911, II:5.

44. *Los Angeles Examiner*, 9 March 1911, 13. See also *Moving Picture World*, Vol. 8, No. 15 (15 April 1911): 826.

45. *Los Angeles Daily Journal*, 5 August 1911, 7; Ordinance No. 23,161, New Series.

46. For example in No. 24,187 (published 27 January 1912) and No. 33,908 (published 4 April 1916): both in the *Los Angeles Daily Journal.*

47. *Billboard*, Vol. 23, No. 25 (24 June 1911): 22.

48. Article from *Pittsburgh Leader*, "Motion Pictures Defended," reprinted in *Photoplay Magazine*, Vol. 2, No. 3 (April 1912): 73.

49. "Recreation Survey, Milwaukee, Wisconsin," *Playground*, Vol. 6, No. 2 (May 1912): 38–59; quotation from p. 48.

50. *Woman's Home Companion*, Vol. 42, No. 11 (November 1915): 52.

51. "Talbot on Motion Photography Unreliable," *Moving Picture World*, Vol. 11, No. 11 (16 March 1912): 942–43; quotations from p. 942.

52. *Los Angeles Times*, July 9 1911, II:5.

53. Ben Brewster, "A Scene at the 'Movies,'" *Screen*, Vol. 23, No. 2 (July-August 1982): 4–15.

54. *The Bioscope*, Vol. 31, No. 499 (4 May 1916): 561.

55. *Film Index*, Vol. 7, No. 15 (15 April 1911): 5.

56. Walter Prichard Eaton, "Class-Consciousness and the 'Movies,'" *Atlantic Monthly*, Vol. 105, No. 1 (January 1915): 48–56; quotation from page 55.

57. Walter Prichard Eaton, "Menace of the Movies," *American Magazine*, Vol. 76, No. 5 (September 1913): 55–60; quotation from p. 60.

58. Garnet Warren, "How the Millions Are Catered to in the Matter of Amusements," *Los Angeles Herald*, 21 March 1909, Feature Section:8.

59. *Nickelodeon*, Vol. 5, No. 4, (28 January 1911): 97.

60. Olivia Howard Dunbar, "The Lure of the Films," *Harper's Weekly*, Vol. 57, No. 2926 (18 January 1913): 20–22.

61. James Oppenheim, "Saturday Night," *Forum*, Vol. 43, No. 2 (February 1910): 97–106, passim.

62. *Motion Picture Patents Co. versus United States. Transcript of Records*, Vol. 3, 1569.

63. James R. Cameron, *Motion Picture Projection* (Manhattan Beach, N.Y.: Cameron Publishing Co., Inc., 1928), 563.

64. *Los Angeles Express*, 2 August 1913, 9.

65. For instance in the *Los Angeles Examiner*, 5 April 1914, American Magazine Section:6.

66. Chicago's Amazonian hiring pattern was emulated on the Zone at the Panama-Pacific Exhibition in the hiring of Blanche Payson as a policewoman. Payson later became a "keystone amazon" and even later a forceful presence, in fact playing an Amazon, in Buster Keaton's *The Three Ages*. Her measurements, a deterrent to most criminals, was reported as being 6 feet, 4 inches and 234 lbs. *Triangle*, Vol. 1, No. 25 (8 April 1916): 3.

67. *Boston Evening Transcript*, 23 August 1913, 2.

68. *Chicago Tribune*, 4 April 1914, 12.

69. *Cleveland Citizen*, 7 March 1914, 2.
70. "Reminiscences of a Policewoman," *Police Reporter*, Vol. 1, No. 6 (September 1929): 23.
71. *New York Evening World*, 19 February 1910, 8.
72. *Los Angeles Express*, 1 December 1911, 13.
73. Clara M. Greening, "Policewoman Number One," *Sunset Magazine*, Vol. 27, No. 3 (September 1911): 304–306.
74. *Chicago Tribune*, 14 October 1912, 1.
75. *Washington Post*, 5 August 1910, 3. The most comprehensive discussions of her work were published by Bertha H. Smith, "The Policewoman," *Good Housekeeping Magazine*, Vol. 52, No. 3 (March 1911): 296–298; *Los Angeles Herald*, 4 June 1911, Magazine Section:3; *New York Times*, 22 December 1912, Sunday Magazine Section:13.
76. *Los Angeles Examiner*, 10 March 1913, 13.
77. *Evening World*, 4 December 1912, 24.
78. *New York Clipper*, Vol. 60, No. 46 (28 December 1912): 4.
79. *Los Angeles Times*, 14 September 1910, II:1.
80. *Los Angeles Examiner*, 6 July 1911, 9.
81. Ibid., 21 September 1911, 9.
82. *Los Angeles Herald*, 10 August 1911, 11.
83. *Chicago Tribune*, 12 February 1915, 1.
84. *Los Angeles Examiner*, 18 July 1912, 8.
85. *Los Angeles Times*, 19 September 1912, I:16.
86. *New York World*, 27 May 1906, Magazine Section:1.
87. *Los Angeles Examiner*, 28 April 1913, 2.
88. *Los Angeles Herald*, 25 April 1913, 14.
89. *Los Angeles Express*, 16 January 1914, 9.
90. Ibid., 24 October 1913, 9.
91. *Los Angeles Examiner*, 26 May 1914, I:3.
92. *Los Angeles Record*, 2 May 1913, 4.
93. *Los Angeles Tribune*, 29 November 1914, 6.
94. *New York Times*, 22 December 1912, Sunday Magazine:13.
95. *Los Angeles Examiner*, 21 May 1913, 25.
96. *Los Angeles Tribune*, 14 August 1914, 10.
97. *Los Angeles Examiner*, 17 June 1914, II:1.
98. For example in the *Los Angeles Tribune*, 12 October 1914, 8; and *Motography*, Vol. 7, No. 18 (31 October 1914): 592.

Chapter 7

1. Charles Dickens, *Martin Chuzzlewit* (Ware, Hertfordshire: Wordsworth Classics, 1997 [1843–44]), 470.
2. For a discussion of Hollywood's subsequent cult of youth, see Heather Addison, "'Must Players Keep Young?': Early Hollywood's Cult of Youth," *Cinema Journal*, Vol. 45, No. 4 (Summer 2006): 3–25.
3. *Cosmopolitan*, Vol. 58, No. 5 (April 1915): 596; *Moving Picture World*, Vol. 32, No. 2 (14 April 1917): 279.
4. An excellent example of such a magazine is *Eve's Film Review* produced by British Pathé from 1921 to 1933, a run discussed in depth by Jenny Hammerton. This run, while specifically targeting women, was also self-consciously aware of its obvious appeal for all the Adams in the audience when showcasing certain aspects of women's world, in an interesting fashion toying with both modes of address and stylistic features and striking a balance between attraction-inflected showing and transparent storytelling. The intertitles are absolutely essential for stitching together and framing the material by way of a distinct type of voice. But overall, man is conspicuously absent from the screen. The success of *Eve's Film Review* in Britain did not spill over to the American market for this particular cinemagazine, and after a short tryout it vanished from U.S. screens.
5. For a multitude of aspects of this process, see Leo Charney and Vanessa R. Schwartz, eds., *Cinema and the Invention of Modern Life* (Berkeley: University of California Press, 1995). Concerning the electrical discourse, see Christoph Asendorf, *Batteries of Life: On the History of Things and Their Perception in Modernity* (Berkeley: University of California Press, 1991); and David E. Nye, *Electrifying America: Social Meanings of a New Technology 1880–1940* (Cambridge, Mass.: MIT Press, 1990).
6. *Moving Picture World*, Vol. 23, No. 4 (23 January 1915): 487.
7. *New York Dramatic Mirror*, Vol. 71, No. 1836 (25 February 1914): 28.
8. *Motion Picture News*, Vol. 9, No. 9 (7 March 1914): 26.
9. The most recent Hearst biography, Nasaw (2000), describes Hearst's newsreel partner, Colonel Selig, as a small-time producer, which is a flagrant mischaracterization. Selig Polyscope was one of the major corporations in the field and a company with impressive resources at its command.
10. Ad in *Billboard*, Vol. 27, No. 2 (9 January 1915): 47. A list of newspapers publishing the Kathlyn synopses can be found in the *New York Clipper*, Vol. 61, No. 49 (17 January 1914): 15. The *Clipper* had already reported on the "wedded art of literary craftsmanship and realistic photoplay" after Harold McGrath's visit to Selig Studios in September 1913. The author "was called to this city from his Eastern home by *The Chicago Tribune*." Vol. 61, No. 33

(27 September 1913): 14. The strategy behind the campaign was outlined by William H. Fields after some of the syndicating papers had complained about being shortchanged—"Is not Press Agent," *Editor, Publisher, and Journalist*, 4 July 1914, 46. Fields claimed that the *Tribune*'s circulation had increased by 50,000 on Sundays, attracting a substantial number of advertisements from local exhibitors; $30,000 was estimated as the extra revenue for the year. Unfortunately, the film exchanges were not able to furnish a sufficient number of film prints to the syndicating cities.

11. See advance notice in *Moving Picture World*, Vol. 12, No. 13 (29 June 1912): 1212.

12. *New York American*, 3 April 1910, City Life Section:1; 10 April 1910, City Life Section:1.

13. "Newspapers Falling in Line," *Variety*, Vol. 35, No. 6 (10 July 1914): 19. Grau (1969 [1914]), 236–37. Grau here seems to echo Will Irwin's well-researched attack on "Zit's" handling of theatrical matters in the *Evening Journal*, particularly the innovative theatrical race-track chart. The power of advertising was attested to in a letter to C.F. Zittel (Zit) published in the *Evening Journal*: "I'm writing you in appreciation of the wonderful returns that we are getting from the advertising which we are placing in the Journal. It is really astonishing that we should get such wonderful results from our advertisements despite the fact that every critic in New York City (with the exception of the New York Journal representative) who reviewed 'To-Day' at the Forty-Eight Street Theater, pronounced it a complete failure./We are selling out every performance and have a wonderful demand for weeks ahead. I am sending you herewith enclosed an order for two half pages for the coming week." (25 October 1913): 7

14. See Dan Streible, "Children at the Mutoscope," *CINéMAS*, Vol. 14, No. 1 (2003): 91–116. The fact that the campaign was confined to Hearst's paper is read by Streible as an indication that the problem was minor irrespective of blazing headlines. It was however not often that a newspaper campaign spilled over from one newspaper to the others in the area. The crusades in the *New York Evening World*, perhaps the longest on record, did not prompt comments from the other dailies in New York City. The 1907 campaign in the *Chicago Tribune* garnered some attention in other Chicago papers primarily due to its broad scope and relation to the overall political situation in the city at the time.

15. For a full account, see Olsson (2004).

16. *New York Dramatic Mirror*, Vol. 71, No. 1836 (25 February 1914): 29.

17. *Los Angeles Examiner*, 8 and 9 February 1914 (*Germinal*); 10 (*The Fat Man's Burden*); 11 (*The Lunatic's Child*); 12 (*In The Mesh of Her Hair*); 13 (*All Account of Polly*); 16 (*The Blighted Son*); 18 (*The Chains of Honor*); 19 (*Whiffles' Balcony*

Buds); 20 (*Won By a Nose*); 21 (*Broken Lives*); 22 (*September Morn*); 24 (*Victims of Vanity*); 25 (*The Winning Hand*); 27 (*Devil's Assistant*); 28 (*Romeo and Juliet*); March 1, 2, and 3 (*The Parasites*); 4, 5, 6, and 9 (*Germinal*); 18 and 19 (*Against Heavy Odds*); 23 and 30 (*The Life of Our Savior*); April 9 and 10 (*The Greater Love*). The first installment of *Perils of Pauline* was published on March 22nd, which after a few weeks obviated publishing stories of other Pathé films.

18. For a discussion of the newsreel's place on a well-balanced variety program, akin to the diversity of the newspaper and its many sections and addresses, see "Periodical Topicals," *Motography*, Vol. 6, No. 2 (August 1911): 56–57; for comments on both *Pathé Weekly* and Vitagraph's monthly magazine *Current Events*.

19. *Motography*, Vol. 11, No. 12 (13 June 1914): 431. Later, a detailed account of the industry's attempt at having films "included in the list of merchandise admitted to the parcel post" was discussed in the wake of a new type of cases, *New York Clipper*, Vol. 62, No. 33 (26 September 1914): 14. *Film Index*, Vol. 6, No. 26 (24 December 1910): 2, reported when the so-called Sulzer Bill passed by Congress, thereby breaking the express companies' monopoly on parcels weighing over four pounds—according to the bill, the government's postal service would be permitted to carry packages weighing up to eleven pounds and reduce the rate to eight cents from 16 per pound. The rates for interstate packages were more expensive than for those to Europe.

20. For a perceptive discussion of the serial format in general and the Pauline series in particular, see Jennifer Bean, "Technologies of Early Stardom and the Extraordinary Body," *Camera Obscura*, Vol. 16, No. 3 (48, 2001): 9–56.

21. For in-depth perspectives on Pathé's strategies see Abel (1999) and Abel (2006) as well as Marina Dahlquist, "Becoming American in 1910?: Pathé Frères' Settlement in New Jersey," *Quarterly Review of Film & Video*, Vol. 22, No. 3 (2005): 251–262; and "Global versus Local: The Case of Pathé," *Film History*, Vol. 17, No. 1 (2005): 29–38.

22. *Moving Picture World*, Vol. 20, No. 6 (9 May 1914): 835.

23. "The Mutual, for the first time in the history of film newspaper advertising, plunged into the daily papers of several cities last Sunday, taking half pages to cry the Mutual's claims to the movie patrons attentions. The Mutual heads believe the opprobrium carelessly meted out to the movies by some newspapers, who ascribe to the films' influence, crime, floods and disaster, will be swung around to a more sympathetic understanding of the moral good of the films when the manufacturers and exhibitors make the newspapers their forum." *Variety*, Vol. 33, No. 2 (12 December 1913): 13. Among metropolitan newspapers, one could find ads even earlier in, for instance, the *Chicago Tribune* on October 26, November 9 and 23, December 7 and 14, 1913 and, finally, on January 4, 1914.

24. Janet Staiger, "Announcing Wares, Winning Patrons, Voicing Ideals: Thinking about the History and Theory of Film Advertising," *Cinema Journal*, Vol. 29, No. 3 (Spring 1990): 3–31; Jane Gaines, "From Elephants to Lux Soap: The Programming and 'Flow' of Early Motion Picture Exploitation," *The Velvet Light Trap*, No. 25 (Spring 1990): 29–43; Moya Luckett, "Advertising and femininity: the case of *Our Mutual Girl*," *Screen*, Vol. 40, No. 4 (Winter 1999): 363–383.

25. *New York Clipper*, Vol. 61, No. 42 (29 November 1913): 15.

26. Bowser (1990), 185.

27. See ad in *Billboard*, Vol. 24, No. 16 (20 April 1912): 52.

28. Raymond Fielding, *The American Newsreel 1911–1967* (Norman, Oklahoma: University of Oklahoma Press, 1972), 37–45.

29. Norma Phillips' biography in *Motography*, Vol. 12, No. 23 (5 December 1914): 779.

30. *New York Times*, (14 June 1914), VII:8.

31. *Reel Life*, Vol. 4, No. 10 (3 January 1914): 6.

32. The *New York Clipper* ventured a witty account of a screening of the first episode for trade critics, hosted by Philip Mindil, who according to the headline "wines and dines the critics." The event was however a lunch, the venue the Masonic Club. Vol. 61, No. 49 (17 January 1914): 16. See also a report in *Billboard*, Vol. 26, No. 4 (24 January 1914): 60. Apart from all the brothers, Mabel Condon of *Photoplay Magazine* was invited. Condon wrote a feature article on "The Statuesque Mutual" for the March issue of the magazine, which featured Norma Phillips on the cover (the article is on pp. 48–52). Condon here covers an array of aspects of the series: the strenuous shooting, the casting of Norma Phillips and her background, and the nuts and bolts of the series. Philips is quoted saying "clothes are not the keynote of the picture," which does not obviate in-depth accounts of the costumes and the tabs picked up by Mutual for the outfits. Furthermore, "that which appeals most intimately to the women devotees of the screen are the elaborate and up-to-the-very-last-minute garments with which the Mutual Girl is outfitted at the cost of good-sized fortune." Vol. 7, No. 4.

33. The *New York Herald* reported that the indisposed Carnegie was reluctant to leave his bed when Norma Phillips and the film troupe arrived, but eventually was coaxed out for some shots in the garden. 1 February 1914, 8.

34. Cobb recounted his film experiences in the *New York Times*, 5 July 1914, X:6.

35. The *New York Herald* carried a featured article when Katherine Davis was about take office as commissioner in early January. In stark contrast to the fashion fiend Margaret, it was reported that "Commissioner Davis doesn't go in for the frills of fashion." 4 January 1914, III:2.

36. Episode 20, *Moving Picture World*, Vol. 20, No. 11 (13 June 1914): 1541.

37. Episode 21, ibid., Vol. 20, No. 12 (20 June 1914): 1689.

38. *New York Times*, 18 January 1914, C:5.

39. Episode 31, *Moving Picture World*, Vol. 21, No. 9 (29 August 1914): 1242.

40. Ibid., Vol. 23, No. 4 (23 January 1915): 516.

41. *Motography*, Vol. 9, No. 11 (30 May 1914): 389.

42. Attributing the new role of press agents to the breakthrough of features, an article in *Variety* notes the emergence of a new type of such agents, "a real executive and man of business as compared to the 'squib writing' publicity man who ran the manufacturer's publicity campaigns in the earlier days of the industry." *Variety*, Vol. 37, No. 4 (25 December 1914): 33.

43. An unsystematic examination of *SF-Journalen*, the Swedish Film Industry newsreel, from the early 1930s reveals that women still introduced fashion via voice-over, and that more or less witty animated sequences were part of the format.

44. Her assignment was soberly mentioned in a notice in *Motography*, Vol. 13, No. 4 (23 January 1915): 133–34.

45. *Moving Picture World*, Vol. 38, No. 11 (14 December 1918): 1242.

46. Ibid., Vol. 23, No. 10 (6 March 1915): 1542.

47. *Motion Picture News*, Vol. 11, No. 9 (6 March 1915): 36.

48. Ibid., Vol. 11, No. 5 (6 February 1915): 30.

49. *New York American*, 20 January 1915, 3.

50. *San Francisco Examiner*, 12 October 1916, 7.

51. Elinor De Wire, "Grace Darling's Daring Deeds," *Mariners Weather Log*, Vol. 38, No. 3 (Summer 1994): 62–63.

52. *New York American*, 24 January 1915, II:3

53. It might have appeared in No. 4, 1915, which was released on January 14, but not published in *Moving Picture World*.

54. *Moving Picture World*, Vol. 23, No. 10 (6 March 1915): 1502.

55. *New York American*, 21 February 1915, II:1.

56. Ibid., 28 February 1915, II:1, 2.

57. *New York Evening Journal*, 11 March 1915, 12.

58. *New York American*, 7 March 1915, II:1.

59. *New York Evening Journal*, 11 March 1915, 12.

60. Ibid., 11 February 1915, 9.

61. Yet another link across America was depicted in a later *News Pictorial* issue showing Hearst and Selig having a long-distance telephone conversation, another novel technological marvel from 1915. Appropriately, the parties for the very first long-distance call were Bell and Watson. The account of the telephone of the transcontinental call between Hearst at his "summer home in California" and Selig "in his private offices in Chicago" was published in

Selig's in-house magazine *Paste-Pot and Shears* (11 October 1915): 1. The call was shown in *Hearst-Selig News Pictorial No. 72*, released on September 9th. A full synopsis for this edition of the News Pictorial can be found in *Moving Picture World*, Vol. 25, No. 13 (25 September 1915): 2230.

62. "Something New Under the Sun. A Pictorial Voyageur Reporter—Grace Darling," *Movie Pictorial*, Vol. 1, No. 25 (March 1915): 7–8.

63. *New York Evening Journal*, 27 February 1915, 4.

64. "Something New Under the Sun."

65. *Los Angeles Examiner*, 15 February 1915, II:1, 5.

66. "Miss Darling finally broke down, and, by the doctor's orders, was compelled to take a rest of several days." *San Diego Union*, 27 February 1915, I:3. In the absence of a Hearst paper in San Diego, the local papers were apparently inhibited in covering her activities. Her first visit to San Diego was commented upon in the *San Diego Tribune*, and appropriately by a female reporter, Lena Falk Gjertsen, aka The Tribune Girl.

67. *Los Angeles Examiner*, 18 February 1915, I:8.

68. *San Francisco Examiner*, 17 February 1915, 8.

69. *Los Angeles Examiner*, 26 February 1915, II:1.

70. Ibid., 27 February 1915, II:1.

71. Ibid., 4 March 1915, II:1.

72. *Moving Picture World*, Vol. 23, No. 13 (27 March 1915): 1907; see also *Motion Picture News*, Vol. 11, No. 13 (3 April 1915): *New York Dramatic Mirror*, Vol. 73, No. 1892 (24 March 1915): 25, and *Motography*, Vol. 13, No. 12 (20 March 1915): 434.

73. *Chicago American*, 8 March 1915, 1.

74. *Movie Pictorial* (March 1915): 7–8.

75. *Los Angeles Examiner*, 9 March 1915, II:10.

76. Ibid.

77. Marie Manning, *Ladies Now and Then, by Beatrice Fairfax (Marie Manning)* (New York: E.P. Dutton & Co., Inc., 1944).

78. One episode has survived at the National Film and Television Archive in London, Chapter 10: "Dolly Plays Detective."

79. "Grace Darling Talks to Girls," *New York Evening Journal*, 24 February 1916, 5; 1 March 1916, 14; 3 March 1916, 20; 8 March 1916, 16; 10 March 1916, 20; 14 March 1916, 14; 17 March 1916, 22; 21 March 1916, 18; 24 March 1916, 24; 28 March 1916, 18; 31 March 1916, 24; 4 April 1916, 20; 7 April 1916, 21; 15 April 1916, 10.

80. *New York Evening Journal*, 4 August 1916, 9.

81. Ibid., 27 July 1916, 3.

82. Ibid., 9 August 1916, 6.

83. Ibid., 23 August 1916, Magazine Page.

84. *Los Angeles Examiner*, 6 August 1916, VI:2. See also *Motography*, Vol. 16, No. 9 (26 August 1916): 495.

85. *New York Evening Journal*, 22 August 1916, Magazine Page.

86. *Moving Picture World*, Vol. 29, No. 9 (26 August 1916): 1391.

87. Ibid., Vol. 29, No. 11 (9 September, 1916): 1683.

88. *Variety*, Vol. 43, No. 13 (25 August 1916): 25. *Motography*, likewise, considered episodes three and four better than the first two; Vol. 16, No. 12 (16 September 1916): 611.

89. *Variety* was at its most corrosive in its dismissive review: "The boy who wrote the titles is not given any program billing. He should have been featured above the ghastly, unattractive feminine person who presumes to be the star and he certainly deserves more credit than the directorial responsible for the creation of a film that mirrors his incompetence in every scene." *Variety*, Vol. 84, No. 10 (21 December, 1927): 24.

Chapter 8

1. "On Style: An Interview with Cinema" [1963], reprinted in Sidney Gottlieb, ed., *Hitchcock on Hitchcock. Selected Writings and Interviews* (Berkeley: University of California Press, 1995), 285–302; quotation from p. 286.

2. For a discussion of the genre, see Anne Morey, "Acting Naturally: Juvenile Fiction Series and the Movies," *Aura. Film Studies Journal*, Vol. 6, No. 2 (2000): 90–112.

3. Tom Gunning, among others, has devoted energy to refute the accuracy of such reactions by looking at reception material from the first screenings. The most in-depth discussion of the "Train Effect," a phrase coined by Yuri Tsivian, is Stephen Bottomore's essay "The Panicking Audience?: Early Cinema and the 'train effect,' " *Historical Journal of Film, Radio and Television*, Vol. 19, No. 2 (June 1999): 177–216. Just to add to Bottomore's roster of early comments about film trains, let me mention an account of the very first film screening in Sweden. Writes the anonymous critic: "[I]t looks as if it [the train] would run out among the spectators—here the film comes to a halt." (*Arbetet*, 29 June 1896, 2) Nothing about panic in the auditorium, however. See also Mrs. Mozart's account of her first screening for Native Americans in Chapter 3.

4. A description from Selig's program leaflet for the film. Entry 3395 in the microfilm run based on Library of Congress, Copyright Office, *Catalog of Copyright Entries. Cumulative Series: Motion Pictures 1912–1939* (Washington, D.C.: Library of Congress, 1951).

5. For a discussion of duplicitous narration, see Kristin Thompson, *Breaking the*

Glass Armor: Neoformalist Film Analysis (Princeton: Princeton University Press, 1988), 135–161.

6. Michel Foucault, "Of Other Spaces," *Diacritics*, Vol. 16, No. 1 (Spring 1986): 22–27.

7. *Chicago Tribune*, 3 November 1907, B:3.

8. For an overview, see Abel (1999), Chapter 6.

9. The key text is still Frederick Jackson Turner, "The Significance of the Frontier in American History" [1893], reprinted in Turner, *The Frontier in American History* (Tucson: University of Arizona Press, 1986), pp. 1–38. In the wake of this closing, such moments could be effectively mass-marketed in genres more in tune with current frontiers offering new forms of cultural challenges. This wisdom was formulated much later in an episode in Selznick's tribute to electricity, *Light's Diamond Jubilee*—a 1954 televisual extravaganza distributed to all Americans across the standard network borders. When the West was conquered, the American frontier spirit had to go elsewhere, looking for challenges in space, or new territories to civilize. Hollywood intervenes only after legends have become facts.

10. J. Berg Esenwein and Arthur Leeds, *Writing the Photoplay* (Springfield, Mass.: Home Correspondence School, 1913), 14.

11. Nancy Brooker-Bowers, *The Hollywood Novel and Other Novels About Film 1912–1982* (New York: Garland, 1985); for a second attempt at bibliographic coverage, see Anthony Slide, *The Hollywood Novel. A Critical Guide to Over 1200 Works with Film-Related Themes or Characters, 1912 through 1994* (Jefferson, N.C., McFarland & Company, 1995).

12. Bruce Kawin, *Mindscreen: Bergman, Godard, and First-Person Film* (Princeton: Princeton University Press, 1978).

13. Later in 1916 Bower published a novel called *Heritage of the Sioux* (Boston: Little, Brown, and Co.); again, no citation in the bibliographies. The film aspect is here less dominant than in the previous texts. The storyline, however, confirms that the studio head made good on his promise to bring Jean of the Lazy A back to the screen.

14. *New York Dramatic Mirror*, Vol. 64, No. 5170 (12 October 1910): 29. Essanay hosted the contest for a new term for the screened product, which resulted in victory for the term photoplay; the result of the contest was discussed in *Film Index*, Vol. 6, No. 16 (15 October 1910): 2–3.

15. *Moving Picture World*, Vol. 12, No. 10 (8 June 1912): 920. For a less temperamental protest, see "Common and Proper Names", *Independent*, Vol. 73, No. 3322 (1 August 1912): 278–280. The anonymous writer hopes that the term "kodak" will eventually prevail.

16. *New York Times*, 26 May 1914, I:10.

17. *Photoplay Magazine*, Vol. 7, No. 5 (April 1915): 129–130.

18. *Motion Picture Magazine*, Vol. 9, No. 3 (April 1915): 119.

19. *Motography*, Vol. 9, No. 4 (1 February 1913): 67.

20. *Los Angeles Tribune*, 18 August 1914, 14.

21. *Motion Picture News*, Vol. 10, No. 10 (12 September 1914): 42. *Moving Picture World*, Vol. 18, No. 9 (29 November 1913): 999; report on semantic dissent from other sources.

22. *Chicago Herald*, 14 March 1915, VI:6.

23. *Exhibitors Herald*, Vol. 1, No. 22 (20 November 1915): 10. W.W. Hodkinson outlined his ideas on picture management during his time as general manager of the Progressive Motion Picture Company in Ogden, Utah, in *Film Index*; the concluding installment was published in Vol. 5, No. 12 (19 March 1910): 8–9.

24. *Chicago Tribune*, 25 November 1915, 20.

25. *Evening Sun*, 4 April 1914, 11.

26. Faulkner's article from the London *Daily Mail* was summarized in *The Literary Digest*, Vol. 47, No. 3 (19 July 1913): 97–98.

27. Henry R. Luce, "The American Century," *Life*, Vol. 10, No. 7 (17 February 1941): 61–65.

28. *New York Review*, Vol. 8, No. 24 (31 January 1914): 4.

29. For a discussion of the increase in film length and the industrial background for multi-reel films, see Bordwell et al. (1985), 128–134.

30. *Current Literature*, Vol. 43, No. 5 (November 1909): 554.

31. O. Winter, "The Cinematograph" [1896], reprinted in *Sight and Sound*, Vol. 51, No. 4 (Autumn 1982), 294–96.

32. DeCordova (1990).

33. *New York Clipper*, Vol. 59, No. 28 (26 August 1911): 17.

34. *Chicago Herald*, 25 November 1917, VII:5.

35. *Moving Picture World*, Vol. 18, No. 9 (29 November 1913): 1004–05.

36. *Philadelphia Record*, 13 October 1912, III:3.

37. Barry Salt, *Film Style and Technology: History and Analysis* (London: Starword, 1992), 90.

38. A featured article in *New York Times* offered an illustrated account of the shooting, 8 February 1914, Sunday Magazine:5; see also 20 February 1914, 11.

39. The Balboa, situated in Long Beach, unsuccessfully contested Hobart Bosworth's rights to Jack London's novels. See the Balboa's scrapbook at the Historical Society, Long Beach.

40. *Motion Picture News*, Vol. 12, No. 14 (9 October 1915): 85.

41. For a detailed analysis of this lost film, see my "Microbes, Animals, and Humans: THE ESCAPE and the Politics of Undesirable Breeding," in Paolo Cherchi Usai, ed., *The D.W. Griffith Project, Volume 12: Essays on D.W. Griffith* (London: BFI Publishing, 2008), 69–82.

42. *Berlingske Tidende*, 26 September 1916, 4; the review is signed "Stifinderen" [Path Finder].
43. *Variety*, Vol. 44, No. 4 (22 September, 1916): 37.
44. *New York Morning Telegraph*, 17 September 1916, V:8.
45. *New York Dramatic Mirror*, Vol. 77, No. 1986 (13 January 1917): 27.

Chapter 9

1. Kitty Kelly, "Flickerings from Film Land," *Chicago Tribune*, 23 March 1915, 10.
2. Stamp (2000).
3. Richard Norton Smith, *The Colonel. The Life and Legend of Robert R. McCormick 1880–1955* (Boston and New York: Houghton Mifflin Company, 1997), 150–51.
4. http://web.ukonline.co.uk/m.gratton/1911-1920/1914.htm
5. *Chicago Tribune*, 12 November 1911, G:7; November 19: Essanay's "A Soldier's Love Story" [title of published synopsis, release title unknown]; November 26: Essanay's *The Long Strike*; December 3: Selig's *The Inner Mind*; December 10: Essanay's *The First Man—A Newspaper Romance*; December 17: Selig's *An Evil Power*; December 24: Essanay's *The Good Fellows Christmas Eve*; December 31: Essanay's "A Tragic Romance"; January 7, 1912: Selig's *Paid Back*; January 14: Selig's *The Prosecuting Attorney*; January 21: Essanay's *The Melody of Love*; January 28: American Film's: *The Real Estate Fraud*; February 4: Essanay's *The Hospital Baby*; February 11: Selig's "The Test"; February 18: Essanay's *An Interrupted Romance*"; February 25: Essanay's "Love Versus Genius"; March 3: American Film's *An Assisted Elopement*; March 10: Essanay's *The Loan Shark*.
6. Ibid., 19 November 1911, B:5.
7. Ibid., 22 February 1914, G:6.
8. Ibid., 24 September 1914, 8.
9. Ibid., 29 March 1914, V:4–5.
10. Vorse (1911).
11. *Chicago Tribune*, 19 April 1914, V:1.
12. *Los Angeles Record*, Katherine M. Zengerle, "Moving Picture Machine Operator Surely Has 'Hot' Time in Turret," 28 June 1909, 4; Katherine M. Zengerle, "Moving Picture Firm 'Cans' Drama by the 1000-Foot Roll at Edendale," 11 November 1909, 4; 14 February 1910, 4 on eye strain (unsigned); 17 March 1910, 4 interview with Hobart Bosworth (unsigned).
13. Ibid., 18 January 1915, 1; 19 January 1915, 1, 2; 20 January 1915, 1, 8.
14. *Chicago Tribune*, 8 March 1915, 13.

15. Ibid., 13 March 1915, 15. The text was dated March 9.
16. Ibid., 15 March 1915, 14. The report included snapshots from a stop at Albuquerque, and on the 16th, Kelly chronicled the experiences from the stop at the Grand Canyon in Arizona (16 March 1915, 10).
17. Ibid., 17 March 1915, 14.
18. Ibid., 20 October 1915, 14.
19. Ibid., 4 October 1914, G:4.
20. Ibid., 18 October 18 1914, G:7. Interventions along similar lines were published on October 25th (G:7), and on November 1st a "Keystone Fan" confessed a disposition antithetic to that of Mr. Travers, namely not appreciating a program without a Keystone title, and especially those featuring Charlie Chaplin and Mabel Normand (F:7). Mr. Lexin, Jr. returned on November 22nd, challenging Mr. Travers to further plead his case or repent in the face of a recent masterpiece like *Dough and Dynamite*. This line of reasoning was repeated in a second intervention with the same date praising Chaplin and Arbuckle (E:11). Live and let live was the motto for the following week's letter (E:4), and then Mr. Travers returned on December 6th (G:9). He tried to lay "the ghost to rest," yielding the point that taste does indeed differ and there's always room for improvement. The value of his first letter was to make clear that "the Keystone is of more importance than any of us had suspected." The debate did not peter out until next week when Tinne published yet another letter, an intervention adding no new perspectives (13 December, E:8).
21. Ibid., 27 October 1915, 10.
22. Ibid., 29 October 1915, 6.
23. Ibid., 1 November 1915, 6.
24. Such gendered polarities have returned in many guises, see for example Raymond Chandler's diatribe against Agatha Christie and Dorothy Sayers, whose female readership allegedly consumed fiction akin to "a cup of lukewarm consommé at a spinterish tea room," as James Naremore reminds us in "Hitchcock at the Margins of *Noir*," in Richard Allen and S. Ishii-Gonzalés, eds., *Alfred Hitchcock: Centenary Essays* (London: BFI Publishing, 1989), 267. For a more general discussion of the gendering of culture, see Andreas Huyssen, *After the Great Divide: Modernism, Mass Culture, Postmodernism* (Bloomington: Indiana University Press, 1986).
25. *Chicago Tribune*, 2 November 1915, 14.
26. Ibid., 11 November 1915, 6.
27. Ibid., 16 November 1915, 14.
28. For a discussion of Asta Nielsen's intervention, see my essay "'Dear Miss Gagner!' – A Star and Her Methods," in Tytti Soila, ed., *Stellar Encounters: Stardom in Popular European Cinema* (London: John Libbey, 2008), 217–229.

29. Richard Henry Little, "The Case for the Defense," *Chicago Herald*, 7 November 1915, VI:4; followed up an earlier piece, "Keeping Alight the Fires On the Altar of Thespis," ibid., 31 October 1915, VI:4; Louella O. Parsons retorted with "The Case for the Defense," ibid., 14 November 1915, VI:4; Little closed the debate with "In Re Drama vs. Movies," ibid., 21 November 1915, VI:4. For an overview of Parsons' career, see Samantha Barbas, *The First Lady of Hollywood: A Biography of Louella Parsons* (Berkeley: University of California Press, 2005).

30. Mae Tinee, *Life Stories of the Movie Stars Volume 1* (Hamilton, Ohio: The Presto Publishing Company, 1916).

31. *Moving Picture World*, Vol. 32, No. 2 (14 April 1917): 279. Kelly had reviewed one of the first attempts in the genre, a volume compiled by Henri Armand de Masi featuring around 300 players. It does not seem that any copies have survived; Kelly offers no title, merely describing the volume as a "Who's Who in Motion Pictures."

Chapter 10

1. Lottie Briscoe, "The Great War," *Motion Picture Magazine*, Vol. 9, No. 1 (February 1915): 81–84; quotation from p. 82.

2. James M. Cain, "Double Indemnity" [1936], *The Postman Always Rings Twice, Double Indemnity, Mildred Pierce, and Selected Stories* (New York: Everyman's Library, 2003), 116.

3. H.G. Wells, *When the Sleeper Wakes* (New York and London: Harper & Brothers, 1899), Chapter 14.

4. *New York Herald*, 30 December 1900, V:10.

5. See Chapter 24, "The Dynamo and the Virgin," Henry Adams, *The Education of Henry Adams* (Washington, D.C.: Adams, 1907).

6. *New York Herald*, 7 June 1914, III:5.

7. *Evening Sun*, 6 June 1914, 4.

8. *Los Angeles Times*, 6 November 1907, II:11.

9. Harry C. Carr, "Directors. The Men Who Make the Plays," *Photoplay Magazine*, Vol. 8, No. 1 (June 1915): 80–85.

10. For an analysis of the context for Griffith's film, see Olsson (2005).

11. *New York Dramatic Mirror*, Vol. 62, No. 1618 (25 December 1909): 15.

12. *Motography*, Vol. 6, No. 2 (August 1911): 90–91. The article was pre-printed by the *New York Times*, 30 July 1911, Sunday Magazine:4.

13. *Los Angeles Times*, 2 December 1910, II:5.

14. *New York Morning Telegraph*, 19 April 1914, V:1.

15. *Evening Sun*, 16 December 1909, 10.

16. Howard B. Grose, *Aliens or Americans?* (New York: Eaton & Main, 1906), 209.

17. Emory S. Bogardus, *Essentials of Americanization* (Los Angeles: University of Southern California Press, 2nd revised edition, 1920), 101–02.

18. *Los Angeles Times*, 25 June 1911, II:4.

19. Bogardus (1920), 101.

20. Thorstein Veblen, *The Theory of the Leisure Class: An Economic Study of Institutions* (New York: Macmillan, 1908 [1899]); Georg Simmel, *The Philosophy of Money* [1900], ed. David Frisby, (London and New York: Routledge, 2004); Georg Simmel, "The Metropolis and Mental Life" [1903], in Donald N. Levine, ed., *Georg Simmel on Individuality and Social Forms*, (Chicago: University of Chicago Press, 1971), 324–339.

21. *Playground*, Vol. 3, No. 12 (March 1910): 24.

22. *Los Angeles Times*, 27 August 1911, V:17.

23. Ibid. For general perspectives on Southern California's "dreamscape," see Kevin Starr, *Material Dreams: Southern California through the 1920's* (Oxford and New York: Oxford University Press, 1990).

24. *Moving Picture World*, Vol. 9. No. 1 (15 July 1911): 52; see also *Moving Picture News*, Vol. 5, No. 7 (17 February 1912): 29 on the campaigns of three railroad companies, Santa Fe, Salt Lake, and Southern Pacific, to lure "colonists" and tourists to Los Angeles.

25. For instance in *Los Angeles Herald*, 22 August 1913, 15.

26. *Los Angeles Record*, 9 December 1913, 9.

27. *Los Angeles Express*, 3 March 1915, 12.

28. *Moving Picture World*, Vol. 8, No. 22 (3 June 1911): 1244.

29. *Los Angeles Times*, 12 March 1911, II:1, 7.

30. The *Express* published an extensive account of its reform struggles and successes over the years, "Early History of Express Shows Struggles of City," *Los Angeles Express*, 31 January 1914, 13–14.

31. *Los Angeles Express*, 28 February 1913, 16.

32. *Los Angeles Times*, 27 February 1913, 6.

33. *Los Angeles Herald*, 18 September 1913, II:1.

34. *Los Angeles Times*, 12 March 1913, III:4.

35. James A.B. Scherer, "What Kind of Pittsburgh is Los Angeles?", *World's Work*, Vol. 41, No. 4 (February 1921): 382–392; quotation from p. 391.

36. Harry Carr, *Los Angeles. City of Dreams* (New York: Grosset & Dunlap, 1935), 124.

37. John O'Hara, *Hope of Heaven* (New York: Harcourt, Brace and Company, 1938), 52. In the beginning of the 1930s—and with an acerbic slant—Robert Benchley echoes Wright's analysis, but with an emphasis on life and night-life in Hollywood (or the lack thereof). From the perspective of New York

City's bohemian culture, Benchley considers Hollywood to be "one of the dullest centres of its size in the country." Robert Benchley, "A Possible Revolution in Hollywood," *Yale Review*, Vol. 21, No. 9 (September 1931): 100–110; quotation from p. 102.

38. George Jean Nathan and H.L. Mencken, *The American Credo: A Contribution toward the Interpretation of the National Mind* (New York: A.A. Knopf, 1920), 94.

39. Sarah Comstock, "The Great American Mirror. Reflections from Los Angeles," *Harper's Monthly Magazine*, Vol. 156, No 936 (May 1928): 715–723; quotation from p. 716. Comstock's analysis is closely foreshadowed in George P. West, "California the Prodigious," *The Nation*, Vol. 115, No. 2987 (4 October 1922): 325–328.

40. Carr (1935), 133.

41. Bruce Bliven, "Los Angeles. The City That is Bacchanalian—in a Nice Way," *New Republic*, Vol. 51, No. 658 (13 July 1927): 197–200; quotation from p. 197.

42. *Motion Picture News*, Vol. 11, No. 5 (6 February 1915): 2.

43. *New York Times*, 9 July 1913, 5. The background for her ambition to protect children at movie theaters was outlined in ibid., 4 July 1913, 1.

44. *New York Tribune*, 7 June 1914, III:7. The glowing review of Griffith's film was published by the *Tribune* on 29 March 1915, III:9.

45. Ibid., 15 March 1914, III:11.

46. The unsigned column in *Los Angeles Tribune* was inaugurated on Friday, July 18, 1913. The five paragraphs were devoted to director Otis Turners' (Rex) troubles on location, dangers faced by Henry Van Meter when acting in a film for Bison-101, actress Pauline Bush's series of scenarios written as spin-offs from her magazine stories, Marshall Neilan was reported to have composed "The Photoplayers Rag," and, finally, the following week one could see Essanay's newspaper drama *Tapped Wires* at Clune's Broadway, and at Clune's Fifth street Theater Selig's two-reel drama *The Never to Return Road*. The column was subsequently published on July 19th, 21st, 22nd, 24th, 25th, 26th, 29th, 30th, August 2nd, 4th, 7th, 9th, 15th, 18th, 23rd, 25th, 26th, 27th, 28th, 30th, September 1st, and, finally, on September 8th.

47. *New York Tribune*, 15 March 1915, III:11.

48. *Chicago Tribune*, 18 January 1915, 10.

49. *New York Herald*, 28 March 1915, III:10. For an analysis of Griffith's poetics, see Anon., "A Poet Who Writes on Motion Picture Films," *Theatre Magazine*, Vol. 19, No. 160 (June 1914): 311–312, 314, 316, and James Shelley Hamilton, "Putting a New Move in the Movies", *Everybody's Magazine*, Vol. 32, No. 6 (June 1915): 677–686.

50. For an account of eugenics with an emphasis on California, see Alexandra

Stern, *Eugenic Nation: Faults and Frontiers of Better Breeding in Modern America* (Berkeley: University of California Press, 2005).

51. *New York Review*, Vol. 9, No. 13 (16 May 1914): II:4.

52. *Variety*, Vol. 35, No. 1 (5 June 1914): 19.

53. *Caucasian*, 24 August 1915, 6.

54. W.T. Stead, *The Americanisation of the World, or The Trend of the Twentieth Century* (London: Review of Reviews, 1902).

55. *Globe and Commercial Advertiser*, 5 March 1915, 12.

56. *New Republic*, Vol. 2, No. 20 (20 March 1915): 185.

57. *Globe and Commercial Advertiser*, 6 April 1915, 10. Replies from Griffith and Dixon were published on April 10th. The debate is reprinted in Robert Lang, ed., *The Birth of a Nation: D.W. Griffith, Director* (New Brunswick, N.J.: Rutgers University Press, 1994), 164–170.

58. Janet Staiger, *Interpreting Films: Studies in the Historical Reception of American Cinema* (Princeton, N.J.: Princeton University Press, 1992), Chapter 7; see also Cripps (1977), Chapter 2.

59. City Council of Los Angeles, *Petitions*, Vol. 99 (letter dated 11 February 1915).

60. The Public Welfare Committee of the City Council of the City of Los Angeles, File 2124 (1913), "Afro-American Race Discrimination," Transcript of Testimony.

61. *Los Angeles Record*, 6 March 1914, 2.

62. U.S. Supreme Court, PLESSY v. FERGUSON, 163 U.S. 537 (1896). The doctrine upheld by this case was not overruled by the Supreme Court until 1954 in the landmark ruling in the case Brown vs. Board of Education of Topeka, U.S. Supreme Court BROWN v. BOARD OF EDUCATION, 347 U.S. 483 (1954).

63. Carr (1935), 137.

64. *Los Angeles Times*, 7 February 1913, III:1.

65. Ibid., 5 February 1911, III:15.

66. Ibid., 7 February 1913, III:1.

67. Ibid., 20 March 1913, III:1.

68. Ibid., 4 May 1915, III:1

69. See his write-up of *Orphans of the Storm* just after he had the left studio and prior to the release of the film. Ibid., 16 October 1921, III:1.

70. *Los Angeles Herald*, 27 February 1915, 11.

71. *Los Angeles Examiner*, 11 January 1915, I:7.

72. *Los Angeles Express*, 11 January 1915, 4.

73. *Los Angeles Times*, 1 January 1915, 146.

74. *Los Angeles Examiner*, 24 December 1911, 8.

75. *Los Angeles Tribune*, 11 January 1915, 2.

76. Ibid., 17 January 1915, I:4.
77. *Los Angeles Times*, 24 January 1915, III:3, 12.
78. *New York Times*, 15 December 1916, 12; 17 December 1916, IV:5.

BIBLIOGRAPHY

Abel, Richard. *Americanizing the Movies and "Movie-Mad" Audiences, 1910–1914*. Berkeley: University of California Press, 2006.

——. *The Ciné Goes to Town: French Cinema, 1896–1914*. Berkeley: University of California Press, 1994.

——. "The Passing (Picture) Show in the Industrial Heartland: The Early 1910s." In *Allegories of Communication. Intermedial Concerns from Cinema to the Digital*, edited by John Fullerton and Jan Olsson, 321–332. Rome: John Libbey, 2004.

——. *The Red Rooster Scare: Making Cinema American, 1900–1910*. Berkeley: University of California Press, 1999.

——, ed. *Encyclopedia of Early Cinema*. London and New York: Routledge, 2005.

Adams, Henry. *The Education of Henry Adams*. Washington, D.C.: Adams, 1907.

Addams, Jane. *Spirit of Youth and the City Streets*. New York: Macmillan, 1909.

Addison, Heather. "'Must Players Keep Young?': Early Hollywood's Cult of Youth." *Cinema Journal* 45, no. 4 (Summer 2006): 3–25.

Allen, Robert C. "Contra the 'Chaser Theory.'" *Wide Angle* 3, no. 1 (1979): 4–11.

——. "Looking at 'Another Look at the Chaser Theory.'" *Studies in Visual Communication* 10, no. 4 (1984): 45–50.

——. "Manhattan Myopia; or, Oh! Iowa!" *Cinema Journal* 35, no. 3 (Spring 1996): 73–103.

——. "Motion Picture Exhibition in Manhattan 1906-1912: Beyond the Nickelodeon." *Cinema Journal* 18, no. 2 (Spring 1979): 2–15.

447

——. "Relocating American Film History: The 'Problem' of the Empirical." *Cultural Studies* 20, no. 1 (January 2006): 48–88.

——. *Vaudeville and Film, 1895–1915: A Study in Media Interaction*. New York: Arno Press, 1980 [1977].

Altman, Rick. "The Silence of the Silents." *Musical Quarterly* 80, no. 4 (1996): 648–718.

The Amusement Situation in Boston. Boston: The Drama Committee of the Twentieth Century Club, 1910.

Amusements and Recreation in Milwaukee: A Bulletin of the City Club, 1914. Milwaukee, Wis.: The Club, 1914.

Appleton, Victor. *The Motion Picture Boys*. New York: Grosset & Dunlap, 1913.

Asendorf, Christoph. *Batteries of Life: On the History of Things and Their Perception in Modernity*. Berkeley: University of California Press, 1991.

Baehr, Harry W., Jr. *The New York Tribune Since the Civil War*. New York: Dodd, Mead & Co., 1936.

Baldasty, Gerald J. *The Commercialization of News in the Nineteenth Century*. Madison, Wis.: University of Wisconsin Press, 1992.

——. *E.W. Scripps and the Business of Newspapers*. Urbana: University of Illinois Press, 1999.

Balides, Constance. "Cinema under the Sign of Money: Commercialized Leisure, Economies of Abundance, and Pecuniary Madness, 1905–1915." In *American Cinema's Transitional Era: Audiences, Institutions, Practices*, edited by Charlie Keil and Shelley Stamp, 285–314. Berkeley: University of California Press, 2004.

Barbas, Samantha. *The First Lady of Hollywood: A Biography of Louella Parsons*. Berkeley: University of California Press, 2005.

Barnum, P.T. *The Life of Barnum, the World-Renowned Showman*. Buffalo, N.Y.: Callahan & Connealy, 1899 [1855].

Barth, Gunther. *City People: The Rise of Modern City Culture in Nineteenth-Century America*. Oxford and New York: Oxford University Press, 1982 [1980].

Bartholomew, Robt. O. *Report of Censorship of Motion Pictures and of Investigation of Motion Picture Theaters of Cleveland*. Cleveland: Council of City of Cleveland, 1913.

Bean, Jennifer. "Technologies of Early Stardom and the Extraordinary Body." *Camera Obscura* 16, no. 3 (48, 2001): 9–56.

Benchley, Robert. "A Possible Revolution in Hollywood." *Yale Review* 21, no. 9 (September 1931): 100–110.

Blackall, C.H. "New York Moving Picture Theater Law," *Brickbuilder*, Supplement to 23, no. 3 (February 1914): 47.

Bleyer, Willard Grosvenor. *Main Currents in the History of American Journalism*. Boston: Houghton Mifflin Co., 1927.

448

Bliven, Bruce. "Los Angeles. The City That Is Bacchanalian–in a Nice Way." *New Republic* 51, no. 658 (13 July 1927): 197–200.

Bogardus, Emory S. *Essentials of Americanization*. Los Angeles: University of Southern California Press, 2nd revised edition, 1920.

Bordwell, David. *On the History of Film Style*. Cambridge, Mass.: Harvard University Press, 1997.

Bordwell, David, Janet Staiger, and Kristin Thompson. *The Classical Hollywood Cinema: Film Style & Mode of Production to 1960*. New York: Columbia University Press, 1985.

Bottles, Scott L. *Los Angeles and the Automobile: The Making of the Modern City*. Berkeley: University of California Press, 1987.

Bottomore, Stephen. "The Panicking Audience?: Early Cinema and the 'Train Effect,' " *Historical Journal of Film, Radio and Television* 19, no. 2 (June 1999): 177–216.

Bower, B.M. *Heritage of the Sioux*. Boston: Little, Brown, and Co., 1916.

——. *Jean of the Lazy A*. Boston: Little, Brown, and Co., 1915.

——. *The Phantom Herd*. Boston: Little, Brown, and Co., 1916.

Bowser, Eileen. *The Transformation of Cinema, 1907–1915*. New York: Scribner, 1990.

Brady, Anna, Richard Wall, and Carolyn Newitt Weiner. *Union List of Film Periodicals: Holdings of Selected American Collections*. Westport, Connecticut: Greenwood Press, 1984.

Brewster, Ben. "A Scene at the 'Movies,'" *Screen* 23, no. 2 (July-August 1982): 4–15.

Brewster, Ben, and Lea Jacobs. *Theatre to Cinema: Stage Pictorialism and the Early Feature Film*. New York: Oxford University Press, 1997.

Briscoe, Lottie. "The Great War." *Motion Picture Magazine* 9, no. 1 (February 1915): 81–84.

Brooker-Bowers, Nancy. *The Hollywood Novel and Other Novels About Film 1912–1982*. New York: Garland, 1985.

Bruno, Giuliana. *Streetwalking on a Ruined Map: Cultural Theory and the City Films of Elvira Notari*. Princeton, N.J.: Princeton University Press, 1993.

Cain, James M. *Double Indemnity* [1936]. In Cain, *The Postman Always Rings Twice, Double Indemnity, Mildred Pierce, and Selected Stories*. New York: Everyman's Library, 2003.

Cameron, James R. *Motion Picture Projection*. Manhattan Beach, N.Y.: Cameron Publishing Co., Inc., 1928.

Carbine, Mary. "'The Finest outside the Loop': Motion Picture Exhibition in Chicago's Black Metropolis, 1905–1928." *Camera Obscura 23* (May 1990): 9–41.

Carr, Harry. *Los Angeles. City of Dreams*. New York: Grosset & Dunlap, 1935.

——. "Directors. The Men Who Make the Plays." *Photoplay Magazine* 8, no. 1 (June 1915): 80–85.

449

Casetti, Francesco. *The Theories of Cinema 1945–1995*. Austin: University of Texas Press, 1999.

Charney, Leo, and Vanessa R. Schwartz, eds. *Cinema and the Invention of Modern Life*. Berkeley: University of California Press, 1995.

"The Chinese Theater, Law and Order in Los Angeles; Jew Ah Mow and His Congressional Testimony." *Chinese Historical Society of Southern California* 7, no. 2 (December 1984): 1–4.

Clapp, Elizabeth J. *Mothers of All Children: Women Reformers and the Rise of the Juvenile Courts in Progressive America*. University Park, Pa.: Pennsylvania State University Press, 1998.

Clarke, Frederic Colburn. "Moving Picture Tricks." *Vanity Fair* 3, no. 1 (September 1914): 63.

Clement, Josephine. "Standardizing the Picture Theater." *Motography* 8, no. 13 (21 December 1912): 457–460.

——. "What the Public Wants." *Playground* 7, no. 1 (April 1913): 60–66.

Collier, John. "Leisure Time, the Last Problem of Conservation." *Playground* 6, no. 1 (June 1912): 93–106.

——. " 'Movies' and the Law." *Survey* 27, no. 16 (20 January 1912): 1628–29; reprinted in *Moving Picture News* 5, no. 8 (24 February 1912): 13–14.

——. "Moving Pictures: Their Function and Proper Regulation." *Playground* 4, no. 7 (1910): 232–240.

"Commonwealth vs. Edward K. Mozart." *Lancaster Law Review* 30 (Lancaster, Pa. Wickersham Printing Co., 1913): 147–148.

Comstock, Sarah. "The Great American Mirror. Reflections from Los Angeles." *Harper's Monthly Magazine* 156, no. 936 (May 1928): 715–723.

Cripps, Thomas. *Slow Fade to Black: The Negro in American Film, 1900-1942*. New York: Oxford University Press, 1977.

Czitrom, Daniel. "The Redemption of Leisure: The National Board of Censorship and the Rise of Motion Picture in New York City, 1900–1920." *Studies in Visual Communication* 10, no. 4 (1984): 2–6.

Dahlquist, Marina. "Becoming American in 1910?: Pathé Frères' Settlement in New Jersey." *Quarterly Review of Film & Video* 22, no. 3 (2005): 251–262.

——. "Global versus Local: The Case of Pathé." *Film History* 17, no. 1 (2005): 29–38.

Davis, Lennard. *Factual Fictions: The Origins of the English Novel*. New York: Columbia University Press, 1983.

Davis, Michael M., Jr. *The Exploitation of Pleasure*. New York City: Russell Sage Foundation, 1911.

DeCordova, Richard. *Picture Personalities: The Emergence of the Star System in America*. Urbana: University of Illinois Press, 1990.

de Koven Bowen, Louise. *Five and Ten Cent Theaters. Two Investigations*. Chicago: Juvenile Protective Association of Chicago, 1909 and 1911.

De Wire, Elinor. "Grace Darling's Daring Deeds." *Mariners Weather Log* 38, no. 3 (Summer 1994): 62–63.

Dickens, Charles. *Martin Chuzzlewit*. Ware, Hertfordshire: Wordsworth Classics, 1997 [1843–44].

Dunbar, Olivia Howard. "The Lure of the Films." *Harper's Weekly* 57, no. 2926 (18 January 1913): 20–22.

Eaton, Walter Prichard. "Class-Consciousness and the 'Movies.'" *Atlantic Monthly* 105, no. 1 (January 1915): 48–56.

——. "Menace of the Movies." *American Magazine* 76, no. 5 (September 1913): 55–60.

Edwards, Richard Henry. *Popular Amusements*. New York: Association Press, 1915.

Esenwein, J. Berg, and Arthur Leeds. *Writing the Photoplay*. Springfield, Mass.: Home Correspondence School, 1913.

Ewen, Stuart. *Captains of Consciousness: Advertising and the Roots of the Consumer Culture*. New York: McGraw-Hill, 1976.

Fielding, Raymond. *The American Newsreel 1911–1967*. Norman, Oklahoma: University of Oklahoma Press, 1972.

Fogelson, Robert M. *The Fragmented City: Los Angeles, 1850–1930*. Berkeley: University of California Press, 1993 [1967].

Fosdick, Raymond B. "Report on New York Picture Theaters." *Motography* 5, no. 4 (April 1911): 27–31.

Foster, William Trufant. *Vaudeville and Motion Picture Shows: A Study of Theaters in Portland, Oregon*. Reed College: Social Services Series 2, 1914.

Foucault, Michel. "Of Other Spaces." *Diacritics* 16, no. 1 (Spring 1986): 22–27.

Fox, Daniel M. *The Discovery of Abundance: Simon N. Patten and the Transformation of Social Theory*. Ithaca: Cornell University Press, 1967.

Fox, Stephen. *The Mirror Makers: A History of American Advertising and Its Creators*. New York: William Morrow and Company, Inc., 1984.

Fuller, Kathryn H. *At the Picture Show. Small-Town Audiences and the Creation of Movie Fan Culture*. Washington, D.C.: Smithsonian Institution Press, 1996.

Gaines, Jane. *Fire and Desire: Mixed-Race Movies in the Silent Era*. Chicago: University of Chicago Press, 2001.

——. "From Elephants to Lux Soap: The Programming and 'Flow' of Early Motion Picture Exploitation." *The Velvet Light Trap*, no. 25 (Spring 1990): 29–43.

Gardette, L. "Some Tricks of the Moving Picture Maker." *Scientific American* 100, no. 26 (26 June 1909): 476–477, 487.

Gelfand, Mitchell Brian. "Chutzpah in El Dorado. Social Mobility of Jews in Los Angeles, 1900-1920." Ph.D. diss., Carnegie-Mellon University, 1981.

Goodman, Daniel Carson. *Hagar Revelly*. New York: M. Kennerley, 1913.

Gottlieb, Robert, and Irene Wolt. *Thinking Big: The Story of the Los Angeles Times,*

Its Publishers and Their Influence on Southern California. New York: Putnam, 1977.

Grau, Robert. *The Business Man in the Amusement World: A Volume of Progress in the Field of the Theater.* New York: Broadway Publishing Co., 1910.

——. *Forty Years Observation of the Music and the Drama.* New York and Baltimore: The Broadway Publishing Company, 1909.

——. *Theater of Science.* New York: Benjamin Blom, Inc., 1969 [1914].

Greening, Clara M. "Policewoman Number One." *Sunset Magazine* 27, no. 3 (September 1911): 304–306.

Grieveson, Lee. *Policing Cinema: Movies and Censorship in Early-Twentieth-Century America.* Berkeley: University of California Press, 2004.

Griffths, Alison. " 'THEY GO TO SEE A SHOW': Vicissitudes of spectating and the anxiety over the machine in the nineteenth century science museum." *Early Popular Visual Culture* 4, no. 3 (November 2006): 245–271.

——. *Wondrous Difference: Cinema, Anthropology, and Turn-of-the-Century Visual Culture.* New York: Columbia University Press, 2002.

Grose, Howard B. *Aliens or Americans?* New York: Eaton & Main, 1906.

Gullason, Thomas A., ed. *The Complete Short Stories and Sketches of Stephen Crane.* Garden City, N.Y.: Doubleday & Company, Inc., 1963.

Gunning, Tom. "The Cinema of Attraction: Early Film, its Spectator and the Avant-Garde." *Wide Angle* 8, no. 3/4 (1986): 63–67.

——. *D.W. Griffith and the Origins of American Narrative Film: The Early Years at Biograph.* Urbana: University of Illinois Press, 1991.

——. "Modernity and Cinema: A Culture of Shocks and Flow." In *Cinema and Modernity*, edited by Murray Pomerance, 297–315. New Brunswick, N.J.: Rutgers University Press, 2006.

Hamilton, James Shelley. "Putting a New Move in the Movies." *Everybody's Magazine* 32, no. 6 (June 1915): 677–686.

Hansen, Miriam. *Babel and Babylon. Spectatorship in American Silent Film.* Cambridge, Mass.: Harvard University Press, 1991.

Hapgood, Hutchins. *Types from City Streets.* New York: Funk & Wagnalls, 1910.

Heaton, John L. *The Story of a Page: Thirty Years of Public Service and Public Discussion in the Editorial Columns of the New York World.* New York: Harper & Brothers, 1913.

Hoff, James L. "The Era of the Motion Picture." *The Chautauquan* 71, no. 1 (7 June 1913): 1–10.

Hopper, James, and Fred R. Bechdolt. *9009.* New York: The McClure Co., 1908.

Howells, William Dean. "Editor's Easy Chair." *Harper's Monthly Magazine* 106, no. 5 (April 1903): 811–815.

Hughes, Helen MacGill. *News and the Human Interest Story.* Chicago: University of Chicago Press, 1940.

Huyssen, Andreas. *After the Great Divide: Modernism, Mass Culture, Postmodernism*. Bloomington: Indiana University Press, 1986.

Indianapolis Recreation Survey. Indianapolis: General Civic Improvements Committee of the Indianapolis Chamber of Commerce, 1914.

Irwin, Will. "The American Newspaper." Published as a series of fifteen articles in *Collier's* in 1911, vol. 46; reprinted as *The American Newspaper*. With comments by Clifford F. Weigle and David C. Clark for The Iowa State University Press (Ames, Iowa), [1969].

James, David E. *The Most Typical Avant-Garde: History and Geography of Minor Cinemas in Los Angeles*. Berkeley: University of California Press, 2005.

Jowett, Garth. *Film: The Democratic Art*. Boston: Little, Brown, and Co., 1976.

Juergens, George. *Joseph Pulitzer and the New York World*. Princeton, N.J.: Princeton University Press, 1966.

Jump, Herbert A. "The Social Influence of the Moving Picture." *Playground* 5, no. 3 (June 1911): 74–84.

Kawin, Bruce. *Mindscreen: Bergman, Godard, and First-Person Film*. Princeton, N.J.: Princeton University Press, 1978.

Keil, Charlie. *Early American Cinema in Transition: Story, Style, and Filmmaking, 1907–1913*. Madison, Wis.: University of Wisconsin Press, 2001.

Keil, Charlie, and Shelley Stamp, eds. *American Cinema's Transitional Era: Audiences, Institutions, Practices*. Berkeley: University of California Press, 2004.

Kellogg, Daniel F. "The Changed American." *North American Review* 200, no. 704 (July 1914): 59–70.

Kingsley, Sherman C. "The Penny Arcade and the Cheap Theatre." *Charities and the Common* 18, no. 10 (8 June 1907): 295–297.

Kirby, Lynne. *Parallel Tracks: The Railroad and Silent Cinema*. Durham, N.C.: Duke University Press, 1997.

Koszarski, Richard. *An Evening's Entertainment: The Age of the Silent Feature Picture, 1915-1928*. New York: Scribner, 1990.

Lang, Robert, ed. *The Birth of a Nation: D. W. Griffith, Director*. New Brunswick, N.J.: Rutgers University Press, 1994.

Lant, Antonia, ed. *Red Velvet Seat: Women's Writing of the First Fifty Years of Cinema*. New York: Verso, 2006.

Leab, Daniel J. *From Sambo to Superspade: The Black Experience in Motion Pictures*. Boston: Houghton Mifflin, 1975.

Leach, William. *Land of Desire. Merchants, Power, and the Rise of New American Culture*. New York: Pantheon Books, 1993.

Levine, Lawrence W. *Highbrow/Lowbrow: The Emergence of Cultural Hierarchy in America*. Cambridge, Mass.: Harvard University Press, 1988.

Library of Congress. Copyright Office. *Catalog of Copyright Entries. Cumulative Series: Motion Pictures 1912–1939*. Washington, D.C.: The Library of Congress, 1951.

453

Lindstrom, Julie Ann. " 'Almost worse than the restrictive measures is our apparent belief that the city itself has no obligation in the matter': Chicago Reformers and the Nickelodeons." *Cinema Journal* 39, no. 1 (Fall 1999): 90–112.

——. " 'Getting a Hold Deeper in the Life of the City': Chicago Nickelodeons, 1905–1914." Ph.D. diss., Northwestern University, 1998.

Luce, Henry R. "The American Century." *Life* 10, no. 7 (17 February 1941): 61-65.

Luckett, Moya. "Advertising and femininity: The case of *Our Mutual Girl*." *Screen* 40, no. 4 (Winter 1999): 363-383.

——. "Cities and Spectators: A Historical Analysis of Film Audiences in Chicago, 1910-1915." Ph.D. diss., University of Wisconsin-Madison, 1995.

McCarthy, Kathleen D. "Nickel Vice and Virtue: Movie Censorship in Chicago, 1907–1915." *Journal of Popular Film* 5, no. 1 (1976): 37–55.

MacFarlane, Peter Clark. "What is the Matter with Los Angeles?" *Collier's* 8, no. 11 (2 December 1911): 28, 30.

McKeever, William A. "A Primary School for Criminals." *Good Housekeeping Magazine* 51, no. 2 (August 1910): 184–186.

Madison, 'the Four Lake City,' Recreational Survey Prepared by a Special Committee of the Madison Board of Commerce. Madison, Wis.: Tracy & Kilgore, printers, 1915.

Manning, Marie. *Ladies Now and Then, by Beatrice Fairfax (Marie Manning)*. New York: E.P. Dutton & Co., Inc., 1944.

Marks, Martin Miller. *Music and the Silent Film: Contexts and Case Studies, 1895-1924*. New York: Oxford University Press, 1997.

Moore, Paul S. "Everybody's Going: City Newspapers and the Early Mass Market for Movies." *City & Community* 4, no. 4 (December 2005), 339-357.

Morey, Anne. "Acting Naturally: Juvenile Fiction Series and the Movies." *Aura. Film Studies Journal* 6, no. 2 (2000): 90–112.

Morosco, Oliver. *Life of Oliver Morosco: The Oracle of Broadway Written from His Own Notes and Comments by Helen M. Morosco and Leonard Paul Dugger*. Caldwell, Id.: Caxton Printers, 1944.

Musser, Charles. "Another Look at the 'Chaser Theory.' " *Studies in Visual Communication* 10, no. 4 (1984): 24–44, 51.

——. *The Emergence of Cinema: The American Screen to 1907*. New York: Scribner, 1990.

——. "Introducing Cinema to the American Public: The Vitascope in the United States, 1896–7." In *Moviegoing in America*, edited by Gregory A. Waller, 13–26. Malden, Mass.: Blackwell Publishers Inc., 2002.

Musser, Charles, and Carol Nelson. *High-Class Moving Pictures: Lyman H. Howe and the Forgotten Era of Traveling Exhibition, 1880-1920*. Princeton, N.J.: Princeton University Press, 1991.

N.W. Ayer & Son's American Newspaper Annual and Directory. Philadelphia: N.W Ayer & Son, 1910–1915.

Naremore, James. "Hitchcock at the Margins of *Noir*." In *Alfred Hitchcock: Centenary Essays*, edited by Richard Allen and S. Ishii-Gonzalés, 263–277. London: BFI Publishing, 1989.

Nasaw, David. *The Chief: The Life of William Randolph Hearst*. Boston: Houghton Mifflin, 2000.

Nathan, George Jean, and H.L. Mencken. *The American Credo: A Contribution Toward the Interpretation of the National Mind*. New York: A.A. Knopf, 1920.

Nye, David E. *Electrifying America: Social Meanings of a New Technology 1880–1940*. Cambridge, Mass.: MIT Press, 1990.

O'Brien, Frank M. *The Story of The Sun: New York 1833–1928*. New York: Greenwood Press, 1968 [1928].

O'Connor, Richard. *The Scandalous Mr. Bennett*. Garden City, N.Y.: Doubleday & Company, Inc., 1962.

O'Hara, John. *Hope of Heaven*. New York: Harcourt, Brace and Company, 1938.

Olsson, Jan. " 'Dear Miss Gagner!'—A Star and Her Methods." In *Stellar Encounters: Stardom in Popular European Cinema*, edited by Tytti Soila, 217–229. London: John Libbey, 2008.

——. "Microbes, Animals, and Humans: THE ESCAPE and the Politics of Undesirable Breeding." In *The D.W. Griffith Project, Volume 12: Essays on D.W. Griffith*, edited by Paolo Cherchi Usai, 69–82. London: BFI Publishing, 2008.

——. "Pressing Inroads: Metaspectators and the Nickelodeon Culture." In *Screen Culture: History and Textuality*, edited by John Fullerton, 113–135. Eastleigh: John Libbey Publishing, 2004.

——. *Sensationer från en bakgård: Frans Lundberg som biografägare och filmproducent i Malmö och Köpenhamn* ["Sensations from a Backyard: Frans Lundberg as Exhibitor and Film Producer in Malmö and Copenhagen"]. Stockholm: Symposion, 1989.

——. "Sound Aspirations: The Two Dimensions of Synchronicity." In *Le son en perspective: nouvelles recherches/New Perspectives in Sound Study*, edited by Didier Huvelle and Dominique Nasta, 99-114. Brussels: P.I. E,-Peter Lang, 2004.

——. "Trading Places: Griffith, Patten and Agricultural Modernity." *Film History* 17, no. 1 (2005): 39–65.

"On Style: An Interview with Cinema" [1963]. Reprinted in *Hitchcock on Hitchcock. Selected Writings and Interviews*, edited by Sidney Gottlieb, 285–302. Berkeley: University of California Press, 1995.

Oppenheim, James. "Saturday Night." *Forum* 43, no. 2 (February 1910): 97–106.

Otis, Harrison Gray, ed. *California "Where Sets the Sun": The Writings of Eliza A. Otis in Poetry and Prose*. Los Angeles: Times-Mirror Co., 1905.

Palmer, Lewis E. "The World in Motion." *Survey* 22, no. 10 (5 June 1909): 355–365.

Patten, Simon N. "The Making of Economic Literature: Annual Address of the President." *American Economic Association. Publications (1886–1911)* 10, no. 1 (April 1909): 1–14.

———. *The New Basis of Civilization*. New York: The Macmillan Co., 1907.

———. *Product and Climax*. New York: B.W. Huebsch, 1909.

Perry, Bliss. *The American Mind*. Boston and New York: Houghton Mifflin Co., 1912.

Pearson, Roberta E. *Eloquent Gestures: The Transformation of Performance Style in the Griffith Biograph Films*. Berkeley: University of California Press, 1992.

Peterson, Jennifer. "World Pictures: Travelogue Films and the Lure of the Exotic, 1890–1920." Ph.D. diss., University of Chicago, 1999.

Pirandello, Luigi. *Shoot! (Si gira): The Notebooks of Serafino Gubbio, Cinematograph Operator*, authorized translation from the Italian by C.K. Scott Moncrieff. New York: E.P. Dutton & Co., 1926 [1914]); reprinted by the University of Chicago Press in 2005.

The Pittsburgh Survey: Findings in Six Volumes. New York: Charities Publication Committee, 1909–1914.

Quinn, Michael. "Distribution, the Transient Audience, and the Transition to the Feature Film." *Cinema Journal* 40, no. 2 (Winter 2001): 35–56.

Rabinovitz Lauren. *For the Love of Pleasure: Women, Movies, and Culture in Turn-of-the-Century Chicago*. New Brunswick, N.J.: Rutgers University Press, 1998.

Ramsaye, Terry. *A Million and One Nights: A History of the Motion Picture*. New York: Simon & Schuster, Inc., 1926.

"Recreation Program For a Million Children." *Charities and the Commons* 21, no. 23 (6 March 1909): 1037–1039.

Report and Recommendations of the Morals Efficiency Commission. Pittsburgh: The Morals Efficiency Commission, 1913.

Report of the Recreation Conditions and Problems of Peoria, with Recommendations and Suggested System. Peoria: Peoria Association of Commerce, 1916.

Rhodes, John Ford. "Newspapers as Historical Sources." *Atlantic Monthly* 103, no. 5 (May 1909): 650–657.

Richardson, Anna S. "The Menace of the Moving Picture Theater." *Pictorial Review* 12, no. 1 (October 1910): 9, 67.

Rischin, Moses, ed. *Grandma Never Lived in America: The New Journalism of Abraham Cahan*. Bloomington: Indiana University Press, 1985.

Robertson, Michael. *Stephen Crane, Journalism and the Making of Modern American Literature*. New York: Columbia University Press, 1983.

Rodgers, Daniel T. "In Search of Progressivism." *Reviews in American History* 10, no. 4 (December, 1982): 113–132.

Rogin, Michael Paul. *"Ronald Reagan," the Movie: and Other Episodes in Political Demonology*. Berkeley: University of California Press, 1987.

Rosebault, Charles. *When Dana Was The Sun*. New York: Robert M. McBride & Co., 1931.

Rosenblom, Nancy J. "Between Reform and Regulation: The Struggle over Film Censorship in Progressive America, 1909–1922." *Film History* 1, no. 4 (1987).

Rosenzweig, Roy. *Eight Hours for What We Will: Workers and Leisure in an Industrial City, 1870–1920*. Cambridge and New York: Cambridge University Press, 1983.

Ross, Steven J. *Working-Class Hollywood: Silent Film and the Shaping of Class in America*. Princeton, N.J.: Princeton University Press, 1998.

Rowell's American Newspaper Directory. New York: Printers' Ink Publishing Co., 1905–1909.

Royle, Edwin Milton. "The Vaudeville Theater." *Scribner's Magazine* 26, no. 4 (October 1899): 485–495.

Salt, Barry. *Film Style and Technology: History and Analysis*. London: Starword, 1992.

Sánchez, George J. *Becoming Mexican American: Ethnicity, Culture and Identity in Chicano Los Angeles, 1900–1945*. New York: Oxford University Press, 1993.

Scherer, James A.B. "What Kind of Pittsburgh is Los Angeles?" *World's Work* 41, no. 4 (February 1921): 382–392.

Schivelbusch, Wolfgang. *The Railway Journey: Trains and Travel in the 19th Century*. New York: Urizen Books, 1979.

Scudson, Michael. *Discovering the News: A Social History of American Newspapers*. New York: Basic Books, Inc., 1978.

Seitz, Don C. *The James Gordon Bennetts, Father and Son: Proprietors of the New York Herald*. Indianapolis: Bobbs-Merrill, 1928.

Simmel, Georg. "The Metropolis and Mental Life" [1903]. In *Georg Simmel on Individuality and Social Forms*, edited by Donald N. Levine, 324–339. Chicago: University of Chicago Press, 1971.

——. *The Philosophy of Money* [1900], edited by David Frisby. New York: Routledge, 2004.

Singer, Ben. "Manhattan Melodrama." *Cinema Journal* 36, no. 4 (Summer 1997): 107–112.

——. "Manhattan Nickelodeons: New Data on Audiences and Exhibitors." *Cinema Journal* 34, no. 4 (Spring 1995): 5–35.

——. *Melodrama and Modernity: Early Sensational Cinema and Its Contexts*. New York: Columbia University Press, 2001.

——. "New York, Just Like I Pictured It." *Cinema Journal* 35, no. 5 (Spring 1996): 104–128.

Singer, Stan. "The Orpheum Theater of Los Angeles: A Chronology." *Southern California Quarterly* 72, no. 4 (Winter 1990): 339–372.

Sklar, Robert. *Movie-Made America: A Cultural History of American Movies*. New York: Random House, 1975.

——. "Oh! Althusser!: Historiography and the Rise of Cinema Studies." In Resisting Images: Essays on Cinema and History, edited by Robert Sklar and Charles Musser, 12–35. Philadelphia: Temple University Press, 1990.

Slide, Anthony. The Hollywood Novel. A Critical Guide to Over 1200 Works with Film-Related Themes or Characters, 1912 through 1994. Jefferson, N.C.: McFarland & Company, 1995.

Smith, Bertha H. "The Making of Los Angeles." Sunset Magazine 19, no. 3 (July 1907): 237–254.

——. "The Policewoman." Good Housekeeping Magazine 52, no. 3 (March 1911): 296–298.

Smith, Richard Norton. The Colonel. The Life and Legend of Robert R. McCormick 1880–1955. Boston and New York: Houghton Mifflin Co., 1997.

Söderberg, Hjalmar, "En barnföreställning" ["A Matinee for Children"]. Svenska Dagbladet, 27 April 1904, 8.

Staiger, Janet. "Announcing Wares, Winning Patrons, Voicing Ideals: Thinking about the History and Theory of Film Advertising." Cinema Journal 29, no. 3 (Spring 1990): 3-31.

——. "Combination and Litigation: Structures of U.S. Film Distribution, 1896-1917." Cinema Journal 23, no. 2 (Winter 1984): 41–72.

——. "The Future of the Past." Cinema Journal 44, no. 1 (Fall 2004): 126-129.

——. Interpreting Films: Studies in the Historical Reception of American Cinema. Princeton, N.J.: Princeton University Press, 1992.

Stamp, Shelley. Movie-Struck Girls: Women and Motion Picture Culture after the Nickelodeon. Princeton, N.J.: Princeton University Press, 2000.

Starr, Kevin. Material Dreams: Southern California through the 1920's. New York: Oxford University Press, 1990.

Starr, Paul. The Creation of the Media: Political Origins of Modern Communications. New York: Basic Books, 2004.

Stead, W.T. The Americanisation of the World, or The Trend of the Twentieth Century. London: Review of Reviews, 1902.

Steffens, Lincoln. The Autobiography of Lincoln Steffens. New York: Literary Guild, 1931.

Stern, Alexandra. Eugenic Nation: Faults and Frontiers of Better Breeding in Modern America. Berkeley: University of California Press, 2005.

Stoddard, Bessie D. "Recreative Centers of Los Angeles, California." The Annals of the American Academy of Political and Social Science 35, no. 2 (March, 1910): 426–435.

Stone, Herbert S. The Chap-Book 5, no. 6 (July 15 1896): 239–240.

Stewart, Jacqueline Najuma. Migrating to the Movies: Cinema and Black Urban Modernity. Berkeley: University of California Press, 2005.

Strauven, Wanda, ed. The Cinema of Attractions Reloaded. Amsterdam: Amsterdam University Press, 2006.

Streible, Dan. "Children at the Mutoscope." *CINéMAS* 14, no. 1 (2003): 91–116.

———. *Fight Pictures: A History of Boxing and Early Cinema*. Berkeley: University of California Press, 2008.

Suggestions for a Model Ordinance for Regulating Motion Picture Theaters. New York: National Board of Censorship of Motion Pictures, 1913.

Talbot, Frederick A. *Moving Pictures—How They Are Made and Worked*. Philadelphia: J.B. Lippincott Co., 1912.

Thissen, Judith. "Oy, Myopia!" *Cinema Journal* 36, no. 4 (Summer 1997): 102–107.

Thompson, Kristin. *Breaking the Glass Armor: Neoformalist Film Analysis*. Princeton, N.J.: Princeton University Press, 1988.

———. "The Concept of Cinematic Excess." In *Narrative, Apparatus, Ideology: A Film Theory Reader*, edited by Philip Rosen, 130–142. New York: Columbia University Press, 1986.

———. "The International Exploration of Cinematic Expressivity." In *Film and the First World War*, edited by Karel Dibbets and Bert Hogenkamp, 65–85. Amsterdam: Amsterdam University Press, 1995.

Tinee, Mae. *Life Stories of the Movie Stars Volume 1*. Hamilton, OH.: The Presto Publishing Company, 1916.

Transcript of Record. Supreme Court of the United States, October term, 1917, no. 155. Motion Picture Patents Company, General Film Company, Biograph Company, et al., Appellants vs. the United States. Appeal from the District Court of the United States for the Eastern District of Pennsylvania. Filed April 22, 1916. New York: Appeal Printing Co., 1916.

Turner, Frederick Jackson. "The Significance of the Frontier in American History" [1893]. Reprinted in Turner, *The Frontier in American History*, 1–38. Tucson: University of Arizona Press, 1986.

Uricchio, William, and Roberta E. Pearson. "Manhattan's Nickelodeons: New York? New York!" *Cinema Journal* 36, no. 4 (Summer 1997): 98–102.

———. *Reframing Culture: The Case of the Vitagraph Quality Film*. Princeton, N.J.: Princeton University Press, 1993.

Ury, Mabel B. "The Evolution of a Moving-Picture Show: An Interview with Josephine Clement." *Twentieth Century Magazine* 5, no. 2 (December 1911): 135–141.

Uzanne, Octave. "The End of Books." *Scribner's Magazine* 16, no. 2 (August 1894): 221–232.

Veblen, Thorstein. *The Theory of the Leisure Class: An Economic Study of Institutions*. New York: Macmillan, 1908 [1899].

Vorse, Mary Heaton. "Some Picture Show Audiences." *Outlook* 98, no. 8 (June 24 1911): 441–447.

Waller, Gregory A. *Main Street Amusements. Movies and Commercial Entertainment in a Southern City, 1896–1930*. Washington, D.C.: Smithsonian Institution Press, 1995.

——. ed. *Moviegoing in America*. Malden, Mass.: Blackwell Publishers Inc., 2002.

Waters, Theodore. "Out With a Moving Picture Machine." *Cosmopolitan* 40, no. 3 (January 1906): 251–259; reprinted in *Film History* 15, no. 4 (2003): 396–402.

Wells, H.G. *When the Sleeper Wakes*. New York: Harper & Brothers, 1899.

West, George P. "California the Prodigious." *The Nation* 115, no. 2987 (4 October 1922): 325–328.

White, Stewart Edward. *The Rules of the Game*. New York: Doubleday, Page & Co., 1910.

Williams, Linda. *Playing the Race Card: Melodramas of Black and White from Uncle Tom to O.J. Simpson*. Princeton, N.J.: Princeton University Press, 2001.

Williams, Raymond. "Dominant, Residual and Emergent." In Williams, *Marxism and Literature*, 121–127. New York: Oxford University Press, 1977.

Winter, O. "The Cinematograph" [1896]; reprinted in *Sight and Sound* 51, no. 4 (Autumn 1982): 294–96.

Wolf, Jerome. "The Los Angeles Times, Labor, and the Open Shop, 1890–1910." Ph.D. diss., University of Southern California, 1961.

INDEX

Page numbers in italics refer to figures.

461